Personal Injury Handbook

Related titles by Law Society Publishing

Child Abuse Compensation Claims
Elizabeth-Anne Gumbel, Malcolm Johnson and Richard Scorer
1 85328 717 2

Criminal Injuries Compensation Claims
Clare Padley and Laura Begley
1 85328 882 9

Fatal Accidents: Law and Practice
Clive Thomas
1 85328 957 4

Criminal Contracting: A Compliance Guide
Andrew Keogh and Brian Craig
1 85328 987 6

Titles from Law Society Publishing can be ordered from all good bookshops or direct from our distributors, Marston Book Services (tel. 01235 465656 or e-mail law.society@marston.co.uk). For further information or a catalogue, e-mail our editorial and marketing office at publishing@lawsociety.org.uk.

PERSONAL INJURY HANDBOOK

Nicholas Waller

The Law Society

ISBN 1–85328–942–6

Published in 2005 by Law Society
113 Chancery Lane, London WC2A 1PL

Typeset by J&L Composition, Filey, North Yorkshire
Printed by Antony Rowe Ltd, Chippenham, Wiltshire

Contents

Preface

This handbook examines liability, quantum and tactics, and contains enough procedure to put them in context. It relates to personal injury work in England and Wales. Northern Ireland, the Channel Islands, the Isle of Man and Scotland all have a different approach.

Personal injury (PI) law, procedure and funding have undergone dizzying changes in the last 10 years. One always owes the client a full professional duty, but now one can investigate and prepare only in proportion to the value of the claim. This may require a leap in the dark when deciding whether to take on a case or obtain expert evidence on a particular topic. To survive, never mind earn anything like members of the other professions, one must work smart.

PI is one of the most diverse areas of legal practice. How to interpret skid marks and debris? Can one measure pain? How would the claimant's business have developed? Does he need treatment the NHS won't give him? Various websites offer an opportunity to keep up to date. For a free e-mail newsletter, go to **www.lawinclear.co.uk**.

A handbook provides a map to assist in navigating legal territory. It is not a substitute for exploring the territory itself, by reading the case law and legislation cited in the text. Within five years it will be possible to find practically all this source material at the click of a mouse, free. Most legislation and case law from 1996 onwards is already freely available on the Internet (see **Appendix 3**).

To help readers find free case law, this handbook uses the court's neutral citation system as far as possible. A neutral citation for a decision of the Court of Appeal appears as *Smith* v. *Jones* [2004] EWCA Civ 99. For the House of Lords the reference is UKHL, and for the High Court, EWHC.

Save for the fortunate few with easy access to an excellent law library, neutral citation is the most useful system when preparing a case. However, when citing case law to the court, one should still use the Law Reports reference from the Incorporated Council of Law Reporting's AC, QB, Ch, Fam or P series. For example, *Donoghue* v. *Stevenson* [1932] AC 562. If the case did not appear in the Law Reports, one may fall back on the WLR series, failing that the All ER series (*Practice Direction (Judgments: Form & Citation)*

(Supreme Court) [2001] 1 WLR 194). If the case is reported only in *The Times*, *Current Law*, PIQR, Lloyd's Medical Reports, the *Gazette* or the *Estates Gazette*, one can only give that citation.

The author is most grateful to the following, for kindly guiding him in the right direction. In alphabetical order: Tom Bucher FRCS (orthopaedics), Stuart Cowen of Francis Clark, accountants of Exeter (forensic accounts and pension loss), Drs Ingrid Gooch and Tony Davis (chronic pain), Henry Scrope of **www.emplaw.co.uk** (employment law) and Dr Duncan Veasey MRCPsych (psychiatry).

It is hard to over praise the Association of Personal Injury Lawyers and its newsletter *PI Focus*. Membership is currently restricted to those who do more claimant than defendant work (APIL, 11 Castle Quay, Nottingham NG7 1FW (0115 958 0585) or **www.apil.com**).

The author hopes that nobody will be offended that he has written as if everybody in the world is male. The his/her/their/its alternatives are too clumsy.

If you find an error in the text, do please let the author know, preferably by e-mail to **erratum@lawinclear.co.uk**.

Nicholas Waller, August 2004

Table of cases

Table of statutes

Table of Secondary, European and International legislation

SECONDARY LEGISLATION

EUROPEAN LEGISLATION

INTERNATIONAL LEGISLATION

CHAPTER 1

First instructions – claimant lawyer

1.1 INITIAL ENQUIRY

A potential claimant rings up. One writes down his name, address, date of birth, phone number, type of accident, date of accident, when reported to the police, the nature of his injuries to assess whether it is worth more than the Small Claims limit, and the name of the proposed defendant.

Although a claimant generally has three years to decide whether to claim, some things do require that he take immediate action. Even if one doubts he has a good claim, it is good public relations and a useful precaution to send out a leaflet containing some general advice about items 1 to 9 in **section 1.2**.

One's career and the survival of the firm's personal injury department depend on working profitably. That means handling only good claims. For every claim taken on, one may have to turn 10 away. Probably one rejects Small Claims, time-barred claims, those with nobody at fault, and those with a shifty or evidently deranged claimant. Firms without relevant experience may also turn away claims involving uninsured or untraced defendants, holiday accidents, foreign claimants, industrial disease, criminal injuries, claims against the police, clinical negligence, product liability, housing disrepair, child abuse, appeals by claimants who failed at first instance, and claims against negligent solicitors.

If it takes two hours to obtain instructions on each of 10 claims, consider the position and write to the claimants to turn them down, half the working week is gone. Have no qualms about turning away an unpromising claim during the initial phone call. It is difficult to give perfect legal advice based on a short phone call, and it is best not to try. Rather than tell the enquirer that he does not have a claim at all, one can say that one's firm's policy is not to take on claims of this sort but he might like to try elsewhere. Whether or not one gave advice or accepted the claim, one must keep a note of what was said. For one's own protection, one should keep this note for at least six years, even if the claim goes nowhere.

If one is lucky enough to have somebody else take incoming calls, one can devise a questionnaire to filter out unwanted new claims. This could be based on the Initial Enquiry Questionnaire on the CD-ROM which accompanies this book.

Some firms specialise in one or more types of difficult claim, even uninsured driver and foreign accident claims, and pay other firms to refer business to them. One can often find advertisements to this effect in the *Gazette* and APIL's *PI Focus*.

1.2 FOLLOW UP AND FIRST INTERVIEW

The initial source of information will be one's client. For questionnaires that may help with a streamlined interview in road, trip, slip, workplace and fatal accident cases, and as to pain and disability, see the CD-ROM. Any questionnaire may need to be adapted to take account of procedural or legal changes, or to reflect a particular firm's systems or the demands of a legal expenses insurer.

It is highly likely that one will need to make or remake most of the following points to the claimant, usually the earlier the better. To save time, one can do this by handing out advice leaflets. To avoid complaints and claims, keep a tick-box form on each file to show which leaflets one gave the claimant.

1. The basic time limit for making a claim is three years from the date of the accident (see **Chapter 18**). However, there are many shorter time limits. Missed deadlines are the main reason for professional negligence claims in personal injury work. The summary in this handbook cannot be a substitute for your responsibility to check the relevant periods when first notified of any claim. Note that:
   (a) If it seems possible that injury was caused by one of the 5 per cent of drivers who are uninsured, the claimant must take prompt steps to identify him (see **sections 7.1** and **7.3**).
   (b) Even prompter action is needed if the injury was caused by an untraced driver, whether this be a hit and run, a collision with cargo dropped on the road, a skid on spilt oil or diesel, or where it turns out that the other driver gave a false name or address. The Motor Insurers' Bureau (MIB) Untraced Drivers Agreement 2003 states that the MIB will pay for damaged property only if the incident was reported to the police within five days and the application is made within nine months. Even if there is no claim for property damage, the incident must have been reported to the police within 14 days (see **section 7.2**).
   (c) To make a Criminal Injuries Compensation Scheme claim the victim must report the incident promptly to the police, cooperate promptly with their investigation, and bring his claim within two years. If the

claim is for minor multiple physical injuries, he must see a doctor twice in the first six weeks (see **Chapter 8**).

(d) If the claimant needs to make a claim in the Employment Tribunal for dismissal or discrimination the time limit may be three or nine months (see **section 6.20**).

(e) If he may need to bring proceedings in a foreign country, the time limit may be 12 months or less.

(f) Some time limits apply even if the claimant is a young child (see **section 18.2**).

2. The claimant may have a statutory obligation under s.170 Road Traffic Act 1988 to report the accident to the police. If 'owing to the presence of a motor vehicle on a road, an accident occurs by which . . . personal injury is caused to a person other than the driver of that motor vehicle' or there is damage to any other vehicle, trailer, animal, the road itself or roadside property 'the driver of the motor vehicle must stop and, if required to do so by any person having reasonable grounds for so requiring, give his name and address and also the name and address of the owner and the identification marks of the vehicle'. If the driver of a motor vehicle does not give his name, address and evidence of insurance at the time, he must report the accident. He 'must do so at a police station or to a constable, and . . .must do so as soon as is reasonably practicable and, in any case, within twenty-four hours of the occurrence of the accident'.
3. The claimant should preserve evidence of his accident (see **section 4.18**).
4. If the claimant is insured for losses or liabilities arising out of the accident he must tell his insurers at once, whether or not he wants to make a claim. He must also tell them at once if the other party indicates that it plans to make any claim against him.
5. If the claimant's vehicle was damaged in the accident, he needs to know how to go about hiring a vehicle. Car hire causes a lot of avoidable disputes (see **section 14.6**).
6. The claimant should keep receipts for his expenses such as prescriptions. He should also keep a list of extra travel stating the destination and reason for each trip he made by car, taxi, etc (see **section 14.8**).
7. If the claimant was injured at work, there are special considerations in the early stages of the claim (see **section 6.1**).
8. The claimant may need to obtain specialist legal advice from an employment lawyer if he suffers discrimination at work, has been dismissed or is under threat of dismissal from work. Some personal injury claims may become barred if the claimant makes a Tribunal claim (see **section 6.20**).
9. The claimant must check at once whether he is entitled to rely on legal expenses insurance. Many forget they have this as an add-on to a car, house contents, travel, business or sports insurance policy, or hidden

within a credit card agreement. The claimant may be entitled to benefit from a policy held by a member of his family. The same applies to trades union membership, which often includes legal expenses cover for the member and his family. He should bring copies of all such agreements to the first interview. Particularly if the claimant was a passenger in the defendant's car when he was injured, one should ask the defendant whether he has any legal expenses insurance that might cover the claimant, as in *Sarwar* v. *Alam* [2001] EWCA Civ 1401. Take reasonable steps to find out whether the claimant has legal expenses cover before offering a client a conditional fee agreement (see **section 19.5**). If there is legal expenses cover, the insurer or union may insist that he instructs a law firm on its panel.

10. If the claim is worth less than the Small Claims limit, few, if any, law firms will give a claimant more than very limited assistance (see **section 21.1**).
11. The claimant should consider giving instructions for an immediate offer, if his insurers agree, to settle liability on a 95:05 basis in his favour, as in *Huck* v. *Robson* (see **section 16.7**).
12. The claimant should preserve evidence of his injuries. It can be useful if he keeps a concise pain diary (see **Chapter 11**).
13. The claimant needs to be aware of his duty to mitigate his losses, and the need to prove that he took appropriate steps. If he loses his job because of his injuries, it is important that he be able to prove he put effort into looking for jobs, and retraining if necessary (see **section 9.6**).
14. Many claimants are confused about the difference between insured losses that their own insurers will pay for, usually vehicle damage and car hire, and what they must claim from the defendant's insurers. It may be worth explaining the meaning of uninsured losses.
15. If the claimant was an employee, was injured in a road accident and receives sick pay on the basis that he must repay it out of his compensation, there can be problems if the other driver turns out to be untraceable (see **section 7.2**).
16. Special care is needed from the outset if the claimant is receiving care provided by the defendant. For a discussion of *Hunt* v. *Severs* [1994] 2 All ER 385, see **section 14.18** The same applies if he receives assistance from family or friends to keep his business going. As to *Hardwick* v. *Hudson* [1999] EWCA Civ 1428, see **section 13.3**.
17. Special care is also needed from the outset if a self-employed claimant is losing earnings from his partnership or from a limited company of which he is part owner. He should consider rearranging the distribution of profits immediately, so that he bears all the loss (see **section 13.3**).
18. It is as well to manage the claimant's expectations about how long a claim takes. One might wish to tell him that it will not be safe to settle his claim until either he has fully recovered from his injuries, or the doctors

have said exactly what the future holds for him. Point out, also, that the defendant will not make a realistic offer until he has all the evidence, including a final medical report, and that it is better to negotiate, because issuing proceedings raises the stakes for everybody (see **section 3.3**). The claimant also needs to know that depending how the claim is funded, he will not receive his compensation until either the defendant has agreed what contribution he will make towards his legal costs, or the court has assessed them. Essentially, the claimant should not spend his compensation until he gets it.

19. The claimant's expectations about the amount of compensation may also need management at a fairly early stage if he is not to be disappointed. A disappointed client can be a problem.
20. One may wish to tell the claimant to make an honest claim, on the basis that the defendant is likely to realise if he does not.
21. Clients assume, as was the case until recently, that anything they tell their lawyer is in perfect confidence. It may be worth telling him that evidence of fraud or other criminal activity may result in one having to report him to the police without warning (Proceeds of Crime Act 2002).
22. If the defendant makes it clear that he doubts the extent of the claimant's disability, and the claim is worth a good deal of money, one may wish to tell the claimant how covert video surveillance works (see **section 11.12**).

One needs to carry out a conflict check, to ensure that the firm does not already act for the defendant. Some firms also carry out bankruptcy checks against all new claimant clients. As to why, see **section 9.17**.

Consider whether the claimant is eligible for Legal Aid, or Community Legal Service funding as it is now known. If so, the court will almost certainly expect one to go down that road rather than give the claimant a conditional fee agreement. See, for example, the housing disrepair case *Bowen* v. *Bridgend County Council* [2004] EWHC 9010 (Costs). For full information on Legal Aid see the Legal Services Commission Manual, published by HM Stationery Office, or the Legal Aid Manual, published by Sweet & Maxwell. Each costs a little less than £200 and is frequently updated. The Access to Justice Act 1999 withdrew Legal Aid outright for 'negligently caused injury, death or damage to property'. Funding for full representation may still be available for personal injury claims:

- For clinical negligence, which was expressly exempted from withdrawal in the 1999 Act.
- For assault, child abuse and certain forms of harassment, as these involve injuries that were not negligently caused.
- Against a care organisation for negligently permitting an employee to carry out deliberate abuse. Although a negligence claim, it is within the scope if the abuse was deliberate.

- For proceedings against public authorities concerning serious wrong-doing, abuse of position or power, or significant breach of human rights. This might include a claim against a school for failing to deal with dyslexia, or against the police for assault, trespass, wrongful arrest, false imprisonment or malicious prosecution.
- For housing proceedings. These are not removed from the scope merely because they include a subordinate claim for personal injury caused by housing disrepair.

Full representation is also theoretically available for the following, but will very seldom be granted because these cases are generally suitable for a conditional fee agreement:

- Claims for breach of a strict statutory or contractual duty.
- Professional negligence proceedings. Claims relating to negligent handling of personal injury actions are within the scope.
- Proceedings which have a significant wider public interest, such as litigation about the safety of oral contraceptives; or to obtain a decision as to whether South African miners could proceed against the UK parent company of an asbestos company; or for judicial review of the Criminal Injuries Compensation Authority's definition of a crime of violence, or a local authority's refusal to allow its staff to be interviewed by solicitors in the context of child care proceedings.

1.3 COSTS AND CASE PLANS

The legal costs may be more than the damages. It is well worth anticipating the ways in which the defendant may challenge one's costs claim at the end of the day (see **section 19.5**).

The claimant's lawyer is 'under a heavy duty to conduct . . . litigation in as economic a manner as possible' especially in claims worth only a few thousand pound: *Jefferson v. National Freight Carriers* [2001] EWCA Civ 2082. This means starting each claim by preparing a case plan. One assesses the likely value of the claim, decides which grade of fee earner should handle it, and budgets what to spend: *Lownds v. Home Office* [2002] EWCA Civ 365.

One should decide not only the maximum that one will spend in total but also the amount to be spent on each stage:

- establishing liability;
- medical issues;
- calculating and proving financial losses;
- issuing proceedings and taking the claim to trial.

It is essential to check at intervals to see that the case is still within budget. Even those who have developed an ability to work in a lean and efficient way, must always be aware what costs and disbursements have accrued on the file open on the desk, and consider what tasks remain. It is time to start worrying if liability has eaten up half of the total budget and there is still no medical report.

CHAPTER 2

First instructions – defendant lawyer

If one takes the view that personal injury litigation is a quest for justice, some of the tactics in this chapter may appear cynical. If one takes the view that PI is a tough game played by rules, the best thing for both sides is to be able to anticipate the moves.

2.1 FIRST STEPS ON LIABILITY

By the time one is instructed, it is generally far too late to see anything useful at the accident site. Nonetheless, there may be positive steps that can be taken to investigate liability. If the value of the claim justifies it, one can make a site visit. If it does not, consider having somebody take photos of the site. The amount of investigation appropriate depends on:

- the value of the claim;
- the message that one's insurance company client wants to send to people who may be thinking about making similar claims; and
- whether one knows an affordable investigator for site visits and interviews.

Workplace claims require special treatment (see **section 6.2**).

In light of *Sarwar* v. *Alam* [2001] EWCA Civ 1401 check whether the defendant has legal expenses insurance that provides cover to the claimant. If so, notify the claimant that if he proceeds instead under a conditional fee agreement (CFA) the defendant may well not be liable to pay the additional liability under a CFA, that is to say, the success fee or the premium for an after the event legal expenses insurance policy (**section 19.5**).

A similar position exists where the claimant could have obtained Legal Aid but proceeded under a CFA instead. The defendant will not have to pay the additional liability (see **section 1.2**).

One may wish to suggest to the claimant that the claim should be dealt with by arbitration or mediation (see **section 3.5**). One may be able to shift some or all of the blame to another defendant (see **section 4.17**).

If one has no defence, the Pre-action Protocol for personal injury claims requires one to admit liability promptly. To do so often saves one's client the cost of a continuing investigation into liability by the claimant, and may well save the client the cost of proceedings. Some defendants feel they may benefit from doing the opposite (see **section 4.19**).

Is the claimant still receiving state benefits as a result of the accident? And can one justify an allegation of contributory negligence? If so, consider whether the allegation may be more trouble than it is worth. Alternatively, consider whether contributory negligence may be a reason to settle the claim swiftly even if this means offering the claimant a little more. These points arise because the defendant has to reimburse the Compensation Recovery Unit (CRU) for all the state benefits paid in respect of the accident but he may not, if there is an allegation of contributory negligence, be able to offset all this against the claimant's damages (see **section 9.7**).

Defendant lawyers are occasionally consulted by an individual who has caused an injury but has not yet had a letter of claim and therefore has not notified his insurers. He should do so at once. It is a condition precedent in most insurance contracts that the insured notify his insurers promptly of any circumstances that may give rise to a claim.

2.2 QUANTUM TACTICS

It is essential to weed out Small Claims as soon as possible, and refer them to a junior member of the team (see **section 21.1**). One can bury many Small Claims by pointing out to the claimant's solicitor that this is what they are. If the claimant has no solicitor, one might send him an advice leaflet to give him a fair and accurate account of the risks of issuing proceedings, especially in terms of legal costs.

If the claimant's vehicle was damaged in the accident, it may be worth immediately offering him a hire car at no cost to him if one's insurer client has set up a system to do so. In any case check that repairs, or any decision about writing off the claimant's vehicle, proceed swiftly. If this has been overlooked there may be an enormous claim for vehicle storage, car hire or loss of use (see **sections 14.1, 14.2** and **14.6**).

Consider offering rehabilitation facilities to the claimant. It may save a good deal of money to organise prompt physiotherapy or chiropractic for a whiplash victim. In cases of very serious injury, great savings can be made by arranging more sophisticated rehabilitation (see **section 14.11**).

If advising an insurance company to admit liability, consider advising it to make an interim payment for the claimant's losses to date. If this reduces the value of the claim below the Small Claims limit, it may halve the defendant's outlay by saving legal costs. It may also have more subtle benefits (see **section 9.3**).

If the claimant is still off work as a result of the accident, one may set out in a letter to his solicitor what training or work he could be doing. If he clearly is not earning as much as he could, this will help stop him blaming all his losses on the defendant (see **section 9.6**).

If the claim is large enough to justify it, one can sometimes achieve good results by examining the claimant's medical records. These may reveal medical problems not caused by the accident, or even that the accident occurred in a different way to that claimed (see **section 20.5**).

Consider obtaining an independent medical report in case the claimant's doctors are too quick to say that the accident caused all his symptoms, or too pessimistic about his chances of recovery. Do this especially in cases of whiplash, low back injury, RSI/WRULD, brain injury, and chronic pain syndrome. As to whiplash, low back injuries, chronic pain and psychiatric injuries, see **sections 11.8–11.11**.

If the claim involves an injury which is likely to resolve completely within a few years at most, but notoriously carries a risk that symptoms will continue and will eventually be said to be permanent, consider making an offer within the first year based on the assumption that the claimant will get better. The claimant may be very reluctant to accept, but feel that he has no choice because of the potential costs consequences. Such an offer should at least put pressure on the claimant's lawyer to do as little as possible while waiting until a final medical report is available. As to whiplash, see **section 11.8**. As to low back injuries, see **section 11.9**. As to the effect of a settlement offer, see **section 16.3**.

On all the following expert evidence tactics, see **sections 20.7–20.15**:

- One should not always instruct an expert jointly with the claimant.
- If one may want to obtain an independent report at any stage, one should object promptly to the experts proposed by the claimant.
- Even if one is sure one will not wish to instruct an independent expert, tactically, one should object to all but one of the claimant's proposed experts. That will make it harder for him to try a different expert if he finds the first expert's report unhelpful.
- When one sees the claimant's expert's report, check whether one has all the documents the expert saw.
- If one wants to raise questions with the expert, try to do so (via the claimant's lawyer) within 14 days of seeing the report.
- The court will often refuse to consider a defendant's expert evidence unless it is exchanged with the claimant according to the court's directions timetable. That probably means having to exchange little more than three months after serving a defence. It may be necessary to chase one's expert vigorously to get the report in time.
- If the claimant says that he intends to obtain a medical report to deal with a new point after proceedings are issued, there is probably insufficient

time to wait and see what it says before deciding whether to obtain one's own report on the point.

- One need not necessarily expect the court to accept everything the claimant's medical expert says, even if one has no expert evidence of one's own.
- If the claimant's medical problem was caused by an apparently trivial incident, one could ask the experts 'Given the nature of the force that caused the injury, and the demands of the claimant's everyday life, how long would it have been before some everyday load or impact caused these symptoms anyway?'
- Where the claimant's case is that he will have a particular problem in future, it may be worth checking whether the experts think the problem is certain to exist. If there is a 25 per cent chance that it will not, the court may give the defendant a discount of up to 25 per cent (see **section 9.5**).
- If the claimant's medical expert advises that the accident accelerated by five years the onset of a medical condition he would have had anyway, it may well be that another expert will say that the acceleration period was two or three years. This could save £30,000 on a loss of earnings claim (see **section 11.5**).

If there is a substantial future loss or expense which will be calculated on a multiplier/multiplicand basis, it may be best for the defendant to settle the claim swiftly even if this means offering the claimant a little more (see **section 9.4**).

If the claimant is still receiving state benefits that the Certificate of Recoverable Benefits attributes to the accident, and the defendant will not be able to offset all of them against damages, it may in some situations be worth going to trial rather than settling if one feels that some or all of those benefits were paid because of medical problems that do not exist or were not caused by the accident. This is because the CRU may not revise their Certificate voluntarily, so one will need to appeal it after settling the claim. The appeal body is required by statute to take account of any decision of the court. If the court finds that the claimant was malingering or that the accident merely accelerated the onset of symptoms by a short period, the appeal stands a much better chance of success than if one merely submits medical reports (see **section 9.7**).

It may be possible to save thousands of pounds by asking the claimant whether he received benefits as a result of the accident that are not covered by the Social Security (Recovery of Benefits) Act 1997 (see **section 9.10**).

If the claimant needs care, equipment or accommodation as a result of his injuries, several tactical points arise:

- If he has in fact managed without these things for some years since the accident, one has a good argument that they are not reasonably necessary. This may mean that the defendant should resist making an interim payment (see **section 14.16**).

- A claim for the value of unpaid care may sink without trace if the carer would not accept a reward under any circumstances (see **section 14.18**).
- If there is a claim for future care, consider whether it will probably be provided free by friends and relatives. If so, one should resist any attempt to claim the value of commercial care (see **section 14.18**).
- If the claimant seeks damages for loss of earnings, consider whether some of his everyday expenses have been met by the state because he is in an institution, or are being sought from the defendant as part of a care package. If so, the defendant is entitled to a discount from the loss of earnings claim (see **section 14.16**).

A settlement offer may be withdrawn at any time until acceptance, and the apparent value of a claim may go up or down after an offer is made. Like a claimant, a defendant making an offer should note it on the file cover so he remembers to withdraw it if the apparent value of the claim goes down; and if he receives an unattractive offer he should not positively reject it. If the defendant has paid money into court and the apparent value of the claim goes down, he will have to apply to the court to withdraw some of the money (see **section 16.7**).

If the claimant issues proceedings after the defendant makes a settlement offer, one should obtain a CRU certificate and get the money from one's insurance company client, in order to back up the offer by making a payment into court within 14 days of service of the claim form (see **section 16.2**).

An employer defending a damages claim made by an employee who has committed fundamental breaches of the employment contract may be entitled to dismiss him. Certainly a worker who is dismissed for wilfully breaching safety rules or fraud has limited future earnings prospects, and this will slash his claim for loss of future earnings. The employer will need advice from an employment law specialist (see **section 6.20**).

It is worth looking for evidence of inaccuracy. If a claim goes to trial, the outcome will depend very much on the claimant's own evidence and credibility. If the defendant can show that by careless exaggeration he claimed 22 trips to physiotherapy at 5 miles each, but had only 17 at 3 miles each, the defendant may save only £20 directly, but it will cast a shadow over all the claimant's evidence.

2.3 COSTS TACTICS

Be as aware of costs tactics as of liability and quantum. Indeed, the costs may be more than the damages. For some pointers, see **section 19.5**.

CHAPTER 3

Negotiating under the Protocols

3.1 CIVIL PROCEDURE RULES 1998

Under the Civil Procedure Rules 1998 (CPR) Part 1.1 the overriding objective of the courts is to deal with cases justly. The courts are determined to prevent delay and wasted legal costs, which generally means penalties in legal costs or interest for a party that fails to comply with the court's timetable. The court may refuse to consider a party's witness statements or medical evidence if they are produced much after the date set under the CPR's case management powers, even if this causes the other side to win at trial (see **sections 20.6** and **20.14**).

The CPR governs proceedings in the county court, High Court and Court of Appeal. The CPR is made up of the rules themselves and corresponding Practice Directions such as CPR PD 1. As the CPR has already been amended 35 times, it makes sense to check that one has the latest version before taking any major step. For an up-to-date copy, go to the website of the Department for Constitutional Affairs at **www.dca.gov.uk**.

Perhaps the most important effect of the CPR on personal injury work is that it requires the parties to observe, from the outset, Pre-action Protocols for:

- Personal injury claims.
- Resolution of clinical disputes.
- Disease and injury claims. This Protocol applies to injury claims where 'the injury is not the result of an accident but takes the form of an illness or disease [unless it was] solely caused by an accident or other similar single event'.
- Housing disrepair cases. This Protocol applies to any civil claim 'arising from the condition of residential premises and may include a related personal injury claim . . .'.
- Judicial review, relevant if challenging a decision of the Criminal Injuries Compensation Appeal Panel.
- Professional negligence, say for a claim against solicitors who dealt negligently with a personal injury claim.

The Protocols Practice Direction says that the Protocols are 'the normal, reasonable way of dealing with disputes'. Each Protocol requires one to warn, inform and negotiate with the opponent, not just charge on towards trial. The claimant must put at least some of his cards on the table at the very start of correspondence. Either party may be penalised for failing to make enough efforts to settle the claim. Both parties should do most of their preparation before proceedings are issued (frontloading). There may not be time afterwards.

The Protocols are primarily designed for claims worth under £15,000, but the Practice Direction says: 'In cases not covered by any approved Protocol, the court will expect the parties, in accordance with the overriding objective . . . to act reasonably in exchanging information and documents relevant to the claim and generally in trying to . . . [settle] the claim promptly and without court proceedings.' The Practice Direction was further amended in 2003 to include a further nine paragraphs about general behaviour in cases 'not governed by any approved protocol'.

Particularly if the breach of the Protocol means that proceedings were issued when this might possibly have been avoided, or costs have been wasted in or by the proceedings, the court may penalise the guilty party either when assessing legal costs, or when awarding interest. This could mean the loser having to pay every penny of the winner's legal costs rather than benefiting from the usual discount. If a party fails to comply with a relevant Protocol but then has to ask the court for leave to do something, the court may well refuse.

In Spring 2001, 68 per cent of solicitors surveyed by the Law Society stated that the courts did not apply penalties following breaches of the Protocols, but the trend led by the Court of Appeal is towards greater firmness.

In *Smith* v. *Havering Hospitals NHS Trust* [2003] EWHC 9002 (Costs) the Supreme Court Costs Master considered the defendant's complaint that the claimant had issued proceedings before sending a letter of claim. He did not impose a penalty because the claimant had in fact given the defendant more time than was required by the Protocol to decide whether to defend the claim. Also, the defendant itself had taken over a year to admit liability.

Most disputes about Protocol points lose their relevance as the claim progresses. If one takes the view that one's opponent is in breach of the Protocol, the best approach is usually just to tell him so for the record. Leave any dispute until liability and quantum have been agreed, and only costs are outstanding. The main exception is a failure by one's opponent to provide copy documentation as required by a Protocol. Claimants often fail to provide adequate evidence about the value of the claim; and defendants often deny liability but try to withhold documents such as accident reports (see **section 20.4**).

3.2 THE PERSONAL INJURY PROTOCOL

The Pre-action Protocol for personal injury claims governs general personal injury work, including road traffic accidents, slips and trips, occupiers' liability, and accidents at work other than industrial disease claims.

Its main aim is 'to enable parties to avoid litigation by agreeing a settlement of the claim before the commencement of proceedings'. It does this by imposing a timetable on the parties, within which they should provide information and documents to their opponent.

As soon as the claimant has enough information to 'substantiate a realistic claim and before issues of quantum are addressed in detail,' he should send a letter of claim to the defendant, in duplicate. This should contain:

- Sufficient concise details to enable the recipient to understand and investigate the claim without extensive further information.
- Copies of the essential documents that the claimant relies on.
- A request for a prompt acknowledgment, and a full written response within a reasonable stated period. Until the Protocol is amended to say otherwise, the periods it prescribes must be adequate for any normal claim. These are 21 days for the acknowledgement, plus three months from the acknowledgment for the full written response.
- An indication whether proceedings will be issued if a full response is not received within that period.
- A request for documents. The claimant should identify and ask for copies of any essential documents that he does not have, but wishes to see.
- A proposal, if the claimant wants to make one, that the claim be dealt with by alternative dispute resolution (see **section 3.5**).
- A warning that the court may impose sanctions if a party fails to comply with the Protocols Practice Direction. If the defendant is likely not to be represented by a lawyer, the claimant should send him a copy of the Protocols Practice Direction. It might also be at least as helpful to send him a copy of the Protocol itself.

In a normal personal injury matter, the claimant should give:

- A clear summary of the facts on which the claim is based, giving sufficient information for the defendant to commence investigations.
- The nature of any injuries suffered.
- The financial loss incurred. The Protocol requires the claimant to give, about injuries and losses alike, sufficient information for the defendant at least to put a broad valuation on the risk. Although the Protocol does not actually say so, the wording of the Practice Direction suggests that the claimant should disclose evidence of his main losses.

- In the case of a road accident, the name and address of the hospital where treatment has been obtained, and the claimant's hospital reference number. This is for recovery of NHS charges from the defendant.
- An indication of the way the claim is being funded (see later in this section).

Can the claimant give minimal information about the circumstances of the claim? The sample letter contained within the Protocol suggests that 'defective machine' or 'broken ground' would be enough. Many judges would consider this inadequate today, particularly since in both cases the defendant may not even know there has been an accident.

Can the claimant give minimal information about the value of the claim ('back injury, and losses to be particularised in due course')? Or should he really put his cards on the table by saying 'back strain requiring three weeks off work, four weeks off heavy housework, eight weeks off rugby, and still causing significant but fading symptoms today. Losses and expenses to date and estimates for the future are set out in the attached Schedule'.

The answer is not yet entirely clear. The Protocol gives two examples of conduct by a claimant that may lead to his being penalised. One is 'not having provided sufficient information to the defendant'. If the claimant tells the defendant that the extent of his pain, suffering and losses is already clear, and makes a settlement offer, he may be able to dispose of the claim at once. However, the claimant is probably not yet sure what his claim is worth, and will keep the letter very brief to prevent the defendant making an early settlement offer. In reality, very few defendants make early offers based on guesswork. As a general rule, it is best for the claimant if he provides as much information as possible from the outset.

Neither the claimant's date of birth nor his National Insurance number should appear in the letter of claim. The more this information is spread around, the more vulnerable the claimant becomes to identity theft. The defendant's insurers need to insert this information in the CRU1 when they register the claim with the Compensation Recovery Unit, and they will ask for it when they get their copy of the letter of claim.

The defendant should acknowledge the letter of claim within 21 days of the date when it was posted. Failing this, the claimant is entitled to issue proceedings. The defendant should state when he will give a full written response to the allegations. If this is longer than the period stated by the claimant, he should say why he needs more time.

The Protocol expects the defendant to supply a full written response within three months of acknowledgment. The defendant should accept the claim in whole or in part, and make proposals for settlement; or state that the claim is not accepted. If he does not accept full liability, or is unwilling to accept that the accident caused all the alleged injuries and losses, he should:

- give detailed reasons for the denial, and say which parts of the claim he accepts, and which he does not;
- enclose copies of essential documents that he relies on;
- enclose copies of documents requested by the claimant, or explain why they are not enclosed;
- ask for copies of essential documents that he does not possess but wishes to see;
- say whether he is willing to enter into alternative dispute resolution.

The parties should then 'promptly engage in appropriate negotiations with a view to settling the dispute and avoiding litigation'. If the defendant admits liability, the claimant should disclose to him any medical report already obtained.

Protocol 3.13 requires the claimant to send the defendant as soon as practicable a 'Schedule of Special Damages with supporting documents,' particularly where the defendant has admitted liability. This language harks back to the old County Court Rules. It seems generally understood that what is really needed is what is now a CPR PD 16.4.2 Schedule of Loss, which sets out 'details of any past and future expenses and losses'. There is seldom any reason why at least a partial Schedule should not be set out in the letter of claim.

Before any party instructs a medical or liability expert he should give the other party a list of the names of one or more experts who he says are suitable, and try to instruct an expert who is acceptable to the other party. If the other party objects to all the proposed experts, the Protocol indicates that the parties can instruct experts of their own choice. Where a medical expert is to be instructed, the Protocol says the claimant's lawyer will organise access to relevant medical records for the expert. When an agreed expert has produced his report, either party may send written questions to that expert. For much more on these apparently harmless points, see **sections 20.10–20.15**.

The claimant should not issue proceedings, where the defendant admits liability in whole or in part, before giving the defendant 21 days to consider medical evidence and perhaps make an offer of settlement (Protocol 3.21). A defendant may settle a modest claim where he would resist a larger one. Whether liability is admitted or not, it makes sense for the claimant to ensure that the defendant sees the medical evidence, a proper schedule of loss, and the documents with which he intends to prove his loss. Note that:

- the notes for guidance state 'litigation should be a last resort, and ... claims should not be issued prematurely when a settlement is in reasonable prospect';
- under CPR Part 44 the courts will consider, when deciding who pays the costs, whether a party made reasonable attempts to settle the claim;

- the Court of Appeal has referred to 'the paramount importance of avoiding litigation whenever this is possible' (*Cowl* v. *Plymouth City Council* [2001] EWCA Civ 1935).

If the claimant can do so, it is best to give the defendant several months to make an offer. If the defendant intends to make an offer but needs more than 21 days, he should ask for it in open correspondence.

The Protocols Practice Direction says at paragraph 4A.1: 'When a person enters into a funding arrangement ... he should inform other potential parties to the claim that he has done so.' Paragraph 4A.2 says that this 'applies to all proceedings whether . . . a pre-action protocol applies or otherwise'. This includes negotiations leading to settlement before proceedings are issued, as the claimant will want costs as well as damages (see, for example, *Crosbie* v. *Munroe* [2003] EWCA Civ 350). If the claim is being run under a conditional fee agreement with after-the-event legal expenses insurance (ATE or AEI), it would be prudent to send all the information required for a court form N251 Notice of Funding. One does not at this stage tell one's opponent the size of the success fee, or the cost of ATE, as these reveal one's assessment of the strength of the claim.

If the claim is publicly funded under the Community Legal Service, the defendant may not be able to recover his costs from the claimant if the claim fails. The claimant should notify the defendant as soon as possible that he has legal aid.

3.3 WHEN TO SETTLE

Early settlement is generally good for the defendant, not the claimant. It may look attractive to a claimant or his lawyer if:

- The claimant is off work, as he may be desperate for money. It may be possible for his lawyer to get him an interim payment so that he stays afloat until the claim can be settled properly (see **section 9.3**).
- The claimant is still receiving state benefits as a result of the accident. The defendant has to repay to the state any benefits paid to the claimant in respect of his injuries, but can offset most or all of these benefits against the claimant's damages (see **section 9.7**). If the claimant is off work for a year or three years, his loss of earnings claim will be the same whether the claim is settled early or late, but the repayable state benefits stop accruing when the claim settles.
- The claimant wants full interest on damages. If settlement is delayed more than three or four years after the accident, there is an increasing risk that the court will deduct interest as a penalty.
- The claimant is stressed about the claim.

- The claimant's lawyer wants to get paid. An interim payment can at least reimburse him the cost of medical reports, etc., that he has purchased on behalf of the claimant.

Whatever the reason for settling early, from the claimant's point of view there are usually better reasons to delay:

- The claim should not be settled while there is too much uncertainty about the claimant's medical future. Provisional damages aside, the claimant gets only one opportunity to settle his claim. Most victims of whiplash, low back injuries and travel anxiety make a complete recovery within two years of the accident. A percentage, say 10 per cent, suffer long-term or permanent symptoms. It is not possible to predict who the long-term sufferers will be. A doctor who is asked to give a prognosis within two years of the accident can only assume that the claimant will recover. If the claimant still has symptoms three years after the accident, it means he is one of the 10 per cent. Only the most straightforward claim should be settled within 18 months of the accident.
- If there is a claim for many years of future losses, the multiplier/multiplicand calculation often gives an extra year's worth of earnings or care compensation for every year's delay in settling (see **section 9.4**).

If the claimant has reasons to delay settling the claim, he has reasons to delay issuing proceedings. These are because:

- Once proceedings are issued, the court imposes a strict timetable that will get the claim to trial in about seven months in the fast track, or less for a Small Claim. It may be hard to comply, particularly with the time limits for exchanging expert evidence. If one fails to comply the judge may impose cost penalties or rule the evidence inadmissible.
- The courts may apply costs penalties to a claimant who issues proceedings without first going through the evidence and arguments in a genuine effort to settle the claim.
- A defendant has to pay most of a successful claimant's legal costs, but there are many reasons why he may not have to pay all of them. The more legal costs run up by the claimant's team, the greater the risk of a costs shortfall.

For a claimant, the only clear disadvantage of delay in issuing proceedings is the negligible one that interest does not start to accrue on damages for pain and suffering until proceedings are served.

Claims have a time limit, usually three years from the date of the accident (see **Chapter 18**). The claimant should settle the claim, or issue and serve proceedings, at least four months before the limitation period expires, but six months is better. This gives time to sort out any unexpected problems.

If the defendant was an uninsured driver and the claimant presently knows where he can be found, he should issue and serve proceedings as early as possible. Losing sight of an uninsured defendant can be a real problem (see **section 7.3**).

3.4 WITHOUT PREJUDICE SAVE AS TO COSTS

A solicitor does, in some situations, have ostensible authority to make binding agreements without instructions from his client. Whether negotiating by letter or speech, it is usually best, unless the client has said what may be agreed, to tell the other side at the outset that one has no authority to make any agreement, and will have to go back to the client for instructions before any agreement is reached. If one party is under a disability, it may be that any agreement also requires the court's approval (see **section 17.7**).

One should also make it clear that the negotiations are 'without prejudice save as to costs'. Certainly any settlement proposals, whether on liability or quantum, should either be in a letter headed without prejudice save as to costs, or made under CPR Part 36. An offer made without prejudice or pursuant to Part 36 is privileged, and the trial judge will not see it until he has determined liability and damages.

The without prejudice privilege is designed to let the parties put their cards on the table in a full and frank way. As long as the material is part of a genuine process of negotiation, it can contain not only discussions of the law and what one is willing to offer, but also admissions about the strengths of the other side's case and the weaknesses of one's own. Only in the most extreme case will the court override the privilege so that the other party may bring without prejudice material to the attention of the trial judge. The test is whether this privilege would act as a cloak for 'blackmail, perjury or other unambiguous impropriety' (*Unilever* v. *Proctor & Gamble* [2000] FSR 344).

The courts are quite ready to find that a letter is without prejudice although it is not so headed, if the party started negotiations expressly on a without prejudice basis and then omitted these words from one letter in the series (*Cheddar Valley Engineering* v. *Chaddlewood Homes* [1992] 4 All ER 942). The court will find that a letter is without prejudice in any case if it was sent as part of a genuine process of negotiation.

Where agreement is reached on all or part of the claim by offer and acceptance within without prejudice letters, and where there is consideration for the agreement, as a rule this creates a contract. If one party breaches the agreement, the other can sue on the contract (see **section 4.19**).

CPR Part 36.19 says: 'A Part 36 offer will be treated as Without Prejudice except as to costs . . . the fact that a Part 36 payment has been made shall not be communicated to the trial judge until all questions of liability and the amount of money to be awarded have been decided.' Neither Part 36 nor without prejudice material should be included in the trial bundle or in an appeal bundle. This rule does not seem to prevent a party referring to a Part 36 offer when applying for an interim payment, as this will not be dealt with by the trial judge. In support of this, under CPR Part 25.9 a similar non-disclosure rule applies to interim payments, so that they cannot be brought to the attention of the trial judge until the end of the trial.

If a party accidentally brings Part 36 or without prejudice material to the attention of the trial judge, the consequences are not always disastrous (*Garratt* v. *Saxby* [2004] EWCA Civ 341). It is for the judge to decide in each case whether a fair trial is still possible.

If one wants to refer the judge to without prejudice material at the end of the trial, with a view to obtaining a better outcome on costs, one should agree a separate bundle of it with the other side beforehand. If one wants to make an offer and also pass on some open material, he should write two letters, one privileged and one open.

If an offer is made in open correspondence, the trial judge will see it and may be influenced by it. A defendant might make an open offer to settle one part of the claim in full and reduce the total below the Small Claims limit. There is no reason why the judge should not know of this.

3.5 ALTERNATIVE DISPUTE RESOLUTION

The main types of alternative dispute resolution (ADR) are arbitration and mediation. The idea is to avoid a trial by encouraging the parties to look for a practical solution to the claim in a mini hearing.

Arbitration is an informal trial. The arbitrator may have some experience as a judge or as a tribunal chairman. The parties hear how the arbitrator proposes to deal with their evidence (whether to hear oral evidence, whether to carry out a site visit, etc.). If satisfied, they agree to be bound by whatever decision the arbitrator reaches.

Mediation is a without prejudice meeting at which a neutral mediator assists the parties to reach agreement. He may help them reach common ground by telling each party how convincing he finds their evidence. If the parties can agree, the mediator helps them embody this in a contract that ends the personal injury dispute. If the paying party fails to honour the contract, the other simply sues on the contract.

In *Cowl* v. *Plymouth City Council* [2001] EWCA Civ 1935 the Court of Appeal stated that 'insufficient attention is paid to the paramount importance of avoiding litigation whenever this is possible' and 'the parties should be asked why a complaints procedure or some other form of ADR has not been used'.

In *Dunnett* v. *Railtrack plc* [2002] EWCA Civ 303 the court had recommended that the parties submit to ADR. The defendant did not do so, and although it won on appeal, it did not get costs. The court said that ADR did not necessarily mean reaching a compromise somewhere between the positions taken by claimant and defendant. A mediator might enable the parties to reach a better result than they could obtain through the courts.

If a party invites its opponent to ADR, the opponent may refuse. If he refuses unreasonably and then wins the case, he can expect the court to impose a costs penalty, departing to some extent from the usual rule that the loser pays the winner's costs. It is for the party who asserts that there was unreasonable refusal to satisfy the court that this was the case (*Halsey* v. *Milton Keynes General NHS Trust* [2004] EWCA Civ 576, also reported as *Steel* v. *Joy*). This case set out the factors to consider when deciding whether a party has unreasonably refused ADR:

- The nature of the dispute. Most cases are suitable for ADR, unless one wants the court to determine issues of law, or to interpret documents.
- The merits of the case. A belief that one's case is watertight may justify refusing ADR, but only if it was reasonable. The court will be alert to the claimant with a weak case who invites the defendant to mediate because he calculates that the defendant 'may at least make a nuisance-value offer to buy off the cost of a mediation and the risk of being penalised in costs for refusing a mediation even if ultimately successful'.
- Whether there had been other attempts at settlement. If an unreasonable settlement offer had been made, or a reasonable offer has been rejected, it may suggest that ADR had little chance of success.
- Whether the cost of the ADR would have been disproportionately high.
- Whether any delay in setting up and attending the ADR would have been prejudicial. This is particularly likely if ADR is proposed late in the day.
- Whether the ADR had a reasonable prospect of success. This is relevant but not crucial. One might reasonably reject ADR if the other party's combative attitude makes it clear that ADR will be a waste of time (*Hurst* v. *Leeming* [2002] EWHC 1051 (Ch)).

In Spring 2003 the Association of British Travel Agents set up the ABTA mediation scheme for compensation claims arising out of package holidays. The scheme provides ADR (at a small fee) for claims of any size.

CHAPTER 4

Liability

A personal injury claim may be based on a tort (negligence, breach of statutory duty, trespass against the person, or possibly nuisance) committed by a tortfeasor. Alternatively, it may be based on breach of contract (see **section 4.7**).

This chapter, as with the rest of the handbook, looks at the law very much in a personal injury context.

Most personal injury claims are based on negligence.

4.1 NEGLIGENCE AND OTHER CLAIMS

The elements of negligence are that the defendant owed the claimant a duty of care; he committed a breach of that duty by act or omission; the foreseeable result of the breach was that the claimant would suffer injury or loss; and the injury and loss were caused by the breach of duty and were not too remote from it. These elements are discussed below in the context of personal injury work (see **sections 4.2–4.5**).

If the claimant can rely on a statutory duty, particularly one for which liability is strict, he has an easier route to compensation than if he can base it only on negligence. Statutory duties include:

- Those relating to workplace health and safety. Some of these duties are strict (see **section 6.6**).
- Section 41 Highways Act 1980, which imposes a duty on highway authorities to maintain highways (see **section 5.2**).
- The Consumer Protection Act 1987 and General Product Safety Regulations 1994. These impose strict liability on manufacturers, providers and sellers for injuries resulting from defective products and services (see **section 5.7**).
- The Animals Act 1971 makes the keeper of an animal, in some situations, strictly liable for any injury it causes (see **section 5.9**).

Nuisance is a rather vague concept. *Cambridge Water Co* v. *Eastern Counties Leather* [1994] 2 AC 264 and *Hunter* v. *Canary Wharf* [1997] UKHL 14 *obiter dicta* by Lord Goff of Chieveley throw doubt on whether damages for personal injuries can now be recovered in nuisance or under the rule in *Rylands* v. *Fletcher* (1868) LR 3 HL 330. In *Hunter* he said 'there is now developing a school of thought that the appropriate remedy for [personal injury claims] should lie in our now fully developed law of negligence, and that personal injury claims should be altogether excluded from the domain of nuisance'. In *Transco* v. *Stockport Borough Council* [2003] UKHL 61 Lord Bingham said, and Lord Hoffman agreed, that a *Rylands* v. *Fletcher* claim 'cannot include a claim for death or personal injury, since such a claim does not relate to any right in or enjoyment of land'. However, as nuisance does not necessarily require fault on the part of the defendant, it still attracts claimants who despair of proving negligence.

There are two sorts of nuisance, private and public. Private nuisance is an interference with a right of enjoyment of land. 'Private nuisance arises out of a state of things on one man's land whereby his neighbour's property is exposed to danger' (*Spicer* v. *Smee* [1946] 1 All ER 489 in which the claimant's bungalow was destroyed by fire caused by defective wiring on his next-door neighbour's property). In *Halsey* v. *Esso Petroleum* [1961] 1 WLR 683 the claimant landowner suffered from inhalation of fumes and noise day and night produced on his neighbour's premises. In *Malone* v. *Laskey* [1907] 2 KB 141 the claimant was a licensee, and vibration from an engine installed by her neighbour caused a tank bracket to give way and injure her. Note that a claim in private nuisance can be made only by somebody having a right to exclusive possession of the property on which the injury occurred: owner, yes; tenant, yes; other members of the family, no. *Hunter* v. *Canary Wharf* [1997] UKHL 14 said '*Khorasandjian v. Bush* [1993] QB 727 must be overruled insofar as it holds that a mere licensee can sue in private nuisance. . .'.

Public nuisance is an unreasonable interference with the reasonable comfort and convenience of some part of the public. It must generally be a continuing problem, a state of affairs rather than an isolated incident. Several classic personal injury cases were based on public nuisance. In *Dymond* v. *Pearce* [1972] 1 All ER 1142 the defendant had left a lorry parked on the highway without good reason for so long that it constituted a public nuisance. The claimant collided with it but his claim failed as the true cause of the accident was his failure to look where he was going. It may be a public nuisance to obstruct the highway by digging an unfenced trench across it, or by causing or permitting any unreasonable obstruction that puts road users at risk. Putting a half inch hosepipe across a country lane for a couple of hours during daylight to provide water during dry weather is not unreasonable (*Trevett* v. *Lee* [1955] 1 WLR 113). Designing a golf course in such a way that balls slice onto the highway may be unreasonable (*Castle* v. *St Augustine's Links* (1922) 38 TLR 615). One modern situation in which a claimant might wish to rely on nuisance is where he is injured, while using the highway, by a slate falling off an apparently sound roof. In the 'latent defect' case *Wringe* v. *Cohen* [1940] 1 KB

229 the Court of Appeal said 'if owing to lack of repair, premises on a highway become dangerous and therefore a nuisance, and a passer-by or an adjoining owner suffers damage by their collapse the occupier, if he has undertaken the duty of repair, is liable whether he knew of the danger or not' (see also *Mint* v. *Good* [1951] 1 KB 517).

As to the rule in *Rylands* v. *Fletcher* (1868) LR 3 HL 330, if someone assembles something dangerous on his property, or he permits something to collect on his property, he can be liable for its escape even if he was not to blame for the escape. Misfeasance, as in *Rylands* v. *Fletcher* (1868) LR 3 HL 330, might involve bringing toxic chemicals onto his land, or collecting water behind an unsound dam. Nonfeasance, as in *Sedleigh-Denfield* v. *O'Callaghan* [1940] AC 880, might involve a trespasser laying a drainage pipe on the defendant's land, the defendant knowing it was blocked but doing nothing about it until floodwater affects his neighbour.

Nuisance presents some thorny problems, so it is unusual for it even to be mentioned in particulars of claim by way of 'belt and braces'. A claimant who adds complex and unnecessary issues may face a hostile costs order.

The other main tort in personal injury work is trespass to the person. A claim relating to deliberate injury must be based on trespass (see **section 4.6**).

In any personal injury claim based on tort:

- damages are calculated in the same way, apart from a slight difference for trespass claims;
- contributory negligence applies to reduce the damages of a claimant whose own negligence contributed to the accident or his injury, again with a slight difference for trespass cases;
- *volenti non fit injuria* applies, so that a claim may fail altogether if the claimant knowingly and freely accepted the risk of injury.

4.2 DUTY OF CARE IN NEGLIGENCE

The defendant may be liable in negligence if:

- he had a duty of care towards the claimant;
- he committed a breach of that duty, by act or omission (see **section 4.3**);
- the foreseeable result of the breach was that the claimant suffered injury or loss;
- the injury and loss were caused by the breach of duty and were not too remote from it (see **section 4.4**).

A duty of care exists in almost all situations where a reasonable person would foresee that his acts or omissions might cause some significant damage or injury to his 'neighbour'. However, the reasonable man would not anticipate every remote possibility, and need pay no attention to a risk of insignificant injury.

A driver owes a duty to pedestrians and other drivers not to injure them by careless driving. An employer owes a duty of care to his employees not to allow them to be injured by the way he runs his business. A manufacturer of goods owes a duty of care to the ultimate user of his products not to manufacture the goods in a negligent way. An occupier of land owes a duty of care to both visitor and trespasser not to injure them or allow them to be injured.

The courts are very ready to find a duty of care not to cause injury by actions, but rather less so where injury is caused by an omission. There is no common law duty to throw a lifebelt to a drowning man, or to shout a warning if one sees that an accident is about to occur. However, many omissions can be seen as negligent ways of carrying out acts, for example failing to refrigerate fresh fish in hot weather before selling it to customers. The courts may find a duty of care for an omission if it arises only within circumstances someone has created. A driver of a vehicle that breaks down while he is driving may be found to have breached his duty of care if he leaves it in a place where it may cause an accident. A shopkeeper must clear up things spilt on his floor, even if his customers spilt them. If someone has control of a child, patient or prisoner, they generally have a duty not to allow that person to be harmed by omission.

In a borderline case, the court will apply the three-fold test stated by Lord Bridge in *Caparo* v. *Dickman* [1990] 2 AC 605. A duty of care will be imposed if the injury or loss was a foreseeable consequence of the defendant's acts or omissions; there is sufficient proximity between defendant and claimant; and it is just and reasonable to impose a duty of care. In other words, any new duty of care must reflect the court's view of public policy.

The courts are generally unwilling to find a duty not to cause injury by negligent misstatements or gestures. For example, a driver beckoning another road user may mean 'It's definitely safe for you to pull out,' but the courts will take the view that he is merely saying 'You can pull out as far as I'm concerned'.

A professional who gives a negligent misstatement in advice to a client, in terms that might foreseeably result in injury, will certainly be liable if the client is injured. A professional may well be held to have a duty of care to third parties. In *Clay* v. *Crump & Sons* [1964] 1 QB 133 building and demolition work was being carried out in accordance with plans drawn up by an architect. The claimant building worker was injured when a wall fell on him as a result. Although the architect drew up the plans for the developer, he had a duty of care to contractors who might be injured by his negligence.

Any defendant may be liable for a negligent misstatement if he had special knowledge and was aware that the claimant was relying on him. For example 'Yes, your safety harness is done up at the back' or 'I cooked the lemon meringue myself and it definitely doesn't have nuts in it.' Consider *Blantern* v. *William Birch Ltd* [1998] EWCA Civ 575.

The legal concept of the neighbour seldom creates any practical problems. Our 'neighbour' in the law of negligence is any person who is so closely and directly affected by our act that we ought reasonably to have them in contemplation as being so affected when we are directing our minds to the acts or omissions in question. If we throw a rock off a cliff, there may be a neighbour standing underneath. If we drive round a blind bend there may be some unknown neighbour coming round the other way (see *Donoghue* v. *Stevenson* [1932] AC 562).

There are still some situations where one might think that a duty of care is owed but in fact it is not. Public bodies are allowed to get away with a great deal. As a matter of public policy, the courts prefer them to be free to carry out their tasks without a constant and disabling fear of litigation (see **section 4.10**).

Somebody who causes a horrifying disaster has a duty of care to those who might be physically injured in it. The courts feel that it would be contrary to public policy to open the floodgates to a torrent of claims by friends, workmates and bystanders who have foreseeably sustained psychiatric injury as a result of witnessing the disaster (see **section 11.11**).

Somebody who employs an independent contractor does not generally owe a duty of care to his neighbours in respect of injury caused by the contractor (see **section 4.9**).

A landlord does not owe a common law duty to his tenant's customers or guests to protect them from injury by the dilapidated state of the premises (*Cavalier* v. *Pope* [1906] AC 428). His statutory duties are quite limited too (see **section 5.6**).

One owes a duty to Mr X not to injure him, but not a duty of care to his employer, business partner, employees or spouse not to cause loss to them by injuring him. Section 2 Administration of Justice Act 1982 says: 'No person shall be liable in tort . . . to a husband on the ground only of his having deprived him of the services or society of his wife [nor] to a parent (or person standing in the place of a parent) on the ground only of his having deprived him of the services of a child; or on the ground only of having deprived another of the services of his menial servant.' Likewise, although one probably owes a duty of care to Mr X not to injure him, one does not owe a duty of care to his son not to deprive him of Mr X's parental services (*Buckley* v. *Farrow* [1997] EWCA Civ 918). Claims under the Fatal Accidents Act 1976 are, in a sense, an exception to this (see **Chapter 15**).

The claim cannot succeed unless a person in the defendant's position would reasonably have foreseen at the time of his act or omission a risk that some injury, loss or damage might result from it. The claim may succeed although the risk was slight. It will not succeed if the risk of an accident was insignificant. In *Bolton* v. *Stone* [1951] 1 All ER 1078 there had been only a 'remote possibility' that a passer-by would be struck by a cricket ball hit out of the defendant's ground. That was not enough. If a situation has existed for some time without causing any injury, the courts may feel it was not reasonably foreseeable that it would. In *C (a child)* v. *Nottingham City Council*

[2000] CL November, the claimant was injured because a door had been glazed with thin glass. The door had been like that since 1948, with no other similar accident ever reported, and thus the claim failed.

Neither will the claim succeed if the injury that any foreseeable accident might produce would have been insignificant. In *Burke* v. *Lancashire County Council* [2001] EWCA Civ 1679, the claimant was severely injured when chairs stacked by a student toppled onto her at college. Her claim failed, partly because no reasonably careful member of staff would have thought that if the chairs fell over 'they would cause any injury of any seriousness' (see also *Fryer* v. *Pearson* (2000) *The Times*, 4 April).

4.3 STANDARD OF CARE IN NEGLIGENCE

If the defendant had a duty of care, did he breach that duty? How careful should he have been?

Certainly he must not be reckless. A person is reckless if they recognise an obvious risk of damage or loss, but instead of giving any thought to it, take the risk. This is the threshold for the liability of a landowner to people exercising the statutory right to roam over his land (see **section 5.5**).

However, the threshold for liability in negligence is set much lower than that. 'Negligence is the omission to do something which a reasonable man, guided upon the considerations which ordinarily regulate the conduct of human affairs, would do; or doing something which a prudent and reasonable man would not do' (*Blyth* v. *Birmingham Waterworks* (1856) 11 Exch 781). In other words, to satisfy a duty of care, a person must take reasonable care judged by the standard of the ordinary reasonable man. The reasonable man is reasonably prudent. He knows what the ordinary man knows, but has no special skill in predicting the future.

Children are allowed some leeway, being required only to reach the standard of the ordinarily prudent and reasonable child of that age (see **sections 4.12** and **4.13**).

In some situations, a slightly higher standard of care applies than that of the reasonable man. A doctor or other professional with special skills is judged by the standard of the ordinary person who has that particular skill, so a GP's work is judged by the standard of the ordinary GP (see **section 5.11**). A parent, or a teacher looking after pupils, is judged by the standard of the reasonably careful parent. A teacher is also a professional, and the success of his teaching will be judged by the professional standard (see section 5.12). An employer is judged by the standard of the reasonably prudent employer (see **section 6.5**).

Is there any leeway for those who are learning a new skill, and have no choice but to do so in the real world? It is no answer for the defendant to say '"I was a learner driver under instruction. I was doing my best and I could not help it" . . . he must drive in as good a manner as a driver of skill, experience and care, who is sound in wind and limb, and who makes no errors of judgement, has good eyesight and hearing, and is free from any infirmity' (*Nettleship* v. *Weston* [1971] 3 All ER 581). The same applies to a doctor learning the ropes in a new job (*Wilsher* v. *Essex Area Health Authority* [1987] 2 WLR 425).

It is seldom a defence to say 'I only did what everybody else does in this industry/at this road junction'.

The common sense of the reasonable man doesn't always enable one to say whether a defendant satisfied his duty of care. If the situation is outside the common routine of householder, road user or pedestrian, one may need to refer to written standards. These can be found in regulations, British Standards, a code of practice, or similar cases already decided by the courts (see **section 5.14**). Occasionally one needs expert evidence (see **section 20.8**).

4.4 CAUSATION OF INJURY AND LOSS

A claimant must show that his injury and loss were caused by the defendant's act or omission, and that they were sufficiently proximate to the act or omission.

It is not enough to show that the damage occurred after the act or omission, although where causation is unclear and the damage occurred soon enough after the event (a temporal connection), the court is sometimes willing to infer that the event caused the damage.

The test is that the damage would not have occurred 'but for' the defendant's act or omission. The claimant's standard of proof is the balance of probabilities. In other words: 'The plaintiff gets nothing if he fails to establish that it is more likely than not that the accident resulted in the injury' (*Allied Maples Group* v. *Simmons & Simmons* [1995] 1 WLR 1602). If the defendant's negligence deprived the claimant of a 51 per cent chance of escaping injury, he is entitled to full compensation.

In *Hotson* v. *East Berkshire Health Authority* [1987] AC 750 the claimant fractured his femur falling out of a tree. This ruptured enough blood vessels to give a 75 per cent chance of necrosis in the joint. He was taken to the defendant's hospital. It took them five days to diagnose the injury correctly, and this negligence made necrosis inevitable. The House of Lords held that: 'Unless the plaintiff proves on a balance of probabilities that the delayed treatment was at least a material contributory cause of the avascular necrosis he fails on the issue of causation and no question of quantification can arise.'

Hotson means that there can be no claim for merely losing a chance of escaping injury. If someone would probably have suffered the injury anyway, they are not entitled to any compensation. The trial judge in *Hotson* remains unconvinced by this. 'If I consult a doctor about a specific condition and, through the doctor's negligence in diagnosis or treatment, reduce from 49 per cent to 5 per cent my chance of averting an adverse outcome, not everyone would think it "just and reasonable" that my claim must inevitably fail on the issue of causation' (Simon Brown LJ in *Gregg* v. *Scott* [2002] EWCA Civ 1471).

The 'but for' test applies in the overwhelming majority of cases. But for the defendant driver's failure to look where he was going, probably he would not have collided with the claimant. But for the defendant spilling oil on the floor, probably the claimant would not have slipped and fallen.

Where there is scientific uncertainty about the nature of the claimant's injury, the court may well not accept that the defendant's negligence caused it. In the multiple sclerosis case *Dingley* v. *Chief Constable of Strathclyde Police* [2000] UKHL 14 the House of Lords confirmed that a claim cannot succeed on the balance of probabilities unless there is a satisfactory explanation of the way the negligence caused the injury.

The courts are willing to make an exception to the 'but for' test in some situations. These are usually cases of industrial disease. The problem with these cases is that the injury is caused not by one incident, but by steady exposure to hazardous substances over a period of time, and often by a succession of different employers. The claimant cannot prove that 'but for' the negligence of any single employer, he would not have the disease. If he cannot satisfy the 'but for' test, he has to show only that his employer materially contributed to his injury.

The material contribution test is also used if the claimant has industrial disease from exposure to a particular substance or process where part of the exposure was permitted by law. In *Bonnington Castings* v. *Wardlaw* [1956] AC 613 the claimant was exposed to silica dust at work by two machines. As a result he got pneumoconiosis. The employer was negligent in respect of only one of the machines, which did not have an adequate dust extractor. There was 'innocent dust' and 'guilty' or 'tortious' dust. Although most of the dust was 'innocent', the defective machine had contributed to the injury in a way that was not trivial. 'I think the natural inference is that had it not been for the cumulative effect, the Pursuer would not have developed pneumoconiosis when he did, and might not have developed it at all.' The employer was liable to compensate him for all his pain, suffering and loss.

In some cases where the claimant cannot even prove that the defendant materially contributed to his injury, the court may be willing to find liability if the defendant merely 'materially contributed' to the risk that the claimant might be injured. In *McGhee* v. *National Coal Board* [1972] 3 All ER 1008 the claimant's workplace contained a lot of brick dust. Although this can cause dermatitis, it was acceptable as the law stood at the time. However, his employers negligently failed to provide a shower for use at the end of his shift, so he had it on his skin for longer than necessary. The dermatitis was clearly caused by brick dust and nothing else. The claim was allowed on the basis that the negligence had materially contributed to the risk of dermatitis.

In *Wilsher* v. *Essex Area Health Authority* [1988] AC 1074 the claimant was a premature baby who contracted RLF (retrolental fibroplasia). The defendant had negligently exposed him to excess oxygen, which can cause RLF. However, at about the same time, the baby also suffered hypercarbia, intraventricular haemorrhage, apnoea and patent ductus arteriosus, which were just as likely as the excess oxygen to have caused the RLF. These were not the defendant's fault. The House of Lords held that the *McGhee* principle could not apply if all the claimant can prove is that his injury could have been caused by a number of things, only one of which was the defendant's negligence.

In *Fairchild* v. *Glenhaven Funeral Services Ltd* [2002] UKHL 22, the claimant contracted mesothelioma from exposure to asbestos. He was unable to prove that his injury would not have occurred but for the defendant's negligence. He could not even prove that the negligence had contributed to the mesothelioma, as it might have been caused by a single strand of asbestos that was nothing to do with the defendant. The House of Lords awarded damages as the defendant had a duty of care which was specifically intended to protect employees from being unnecessarily exposed to asbestos; the duty was intended to create a right to compensation; the defendant had breached its duty in a way that may have caused the injury; mesothelioma can be caused only by asbestos; medical science could not prove how the injury occurred; the greater the exposure to asbestos, the greater the risk of mesothelioma; and the claimant had the very disease from which the defendant should have protected him.

There are a few material contribution cases that do not involve industrial disease. *Hutchinson* v. *Epsom & St Helier NHS Trust* [2002] EWHC 2363 (QB) arose from the death of a patient who died of liver disease caused by years of alcoholism and extreme obesity. The defendant's failure to warn him to give up drinking had materially contributed to his death at the age of 51. Had he been warned to give up drinking and lose weight he would have lived to 60. The defendant had to pay the fatal accident claim in full. Less controversially, see *Chapman* v. *Tangmere Airfield Nurseries* [1998] EWCA Civ 1730 (a fall at work) and *Durnford* v. *Western Atlas* [2003] EWCA Civ 306 (a prolapsed disc at work).

The second part of the causation test is whether the damage was sufficiently proximate to the negligence. To put it another way, was the damage too remote? If a reasonable man would have foreseen any damage to the claimant as likely to result from his act or omission, then he is liable for all the direct consequences of it suffered by the claimant, whether a reasonable man would have foreseen them or not (*Bradford* v. *Robinson Rentals* [1967] 1 WLR 337 and *Page* v. *Smith* [1996] AC 155).

Say a garage does a negligent job of repairing the claimant's motorbike, so that it might foreseeably seize up while he is riding along. It is plainly foreseeable that some injury or damage might result. The bike seizes up, the claimant comes off and gets a broken rib when he hits the tarmac. The garage is liable for this injury. While still tumbling along the motorway, he is hit by a vehicle that had no chance to avoid him, and gets a broken wrist. This is a direct consequence of the negligence, and the garage is liable. He then continues his journey by train. Before he gets to London the train crashes and he gets a broken leg. This would not have happened but for the negligence, but it is too remote from it.

The chain of causation may be broken by the intervention of a third party. If the claimant steps on a rusty nail through the defendant's negligence, goes to hospital for a tetanus injection and is given a lethal injection by a drunken doctor, the chain of causation is broken by this *novus actus interveniens* (intervening new cause). The more wilful or serious the intervention, the more likely it is to break the chain.

The rules of remoteness say that 'a defendant has to take his victim as he finds him'. Otherwise known as the eggshell skull rule, this applies to any sort of vulnerability. The classic case is *Smith* v. *Leech Brain & Co Ltd* [1962] 2 QB 405 in which the claimant suffered a burn to his lip owing to the defendant's negligence. Because he happened to be particularly vulnerable, the burn turned into a fatal cancer. As there was an unbroken chain of causation from negligence to death, the defendant was liable although the extent of the claimant's injury and loss was unforeseeable.

In *Pigney* v. *Pointer's Transport Services Ltd* [1957] 1 WLR 1121, the victim suffered physical injuries as a result of which he became depressed. The effect of the depression on his pre-accident personality was to make him commit suicide. The defendant was held liable for the suicide which was found not to have broken the chain of causation.

In *Lagden* v. *O'Connor* [2003] UKHL 64 the House of Lords extended the eggshell skull rule so that it now also applies to the victim's finances. If the claimant was too poor to take cost-effective steps to limit the damage caused by the defendant, the defendant cannot expect damages to be assessed as if the claimant did take those steps. If the defendant damaged the claimant's car and he had neither savings nor fully comprehensive insurance to have it repaired promptly, the defendant will have to pay the car hire bill.

4.5 MULTIPLE TORTFEASORS

If two tortfeasors cause two different injuries to the claimant, each is responsible only for the injury he caused. Each is a several tortfeasor. In *Rahman* v. *Arearose* [2000] EWCA Civ 190 the claimant suffered an eye injury because of his employer's negligence. The employer had to compensate him for an eye injury and a phobia. The claimant went to hospital for treatment and received negligent medical treatment that left him blind in the injured eye and worsened his psychiatric problems. The court found that the injuries could, with difficulty, be divided between the two tortfeasors, and did so.

If the combined negligence of two tortfeasors caused the claimant's injuries, and one cannot realistically attribute part of the injury to one particular tortfeasor, they are joint and several tortfeasors and are both liable for all the claimant's injuries. For example, the claimant is a passenger in the first defendant's car, and is injured when there is a collision with the second defendant's vehicle. The collision was caused by the negligent driving of both, and can sue either of them for the full amount of his loss.

If two tortfeasors are liable for the same injuries, but for different reasons, their liability is said to be concurrent. In *Grant* v. *Sun Shipping Co Ltd* [1948] AC 549 the claimant fell through an open hatch while unloading a ship. The hatch had been negligently left open by the ship repairers, who were liable concurrently with the shipowners as the latter had breached their duty to provide the claimant with a safe place of work. As with joint and several liability, the claimant can recover all his damages from either or both of concurrent tortfeasors.

Say the claimant suffers industrial disease because he was exposed to risk by several employers in succession. Can he sue just one of them, and get all his damages from that one? The question is whether the injury is divisible or indivisible. Industrial deafness is divisible. The longer the exposure goes on, the deafer someone gets, so no defendant will be liable to pay for more than its share of the deafness (*Thompson* v. *Smiths Ship Repairers* [1984] 1 QB 405).

Asbestosis is also divisible. In *Holtby* v. *Brigham & Cowan (Hull) Ltd* [2000] EWCA Civ 111 the claimant spent half his working life exposed to asbestos by the defendant's negligence. The defendant was liable because it had materially contributed to his injury, but he had also been exposed to asbestos elsewhere. He would have got asbestosis, although not as badly, even if the defendant had not been negligent. His case was that if the defendant had made a material contribution to the disease, it should pay for all the injury and loss caused by the disease. The Court of Appeal said that a tortfeasor should pay only for the part that it had caused. Mr Holtby lost 25 per cent of his potential damages.

Mesothelioma is indivisible, because it could be caused by a single strand of asbestos. In the fatal case of *Barker* v. *St Gobain* [2004] EWCA Civ 545, the deceased had been exposed to asbestos by the negligence of the defendant. At other times in his career he had also been exposed to it by another employer and by his own negligence while self-employed as a plasterer. The Court of Appeal refused any deduction to allow for the other employer's contribution. (However it approved a 20 per cent deduction for the claimant's own contributory negligence.)

4.6 LAW OF TRESPASS

The tort of trespass against the person includes:

- Assault. Technically, an act of the defendant that causes the claimant reasonable fear that the defendant will commit a battery on him. Everywhere else in this handbook, assault is used in its everyday meaning.
- Battery. The intentional and direct application of force to another person. 'Any touching of another's body is, in the absence of lawful excuse, capable of amounting to a battery and a trespass' (*F* v. *West Berkshire Health Authority* [1990] 2 AC 1). Lawful excuses include self-defence, a parent's wish to control his or her child, a right to eject a trespasser, and the claimant's having consented to the general circumstances within which the force was applied, as in *Blake* v. *Galloway* [2004] EWCA Civ 814. Of course a police officer has wide powers to use force. Even where there is a lawful reason for using force, the amount and type must not be excessive. The damages for a very trivial battery would be very low, and might be outweighed by the claimant's share of the legal costs.
- False imprisonment. The infliction of bodily restraint that is not authorised by the law (see **section 5.10**).
- Making false statements calculated to cause harm as in *Wilkinson* v. *Downton* [1897] 2 QB 57, or *Janvier* v. *Sweeney* [1919] 2 KB 316 where the defendant wanted to get hold of letters written by the claimant's employer, and so told her that she was wanted for corresponding with a German spy. The shock to the claimant caused neurasthenia and shingles, and her compensation claim was successful. The defendant will be liable if he intended physical or psychiatric injury; or if he knew such injury was likely; or if such injury was so likely to occur that he cannot fairly say: 'I didn't mean any harm.'
- Harassment. It is an offence under the Protection from Harassment Act 1997 to carry out 'a course of conduct which amounts to harassment of another and which [the defendant] knows or ought to know amounts to harassment of the other'. This includes stalking, threatening phone calls, and bullying at work. It is a defence if the conduct was to prevent or detect crime, was required by law, or was reasonable in the circumstances. To amount to a course of conduct, there must be at least two incidents. Section 3(2) of the Act says that the civil courts may award damages for suffering and loss including 'any anxiety caused by the harassment and any financial loss resulting from the harassment' (see CPR Part 65.27–30).

If the defendant intended to injure the claimant, the claimant cannot sue in negligence. A civil claim can only be based on trespass (*Stubbings* v. *Webb* [1993] AC 498). Neither malice nor an intention to injure the claimant are essential elements of trespass. It seems that a claim for negligent trespass to the person must be based on negligence and not trespass (*Letang* v. *Cooper*

[1965] 1 QB 232 in which the claimant was accidentally run over while sunbathing).

As with negligence, the burden of proof is on the claimant. He must prove what he asserts. As with negligence, the standard of proof is the balance of probabilities. The claimant must prove that his version of events is more likely than not to be the true one. Although the standard of proof is exactly the same as in negligence, it is often harder to satisfy. This apparent contradiction arises because negligence generally relates to events that are easy to believe, for example that the defendant was driving too fast to be safe. A serious allegation of trespass, however, alleges that the defendant did something socially quite unacceptable, something that only a tiny percentage of the population would do. Child abuse is an example. If an allegation is improbable, it is harder to persuade a court that it probably happened.

Damages for trespass are calculated in the same way as for other torts, save that the claimant can recover for injury and losses that would be too remote if caused by another tort, and he may be entitled to aggravated or exemplary damages. The major difference between trespass and other torts is that in cases of accidental injury, the Limitation Act 1980 gives the claimant three years to bring a claim and gives the court discretion to extend this period, but in a trespass case the time limit for bringing a claim is six years with no extension. This has implications in child abuse cases (see **section 5.13**).

It is unclear whether the court will reduce the claimant's compensation because, for example, he taunted his assailant. Compensation was reduced in *Murphy* v. *Culhane* [1977] QB 94 because the victim voluntarily participated in a fight that led to his death, and in *Revill* v. *Newberry* [1996] 1 All ER 291 where the claimant was a burglar who was shot by his intended victim. However, *Standard Chartered Bank v. Pakistan National Shipping* [2002] UKHL 43 casts doubt on *Murphy*.

For a successful claim based on domestic violence, see *Richardson* v. *Howie* [2004] EWCA Civ 1127. In this case, the court considered the status of aggravated damages, and concluded that in a case of deliberate injury they are compensatory. The victim is entitled to expect aggravated damages to compensate for injury to his feelings from 'the indignity, mental suffering, humiliation or distress that might be caused by such an attack, as well as anger or indignation arising from the circumstances of the attack'.

When a claimant lawyer is deciding whether to take on a domestic violence claim, it is as well to note that a claimant who knows the assailant may decide to drop the claim when the initial outrage subsides. Only 3 per cent of domestic violence complaints to the police end in a conviction. Compensation under the Criminal Injuries Compensation Scheme is seldom available for an adult victim where assailant and victim were living together at the time of the assault and are still doing so.

Particularly in cases of domestic violence, it may be necessary to obtain an injunction to reduce the risk of further assaults. If there is much delay in requesting an injunction, the court may be unwilling to grant one.

A defendant's insurance policies are unlikely to cover him for inflicting deliberate injury. Even if the defendant's insurance appears to cover him for the effects of his own wilful acts, the law may prevent this (see *Gray* v. *Barr* [1971] 2 QB 554 (fatal shooting when insured used a shotgun in threat) and *Churchill Insurance v. Charlton* [2001] EWCA Civ 112 (insured motorist rammed another vehicle in a car park)). However, if the incident was one that required the culprit to have insurance under s.151 Road Traffic Act 1988, the insurers must satisfy the victim's claim.

Apart from being a tort, trespass to the person is likely to be a crime. The main offences are actual bodily harm (ABH) and grievous bodily harm (GBH). ABH is an offence under s.47 Offences Against the Person Act 1861, and GBH is an offence under s.18 of that Act.

A prosecution may bar a civil claim. In *Wong* v. *Parkside Health NHS Trust* [2001] EWCA Civ 1721 the Court of Appeal said: 'If the authorities choose to prosecute, there is no problem. But if they do not, [the claimant] must choose between bringing a private prosecution or a civil action. The former will destroy [the claimant's] right to bring the latter, irrespective of the outcome' (see s.42–45 Offences Against the Person Act 1861).

It is unusual for a victim to make a civil claim for damages for trespass. Most prefer an award under the Criminal Injuries Compensation Scheme (see **sections 8.1–8.6**). There is also the possibility of a Compensation Order through the criminal courts (see **section 8.7**).

4.7 LAW OF CONTRACT

Liability for breach of contract can be easier to establish than liability for a tort. Injury and loss may arise from a breach of contract between consumer and retailer, holidaymaker and tour operator, employer and employee, or landlord and tenant, a lease being a contract.

The breach may be of an express term (I give you £10, in return you ferry me over to the Hebrides) or an implied term (you will perform this service with reasonable care and skill). Some implied terms are inserted by the common law because they are normal and necessary (the car is mine to sell), others by consumer protection statutes.

Claims for breach of contract can be brought only between the parties to the original contract. This privity of contract has a few exceptions:

- Under the Contracts (Rights of Third Parties) Act 1999, a seller's liability to his original buyer can be extended to any third party.

- The purchaser may have been acting as the claimant's agent. For example one member of a family buys a meal for the whole family and it is somebody else in the party who gets the 'salmonella sandwich'.
- The seller may have been acting as the defendant's agent. A travel agent can commit a tour operator to a binding contract with a holidaymaker, so the tour operator can be sued.

The defendant may be able to rely upon an express term in the contract that limits his liability. This will be effective unless it is unfair. A term excluding liability for death or personal injury will usually be ineffective (see **section 4.16**).

Ambiguity in a contract is construed *contra proferentem* – against the interests of the party who drew it up.

Specialist textbooks describe the various possible defences to a claim for breach of contract. It is in general no defence that the defendant took all reasonable care to avoid breaching the contract. One defence that arises from time to time in personal injury work is that the contract was for an illegal purpose and is therefore unenforceable. In Latin, *ex turpi causa non oritur actio*, which means roughly 'the courts won't help anybody recover compensation or indemnity if the claim is founded in his own crime'. A contract to do something illegal, for example, to launder money, is wholly unenforceable. An employee with a contract to do this could not claim compensation for personal injury based on breach of it.

Exceptionally, a contract that was legal at the outset could become wholly unenforceable if its performance comes to depend on something illegal. Far more often there will be some incidental illegality about the way a contract is performed, for example a modest amount of tax evasion in the performance of an employment contract. This does not bar a personal injury claim (see **section 13.4**).

Contributory negligence does generally apply to personal injury claims based on contract. It applies to claims based on breach of a contractual duty of care (*Artingstoll* v. *Hewen's Garages* [1973] RTR 197). It does not apply to claims based on breach of a strict contractual duty, unless the claim could just as well have been based on tort.

If the defendant's breach of contract caused an injury, the facts generally show that he was negligent too. Since the CPR 1998 the courts have begun deducting a percentage of the claimant's costs if he pursues issues on which he is unsuccessful, or which he does not rely on at trial. However, a personal injury claimant who relies on breach of contract will still usually state in his particulars of claim that the defendant acted negligently and in breach of contract.

Damages for a claim based on breach of contract are calculated in broadly the same way as damages for any other personal injury claim, with four main exceptions:

1. In contract, the defendant is liable only for losses 'arising naturally, i.e. according to the usual course of things, from [the] breach of contract itself, or such as may reasonably be supposed to have been in the contemplation of both parties, at the time they made the contract, as the probable result of breach of it' (*Hadley* v. *Baxendale* (1854) 9 Exch 341). Contrast this with the eggshell skull rule which applies to claims based on tort, and which makes the defendant liable for injury and loss arising from an unknown vulnerability. In *Kemp* v. *Intasun Holidays Ltd* (1988) 6 Tr L 161 the claimant holidaymaker had been given dusty accommodation that caused a serious asthma attack. The claimant could not succeed in a personal injury claim based on breach of contract as the defendant had not known that the claimant had asthma.
2. Although in contract a claimant can recover damages for 'a loss of a kind which the defendant, when he made the contract, ought to have realized was not unlikely to result from a breach of contract' this does not mean that the defendant will be liable for 'loss or damage which on the knowledge available to the defendant would appear to him as only likely to occur in a small minority of cases' (*Koufos* v. *Czarnikow* [1969] 1 AC 350). This case is sometimes cited as *The Heron II*. This test of remoteness of damage seems slightly different to that used in tort. Consider *Berryman* v. *Hounslow London Borough Council* [1996] EWCA Civ 1001 and see **section 4.4**.
3. In claims based on tort, the claimant is not entitled to extra damages for inconvenience and mental distress that fall short of being a recognisable psychiatric disorder. In a claim based on breach of contract, the claimant may be entitled to damages for these things if the contract was designed to give pleasure, relaxation, peace of mind or freedom from molestation.
4. Pure economic loss. A loss which is not connected with or flowing from any damage to person or property is more likely to be recoverable in contract than in tort. A claim against a defendant alleging that he caused injury does not, by definition, include pure economic loss. A negligence claim against a company director for failing to take out employer's liability insurance, so that when the company was insolvent there was no money to compensate an injured employee, is a claim for pure economic loss (see *Richardson* v. *Pitt-Stanley* [1995] 1 All ER 460).

4.8 VICARIOUS LIABILITY

At common law, an employer or vehicle owner may be liable for the tort of his employee or driver without being blameworthy himself.

Employers are very often vicariously liable for torts committed by their employees in the course of employment, for example, the claimant who is knocked down by the defendant's company vehicle because of the negligent driving of the defendant's employed driver.

Employers are also liable for torts done by an employee with the employer's express or implied permission. Although this is often said to be an example of vicarious liability, it could equally be said that the employer who authorises a tort is directly liable to anybody injured by it.

'Employee'? An employer is vicariously liable for his employees, but not for self-employed people who work for him as independent contractors. It is often difficult even for the people concerned to work out whether the relationship is employer-employee, or employer-independent contractor. It seems the courts will apply the same test when deciding whether a worker was an employee for health and safety purposes and for vicarious liability purposes. See the speeches of Mummery and Sedley LJJ in *Brook Street Bureau* v. *Dacas* [2004] EWCA Civ 217. In general, see **section 6.16**.

A claimant can easily reach the stage of issuing proceedings without knowing whether the culprit was an employee acting in the course of employment. He could sue both the culprit and the apparent employer, but may suffer a costs penalty if it proves that the employer is not liable. Well before the time when he must issue proceedings, the claimant should ask the employer's insurers to give a simple open admission that the culprit was at all material times acting in the course of his employment with their insured. If they do, the claimant can leave the employee out of the proceedings. If they do not, the record will show that the claimant tried to save these costs.

'In the course of his employment'? The employer will not be vicariously liable if the employee was using the vehicle for his own personal purposes, for example, to move his belongings to a new flat on a Sunday. He is then said to have been off on a frolic of his own. In *Hilton* v. *Thomas Burton Ltd* [1961] 1 WLR 705, employees were allowed to use the employer's van to go to a cafe when they had finished the day's tasks. There was a fatal accident, and the employer was not vicariously liable.

An employee is not in the course of his employment when using his own car to drive to the office for a 9 a.m. start. He may be if he uses it during the working day to pick up some stationery or go to a meeting. Was he being paid wages for the time he is behind the wheel? See *Smith* v. *Stages* [1989] 2 WLR 529, where some insulation fitters were paid for travelling time, and the employer was liable when one of them caused a fatal car crash on the way back from a job.

The main test is whether the employee was carrying out the employer's business or not. An employer cannot escape liability by arguing that the employee was carrying out his duties in an improper way. A nightclub bouncer who kicks a customer down the club steps may be acting in an unauthorised way, but is still carrying out his employer's business.

It seems that an employer may be vicariously liable for the act of an employee even if he had forbidden the act, e.g. where an employed delivery driver causes an accident by speeding or taking a forbidden short cut. In *Rose* v. *Plenty* [1976] 1 WLR 141 a milkman was carrying a boy on his milk float to help with deliveries. The employer had forbidden this, but was nonetheless liable for the milkman's negligence when he negligently injured the boy.

The employer will not be liable if the employee was outside the scope of his employment. This is where the law of vicarious liability gets unpredictable. An employee is not in the course of his employment if he is doing something that was not his job. For example, a man employed to work on the door of a nightclub as a bouncer may not be in the course of his employment if he offers to park a customer's car on his own initiative.

However, the court is prepared to take a pretty broad view, and might well accept that the bouncer had implied authority to drive and park the car if a drunken customer had left it in a place amounting to a security risk, or if the employer knew he had done it before but had not said anything.

If the injury caused by the employee's act was covered by the employer's insurance, it is highly likely that the court will find the employer vicariously liable, one way or another.

For a survey of the case law, see the Court of Appeal case of *Fennelly* v. *Connex South Eastern* [2001] IRLR 390. In *Fennelly* a railway ticket inspector asked a passenger for his ticket. There was a confrontation, which escalated into a headlock. The judge at first instance thought that a point was reached where the inspector was no longer in the course of his employment as he was merely getting his own back. The Court of Appeal disagreed.

See also *Mattis* v. *Pollock* [2003] EWCA Civ 887, in which the defendant nightclub owner was vicariously liable for a stabbing carried out by a bouncer. The defendant had 'wished to employ someone as a doorman who could be relied upon to intimidate customers,' and the stabbing was closely connected with his duties.

Since *Fennelly*, the ambit of vicarious liability has been widened by *Lister* v. *Hesley Hall Ltd* [2001] UKHL 22. In *Lister* the House of Lords found that the operators of a residential school were vicariously liable for sexual abuse carried out by a warden they employed because there was enough connection between the work he was employed to do and the abuse itself. Sexually abusing a child could never represent carrying out the employer's business in an unauthorised way. However, the House of Lords found that in a children's home 'there is an inherent risk that indecent assaults on the residents will be committed by those placed in authority over them'. A special relationship exists between the operator of the home and the children. This justifies making the operator liable for abuse of residents by employees. This special relationship also exists between school and pupil, and prison and prisoner. It may exist between hospital and patient, especially if the patient is elderly.

The principle of vicarious liability also applies to some road traffic situations where the culprit is not an employee. If the owner of a vehicle asks or allows a friend to drive it for the owner's purposes, the owner is vicariously liable for his torts (see *Ormrod* v. *Crosville Motor Services Ltd* [1953] 1 WLR 1120, or *Candler* v. *Thomas* [1996] EWCA Civ 1222).

After an accident in which an uninsured person was driving somebody else's car, often neither the driver nor the owner will respond to letters or phone calls. Where nobody will say why the vehicle was being used, there is a presumption that the driver was acting as the owner's agent (*Morgans* v. *Launchbury* [1973] AC 127).

Section 143 of the Road Traffic Act 1988 makes it an offence to 'cause or permit any . . . person to use a motor vehicle on a road unless there is in force in relation to the use of the vehicle by that other person . . . a policy of insurance' as required by the Act in respect of third party risks. Although breach of the Act cannot generally be used to found a civil claim for compensation, it seems that this is an exception. A person injured by the negligence of an uninsured driver may claim against the owner who permitted the uninsured use, whether the use was for the benefit of driver or owner (*Monks* v. *Warbey* [1935] 1 KB 75).

The owner of a taxi firm can be liable for the acts and omissions of his drivers (London Hackney Carriages Act 1843 and Town Police Clauses Act 1847).

Financial services companies can be liable for defects in goods purchased on credit or hire purchase. See s.75 of the Consumer Credit Act 1974, which says that 'if the debtor under a debtor-creditor-supplier agreement falling within s.12(b) or (c) has, in relation to a transaction financed by the agreement, any claim against the supplier in respect of a misrepresentation or breach of contract, he shall have a like claim against the creditor who, with the supplier, shall accordingly be jointly and severally liable to the debtor'. In other words, where a purchase has been made using a credit card, the credit card company is liable for misrepresentation and breach of contract alongside the actual seller. This applies to purchases between £100 and £30,000.

4.9 LIABILITY FOR INDEPENDENT CONTRACTORS

The claimant was sitting in his garden when he was hit by a slate dropped off his neighbour's roof by a roofing contractor. The contractor is uninsured, has no assets, and disappears to avoid being sued. Can the claimant sue his neighbour instead?

An employer may be vicariously liable for the torts of his employees (see **section 4.8**). As a rule a person is not liable for things done by an independent contractor. To tell the difference, see **section 6.16**.

A person can be liable for operations carried out on the highway by his independent contractor if they cause danger to people using it, for instance when repairing a lamp bracket (see the comments on *Tarry* v. *Ashton* (1876) 1 QBD 314 in *Wringe* v. *Cohen* [1940] 1 KB 229). If a contractor is asked to excavate earth from a trench in the highway and leaves the spoil in an unlit heap on the road, dealing with the spoil is an integral part of the activity for which the contractor was employed and one can be liable to a pedestrian who trips over it (*Penny* v. *Wimbledon Urban District Council* [1899] 2 QB 72). However, if the pedestrian is injured when he trips on tools carelessly left on the pavement by the contractor, or the contractor reverses a vehicle into him, that cause of the injury is merely incidental to the work and only the contractor himself can be liable (*Rowe* v. *Herman* [1997] EWCA Civ 1633).

An employer can be liable for extra-hazardous things done by his independent contractor, as the court will expect the employer to ensure that the contractor goes about the job carefully. The court in *Salsbury* v. *Woodland* [1969] 3 All ER 863 said that activities are extra hazardous if they are 'dangerous even if carried out with caution by those skilled in the activity'. This generally means a risk of fire or explosion, as in *Honeywell & Stein* v. *Larkin Bros* [1934] 1 KB 191.

Under the Occupiers' Liability Act 1957, if a visitor to premises is injured as a result of work done by an independent contractor on behalf of the occupier, the occupier will be liable if he was unreasonable to entrust the job to the contractor, or should have checked the work himself. This may require the occupier to check whether the contractor is insured against personal injury claims (see **section 5.5**).

A person can always be liable for his own negligence, of course. To return to the example at the start of this section, if the roofer dropped the slate because the householder got in his way, or because the householder told him it was safe to do so, the householder himself was negligent. The householder might be liable if he has reason to suspect that the roofer is using an unsafe system of work but does nothing (*Ferguson* v. *Welsh* [1987] 1 WLR 1553 and *Clark v. Hosier & Dickson* [2003] EWCA Civ 1467).

4.10 LOCAL AUTHORITY AS DEFENDANT

Although a local authority is made up of various departments, it is a single body corporate and not a collection of separate legal entities.

Some acts by a local authority, for example a decision to give £100,000 to a free pop festival rather than to fire prevention or to the highways department, are non-justiciable. The courts will not decide how a local authority should exercise its discretion on matters of policy (*Phelps* v. *London Borough of Hillingdon* [2000] UKHL 47). There are, however, many ways in which a local authority may be liable to pay compensation for injury.

If it does acts, or enters into relationships, or undertakes responsibilities, these things may give rise to a common law duty of care just as when an individual does them. It may be liable in its capacity as an occupier of land or landlord. As an employer, it has all the usual common law and statutory duties to its employees. It can be vicariously liable for the torts of its employees. It can be liable for breach of contract. Being a public authority, it can be liable for injury caused by acting in a way incompatible with human rights (see the European Convention on Human Rights 1950 and Human Rights Act 1998).

The courts are reluctant to impose liability on a public body in connection with its statutory powers and duties. Local authorities have powers and duties under dozens of statutes and regulations such as the Public Health Acts 1875 and 1936, various Local Government Acts, Highways Act 1980, Road Traffic Act 1988, Children Act 1989, and Education Act 1996. Statutory duties very often impose broad public duties that require the authority, for example, to set up and run a satisfactory education or child-care system, or to promote road safety. One would not expect the draftsman of a statute setting up such a target duty to provide for compensation for those aggrieved because the authority failed to hit the bullseye. Where there is a more specific duty, such as s.41 Highways Act 1980, the draftsman may provide that the authority is to compensate those injured by breach of duty (see **sections 5.2** and **5.3**). If the statute itself does not provide for compensation, the courts are unlikely to give an aggrieved person a common law remedy for breach of statutory duty by a public body.

If legislation gives a statutory power but no duty to exercise it, a local authority 'cannot be made liable for any damage sustained by a member of the public by reason of a failure to exercise that power. . . So long as they exercise their discretion honestly, it is for them to determine the method by which and the time in which and the time during which the power shall be exercised' (*East Suffolk Rivers Catchment Board* v. *Kent* [1941] AC 74).

The House of Lords said in *Stovin* v. *Wise* [1996] AC 923: 'If the policy of the Act is not to create a statutory liability to pay compensation, the same policy should ordinarily exclude the existence of a common law duty of care,' and that the courts would not impose a duty of care to exercise a statutory power unless 'it would in the circumstances have been irrational not to have exercised the power, so that there was in effect a public law duty to act' and it seemed that 'the policy of the statute requires compensation to be paid to persons who suffer loss because the power was not exercised'. As to public law, in *Associated Provincial Picture Houses* v. *Wednesbury Corpn* [1948] 1 KB 223 the local authority had exercised a statutory power, and the claimant complained of the way it had done so. The court could intervene only if 'a decision on a competent matter is so unreasonable that no reasonable authority could ever have come to it'.

Today it is difficult to imagine a case in which a common law duty might be founded simply on a failure, even an irrational failure, to provide some benefit that a public authority merely had a power to provide, or a public authority's failure to comply with a broad public law duty (*Gorringe* v. *Calderdale Metropolitan Borough Council* [2004] UKHL 15, which also casts doubt on the use of *Wednesbury* unreasonableness as a preliminary test for liability in negligence).

Gorringe is the leading case on a local authority's liability for injuries caused by highway repairs, a subject discussed later on in more detail (see **sections 5.2** and **5.3**). The following are the main cases on local authority liability for personal injury:

- Adoption agency. *A* v. *Essex County Council* [2003] EWCA Civ 1848.
- Education authority. See the special educational needs cases of *Phelps* v. *London Borough of Hillingdon* [2000] UKHL 47 and *Carty* v. *London Borough of Croydon* [2004] EWHC 228 (QB), and see **section 5.12**.
- Social services body. *X (Minors)* v. *Bedfordshire County Council* [1995] 2 AC 633, *Z & others v. United Kingdom* [2001] ECHR 329 and *Barrett* v. *Enfield London Borough Council* [1999] UKHL 25, and see **section 5.13**.
- Landlord. *Lee* v. *Leeds City Council* and *Ratcliffe* v. *Sandwell Metropolitan Borough Council* [2002] EWCA Civ 6.

There are many specialist books and law reports on local government law.

4.11 THE STATE AS DEFENDANT

Until 1947, somebody injured by the negligent driving of a Crown employee might get an *ex gratia* payment but had no right to sue. Crown immunity was largely removed by the Crown Proceedings Act 1947. The Crown can now be liable as occupier of land, to its employees, or vicariously for the torts of its employees.

Policing and health care are organised on a regional rather than central level (see **sections 5.10** and **5.11**). This leaves the Ministry of Defence and Home Department as the usual central government defendants. The latter is responsible for prisons and detention centres. It owes a duty of care to prisoners, and can be liable for personal injury caused by its negligence or misfeasance in public office. The level of control it exercises over prisoners means that it is likely to be vicariously liable for negligence and even assault committed by a prison officer (*Lister* v. *Hesley Hall Ltd* [2001] UKHL 22).

The courts may be willing to find that the Home Department owes a duty of care if it allows a dangerous inmate to escape. The well-known case of *Dorset Yacht Co Ltd* v. *Home Office* [1970] AC 1004 is relevant, but for a more general rule see *K* v. *Secretary of State for the Home Department* [2002] EWCA Civ 775.

As to the MoD, s.10 of the Crown Proceedings Act 1947 preserved the Crown's immunity against personal injury claims by members of the armed forces, whether caused by fellow servicemen or the condition of premises or equipment. Instead, there was a no fault pension scheme for servicemen injured while on duty, or on land, premises, ship, aircraft or vehicle used for the purposes of the armed forces. The pensions tended to pay much less than a court would award by way of compensation. The Crown Proceedings (Armed Forces) Act 1987 removed this immunity, but is not retrospective (*Matthews* v. *Ministry of Defence* [2003] UKHL 5).

4.12 CHILDREN AS DEFENDANTS

A child may be liable in the ordinary way if it causes injury by acts or omissions that fall below the standard expected of an ordinarily prudent and reasonable child of that age. It follows that a very young child cannot be negligent.

In *Mullin* v. *Richards* [1997] EWCA Civ 2662 two 15-year-olds were play fighting with plastic rulers and one received a serious eye injury from a fragment of ruler. A prudent and reasonable child of that age would not have foreseen any significant injury.

A child who has caused injury will very seldom be able to pay compensation, whether from insurance, income or savings. The claimant cannot demand that the child's parents pay the judgment. Household insurance policies will often pay up if the children of the family have been negligent. The child's parent may pay up. If the injury was caused by a road accident there is the MIB Uninsured Drivers Agreement. If it was caused by a crime of violence, there is the Criminal Injuries Compensation Scheme. Failing that, the claimant may have to wait many years before enforcing the judgment.

Given the difficulty of proving liability against a child and then enforcing a judgment, the claimant will naturally prefer to bring his claim against an adult or organisation if he can. Potential targets are the child's parents, or the school if that is where the injury occurred.

Parents are not vicariously liable for injuries caused by their children, but an adult who encourages or permits a child to do potentially dangerous activities such as shooting can be directly liable if he was negligent to do so.

A parent who parks his car on a slope and leaves a young child in it may be directly liable for injury caused when the child knocks off the handbrake. The same applies if a parent allows a toddler to wander in the road and cause an accident. Consider *Carmarthenshire County Council* v. *Lewis* [1955] AC 549.

If the defendant is still under 18 when proceedings are started against him, a litigation friend must be appointed to accept service (see CPR Parts 6 and 21).

4.13 CHILDREN AS CLAIMANTS

A child's parent owes the child a duty to take as much care as the reasonably careful parent. This is not an absolute duty to prevent injury. It does not require a parent to supervise even young children constantly. It is a duty to treat children according to their age and characteristics.

It is, however, a higher duty than is owed to a child by a stranger. Many claims brought by younger children against third parties would have a better chance of success if brought against their own parents for allowing them to get into the situation in the first place. It is difficult to broach this with a parent who has just brought the child to a first interview with a view to making a claim. If the parent is not certain that he is insured for such a claim, there may be no second interview. However, if the claimant's lawyer does not raise this point, the third party defendant may do so by seeking contribution or indemnity from the parents (see **section 4.17**).

The standard of care owed by a stranger towards a child is to take reasonable care, judged by the standard of the reasonable man. The reasonable man is alert to the risk that a child will behave unpredictably, and so takes more care if he knows there are children around.

A driver may be liable in negligence if he drives too fast past a roadside place where a child might foreseeably be hidden, such as between parked cars on a housing estate (*Fielding* v. *Greenhalgh* [1999] EWCA Civ 1799). He may also be liable if he fails to take extra care after seeing a child playing a game that might involve jumping into the road. This does not mean that a driver will be liable if he was going at a sensible speed, paying due attention, and had no chance to miss the child (*Miller* v. *C&G Coach Services* [2002] EWHC 1361 (QB)).

The question is whether it would have been 'apparent to a reasonable man, armed with the common sense and experience of the way pedestrians, particularly children, are likely to behave in the circumstances which were known by the defendant to exist . . . that there was a possibility of a danger emerging, to avoid which he should slow down or sound his horn or both' (*Moore* v. *Poyner* [1975] RTR 127 and see *J (a child)* v. *West* [1999] EWCA Civ 1813, a successful claim by a nine-year-old).

A child's compensation may be reduced for contributory negligence. The test is whether the claimant took as much care as the ordinary child of his age. The younger the child, the less likely it is that there will be any deduction. It seems that a child up to the age of three or four cannot be contributorily negligent at all. In one Scottish case decided by the Outer House, a five-year-old who ran across the road and was hit by a car suffered a 50 per cent deduction (*McKinnell* v. *White* [1971] SLT 61). Generally, one would not expect a deduction if the claimant was only five.

With slightly older children, it is helpful to distinguish between momentary forgetfulness and deliberate acts. A seven-year-old who runs into the path of a motorist will not suffer any discount if the court finds that this was what would be expected in a normal child of his age momentarily forgetful of the perils of crossing a road (see *Jones* v. *Lawrence* [1969] 3 All ER 267). The same result is likely for a nine-year-old who jumps into the road to escape a pavement scuffle (*J (a child)* v. *West* [1999] EWCA Civ 1813). A 12-year-old who suddenly dashes across the road may suffer a 75 per cent deduction (*Willbye* v. *Gibbons* [1997] EWCA Civ 2123). In *Eagle* v. *Chambers* [2003] EWCA Civ 1107 the Court of Appeal treated the deliberate acts of a distraught 17-year-old pedestrian very much as they would those of an adult.

Many claims are the result of adventurous play. Obvious dangers are not always obvious to children, and the reasonable man knows that children walk and climb where they should not. There is a statutory duty of care to child trespassers, although one is entitled to expect that very young children will be accompanied by their parents who will keep them away from evident dangers (see **section 5.5**).

An adult must allow for the risk of trespass and even theft by slightly older children. The owner of a garage may be liable for injuries if he leaves petrol where it is reasonably foreseeable that a trespassing child may take it and start a fire with it (see *S (a child)* v. *A&E Autos* [2002] 4 CL 345).

In *Gabriel* v. *Kirklees Metropolitan Council* [2004] EWCA Civ 345 the Court of Appeal noted that children's ingenuity in finding unexpected ways of doing mischief to themselves and others should never be underestimated. The defendant had left a pile of rubble on a building site occupied by the defendant. Part of the site had been excavated, making it an interesting place to play. The site was next to a pavement, and the claimant was walking along the pavement when injured by rubble thrown by children playing on the site. The occupier was potentially liable. The questions to ask were whether it was reasonably foreseeable that if the site were not properly fenced, children would enter it; if, when on the site, they would play there; if, as part of their play, they would throw anything that came to hand; and if in throwing the rubble, they would injure passers-by on the pavement.

If an adventurous play claim succeeds, there will be a deduction for contributory negligence according to the claimant's age at the time. A 'bright lad' of nine who persuades a garage to sell him petrol 'for mother' but in fact for a game of Red Indians is negligent if he knew the potential dangers, and is likely to be blameworthy by today's standards. Consider *Yachuk* v. *Oliver Blais* [1949] AC 386 in the light of *Chappell* v *Imperial Design* [2000] EWCA Civ 370.

In *Evans* v. *Souls Garage* (2001) *The Times* 23 January two boys of 13 bought petrol from a garage in order to sniff it as some children sniff glue. One spilt it on his trousers, and was very badly burned when he and his friend lit cigarettes. He established primary liability against the garage as it had breached a statutory duty not to sell petrol to under-16s. There was a one-third deduction for the claimant's own contributory negligence. The defendant did not appeal.

In *Adams* v. *Southern Electricity* (1993) *The Times* 21 October, a boy of 15 managed to bypass a defective anti-climbing device on an electricity pylon and came into contact with the transformer. There was a two-thirds discount for contributory negligence.

A minor cannot be a party to litigation, so a litigation friend must be appointed before proceedings are issued. If a claim may well be brought against the claimant's parent, one should not appoint the parent as litigation friend. Any settlement of the claim must be approved by the court (CPR Part 21 and PD 21). The court will invest the compensation until the child is 18 (see **section 17.7**).

4.14 CONTRIBUTORY NEGLIGENCE

If the claimant can show that the defendant was negligent and this caused his injury, he has established primary liability. It may be that the claimant was very much more at fault than the defendant. In *Green v. Bannister* [2003] EWCA Civ 1819 the defendant was negligent in that she did not look behind carefully when reversing her car. The claimant thus established primary liability, although the most obvious cause of the accident was that he had passed out in the road after a night of drinking.

However, a claimant whose own negligence contributed to some extent to the accident or to his injuries by being careless himself will face a deduction under the Law Reform (Contributory Negligence) Act 1945: 'Where any person suffers damage as the result partly of his own fault and partly of the fault of any other person or persons, a claim in respect of that damage shall not be defeated by reason of the fault of the person suffering the damage, but the damages recoverable in respect thereof shall be reduced to such extent as the court thinks just and equitable having regard to the claimant's share in the responsibility for the damage.'

The court cannot reduce damages by 100 per cent on the basis of contributory negligence, as this would defeat the claim (*Pitts* v. *Hunt* [1991] 1 QB 24).

Contributory negligence may reduce the compensation in claims based on negligence, nuisance, and breach of statutory duty, even if the duty breached is one for which liability is strict. Contributory negligence applies to most personal injury claims based on breach of contract. It probably applies to claims based on trespass.

'A person is guilty of contributory negligence if he ought reasonably to have foreseen that, if he did not act as a reasonable, prudent man, he might be hurt himself. . .' (*Jones* v. *Livox Quarries* [1952] 2 QB 608). It is for the defendant to prove this. A defendant who wishes to rely on an allegation of contributory negligence must state it in the defence.

A contributory negligence calculation '. . . involves a consideration not only of the causative potency of a particular factor, but also of its blameworthiness' (*Davies* v. *Swan Motors* [1949] 2 KB 291).

In *Eagle* v. *Chambers* [2003] EWCA Civ 1107 the teenage claimant was emotional and behaving erratically. She was walking in a fairly straight line down the middle of the carriageway at midnight. An onlooker had told her to get off the road, and she had told him to 'F**k off'. The road was, however, straight and well lit. The defendant was driving along the road at 30–35mph. He had been drinking and accepted that this had affected his driving, although his blood alcohol level was a little below the level permitted by the criminal law. He should certainly have seen the claimant, and should have had no difficulty whatever in avoiding her. In fact he ran her over. The court deducted 40 per cent for her own contribution.

In *Brannan* v. *Airtours* [1999] EWCA Civ 588, the claimant was at a package holiday party organised by the defendant, which provided free alcohol. There was a ceiling fan seven feet above the ground, which the defendant had drawn to the attention of guests. The claimant wanted to get out of his seat without getting his neighbours to stand up, so he climbed on the table, and the fan hit him on the head. There was a 50 per cent deduction.

In *Green v. Bannister* [2003] EWCA Civ 1819 (see above) the deduction was 60 per cent.

In *Revill* v. *Newberry* [1996] 1 All ER 291 the claimant went to break into an allotment shed. This not being the first time, the defendant owner was waiting for him, and shot him. The claimant's damages were reduced by two-thirds.

In *Goddard v. Greenwood* [2002] EWCA Civ 1590, the claimant joggers were crossing a multi-lane road at traffic lights in front of a stationary lorry. The lorry driver had seen them, so he did not pull away when the lights turned to green. On clearing the lorry, the claimants collided with a car that was overtaking the lorry in the next lane. The car driver was liable, as he had been going too fast in the circumstances. There was an 80 per cent deduction.

In *Grealis* v. *Opuni* [2003] EWCA Civ 177 the claimant tried to ride his employer's moped across a main road despite oncoming traffic which had right of way. He nearly made it, but his back wheel was hit by a car. The car driver was primarily liable because he should have known that traffic waiting to pull out might misjudge his approach speed, and was doing 38mph in a 30mph zone. If the car driver had been travelling at a safe, not to say legal, speed, the claimant would have got across the road safely. However, the claimant's damages were reduced by 80 per cent.

Cases where the claimant was a passenger in a car and knew that the driver was drunk are quite common. There should be a deduction from the passenger's damages if he knew or should have known that the driver has drunk so much that his ability to drive safely was likely to be impaired; or if he went out for 'a bout of drinking which has the effect, eventually, of robbing the passenger of clear thought and perception and diminishes the driver's capacity to drive properly and carefully' (*Owens* v. *Brimmell* [1977] 1 QB 859, in which both driver and passenger had drunk eight or nine pints of beer). There was a 20 per cent deduction. The courts apply an objective standard, so a passenger cannot argue that he himself was too drunk to make the assessment. If a reasonable person would have appreciated, from all he saw or heard, that the driver was not safe to drive, an injured passenger can expect a finding of contributory negligence. It may be sensible to ask a driver how much he has drunk, but the law does not expect one to interrogate him (*Booth* v. *White* [2003] EWCA Civ 1708).

In *Stinton* v. *Stinton & MIB* [1995] RTR 167 the passenger saw his driver have four drinks during the evening, so he knew him to be over the legal limit, but thought he was capable of driving safely. There was a one-third deduction.

The classic case of contributory negligence is failure to wear a seat belt. Seat belt use has been compulsory even in the rear of a car since 1991, although some vehicles and some drivers are exempt (Wearing of Seat Belts Regulations 1983 and Motor Vehicles (Wearing of Seat Belts in Rear Seat by Adults) Regulations 1991).

If the driver was required to wear a seat belt and did not, there will be a deduction as follows. If wearing a seat belt would have prevented any injury, 25 per cent. If the injuries would have been reduced by use of a seat belt, 15 per cent. If a seat belt would not have reduced the severity of the injuries, there should be no deduction (*Froom* v. *Butcher* [1976] QB 286). This is only a guideline. However, it was endorsed by the Court of Appeal in *Jones* v. *Wilkins* (2001) *The Times* 6 February.

What if the claimant was injured in a car crash because he was not wearing a seat belt, but the evidence is that he would have suffered other injuries if he had been? In *Patience* v. *Andrews* [1983] RTR 447 the court declined to consider what other injuries the claimant might have had. Simon Brown, LJ doubted the correctness of this in *Mutch* v. *Allen* [2001] EWCA Civ 76.

Less common but still with its own rule of thumb is the situation where a motorcyclist fails to do up his crash helmet and it comes off in an accident. *Capps* v. *Miller* [1989] 1 WLR 839 indicates that the conventional discount is to be 10 per cent if doing up the helmet properly might have prevented injury. If the motorcyclist simply fails to wear a crash helmet, conventionally there is a 25 per cent/15 per cent deduction as in *Froom* v. *Butcher* [1976] QB 286.

Children can be guilty of contributory negligence (see **section 4.13**).

When the claimant was injured at work, the court's attitude is somewhat different (see **section 6.14**).

4.15 CONSENT TO RISK

If the claimant consented to the situation that caused the injury, he may get no compensation.

Volenti non fit injuria is Latin for, roughly, 'if one consents to a situation which results in one being injured, one cannot claim compensation'.

Before the courts refuse a claim on the basis of *volenti* they want to know that the victim truly consented. It is unlikely, for example, that an employee freely consented to hazards at his workplace (see **section 6.15**).

In *Smoldon* v. *Whitworth & Nolan* [1996] EWCA Civ 1225 the Court of Appeal gave a reminder that by taking part in a game of rugby, one consents to the ordinary risks of the game. However, a player could claim if injured by a reckless and dangerous tackle, or in an off-the-ball incident (see **section 5.8**).

An adult who chooses to step off a bus before it has come to a complete standstill at a bus stop has only himself to blame. In the absence of any evidence that he was somehow deceived about what the bus was doing, the fact that the driver had opened the bus door while the bus was still moving did not make the bus company liable (*Marshall* v. *Lincolnshire Road Car Co* (CA 7 December 2000).

Under the Occupiers' Liability Acts 1957 and 1984 the common law duty of care that an occupier would otherwise owe to visitors and others on his premises is replaced by a duty of care under the statute (see **section 5.5**). This 'does not impose on an occupier any obligation to a visitor [or trespasser] in respect of risks willingly accepted as his' (s.2(5) of the 1957 Act and s.1(6) of the 1984 Act). So 'high-spirited young men who take risks with their own safety and do things that they know are forbidden . . . cannot blame others for their rashness'. The Court of Appeal said this in a case where the claimant had been drinking, climbed into a locked swimming pool he knew to be out of bounds, dived in and was injured when his head hit the bottom (*Ratcliff* v. *McConnell* [1997] EWCA Civ 2679).

Rescuers are generally an exception to *volenti non fit injuria*. Attempting to rescue somebody from drowning does not mean one accepts the risk of drowning oneself.

4.16 EXCLUDING LIABILITY

Businesses are regulated by the Unfair Contract Terms Act 1977 and the Unfair Terms in Consumer Contracts Regulations 1999. Section 2(1) of the Act says: 'A person cannot by reference to any contract term or to a notice given to persons generally or to particular persons exclude or restrict his liability for death or personal injury resulting from negligence'; and s.2(2): 'In the case of other loss or damage, a person cannot so exclude or restrict his liability for negligence except in so far as the term or notice satisfies the requirement of reasonableness.'

The Act and Regulations make ineffective any contract terms and notices that purport to limit liability for death or injury resulting from negligence if:

- they are made in the course of a business; or
- they relate to land that is occupied for business purposes, unless the claimant was on the land for recreational or educational purposes that are unconnected with the occupier's business and was injured by the dangerous state of the premises (for example, a rambler on farmland).

The 1977 Act also prevents exclusion of liability for injury caused by goods and services under the Sale of Goods Act 1979 and the Supply of Goods and Services Act 1982.

Any attempt by a taxi or minicab company to exclude liability is ineffective as regards any liability required by the Road Traffic Act 1988 to be covered by insurance (see s.149 of the Act). Public service vehicle operators cannot exclude their liability for death or personal injury (see the Public Passenger Vehicles Act 1981).

An occupier of premises who puts up a warning sign still has a duty of care to visitors and others. However, if it provided enough information to enable the claimant to escape injury, the defendant may be able to escape liability (see **section 5.5**).

4.17 CONTRIBUTION AND INDEMNITY

A defendant may be liable to the claimant, but be entitled to recoup part (contribution) or all (indemnity) of the damages and legal costs from another person who contributed to or caused the injury.

The Civil Liability (Contribution) Act 1978 says 'any person liable in respect of any damage suffered by another person may recover contribution from any other person liable in respect of the same damage (whether jointly with him or otherwise)', and 'the amount of the contribution . . . shall be such as may be found by the court to be just and equitable having regard to the extent of that person's responsibility for the damage in question'.

Some typical examples are:

- A young child claimant was injured when his mother's car was hit by the defendant's vehicle, but the defendant sought a contribution from the mother because she did not strap him in properly (*Jones* v. *Wilkins* (2001) *The Times* 6 February).
- A child of five was injured when trespassing on the defendant's wasteland, in circumstances where his parents knew or should have known that he was not playing somewhere safe (*Phipps* v. *Rochester Corporation* [1955] 1 QB 450).
- The claimant had three successive tail-end shunt accidents, each causing or exacerbating whiplash and low back pain. The lingering effects of these accidents eventually forced the claimant to take early retirement. One of the defendants sought a contribution from the other two (*Pearce* v. *Lindfield* [2003] EWCA Civ 647).
- The claimant worked as a manager for an office cleaning company. She worked at a client's office block, where a sink one day fell off the wall and knocked her over. Although the occupier was in actual control of the premises, the main responsibility for ensuring a safe place of work lies

with a person's employers. The employer knew the sink was loose but had not said anything to the occupier. The employer was 75 per cent liable, but the occupier bore 25 per cent (*Andrews* v. *Initial Cleaning Services* [1999] EWCA Civ 1831).

- The claimant was injured at work on a building site when he dug into an electric cable. The danger was created by a sub-contractor but suspected by the site's owner. The owner was liable in part as he had not acted on his suspicions (*Clark v. Hosier & Dickson* [2003] EWCA Civ 1467).

If an employer is vicariously liable for the carelessness of an employee, he may in theory recover his outlays from the culprit (*Lister* v. *Romford Ice & Cold Storage Co* [1957] AC 555). *Lister* claims are very rare, because the case prompted the insurance industry to reach an internal agreement not to pursue them unless there is evidence of conspiracy between the parties, or wilful misconduct by the culprit.

The claimant may sue all the tortfeasors, as first defendant, second defendant, etc. If the claimant does not sue all of them, a defendant may himself join a wrongdoer from whom he wants a contribution or indemnity (CPR Part 20).

On the face of it, the maxim *ex turpi causa non oritur actio* could act as a defence to most Part 20 proceedings. It means, roughly, 'the courts will not help anybody recover compensation or indemnity if the claim is founded in his own crime'. It does not apply to road traffic offences, except perhaps those of specific intent where the Part 20 applicant was more than just careless or reckless (*Great North Eastern Railway Ltd* v. *Hart* [2003] EWHC 2450).

Contribution and indemnity claims have a special limitation period under s.10 of the Limitation Act 1980. 'No action to recover contribution . . . shall be brought after the expiration of two years from the date on which that right accrued.' The right accrues when judgment is given against the defendant, or an arbitration award is made against him, or he pays or agrees to pay compensation to the claimant, whether or not he admits any liability in respect of the damage.

However, it is better for the defendant to seek contribution or indemnity at the same time that he files a defence in the main action. The court may not permit him to do so if it would mean the court having to examine the facts of the case a second time in litigation between defendant and Part 20 defendant (CPR Part 20.6 and *Roe* v. *Sheffield City Council* [2004] EWCA Civ 329).

4.18 LIABILITY PHOTOGRAPHS AND MEASUREMENTS

The site of the accident is still very often referred to as the *locus in quo*. Photographs of the *locus* are often crucial. When a client takes photographs, they tend to be very disappointing. If not taking the photographs yourself, it is worth giving detailed instructions as set out below. If the accident took place at work, see **section 6.1**.

Ideally, the office will have a site kit consisting of:

- digital camera, capable of focusing down to 50cm;
- surveyor's 25m tape;
- six inch ruler;
- metre rule.

Taking site photographs is a potentially hazardous activity. It would not only be very upsetting if a trainee solicitor were to get hit by a car while standing in the road with a camera, but the employing firm could also be prosecuted. If taking photographs involves a member of staff standing in the road, he should have an assistant to warn of oncoming vehicles, and a fluorescent waistcoat. If working on a high speed road (over 50mph) he needs non-slip safety footwear and EU Class 3 reflective clothing, which means a jacket. Some situations will need folding 'Slow – Surveying In Progress' roadsigns, traffic cones and torches. If these tasks are to be carried out by an employee ask the firm's health and safety officer to risk assess the activity and produce a safety code and organise training.

If the site of the accident is private property and the owner will not give permission for a site visit, consider obtaining a court order under CPR Part 25.

Road traffic accidents

Photographs of the site of the accident, its approaches, and all damaged vehicles are required. Take 30 or so.

Skid marks on a road, except in wet weather when there may be none, are excellent evidence of speed and direction. They fade and disappear within days on a busy road. At the point of impact, mud is dislodged from under the wheel arches and broken glass is scattered. There may be gouges in the road surface. Where a vehicle comes to rest, there may be more debris, or liquid from a damaged radiator or sump. With luck, most of this will be shown on the sketch plan in the police accident report, but photographs are better.

Ideally, photographs should show what the drivers saw in the last 150 metres before impact. This means two sets of approach photographs, one showing things from the claimant's perspective at 25-metre intervals as he drove towards the site of the accident, and the other from the perspective of the defendant. Ideally, take the photographs from the height of a driver's eyes. This can give an intuitive understanding of what happened on the day of the accident. Approach photos show how far up the road the drivers could see; any distractions like a pelican crossing or rows of parked cars; and any bushes, trees or signs that would have affected visibility. The background may be more important than one thinks, for instance if it includes temporary road signs.

If general traffic conditions are relevant, try to take photographs of the site of the accident at the time of the week when the accident took place, for example, 8.50 a.m. on a Tuesday. The results may be useful if at that time there is normally heavy traffic, or a row of cars parked right along the road.

If possible, and if the value of the claim justifies making a trip to see the opposition's vehicle, try to get photographs of all damaged vehicles. The damage may tell an expert something about the force involved, and how the accident occurred. If there is damage to the front wings, lift the bonnet and photograph the inner wings.

There is another reason for having the claimant's vehicle photographed before it is repaired or scrapped. It helps resolve disputes about whether its pre-accident condition was A1, good or fair; and about the proper cost of repairs or value of the salvage.

If the claimant was seriously injured, consider getting a road accident reconstruction consultant to do a preliminary site visit. The Pre-action Protocol gives the defendant nearly four months within which to admit or deny liability, and the parties' positions on liability may have changed a good deal by then. A preliminary site visit might cost £300.

Pavement trip accidents

The most important shot is the one showing the height or depth of the trip. The person with the camera needs to get down on his stomach on the pavement. This photograph must be taken with the camera no more than 25cm above ground level, and no more than 1 metre from the trip at most. It requires a camera that can focus fairly close to its subject, perhaps through a macro lens setting.

It is essential to have something in the photograph that shows the scale of the trip. The usual thing is to stand a six inch ruler on end with its lowest marking on the bottom of the trip, and the trip visible behind it. Most rulers have a blank section at each end before the markings begin – cut it off. Avoid engraved steel rules, as the marking does not show up on photographs.

The next most important photograph is the sympathy shot, to help the court appreciate why the claimant tripped. This means holding the camera at about knee height, 2 metres off to the side, showing the claimant's toe engaging the trip.

Take some photographs from a standing position 2 metres away, to show how the defect looked to the claimant as he walked towards it.

If the photographs are intended to show that an area had sunk, take along a metre rule to use as a straight edge. Put this across the hollow, bridging it from one side to the other, and then prop the ruler up against it to show the maximum depth.

Take some general photographs of the area to show the location of the trip, especially if its location means that a fall could be serious, or that a pedestrian had to pay more attention to traffic at that point than to his own feet. The general state of the pavement can be relevant (*Dibb* v. *Kirklees Metropolitan Borough Council* [1999] EWCA Civ 1180).

Verification

To avoid any dispute over authenticity, prepare a short witness statement for signature by the photographer giving his name, date of birth, address, occupation, relationship to the claimant or defendant, date when the photographs were taken, and that they have not been altered. Attach a set of prints signed by the photographer.

CCTV

Was the accident recorded on closed circuit TV? There are now traffic and security cameras in many places, especially at road junctions, high streets and workplaces. If there is a CCTV recording, one should get it straight away. It probably will not be kept for more than a month.

Although these recordings are generally on standard VHS videotape, it is not possible to view them on an office VCR as they are multiplexed to accept simultaneous input from several different cameras. There are half a dozen different multiplexing systems, and it takes a specialist to provide a decoded tape which can be watched on an ordinary VCR, or take still photographs from it. The author has not used the following, but they advertise a decoding service for lawyers (see **Appendix 4** for contact details):

- Symbiosis Forensic Systems (**www.symbiosis.com**);
- P G Video.

In Small Claims, the court will not order the loser to reimburse the winner for the cost of photographs or scale plans of the *locus*, or the police accident report.

4.19 NEGOTIATING LIABILITY

At the start of any negotiation one should make it clear that one's letters and conversations are without prejudice save as to costs, and that the client's instructions will have to be sought before any point is agreed (see **section 3.4**).

Admissions

The Personal Injury Protocol requires the claimant to send the defendant a letter of claim setting out his allegations and requesting copies of any relevant documents. It requires the defendant to respond by saying whether he denies liability or causation. If he does, he is required to give detailed reasons and provide copies of documents.

'Liability is admitted' or 'liability will not be an issue' are admissions, but insurers may merely say 'we are prepared to negotiate' or 'we are instructed to seek an amicable settlement'. These are not admissions. They leave the defendant free to change his mind and either reject liability altogether or make a surprise allegation that the claimant was 50 per cent to blame for his own injuries, or had no injuries. Where a defendant had no real defence, or intended to settle the claim in full, the court has the power to punish a failure to make an admission when it assesses legal costs in any claim, large or small. It can amount to unreasonable behaviour, which would justify a court ordering the defendant to pay the claimant's legal costs in a Small Claim.

The claimant's problem, if the defendant will not give more than a vague assurance on liability, is that he may find, when necessary evidence is no longer available, that liability or causation are disputed. Documents may have been destroyed, machinery scrapped, or road or factory layouts altered. Witnesses may have moved, died or just forgotten what they saw. The claimant will have been provided with legal services and/or after the event (ATE or AEI) legal expenses insurance cover on a mistakenly optimistic view of the claim. The part of the costs budget allocated to liability may have been used in other aspects of the case.

If the defendant breaches the Protocol and fails to make a positive denial or admission, the claimant should certainly tell the defendant that he wants him to do so within two weeks, and that as long as the defendant fails to commit himself, he is in breach of the Protocol and may face costs penalties. If this does not produce the desired admission, is the assurance of an amicable settlement enough?

If all the evidence has been safely gathered in, and the liability issues are straightforward, the claimant should generally accept the assurance. There is a small risk that the defendant will raise an issue that the claimant's investigation did not consider, but this will seldom be enough to justify doing more work on liability, still less issuing proceedings. One should explain this to the client, and if necessary to his legal expenses insurer.

If the claimant cannot afford to proceed without a firm admission, he should send the defendant a demand for any outstanding liability documents; an outline of the work he needs to do to preserve the liability evidence; and an estimate of the costs involved. He should say that this work is needed only because the defendant has failed to admit liability as required by the Protocol, and that if an admission is not received in another 14 days he will continue the liability investigation with a view to issuing proceedings.

From the defendant's point of view, the main attraction of an admission is that the claimant stops work on liability, and if the claimant has a conditional fee agreement his solicitor's success fee may go down from 100 per cent to 5 per cent.

What makes an admission unattractive for the defendant is that the court's permission is necessary to withdraw it. Failing to admit liability where there is no real defence may be a breach of the Protocol, but it probably will not result in a costs penalty for the defendant. It is virtually standard practice for many insurers and law firms in cases of clinical negligence and industrial disease. If a defendant does not give an admission, a determined claimant may issue proceedings, at the defendant's expense. However, lack of an admission makes some claimants give up altogether. Some claimants, with or without a solicitor, simply do not want the fuss of issuing proceedings. In a very difficult case, an inexperienced claimant solicitor may not have the courage either to issue proceedings or to send the client elsewhere.

A defendant may be happy to admit that it was liable for an accident, but not that the accident caused the injury and damage complained of by the claimant, or indeed any damage. Unless both liability and causation are admitted, the claimant is not automatically entitled to judgment on admission. 'Nothing short of a clear admission of liability, both of negligence causing the accident and of damage resulting from the accident caused by the negligence, is enough to . . . entitle the plaintiff to judgment' (*Rankine* v. *Garton* [1979] 2 All ER 1185). If the defendant admits liability but not causation, where the accident was of a sort that clearly would have caused some sort of injury, the claimant can seek summary judgment under CPR Part 24.

Withdrawing an admission

An insurer may wish to withdraw an admission if new evidence emerges, or more often if the file is handed to a new claims handler who feels the claim could and should be defended. He can do so only if the court gives him leave.

CPR Part 14.1.5 says 'The court may allow a party to amend or withdraw an admission', and CPR Part 3.1.3 says 'When the court makes an order, it may . . . make it subject to conditions, including a condition to pay a sum of money into court'.

How will the court exercise its Part 14 discretion? Prior to the CPR there was *Gale* v. *Superdrug Stores* [1996] 1 WLR 1089. This was an employer's liability claim. The court would 'restrain the privilege which every litigant enjoys of freedom to change his mind' only if there was 'clear and cogent evidence of prejudice' to the claimant that could not be adequately compensated, for example by an award of legal costs. It appears from *Sollitt* v. *DJ Broady Ltd* (2000) LTL 23 February, an employer's liability case after the CPR, that one must balance the prejudice to the claimant if the court allows the admission to be withdrawn, and the prejudice to the defendant if it does not. It seems that:

- It will not necessarily be enough for the defendant to show that he has a complete defence to the claim, as the defendant did in this case albeit in somewhat odd circumstances.

- The defendant must come up with a very good reason for withdrawing his admission, for example, that the claimant had misled him about significant facts.
- It will seldom be enough that the defendant has simply changed his mind about facts which he knew when he made the admission, or which he could with reasonable diligence have discovered beforehand.
- If the defendant gets over these hurdles, the court will then consider whether giving leave to withdraw the admission will result in undue prejudice to the claimant. The claimant may suffer particular prejudice if the admission is withdrawn and in the meantime he has lost touch with witnesses; or their memory of the accident is likely to have faded; or the withdrawal means that the claimant may wish to proceed against a different defendant but the claim is now time barred; or physical evidence has been destroyed, for example a damaged car has been repaired where the damage might have shed light on the accident. The court may be willing to consider the claimant prejudiced if withdrawal would mean repaying an interim payment.

The Personal Injury Protocol states: 'Where liability is admitted, the presumption is that the defendant will be bound by this admission for all claims with a total value of up to £15,000.' In *Hamilton* v. *Hertfordshire County Council* [2003] EWHC 3018 (QB) the claimant alleged that she had injured her back at work, lifting a handicapped child out of a swimming pool. The defendant admitted liability, but then sought to withdraw the admission on hearing a different version of the accident. The case was worth over £15,000, so there was no presumption that the defendant's admission was binding. The burden of proof regarding prejudice rested on the claimant. She was unable to show any particular prejudice, and the defendant was given leave to withdraw its admission, even though it could have seen the other version of events before admitting liability if it had read the accident report carefully.

The court in *Hamilton* noted that if a defendant is permitted to withdraw an admission and the claimant is represented under a conditional fee agreement, the claimant's solicitor may decline to continue acting, or the claimant's ATE insurer may withdraw cover. Either of these might arguably represent a very significant prejudice to the claimant.

As the court has discretion to allow a party to withdraw an admission, it would seem that a simple admission cannot create a binding agreement between the parties. However, an agreement about liability, say to divide liability 75:25 in the claimant's favour, does create a binding contract unless the claimant is under a disability and the court has not yet approved the agreement (*Drinkall* v. *Whitwood* [2003] EWCA Civ 1547).

Unrepresented claimants

If the claimant is negotiating without a solicitor, this is probably because he has tried without success to get one. Without a solicitor, he will not be able to get legal expenses insurance. A defendant can legitimately write to an unrepresented claimant to point out how much money he could lose if he issues proceedings and the claim fails.

Even in Small Claims, a lack of legal expenses insurance is worrying for a claimant. If the claim is worth more than the Small Claims limit, only the most determined claimant would issue proceedings without a solicitor, because of the risk that he might end up paying the defendant's costs and disbursements.

CHAPTER 5

The main injury scenarios

5.1 ROAD TRAFFIC ACCIDENTS – CLAIMS AGAINST DRIVERS

Injuries to drivers, passengers and pedestrians are responsible for about two-thirds of personal injury claims.

As many as 5 per cent of drivers in the UK are uninsured. The Motor Insurers' Bureau (MIB) provides some cover for their victims, but requires the claimant to take prompt action to identify the driver and his insurers (see **section 7.1**). Any road traffic accident could, some months down the line, turn out to involve an uninsured defendant, so any claimant lawyer should attend to the MIB requirement at once whenever he receives new instructions in a road traffic case, unless these details have already been provided and verified. If it turns out that the details provided by the driver are not accurate one must deal, at once, with the MIB requirement.

Claimant lawyers should be wary of accepting instructions from both driver and passenger. If it emerges that the driver may have contributed to the accident, there is a conflict of interest and one may have to stop acting for one or both. A driver can be negligent in the way that he drove the car, by drink driving, by failing to maintain the car properly, or by failing to ensure that a young child passenger wore a seat belt as in *Jones* v. *Wilkins* (2001) *The Times* 6 February.

The initial source of information will be one's client. For a questionnaire that may help with a streamlined interview, see the accompanying CD-ROM.

If the accident involved injury, the police will usually have attended and there should be a police accident report. This will contain statements by both drivers and any other witnesses; and maybe a sketch plan showing distances, skid marks, the position of debris, and the place where the cars came to rest.

The police fee for providing a copy of the accident report is, at the time of writing, £60 to £80 depending whether the force in question follows the ACPO guidelines on fees. From the claimant's point of view, it is usually best to postpone getting a copy until the defendant has said whether he intends to admit liability.

If one receives the report before the opposition, one can offer to send them a copy if they pay half the fee. If the opposition receive the report first and offer to provide a copy, does one trust them? It is easy to leave out vital parts when photocopying. Check for missing page numbers. In a large claim with disputed liability, get a copy directly from the police and do not worry about the money.

In a Small Claim the court will not order the loser to reimburse the winner for the cost of the police accident report, nor for the cost of photographs or a plan of the accident site.

In road traffic cases, there are seldom any relevant documents for the defendant to disclose. If he was driving a vehicle fitted with a tachograph and there is a dispute about liability, the claimant should request the tachograph disc. It will show what speeds the vehicle was doing immediately before the accident. It will probably be necessary to have the disc analysed by an expert, and a photocopy of the disc is no use for this. The system is now moving towards digital tachograph recording.

If the accident occurred because the defendant's vehicle had brake failure or shed a wheel, the claimant will need copies of maintenance records and MOT test certificates.

If the precise timing of the changes at traffic lights is important, the highway authority will be able to provide details of the light sequence.

Liability depends on common sense, case law, and the *Highway Code*. The latest edition can be seen online at **www.highwaycode.gov.uk**.

Section 38(7) of the Road Traffic Act 1988 says: 'A failure on the part of a person to observe a provision of the Highway Code . . . may in any proceedings (whether civil or criminal) be relied upon by any party as tending to establish or negative any liability which is in question in those proceedings.'

The courts have said:

> In law a breach of the Highway Code has a limited effect . . . a breach creates no presumption of negligence calling for an explanation, still less a presumption of negligence making a real contribution to causing an accident or injury. The breach is just one of the circumstances on which one party is entitled to rely in establishing the negligence of the other and its contribution towards causing the accident or injury.
>
> (*Powell* v. *Phillips* [1972] 3 All ER 864)

For example, a cyclist is going down a cycle lane on the nearside of slow-moving traffic. A lorry turns left into a garage, and he goes under its wheels. The *Highway Code* says that the lorry driver should:

- use his mirrors often so that he knows what is to each side of him;
- keep a special look-out for cycles, especially when turning;
- being a long vehicle, leave plenty of room for pedal cyclists;
- indicate before turning left;
- always check that a cyclist is not coming up behind before turning left.

However, the cyclist himself has certain responsibilities under the *Code*. The fact of his overtaking the rear part of the lorry on its left is likely to lead to a substantial reduction for contributory negligence. For a real case of this sort, see *Clenshaw* v. *Tanner* [2002] EWHC 184 (QB). This case went to appeal under the neutral citation [2002] EWCA Civ 1848.

The outcome of a case will always depend on all the facts, not on a rule or guideline. To get a feel for the courts' approach to liability and contributory negligence, look at the case summaries in Bingham's Motor Claims Cases. The following rules of thumb are based on comments by judges in various cases:

- The speed limit is a maximum, not a recommended figure. The speed limit in a housing estate may be 30 mph, but the maximum safe speed in all the circumstances may be only 15 mph (*Fielding* v. *Greenhalgh* [1999] EWCA Civ 1799).
- Driving faster than the speed limit is not necessarily negligent. The question is whether the defendant was driving faster than was safe in all the circumstances. Did excess speed prevent the speeding driver stopping in time to avoid a collision, or at least slowing down enough to reduce the effects of the impact (*Grealis* v. *Opuni* [2003] EWCA Civ 177)?
- A vehicle should be driven at a speed that permits the driver to stop within the limits of his vision, especially in adverse weather (*Arnot* v. *Sprake & Batchelor* [2001] EWCA Civ 341).
- Drivers are expected to slow down so as to be safe despite problems with the road surface, taking account of snow and rain. A driver may not be negligent if he loses control because of a slippery patch that the reasonably skilled driver would not have expected (*Rogers* v. *National Assembly for Wales* [2004] EWCA Civ 250).
- If there is a head-on collision whilst one driver is over the centre line dividing his carriageway from oncoming traffic, it is likely that he bears most of the responsibility.
- At a junction which is not marked to show who has priority, a motorist should generally give way to traffic coming from the right.
- If a driver has right of way and another vehicle pulls out in front of him, that does not mean that the driver with right of way will necessarily escape all liability if he could have prevented the collision by taking evasive action, such as braking (*Jenkins* v. *Holt* [1999] EWCA Civ 1240).
- Refusing to slow down to allow an overtaking vehicle to pull into one's lane can be negligence if there is, or may be, oncoming traffic or the lane(s) will soon start to narrow although see *Smith* v. *Cribben* [1994] PIQR P218.
- Failing to take steps to move a vehicle that has broken down in a dangerous location can be negligent.
- Drivers are not entitled to assume, without looking and listening, that they can proceed through traffic lights when they have a green light (*Goddard* v. *Greenwood* [2002] EWCA Civ 1590).

- A road user has to keep a good look-out, especially at junctions. If he is hit by an ambulance or fire engine he may bear most of the blame. It depends whether the emergency services vehicle was using both lights and siren; how fast each vehicle was going; whether the car was first away from the lights or following other vehicles; and visibility at the junction (see *Griffin* v. *Mersey Regional Ambulance* [1997] EWCA Civ 2441, *Purdue* v. *Devon Fire & Rescue* [2002] EWCA Civ 1538, and reg. 33(1)b Traffic Signs Regulations & General Directions 1994).
- If a driver is proceeding along a main road and another car is coming up a minor road to join the main road, it is reasonable to expect the other car to stop at the stop line.
- A driver who is in the outside lane of a roundabout (but does not intend to leave by the next exit) must bear in mind that this may lull other traffic into believing that he will take the next exit.
- If a vehicle is emerging blind onto a road, either because of the shape of the junction or (as with some vans) because of restricted nearside visibility, there is no rule that says that the vehicle is always entitled to inch forward into the road. As always, assessing liability if an accident ensues means looking at all the circumstances.
- A driver is not entitled to assume that another driver who has an indicator flashing actually intends to turn. He may have forgotten to cancel the indicator after turning earlier.
- A driver is not entitled to assume that anybody flashing his headlights means any more than 'I am here'.
- If somebody beckons you to come on, you are not entitled to assume that he has taken account of all oncoming vehicles. He is saying only 'you can come on as far as I am concerned'. You must still take the usual precautions in case there is any other vehicle coming.
- If traffic stops on a major road to let a car enter it from a minor road, and a vehicle overtaking along the outside keeps going and hits the car, it is likely that the overtaker bears most of the responsibility.
- A driver who knows he has a relevant medical condition (such as uncorrected short sight) is negligent and commits an offence if he drives anyway. It is most unlikely that a claimant will get the opportunity to trawl through the defendant's medical records unless the defence is based on an unsuspected medical condition (*Mansfield* v. *Weetabix Ltd* [1998] EWCA Civ 1352).
- If a pedestrian is hit on a zebra crossing it will generally be the car driver's fault, but there is no magic to a zebra crossing. The pedestrian will be at least partly to blame if he stepped onto the crossing without giving an oncoming driver any reasonable chance to stop (see the Zebra Pedestrian Crossing Regulations 1971).

- Wearing dark clothing and walking down a dark lane is a significant breach of the *Highway Code* and can be contributory negligence (see, *Powell* v. *Phillips* [1972] 3 All ER 864 and *Widdowson* v. *Newgate Meat Corp* [1997] EWCA Civ 2763).
- A driver is not entitled to expect that other drivers and pedestrians will behave sensibly. The Court of Appeal said in *Moore* v. *Poyner* [1975] RTR 127 that if it would be 'apparent to a reasonable man, armed with the common sense and experience of the way pedestrians . . . are likely to behave in the circumstances which were known by the defendant to exist . . . that there was a possibility of a danger emerging' then the defendant had a duty to avoid this danger by slowing down or sounding his horn or both. A driver going up a street lined with pubs, clubs and bars late on a Saturday night should certainly realise that the pedestrians milling around on the pavement are likely to be drunk and careless (*Ratcliffe* v. *Barnes* [1997] EWCA Civ 1930).

Lord Reid in *Baker* v. *Willoughby* [1969] 3 All ER 1528 considered how to apportion blame when a sober pedestrian crossing the road has been hit by a car, and commented that the car driver may be very much more to blame. He said:

> A pedestrian crossing the road has to look to both sides as well as forwards. He is going at perhaps 3 mph and at that speed he is rarely a danger to anybody else. The motorist has not got to look sideways, although he may have to observe over a wide angle ahead, and if he is going at a considerable speed he must not relax his observation. . .

On the other hand, Hodson LJ said in *Brown* v. *Bramley* [1960] AC 145 that the car driver:

> has to look not only in front but also to right and to left and in his mirror behind. He cannot look in all these places at the same time. His primary duty is to look at the part of the road on which he is himself travelling. That does not mean that he is absolved from keeping observation even on pavements as well as on the other half of the road. But that is a matter really of degree.

As to contributory negligence, see **section 4.14**.

If one has only the flimsiest evidence, mere hints at liability, how far can one rely upon it? The Court of Appeal has said '. . . the opinion of a third party as to the driving ability of either party is . . .completely worthless . . . Even for a driver with an impeccable driving reputation there is always the possibility of inattention for whatever reason which may lead to a collision' (*Cooper* v. *Hatton* [2001] EWCA Civ 623). However, in *Cooper* v. *Floor Cleaning Machines Ltd* [2003] *The Times* 24 October the Court of Appeal found against the claimant on the basis that the defendant knew the road quite well but the claimant did not, and that certain photographs of the vehicle damage, although they could not have been said to provide compelling evidence, were not entirely consistent with the claimant's story.

The accident had taken place when a driver fouled another at a multi-lane interchange.

With thought, it may be obvious that one version of events is impossible, or at least less likely than the other version. It is often possible to come to some convincing conclusions using just:

- a rough plan of the site of the accident;
- a few measurements (such as road width);
- your own experience as a pedestrian and driver;
- some common knowledge, such as that ordinary walking speed is 3 mph or 1.34 metres/second;
- the table of stopping distances in the *Highway Code*.

Judges deciding road traffic cases are often referred to the table of stopping distances, and are usually happy to consider arguments based on it. Note that the distances in the table are for a car on a dry road. A van on a wet road might take much longer to stop. By breaking the stopping distances down into thinking time (which does not change) and stopping time, and drawing a graph, you can find the stopping distance for whatever speed a vehicle was doing. It is safe to use a graph to project a stopping distance between two of the values given in this table (e.g. the table gives 30 mph and 40 mph, but 35 mph is required). It is not safe to do so for a speed much below the lowest speed in the table, as the stopping distance for a really slow-moving car is negligible.

Carry out the calculations in metres per second. To convert from miles per hour to kilometres per hour, multiply by 1.6093. To convert kilometres per hour to metres per second, divide by 3.6. For a real example of rough and ready calculations, see *James* v. *Fairley* [2002] EWCA Civ 162. The claimant lost £400,000 because the Court of Appeal found them convincing.

5.2 ROAD TRAFFIC ACCIDENTS – HIGHWAY AUTHORITY CLAIMS

This section relates to accidents caused by a highway authority's failure to maintain the public highway. For accidents caused by street works or occurring off the public highway, see **section 5.3**.

Section 41 Highways Act 1980 requires the highway authority 'to maintain the highway'. It applies to highways that are 'maintainable at public expense'. A person injured by breach of this duty is entitled to compensation, subject to a statutory defence under s.58 of the Act.

'Highway Authority'? Under the 1980 Act and the Local Government Act 1972 the duty is non-delegable. All motorways and trunk roads are the responsibility of the Secretary of State, and are administered nationally by the Highways Agency or the National Assembly for Wales. Otherwise, in London, the highway authority is the Borough Council, the Common Council of the City of London, or Transport for London in the case of designated Greater London Authority roads. Outside London, the highway authority is the Metropolitan District Council or the County Council.

'Maintain'? At s.329, the 1980 Act states that maintenance includes repair, and the word maintain should be read in that light.

Maintenance means putting and keeping the highway in repair. It does not include improvement (see dissenting judgment of Lord Denning MR in *Haydon* v. *Kent County Council* [1978] QB 343, approved in *Goodes* v. *East Sussex County Council* [2000] UKHL 34). Nor does it include putting up warning signs, or painting warning signs on the road surface (*Gorringe* v. *Calderdale Metropolitan Borough Council* [2004] UKHL 15).

The s.41 duty extends to maintaining manhole covers and other installations, whether they are the property of the council or of a statutory undertaker such as a water board (*Walton* v. *Torfaen County Borough Council & Hyder Group* (CA 9 June 2003).

The duty is:

> reasonably to maintain and repair the highway so that it is free of danger to all users who use that highway in the way normally to be expected of them . . . The highway authority must provide not merely for model drivers, but for the normal run of drivers to be found on their highways, and that includes those who make the mistakes which experience and common sense teaches are likely to occur
>
> (*Rider* v. *Rider* [1973] 1 QB 505)

The test is whether the road is foreseeably dangerous to vehicles being driven in the way vehicles normally are driven on that road.

Therefore the claimant must show that:

- danger was reasonably foreseeable from the state of the highway;
- the danger was caused by a failure to maintain or repair the highway;
- the injury was caused by this failure.

If the claimant can do this, his claim against the highway authority will succeed unless the latter can set up a defence. Under s.58 of the 1980 Act it is a defence to a claim based on failure to maintain a highway maintainable at public expense if the highway authority had taken such care as in all the circumstances was reasonably required to secure that the part of the highway to which the claim relates was not dangerous for traffic.

In order to ensure you take account of all the circumstances, consider:

- The character of the highway and the traffic that was reasonably to be expected to use it. Was the highway heavily used by articulated lorries or construction site traffic, which would cause it to wear out quickly?
- The standard of maintenance appropriate for a highway of that character and used by such traffic.
- The state of repair in which a reasonable person would have expected to find the highway.

- Whether the highway authority knew, or could reasonably have been expected to know, that the condition of the highway to which the action relates was likely to cause danger to users of the highway. Was the defect already there at the time of the last highways inspection, and had there been any other complaints or accidents?
- Where the highway authority could not reasonably have been expected to repair that part of the highway before the cause of action arose, what warning notice of its condition had been displayed.
- For the purposes of such a defence it is not relevant to prove that the highway authority had arranged for a competent person to carry out or supervise the maintenance of the part of the highway to which the action relates unless it is also proved that the authority had given him proper instructions with regard to the maintenance of the highway and that he had carried out those instructions.

Essentially, s.58 gives a defence if the highway authority did not know that a danger existed, and had a proper system for inspecting the highway, and then for carrying out necessary repairs reasonably swiftly. A good system for inspecting road carriageways might be to look at strategic routes and distributor roads monthly; local interconnecting roads every three months; and local access roads every four months. The Court of Appeal indicated in *Pridham* v. *Hemel Hempstead Corporation* (1971) 69 LGR 523 that the system should include recording and acting on complaints by the public. The Court also said that there was no point obtaining evidence from an expert engineer as to the ideal interval between inspections: 'One must instead determine what is reasonable by a suitable compromise between conflicting considerations.' Ideally there would be very frequent and thorough inspections, but a local authority's resources are limited. If it spends too much on inspections it will have less not only for road maintenance but also for its many other functions.

The highway authority has a good defence if it really had suitable, effective systems for inspection and repair – not just because it claims it did.

Did the defect exist at the time the highway inspector last patrolled, but he failed to notice it? The claimant may need to argue that, given the nature of the defect, it must have been there for years, rather than having become dangerous since the last inspection. The defendant may wish to argue that damage of that kind and in that location could easily have been caused by an articulated lorry or a drought, and may not have been apparent even a week before the claimant's accident. The court will be interested in common sense argument about these things, but not in mere guesswork based on dubious presumptions. Certainly in the fast track, it is most unlikely that the court will be willing to consider expert evidence about the length of time a defect must have been there.

Many highway authorities operate a Code of Practice that permits drive-by highways inspection. In other words, the inspector cruises along the road looking out of his car window (see, for example, *Thompson* v. *Hampshire County Council* [2004] EWCA Civ 1016). Amongst the many things this will not reveal are cracks in a manhole cover. If there is reason to doubt the value of the defendant's system, ask:

- for a copy of the Code of Practice in use at the time;
- whether the inspection was drive by;
- how long before the accident was the last inspection;
- what defects the inspector noted at that time;
- when he did find a defect, how long it took the defendant to repair it.

If the defect in the highway was actually created or installed by the authority, it will not be a defence for the authority to show that it had a proper system for inspection. This also applies if a member of the public had complained to the authority of a dangerous defect and it failed to act on the complaint.

The Highways Act 1980 imposes on the highway authority an absolute duty to maintain the highway, but allows it a reasonable amount of time in which to respond to a need for maintenance. If there has been unreasonable delay, the question is whether the claimant would have been injured had the highway authority carried out the repair in a reasonable time. What is reasonable depends on the circumstances. If a large hole suddenly appears in the High Street, that calls for a faster response than if the same happens on the coast path. In *Rogers* v. *National Assembly for Wales* [2004] EWCA Civ 250 the highway authority had known for some time that a certain road surface was dangerously slippery, and had scheduled repairs. These were postponed, and in the meantime the slipperiness caused a fatal accident. The claim succeeded.

If the highway authority denies liability for the accident, the Personal Injury Protocol requires it to disclose liability documents. The standard disclosure list of the Pre-action Protocol highlights various documents for disclosure by the defendant if it denies liability for a pavement trip accident. If a road accident was caused by a failure to maintain the highway, the same documents are relevant. They are, for the 12 months before the accident, records of:

- inspections for the relevant stretch of highway;
- maintenance including records of independent contractors working in relevant area;
- the minutes of highway authority meetings where maintenance or repair policy has been discussed or decided;
- complaints about the state of the highways;
- other accidents that have occurred on the relevant stretch of highway.

There is no point a claimant arguing that the local authority should have spent less on frivolous matters and more on the highways, as policy matters are non-justiciable (see the discussion in *Phelps* v. *London Borough of Hillingdon* [2000] UKHL 47). Neither can shortage of money be raised as a defence to a claim based on failure to maintain under s.41 of the 1980 Act (*Goodes* v. *East Sussex County Council* [2000] UKHL 34).

A highway authority may be liable for its acts, but is seldom liable simply for failure to exercise a statutory power. In *Stovin* v. *Wise* [1996] AC 923 the highway authority had a statutory power to remove a bank of earth on private land, which dangerously restricted visibility at a road junction. It did not exercise the power. The claimant was injured when the defendant negligently drove out of a minor road and into collision with him. The defendant's insurers sought a contribution from the highway authority. The House of Lords refused to find that the highway authority had a common law duty of care to exercise the statutory power, saying: 'If the policy of the Act is not to create a statutory liability to pay compensation, the same policy should ordinarily exclude the existence of a common law duty of care.'

Section 62 of the Highways Act 1980 gives highway authorities a power to improve highways, but if it does not do so and a road user is injured as a result, he has no right to compensation (*Sandhar* v. *Department for Transport* [2004] EWHC 28 (QB)).

Section 39 of the Road Traffic Act 1988 says that highway authorities:

> must prepare and carry out a programme of measures designed to promote road safety [and] carry out studies into accidents arising out of the use of roads . . . [and] take such measures as appear to the authority to be appropriate to prevent such accidents, including . . . the construction, improvement, maintenance or repair of roads . . . and other measures taken in the exercise of their powers for controlling, protecting, or assisting the movement of traffic on roads.

The standard disclosure list therefore expects a highway authority to disclose documents about such matters. However s.39 imposes a broad public law duty. The House of Lords considers it difficult to imagine a case in which a common law duty of care might be founded on a target duty of that sort, or on failure to provide some benefit that a public authority merely had a power to provide (*Gorringe* v. *Calderdale Metropolitan Borough Council* [2004] UKHL 15).

As to accidents caused by flooding, s.41 imposes:

> a duty not merely to keep a highway in such a state of repair as it is at any particular time, but to put it in such good repair as renders it reasonably passable for the ordinary traffic of the neighbourhood at all seasons of the year without danger caused by its physical condition.

That does not mean that the highway authority will always be liable for accidents caused by water collecting on the road, especially in a major storm (*Burnside* v. *Emerson* [1968] 1 WLR 1490).

What if an accident results from a skid on snow or ice? Gritting of roads in icy weather and clearing snow from roads are tasks carried out by the highway authority, and there were various successful compensation claims when injury resulted from winter skids. The House of Lords stopped this temporarily with its judgment in *Goodes* v. *East Sussex County Council* [2000] UKHL 34.

Goodes said that when s.41 of the Highways Act 1980 requires the highway authority to maintain the highway, this means to keep the fabric of the highway in a good state of repair. Therefore it was irrelevant that the highway may be covered in a slippery layer, and a highway authority had no duty to grit or clear the highway in winter. Parliament responded by imposing a new s.41 of the Highways Act 1980, applicable from 1 November 2003: 'In particular, a highway authority is under a duty to ensure, so far as is reasonably practicable, that safe passage along a highway is not endangered by snow or ice.'

If the claimant was injured by a skid on snow or ice before 1 November 2003, can he get around *Goodes* by arguing that the highway authority had a duty of care at common law to keep the highway clear of these hazards? It seems not. See *Sandhar* v. *Department for Transport* [2004] EWCA Civ 1440 in which the claimant might not have been injured if the highway authority had adhered to the Trunk Roads Maintenance Manual, and the claimant argued unsuccessfully that its common law duty of care required it to do so. The Manual is now the Statement of Service and Code of Practice for the Winter Maintenance of Motorways and Trunk Roads. The equivalent for other highway authorities is the Local Authority's Association's Highway Maintenance – a Guide to Good Practice.

The principle in *Goodes* presumably applies equally to deposits of mud, gravel or leaves. The post-*Goodes* amendment to s.41 of the Highways Act 1980 does not apply to these things, and *Sandhar* suggests that the highway authority will not be found to have any common law duty of care to remove them.

Where snow or mud has collected so as to form an obstruction rather than a slippery surface, note s.150 Highways Act 1980: 'If an obstruction arises in a highway from accumulation of snow or from the falling down of banks on the side of the highway, or from any other cause, the highway authority shall remove the obstruction.' This appears to be a duty that could be used as the basis for a damages claim.

If an accident is caused because somebody has spilt mud or oil on the road, one should proceed against the actual culprit based on the normal rules of negligence. If he is untraceable, consider a claim under the Motor Insurers' Bureau Untraced Drivers Agreement.

5.3 PEDESTRIAN TRIPPING ACCIDENTS

Trips usually cause just grazed palms and squashed shopping. However, they can cause a broken wrist or a tear of the rotator cuff in the shoulder even if the victim is young and active. An elderly trip victim may suffer a facial fracture or fractured hip.

Trip defendants are reluctant to settle even small claims, and some highway authorities have a 70 per cent success rate in resisting them.

For the sake of clarity, there is some overlap between this section and the previous one. That section relates to road traffic accidents that are the fault of the highway authority, and so deals with the public highway. Pedestrian tripping accidents often occur in other situations, and have other defendants and other crucial facts.

A tripper claim may be based on:

- Section 41 Highways Act 1980, which imposes a duty on highway authorities to maintain public highways as discussed below.
- An act of negligence, if the trip was created by the act of a known person. Typical situations include an articulated lorry breaking a manhole cover, or a fish and chip shop spilling oil on the pavement. An employer may be vicariously liable for the torts of his employees, and in the case of works to the highway, he may be liable for the torts of his independent contractors.
- Negligence, or possibly nuisance, emanating from land adjoining the highway. The occupier or owner of the land may be liable even if he did not create the hazard. The classic example is a trip caused by the roots of a tree on land adjoining the highway. If the trip has existed for any length of time on the public highway, the claimant may be able to pursue the culprit for causing it or failing to cure it, or the highway authority for failing to intervene (see **section 4.1**).
- Occupiers' liability, if the trip occurred on private land and not on a public highway (see **section 5.5**).
- An employer's breach of statutory duty, if the claimant was injured by tripping at work (see **section 6.26**).
- The duty of care of the concessionaire of a toll road. Unless privately owned, these roads are created under some sort of agreement, usually under the New Roads & Street Works Act 1991 or a predecessor.
- The Docks Regulations 1988. These impose a statutory duty on dock operators to provide and maintain a safe means of access to every part of dock premises; to ensure that all floors, decks, surfaces, stairs, steps, passageways and gangways are kept free of substances likely to cause a person to slip or fall or vehicles to skid; lighting, and marking of hazards.

'Public highway'? Under s.36(6) Highways Act 1980 and under the Wildlife and the Countryside Act 1981 each county council, metropolitan district council, London borough council and the Common Council must keep a list of the public highways within its area. This is available for inspection at the office of the relevant district council, free of charge at reasonable hours. One could go along and inspect the list. It is easier for the claimant, and probably the authority, to send in a map showing the location of the accident and ask for a written response.

Disputes about whether or not a particular place is part of the highway are fearsomely complex. Fortunately, they are also rare. If problems arise about this or any other very technical point in a highway claim, one must refer to a specialist textbook.

Very briefly, anything used as a highway is likely to be a public highway, maintainable at public expense. A road, a pavement or footway, a bridleway, or even a field path may become a public highway in various ways, principally:

- By dedication and acceptance at common law.
- Under the National Parks and access to the Countryside Act 1949 because it was already in use as a footpath or bridleway at 16 December 1949.
- By agreement between the landowner and highway authority under s.35 Highways Act 1980, as for example with many pedestrian precincts and walkways in town centres.
- Under s.36(1) Highways Act 1980 because it was already '. . .maintainable at public expense ... immediately before the commencement of this Act. . .'.
- By agreement, adoption or declaration under s.30 of the 1980 Act or otherwise.
- By long user. Section 31 of the 1980 Act says: 'Where a way over any land, other than a way of such a character that use of it by the public could not give rise at common law to any presumption of dedication, has been actually enjoyed by the public as of right and without interruption for a full period of 20 years, the way is to be deemed to have been dedicated as a highway unless there is sufficient evidence that there was no intention during that period to dedicate it.'
- Because it was built by a highway authority or local authority. Section 36(2) of the 1980 Act says ' . . . the following highways . . . shall for the purposes of this Act be highways maintainable at public expense: a) A highway constructed by a highway authority, otherwise than on behalf of some other person who is not a highway authority; b) A highway constructed by a council within their own area under Part V of the Housing Act 1957'. Part V is now Part II of the Housing Act 1985.
- Because in fact the highway authority has maintained the path. This is what s.38(1) of the 1980 Act means when it refers to the old law of tenure.

In *Gulliksen* v. *Pembrokeshire County Council* [2002] EWCA Civ 968 the claimant tripped over a defect in a path on the defendant's council estate. Given that the defendant could not be liable at common law for nonfeasance, the question was whether the path was a highway maintainable at public expense so that the defendant had a s.41 duty to maintain. The path had been built by the defendant's predecessor as part of a housing estate. Although it was not a through route, the court found that all members of the public had had the right to pass and repass without hindrance since the estate first opened in 1974. Therefore at common law it had been a highway by dedication since it first opened. The Highways Act applicable in 1974 was the 1959 Act, s.38(2)(*c*) of which was very similar to s.36(2)(*c*) of the 1980 Act. As the path had been built by the council in its housing role, s.38(2)(*c*) made the path a highway maintainable at public expense. By s.36(1) of the 1980 Act, it continued to be so after 1980. See also the House of Lords judgment in *McGeown* v. *Northern Ireland Housing Executive* [1995] 1 AC 233.

If a highway authority is liable to maintain a particular carriageway, it is liable to maintain any footway that runs alongside it and forms part of the highway. It is a question of fact in each case whether the grass verge is part of the highway. The highway authority is responsible for grass or waste ground that, as a matter of fact, forms part of the highway. See the wording of s.130 of the Highways Act 1980. Therefore a narrow, smoothly mown grass strip running between the road and the pavement is probably part of the highway, not least because pedestrians have to cross it to get to the road. Rough, tussocky waste ground probably is not part of the highway. See, for example, *Thompson* v. *Hampshire County Council* [2004] EWCA Civ 1016 where the highway authority accepted that a metre-wide strip of verge, mown twice a year, was part of the public highway.

A gate or stile that exists so pedestrians can use a public path is probably part of the highway and maintainable by the highway authority, but again this is a question of fact. It may still belong to the successors in title of the land on which the highway was created.

The s.41 (Highways Act 1980) duty requires the highway authority 'to maintain the highway'. It applies to highways that are 'maintainable at public expense'. A person injured by breach of this duty is entitled to compensation, subject to a statutory defence under s.58 of the Act.

'Highway authority'? Under the 1980 Act and the Local Government Act 1972 the s.41 duty is non-delegable. All motorways and trunk roads are the responsibility of the Secretary of State, and are administered nationally by the Highways Agency or the National Assembly for Wales. Otherwise, in London, the highway authority is the borough council, the Common Council of the City of London, or Transport for London in the case of designated Greater London Authority roads. Outside London, the highway authority is the Metropolitan District Council or the County Council.

'Maintain'? At s.329, the Act states that maintenance includes repair, and the word maintain should be read in that light. Maintenance means putting and keeping the highway in repair. It does not include improvement (*Haydon* v. *Kent County Council* [1978] QB 343, approved in *Goodes* v. *East Sussex County Council* [2000] UKHL 34).

The s.41 duty extends to maintaining manhole covers and other installations, whether they are the property of the council or of a statutory undertaker such as a water board. See *Walton* v. *Torfaen County Borough Council & Hyder Group* (CA 9 June 2003), in which the claimant fell into a manhole in a grass verge when its cover and frame gave way underneath him. His claim succeeded against both highway authority and water board.

In *Mills* v. *Barnsley Metropolitan Borough Council* [1992] PIQR 291 the Court of Appeal said that in a tripper claim against the highway authority, the claimant must prove that:

> The highway was in such a condition that it was dangerous to traffic or pedestrians in the sense that, in the ordinary course of human affairs, danger may reasonably have been anticipated from its continued use by the public; the dangerous condition was created by the failure to maintain or repair the highway; and the injury or damage resulted from such a failure.

If the claimant can do this, his s.41 claim will succeed unless the highway authority can set up a defence under s.58 of the 1980 Act as discussed below.

'Dangerous condition'? The typical pedestrian does not always walk with his eyes on the ground, especially in areas where one would reasonably expect the ground to be level and safe or where he has to pay attention to traffic in a road he wants to cross. In *Rider* v. *Rider* [1973] 1 QB 505 the Court of Appeal indicated that the highway authority's duty under s.41 is reasonably to maintain and repair the highway so that it is free of danger to all who use it in the way normally to be expected; and that the highway authority is not entitled to assume that everybody is prudent and alert. It must take account of people who make the mistakes that experience and common sense suggest are likely to occur. As the claimant in *Rider* was a motorist, not a pedestrian, the test was whether the road is foreseeably dangerous to vehicles being driven in the way vehicles normally are driven on that road.

Although the courts do not expect a pedestrian to watch the ground constantly, it is good practice for the defendant to allege in every case that the claimant failed to look where he was putting his feet. It may result in a deduction from the compensation on the basis of contributory negligence.

The highway authority is not entitled to assume that every pedestrian will be able to see. In *Haley* v. *London Electricity Board* [1965] AC 778 the claimant was blind, and fell into a trench in a pavement. It was reasonably foreseeable that blind people would use that pavement. The works should have been marked in such a way that a blind person would have found them with his cane.

If a highway defect arises from wear and tear, the courts say:

- 'There may be a ridge of half an inch or three-quarters of an inch occasionally but that is not the sort of thing which makes [a pavement] dangerous or not reasonably safe' (*Meggs* v. *Liverpool City Corporation* [1968] 1 All ER 1137).
- 'Uneven surfaces and differences in levels between flagstones of about an inch may cause a pedestrian temporarily off balance to trip and stumble, but such characteristics have to be accepted. A highway is not to be

judged by the standard of a bowling green' (*Littler* v. *Liverpool Corporation* [1968] 2 All ER 343).

- 'It would not be right to say that a depression of one inch will never be dangerous but a depression of more than one inch will always be dangerous. The test of dangerousness is one of reasonable foresight of harm to users of the highway. The question is whether a reasonable person would regard it as presenting a real source of danger' (*Mills* v. *Barnsley Metropolitan Borough Council* [1992] PIQR 291) (CA). This unsuccessful claim was based on a slab which had a 2 inch wide gap, 1¼ inches deep.
- *Winterhalder* v. *Leeds City Council* [2002] LTL 26 September. A finding in favour of any particular claimant 'certainly does not mean that if a pedestrian trips on or over a gap of 2½ inches, or any other measurement, that he or she is likely or unlikely to be successful in recovering damages. As has been said in previous cases, it is quite impossible and very misleading to state that a depression or a gap or a dip of any particular dimension forms a danger to pedestrians'.
- 'There are two aspects to the exercise of determining dangerousness. First, it is one of ". . . reasonable foresight of harm to users of the highway". Secondly . . . "whether a reasonable person would regard it as presenting a real source of danger". Both criteria have to be fulfilled' (Eady J in *Galloway v. London Borough of Richmond upon Thames* (QBD 20 February 2003). The second criterion balances the private interest of the accident victim with the public interest in making good use of limited maintenance funds. This claim, which related to a 1¼ inch deep hole in a kerbstone, failed. The judge concluded that pedestrians were more alert when stepping onto kerbstones than when just making their way along the pavement. As to the second criterion, he noted that the defect was 'unremarkable' and that within the borough there were thousands of similarly chipped kerbstones.

Clearly there is no rule that a ½ inch (13mm) high trip is acceptable and 1 inch (26mm) is not. The courts often emphasise that each case turns on its own facts.

A ½ inch trip may well be unacceptable if it is located where it might cause somebody to trip and fall down a flight of steps, or where many old people walk over it. *Wright* v. *London Borough of Greenwich* [1997] JPIL 01/97 61 is interesting, this was a county court case, actually brought under the Occupiers' Liability Acts as the trip occurred on a path on the defendant's premises. There was quite a small defect in an old York stone path. In this sort of path, irregularities are to be expected and are arguably part of its charm. The defendant was liable, however, because it knew that many old people used the path, there had been previous trip accidents, and it could have repaired the defect easily and cheaply. The Occupiers' Liability Act 1957 requires the occupier to have regard to the degree of care, or want of care, which one would expect from a visitor. Section 58 of the Highways Act 1980 contains a similar provision.

A ¾ inch trip may be unacceptable if it is somewhere busy (say at a school entrance or by a Pelican crossing perhaps) or badly lit.

The court may be readier to find the defendant liable if it actually created the trip. If council workmen install a new pavement and leave one paving slab sticking up it seems arguable that a relatively small trip should result in a successful claim. There seems to be an element of this in *Dibb* v. *Kirklees Metropolitan Borough Council* [1999] EWCA Civ 1180 (later in this section) but one should not bet on it too heavily.

The courts have sometimes found that something suddenly introduced into the highway may be a significant danger even if it is quite a low trip, for example a ⅛ inch thick metal sheet laid on a pavement that caused an elderly lady familiar with the pavement to trip when she encountered it at dusk (*Pitman* v. *Southern Electricity Board* [1978] 2 All ER 901).

The claimant may have tripped while walking on the carriageway. Do the courts apply the same standards to the surface of roads as they do to the pavement? In *Bird* v. *Tower Hamlets London Borough Council* (1969) 67 LGR 682 the court said pedestrians had to cross the road, and the highway authority had to keep the highway safe for them to do so. However, in *Ford* v. *Liverpool Corporation* (1972) 117 SJ 167 the court found the highway authority not liable after a pedestrian tripped over a defect in the carriageway which was more than an inch high.

What will the court consider when dealing with a highway authority's s.58 defence to a s.41 claim? It is a defence under s.58 if the highway authority had taken such care as in all the circumstances was reasonably required to secure that the part of the highway to which the claim relates was not dangerous for traffic. Consider:

- The character of the highway and the traffic that was reasonably to be expected to use it. Did it have a high density of pedestrians including prams and elderly people?
- The standard of maintenance appropriate for a highway of that character and used by such traffic. Normal conditions on a country lane or field path would be unacceptable in a city centre.
- The state of repair in which a reasonable person would have expected to find the highway. By today's standards, not those of 50 years ago.
- Whether the highway authority knew, or could reasonably have been expected to know, that the condition of the highway to which the action relates was likely to cause danger to users of the highway. Was the defect already there at the time of the last highways inspection, and had there been any other complaints or accidents.

- Where the highway authority could not reasonably have been expected to repair that part of the highway before the cause of action arose, what warning notice of its condition had been displayed.
- For the purposes of such a defence it is not relevant to prove that the highway authority had arranged for a competent person to carry out or supervise the maintenance of the part of the highway to which the action relates unless it is also proved that the authority had given him proper instructions with regard to the maintenance of the highway and that he had carried out those instructions.

Essentially, s.58 gives a defence if the highway authority did not know that a danger existed, and had a proper system for inspecting and repairing the highway. A good system for inspecting pavements might be to examine footways in main shopping areas every month; pavements in busy urban areas every three months; other urban and busy rural areas every six months; and little-used rural footways once a year. The Court of Appeal indicated in *Pridham* v. *Hemel Hempstead Corporation* (1971) 69 LGR 523 that the system should include recording and acting on complaints by the public. The court also said that there was no point obtaining evidence from an expert engineer as to the ideal interval between inspections. 'One must instead determine what is reasonable by a suitable compromise between conflicting considerations.' Ideally, there would be very frequent and thorough inspections, but a local authority's resources are limited. If it spends too much on inspections it will have less not only for road maintenance but also for its many other functions.

If a highway authority denies liability for a trip accident, the Pre-action Protocol requires it to make disclosure of documents relating to liability. The documents highlighted by the Standard Disclosure list of the Protocol are, for the 12 months before the accident:

- records of inspection for the relevant stretch of highway;
- maintenance records including records of independent contractors working in relevant area;
- records of the minutes of highway authority meetings where maintenance or repair policy has been discussed or decided;
- records of complaints about the state of the highways;
- records of other accidents that have occurred on the relevant stretch of highway.

If there is any doubt whether the highway authority's inspectors were applying the correct standards, the claimant should ask for copies of the guidelines used by the authority. These might, for example, say that for pavements outside busy urban areas a trip of three quarters of an inch or more would be regarded as needing urgent repair. In setting their standards, highway authorities usually follow the Local Authority's Association's

Highway Maintenance – a Guide to Good Practice. If the defendant had set itself higher standards than usual, and then failed to meet those standards, it may well be liable even if it did meet the usual standard. However, in *Sandhar* v. *Department for Transport* [2004] EWHC 28 (QB), the defendant was not found liable despite having failed to follow the Trunk Roads Maintenance Manual. A claimant who doubts that the defendant was actually operating a suitable, effective system of inspection and repair should also refer to the previous section (**section 5.2**).

There is no point a claimant arguing that the local authority should have spent less on frivolous matters and more on the highways, as policy matters are non-justiciable. See the discussion in *Phelps* v. *London Borough of Hillingdon* [2000] UKHL 47. Neither can shortage of money be raised as a defence to a claim based on failure to maintain under s.41 of the 1980 Act (*Goodes* v. *East Sussex County Council* [2000] UKHL 34).

As to street works, 'the duty imposed by the common law on a person who carries out works to a public highway, including a footway, is to take reasonable care to carry out those works in such a way that they are not dangerous to persons who use the highway with reasonable care for their own safety' (*Brett* v. *Lewisham London Borough Council* (CA 20 December 1999), which related to a temporary tarmac patch).

Street works may be carried out on behalf of private individuals. If carried out by employees, the employer will be liable for their negligence under the normal principles of vicarious liability. Generally, there is no liability for the torts of independent contractors, but one may be liable alongside them if they carry out street works on one's behalf. The question is whether the cause of the accident was something integral to the works, or merely incidental (see **section 4.9**).

Generally, street works are carried out by the highway authority under non-delegable duties, and the authority is the correct defendant under s.41 Highways Act 1980. The highway authority may have asked a contractor to do maintenance work, or arranged for another local authority to act as its agent and carry out the work under an agency agreement. Even so, the highway authority remains the correct defendant. See s.58(2) Highways Act 1980 and the Local Government Act 1972.

Some street works are carried out not by the highway authority, but by a statutory undertaker such as the water, electricity or gas company. When a statutory undertaker does work on or under the highway, it does so under statutory powers and duties. Street works carried out by a water board are regulated by the Water Act 1945 and the New Roads and Street Works Act 1991. The 1991 Act requires the statutory undertaker to liaise with the street authority. If the work was to a highway maintainable at public expense, the highway authority is the street authority. The 1991 Act requires statutory undertakers to guard, sign and light street works such as excavations in the road or pavement. It also requires them to complete their work and reinstate the street as soon as possible, and tell the street authority it is done.

There is a Code of Practice under the 1991 Act, made by the Secretary of State for Transport – Safety at Street Works and Road Work. Amongst other detailed requirements, it says that signs must be secured with sandbags so that they do not blow over, and gives guidance about use of traffic cones and pedestrian safety barriers.

The street authority has to keep a Street Works Register, which makes it easy for a claimant's lawyer to find out what his client tripped over/fell into. The street authority may itself be liable if it knew or should have known that the statutory undertaker failed to reinstate the street properly.

A statutory undertaker such as a gas, electricity or water board has a duty of care to maintain its installations. It may not be realistic for the water board to carry out regular inspections of the highway over each of its manholes and sewers. It will often rely on the highway authority to report any defects it notes during inspections. If so it will be taken to know about anything it would have known if it had carried out its own inspection (*Reid* v. *British Telecommunications* (1987) *The Times* 27 June).

Say the claimant tripped over a hole in the pavement a week after some works were completed by the water board; or put a foot into a stopcock hole because the cover had been smashed by vandals. He is going to be in some doubt whether the appropriate defendant is the highway authority, the water board, or both as in *Walton* v. *Torfaen County Borough Council & Hyder Group* (CA 9 June 2003). He should send his letter of claim to both, and ensure they both get copies of all correspondence and documents. He should ask them to save legal costs by resolving liability between themselves. Generally, they will tell the claimant that one or other will act as defendant. If not, he can apply pressure by issuing proceedings naming both as defendants. This additional pressure will, with luck, cause the defendants to agree liability between themselves, so that the claimant can amend the proceedings and serve them on only one defendant.

The claimant must have evidence (see **section 4.18**), and the tripper questionnaire on the accompanying CD-ROM. If the claimant cannot prove exactly what he tripped over, and how high/deep it was, it is most unlikely that the claim will succeed.

> The question in each case is whether the particular spot where the plaintiff tripped or fell was dangerous. If it was, then the defendant authority concedes that there was a failure to maintain the highway and the plaintiff would be entitled to recover. But if the particular spot was not dangerous, then it is irrelevant that there were other spots nearby that were dangerous or that the area as a whole was due for resurfacing
>
> (*James* v. *Preseli Pembrokeshire District Council* [1993] PIQR 114)

It is worth noting *Dibb* v. *Kirklees Metropolitan Borough Council* [1999] EWCA Civ 1180, in which the claimant tripped on or near a pavement defect but was unable to say exactly what she did trip on. This stretch of pavement was steep, narrow, badly designed and broken. The claimant at one point said she turned her ankle when she stepped on an area of broken concrete, and at another that it happened when she caught her heel in a grating just beside the broken area. At trial she confessed that she could not remember, if she had ever known, exactly what caused the injury. The Court of Appeal said 'where the plaintiff undoubtedly fell on a piece of pavement which was plainly dangerous it is . . . open to the judge to draw the inference. . . that the plaintiff's fall and her consequent injuries were indeed caused by the defective pavement'. The court was perhaps influenced by the evidence of the claimant's expert witness, which appears to have been accepted, that the defect did not arise from wear and tear but was created by the defendant as 'a very botched piece of engineering'.

Even if the highway authority has repaired the trip already the claimant should carry out a site visit with a camera. Other features in the vicinity may strongly suggest that the highway authority did not, in fact, operate effective systems. For example, there may be many 1 inch trips near the one that caused the accident, or faded yellow paint marks showing defects that the highway authority noted a long time ago but have not repaired. It is clear from *Dibb* v. *Kirklees* that the general state of the highway in the area may be relevant.

Where an allegedly dangerous situation has existed for some time, the court will be impressed by evidence that there had been previous trips. Conversely, if the defendant's witnesses are believable, the court will be very impressed to learn that there have been no previous similar incidents despite many thousands of pedestrian visits.

5.4 PEDESTRIAN SLIPPING ACCIDENTS

If the claimant slipped on private premises his claim will be against the occupier, based on breach of a duty of care under the Occupiers' Liability Acts. An occupier owes the common duty of care to his visitors, which is a duty to take such care as in all the circumstances of the case is reasonable to see that his visitors are reasonably safe in using the premises for the purposes for which he was invited or permitted by the occupier to be there. He owes a rather lower duty to persons other than his visitors (see **section 5.5**).

Employers have additional statutory duties to prevent slips (see **section 6.26**).

If the slip took place on a dock, see the Docks Regulations 1988. These impose a statutory duty on the dock company to provide and maintain a safe means of access to every part of the dock premises, and to ensure that all floors, decks, surfaces, stairs, steps, passageways and gangways are kept free of substances likely to cause a person to slip or fall.

If the slip occurred on the public highway because the surface was too smooth, the claim will be against the highway authority under s.41 Highways

Act 1980. If the slip occurred because of winter conditions on the highway, note that since 1 November 2003, highway authorities have had a duty under s.41 Highways Act 1980 'to ensure, so far as is reasonably practicable, that safe passage along a highway is not endangered by snow or ice'. If injury results from a breach of this duty, the victim is entitled to compensation. A highway authority's liability for other slippery substances on the highway is very limited, and it may be that a claim can only be brought against the person whose negligence caused the spill (see **section 5.2**).

It is possible to measure the coefficient of friction of a particular shoe on a particular floor. The amount of friction depends on:

- what the two surfaces are made of;
- how rough the surfaces are;
- the contours of the surfaces, for example, whether the shoe has tread or the floor has ridges;
- whether there is any dry lubricant such as flour or sand;
- whether there is any wet lubricant such as water or grease;
- how much pressure brings the surfaces together;
- and (if one or both is moving) the speed and direction of any movement.

The slip resistance of a floor depends mainly on microscopic peaks on its surface. The height of these peaks is measured in microns. With less than 10 microns of roughness, even a spill of water can create a hydrodynamic film on the floor and cause an aquaplaning slip. Peaks measuring less than 10 microns will not stick through the film to prevent this. Peaks of 20 microns or more are needed to prevent a slip if oil or fruit pulp gets on the floor. The qualities of the floor can be measured with:

- A roughness meter (which works in the same way as a record-player stylus).
- A skid resistance tester designed by the Transport and Road Research Laboratory. This portable device includes a pendulum, on the bottom of which is a piece of rubber, such as the Simulated Standard Shoe Sole prepared for the purpose by the Rubber and Plastics Research Association. When the device is set up on a flat surface, the pendulum scuffs the rubber along the floor surface for 5 inches.

Other systems can be used, but any device that pulls a weight across the floor is likely to underestimate the slipperiness of the surface in wet conditions. The weight sweeps away the hydrodynamic film.

The results can be assessed using the guidelines of the UK Slip Resistance Group, which includes the Health and Safety Executive (HSE). See also the HSE publications *Watch your Step* (which deals with slip resistance for different floor coverings) and *Slips and Trips*, and the *British Standards Institution Code of Practice for Stairs*, BS5395.

It is hard to imagine addressing a court on these points, however. The claimant may be able to get the defendant to agree that the floor was dangerously slippery. If the defendant is reluctant to agree, consider arranging a joint site visit at an early stage in the claim. The parties can put some of the guilty substance on the floor, and see how slippery it was. If the claim goes to trial on liability, the judge will simply decide for himself whether he thinks the surface was slippery. It is very unlikely that he will feel the need for measurements or expert help. He will make his own decision based on a description of the floor (unless he is minded to visit the scene of the accident himself), the length of time for which it has been in that state, and whether there have been any other accidents or complaints.

The courts seem generally willing to accept that very smooth floors and stairs become dangerously slippery if wetted with oil or washing up liquid, or they have just been polished and buffed. See, for example, *Jacob* v. *Tesco Stores* [1998] EWCA Civ 1793 and *McGhee* v. *Strathclyde Fire Brigade* [2002] Scot CS 16. The court may accept that a spill of water or coffee makes a very smooth floor dangerous, and there is an excellent chance it will take that view of a spill of grease or fruit pulp.

Where there is a history of frequent spillages, as in any supermarket, the occupier should instruct its staff to look for spills and to deal with them promptly. The occupier has:

> a duty to use reasonable care to see that the shop floor, on which people are invited, is kept reasonably safe . . . there is a burden thrown on the defendants either of explaining how this thing got to the floor or giving [adequate] evidence. . . as to the state of the floor and the watch that was kept on it immediately before the accident.
>
> (*Turner* v. *Arding & Hobbs Ltd* [1942] 2 All ER 911)

In *Ward* v. *Tesco Stores* [1976] 1 WLR 801 the claimant slipped on a spill of yogurt in a supermarket. There was no evidence that the spill had been caused by the defendant. The defendant cleaned the floor five or six times a day. The Court of Appeal held that the claimant was not required to show how long the spill had been on the floor. The floor was under the defendant's management. This sort of accident did not happen in the ordinary course of events if the floor was kept clean and spillages dealt with as soon as they occurred. The spill had probably been on the floor for long enough to be dealt with. To escape liability, the defendant had to show that the accident had not occurred because of a want of proper care on its part. This meant showing that it operated 'a reasonably effective system for clearing dangers which may, from time to time, exist', or that the accident 'would have been at least equally likely to have happened despite a proper system designed to give reasonable protection to customers'. *Ward* has been approved on a regular basis for nearly 30 years, for example in *Jacob* v. *Tesco Stores* [1998] EWCA Civ 1793.

A shop's usual defence is in four parts:

1. The thing was not spilt by the defendant's employees. If it was, the defendant will be vicariously liable.

2. The defendant had an adequate system for inspecting the floor at frequent enough intervals.
3. Staff were properly trained and knew what dangers to look for.
4. A competent person was actually implementing the system in full at the time of the accident. Ideally, this means referring to an inspection log that was signed at regular intervals on the day of the accident.

Another possible defence is that the accident would have occurred even if the defendant had an effective cleaning system. For example, positive proof that the spill was created by a member of the public only seconds before the accident.

The claimant may want to call evidence from independent witnesses about the number of spills on the floor before or after the accident, and the time it took staff to clean them up. If there have been many customer visits and very few slip accidents, this is good evidence that the defendant generally had an adequate system. If there have never been any slip accidents, this may show that the defendant was doing all that was necessary even if it had no system for checking the floors. This might be the case in a museum or library.

Shops and cafés argue that they need smooth, slippery flooring in order to comply with hygiene standards. However, there are industrial flooring materials that are both easy to clean and non-slip. One pharmacy chain in the USA reported a 75 per cent reduction in the number of slipping accidents after using a proprietary floor coating with quartz crystals. Some flooring materials, such as carborundum-faced floor tiles, are less easy to clean but are suitable for high-risk areas. Many supermarkets place washable matting in the aisle where fruit is displayed.

An occupier has no duty to guarantee a visitor's safety. The court decides in each case, based on the particular facts of the case, whether the common duty of care has been satisfied. A court might find, for example, that a householder who knows he might have visitors has a duty to clear snow from his doorstep.

If the risk was obvious, and the accident would not have occurred if the claimant took reasonable care, the claim may well fail (*Laverton* v. *Kiapasha* [2002] EWCA Civ 1656). There is a questionnaire about this sort of accident on the accompanying CD-ROM.

Although wearing smooth-soled shoes may not be a good idea, it is such common practice that it probably will not be seen as contributory negligence on the part of a claimant.

Slipper claims are riskier than routine road traffic claims. Thus in *Abrew* v. *Tesco Stores* [2003] EWHC 9003 (Costs) the Supreme Court Costs Master allowed a 50 per cent success fee on the claimant's conditional fee agreement, even though there were eyewitnesses to the claimant's slip on dried spaghetti.

5.5 OCCUPIERS' LIABILITY

The Occupiers' Liability Act 1957 regulates the duty of care that is owed by any occupier towards his visitors, and the Occupiers' Liability Act 1984 regulates his duty towards persons other than his visitors. The same definitions of occupier, premises and visitor are used in both Acts, but those who are invited by the occupier to enter his premises, or are treated as having been invited, enjoy more protection than others.

The Acts replace any common law duty of care 'in respect of dangers due to the state of the premises or to things done or omitted to be done on them' (s.1(1) 1957 Act). To avoid failing on a technicality, claimants generally state in the particulars of claim that the defendant acted 'negligently and in breach of the common duty of care under the Occupiers' Liability Act 1957' or as the case may be. The court may impose a costs penalty if one makes superfluous allegations, but the common law and the Acts have so much in common that a penalty is unlikely.

To start with, we will look at the situation with regard to visitors under the 1957 Act. Section 2(2) says that an occupier's common duty of care to his visitors is 'a duty to take such care as in all the circumstances of the case is reasonable to see that the visitor will be reasonably safe in using the premises for the purposes for which they are invited or permitted by the occupier to be there'.

'Occupier'? The Acts do not alter the common law rules as to who is an occupier. The occupier may be the owner, a tenant, somebody running a business on the land, somebody who has a right over the land such as a right to drive over it, a building or demolition contractor developing the site, etc. Several people may simultaneously occupy premises in different ways.

To be an occupier, a person must have some control over the premises or the activities carried out there. In *Wheat* v. *Lacon* [1966] 1 All ER 582 the premises were owned by a brewery and managed by a couple who had a licence to live in a flat on the premises. A guest fell down the dark and dangerous stairs outside the flat and was killed. The Court of Appeal said:

> an occupier is the one who has immediate supervision and control and the power of permitting or prohibiting the entry of other persons . . . wherever a person has a sufficient degree of control over premises that he ought to realise that any failure on his part to use care may result in injury to a person . . . lawfully there

that person was an occupier. The brewery was responsible for maintaining the premises, and was an occupier to that extent. Its duty of care required it to provide a lighting system and a sound staircase. As managers, the couple were occupiers with a duty to make sure that the lights were on. In fact, neither was liable, as the brewery did not know the stairs were dangerous and the couple did not know the bulb was missing.

The court in *Wheat* v. *Lacon* also discussed other common situations. If a landlord rents premises to a tenant but does not demise the roof, boiler room, or parts that are shared between several tenants (hallway, stairwell, car parking area) the landlord is still the occupier of the parts not demised. A tenant cannot be liable for failing to do something he had no legal power to do, such as installing lighting in a common stairwell. If a landlord employs an independent contractor to carry out work to premises it owns, the landlord retains a degree of control and continues to be an occupier even when absent.

'Premises'? Premises includes workplaces, building sites, shops, homes, gardens, farmland, wasteland. Indeed by s.1(3) of the 1957 Act the occupier of 'any fixed or moveable structure, including any vehicle, vessel or aircraft' owes his visitors the common duty of care. In effect, the word premises includes electricity pylons, diving boards, lifts and even an ordinary ladder, although it may be hard to show that anybody occupies a ladder other than the person climbing it (*Wheeler* v. *Copas* [1981] 3 All ER 405). It does not include a vehicle, vessel or aircraft that the claimant had hired, or in which he was being transported under a carriage for reward agreement.

'Visitor'? A visitor under the Acts is a person who, under the common law rules, would be the occupier's invitee or licensee. This includes anybody who is invited or permitted to enter the occupier's property, or who has a contractual right to enter.

Somebody using a park provided for the use of the public is a visitor. Most people who visit commercial or domestic premises are visitors because there is an implied invitation to enter the public part of commercial premises during business hours. There is also an implied invitation to walk up the front path of a private home with the intention of posting a letter or speaking to the occupier. Somebody doing these things is a visitor unless he knew that he did not have permission, or his intentions were unlawful, or he was not there as the visitor of the occupier. For example, in *Holden* v. *White* [1982] 2 WLR 1030 the claimant was a milkman making a delivery, but he was not delivering to the occupier's premises. He was delivering next door, and was merely using the occupier's land as a shortcut.

An invitee or visitor becomes a trespasser if he strays onto part of the premises where he had no business to be, or enters them outside opening hours. In the well-known expression of Scrutton LJ in *The Calgarth* [1927] P 93 '. . . when you invite a person into your house to use the stairs, you do not invite that person to slide down the banisters'.

Under s.2(6) of the 1957 Act, somebody exercising a legal right to enter is a visitor, even if the occupier objects to their entering. For example, a fireman or police officer in an emergency, or a High Court bailiff with a warrant.

Note the following points on visitors on paths and rights of way:

- Somebody using a private path is a visitor, save as above.
- Somebody using a common path by permission (e.g. on a housing estate where the occupier of the common parts gives a licence to tenants and their guests to use the estate paths) is the occupier's visitor.
- Somebody exercising a private right of way over land does so as of right. Therefore he is not a visitor and does not have the protection of the 1957 Act (*McGeown* v. *Northern Ireland Housing Executive* [1995] 1 AC 233). The 1984 Act would apply.
- Using a public right of way or highway does not make someone a visitor, for purposes of the 1957 Act, of the person who occupies the land over which the right of way happens to run. See the House of Lords judgment in *McGeown*, in which the claimant tripped over a hole in a footpath on the defendant's housing estate. This had become a public right of way, and this extinguished any licence that previously existed. The Lords felt that it would be unreasonable if landowners not only had to submit to the passage over their land of anyone who chose to exercise the right to do so, but were also under a duty to maintain it in a safe condition. They were not to be liable for mere nonfeasance. As to the 1984 Act, under s.1(7) no duty is owed to persons using the highway. For accidents on the highway see **sections 5.2** and **5.3**.
- Note also what is known as the right to roam. Section 1(4) of the 1957 Act was amended by the Countryside and Rights of Way Act 2000 to say: 'A person entering any premises in exercise of rights conferred by virtue of s.2(1) of the Countryside and Rights of Way Act 2000 or an access agreement or order under the National Parks and Access to the Countryside Act 1949 is not, for the purposes of this Act, a visitor of the occupier of the premises', and s.1(6)A says that when somebody is injured while exercising the right to roam, the occupier will not be liable for injuries 'resulting from the existence of any natural feature of the landscape, or any river, stream, ditch or pond whether or not a natural feature . . . or a risk of that person suffering injury when passing over, under or through any wall, fence or gate, except by proper use of the gate or of a stile . . .' unless the occupier created the risk deliberately or was reckless as to whether it was created.

'Such care as . . . is reasonable'. Unless there is a foreseeable risk of significant injury, the common duty of care does not require the occupier to take any steps.

The court will take account of all the circumstances, including the era when the premises were constructed (*Hogg* v. *Historic Buildings & Monuments Commission* [1988] 3 CL 285). The Countryside and Rights of Way Act 2000 likewise requires the courts to consider the importance of maintaining the character of the countryside, including features of historic, traditional or archaeological interest.

'Reasonably safe'? Claims under the Acts very often relate to trips and slips (see **sections 5.3** and **5.4**). Workplace accident statistics show over 100,000 injuries caused by stairs, 100 of which are fatal, every year. However, stairs are reasonably safe, unless there is a special reason as in *Wheat* v. *Lacon*. Steps leading down into a swimming pool are usually wet and therefore more slippery than if they were dry. Although a careless or awkward swimmer may slip on them, the need to take care is quite obvious, so these steps are reasonably safe. They might be unsafe if surfaced with ultra-slippery tiles with a vitreous glaze, designed for use on walls only.

Ordinary doors cause a lot of injuries. The courts would hardly consider it a breach of duty to allow a visitor to use a door. However, if there is a corridor through a building with a door at each end, opening both at the same time can lead to a through-draft that will slam a door with shattering force. In a public building, where a door may be opened unpredictably by one of many residents or visitors, this may well be unsafe unless the doors are both fitted with pneumatic closers, or the situation has existed for many years without accidents.

Say the claimant was standing in a bath at the defendant's premises, using an overbath shower. There was a rubber non-slip mat in the bath, but he slipped, fell sideways and was injured when he hit the floor. Were the premises reasonably safe? If this washing arrangement had been fitted in a workplace, the employer would probably have been in breach of statutory duty. If the premises were intended for use by the elderly, this arrangement would probably not be reasonably safe. The DTI/ROSPA home accident surveillance system (HASS) shows 595 accidents a year involving non-slip bath mats, and many more involving falls in and from the bath. It is a question of fact in all the circumstances whether the premises were reasonably safe. Some judges would accept the claim on the basis that expecting anybody to stand on a wet, curved surface with a face full of soap involves an unacceptable risk of injury, which could have been avoided by fitting a guardrail or a separate shower cubicle. Others would consider that the premises were reasonably safe, and that in any case any danger was obvious and an able-bodied claimant could have avoided it by having a bath instead. For HASS data (which incidentally shows 677 people injured each year by CDs and audio cassettes, 800 by parts of flowers, 1,784 by sheets and 10,127 by telephones) see **www.dti.gov.uk**.

Premises do not have to be safe for woolgathering or horseplay. If the only risk is obvious and avoidable, the premises are not unsafe. Compare *Peskett* v. *Portsmouth City Council* [2002] EWCA Civ 1175, and *Tomlinson* v. *Congleton Borough Council* [2003] UKHL 47, both of which are summarised later in this section.

'All the circumstances'? The occupier has to take such care as in all the circumstances of the case is reasonable. It seems that one considers the defendant's resources, so a rich defendant should take more care (*Laverton* v. *Kiapasha* [2002] EWCA Civ 1656).

Section 2(3)(*a*) of the 1957 Act echoes the common law by saying that the occupier must be prepared for children to be less careful than adults. Case law predating the Act is still useful when interpreting it today, in particular about an occupier's liability for things on its land that are either alluring to children, or represent a concealed danger.

It may not be apparent to a child that something is in fact dangerous. In *Glasgow Corporation* v. *Taylor* [1922] 1 AC 44 the defendant local authority was the occupier of a botanical garden, open to the public, in which there was a bush with poisonous berries. A seven-year-old visitor ate some and died. The defendant was liable. It was highly relevant that the berries were shiny and attractive to children, who might well pop them into their mouths. If one can reasonably expect children to find a hazard on the occupier's premises alluring, this circumstance requires the occupier to take more care for their safety.

An occupier is entitled to expect that 'little children' (zero to six years?) will be accompanied by their parents, who will keep them away from any evident dangers. It:

> would not be socially desirable if parents were . . . able to shift the burden of looking after their children from their own shoulders to those of persons who happen to have accessible bits of land. Different considerations may well apply to public parks or to recognised playing grounds where parents allow their children to go unaccompanied in the reasonable belief that they are safe

(*Phipps* v. *Rochester Corporation* [1955] 1 QB 450)

Note that in such a case the child would often have more chance in a negligence claim against his parents, the defendant may seek contribution or indemnity from the parents, and it may be best to avoid appointing the parent as litigation friend in case of a conflict of interest (see **section 17.7**).

Case law both before and after the 1957 Act supports the idea that an occupier is very likely to be liable to a child injured by a hazard on its land if it represented a concealed danger, such as a pile of coal waste which is scalding hot under a thin crust. The other side of the coin is *Simkiss* v. *Rhondda Borough Council* (1981) LGR 460. The claimant, aged seven, found a steep bit of ground on council property and slid down it for fun. She was injured, and it was claimed on her behalf that the council should have fenced off the land. The claim failed. There was no concealed danger, and the claimant's father conceded that he would not have thought that the area was dangerous.

Children play with more enthusiasm and less care than adults, and often fall off playground equipment provided for them in parks. The British Standard EN1977 recommends the user of rubberised surfaces in playgrounds, apparently not to reduce the risk of broken arms and legs but to reduce head injuries. The courts may well consider that a local authority is in breach of its common duty of care if it fails to provide an impact-absorbing surface under and around swings and slides. If a child claimant is injured in a fall and wants to claim against the occupier, the questions are whether he was of an age at which the British Standard was aimed, and whether the medical evidence says that an impact-absorbing surface would probably have prevented or reduced the injury?

British Standard EN1176 relates to the design of playground equipment, which again may be relevant to an injury. As to the status of British Standards in court, and some other BSI and HSE guidance on play equipment, see **section 5.14**. Depending on the nature of the equipment and the age of the child, the courts might feel that the occupier's duty of care requires him to provide trained adult supervision.

In *Simonds* v. *Isle of Wight* (2003) *The Times* 9 October, a five-year-old at a school sports day was told by his mother to go and join a group supervised by teachers so she could go shopping. Instead, he climbed onto a swing and jumped off pretending to be Superman. He broke his arm. On appeal, the court found that it would be madness to make the occupier liable. The school had provided a reasonable level of supervision, an occupier has no duty to guarantee a child's safety on a playing field, and it would be unreasonable to require an occupier to impose a duty to warn mothers that swings are dangerous.

In *Jolley* v. *London Borough of Sutton* [2000] UKHL 31 a third party had dumped an old boat on the defendant's land. It was reasonably foreseeable that children might play on it and get cuts and bruises by putting a foot through a rotten plank. The defendant accepted that it should have removed the boat for this reason. What actually happened was that the claimant jacked the boat up to repair it and it fell on him. The Court of Appeal found the defendant not liable because the claimant was not carrying out a normal play activity. However, the House of Lords said it had been foreseeable that children would 'meddle with the boat at the risk of some physical injury,' and the care needed to prevent the minor injury was just the same as to prevent the serious injury. The actual meddling was not all that different to what had been foreseeable, so it was still within the scope of the defendant's duty of care.

Section 2(3)(*b*) of the 1957 Act says that the occupier may expect that a person, in the exercise of his calling, will appreciate and guard against any special risks ordinarily incident to it, so far as the occupier leaves him free to do so. This affects the emergency services and tradesmen. In both *Salmon* v. *Seafarer Restaurants* [1983] 1 WLR 1264 and *Ogwo* v. *Taylor* [1988] 1 AC 431 the claimants were firemen who sued the person who negligently started the fire. The defendants could have foreseen that their negligence would lead to the fire brigade attending, to firemen using their skills to do whatever was both necessary and reasonably practical to extinguish the fire, and to one of them being injured by the inherent risks of doing so.

Tradesmen are not expected to be able to avoid unusual concealed hazards on a customer's premises, but are expected to be competent enough to access awkward areas without injury (*Hughes* v. *Midnight Theatre Company* [1998] EWCA Civ 595).

If injury is caused by faulty building, maintenance or repair work done by an independent contractor on behalf of the occupier, s.2(4)(*b*) of the 1957 Act says that:

> the occupier is not to be treated without more as answerable for the danger if in all the circumstances he acted reasonably in entrusting the work to an independent contractor and had taken such steps (if any) as he reasonably ought in order to satisfy himself that the contractor was competent and that the work had been properly done.

Haseldine v. *Daw* [1941] 2 KB 343 pre-dates the 1957 Act but still provides a useful illustration of its independent contractor provisions. The claimant was injured when a lift at the occupier's premises fell down the lift shaft. The occupier did not maintain the lift himself. He had signed a maintenance contract with 'a first class firm of lift engineers' to inspect it at intervals, service it and provide a report. Although apparently competent, the contractor did a bad job. The occupier had no way of checking, and no reason to believe there was a problem. The contractor might be liable, the occupier was not.

If his work may foreseeably cause injury, the competent contractor is insured for third party liability. One may be liable to somebody injured by an independent contractor if one did not enquire whether he had suitable insurance arrangements (*Gwilliam* v. *West Hertfordshire NHS Trust* [2002] EWCA Civ 1041 and *Bottomley* v. *Todmorden Cricket Club* [2003] EWCA Civ 1575). As to the precise nature of this duty, see also *Naylor* v. *Payling* [2004] EWCA Civ 560.

If the occupier asks an independent contractor to do a job and can perfectly well see for himself whether it has been properly done, he may be liable if it is done badly and injury results (*Woodward* v. *Mayor of Hastings* [1944] 1 KB 174, where the work was shovelling snow off a step).

Under s.2(4)(*a*) of the 1957 Act an occupier generally has a good defence to a claim if he had previously given warning of the danger, as long as 'in all the circumstances it was enough to enable the visitor to be reasonably safe'. A sign saying Beware of the Dog would not enable a visitor to be reasonably safe. *White* v. *Blackmore* [1972] 2 QB 651 was a claim in respect of a spectator killed when a car left the track. The Court of Appeal considered whether the warning notice put up by the occupier could provide an effective defence under s.2(4)(*a*). A notice saying 'Motor Racing Is Dangerous' does not necessarily tell a spectator that he is personally at risk, or that the risk goes beyond being pelted with gravel. Today one would expect a warning notice to provide an effective defence only if the claimant saw it or should in all the circumstances have seen it, and if it should have been clear to him from the notice and/or the surrounding circumstances that he would be in danger, the nature of the danger and what he could do to keep safe.

There is no duty to put up a warning sign relating to any possible hazard. In *Staples* v. *West Dorset District Council* [1995] PIQR 439 the claimant slipped while walking on the Cobb at Lyme Regis. There was no warning sign, but the Cobb is primarily a sea defence, not a promenade. An occupier would have a duty to put up a warning: 'if, without a warning, the visitor in question would have been unaware of the nature and extent of the risk . . . but if the danger is obvious, the visitor is able to appreciate it, he is not under any kind of pressure and he is free to do what is necessary for his own safety, then no warning is required'.

See also *Darby* v. *National Trust* [2001] EWCA Civ 189, a fatal claim relating to a drowning in a pond on the defendant's land. The pond was 60 feet across, muddy in places and up to 6 feet deep. It was not clear why the deceased drowned. The pond was no different to thousands of others across the UK, and the occupier had no duty to warn visitors of obvious risks.

An occupier's right to exclude liability, for example by including a disclaimer on an entrance ticket if the public have to pay to enter his premises, is restricted by the Unfair Contract Terms Act 1977. This renders ineffective most terms that exclude liability for injury arising from the conduct of a business. An occupier cannot exclude liability to persons who enter his premises because they have a legal right to do so, for example a police officer executing a warrant.

Cases

Some cases on the modern law of occupier's liability to visitors are given below.

In *Peskett* v. *Portsmouth City Council* [2002] EWCA Civ 1175 the claimant tripped when hurrying along a well-worn short cut across a grassed area. At either end of the short cut was a trip, perhaps 3–4 inches high. The claim succeeded because the occupier had failed to take such care as was reasonable in all the circumstances to ensure that its visitors were reasonably safe. It knew the short cut was in use and that although there had been no previous accidents the trip was getting deeper. At the time of the accident the trip hazard should have been obvious to the occupier and it would have been easy to reduce the risk by paving the short-cut. This was very much a borderline case, and the court deducted 50 per cent for contributory negligence.

In *Beaton* v. *Devon County Council* [2002] EWCA Civ 1675 the claimant was cycling with her family on a local authority cycle track that was used by about 30,000 cyclists a year, and had been used for many years. She entered a tunnel, which had electric lighting and drainage gullies 6 inches deep running along each side close to the wall. Distracted by her children's activities, the claimant stopped by the wall of the tunnel and put a foot down. Her foot went into one of the gullies and she was injured. There was no grille on the gully to prevent this sort of accident but it was filled with chippings to within 2½ inches of the level of the cycle track. The Court of Appeal noted that the 1957 Act did not impose a duty to ensure the safety of all, but a duty to take such care as was reasonable. There had been no previous accidents. The claim failed.

The Occupiers' Liability Act 1984 may make an occupier liable for injuries suffered by people 'other than his visitors'. For convenience, in this handbook they are referred to as trespassers, although the Act also covers somebody exercising a right of way.

The duty owed to trespassers is not as high as that owed to visitors. Under s.1(4) it is a duty 'to take such care as is reasonable in all the circumstances of the case to see that [people other than visitors do] not suffer injury on the premises by reason of the danger concerned'. The courts would not consider it reasonable for an occupier to take much care to avoid injury to a poacher or burglar. The 1984 Act relates to injury, and does not impose any liability in respect of loss of or damage to property.

Under s.1(3) of the 1984 Act an occupier of premises owes a duty to a trespasser who is injured by reason of any danger due to the state of the premises or to things done or omitted to be done on them, if:

> he is aware of the danger or has reasonable grounds to believe that it exists . . . he knows or has reasonable grounds to believe that [a trespasser] is in the vicinity of the danger concerned or that he may come into the vicinity of the danger . . . and . . . the risk is one against which, in all the circumstances of the case, he may reasonably be expected to offer [a trespasser] some protection.

An occupier is not expected to believe that a trespasser will come into the vicinity of a hazard merely because it is possible. In *Swain* v. *Puri* [1996] PIQR 442 the claimant was a child who fell through a factory skylight while trespassing on the roof. The claim failed as there had been no previous instances of children getting onto the roof, or trying to do so.

In *Higgs* v. *WH Foster* [2004] EWCA Civ 843 the claimant was a police officer who climbed into the defendant's coach park to investigate a suspected stolen trailer. It was dark, he was not using a torch, and in walking round the back of some parked coaches he fell into an uncovered open-air inspection pit. The court found that there was nothing alluring about the coach park, no reason to expect anybody to enter it merely because it was quite easy to do so, and no reason to expect that, if somebody did, they would go round the back of the coaches. The occupier would have reasonable grounds to expect this only if 'there was evidence to show that trespassers had indeed been on the premises in the past and in doing so had trespassed on the part of the premises which exposed them to the risk of injury from the pit'.

Even if the occupier knows that trespassers have been on the relevant part of the premises in daylight in summer, the court will not necessarily expect him to believe that one will be there at night in winter (*Donoghue* v. *Folkestone Properties* [2003] EWCA Civ 231).

An occupier can generally satisfy his duty under the 1984 Act by putting a fence around his land, or at least around the hazard. He may be able to satisfy his duty by taking 'such steps as are reasonable in all the circumstances of the case to give warning of the danger concerned or to discourage persons from incurring the risk' (s.1(5)). However, there have been many successful claims by children who got into places where they should not be, such as industrial wasteland. It takes a pretty good fence to keep a child out, especially if the things on the other side are particularly alluring.

Claims by trespassers under the Occupiers' Liability Act 1984 tend to succeed best for children of seven to 12 years of age. As regards younger children, an occupier is entitled to expect that very young children (zero to six years?) will be accompanied by their parents, who will keep them away from any evident dangers (see *Phipps* earlier in this section).

As regards older children, if the claim succeeds one can expect a large deduction for contributory negligence. In *Adams* v. *Southern Electricity* (1993) *The Times* 21 October a 15-year-old managed to bypass a defective anti-climbing device on an electricity pylon and came into contact with the transformer. The electricity company were liable but there was a two-thirds discount for the boy's own negligence.

The tide has turned against cases like *Adams*. See *Ratcliff* v. *McConnell* [1997] EWCA Civ 2679, in which a young man climbed into a locked swimming pool that he knew to be out of bounds, dived in and was seriously injured when he hit the bottom. His claim failed. See also *Tomlinson* v. *Congleton Borough Council* [2003] UKHL 47. The claimant dived into a lake in the defendant's public park, hit his head and suffered spinal injuries. Having seen and ignored the occupier's 'No swimming' signs, the claimant became a trespasser when he entered the water, so his claim was regulated by the 1984 Act. The occupier knew there was a danger, and had reasonable grounds to believe that a trespasser would come into its vicinity. It had decided to take steps to discourage swimmers. The House of Lords found that the shallowness of the lake was a natural feature or the landscape, and as a danger it was obvious and avoidable even without the warning signs. The risk was not one against which the occupier might reasonably have been expected to offer the claimant any protection.

5.6 DEFECTIVE PREMISES

Typical injury scenarios are:

- a trip on defective stairs leading to the claimant's front door;
- cut from glazing that broke when the claimant bumped into it.

If the accident was the occupier's fault see **section 5.6**. An absentee landlord is not usually an occupier, although he may be taken to occupy any parts of the premises which he did not demise to the tenant, such as the roof or a common parking area.

In this section we are looking at accidents caused by a dangerous defect which is the responsibility of a non-occupying landlord or 'bare landlord'. Liability depends on whether the defect arose because of a lack of maintenance or from the way the property was designed and built, and whether the claimant is the tenant or merely a member of the tenant's family or a visitor.

If the claimant is the tenant of the premises, he may well be able to sue the landlord for breach of contract, the contract being the lease. If the claimant was not a party to the lease, the doctrine of privity of contract means he cannot sue for breach of it.

Neither does anybody other than the tenant have any common law right to sue a bare landlord for injury suffered on the premises as a result of lack of maintenance. In *Cavalier* v. *Pope* [1906] AC 428 the House of Lords endorsed the comments in *Robbins v. Jones* (1863) 15 CB (NS) 21 that: 'A landlord who lets a house in a dangerous state is not liable to the tenant's customers or guests for accidents happening during the term, for, fraud apart, there is no law against letting a tumbledown house.' In this case the landlord had agreed with the tenant that he would repair a dangerously defective floor. Before he did, the tenant's wife fell through it. The landlord was not liable to the wife.

Parliament partly filled this gap in the common law with s.4 of the Defective Premises Act 1972 (DPA), as amended by the Housing Act 1988. The DPA imposes a duty on landlords to people other than their tenants.

Section 4(1) of the DPA says:

> Where premises are let under a tenancy which puts on the landlord an obligation to the tenant for the maintenance or repair of the premises, the landlord owes to all persons who might reasonably be expected to be affected by defects in the state of the premises a duty to take such care as is reasonable in all the circumstances to see that they are reasonably safe from personal injury or from damage to their property caused by a relevant defect.

Section 4(2) says: 'The said duty is owed if the landlord knows (whether as a result of being notified by the tenant or otherwise) or if he ought in all the circumstances to have known of the relevant defect.' In *Sykes* v. *Harry* [2001] EWCA Civ 167, the gas fire at the claimant's rented property had a partly blocked flue and a cracked heat exchanger. Fitted eight years earlier, it had never been serviced. Under the lease, it was the landlord's duty to maintain the fire. It was no defence to a claim based on s.4 for the landlord to say he had no actual knowledge that the appliance was defective. He ought to have known of the defect, as it would have been revealed had he done proper inspection and maintenance.

'Relevant defect'? A 'defect in the state of the premises existing at or after the material time and arising from, or continuing because of, an act or omission by the landlord which constitutes or would if he had notice of the defect have constituted a failure by him to carry out his obligation to the tenant for the maintenance or repair of the premises'. DPA 1972, (s.4(3)).

'Material time'? '. . . the earliest of the following times, that is to say . . . the time when the tenancy commences; [or] the time when the tenancy agreement is entered into'. DPA 1972, (s.4(3)).

'Obligation . . . for maintenance or repair'? The DPA's protection is geared to the landlord's obligation to repair the premises, and goes no wider than that. Most long leases contain a covenant requiring the landlord to maintain the structure and exterior of the property. In a lease for less than seven years, see s.11 Landlord and Tenant Act 1985:

> In a lease to which this section applies . . . there is implied a covenant by the lessor:
> (a) To keep in repair the structure and exterior of the dwelling-house (including drains, gutters and external pipes),
> (b) To keep in repair and proper working order the installations in the dwelling-house for the supply of water, gas and electricity and for sanitation (including basins, sinks, baths and sanitary conveniences, but not other fixtures, fittings and appliances for making use of the supply of water, gas or electricity), and
> (c) To keep in repair and proper working order the installations in the dwelling-house for space heating and heating water.

It seems the structure and exterior can include routes that have to be used to get to and from the property (*Brown* v. *Liverpool Corporation* [1969] 3 All ER 1345).

Repair does not include improving the property, and s.11 does not require the landlord to ensure that the premises were fit for the purpose for which they had been let (*Quick* v. *Taff-Ely Borough Council* [1986] QB 809).

If there is no actual duty to maintain or repair, s.4(4) of the DPA states that a landlord who has an express or implied right 'to enter the premises to carry out any description of maintenance or repair of the premises' will be treated under the Act as if he had an obligation to do them (unless the lease said the tenant had to do them). The Court of Appeal held in *McAuley v. Bristol City Council* [1992] 1 QB 134 that an express right in a lease to enter 'for any purpose which may from time to time be required by the landlord' amounted to such a power. It seems that a landlord who has a right to enter the garden in order to carry out maintenance and repair to the house may be treated under the DPA as if he had a duty to maintain and repair the garden too.

The court may be willing to imply into the lease a repairing obligation on the landlord that was not actually agreed between the landlord and tenant. See the rather controversial House of Lords case of *Liverpool City Council* v. *Irwin* [1977] AC 239 in which the landlord was found to be responsible for maintaining the only means of access to flats in a tower block.

In *Boldack* v. *East Lindsey District Council* [1998] EWCA Civ 191 the defendant had inspected one of its council houses when the last tenant left. The claimant, a young child, then moved in with his mother. The lease contained the usual landlord's covenant to maintain the structure and exterior in good repair. The claimant was injured when a paving slab leaning against the wall of the house fell on him. The claimant's case was that the landlord should have removed the slab during its inspection. However, the slab was not part of the structure or exterior of the premises, and the landlord had no more duty to remove it than to remove rubbish from the garden. The child's DPA claim failed. He also alleged that the landlord had been negligent, but he was not a party to the lease so the rule in *Cavalier* v. *Pope* applied. Note that in such a case the child would often have more chance in a negligence claim against his parent, and it may be best to avoid appointing the parent as litigation friend in case of a conflict of interest (see **section 17.7**).

Section 8 of the Landlord and Tenant Act 1985 says:

> In a contract to which this section applies for the letting of a house for human habitation there is implied . . . a condition that the house is fit for human habitation at the commencement of the tenancy, and . . . an undertaking that the house will be kept by the landlord fit for human habitation during the tenancy.

However, the definition of 'contract to which this section applies,' means that s.8 is seldom effective.

The injury may be the result not of defective maintenance, but of the way the property was designed and constructed. A landlord who designs and builds premises does owe a common law duty of care to do so with due regard to the safety of occupiers and visitors (*Rimmer* v. *Liverpool City Council* [1985] QB 1). This is an exception to the rule in *Cavalier* v. *Pope*.

There is a statutory duty too. Section 1 of the DPA 1972 imposes a duty on the architect, surveyor, engineer, builder and any sub-contractors to carry out work 'for or in connection with the provision of a dwelling . . . in a workmanlike or, as the case may be, professional manner, with proper materials and so that as regards that work the dwelling will be fit for habitation when completed'. Provision of a dwelling includes building a house from scratch, but also dividing a property into flats, building an extension, etc.

The statutory duty is owed not only to the original purchaser, but also along the chain of purchasers and tenants. Section 3(1) of the DPA says:

> Where work of construction, repair, maintenance or demolition or any other work is done on or in relation to premises, any duty of care owed, because of the doing of the work, to persons who might reasonably be expected to be affected by defects in the state of the premises created by the doing of the work shall not be abated by the subsequent disposal of the premises by the person who owed the duty.

It may be necessary to obtain expert evidence from an architect or surveyor, but avoid this if possible. One might start by asking the building control department of the local council what they think. They may be prepared to give some free advice on the Building Regulations 2000, which are very helpful with specific issues like this. Probably the local further education college library will let you look up the Regulations on CD-ROM. If successful such research will be more cost effective than obtaining expert evidence.

Does a breach of the Building Regulations give the injured person a civil right to claim for breach of statutory duty? This depends on whether the injury occurred in a workplace. The Building Regulations are made under the Building Act 1984. Section 38 of the Act says that a breach of duty imposed by the regulations will be actionable at civil law, where damage is caused, except where the regulations otherwise provide. Damage includes death and injury. However, at the time of writing this section is not yet in force and the Building Regulations are only part of the evidence to be considered when deciding whether the premises were reasonably safe (*Green* v. *Building Scene Ltd* [1994] PIQR 259).

In the workplace, s.71 of the Health & Safety at Work Act 1974 says 'breach of a duty imposed by Building Regulations shall, so far as it causes damage, be actionable except insofar as the regulations provide otherwise . . . in this section "damage" includes the death of, or injury to, any person'. In addition, the Workplace (Health, Safety & Welfare) Regulations 1992 and other regulations require particular safety features, such as banisters, in workplaces.

If the defendant was in breach of British Standards, it may help the claim (see **section 5.14**).

One hot topic in personal injury work is condensation and mould growth, generally in public sector housing. See *Quick* v. *Taff-Ely Borough Council* [1986] QB 809, *Stent* v. *Monmouth District Council* (1987) 19 HLR 269, *Staves* v. *Leeds Council* (1992) 29 EG 119, *Issa* v. *Hackney London Borough Council* [1996] EWCA Civ 998, *Welsh* v. *Greenwich London Borough Council* [2000] 3 EGLR 41, the conjoined appeals in *Lee* v. *Leeds City Council* and *Ratcliffe* v. *Sandwell Metropolitan Borough Council* [2002] EWCA Civ 6, and *Bowen* v. *Bridgend County Council* [2004] EWHC 9010 (Costs).

5.7 PRODUCT LIABILITY

Malfunctioning toys, tools, electrical goods, medications, foodstuffs and vehicles can all cause injury.

Because a single product may injure thousands of people, many product liability claims are dealt with as group actions. The generic (shared) issues are handled by one or two nominated claimant lawyers, and it is more or less compulsory to join in (CPR Part 19 and *Taylor* v. *Nugent Care Society* [2004] EWCA Civ 51). You can find out if a case you are handling has to be dealt with in this way by contacting the Law Society's Multi-Party Actions Information Service on 0870 606 2522. Alternatively, search for Group Litigation Orders on the Court Service website at **www.courtservice.gov.uk**.

A product liability claim can be based on breach of contract, and/or negligence, and/or the Consumer Protection Act 1987. Breach of contract provides the strongest claim. The defences open to the defendant vary according to the legal basis chosen by the claimant, but basically any product liability claim will fail if:

- The claimant cannot prove that the defect caused the damage.
- The goods were not defective when the claimant bought them. They may have been damaged subsequently by transport, storage or use.
- The seller had given sufficient warning of the defect to the buyer.
- The buyer had already discovered the defect at the time of purchase, or he did so before the accident and consented to the risk by continuing to use the product.
- The injury happened because the goods were being used for a purpose that the seller had, reasonably, not expected, and would not have happened but for this unexpected use.
- The claim is time barred.

Whatever legal basis the claimant relies on, damages may be reduced to reflect his own contributory negligence (see **section 4.14**).

Breach of contract

The original purchaser of goods can claim damages from the seller for breach of contract if injury occurs because the seller breached an express or implied term of the purchase contract. Occasionally, others are entitled to step into the shoes of the original purchaser. It is no defence for the seller to say that he took all possible care to ensure that the goods were as specified. The defendant is liable only for losses flowing naturally from the breach, or which 'may reasonably be supposed to have been in the contemplation of both parties, at the time they made the contract, as the probable result of breach of it'. On all these points, see **section 4.7**.

The term breached by the defendant may be express or implied. The Sale of Goods Act 1979 (as amended by the Sale and Supply of Goods Act 1994 and the Sale and Supply of Goods to Consumers Act 2002) implies three main terms into contracts for the sale of goods. The second and third are implied only into contracts where the vendor sells in the course of a business. Goods must:

- correspond with the way they have been described;
- be of satisfactory quality, unless the seller or supplier had drawn the buyer's attention to a defect, or the buyer had examined the goods and should have discovered the defect;
- be reasonably fit for the purpose for which they are ordinarily used, or for any particular purpose that the buyer made known to the seller.

Goods are of satisfactory quality if they meet the standard that a reasonable person would regard as satisfactory, taking into account any description of the goods, the price and all other relevant circumstances. This condition does not apply to any defect that is specifically brought to the purchaser's attention before sale. Neither, if the purchaser inspected the goods before buying, does it apply to anything that the inspection ought to have revealed.

It is possible for goods to be physically of satisfactory quality and fit for their purpose, but defective in their packaging or instructions, for example, a drug packet that gives the wrong dose.

If the goods are not of satisfactory quality and fit for their purpose then the seller's liability is strict, as the goods he supplied were not the agreed goods. The seller is liable for any injury, death or damage caused by the breach as long as it would have been within the contemplation of the parties when the contract was made.

For similar terms relating to the quality and fitness of services and of goods sold on hire purchase, see the Supply of Goods (Implied Terms) Act 1973, Sale and Supply of Goods Act 1994 and Supply of Goods and Services Act 1982.

The seller may in some circumstances validly exclude liability in the contract. The statutory implied terms can be excluded, but the Unfair Contract Terms Act 1977 restricts a seller's ability to exclude liability for death or personal injury.

Negligence

Those injured by goods that turn out to be dangerously defective can claim damages for negligence. The usual principles of negligence apply, so the claimant must show that the defendant owed him a duty of care; the defendant committed a breach of that duty by act or omission; the foreseeable result of the breach was that the claimant would suffer injury or loss; and the injury and loss were caused by the breach of duty and were not too remote from it (see **sections 4.2–4.5**).

The defendant has a good defence to a negligence claim if he can show that he used all reasonable care and skill, or that no injury was foreseeable. If any significant injury was foreseeable, the defendant will be liable for all injury and loss actually suffered, even if this went beyond the foreseeable.

As to the duty of care, this is not owed only to the original purchaser.

> A manufacturer of products, which he sells in such a form as to show that he intends them to reach the ultimate consumer in the form in which they left him with no reasonable possibility of intermediate examination, and with the knowledge that in the absence of reasonable care in the preparation or putting up of products will result in an injury to the consumer's life or property, owes a duty to the consumer to take that reasonable care.
>
> (*Donoghue* v. *Stevenson* [1932] AC 562)

That principle has since been expanded to include not just manufacturers but wholesalers, distributors, retailers, repairers and hirers; not just the product itself but its packaging and instructions; and not only consumers but even unconnected bystanders.

The negligence might lie in the manufacture; in packaging goods with dangerously misleading instructions; in creating a dangerous defect created by negligent transport or storage of goods; or in sale of goods for a purpose for which they were dangerously inadequate or inappropriate.

As to the defendant's standard of care, it is often helpful to show a breach of statutory duty. Regulations set specific standards for many products. There are many regulations for the safety of gas and electrical appliances, and many fire regulations, some of which govern goods such as clothing and foam and fabric furniture. Suppliers of chemicals must comply with the Chemicals (Hazard Information and Packaging for Supply) Regulations 2002 (CHIP), which require them to use warning labels on containers of chemicals that are flammable, toxic, corrosive, etc; to package them safely, and supply them with information sheets. Bicycles have to comply with the Pedal Bicycles (Safety) Regulations 1984, which require them to meet British Standard BS 6102. The brakes and stability of prams are regulated by the Perambulators and Pushchairs (Safety) Regulations 1978 and the Pushchair (Safety) Regulations 1985. Toys are regulated by the Toys (Safety) Regulations 1974 and 1995. Joke shop supplies are regulated by the Dangerous Substances and Preparations (Safety) (Consolidation) Regulations 1994. Oil heaters and fireworks are governed by the Oil Heaters (Safety) Regulations 1977 and the Fireworks Act 2003. In fact, the list of product regulations is seemingly endless.

A claimant injured by breach of statutory duty may in some situations base his claim on that breach (see **section 6.7**). Regulations that ban sales of dangerous items to under-age purchasers are of particular interest in personal injury work. For example, petrol as in *Evans* v. *Souls Garage* (2001) *The Times* 23 January.

Consumer Protection Act 1987

The Consumer Protection Act 1987 as amended by the General Product Safety Regulations 1994 imposes strict liability on various people for injuries resulting from defective products. Somebody injured by a product because of a defect in its design, manufacture, packaging, marketing or instructions may make a claim under the Act, even if he was not the purchaser.

If the claimant can show the product was defective in terms of design, construction, failure to provide suitable information or otherwise, and that the defect caused injury, the Act shifts the burden of proof to the defendant.

The 1987 Act provides that where any injury or damage to property is caused by a defect in a product, 'every person to whom s.2(2) applies shall be liable for the damage'. This means the producer (manufacturer, miner, fisherman and farmer); anybody who adds his own-brand label to goods; if the goods were imported into the EC, the importer; and any supplier in the chain of supply who will not or cannot identify the person from whom he got the goods.

'Defect'? Goods are defective under the Act if 'the safety of the product is not such as persons generally are entitled to expect,' including whether or not adequate instructions were supplied with it. The product must be safe for any purpose for which one might legitimately expect it to be used. Note that if the purchaser had unrealistic expectations, or bought a relatively cheap product that did not have all the latest safety attachments, the test under the Act is what he was entitled to expect. The Act does not require that a cheap small car bought five years ago should provide the same accident protection as the latest large heavy car with ABS and twin airbags.

'Product'? The Act applies to almost anything that can be bought. For example, a toy that puts a child's eye out, a ladder that breaks while the owner is half way up, or a yogurt that causes botulism. The Act specifically includes vehicles, aircraft and ships. Following the Consumer Protection Act 1987 (Product Liability) (Modification) Order 2000, the Act now covers game and agricultural products which have not undergone any industrial process.

'Consumer'? The Act protects the injured consumer even if he is not the person who purchased the goods.

Although the 1987 Act shifts the burden of proof to the defendant as soon as the claimant proves that the product was defective and the defect caused injury, it does provide the defendant with some special defences. Some relate to unusual circumstances for which there is no space in this handbook, but note that a claim will fail if:

- The product was not actually sold by the defendant, but given away or lent.
- The defendant is a producer, own brander or importer and can prove on the balance of probabilities that the defect did not exist in the product when he put it into circulation.
- The defendant can show that 'the state of scientific and technical knowledge at the time when he put the product into circulation was not such as to enable the defect to be discovered'. This is the development risk defence.

It is not possible to exclude liability under the 1987 Act for injury or damage.

Cases

Some cases on the 1987 Act are given below.

In *Abouzaid* v. *Mothercare* [2000] EWCA Civ 348 the claimant was hit in the eye by a buckle on the end of an elasticated strap while fitting an accessory to a pushchair, and suffered a detached retina causing a permanent vision problem. The defendant relied on the development risk defence, on the basis that the product was not known to have caused injury and did not appear on the Department of Trade and Industry database of products that have caused injury. The Court of Appeal doubted whether lack of knowledge of accidents counted as 'scientific and technical knowledge'. This product was defective because the strap could have done its job without being elasticated; and because the defendant had not provided a warning. The claim succeeded under the 1987 Act. It would have failed if based solely on negligence, as there had not been a reasonably foreseeable risk of significant injury.

In *A* v. *National Blood Authority* [2001] EWHC 446 (QB) the claimants contracted Hepatitis C as a result of blood transfusions between the date when the 1987 Act came into force and the time when the defendant started screening blood for this virus. At the start of this period, Hepatitis C had not been discovered. There was no possible test for the virus until summer 1989. The defendant started screening with the test in April 1991. In the meantime, screening had started in other western countries. The claimants did not allege that the defendant had been negligent, but that they had legitimately expected the blood to be safe. Under the Act it made no difference whether it would have been cost effective to screen for the virus at an earlier stage. It made no difference that the product had benefits for society. As soon as the manufacturer knew that there was a general risk that its blood products might be infected, it could no longer rely on the development risk defence.

Bogle v. *McDonalds* [2002] EWHC 490 (QB) was a group action, the claimants mainly being young children. Typically they had suffered a severe scald when somebody knocked a cup of McDonalds coffee onto them while manoeuvring to get to a table. Many needed skin grafts. They alleged negligence by the restaurant, and a breach of the 1987 Act. The coffee was served at a temperature which was too high to drink and capable of causing severe burns in seconds. Field J found that the drinks did meet the legitimate expectations of persons generally. He accepted that 'the insulation efficiency of the cups meant that purchasers could not tell by holding the cup just how hot the contents were' but the great majority of purchasers 'could be expected to know that tea and coffee served by McDonalds was hot, and would cause a serious scalding injury if spilt on someone. They accordingly know that care must be taken to avoid such spills, especially if they are with young children'. Note that in such a case the child would often have more chance in a negligence claim against his parents, the defendant may seek contribution or indemnity from the parents, and it may be best to avoid appointing the parent as litigation friend in case of a conflict of interest (see **section 17.7**).

The 1987 Act is based on the European Union Product Liability Directive 85/374. The General Product Safety Directive 2001/95 applies from 16 January 2004 and governs all consumer goods except food. It imposes a duty on manufacturers and distributors of goods that they know to be dangerous to report the hazard, and co-operate in product recall. The full implications of the Directive are not yet clear.

5.8 SPORTS INJURIES

A player is not entitled to damages for the risks that are incidental to any sport even where it is properly organised and played. He is taken to accept these risks voluntarily. As to the *volenti non fit injuria* rule, see **section 4.15**.

Dangerous play

If a player is injured during a team game as a result of negligence on the part of a fellow player, he is entitled to damages. It is sometimes said that negligence is not enough, and a player will be liable only if he is reckless. Strictly speaking, recklessness is not required as a matter of law, but the courts do not expect a competitor in an active sport to have time to take very great care. An error of judgement or momentary lapse of skill in the heat of the moment will seldom amount to negligence.

Caldwell v. *Maguire* [2001] EWCA Civ 1054 involved an injury to a rider in a horse race. A stewards' enquiry into the incident had found two jockeys guilty of careless riding. The Court of Appeal found that they had not been negligent, and that:

- A contestant in a race owes a duty of care to all the other contestants.
- The duty is to take all care that is objectively reasonable in the circumstances to avoid causing them injury.
- The circumstances include the desire to win; the physical and mental demands of the race; any inherent dangers; the rules and customs of the sport; and the skills and judgement reasonably to be expected of a contestant. In a race run under professional rules, the rules will be relevant.
- In practice the threshold for liability in a fast-moving race is high. A contestant will not be liable for injury resulting from a mere error of judgement or momentary lapse of skill while under the stress of a race.
- In practice it will be difficult to show that a contestant breached his duty of care without reckless disregard for the safety of a fellow contestant. You are reckless if you recognise an obvious risk of damage or loss, but instead of giving any thought to it, you take the risk.

In *Condon* v. *Basi* [1985] 1 WLR 866 a football tackle caused a broken leg. The judge described the tackle as 'made in a reckless and dangerous manner not with malicious intent towards the [claimant] but in an excitable manner without thought of the consequences' and emphasised that: 'By engaging in a sport . . . the participants may be held to have accepted risks which are inherent in that sport . . . but this does not eliminate all duty of care of the one participant to the other.' The claim succeeded.

Turning to more leisurely games, in *Pearson* v. *Lightning* [1998] EWCA Civ 591 the claimant was on a golf course when he was struck in the eye by a ball hit by a player some distance away. The test was 'whether there was a real foreseeable risk that by playing the shot the defendant might injure the claimant'. Given the defendant's competence as a player of golf, that he knew where the claimant was, and that he was trying to loft his ball over a tree, he should have known that there was such a risk. He should either have waited until the claimant was clear, or shouted a warning before playing the shot and asked the defendant if he minded him proceeding. The risk had been small but enough to make the defendant liable.

The rules of a game or sport will always be influential. In non-competitive sports, the court may be influence by a code of practice drawn up either by the national governing body such as the British Canoe Union, or by a regulating body such as the Civil Aviation Authority. There are many examples such as the Fédération Internationale de Ski Code of Practice for Skiers' Behaviour, and the British Parachute Association Operations Manual (and Civil Aviation Authority CAP660) about parachute safety.

If the incident amounted to a wilful trespass against the person, any claim against the assailant must be based on trespass, not negligence. Any house contents or sports insurance the defendant may have is unlikely to pay up (see **section 4.6**).

Officials

Sports organisers and referees owe a duty of care to players in hazardous sports such as boxing or rugby. They also owe a duty to spectators who may foreseeably be injured at a hazardous sporting event.

White v. *Blackmore* [1972] 2 QB 651 was a claim in respect of a spectator at a motor racing event, who was killed when a car left the track. Other than issues which have since been overtaken by the Unfair Contract Terms Act 1977, the main question was whether the occupier of the track had given the deceased enough information to avoid danger. If he had done so he would have had a defence to a claim under the Occupiers' Liability Act 1957, as long as 'in all the circumstances it was enough to enable the visitor to be reasonably safe' (see **section 5.5.**). *Volenti* can provide an effective defence, if the deceased knew where the danger was and could readily have avoided it.

Watson v. *British Boxing Board of Control* [1999] EWCA Civ 2116 was based on a lack of effective ringside medical cover. The defendant was liable for unnecessary brain damage. Key points were that physical injury is inevitable in boxing, and brain injury is foreseeable; the defendant sponsored, encouraged and controlled an activity that was likely to give rise to the injury; it imposed safety rules, including rules about medical cover; boxers reasonably relied upon the defendant to protect their interests; and it could have obtained insurance for £11,000 p.a.

In *Smoldon* v. *Whitworth & Nolan* [1996] EWCA Civ 1225 the claimant was a minor, and was severely injured by a scrum collapse in a Colts (under 19) rugby game. The referee was liable as he had had the opportunity to prevent it, and under the rules of the game he should have done so. The Court of Appeal said:

> The plaintiff had of course consented to the ordinary incidents of a game of rugby football of the kind in which he was taking part. Given, however, that the rules were framed for the protection of him and other players in the same position, he cannot possibly be said to have consented to a breach of duty on the part of the official whose duty it was to apply the rules and ensure so far as possible that they were observed.

Vowles v. *Evans & Welsh Rugby Union* [2003] EWCA Civ 318 confirms that a referee also owes this duty of care to all players, colt or adult.

In *Fowles* v. *Bedfordshire County Council* [1995] *The Times* 22 May the Court of Appeal found in favour of a 21-year-old athlete who was seriously injured when practising forward somersaults at a sports centre, using a crash mat placed against the wall. As a gym student he should have been warned not to practice this hazardous exercise without a trained supervisor, who would have placed the student and the mat to ensure a safe outcome.

5.9 INJURIES BY ANIMALS

Animal-related injuries typically occur when somebody is bitten by a dog, kicked by a horse, or is in collision with a stray cow while driving at night.

A personal injury claim may be based on negligence, occupiers' liability, trespass to the person, or strict liability under the Animals Act 1971.

Negligence

A claim may be based on negligence if an animal causes injury, loss or damage because the person in charge of it failed to take reasonable care (*Fardon* v. *Harcourt-Rivington* [1932] All ER 81).

The law of negligence is important where it is alleged that the owner of an animal negligently allowed it to stray onto a highway. Owners of large animals clearly have a duty to take reasonable care to prevent them ending up on the road. If the defendant argues that he constructed adequate fences and the gate was shut last time he saw it, the claimant will be hard put to prove that the animal strayed because of the defendant's negligence. For a successful claim involving a dilapidated farm, see *Wilson* v. *Donaldson* [2004] EWCA Civ 972. For two unsuccessful claims see *Dunnett* v. *Railtrack plc*

[2002] EWCA Civ 302 and *Hole* v. *Ross-Skinner* [2003] EWCA Civ 774. Such claims are likely to fail unless they can be brought within the Animals Act 1971.

In *Ellis* v. *Johnstone* [1963] 2 QB 8 the court found that there is no general duty to prevent one's dog straying onto the road. Four decades on, with more traffic and higher road speeds, *Ellis* might be decided differently.

Occupiers' liability

If an animal accident occurs when the claimant is on somebody else's premises, it may well be that the claim should be based on the duty of care owed by an occupier of premises to visitors and others under the Occupiers' Liability Acts (see **section 5.5**). This is almost identical to the duty of care in negligence.

Trespass

If injury occurs because a dog owner encourages his animal to attack, or a horseman deliberately rides somebody down, the person in charge of the animal is liable for the resulting injuries under the law of trespass, not negligence (see **section 4.6**).

Animals Act 1971

Under the 1971 Act, the keeper of an animal may be strictly liable for any injury it causes.

In the case of livestock which ends up on the road, the effect of the 1971 Act is that a person who puts grazing animals on roadside land is not responsible for loss or damage if he had a right to put them there and the land is common land, or a village green, or an area such as Dartmoor or the North Yorks Moors where fencing is not customary.

If an animal of a dangerous species causes injury or damage, the 1971 Act makes its keeper strictly liable for the damage. A claim against the owner would succeed even if the injury occurred because the animal was released by burglars.

'Dangerous species'? One that is not usually domesticated in Britain, fully-grown members of which are likely, unless restrained, to cause severe damage, or any damage that they may cause is likely to be severe. A camel is domesticated in many parts of the world but not Britain, not likely to cause any damage, but if it does cause damage it will be severe, so it is 'dangerous'. Horses or dogs are responsible for many serious injuries every year but not likely to cause severe damage if unrestrained. They are domesticated in Britain and so not dangerous as defined.

'Keeper'? Anybody who owns an animal or has it in his possession, or is head of a household in which a person under 16 owns or possesses it. If nobody owned or possessed it at the time of the incident (e.g. it had been abandoned) the keeper is the last person who did own or possess it.

If an animal not of a dangerous species causes an injury the keeper will still be strictly liable for the injury if:

- the damage was of a kind which the animal, unless restrained, was likely to cause, or which, if caused by the animal, was likely to be severe; and
- the likelihood of the damage or of its being severe was due to characteristics of the animal which are not normally found in animals of the same species or are not normally so found except at particular times or in particular circumstances; and
- these characteristics were known to the keeper or were at any time known to a person who at that time had charge of that animal as that keeper's servant or, where that keeper is the head of a household, were known to another keeper of the animal who is a member of that household and under the age of 16.

The defendant who is strictly liable may still rely in his defence on contributory negligence by the victim; trespass by the victim, under s.5(3) of the Act, and *volenti non fit injuria* by the victim, that is, informed consent to the risk posed by the animal. This defence is not available if the victim is the keeper's employee and ran the risk of injury incidental to his employment.

There had long been uncertainty about interpretation of the Act, as demonstrated by the comment of Oliver LJ in *Breeden* v. *Lampard* (CA 21 March 1985): 'I cannot believe that Parliament intended to impose liability for what is essentially normal behaviour in all animals of that species.' The claimant had been kicked by the defendant's horse while foxhunting, and any horse may kick if somebody goes too close behind it without warning.

This was resolved in *Mirvahedy* v. *Henley* [2003] UKHL 16. The claimant had been injured when a runaway horse ran into his moving car. The horse had evidently been panicked by some unknown factor and had crashed through the fence around its paddock. The fence was of a sort quite normal for paddocks, backed up by an inner ring of electric fencing, and there was no evidence that the owner had failed to take reasonable care. The claim could succeed only if the keeper's liability was strict. Horses are not a dangerous species within the meaning of the Act, but:

- given the speed and weight of a horse, if it did cause damage it was likely to be severe;
- it is not normal behaviour for horses to panic and bolt, except in the particular circumstance that they are scared by something;
- the defendant knew that.

The Court of Appeal found the defendant strictly liable because the damage was due to characteristics of this horse that were abnormal as a general rule, even though they were normal for the species in particular circumstances.

Mirvahedy went on to the House of Lords where a 3:2 majority supported this literal interpretation of the Act.

If the horse was standing in the road when hit by a car, as opposed to crashing into the car itself, it seems that strict liability will not attach (*Jaundrill* v. *Gillett* (CA 16 January 1996)).

As to dog bites, the courts do not require a dog owner to impose constant close restraint on the average dog. Consider *Curtis* v. *Betts* [1990] 1 All ER 769. Before liability will attach to the owner, the claimant needs to show either that the dog gave such warning before the bite that the keeper should have prevented the incident by taking reasonable care to get it under control, or that the dog had a history of biting such that the owner should have kept it leashed or even muzzled. One can often establish a history of biting by checking with the police, who keep a register of dog bite incidents, or the keeper's neighbours.

It is seldom appropriate to use expert evidence in animal cases. The judge may not admit expert evidence if he feels he can decide the case effectively without it, and will not order the loser to pay the fees of the winner's expert if he feels that the expert evidence made no real contribution.

Section 5 of the Animals Act 1971 says that a trespasser who is attacked by a guard dog has no claim under the *Act* if 'keeping it there for that purpose was not unreasonable'. In *Cummings* v. *Grainger* [1977] QB 397 the Court of Appeal found it not unreasonable to keep a guard dog in a scrapyard. The Guard Dogs Act 1975 makes it an offence to use or permit the use of a guard dog on business premises (but not domestic or agricultural premises) unless it is at all times under the control of a handler.

The Dangerous Dogs Act 1991/Dangerous Dogs (Amendment) Act 1997 apply if the claimant was attacked by a dog of a sort which, under the Acts, is designated as 'bred for fighting'. The pit bull terrier is so designated. Such dogs must, if they are in a public place, be muzzled and on a lead. If a dog is dangerously out of control in a public place then a criminal offence is committed by the owner and by whoever is in charge of it at the time. If the police prosecute, this will save the claimant the job of collecting evidence on liability, and may be enough to establish liability in the civil claim.

5.10 POLICE CLAIMS

Although legal aid has generally been withdrawn for personal injury matters, public funding under the Community Legal Service may be available for claims against the police. Some firms specialise in these claims.

The police seldom, if ever, owe a duty of care to investigate crime efficiently or at all (*Hill* v. *Chief Constable of West Yorkshire* [1989] AC 53 and *Waters* v. *Commissioner of Metropolitan Police* [2000] UKHL 50).

A police officer may have committed trespass against the person if he struck or restrained the claimant without legal justification, or used excessive force when lawfully restraining him (see **section 4.6**).

The police have powers of arrest with a warrant, and in some circumstances without a warrant. If an officer goes beyond his powers, a claim may be made for wrongful arrest. Powers of arrest arise mainly under ss.24 and 25 of the Police and Criminal Evidence Act 1984 (PACE). See also the Police Reform Act 2002. A police officer has the power to arrest without a warrant somebody who on reasonable grounds the officer suspects has committed, or is about to commit, an arrestable offence. He may also make an arrest where there has been a breach of the peace, or where he is satisfied that a breach of the peace is likely to occur. It can be lawful to arrest an innocent man. An arrest will not be lawful unless/until the officer complies with the relevant procedure.

Following an arrest, detention is lawful only if the police comply with Part IV of PACE. If they do not, there may be a claim for wrongful arrest or false imprisonment.

If a prisoner is brought in ill or drunk, the police have a duty of care towards him, for example to prevent a prisoner asphyxiating on his own vomit. The police also have a duty to prevent a prisoner from committing suicide if they know or should have known that he was a suicide risk. See *Reeves* v. *Commissioner of Police of the Metropolis* [1999] UKHL 35 (suicide risk) and *Orange* v. *Chief Constable of West Yorkshire Police* [2001] EWCA Civ 611 (no apparent risk).

A police constable is an office holder, not an employee, so the normal rules of vicarious liability do not apply. However, the chief constable is vicariously liable under s.88 of the Police Act 1996 for torts committed by his officers 'in the performance or purported performance of their functions'. This liability is wider than the usual liability of an employer for his employees. See, for example, *Weir* v. *Chief Constable of Merseyside Police* [2003] All ER(D) 273 (Jan), in which a police officer was making unauthorised use of a police van while off duty. He got into a row with the claimant while shifting furniture at a block of flats, told the claimant he was a police officer, and then unlawfully forced him down the stairs and locked him in the van. Having told the claimant that he was a police officer, the culprit was in purported performance of his duties as soon as he started taking the claimant out of the building.

The essence of the claim is that the officer exceeded his powers. A precise understanding of police powers, duties and procedure is necessary. Claims against the police also involve specialised civil procedure. A specialist textbook will be required to deal with points such as these:

- What does the claimant have to prove before the burden of proof shifts to the defendant? In false imprisonment, only that he was detained. In malicious prosecution, that he was prosecuted at the instance of the defendant, in the absence of reasonable and probable cause to justify it or without honest belief by the defendant that the prosecution was justified – and malice.

- When are the police entitled to raise the claimant's own history of criminal convictions?
- Claims for malicious prosecution and false imprisonment are dealt with by judge and jury (see s.69 Supreme Court Act 1981 and s.66 County Courts Act 1984). In *Phillips* v. *Commissioner of Police of the Metropolis* [2003] EWCA Civ 382 the Court of Appeal considered when a judge alone should hear such claims, or issues within them.
- How should the judge direct the jury on the issue of exemplary damages?
- As with any other case where an agent of the state is involved with a death, the European Convention on Human Rights 1950 demands that a prompt, effective inquest be held into deaths in police custody, and that the family have the opportunity to be represented.

The Independent Police Complaints Commission investigates complaints against police officers, and takes decisions on disciplinary proceedings. It took over from the Police Complaints Authority in 2004 (**www.ipcc.gov.uk**).

A claimant alleging that he has been assaulted by a police officer would naturally like to see the investigation file, but this will not happen unless disclosure is necessary for the proper discharge of the Commission's functions. The Commission must satisfy the legitimate interest of the complainant and the public that it should be independent and thorough. See *R (Green)* v. *Police Complaints Authority* [2004] UKHL 6 and s.80 of the Police Act 1996.

In cases of assault by the police, compensation for pain and suffering and financial losses is payable in the same way as in other personal injury cases, save that the claimant may also be entitled to aggravated or exemplary damages.

The Court of Appeal laid down guidelines concerning compensation in claims against the police in *Thompson* v. *Commissioner of Police of the Metropolis* [1997] EWCA Civ 1042 and *Hsu* v. *Commissioner of Police of the Metropolis* [1997] EWCA Civ 1042.

- Damages for false imprisonment – £500 for the first hour. £3,000 for 24 hours.
- Damages for malicious prosecution – £2,000, rising to £10,000 if the prosecution was in the Crown Court, and more if there was a conviction.
- Awards of aggravated damages to start at £1,000. Aggravated damages are not generally to exceed twice the amount of damages for pain and suffering.
- Awards of exemplary damages are to be made only in rare cases of particularly oppressive behaviour, and will be from £5,000. If the claimant is blameless, and the police conduct is particularly deserving of

condemnation and directly involved an officer of the rank of superintendent or above, exemplary damages may go up to £50,000. Aggravated damages are not generally to exceed three times the amount for pain and suffering.

5.11 CLINICAL NEGLIGENCE

Clinical negligence is a specialism of its own, and there are many thick and excellent textbooks. It has:

- a separate Protocol – the Pre-Action Protocol for the Resolution of Clinical Disputes;
- a separate Law Society panel of specialist solicitors;
- the possibility of public funding under the Community Legal Service.

The principles in the clinical negligence cases of *Bolam*, *Bolitho* and *Hotson* occasionally affect mainstream personal injury work.

The law does not expect professionals such as doctors to be perfect. An ordinary defendant is expected to take 'reasonable care,' judged by the standard of the ordinary reasonable man. However, where the defendant was exercising some special skill or competence, the test is:

> the standard of the ordinary skilled man exercising and professing to have that special skill. A man need not possess the highest expert skill; it is well-established law that it is sufficient if he exercises the ordinary skill of an ordinary competent man exercising that particular art
>
> (see *Bolam* v. *Friern Hospital Management Committee* [1957] 1 WLR 582)

A doctor is not necessarily negligent if he causes injury because he subscribes to a school of thought which differs from the views held by most of the medical profession. The minority view may be defensible. However, where a school of thought is illogical, the court will not approve it. See *Bolitho* v. *City & Hackney Health Authority* [1997] UKHL 46:

> . . . the court has to be satisfied that the exponents of the body of opinion relied upon can demonstrate that such opinion has a logical basis. In particular in cases involving, as they often do, the weighing of risks against benefits, the judge before accepting a body of opinion as being responsible, reasonable or respectable, will need to be satisfied that, in forming their views, the experts have directed their minds to the question of comparative risks and benefits and have reached a defensible conclusion on the matter.

A major hurdle, in clinical negligence more than anywhere else, is the need to show that but for the negligence the outcome would probably have been better. After all if the claimant had been in perfect health he would not have been receiving treatment. For a brief look at causation, and in particular *Hotson* v. *East Berkshire Health Authority* [1987] AC 750, see **section 4.4**.

5.12 CLAIMS AGAINST SCHOOLS

A school may be a private business or trust, in which case the correct defendants are usually the governors or trustees. More often, it is operated by the local education authority (LEA), and the correct defendant is the local authority.

The defendant may be vicariously liable for the torts of its employees (teachers, educational psychiatrists, education officers). The standard of care in these cases depends on whether the claimant alleges a failure of child care, or a breach of professional duty.

The defendant may also be directly liable for its own failure to operate a safe school environment, generally in its capacity as an occupier of premises (see **section 5.5**).

Public funding may be available under the Community Legal Service. In 2003 the government intended to withdraw it from claims against schools but this had not happened at the time of writing.

Defendant as child carer

A school has day-to-day care of pupils, and therefore a duty of care to safeguard them against physical and psychiatric injuries while they are in its care.

The standard of care is that of the 'reasonably careful parent'. This is not an absolute duty to prevent injury. It does not require one to supervise even young children constantly. It is a duty to treat children according to their age and characteristics. Nobody can guarantee that a child will not injure itself or somebody else by sliding down banisters or throwing stones as soon as the teacher's back is turned.

A teacher is in *loco parentis*, and a teacher's duty as child-carer goes no further than the parents' own duty. Therefore, in *Van Oppen* v. *Trustees of the Bedford Charity* [1990] 1 WLR 235, where a pupil was very seriously injured in a school rugby match, the duty of care did not require the school to take out accident insurance for the benefit of pupils who might be injured.

If a pupil is injured by another pupil, note that young children cannot be negligent, and an older child will be negligent only if its behaviour falls below the standard of the ordinarily prudent and reasonable child of that age. It may be possible to claim against the school based on a failure to provide reasonable supervision.

The following are examples:

- Three or four-year-old pupil: *Carmarthenshire County Council* v. *Lewis* [1955] AC 549. A teacher who left children unsupervised for 10 minutes while giving first aid to another child was not negligent, although children of that age could easily open the door, and she had neither told them to stay where they were nor asked a colleague to keep an eye on them. The case in fact succeeded on the basis that the school should have kept the playground gate locked, and if they had the child would not have got onto the road and caused a fatal accident.

- Eight-year-old pupil: *Gough* v. *Upshire Primary School* [2002] CL August. In this High Court case, the claimant had fallen off a banister while sliding down it. The banisters conformed to building regulations. It had been foreseeable that children would slide down the banisters, and might be injured. The school could easily have fitted studs to the banister to prevent pupils sliding down it. However, the banister had been there since 1936, there had been no previous accidents, and the risk was no greater than many other everyday risks. The claim failed.
- Sixth-former: *Chittock* v. *Woodbridge School* [2002] EWCA Civ 915. The supervising teachers on a school ski trip were not liable for injuries suffered by a sixth-former who they had allowed to continue skiing unsupervised despite having had to reprimand him for skiing off piste. A few days later, the pupil crashed while skiing too fast on the piste. The teachers' duty of care had been that of the reasonably careful parent having experience of skiing and school trips. Given the pupil's age and experience, and his promise to ski more safely, their response had been within the range of reasonable responses.
- Mentally handicapped pupil: Both parents and school are expected to supervise a child more closely than his age would usually require if he is mentally handicapped (*J* v. *North Lincolnshire County Council* [2000] PIQR P84).

A school's duty of care to pupils can extend to periods before and after school hours when they are lawfully on its premises, for example, waiting for lessons to start. See *Kearn-Price* v. *Kent County Council* [2002] EWCA Civ 1539.

The problem of bullying is 'now well enough recognised for it to be reasonable to expect all schools to have policies and practices in place to meet it' as '. . . persistent targeting of one pupil by others can cause lasting damage to the victim'. The duty is to take reasonable steps to protect pupils from bullying, and it will very seldom extend to protecting pupils outside the school gates (*Bradford-Smart* v. *West Sussex County Council* [2002] EWCA Civ 7).

Reasonable steps may include speaking out about bullying during morning assembly; patrolling the school premises frequently, at times and places the bullies cannot predict; keeping a central record of both complaints and reports of bullying; having senior pupils mentor junior ones, so that the juniors confide in somebody resembling a big brother or sister; and disciplining or expelling known bullies.

As to child abuse, in which schools are sometimes implicated, see **section 5.13**.

Defendant as education professional

Apart from being a child carer, a teacher is a skilled professional who must exercise 'the ordinary skill of an ordinary competent man exercising that particular art' (*Bolam* v. *Friern Hospital Management Committee* [1957] 1 WLR 582).

Thus a head teacher has a duty of care to exercise 'the reasonable skills of a headmaster in relation to [the] educational needs' of all his pupils, including those with special educational needs, and a teacher brought in to advise on the educational needs of a specific pupil owes him a duty of care to exercise 'the skill and care of a reasonable advisory teacher' (*Phelps* v. *London Borough of Hillingdon* [2000] UKHL 47).

A school should be alert for special educational needs, and may be vicariously liable if its professional employees fail to take appropriate positive steps where a child is under-performing in class because of problems such as dyslexia, autism, impaired hearing or vision or hyperactivity.

The Education Act 1996 and regulations made under the Act set out the steps to be taken. Codes of Practice from the Department for Education and Skills provide more detail.

A school may make special arrangements itself for the education of a child with special needs. Alternatively, the child's parent or the school may ask the LEA to assess the child in line with the Code of Practice, and perhaps issue a Statement of Special Educational Needs (SSEN). SSENs are prepared in consultation with the child's parents. The SSEN might provide for the child to have more support in his own school, to have therapy at home or at school, or to go to a special school. It is important that the child be sent to the appropriate school. If the school lumps together fit, intelligent but emotionally disturbed teenagers with others who have a very limited ability to communicate and spatter gravy and mashed potato at lunch, they may all fail to thrive. If the parents object to the SSEN, they can appeal it to the Special Educational Needs and Disability Tribunal. The time limit for appeals is short.

If a school's employees fail in their professional duties and this causes a child's education to suffer, he may be entitled to damages. See the dyslexia case *Phelps* v. *London Borough of Hillingdon* [2000] UKHL 47. The claimant alleged breach of statutory duty under the Education Act and regulations, and negligence. The House of Lords found that there was no duty of care to provide an ideal system of education under the Act. However, the defendant could be liable for negligence on the part of its educational psychologist, who failed to diagnose the claimant's dyslexia.

Local government education officers are also involved in decisions about education of pupils with special educational needs, and the LEA may be vicariously liable for harm caused by their decisions if 'after due allowance for the policy background and other constraints, [they] fall outside the scope of acceptability in the eyes of any reasonable body of educational opinion' (*Carty* v. *London Borough of Croydon* [2004] EWHC 228 (QB)).

It may seem odd to include these matters in a personal injury textbook, but in *Phelps* the House of Lords held that these are personal injury claims. Therefore the limitation period will expire three years after the victim's 18th birthday. *Adams* v. *Bracknell Forest* [2004] UKHL 29 was a claim relating to an education authority's failure to diagnose and respond to dyslexia 21 years earlier. The House of Lords found that the claimant's embarrassment about being illiterate did not exempt him from the usual limitation rules. He should have been curious about the reason for his condition and taken appropriate advice. The claim was time-barred and the court would not exercise its discretion in his favour.

Much of the special educational needs case law relates to dyslexia, because this condition is subtle and may not be recognised for some years. A compensation claim is stressful and disruptive to both parties. Assume the claimant can show that his school has breached its duty of care, and that this caused his education to suffer to a significant extent. Is it worth his while to make a claim? For some sufferers, dyslexia makes little financial difference. They would have been manual workers whether they had received special tuition or not, and their damages will be modest. Others overcome their dyslexia by their own determination and obtain highly paid professional jobs. They may get nothing at all. The main losers in cases of undiagnosed dyslexia are those who nearly made it to university and high earnings, but have ended up in relatively menial work.

There are many reasons for poor performance in classroom or examination. The House of Lords in *Phelps* said:

> This is not to open the door to claims based on poor quality of teaching. It is one thing for the law to provide a remedy in damages when there is manifest incompetence or negligence comprising specific, identifiable mistakes. It would be an altogether different matter to countenance claims [that] . . . the child did not receive an adequate education at the school, or that a particular teacher failed to teach properly.

5.13 CHILD ABUSE AND NEGLECT

Abuse and neglect often cause severe psychiatric problems. The victim may be entitled to aggravated or exemplary damages as well as the usual compensatory damages. He may be able to get public funding for his legal costs.

If a claim is brought against an abuser based on rape or assault and battery, it must be for trespass against the person. The abuser is usually hard to trace or unable to pay large amounts of damages. One might expect abuse to be covered by the abuser's household or business insurance, but that would be contrary to public policy (see **section 4.6**).

In practice these claims are dealt with by application to the Criminal Injuries Compensation Scheme, or a civil claim against a care organisation. Such a claim may be based on the care organisation's own negligence in employing a care worker with a history of child abuse, ignoring complaints from victims, or failing to respond to evidence of abuse. Alternatively, it may be based on the organisation's vicarious liability for its care staff. It may be vicariously liable for child abuse carried out by an employee if there is sufficient connection between his job and the abuse he committed, even in the case of sexual abuse that cannot possibly be seen as an attempt to do his job (*Lister* v. *Hesley Hall Ltd* [2001] UKHL 22).

When a local authority takes a child into care, it does so under various statutory powers and duties. Unless the wording or policy of legislation that imposes a statutory duty is that the victim of a breach should be compensated for his injury and loss, the courts will not find any common law duty of care. If the local authority had a statutory power but no statutory duty to exercise it, it would take a truly exceptional claim to succeed on the basis that it failed to exercise the power. The same applies if the claim is founded on breach of a public law duty, as in child care legislation (*Gorringe* v. *Calderdale Metropolitan Borough Council* [2004] UKHL 15).

This explains the claimant's approach in *Barrett* v. *Enfield London Borough Council* [1999] UKHL 25. Having spent his childhood in care managed by the defendant, he alleged that he was given so little stability that he sustained psychiatric injury. He accepted that he could in law have no claim based on breach of the local authority's statutory duties under the Children Act 1989, but argued that it owed him a duty of care because it had assumed parental responsibilities over him by taking him into care. The House of Lords considered that the claimant had a valid argument.

If a child abuse victim is living with his own family, the local authority's social services department may intervene to put him in care after the Child Protection Conference has decided to place him on the Child Protection Register. Rather than being within the sole control of social services, the Conference is required by statute to seek input from police, school, doctors and others. Because of the number of agencies involved, and for other reasons of public policy, in *X (Minors)* v. *Bedfordshire County Council* [1995] 2 AC 633 the House of Lords refused to find that the local authority could owe a duty of care to children who suffer because it did not intervene when it knew they were being neglected, even severely and over a long period. However, it is unlawful for a public authority to act in a way that is incompatible with rights guaranteed by the European Convention on Human Rights 1950. Article 3 gives a right not to be subjected to torture, inhuman or degrading treatment and punishment. In *Z & others* v. *United Kingdom* [2001] ECHR 329 the European

Court of Human Rights (ECtHR) found that the council's failure to act was a breach of Article 3, and the UK had breached Article 13 in that it had failed to give an effective remedy before a national authority. The ECtHR ordered the UK Government to pay to the children a total of £359,000 plus interest.

The situation changed when the Human Rights Act 1998 came into force. *JD* v. *East Berkshire Community Health NHS Trust* [2003] EWCA Civ 1151 states that the decisions such as *X (Minors)* cannot survive the Act, and that a local authority may well owe a duty of care to a child abuse victim living with his own family, depending on the circumstances.

A parent or guardian can defend a criminal assault charge on the basis that he did no more than inflict reasonable chastisement. The courts will consider whether the punishment was in fact reasonable and moderate having regard to the nature and context of the defendant's behaviour, the duration of the behaviour, the physical and mental consequences for the child, the age and personal characteristics of the child, and the reasons for the punishment given by the defendant. In *A* v. *United Kingdom* [1998] ECHR 85 a child had been beaten with a garden cane on various occasions between the ages of six and nine, and his stepfather was acquitted on the basis that he had applied only reasonable chastisement. The UK accepted that the success of this defence had breached Article 3, and 'that this law currently fails to provide adequate protection to children and should be amended'. The ECtHR ordered the UK to pay the applicant £10,000. See also *R* v. *H (reasonable chastisement)* [2001] EWCA Crim 1024.

A teacher is not entitled to inflict any form of corporal punishment. (s.548 Education Act 1996). However, under s.549 and s.550 of the 1996 Act, a member of a school's staff may apply reasonable force to a child to prevent it committing an offence, causing personal injury or damage to the property of any person, or engaging in behaviour prejudicial to the maintenance of good order and discipline at the school.

A common feature in child abuse claims is that many years may go by before a claim is brought. This creates two difficulties. First, the claim may be time barred. If the claim must be brought on the basis of trespass, it will be time barred six years after the claimant's 18th birthday, or the claimant's date of knowledge if later, and the court has no discretion to extend this limitation period (*Stubbings* v. *Webb* [1993] AC 498 and *Stubbings* v. *United Kingdom* [1996] ECHR 44). If the claim can be based on negligence or breach of statutory duty, it will be time barred three years after the claimant's 18th birthday, or his date of knowledge if later. The court has a discretion to extend the three-year time limit.

A court may find that an abuse claim is less about the immediate physical effects of the abuse, and more about the long-term psychiatric consequences; and this may mean that the claimant's date of knowledge is many years after the assault (*K R & others* v. *Bryn Alyn Community Homes* [2003] EWCA Civ 85).

If the claim is against a school or care organisation based purely on its vicarious liability for abuse carried out by an employee, will it be based on trespass or negligence? The answer seems to be trespass. Consider *Lister* and *Bryn Alyn*. A claimant who needs to rely on the court's discretion to proceed with a claim must base his claim on the school's own negligence.

The second difficulty created by a long time lag is that the victim may have spent many years suppressing his or her memories of the abuse, or repeatedly going over them in his or her mind. The legal process involves excavating and laying bare those memories, and establishing which are reliable. In some cases, the claimant had no recollection of childhood abuse until prompted by a therapist, and these recovered memories are felt by many psychiatrists to be highly unreliable.

These claims are extremely difficult for the victim, and can be distressing for the lawyer. If one prefers to give cases of this sort to a lawyer who has a particular interest in the work, there is the Association of Child Abuse Lawyers (ACAL) (**www.childabuselawyers.com**).

5.14 OTHER ACCIDENTS

It is not always clear what standard of care the claimant was entitled to expect from the defendant. Case law can show the way:

- Passengers falling on moving buses or trains: *Fletcher* v. *United Counties Omnibus Co Ltd* [1997] EWCA Civ 2870.
- Tramline accident: *Roe* v. *Sheffield City Council* [2004] EWCA Civ 329.
- Food poisoning: *Giambrone* v. *JMC Holidays* [2004] EWCA Civ 158.
- Fire brigade's duty of care to owner of burning building: *Capital & Counties plc* v. *Hampshire County Council* [1997] 2 All ER 865.
- Police force's duty to protect the public by investigating efficiently: *Hill* v. *Chief Constable of West Yorkshire* [1989] AC 53.
- Police force's duty to investigate allegations: *Waters* v. *Commissioner of Metropolitan Police* [2000] UKHL 50.
- Coastguard's duty to direct rescue competently: *OLL Ltd* v. *Secretary of State for Transport* [1997] 3 All ER 897.
- Ambulance service duty to respond to 999 call: *Kent* v. *Griffiths* [2000] EWCA Civ 25.
- Injury by electromagnetic radiation: *Davis* v. *Balfour Kilpatrick* [2002] EWCA Civ 736.
- Injury by ionising radiation: *Merlin* v. *British Nuclear Fuels plc* [1990] 2 QB 557.
- Contaminated blood transfusion: *A* v. *National Blood Authority* [2001] EWHC 446 (QB).

- Needlestick injury: *Howell* v. *Bolton Hospitals NHS Trust* (Bolton County Court, 16 November 1995, noted in Kemp & Kemp), *Oldham* v. *Sharples* [1997] EWCA Civ 960 and *Toole* v. *Bolton Metropolitan Borough Council* [2002] EWCA Civ 588.

Statutory duties

If the defendant caused the claimant's injury by doing something that was covered by a statute or regulation he may be in breach of statutory duty. In some cases the claimant may be able to base his claim on this as well as, or instead of, negligence (see **section 6.7**).

The cost effective way to find out what regulations apply is often to ask the relevant enforcing body. For example, the trading standards, building control and environmental health departments of local councils are often happy to point one in the right direction if the claim relates to consumer goods, defective premises or food poisoning.

The construction and use of road vehicles is heavily regulated. Note in particular the Road Vehicles (Construction and Use) Regulations 1986, and of course the *Highway Code*.

Fire regulations govern safety precautions in buildings, in the design of appliances and furniture (e.g. use of flame retardants and banning of certain upholstery foams which produce toxic smoke), in transport and storage of flammable materials, and with regard to fireworks. There are about 100, too many to list here.

Outdoor pursuits centres that provide a commercial service for under 18s are required to be licensed under the Activity Centres (Young Persons' Safety) Act 1995.

Codes of practice

Instead of or in addition to a regulation, there may be a Code of Practice or Approved Code of Practice. Neither is binding on the court, but certainly ACoPs are very influential. Some of the best-known codes of practice are the *Highway Code*, and those produced by the Health and Safety Executive for health and safety at work (see **section 6.9**).

Other codes of practice and guidelines include:

- HSE publications such as The Events Safety Guide which relates to fireworks displays, concerts, etc; Managing Crowds Safely, Safe Play on Inflatables and Bouncy Castles, Amusement Devices Inspection, Smoke Effects Used in Entertainment, Working with Animals, Operating Miniature Locomotives.
- Secretary of State for Transport Safety at Street Works and Road Works.

- Department for Transport Practical Guide for Bus Operators and Staff.
- Code of Practice under the Disability Discrimination Act 1995.

British Standards

The British Standards Institution has examined many areas of industrial and domestic life. The Court of Appeal said in *Ward* v. *Ritz Hotel* [1992] 1 PIQR 315 that British Standards 'represent the consensus of professional opinion and practical experience as to the sensible safety precautions'. For example:

- Code of Practice for Stairs BS5395.
- BS EN1977 as to rubberised impact-absorbing surfaces in playgrounds and EN1176 on the design of playground equipment.
- Guidance Note Safe Operation of Passenger Carrying Devices – Inflatable Bouncing Devices.
- Guidance Note Lighting Guide – the Outdoor Environment, which specifies the amount of illumination to be shed on steps and pathways.

Although British Standards represent good practice, a person injured by a breach does not automatically have a right to compensation. In *Green* v. *Building Scene Ltd* [1994] PIQR 259 the Court of Appeal said 'it is one thing to lay down . . . standards with [the] objective [of preventing accidents] and another to define what is reasonably safe in all the circumstances of a particular case'.

CHAPTER 6

Accidents at work

It is harder to predict the outcome of a workplace claim than a road traffic accident. CRU figures show a success rate of 90 per cent for road traffic claims, and 75 per cent for employer's liability. After-the-event legal expenses insurance for employer's liability work is almost twice the price of cover for road traffic work.

If handling workplace claims, one needs some awareness of employment law and disability discrimination, lest the claimant should lose his job or right to compensation or the defendant let himself in for an additional claim (see **sections 6.20** and **6.21**).

6.1 WORKPLACE CLAIMS FOR CLAIMANTS

The claimant is, inevitably, the source of all information for his lawyer at the outset, whether about the accident, the injuries or his employment status. For a questionnaire that may help with a streamlined interview, see the accompanying CD-ROM.

Can one get photographs of the site of the accident and any equipment that was involved? One should obtain permission from the factory owner or site contractor before entering to take photographs. However, this can take months, and the situation may change within days. In a unionised workplace, probably the union's safety representative will be able and willing to take photographs immediately. It might well strengthen the claimant's case if he or a workmate went round at once with a camera under his jacket, but it may represent a breach of an express or implied term of his employment contract. In a high-security workplace it may represent gross misconduct.

If photographs are needed one can fax a request to the employer to confirm urgently that he will not alter the site or any relevant equipment without 14 days' prior warning. If after a reasonable time there is no such confirmation and the claim is valuable, one can ask for a date when one can carry out a site inspection. It may be worth telling the employer at this stage that the layout is evidence, and that if he destroys it the court may refuse to let him give any evidence in his defence (*Malhotra* v. *Dhawan* [1997] EWCA

Civ 1096). A site visit will usually be a joint visit by the claimant in person, his lawyer, a representative of the employer, and the employer's claims handler or lawyer. If all else fails it may be appropriate to obtain a court order under CPR Part 25, requiring the employer to give access to his premises or be in contempt of court.

If the workplace has a safety representative, one can ask the claimant to obtain a copy of the representative's accident report. These reports are included in the Standard Disclosure List so the employer should provide a copy if he denies liability, but it may be useful to get a copy at the outset.

If the claim relates to defective work equipment, ask the claimant to find out whether staff in the maintenance section can say anything useful. A response is unlikely, except in a unionised workplace.

One must observe the relevant Pre-action Protocol, whether this is the Personal Injury Protocol or the Pre-action Protocol for Disease and Injury Claims. This means sending a letter of claim as soon as the claimant has enough information to substantiate a realistic claim, and before issues of quantum are addressed in detail.

If the Health and Safety Executive (HSE) investigated the incident, they may have prepared a report.

The claimant should be able to find out whether the HSE, local authority or trade union is prosecuting the employer.

6.2 WORKPLACE CLAIMS FOR DEFENDANTS

The first point to establish is whether the claimant is employed or self-employed. This allows one to say what duty of care the defendant owed him. If the defendant says that the claimant was self-employed, one must treat this opinion with caution, and usually ask for a copy of the employment contract.

The employer-client should provide one with copies of the documents referred to in the Standard Disclosure List. These should provide one with enough information to advise whether or not liability should be admitted. Under the Pre-action Protocol, unless liability is admitted, documents 1–12 below are to be disclosed to the claimant. Further categories of document are to be disclosed if the claim relates to a trip or slip, work equipment, personal protective equipment, manual handling, display screens, hazardous substances, and other specialised situations.

1. Accident book entry, preferably countersigned by the claimant.
2. First aider's report.
3. If the workplace has a medical surgery, the surgery record of the accident.
4. Foreman/supervisor's signed account of the accident. Ideally, this should include a brief signed statement from all potential witnesses about what happened and what injury the claimant mentioned at the time.

5. Safety representative's accident report.
6. Any report made by the employer to the HSE under the Reporting of Injuries, Diseases and Dangerous Occurrences Regulations 1995 (RIDDOR).
7. Other communications between the defendant and the HSE.
8. Minutes of Health and Safety Committee meetings where the accident or matter was considered. The Standard Disclosure List does not say whether this includes pre-accident discussions of the hazard that allegedly injured the claimant. Many, if not most, judges would think that it does, but few defendants disclose anything in this category unless hounded by a claimant who knows the document exists.
9. BI 76 report to Department for Work and Pensions, if the employee claimed industrial injury benefits as a result of the accident.
10. Documents listed above relative to any previous similar accident identified by the claimant and relied upon as proof of negligence.
11. Earnings information, where the defendant is the claimant's employer. If there is any question that the claimant has lost earnings as a result of the accident, one will be disclosing these to the claimant whether or not liability is admitted.
12. Documents produced to comply with requirements of the Management of Health and Safety at Work Regulations 1999:
    (a) Pre-accident Risk Assessment required by Regulation 3.
    (b) Post-accident re-assessment required by Regulation 3.
    (c) Accident Investigation Report prepared in implementing the requirements of Regulations 4, 6 and 9. If the employer carried out an internal investigation, he is required to disclose his accident investigation report to the claimant unless the dominant purpose for which it was prepared was the conduct of actual or anticipated litigation (see **section 20.4**).
    (d) Health surveillance records in appropriate cases required by Regulation 5.
    (e) Information provided to employees under Regulation 8.
    (f) Documents relating to the employee's health and safety training required by Regulation 11.

Apart from the Standard Disclosure List, one may wish to ask one's employer-client for additional accident documentation:

13. The claimant's signed account of the accident and his injuries. An efficient employer will give all accident victims a standard questionnaire to fill out while waiting for the ambulance, or take one to his home or hospital bed. The safety advantage is that the employer can immediately identify and act on risks before anybody else gets hurt. The litigation advantage is that one pins the claimant down before he has had time to put a spin on the facts.

14. Memo of what the claimant said about his injuries when phoning in sick a day or so after the accident. Sometimes called self-certification.
15. Copy of sick note from the claimant's GP. An employer is entitled to demand that an employee provide a medical certificate after the first week of absence (Statutory Sick Pay (Medical Evidence) Regulations 1985).
16. Copy of the claimant's attendance record since the accident, including whether he returned part time or on light duties before he came back to full normal work.
17. It is often very useful to have a copy of the claimant's attendance record from before the accident, too. If he had had a lot of time off work, this may indicate an ongoing health problem. If the pre-accident problem is similar to the injury caused by the accident, perhaps the accident did no more than exacerbate an existing health problem, or accelerate the onset of symptoms from an existing problem. This is particularly common with back injuries. If the claimant had had a lot of short absences for vague or trivial reasons, this may mean he was already on the slippery slope towards a fair dismissal for incapability. Like evidence of mere acceleration, this would undermine a claim for loss of future earnings. A bad pre-accident attendance record may suggest that the claimant is a malingerer whose claim needs careful thought.
18. Photographs of the accident site and any equipment involved; and a sketch plan of the accident site if necessary.

If one is at risk on liability, one will probably not disclose the photographs and sketch plan at this stage. It makes life too easy for the claimant. It is generally best to disclose items 13–17 to the claimant when sending him copies of the items in the Standard Disclosure List.

If the claim is worth a good deal of money or there is a question mark hanging over it, both sides will be interested to see:

- the claimant's personnel file;
- any occupational health file.

The employer and any works medical staff have free access to these for personnel and health and safety purposes, but that does not mean the employer can copy them to his legal advisers to help them defend a compensation claim. They are shielded by medical ethics and the Data Protection Act 1998, and can be used for another purpose only with the data subject's permission.

Employers frequently avoid all contact with accident victims. It is good tactics to stay in touch and offer sympathy, as long as the employer does not admit liability. He should not discuss the accident with the victim except for the specific purpose of a safety enquiry.

6.3 HEALTH AND SAFETY LAW

A claim by an employee against his employer may be based on:

- Negligence (see **sections 4.1** to **4.5**).
- Trespass. If the injury was caused deliberately, the claim will be based on trespass to the person (see **section 4.6**).
- Breach of the duty of care of an occupier of premises under the Occupiers' Liability Acts (see **section 5.5**).
- Breach of statutory duty (see **sections 6.6** to **6.9**).
- In some cases, breach of European Union law (see **section 6.10**).
- Breach of the employment contract (see **section 6.11**).

There is a sharp distinction between the duties an employer owes to somebody self employed who is working for him, and the much wider duties he owes to his employees at common law and by legislation (see **section 6.16**).

An employer's basic duty to his employees is to operate a safe system of work. He has both a common law duty and various statutory duties to do so. This means setting up a system at boardroom level, not relying on employees to use their skill and common sense to set up a suitable system themselves. Employers know very well that employees are:

> . . . very frequently, if not habitually, careless about the risks which their work may involve. It is . . . for that very reason that the common law demands that employers should take reasonable care to lay down a reasonably safe system of work . . . It is the duty of the employer to consider the situation, to devise a suitable system, to instruct his men what they must do and to supply any implements that may be required . . .
>
> (*General Cleaning Contractors Ltd* v. *Christmas* [1953] AC 180)

A safe system of work takes account of wear and tear on equipment, power failures, floods, computer glitches, misunderstandings, inadvertence or stupidity on the part of employees or the public. It takes account of foreseeable horseplay by colleagues and foreseeable crime by third parties (*Hudson* v. *Ridge Mfg Co* [1957] 2 QB 348 and *Rahman* v. *Arearose* [2000] EWCA Civ 190). It need not take account of unforeseeable criminal acts (*Horton* v. *Taplin Contracts Ltd* [2002] EWCA Civ 1604).

Under the CPR costs regime, the court will seldom order the losing party to pay the costs of issues pursued unsuccessfully by the winner, or alleged in the statements of case but abandoned before trial. It is still normal practice for a claimant who alleges that his employer breached a specific statutory duty to add an allegation that the employer was negligent too. This is unlikely to lead to a costs penalty for the successful claimant.

Ultimately the court is interested only in effective precautions that the employer should have taken. That is to say, precautions that would probably have prevented the accident. However, from the claimant's point of view, it is worth briefly mentioning in witness statements any minor health and safety infractions by the employer, even if they cannot be said to have caused the injury.

The particulars of claim should not specify what precautions the employer should have taken (see **section 17.3**). However, it is prudent for the claimant to tell the defendant in correspondence, well before issuing proceedings, exactly what precautions he should have taken that would have prevented the injury.

6.4 COMMON LAW DUTIES OF EMPLOYERS

An employer will be liable in negligence if he owed the claimant a duty of care; he breached that duty by act or omission; the foreseeable result of the breach was that the claimant would suffer injury or loss; and the claimant's injury and loss were caused by the breach of duty and were not too remote from it.

At common law, an employer owes a duty of care to each of its employees to take reasonable care to operate his business in a way that avoids exposing them to a reasonably foreseeable risk of physical injury. To comply with his duty, he must:

- select competent employees;
- provide the necessary training, tools and materials;
- provide a safe system of work, and supervision to ensure that the system works;
- provide and maintain a safe place of work;
- provide and maintain safe plant and machinery.

See *Wilsons & Clyde Coal* v. *English* [1938] AC 57, *Woods* v. *Durable Suites* [1953] 1 WLR 857 and *Wilson* v. *Tyneside Window Cleaning* [1958] 2 QB 110.

The common law is not static, and in *Walker* v. *Northumberland County Council* [1995] 1 All ER 737 it was recognised that there is a duty to protect employees from a risk of psychiatric injury in certain situations.

The common law duties are non-delegable, so if an employer arranges for them to be carried out by a third party, the employer remains liable to the employee (*Smith* v. *Cammell Laird* [1940] AC 242). The employer may be able to obtain a contribution or indemnity from the person to whom he entrusted the duty.

It is very often a mistake to apply the court's standards of a generation ago to today's workplace. Compare, for example, *Withers* v. *Perry Chain* [1961] 1 WLR 1314 and *Coxall v. Goodyear Great Britain* [2002] EWCA Civ 1010 (see **section 6.19**).

6.5 EMPLOYER'S STANDARD OF CARE IN NEGLIGENCE

The standard of care the employer must reach in order to satisfy his common law duty of care is that of the reasonably prudent employer, and the courts maintain a balance between the cost of safety measures, in money or time, and the likelihood and severity of the risk.

In *Stokes* v. *Guest Keen & Nettlefold (Bolts & Nuts) Ltd* [1968] 1 WLR 1776 the claimant had come into contact every day with mineral oil, which soaked his clothing. It caused cancer of the scrotum, which was ultimately fatal. The works doctor knew that exposure to the oil carried a significant risk of this cancer but had not told the workforce about it, and had not organised regular medical examinations of workers at risk.

> The overall test is still the conduct of the reasonable and prudent employer, giving positive thought to the safety of his workers in the light of what he knows or ought to know . . . [he must] weigh up the risk in terms of the likelihood of injury occurring and the potential consequences if it does; and he must balance against this the probable effectiveness of the precautions that can be taken to meet it and the expense and inconvenience involved.

The employer was in breach of its duty of care to set up a safe system of work.

Conversely in *Latimer* v. *AEC Ltd* [1953] AC 643 the defendant's factory had flooded, and when the water receded the floor was left slippery with oil. The employer took steps to minimise the danger by spreading sawdust while the floor was being cleaned bit by bit. The employer could have closed the factory until the cleaning had been completed, but the cost of doing so would have been disproportionate to the risk of injury. The employer had not been negligent.

6.6 STATUTORY DUTIES OF EMPLOYERS

The relevant law is that which was in force at the time when the alleged breach of duty took place. That may mean looking back at the old law, mainly to be found in:

- Agriculture (Safety, Health & Welfare) Act 1956;
- Factories Act 1961;
- Offices, Shops & Railway Premises Act 1963.

These have been replaced piecemeal over the last three decades by the Health and Safety at Work Act 1974 and regulations made under it. A few provisions are still in force today, such as s.24 Factories Act 1961 which relates to teagle openings and water-sealed gas-holders. The old statutes are seldom relevant to injuries suffered after 1995.

Like the common law duties already described, an employer's statutory duties are non-delegable. If the employer is entitled to delegate performance of a duty to a third party, without remaining liable for breach of the duty, it will be apparent from the statute or regulation concerned.

The Health & Safety at Work Act 1974 (HASAWA) governs nearly all workplaces, including offshore oil rigs and Crown premises. It does not cover domestic servants, or shipping. It contains general duties, and requires that employers should set up safe systems of work. A breach of a duty contained in the Act itself is a criminal offence, but does not give a right to make a civil claim for damages. It may be possible for the victim to get a compensation order in the criminal courts if the offender is convicted.

Regulations made under HASAWA provide detailed statutory duties, and can be found at **www.hmso.gov.uk**.

A breach of health and safety regulations which results in injury generally does give the victim the right to claim damages for his injuries and loss. Some regulations impose strict liability, so that an employer will be liable however much care he took to protect employees. The standard of care is variable (see **sections 6.7** to **6.9**).

The HASAWA regulations usually of interest in personal injury claims are, in date order:

- Health & Safety (First Aid) Regulations 1981. Provision and use of first aid equipment.
- Noise at Work Regulations 1989. Avoiding industrial deafness.
- Electricity at Work Regulations 1989. These require employers and the self-employed to maintain electrical systems so far as reasonably practicable to prevent risk of death or injury.
- Workplace (Health, Safety & Welfare) Regulations 1992 (WorkplaceHSW). These govern most work premises except mines and quarries, building sites and ships (all of which have their own specific regulations) and domestic premises. They are mainly about prevention of slips, trips and falls, and affect any part of work premises where workers may go, including access roads. They impose duties not just on employers but also on anybody who has control of work premises. Doors, gates and lifts must be safe, glass in windows and doors must be appropriate, and lighting must be adequate. The regulations impose a strict duty to maintain (including cleaning as appropriate) the workplace and the equipment, devices and systems to which the Regulations apply 'in an efficient state, in efficient working order and in good repair'. There are strict duties to keep every part of the workplace clean and tidy, and to keep floors free of holes, slopes and slippery sections. There are duties so far as is reasonably practicable to prevent anybody falling a distance likely to cause injury or being struck by any falling object likely to cause injury, and to keep all floors and pedestrian routes 'free from obstruction and from any

article or substance which may cause a person to slip, trip or fall'. As to workplace trips and slips (see **section 6.26**).

- Manual Handling Operations Regulations 1992 (MHOR) (see **section 6.22**).
- Health & Safety (Display Screen) Regulations 1992. Ergonomic use of computers and word processors, in particular relating to keyboards, display screens and monitors (see **section 6.28**).
- Personal Protective Equipment at Work Regulations 1998 (PPE) (see **section 6.23**).
- Provision and Use of Work Equipment Regulations 1998 (PUWER). Covers selection, maintenance and training. Very important (see **section 6.24**).
- Lifting Operations and Lifting Equipment Regulations 1998 (LOLER). Applies to construction work, but this is very widely defined and includes painting, window cleaning, plumbing and demolition. The Regulations relate to the purchase, maintenance and use of ladders, scaffolds and all lifting equipment from rope and pulley, through fork lifts and vehicle hoists, to cranes and goods lifts. Also relates to information and training to be provided to users of lifting equipment.
- Management of Health and Safety at Work Regulations 1999 (ManagementHSW). General provisions on avoiding all risks which can be avoided, and evaluating the others. Requires employers to carry out risk assessments and reassessments; implement any safety measures arising from the risk assessments; appoint competent people to do this; set up emergency procedures; give health and safety information and training to workers. Employers must provide information and monitor health of employees where there is 'a reasonable likelihood that a disease or condition may occur under particular conditions of work' (see **section 6.13**). Provision of training when employees are first taken on, and if the nature of the work changes. Employers to take special care to assess the risks to pregnant women, and protect workers under 18 from injuries resulting from their own inexperience, or from overwork, toxins, radiation, cold, heat, noise or vibration. Breach of these regulations after 27 October 2003 may be used as a basis for a damages claim (Management of Health and Safety at Work and Fire Precautions (Workplace) (Amendment) Regulations 2003).
- Fire Precautions (Workplace) (Amendment) Regulations 1999. As with ManagementHSW, if an employee is injured after 27 October 2003 as a result of his employer's breach of these regulations he has a right to damages.
- Control of Substances Hazardous to Health Regulations 2002 (COSHH) (see **sections 6.8** and **6.27**).

- Dangerous Substances and Explosive Atmospheres Regulations 2002 (DSEAR). These apply at any workplace that has substances that can cause fire or explosion, including sawdust, flour, and paint as well as the more obvious fuels, solvents and explosives. DSEAR require risk assessments and various precautions.

Industries with unique and dangerous working environments have their own regulations. They are usually covered by MHOR, PUWER, LOLER, DSEAR and other general regulations, but some have their own overarching health and safety statute. For example, mining and quarrying, the police, merchant shipping, agriculture, forestry, offshore oil and gas, shipbuilding, dock work, and the railways.

6.7 BREACH OF STATUTORY DUTY

It is generally a criminal offence not to comply with a regulation, so a person injured by the breach may be able to obtain a compensation order in the criminal courts (see **section 8.7**).

Some legislation expressly prevents those injured by a breach from relying on the statutory duty to make a civil claim for compensation, for example the Health and Safety at Work Act 1974 as regards the duties contained within HASAWA itself. Only criminal liability attaches.

Some legislation expressly provides for civil compensation. Section 47(2) HASAWA says: 'Breach of a duty imposed by health and safety regulations or agricultural health and safety regulations shall, so far as it causes damage, be actionable except insofar as the regulations provide otherwise.' Breach of a regulation made under HASAWA, then, is actionable in a civil court.

Most other legislation is silent about compensation. In that case, anybody injured by breach of his statutory right must hope that the common law gives him a remedy. It will do so if the claimant can show that:

1. The regulation upon which he wishes to rely applied to his workplace, employment status and activity at the time of the accident.
2. The claimant's loss was within the mischief envisaged by the statute. If the duty was to fence moving parts of a machine in a workplace in order to prevent an employee coming into contact with moving parts, and the employer failed to do so but the employee was in fact injured because a broken component is flung out of the machine, then the statutory duty is not relevant (even though proper fencing might well have stopped or slowed the component) (*Close* v. *Steel Co of Wales* [1962] AC 367). *King* v. *RCO Support Services & Yorkshire Traction Co* [2002] EWCA Civ 314 suggests that attitudes have changed since *Close*.
3. The defendant owed the duty of care to this claimant. In *Grant* v. *National Coal Board* [1956] AC 649 the House of Lords said: 'The duty

must . . . be to those who ought reasonably to have been in contemplation as likely to be injured as a result of the breach . . . in the ordinary course of their work and without any unusual or unforeseeable occurrence.'

The courts tend to interpret health and safety regulations broadly. In *King* the claimant slipped and fell while gritting an icy coach park with a barrow of grit and a shovel. He was not hurt by the manual handling but by the slip and fall. However, the court found that he was performing a task under the MHOR. Therefore he could rely on MHOR which required his employer, as far as reasonably practicable, to avoid any manual handling operations at work which involve a risk of injury; and to reduce the risk of injury in any remaining tasks to the lowest level reasonably practicable.

4. A breach of this particular duty is actionable in a civil court. Where the legislation itself does not say, the court has to decide. The general rule is that if a regulation provides for something other than damages, such as a fine, a breach is not actionable in a civil court. However, the general rule does not apply where the duty was intended to benefit or protect a particular class of individuals, particularly if it was intended to ensure their health and safety. For recent and very practical examples in personal injury cases, read *Todd* v. *Adams* [2002] EWCA Civ 509 (stability of trawlers) and *Phelps* v. *London Borough of Hillingdon* [2000] UKHL 47 (dyslexia).
5. The defendant committed a breach of that duty. Except where the regulations impose a strict duty, this is the difficult part of the equation. Check the wording of the regulation. For definitions of suitable, reasonably practicable, practicable, adequate and shall, see **section 6.8**.
6. The breach caused the injury and loss. This is the final element to be considered in the liability equation. The rules of causation and remoteness are the same for breach of statutory duty as they are in negligence (see **section 4.4**).

Warner v. *Huntingdon District Council* [2002] EWCA Civ 791 was a manual handling claim. The claimant had always had a vulnerable back, had to do repeated manual handling at work for 10 years, and developed a back problem. He should have been given manual handling training, at the latest after MOHR in 1992. In fact he was not given any training. Nor was he given information about the weight of the sacks as required by MHOR. The claim failed on causation, as there was no evidence that proper training or information would have prevented the damage.

Just as in negligence, the chain of causation between breach of duty and injury can be broken by the intervention of a third party, especially a wilful and blameworthy intervention (*Horton* v. *Taplin Contracts Ltd* [2002] EWCA Civ 1604).

A major difference between claims based on negligence and those based on breach of statutory duty is that with the former, the claimant must show that the accident was a reasonably foreseeable result of the breach. With statutory duty, there is no such requirement (*Larner* v. *British Steel* [1993] ICR 551). This case was based on a breach of the employer's statutory duty under s.29(1) of the old Factories Act 1961 to keep the workplace safe. The claimant did not have to prove that a reasonable defendant in the employer's position should have foreseen the accident. Either the workplace was safe, or it was not.

However, the courts have found that statutory duties sometimes necessarily involve an element of foreseeability. Where the regulation says that an employer must avoid a risk of injury, there cannot be a risk of injury unless it is reasonably foreseeable that some injury could occur. For example, the MOHR say that an employer must 'avoid the need for his employees to undertake any manual handling operations at work which involve a risk of their being injured'. That does not mean he must avoid the need for them to lift a cup of coffee in case it causes a scald or a hernia. The risk of these injuries is so small that it can properly be ignored. In *Koonjul* v. *Thameslink Healthcare Services* [2000] PIQR P123 the claimant was injured while making a child's bed. The Court of Appeal said there had to be at least 'a real risk, a foreseeable possibility of injury, [although] certainly nothing approaching a probability'. *Hawkes* v. *London Borough of Southwark* [1998] EWCA Civ 310 indicates that a slight risk can nonetheless be real.

In *Horton* v. *Taplin Contracts Ltd* [2002] EWCA Civ 1604 the claimant was employed as a carpenter. He was injured when a colleague maliciously tipped over the scaffold tower he was standing on. The employer had not ensured that the scaffold tower was stabilised. If it had, the claimant would not have been injured. However, as far as the employer knew or should have known, there had been no real risk of the tower tipping over, whether because of an assault or an earthquake. Various regulations applied, in particular regulations 5 and 20 of PUWER 1992.

Regulation 5 required 'every employer to ensure that work equipment is so constructed or adapted as to be suitable for the purpose for which it is used or provided'. Suitable was defined as 'suitable in any respect which it is reasonably foreseeable will affect the health or safety of any person'. Evidently this duty must be measured against reasonably foreseeable risks, but what about regulation 20? This said 'every employer shall ensure that work equipment or part of work equipment is stabilised by clamping or otherwise where necessary for purposes of health and safety'. The court found that stabilisation could be necessary only if there was a foreseeable possibility of injury.

Taplin also had a duty under the Construction (Health, Safety & Welfare) Regulations 1996: 'Each place of work shall, so far as reasonably practicable, be made and kept safe for, and without risks of health to, any person at work there.' The court said it would be an affront to common sense not to read this as requiring foreseeability of risk.

An employer may have a defence to an apparent breach of duty where the injured employee was doing something inherently dangerous, if it was socially necessary (*Sussex Ambulance NHS Trust* v. *King* [2002] EWCA Civ 953).

6.8 STANDARD OF CARE IN STATUTORY DUTY

When deciding whether a defendant satisfied a statutory duty, consider how it was phrased. Did the defendant have to do what was suitable; reasonably practicable; or practicable? Did he have to achieve adequate control? Or did the regulation simply say that he shall achieve some result?

A defendant who did all that was reasonably practicable to prevent injury has not been negligent. He may also have a good defence to an alleged breach of statutory duty, but not if the duty was strict.

'Suitable'? The Workplace (Health, Safety & Welfare) Regulations 1992 say: 'Every floor in a workplace and the surface of every traffic route shall be of a construction such that [it] is suitable for the purpose for which it is used.' For a brief summary of *Palmer* v. *Marks & Spencer plc* [2001] EWCA Civ 1528, see **section 6.26**.

The Provision and Use of Work Equipment Regulations 1998 (PUWER). Work equipment must be 'so constructed or adapted as to be suitable for the purpose for which it is used or provided'. For some examples of what is suitable, see **section 6.24**.

'Reasonably practicable'? The Workplace (Health, Safety and Welfare) Regulations 1992 impose a duty as far as is reasonably practicable to keep all floors and pedestrian routes 'free from obstruction and from any article or substance which may cause a person to slip, trip or fall'.

Under the Manual Handling Operations Regulations 1992 an employer has a duty 'so far as is reasonably practicable to avoid the need for his employees to undertake any manual handling operations at work which involve a risk of their being injured'.

The expression implies:

> that a computation must be made by the owner, in which the quantum of risk is placed on one scale and the sacrifice involved in the measures necessary for averting the risk (whether in money, time or trouble) is placed in the other; and if it be shown that there is a gross disproportion between them (the risk being insignificant in relation to the sacrifice) the defendant discharges the onus on them.

This computation should be done in the light of what the employer knew or should have known before the accident, not with hindsight (*Edwards* v. *National Coal Board* [1949] 1 KB 704).

If the employer can show a gross disproportion between:

- the risk of a particular sort of accident (How likely is it to occur? How serious would it be if it did?); and
- the cost of the safety measures required to prevent it (What cost in equipment? What cost in lost productivity?); and
- that the risk is insignificant compared to the cost;

then he has shown that it was not reasonably practicable to take the safety measures. It is difficult for an employer, especially a large and profitable employer, to prove that it was not reasonably practicable to take a particular safety measure.

If the claimant can show that there was apparently a breach of a statutory duty, the burden shifts to the defendant to show that it was not reasonably practicable to do anything more to comply with it. This follows from *Nimmo* v. *Alexander Cowan & Sons Ltd* [1968] AC 107, in which the House of Lords refused to believe 'that Parliament intended to impose on the injured workmen . . . the obligation to aver with the necessary particularity the manner in which the employer should have employed reasonably practicable means to make and keep the place safe for him'.

'Practicable'? A few statutory duties are required to be carried out by the employer as far as practicable. For example, the obligation to guard moving parts of machinery under PUWER 1998. This is a higher standard than 'reasonably practicable,' but something can be impracticable without being impossible.

'Adequate control'? Regulation 7(1) of the Control of Substances Hazardous to Health Regulations 2002 says 'every employer shall ensure that the exposure of his employees to a substance hazardous to health is either prevented or, where this is not reasonably practicable, adequately controlled'. If the employer can show that it was not reasonably practicable to prevent any exposure, what steps will create adequate control? The word, adequate, means that one considers the nature of the substance and the nature and degree of exposure. 'It is by no means incompatible with their purpose that an employer who fails to discover a risk or rates it so low that he takes no precautions against it should nevertheless be liable to the employee who suffers as a result' (*Dugmore* v. *Swansea NHS Trust* [2002] EWCA Civ 1689).

'Shall'? If a regulation simply states that something shall happen, liability is strict. This is so even if a normal and essential activity such as using a grinding wheel cannot be carried out without breach of the duty (*John Summers & Sons Ltd* v. *Frost* [1955] AC 740).

What is now regulation 5 of PUWER requires every employer to 'ensure that work equipment is maintained in an efficient state, in efficient working order and in good repair'. This duty is not qualified by the words, reasonably practicable. In *Stark* v. *The Post Office* [2000] EWCA Civ 64, the defendant employer was held liable for injuries resulting from snapping of a metal component in a postman's bicycle. The defect 'would not and could not have been discovered on any routine inspection . . . a perfectly rigorous examination would not have revealed this defect'. Nonetheless, the claim succeeded, as at the moment of the accident the bicycle was not safe and efficient.

The Workplace (Health, Safety and Welfare) Regulations 1992 provide that 'the workplace and the equipment, devices and systems to which this regulation applies shall be maintained (including cleaned as appropriate) in an efficient state, in efficient working order and in good repair,' just as in the PUWER duty above. Also 'every workplace shall have suitable and sufficient lighting'. If an employee trips in the dark during a power cut, the employer will be liable.

The Personal Protective Equipment at Work Regulations 1998 impose various duties, one of which is that the employer shall maintain the equipment 'in an efficient state, in efficient working order and in good repair'. As to *Fytche* v. *Wincanton Logistics* [2004] UKHL 31, see **section 6.23**.

6.9 STANDARD OF CARE IN PRACTICE

Health and safety revolves around the concept of the safe system of work.

How might a safe system prevent a factory worker getting hit by a passing fork lift truck if he steps backwards without looking? A safe system might arrange for fork lift drivers to be trained, and for the trucks to have a flashing yellow beacon, to travel at a maximum of 5 mph, to travel only within a system of lanes laid out on the factory floor in yellow paint, and to stop if any pedestrians are within 1.5 metres of the lane edge. See the HSE publication Safety in Working with Lift Trucks.

How might a safe system prevent an inexperienced worker causing an explosion in a painting booth? Perhaps by giving a key only to those with a current operator's certificate. The Provision and Use of Work Equipment Regulations 1998 require that:

> where the use of work equipment is likely to involve a specific risk to health and safety, every employer shall ensure that the use of work equipment is restricted to those persons given the task of using it . . . the employer shall ensure that the persons designated [to use it] have received adequate training.

The operator's certificate might be based on refresher training and expire after six months.

Approved codes of practice (ACoPs)

ACoPs are made under s.16 of HASAWA 1974 and are strong evidence of good practice in a particular activity. They include guidance on:

- Safe Use of Work Equipment (about PUWER).
- Safe Use of Lifting Equipment (about LOLER).
- Manual Handling (about the MHOR).
- Control of Substances that Cause Occupational Asthma (about COSHH).

HSE Guidance Notes, etc

Although these are less important than ACoPs, they are nonetheless influential in civil claims. Examples include:

- Sheeting Loads on Tipper Lorries.
- Advice Regarding Call Centre Local Working Practices.
- Manual Handling.
- Manual Handling in the Health Services.
- Safety in Forestry and Arboriculture (chain saws, tree climbing, etc)

An employer, especially a large employer which has staff doctors and scientists, will be taken to know the contents of any HSE publication not long after it is released (*Cartwright* v. *GKN Sankey Ltd* (1973) 14 KIR 349 and *Foster* v. *National Power* [1997] LTL 7 May).

An employer that requires its employees to carry out some industrial activity such as handling asbestos will be taken to know anything about the dangers of the activity that has become common knowledge amongst prudent employers (*Stokes* v. *Guest Keen & Nettlefold (Bolts & Nuts) Ltd* [1968] 1 WLR 1776). '. . . where there is developing knowledge, he must keep reasonably abreast of it and not be too slow to apply it.'

An employer which 'requires employees to use chemicals in the course of their work [must] make enquiries as to the safety hazards which they present' (*Ogden* v. *Airedale Health Authority* [1996] 7 Med LR 153). An employer has 'positive obligations . . . to seek out risks and take precautions against them' (*Dugmore* v. *Swansea NHS Trust* [2002] EWCA Civ 1689).

The Management of Health and Safety at Work Regulations 1999 require employers and the self employed to take reasonable steps to familiarise themselves with the hazards of their industry, for example by reading HSE guidance, the trade press, company and supplier manuals.

Other codes of practice

There are British Standards. For their status in a civil claim, see **section 5.14**. There are also many highly specialised codes of practice known only to experts within a particular industry, such as the Construction Industry Research and Information Association Medical Code of Practice for Work in Compressed Air, and the Maritime and Coastguard Agency Code of Safe Working Practices for Merchant Seamen.

If an employer owes a duty to protect an employee during working hours, it also owes a duty to protect him during activities incidental to work, such as walking across the factory yard to get to his place of work in the morning or having a tea break (*Davidson* v. *Handley Page* [1945] 1 All ER 235). Only in very unusual circumstances would the employer's duty extend to anything occurring off his own premises and outside working hours. Injury while playing for the company football team outside working hours will seldom entitle the employee to damages, although see *Jebson* v. *Ministry of Defence* [2000] EWCA Civ 198.

6.10 EUROPEAN UNION LAW

The basis of the European Union is the Treaty Of Rome 1957. The European Communities Act 1972 makes the Treaty part of UK law and directly enforceable by private individuals.

National courts must interpret domestic law, whether passed before or after a conflicting EU Directive, so as to give precedence to the Directive (*Marleasing* v. *La Comercial Internacional de Alimentacion* [1992] C-106/89).

Where a conflict cannot be avoided in this way, the UK's own courts must recognise the supremacy of EU law, and if necessary make an injunction to prevent enforcement of UK law until Parliament resolves the conflict (*R (Factortame)* v. *Secretary of State for Transport* [1990] ECR I–2433).

European Regulations are directly applicable and binding within the UK, as long as they are clear, unconditional and leave no discretion. An ordinary individual can enforce them vertically (against the UK) and horizontally (against ordinary businesses or his fellow citizens).

European Directives are binding on each member state as to the result to be achieved, and Parliament is obliged to implement them by domestic legislation. However, the member state has a discretion as to the exact way they are implemented. Most of the recent health and safety regulations are based on EU Directives.

At the time of writing, the claimant has no right to enforce a Directive horizontally, but he may have a right to enforce it vertically. In *Francovich* v. *Italy* [1991] ECR C-6/90 the European Court of Justice ruled that a member state can be liable to compensate an individual for its failure to implement a Directive properly and promptly if:

1. The Directive was breached by an emanation of the state.
2. The Directive confers rights on, or protects, individuals such as the claimant.
3. The Directive is clear, unconditional and leaves the state no discretion how it should be applied. To put this another way, the claimant's rights must be identifiable from the Directive itself.
4. The breach amounted to a manifest and grave disregard of the defendant's obligations under the Directive.
5. The breach caused the claimant's loss.

The following are emanations of the state: the armed forces, the civil service, the police, health authorities, local authorities, education authorities, the board of governors of a school accepting financial assistance from the local education authority, and nationalised industries. The European Court of Justice said that the term includes any organisation 'which has been made responsible, pursuant to a measure adopted by the State, for providing a public service under the control of the State and has for that purpose special powers beyond those which result from the normal rules applicable in relations between individuals' (*Foster v. British Gas* [1990] EUECJ C-188/89).

The main EU workplace legislation is:

- Equal Treatment Directive 76/207;
- Asbestos Directive 83/477;
- Noise at Work Directive 86/188;
- Health and Safety Framework Directive 89/391;
- Workplace Minimum Standards Directive 89/654;
- Work Equipment Directive 89/655;
- Use of Personal Equipment Directive 89/656;
- Display Screen Equipment Directive 90/270;
- Carcinogens at Work Directive 90/394;
- Manual Handling Directive 90/269;
- Temporary and Mobile Work Sites Directive 92/57;
- Safety Signs Directive 92/58;
- Pregnant Workers Directive 92/85;
- Protection of Young People at Work Directive 94/33;
- Amending Directive 95/63;
- Biological Agents Directive 2000/54;
- Framework Directive for Equal Treatment in Employment 2000/78;
- Temporary Work at Height Directive 2001/45;
- Physical Agents (Vibration) Directive 2002/44;
- Physical Agents (Noise) Directive 2003/10;
- Physical Agents (Electro-Magnetic Fields) Directive 2004/40.

6.11 EMPLOYMENT CONTRACT

The relationship between employer and employee is necessarily a contractual one, involving mutual obligation. The employee may not have a written employment contract. If he does, the parties should check its express terms. If it confirms that he is an employee, so much the better for the claimant as many health and safety duties are owed only to employees. If the contract is ambiguous, or says he is self-employed, one must consider whether in all the circumstances this is correct (see **section 6.16**).

The claimant should check whether the act or omission that caused the injury could be said to have represented a breach of contract by the employer, enabling him to bring a claim for breach of contract. Claimants do not very often cite breach of contract as the basis for a personal injury claim. It can be easier to prove breach of contract than negligence, but the claimant might well recover more if he based his claim on negligence (see **section 4.7**). He may face a costs penalty if he complicates the claim by adding unnecessary and complex arguments about contract.

The personal injury lawyer needs to be aware that a fundamental or repudiatory breach of the employment contract may entitle the employee to leave and claim compensation for unfair dismissal and/or wrongful dismissal.

The common law implies up to a score of terms into any employment contract. Some are implied by statute, others if they reflect what has actually happened since the employee started the job, or if they are standard in the particular industry. Most implied terms are irrelevant to personal injury claims, for example provision of references. However, the following six may be relevant:

1. That the employer will take reasonable care to provide a safe working environment. As previously mentioned, the employer has a common law duty of care to provide a safe system of work; provide and maintain a safe place of work; provide and maintain safe plant and machinery; select competent employees; and protect employees from reasonably foreseeable risks.

   The common law may imply similar terms into an employment contract. A breach of contract resulting in injury to the employee may well amount to a fundamental or repudiatory breach, entitling the employee to leave and claim unfair dismissal and/or wrongful dismissal (see **section 6.20**).
2. That the employer will comply with its statutory duties, particularly those relating to health and safety.
3. That the employer will not 'without reasonable and proper cause conduct itself in a way calculated and likely to destroy or seriously damage the relationship of trust and confidence between employer and employee' (*Malik* v. *BCCI* [1997] UKHL 23). An employer might breach

the trust and confidence term if he imposes a pay cut; unfairly misses out one employee when giving others promotion, pay rises or training; or abuses or humiliates an employee, especially in public (*Horkulak* v. *Cantor Fitzgerald* [2003] EWHC 1918 (QB)).

If an employee is injured by the fact or manner of dismissal, the courts do not award 'compensation for the manner of dismissal, [or] for his injured feelings . . .' (*Addis* v. *Gramophone Co Ltd* [1909] AC 488). Nor can an employee get round the time limits and financial cap that apply to an unfair dismissal claim in the Employment Tribunal by bringing court proceedings on the basis that the dismissal breached the trust and confidence term (*Johnson* v. *Unisys* [2001] UKHL 13).

However, the courts can award compensation for psychiatric injury in the course of employment, whether this is caused by negligence, breach of statutory duty, or breach of contract. Contract claims are generally based on breach of the trust and confidence term. In *Gogay* v. *Hertfordshire County Council* [2000] EWCA Civ 228 the claimant was a care worker who came under suspicion of child abuse. Although the allegations appeared to be the fantasies of a troubled child, the employer started a formal investigation. In what the court described as a knee jerk reaction, the employer suspended the claimant pending the outcome. The suspension lasted a month, and on top of the investigation it pushed the claimant into clinical depression. The court said the employee had been entitled to better treatment, and that the employer had breached the trust and confidence term.

If the employee suffered psychiatric injury as a result of a mishandled disciplinary investigation or suspension, and is eventually dismissed, he may well have both a court claim for injury in the course of employment, and an Employment Tribunal claim for unfair dismissal. The one does not bar the other (*McCabe* v. *Cornwall County Council* and *Eastwood* v. *Magnox* [2004] UKHL 35).

If an employer refuses to give reasonable sick leave to an injured employee, the refusal may be a repudiatory breach of the trust and confidence term.

4. That the employer will give 'reasonable support to an employee to ensure that the employee can carry out the duties of his job without harassment and disruption by his fellow workers' (*Waters* v. *Commissioner of Metropolitan Police* [2000] UKHL 50).
5. That the employer will abide by terms contained in the staff handbook. These terms may be relevant to health and safety or to the way a disabled employee is treated. They may be part of the employment contract if the parties intended them to be.

   In *Jowitt* v. *Pioneer Technology* [2003] EWCA Civ 411 the contract of employment expressly incorporated the staff handbook. The handbook said that there was a permanent health insurance (PHI) scheme. This would provide an employee who was unable to work with an income, starting 26 weeks after his disability and continuing until retirement if necessary. Mr Jowitt was permanently unable to do his job because of a back injury. After a time, the PHI insurer stopped paying as the insurance contract covered only 'total inability to follow any occupation'. The Court of Appeal found no basis for incorporating the insurance contract into the employment contract. Properly construed, this particular employment contract meant that the employer would provide the employee with an income as long as there was no continuous remunerative full-time work that the employee could realistically be expected to do.

6. That the employer will not dismiss an injured employee, except for gross misconduct, if this will prevent him receiving benefits under a PHI policy that was part of his remuneration package (*Aspden* v. *Webbs Poultry & Meat* [1996] IRLR 521 and *Briscoe* v. *Lubrizol Ltd* [2002] EWCA Civ 508).

In *Crossley* v. *Faithful & Gould* [2004] EWCA Civ 293 the Court of Appeal found that where an employer has not assumed the burden of advising an employee about his rights, it has no general duty to take reasonable care of the employee's economic well being. This claimant was entitled to PHI benefits if he was unable to work, under an insurance policy organised by the defendant. He became disabled. To activate PHI payments he had to apply through the defendant. He had to rely on the defendant to further the application. In the meantime, the defendant amicably encouraged him to resign for medical reasons, and he did so. This ended his right to PHI payments. His claim against the employer failed. The outcome would have been different if the employer had assumed responsibility for advising the employee on his rights, as in *Lennon* v. *Commissioner of Police of the Metropolis* [2004] EWCA Civ 130.

In *Marshall Specialist Vehicles v. Osborne* [2003] IRLR 369 the Employment Appeal Tribunal would not imply into a contract a term that the employer would:

> take such action as (having regard to the availability of its human and financial resources) may be reasonably practicable in the particular circumstances prevailing at the material time to avoid either imposing workload upon you or acquiescing in your assumption of workload which it is reasonably foreseeable may cause you physical or mental injury.

The courts will not imply a term into an employment contract if it directly conflicts with express terms (*Reda* v. *FLAG* [2002] UKPC 38).

If a written employment contract is ambiguous, consider how it has been applied between the parties (*Dunlop Tyres* v. *Blows* [2001] EWCA Civ 1032). Failing that, the courts will construe any ambiguous term *contra proferentem*, against the interests of the party who drew it up.

Section 47(5) of the Health and Safety at Work Act 1974 says: 'Any term of an agreement which purports to exclude or restrict the operation of [s.47(2)] or any liability arising by virtue of that subsection shall be void, except insofar as health and safety regulations, or as the case may be agricultural health and safety regulations provide otherwise.'

Section 47(2) says: 'Breach of a duty imposed by health and safety regulations or agricultural health and safety regulations shall, as far as it causes damage, be actionable except insofar as the regulations provide otherwise.'

Implied terms do not always place the burden on the employer. There is an implied term that an employee will carry out his duties with reasonable care. This may entitle an uninsured employer, vicariously liable for the acts of an employee, to recover his outlays from the guilty employee by way of a claim for contribution and indemnity (*Lister* v. *Romford Ice & Cold Storage Co* [1957] AC 555).

As a matter of employment law, disobedience may amount to conduct or some other substantial reason entitling the claimant's employer to dismiss him without paying compensation for unfair dismissal. A fundamental breach of the employment contract by the employee can have a devastating effect on his claim for loss of future earnings. If the defendant is entitled to fire him, it may greatly reduce his claim for loss of future earnings. Certainly somebody who has been fired for wilful and persistent breaches of safety rules is unlikely to find a good job elsewhere. Neither is a man who got and kept his job by making fraudulent health declarations (*Hewison* v. *Meridian Shipping* [2002] EWCA Civ 1821).

6.12 REPORTING AND ENFORCEMENT

The Reporting of Injuries, Diseases and Dangerous Occurrences Regulations 1995 require an employer to report any accident that causes a death; sick leave for three days or more; a visit to hospital for a member of the public; or a work-related illness. The employer must also report any dangerous occurrence that could have resulted in a reportable injury.

Employers sometimes reveal more in RIDDOR reports than they are later willing to provide in correspondence. The report may also prompt an investigation by the Health and Safety Executive or the environmental health department of the local authority.

A House of Commons select committee found in February 2000 that the HSE was then investigating about 10 per cent of severe workplace injury cases and 20 per cent of fatal cases. It was proposed in 2004 that the HSE should be given funds to triple the number of inspectors.

HSE investigation reports are brief and seldom useful to litigants. Section 28 Health and Safety at Work Act 1974 says no 'relevant information . . . shall be disclosed without the consent of the person by whom it was furnished'. It goes on to say 'the preceding subsection shall not apply to . . . disclosure of information for the purposes of any legal proceedings or any investigation or inquiry held by virtue of s.14(2)'. The HSE seldom lets litigants see witness statements or the reports of its inspector until proceedings have been issued against the employer.

The HSE may be willing to send the claimant, prior to issue of proceedings, a list of the documents on its file, a short statement, and a set of any photographs the inspector took on site.

The HSE (and environmental health departments of local authorities) can prosecute those who cause accidents at work. The trades unions, feeling that the HSE does not use the stick enough, obtained the right in 2003 to bring health and safety prosecutions themselves.

The HSE was not set up to assist claimants and lawyers. Some feel that it is institutionally hostile to personal injury claims. It does not go to sea. In the North Sea oil fields, it shares the health and safety role with the Maritime and Coastguard Agency and the Department for Transport.

It publishes many excellent leaflets, Codes of Practice, Notes for Guidance and books. The smaller documents can be seen free at **www.hse.gov.uk**.

In a unionised workplace, a report may have been prepared by the trade union safety representative, working with management under the Safety Representatives & Safety Committees Regulations 1977. Particularly if the claimant is a union member he should find it easy to get a copy.

The Pre-action Protocol indicates that the defendant should, unless he admits liability, provide the claimant with copies of documents in the Standard Disclosure List. These include the supervisor's accident report, safety representative's accident report, RIDDOR report, other communications between the defendant and the HSE, minutes of health and safety committee meetings where the accident was considered, and the accident investigation report prepared to comply with the Management of Health & Safety at Work Regulations 1992/1999.

If an accident investigation report was required to comply with ManagementHSW, the defendant can hardly argue that it is privileged from disclosure on the basis that its dominant purpose was to conduct actual or anticipated litigation as in *Waugh* v. *British Railways Board* [1980] AC 521 (see **section 20.4**).

Of course, a damning accident investigation report is the last thing most defendants want the claimant to see. They may prefer to risk the court imposing a costs penalty rather than let the claimant have a copy as soon as they deny liability, as required by the Protocol.

6.13 RISK ASSESSMENTS

Various health and safety regulations require the employer to carry out a risk assessment. General ones include the Management of Health & Safety at Work Regulations 1999, as amended by the Management of Health & Safety at Work and Fire Precautions (Workplace) (Amendment) Regulations 2003.

There are also many specific regulations that require a risk assessment in particular circumstances. These include the Manual Handling Operations Regulations 1992, the Health and Safety (Display Screen) Regulations 1992 and the Dangerous Substances and Explosive Atmospheres Regulations 2002.

The Court of Appeal in *Griffiths* v. *Vauxhall Motors* [2003] EWCA Civ 412 said that the point of the risk assessment process is 'that an investigation is carried out in order to identify whether the particular operation gives rise to any risk to safety, and if so what is the extent of that risk, which of course includes the extent of any risk of injury, and what can and should be done to minimise or eradicate the risk'. In some situations, the factors that an employer is required to consider when assessing risk fill many pages.

Many risk assessments assume that all employees are fit, trained people with common sense, but a proper risk assessment must relate to the actual people who are to carry out the task (*O'Neill* v. *DSG Retail Ltd* [2002] EWCA Civ 1139).

There is no need to carry out a risk assessment if there is no real risk. To be real, a risk need not be substantial, and might even be slight (*Koonjul* v. *Thameslink Healthcare Services* [2000] PIQR P123). There is no need for a risk assessment to consider attempts by employees to do a straightforward and well-established job in a novel way that had never been attempted before (*Bennetts* v. *Ministry of Defence* [2004] EWCA Civ 486).

In 2004, a survey of businesses with five to 50 employees found that 24 per cent had never risk assessed any of their activities. From the claimant's point of view it is worth mentioning if the activity which injured him had not been risk assessed. Most courts will be less sympathetic to a slack employer. Can one, however, say that injury was caused by failure to complete a risk assessment? In *Hawkes* v. *London Borough of Southwark* [1998] EWCA Civ 310, the Court of Appeal said that the requirement to carry out a risk assessment is 'merely an exhortation with no sanction attached'.

However, in *Griffiths* v. *Vauxhall Motors* [2003] EWCA Civ 412 the court said that if the employer had carried out a risk assessment 'it is much more likely than not that it would have identified the risk of injury . . . [and therefore] a competent employer would at the very least have instructed [workers] that in order to avoid the risk they must . . . hang on tightly at all times'.

6.14 WORKPLACE CONTRIBUTORY NEGLIGENCE

In the workplace as anywhere else, the effect of the Law Reform (Contributory Negligence) Act 1945 is to reduce damages if the victim's own negligence contributed to the accident or to his injuries, but not to defeat the claim. The court is less ready to discount compensation where the victim was an employee and was injured at work.

The court does not expect employees to walk out if they see anything dangerous. The court does not expect them to complain to the employer about workplace hazards. It does expect them to take risks with their own safety if unsupervised, and will be reluctant to deduct much for an employee's negligence if the employer knew or should have known that the employee was breaking safety rules.

An employer has a duty of care to devise and enforce a safe system of work, and to keep the workplace safe. He cannot expect an employee to remember to duck his head each time he goes around a particular corner, always to look where he is putting his feet, or to test-weigh each sack he lifts in case somebody has put something too heavy in it.

Contributory negligence by the employee can apply to claims based on an employer's breach of statutory duty, even if the duty carries strict liability (*Caswell* v. *Powell Duffryn* [1940] AC 152). However, 'It is not usual for there to be marked findings of contributory negligence in a breach of statutory duty case' (*Toole v. Bolton Metropolitan Borough Council* [2002] EWCA Civ 588), a case in which the Court of Appeal struck down the trial judge's finding that the claimant's own contributory negligence justified reducing his compensation by 75 per cent.

'Unskilled workers'? The courts seldom deduct much from damages for carelessness or breach of safety rules by ordinary employees. Employers are supposed to stamp out dangerous practices. They are not encouraged to blame employees.

If an injury occurs because the claimant did not wear protective equipment which the employer had provided, he may still have a good claim based on a failure by the employer to encourage or coerce him into wearing it, or supervise him to make sure he had the straps done up. This could represent a breach of regulation 10 of the Personal Protective Equipment at Work Regulations 1998. It may also represent negligence on the part of the employer (*Bux* v. *Slough Metals* [1974] 1 All ER 262).

'A person is guilty of contributory negligence if he ought reasonably to have foreseen that, if he did not act as a reasonable, prudent man, he might be hurt himself . . . and in his reckonings he must take into account the possibility of others being careless' (*Jones* v. *Livox Quarries* [1952] 2 QB 608). However, if he is injured because he failed to take into account the possibility that his employer might have breached its own statutory duties, 'it is important to ensure that the statutory requirement placed on the employer is not emasculated by too great a willingness on the part of the courts to find that the employee has been guilty of contributory negligence' (*Cooper* v. *Carillion plc* [2003] EWCA Civ 1811).

It is important 'to give due regard to the actual conditions under which men work in a factory or mine, to the long hours and the fatigue, to the slackening of attention from constant repetition of the same operation, to the noise and confusion in which the man works, to his pre-occupation in what he is actually doing at the cost perhaps of some inattention to his own safety' (*Caswell* v. *Powell Duffryn* [1940] AC 152).

In *White* v. *Lord Chancellor's Department* [1997] EWCA Civ 2451 no deduction was made where a security guard had failed to lift his foot enough to clear a threshold into his kiosk, and had caught his foot in a toecap-sized gap under the sill. The court dismissed the traditional allegation that he had failed to look where he was putting his feet. This was no more than 'inadvertence of the sort that is to be expected of employees'.

In *Williams* v. *Devon County Council* [2003] EWCA Civ 365 the claimant was a canteen manager. She opened the door from kitchen to dining area, walked through the doorway holding a large menu board in a way that prevented her seeing what was in front of her, and fell over a low bench that somebody had foolishly placed across the doorway. The court considered that the 'everyday realities of the working environment' made any deduction inappropriate.

In *Butcher* v. *Cornwall County Council* [2002] EWCA Civ 1640 the claimant was walking in and out of a building all day. As it was a windy day and the employer had not provided any means of latching open the door, he latched it shut each time. On the last occasion he did not quite shut the latch when he went outside, and it blew open and hit him on the head. The Court of Appeal felt that in this sort of case one third to a half was the appropriate discount for contributory negligence.

In *Anderson* v. *Newham College of Further Education* [2002] EWCA Civ 505 the claimant tripped over the leg of a whiteboard that stuck out into the gangway. The leg was bright orange, the lighting was good, and there had been plenty of room for the claimant to walk past safely. The judge at first instance found that the claimant had been so careless himself that he was 90 per cent to blame for his injury. The Court of Appeal reduced this to 50 per cent.

In *King* v. *RCO Support Services & Yorkshire Traction Co* [2002] EWCA Civ 314 the claimant had been spreading grit in an icy coach park with a barrow of grit and a shovel. He had been doing this for two hours when he stepped off the area he had gritted onto the area he had not gritted, and slipped. Although it could be argued that he of all people was in a good position to know which areas were safe to walk on, he suffered only a 50 per cent discount because the task was a long one and the longer the task, the greater the risk of his attention wandering.

In *Jebson* v. *Ministry of Defence* [2000] EWCA Civ 198, soldiers got drunk during a night out organised by their commander. Drunkenness was expected on such an outing. The return journey was in an army lorry. There was no supervision of the young men in the back, and with the lorry doing 50 mph the claimant fell off while trying to climb off the tailgate onto the roof. Given the paternal nature of the army and its attitude to alcohol, the claim succeeded but with a 75 per cent discount for contributory negligence.

If the claimant's own wilful disobedience was 100 per cent to blame for his injuries, the claim will fail altogether even if the employer was in breach of a strict statutory duty (see **section 6.15**).

'Skilled employees'? An employee who has a responsible job and ignores its responsibilities is, in practice, at greater risk of a substantial deduction or of complete failure than an unskilled worker.

In *Cleminson* v. *John Addley Ltd & Croda Resins Ltd* [1999] EWCA Civ 1377 the claimant's job was to clean storage tanks while wearing breathing apparatus that restricted his vision. There was a safe and satisfactory system for getting onto the tank and down through a central manhole and '. . . it was essential not to place himself to the rear of the manhole and between it and the gap. He deliberately chose to go into that area and fell. This was not mere inadvertence or momentary inattention. He placed himself in a position of danger'. A deduction of 20 per cent was made.

In *Griffiths* v. *Vauxhall Motors* [2003] EWCA Civ 412 the claimant was an experienced assembly-line worker, and was injured by the kick of his pneumatic spanner. The injury occurred because he did not grip it tightly enough. He was aware that the tool might kick back if not grasped firmly. The court deducted 50 per cent for contributory negligence.

In *Parker* v. *PFC Flooring* [2001] EWCA Civ 1533, the claimant was injured after climbing onto the roof of his employer's business premises. He went up to remove a cable that had been put up there by a possible burglar, and fell through a skylight. A sales director, he knew that if he had asked his boss he would have been told not to go up there. The court deducted 50 per cent for contributory negligence.

In *Sherlock v. Chester City Council* [2004] EWCA Civ 201 the claimant was a skilled and experienced joiner who consciously chose an obviously risky method of cutting up materials, sooner than take easy precautions. The defendant was in breach of regulations requiring it to instruct him to use equipment that would have made the task safe, and to reduce the risk of injury to the lowest level reasonably practicable. There was, however, a 60 per cent discount.

'Silent employee'? If an employee is one of those who unpredictably develops health problems when his colleagues all seem to be coping, and fails to tell his employer about it until serious damage has been done, the employer may well not have been negligent. However, if the employee can establish primary liability against the employer, the courts will be reluctant to deduct anything from his compensation (*Young* v. *The Post Office* [2002] IRLR 660).

6.15 CONSENT TO RISK AT WORK

If a workman's own carelessness or disobedience contributed to his injury, his damages will be reduced as in the previous section. Damages can be reduced for contributory negligence, but never by 100 per cent.

A claim can be defeated altogether if a claimant knew there was a risk, consented to it, and was injured as a result. The principle is *volenti non fit injuria*. Claims against employers are a special case, as an employee will not be taken to have consented to a risk in the workplace merely because he continues to turn up for work knowing that the risk exists (*Smith* v. *Charles Baker & Sons* [1891] AC 325).

A claim based on negligence may be defeated by *volenti*, but only in very restricted circumstances, for example if the employer can show that the employee voluntarily entered a dangerous place, during working hours but not in connection with his duties (*National Coal Board* v. *England* [1954] AC 403).

In *Woolger* v. *West Surrey & NE Hampshire HA* (1993) *The Times* 8 November, a nurse was injured while lifting a patient in an unsafe way that conflicted with her training. She alleged that her employer should have warned her not to use the unsafe method of lifting. However, the court considered that the method by which a properly trained nurse lifted a patient was a matter for her own judgement.

A claim based on breach of statutory duty may also be defeated by *volenti*, but again only in very restricted circumstances. The general rule is that *volenti* does not apply (*Wheeler* v. *New Merton Board Mills* [1933] 2 KB 669). For an exception, see *ICI* v. *Shatwell* [1965] AC 656. The claimant and his brother were employed as shot firers in a quarry. They knew the explosives regulations but habitually breached them by testing detonators without taking shelter. The claimant was injured when his brother did this, and sued the employer on the basis that it was vicariously liable for his brother's acts. The claim failed.

In *Ginty* v. *Belmont Building Supplies Ltd* [1959] 1 All ER 414 the claimant was an experienced roofer. He was working on site, on a roof he knew to be fragile. His employer had told him to use crawling boards, and in any case he knew that health and safety regulations required him to do so. He did not, and fell through. The employer was morally blameless, and not itself in breach of duty apart from its vicarious liability for the claimant's own breach. The court refused to find the defendant liable, saying that to do so would be absurd where the claimant was 100 per cent to blame.

The claimant may succeed if he can show even the smallest failure on the part of the employer. In *Boyle* v. *Kodak* [1969] 2 All ER 439 the claimant was using a ladder to do some painting. He knew that if possible he should lash the top of the ladder before climbing it. He could have done so by going up a fixed staircase first, but did not, and fell. The House of Lords approved

Ginty but found that the employer should have realised that its employee might not fully appreciate what the regulations required him to do where there was no obvious danger. Thus the employer could have complied with its statutory duty only by giving the claimant more detailed instructions about use of ladders, and the claim succeeded on that basis.

6.16 EMPLOYED OR SELF EMPLOYED

A worker may be an employee, self employed or an office holder. Employment status is important because most of the duties that require employers to train, supervise and protect their workers are for the benefit of employees; anybody with employees also has a heavy burden in terms of employer's liability insurance, employer's National Insurance contributions, unfair dismissal, wrongful dismissal, redundancy, sick pay, holidays and working hours; and employers are vicariously liable for injuries caused by their employees but seldom for those caused by their independent contractors.

An office holder is, simply, somebody who holds an office. Whether or not he is paid to do so, the mere fact of holding the office, such as club secretary or company director, does not make him an employee. He may be an employee too if he has a contract of employment. An office holder may be treated as an employee under a statute. Police cadets and constables are so treated under the Police (Health and Safety) Act 1997. As to civil servants, see s.48 Health & Safety at Work Act 1974. A civil servant may, in addition to his office, have an express or implied contract of employment (*R (Nangle) v. Lord Chancellor's Department* [1991] ICR 743).

As regards his own safety, the self-employed worker is free to do the job as he chooses. His employer is generally under no duty to supervise his work, to advise him on a safe system of work, or to offer him additional safety equipment, although see the extract from the *Associated Octel* case, later in this section.

Like any other member of the public, a self-employed worker or office holder can claim damages if he is injured by another person's negligence, or by breach of the duty of care imposed on occupiers of premises by the Occupiers' Liability Acts (see **section 5.5**). Some health and safety legislation protects the self employed.

Indeed, some workplace regulations protect anybody, regardless of employment status. The Control of Substances Hazardous to Health Regulations 2002 say 'where a duty is placed by these regulations on an employer in respect of his employees, he shall, so far as reasonably practicable, be under a like duty in respect of any other person, whether at work or not, who may be affected by the work carried out by the employer'.

Substantial parts of the Workplace (Health, Safety and Welfare) Regulations 1992, Provision and Use of Work Equipment Regulations 1998,

Construction (Health, Safety and Welfare) Regulations 1996 and Health and Safety (Display Screen) Regulations 1992 are either for the benefit of 'any person at work there' or give some protection to the self employed.

Most regulations, however, protect only employees, for example the Manual Handling Operations Regulations 1992 and the Personal Protective Equipment at Work Regulations 1998.

The European Directives on which our health and safety regulations are based are for the benefit of workers. When the Directives were implemented by regulations made under the Health and Safety at Work Act 1974, the UK regulations referred not to workers but to employees. The European Commission is keen that the self employed should have the same protection from EU law as the employed and is promoting the Self-Employed Workers Proposal 2002/0079.

It is not always obvious whether somebody is employed or self employed. On the one hand there are those who are clearly employees, bound into a master and servant relationship by a contract of service, and on the other those who are clearly independent contractors, working for themselves and providing a service under a contract for services. In the middle is a large grey area. Employees and self-employed workers very often work alongside each other, doing the same work at the same premises for the same employer.

Many employers today give contracts to full-time permanent staff that state that they are self employed. The courts may accept that a worker is self employed for tax purposes but hold that he is an employee for health and safety purposes.

The Health and Safety at Work Act 1974 provides definitions, but nothing very useful. An employee is somebody who works under a contract of employment, whether written or oral whereas a self-employed person works 'for gain or reward otherwise than under a contract of employment'. Essentially, one must fall back on the common law rules.

The label the parties attach to the work relationship is only one of the circumstances when one decides on a worker's status. The courts are keen to find that an injured worker is an employee and therefore entitled to the full benefit of health and safety law. They are about equally keen to do the same in respect of employment protection.

However, 'A man is without question free under the law to contract to carry out certain work for another without entering into a contract of service' (*Calder* v. *Kitson Vickers* [1988] ICR 242). The court will look at the reality of the employer-employee relationship. Was the overall feel of the arrangement that he was his own boss? That he was in business on his own account?

The usual questions were set out by the Court of Appeal in *Hall (Inspector of Taxes)* v. *Lorimer* [1994] ICR 218, a case involving a freelance vision mixer. With a few additions, they are paraphrased below. The main issues are those of control by the employer, mutuality of obligation and whether the worker is bound to provide his services personally:

- How far did the employer control the way in which the worker did his job? Note that many employees have skills their employers do not. The employer of a surgeon, for example, will exercise little day-to-day control over his activities. As long as the worker is relatively unskilled, the control test is both useful and popular with the courts (*Montgomery* v. *Johnson Underwood* [2001] EWCA Civ 318).
- Was there sufficient mutual obligation to show that an employer-employee relationship existed? The irreducible minimum is that the employer is obliged to provide the worker with work (or at least with pay), and the worker is obliged to be ready and willing to work (*Carmichael* v. *National Power* [1999] UKHL 47).
- If he wanted to, could he take time off and arrange for somebody else to do the job for him? Could he hire his own helpers? If a worker is entitled to appoint a substitute except on a limited or occasional basis, he will not be an employee (*Express & Echo Publications Ltd v. Tanton* [1999] EWCA Civ 949 and *Byrne Bros (Formwork) Ltd* v. *Baird* [2002] IRLR 96).
- Was it the worker or his employer who provided and serviced the tools he worked with? Consider not just hammers and brushes but also major items such as compressors and cranes.
- Was it possible for the worker to make a loss on a job?
- Did the worker have to correct unsatisfactory work in his own time, or at his own expense?
- Did the worker have any responsibility for management of the employer's activities, or investment of its funds?
- What benefit would accrue to the worker if he managed his own job well?
- What did the parties understand or intend the relationship to be?
- Did the worker perform the services as part of a businesslike organisation of his own?
- What continuity was there in the relationship between worker and employer? Consider how long he had been continuously with that employer, whether a contract bound him to work for only one employer, whether he had a regular basic wage, whether the employer paid him when there was no work or he was off sick.
- Is it more realistic to say that he was an accessory to the employer's business, or part and parcel of it?

One might also ask whether the worker:

- could choose what hours he worked, or the order in which he did jobs;
- was able to choose to do or not do particular jobs;
- received free training from the employer;

- received holiday pay, although since *R (BECTU)* v. *Secretary of State for Trade & Industry* [2001] IRLR 559 (ECJ) many freelance workers now get holiday pay under the Working Time Directive 93/104/EC.

It is possible for a worker to be a labour-only subcontractor, supply his own tools, work for two or three companies by turns, choose his own working hours and which jobs to do, be paid in cash or work at home, and still have the courts accept that he is an employee when he makes a personal injury claim (see *Lane* v. *Shire Roofing Co (Oxford) Ltd* [1995] IRLR 493).

In some cases the main contractor, for example on a building site, does choose to exercise control over the way in which an independent contractor does his work. It seems at least arguable that the employer may then be liable to pay damages if the contractor works in an unsafe way and is injured. Consider the criminal case of *R* v. *Associated Octel* [1996] UKHL 1, which said:

> whether an employer may leave an independent contractor to do the work as he thinks fit depends upon whether having the work done forms part of the employer's conduct of his undertaking. If it does, he owes a duty under section 3(1) to ensure that it is done without risk, subject, of course, to reasonable practicability, which may limit the extent to which the employer can supervise the activities of a specialist independent contractor.

The Health and Safety (Training for Employment) Regulations 1990 say that certain trainees are to be considered as employees for health and safety purposes.

The HASAWA definition of employee includes apprentices. It has long been accepted that a traditional fixed-term apprenticeship is a contract of service (*Dunk* v. *George Waller & Sons* [1970] 2 QB 163). A modern apprenticeship agreement or MAA is a combination of training and work experience, and will not generally in itself be a contract of employment (*Thorpe* v. *Dul* [2003] UKEAT 0630/02/0107).

6.17 AGENCY WORKERS

In a typical large company, many workers are now supplied week by week through employment agencies. Are they employees of the agency, or of the host company for which they are actually working?

In *Montgomery* v. *Johnson Underwood* [2001] EWCA Civ 318 the applicant was a telephonist-secretary supplied to a host company by the defendant agency. She worked for the host company for two and a half years, until the agency ended the assignment following a complaint from the host. The Employment Tribunal found that she was not employed by the host company. The Court of Appeal found that there was neither control by nor mutuality of obligation with the agency, so she was not employed by them either.

In *Brook Street Bureau* v. *Dacas* [2004] EWCA Civ 217 the worker was paid by the agency, which was entitled to discipline and dismiss her. She had a contract for services with the agency, which expressly stated that she was not an employee, that she was not guaranteed any work and did not have to do work she was offered. There was no mutuality of obligation so she was not employed by the agency. The host exercised day-to-day control over her, telling her where and when to work, and what safe system of work to follow. It supplied her with materials, equipment and an overall. She worked for the host continuously for four years, but her only written contract was with the agency. The contract between agency and host said that the former would provide agency staff on a week-by-week basis, and that the host could ask the agency to remove any particular worker from its service.

Mummery LJ said: 'In dealing with cases of this kind in the future Employment Tribunals should not determine the status of the applicant without also considering the possibility of an implied contact of service' with the host company.

Sedley LJ said it was 'simply not credible' that neither the agency nor the host employed her.

Munby J noted that a worker does not became an employee merely because he works for somebody for a long time under their control, and did not feel (particularly given that the host did not pay the worker) that there was enough mutuality of obligation to find that she was employed by the host.

At the time of writing, a proposed European Union Temporary Workers Directive would give agency workers the same health and safety protection as employees.

6.18 WORKERS AWAY FROM BASE

A carpet fitter or sales representative may spend more time working at the premises of customers than at his employer's own premises. An employer may be liable because something at the customer's premises, over which the employer had no control, was unsafe (*General Cleaning Contractors Ltd* v. *Christmas* [1953] AC 180 and *Andrews* v. *Initial Cleaning Services* [1999] EWCA Civ 1831). The employer has a non-delegable duty concerning the health and safety of employees.

Especially in the construction industry, an employee may be seconded to work for another contractor temporarily. If he is injured, the potential defendants are the victim's employer, the actual culprit, the occupier of the premises, and the other contractor.

In *Morris* v. *Breaveglen* [1993] ICR 766, an employee was seconded to work for S, and worked under the immediate supervision and control of S's foreman. The employee was injured by the negligence of S. As between the employee and his employer, sending him to work for S had amounted to an instruction that he obey S's foreman. There was no basis for implying that the employee had intended to release his employer from its duty to take reasonable care to see that in the operations carried out on the site he was not exposed to unnecessary risk of injury. Although the employer had no manager on site, and no right to send one, it was liable to the employee in negligence and breach of statutory duty. (The employer's claim for contribution from S failed because the contract under which the employer supplied labour to S required the employer to indemnify S if an employee were injured.)

In *Makepeace* v. *Evans Brothers (Reading)* [2000] EWCA Civ 171 the main contractor had subcontracted painting work to the claimant's employers. The main contractor lent the claimant a scaffold tower to do some exterior painting. He had used one in the past, but not for some time. He put it up or used it wrongly, and was injured when it toppled over. He sued his own employers for negligence, and the main contractor for breach of the common duty of care of an occupier of premises (see **section 5.5**). He succeeded against his employers, but the claim under the Occupiers' Liability Act 1957 failed as the common duty of care did not require the occupier, when permitting or encouraging the claimant to use everyday, albeit potentially dangerous, equipment, to check that he was competent. This was a borderline case, and on similar facts *McGarvey* v. *Eve* [2002] EWCA Civ 374 went the other way.

6.19 VULNERABLE WORKERS

The common law rules of negligence state that an employer has a duty to instruct inexperienced workers. Child workers, especially, lack both experience and common sense. An employer cannot just tell an inexperienced worker how to do the task and walk away. He must emphasise the most important points, say why the work has to be done that way, warn of any dangers, and certainly with young people he must supervise the worker for long enough to see that the instruction has sunk in. See *Kerry* v. *Carter* [1969] 3 All ER 723 and the Kurdish refugee case *Tasci* v. *Pekalp of London* [2001] ICR 633.

The working hours and safety of children are governed by the Children and Young Persons Act 1933, Health and Safety (Young Persons) Regulations 1997 and Children (Protection at Work) Regulations 1998.

The Management of Health and Safety at Work Regulations 1999 require employers to provide adequate training when employees are first taken on, and again if the nature of the work changes, and to take special care to protect pregnant women and workers under 18.

If the employer knows that a worker has a relevant health problem then he cannot treat him as if he is able bodied. He has a duty to take special care, for example, of a postman who has a history of back trouble, or a worker who has only one eye meaning an eye injury would be a catastrophe (*Paris* v. *Stepney Borough Council* [1951] AC 367).

Particularly with cases of industrial disease, it may be that only one worker in a thousand is vulnerable and the employer cannot predict who it will be. If the employer knows that the job has 'an inherent, specific and not insignificant risk of [causing] an industrial disease or condition,' he has a common law duty to tell job applicants right at the start so they can decide whether to take up the job (*Presland* v. *G W Padley Ltd* [1979] LTL 29 and *Mountenay* v. *Bernard Matthews plc* [1994] 5 Med LR 293).

Arguably, if an employer is recruiting for a job that he knows carries a risk of industrial disease, he has a duty of care at common law to ask applicants whether they have any history of such problems already. He may well have a statutory duty to do so, under regulations relating to the activity in question. Consider the requirement in the Provision and Use of Work Equipment Regulations 1998 that an employer should provide training where using equipment is likely to involve a specific risk to health.

Unless his employer has told him what to look out for, a worker may not realise that the discomfort he is experiencing is an early warning of industrial disease. Even if he does, he may be reluctant to announce that he has a health problem. If the employer waits to be told about health problems, he may be in breach of a statutory duty to carry out health monitoring. See COSHH and the Management of Health & Safety at Work Regulations 1999.

A worker may even deny that he has a health problem. This will usually prevent him claiming that the employer should have known he had one, as an employer has no real choice but to accept what a worker says. If the employer were to make enquiries with an employee's colleagues or family, or demand to see his medical records, this would conflict with the term of trust and confidence implied into the contract of employment, the Data Protection Act 1998, and an individual's right under Article 8 of the European Convention on Human Rights 1950 to respect for private and family life.

An interesting situation arises if a claimant was injured because he insisted on carrying on with a job that is dangerous for him but safe for the rest of the workforce. A nickel-plating factory's duty of care to employees does not mean it has to stop using nickel because one employee is allergic to it. There is 'no legal duty upon an employer to prevent an adult employee from doing work which he or she is willing to do'. A duty to dismiss vulnerable employees 'would be . . . a restriction on the freedom of the individual which I think is foreign to the whole spirit of the Common Law of our country . . . [and] employer and employee [are] not . . . schoolmaster and pupil' (*Withers* v. *Perry Chain* [1961] 1 WLR 1314).

However, 'cases will undoubtedly arise when, despite the employee's desire to remain at work notwithstanding his recognition of the risk he runs, the employer will nevertheless be under a duty in law to dismiss him for his own good so as to protect him against physical danger' (*Coxall v. Goodyear Great Britain* [2002] EWCA Civ 1010).

If an employer fails to find suitable alternative work for a worker who is incapable of doing his job without injury, this may amount to discrimination under the Disability Discrimination Act 1995 (see **section 6.21**).

6.20 EMPLOYMENT LAW AND THE EMPLOYMENT TRIBUNAL

If an injury occurs at work, the courts can deal with it, whether it was caused by negligence, breach of statutory duty, trespass, harassment or breach of the employment contract. However, the courts cannot deal with claims that fall under the employment legislation.

It is necessary to know when to refer a client to an employment lawyer. Failure to do so could represent negligence, even if one is in a niche personal injury practice, primarily because a claim based on employment legislation can be brought only in the Employment Tribunal and the time limit for making a claim to the Tribunal is very short.

From the employee's point of view, if he is injured at work there is a fair chance that the employer committed a fundamental or repudiatory breach of an express or implied term of the contract of employment (see **section 6.11**). If the employer then fails to give the injured employee reasonable support while he is unable to work, or dismisses him so that he loses the benefit of permanent health insurance, this may again be a fundamental breach of contract (*Aspden* v. *Webbs Poultry & Meat* [1996] IRLR 521 and *Briscoe* v. *Lubrizol Ltd* [2002] EWCA Civ 508). A fundamental breach of the employment contract would entitle the employee to leave and claim constructive dismissal. It might entitle him to compensation for unfair dismissal or wrongful dismissal.

From the employer's point of view, there are various situations in which an employee's conduct or vulnerability before, at or after an accident at work may cause the employer to dismiss him. If so, and the dismissal is not in breach of contract, it is not unfair under the employment legislation and does not breach disability legislation, it will cut back on the employee's rights to sick pay and greatly reduce his claim for future loss of earnings without any extra cost to the employer (*Hewison* v. *Meridian Shipping* [2002] EWCA Civ 1821).

The Employment Tribunal's job, under the Employment Tribunals Act 1996, is to enforce employment legislation including:

- Employment Rights Act 1996;
- Transfer of Undertakings (Protection of Employment) Regulations 1981.

It also has jurisdiction in discrimination cases under the:

- Sex Discrimination Act 1975;
- Race Relations Act 1976;
- Disability Discrimination Act 1995 (see **section 6.21**);
- Employment Equality (Sexual Orientation) Regulations 2003;
- Employment Equality (Religion & Belief) Regulations 2003.

Most employment rights are for the benefit of employees only, but anti-discrimination law also protects the self employed.

The time limit for making an originating application to the Tribunal in respect of a dismissal is currently three months from the effective date of termination of employment. For more about employment law, and to check the latest position on time limits, eligibility and compensation, go to **www.emplaw.co.uk**.

Employment Tribunal decisions are influenced by codes of practice on industrial relations, in particular those produced by the Advisory, Conciliation and Arbitration Service (ACAS). ACAS also has a statutory duty to conciliate in applications before the Tribunal, with a view to settling them without the need for a hearing.

The Tribunal provides statutory remedies for statutory claims. The Industrial Tribunal Extension of Jurisdiction (England & Wales) Order 1994 allows it to deal with certain common law claims.

Unfair dismissal

Unfair dismissal is a purely statutory concept, and only the Tribunal has jurisdiction to hear these claims. Only employees and certain apprentices are entitled to make them. Employees are not generally eligible to claim until they have been in continuous employment with the same employer for a qualifying period of one year.

'Dismissal'? Any kind of dismissal may be unfair, whether it is an ordinary dismissal, or by way of redundancy, expiry of a fixed-term contract, or constructive dismissal. The latter involves a fundamental breach of the employment contract by the employer, which caused the employee to resign fairly promptly 'in circumstances in which he is entitled to terminate [his employment contract] without notice by reason of the employer's conduct'. For example, the employer may impose a pay cut; require him to do something not envisaged by the employment contract; abuse or humiliate him in public; or treat him in an unfair manner by missing him out when giving others promotion, pay rises or training.

Frustration of the contract, for example because the employee is unable to do his duties, is not a dismissal, and so cannot be used to found a claim for unfair dismissal. However, the Employment Tribunal may find a way around this, especially if the reason the employee is off sick is that the employer was negligent or breached his statutory duties (*Hannah Blumenthal, The* [1983] 1 AC 854).

'Unfair'? There may, in common sense terms, be nothing unfair about an unfair dismissal. Certain dismissals are capable of being fair so long as the employer follows the correct procedure; others are automatically unfair.

A dismissal may be fair in all the circumstances:

- If it relates to the capability or qualifications of the employee for performing work of the kind which he was employed by the employer to do. If an employee has had a great deal of time off sick after an accident, it may demonstrate that he is incapable of doing the job, but the Tribunal will focus on whether he will attend adequately in future. Therefore the Tribunal expects the employer to follow a clear disciplinary procedure. An employee who sees he is in danger of dismissal often mends his ways. If the employer dismisses an injured employee without giving him a reasonable time to get back on his feet, or fails to offer him duties that are available and that he is medically capable of doing, the dismissal will probably be unfair in all the circumstances. If the employer caused the disability to start with, the dismissal may be unfair however much thought he puts into overcoming it (*Edwards* v. *Governors of Hanson School* [2001] UKEAT 314/99/1101). The employee may well also have a disability discrimination claim.
- If it relates to the conduct of the employee. Being off sick frequently for unconvincing reasons (flu, then back pain, then diarrhoea, then headache, then a bad cold, then a funeral, then depression) may eventually amount to misconduct. Malingering is serious misconduct (*Hutchinson* v. *Enfield Rolling Mills* [1981] IRLR 318).
- If the employee is redundant. True redundancy exists if the employer gives up the business for which the employee is employed, or gives it up in the place where he is employed; or has a reduced need for employees to do work of a particular kind, or to do work of a particular kind at the place where the redundant employee works. If an employee is dismissed wholly or mainly for reasons of redundancy, and the employer has selected him for appropriate reasons, and gone through the appropriate procedure, he has not been unfairly dismissed. When selecting employees for redundancy, an employer must be careful to follow a fair procedure, in particular selection according to fair criteria. It may be fair today if the employer chooses inefficient employees as the first to be redundant, as long as he can justify his choice objectively. He should be cautious about using redundancy to weed out those with a poor attendance record or ongoing health problems. This may be unfair, especially if it means somebody is selected for redundancy because of disability. So can failing to offer suitable alternative employment, if this could reasonably have been made available within the business or with an associated employer.

- If there is some other substantial reason. If an employee is injured partly because of his own wilful and persistent breaches of health and safety rules it may be fair for the employer to dismiss him.

Since October 2004, both employers taking disciplinary action and employees with a grievance have been required to follow a statutory procedure arising from the Employment Act 2002. The statutory procedure may well be relevant in a case of workplace injury, and can be found in the ACAS handbook on Discipline and Grievances at Work. Any dismissal is automatically unfair if made in breach of the statutory procedure. If an employee resigns without following the procedure, he will not be able to claim unfair dismissal. The procedure requires the aggrieved party to give the other party a written statement of his complaint. The parties must then meet to discuss the problem, and if the outcome of talks is unsatisfactory, there must be scope for an appeal. Where an employer is thinking of dismissing an employee for medical inability to do the job, the Tribunal may also expect him to obtain and consider a medical report. The statutory procedure applies in cases of dismissal for conduct and capability, redundancy, long-term incapacity, etc. The time limit for making an application to the Tribunal may be extended to let talks take place.

Under s.108 of the Employment Rights Act 1996, certain dismissals are automatically unfair even if the employee has not been in continuous employment for the normal qualifying period. Some of these are relevant to personal injury work, that is, those for:

- carrying out health and safety duties for the employer or as a trade union safety representative;
- bringing health and safety hazards to the employer's attention;
- walking out if they reasonably believe that there is serious and imminent danger that they cannot reasonably be expected to avert themselves;
- taking reasonable steps to avert serious and imminent danger;
- a reason connected with pregnancy, childbirth or maternity;
- whistle-blowing, in the sense of reporting the employer for illegal or dangerous practices (see the Public Interest Disclosure Act 1998).

The Tribunal can order reinstatement, re-engagement and compensation. Compensation for unfair dismissal is made up of the basic award (calculated from the employee's actual pay using a formula) and the compensatory award (a sum which is 'just and equitable in all the circumstances'). At the time of writing, the basic award is capped at a little over £7,500, and the compensatory award is capped in most cases at a little over £55,000. These figures go up at intervals, in line with inflation.

The compensatory award cannot take account of injury to feelings. See s.123 Employment Rights Act 1996 and *Dunnachie* v. *Kingston upon Hull City*

Council [2004] UKHL 36 in which the House of Lords held that 'the plain meaning of the word "loss" in s.123(1) excludes non-economic loss'.

Redundancy

Redundancy may entitle an employee to compensation even if it does not amount to unfair dismissal. An employee who is made redundant after having been in continuous employment for a qualifying period of two years is entitled to paid leave to look for work, and a redundancy payment. At the time of writing this may be as much as £7,500.

Wrongful dismissal

Wrongful dismissal is a common law concept, meaning dismissal in breach of contract. Typically, it involves dismissal without adequate notice, or constructive dismissal where the employer breaches the contract without necessarily wishing to get rid of the employee.

Wrongful dismissal does not necessarily amount to unfair dismissal. Both the courts and the Tribunal have jurisdiction to deal with wrongful dismissal.

Generally, compensation consists of the pay the employee should have got had he been dismissed according to the employment contract. The employee must take reasonable steps to mitigate his loss, and if his skills are so sought-after that he can simply walk into a new job, compensation may be very modest.

The Tribunal does not follow the common law damages regime precisely when calculating the compensation, and the amount it can award is capped.

Discrimination claims

The Tribunal can award compensation for unlawful discrimination in the course of the victim's employment. The legislation listed towards the start of this section outlaws discrimination on grounds of race, sex, disability, religion or beliefs, or sexual orientation. From 1 October 2006 there will also be a ban on discrimination on the basis of youth or age unless it can be justified objectively.

In a discrimination case the Tribunal can award compensation for loss of earnings and compensation for injury to feelings. This might amount to a recognised psychiatric injury such as clinical depression, but it could equally well be mere distress, humiliation, damage to reputation, or damage to family life. See, for example, *Sheriff* v. *Klyne Tugs (Lowestoft) Ltd* [1999] EWCA Civ 1663 and *Essa* v. *Laing Ltd* [2004] EWCA Civ 02. The courts, when assessing damages for personal injury, do not award compensation for distress falling short of a recognisable psychiatric disorder (see **section 11.11**).

In a case of unlawful discrimination that caused a recognisable psychiatric disorder, the victim has the choice of either a personal injury claim through the courts, or a Tribunal claim including an element of injury to feelings. To make the choice, he will probably need input from both personal injury and employment law specialists. Usually, the crucial factor is that in the Tribunal the loser seldom has to pay the winner's legal costs. The Tribunal does offer a quicker procedure, but in practice it is not always much cheaper than court proceedings, especially if the claim goes to appeal.

An employee who needs to rely on oral expert evidence, or on documents held by the employer, may be better off issuing court proceedings. It is uncertain at present how the Tribunal will deal with a claim for future losses, or loss of a chance of obtaining some benefit. The Tribunal will often assess the value of the claim within six months of the originating application, on the basis of medical evidence obtained less than a year after the dismissal. However, a medical expert who is asked to give a firm prognosis is virtually bound to predict a full recovery unless symptoms have resisted treatment for several years.

Something that may tip the balance in favour of a Tribunal claim is that it will award compensation for injury to feelings without requiring the applicant to show that the injury or loss was foreseeable, or was in the reasonable contemplation of the parties when the contract was made. See *Essa* v. *Laing Ltd* [2004] EWCA Civ 2, where the applicant was very severely affected by a relatively mild instance of racial abuse. The Tribunal will award £15–£25,000 for injury to feelings in the most serious sex and disability cases, or as little as £500 if there was an isolated instance of mild discrimination (*Vento* v. *Chief Constable of the West Yorkshire Police* [2002] EWCA Civ 1871). Awards for race discrimination are more generous.

Res judicata

Where the Tribunal and the courts have an overlapping jurisdiction, and the victim brings a case in the Tribunal, this usually prevents any further claim through the courts.

Under the rule in *Henderson* v. *Henderson* [1843–1860] All ER 378 a Tribunal applicant is generally barred from making any subsequent court claim for matters which were or could have been included in the Tribunal claim, whether the claim succeeded before the Tribunal or was dismissed.

In the conjoined appeals in *McCabe* v. *Cornwall County Council* and *Eastwood* v. *Magnox* [2004] UKHL 35, the House of Lords found that if an employee acquires a common law right to compensation because of the way he is treated in the course of his employment, his right to seek compensation through the courts is not barred merely because he is subsequently dismissed and claims unfair dismissal.

An agreement in full and final settlement of a Tribunal claim that purports to reserve a personal injury claim to subsequent court proceedings should be treated with caution.

In *Sheriff* v. *Klyne Tugs (Lowestoft) Ltd* [1999] EWCA Civ 1663 the claimant was a Somali engineer who suffered racial discrimination leading to a nervous breakdown. He made a discrimination claim through the Tribunal in which he could have claimed compensation for injury to feelings but did not. The claim was settled on the standard terms of the Commission for Racial Equality, which were that: 'The applicant accepts the terms of this Agreement in full and final settlement of all claims which he has or may have against the respondent arising out of his employment or the termination thereof being claims in respect of which an Industrial Tribunal has jurisdiction.' After this, he could not bring court proceedings for psychiatric injury.

Section 203 of the Employment Rights Act 1996 may make settlement of a Tribunal claim void as regards employment rights if it fails to comply with certain procedures, but will not prevent it barring a subsequent court claim for personal injury (*Sutherland* v. *Network Appliance Ltd* [2001] IRLR 12).

6.21 DISABILITY DISCRIMINATION

The Disability Discrimination Act 1995 makes it unlawful for an employer to discriminate against a disabled person. The Act is backed up by a statutory Code of Practice.

The Employment Tribunal has jurisdiction to deal with these cases. There is a short time limit for bringing a claim – at the time of writing, three months.

'Disabled person'? A 'person who has a physical or mental impairment which has a substantial and long term adverse effect on his ability to carry out normal day to day activities'.

'Person'? Employees, but also job applicants, apprentices and independent contractors.

'Mental impairment'? This must be an illness which is clinically recognised, probably something defined under ICD-10 (World Health Organisation International Classification of Mental and Behavioural Disorders) or DSM-IV (American Psychiatric Association Diagnostic and Statistical Manual).

'Long term' means at least 12 months in total.

'Normal day-to-day activities' include mobility, manual dexterity, co-ordination, lifting and carrying of everyday objects, speech, hearing, eyesight, memory and concentration. Strangely, in assessing whether somebody is disabled one must disregard any medical treatment (see Schedule 1).

Therefore a person who functions quite normally because of medication or other treatment can nonetheless be a disabled person for the purposes of the Act.

An employer discriminates against a disabled person if 'for a reason which relates to the disabled person's disability he treats him less favourably than he treats or would treat others to whom that reason does not or would not apply' and 'he cannot show that the treatment in question is justified'. This applies both to job applicants and to existing employees. The disabled are generally entitled to equal treatment in terms of job offers, pay and other terms of employment, promotion, training, and dismissal.

Under s.6 the employer has a duty to take 'such steps as are reasonable' to overcome problems where 'any arrangements made by or on behalf of an employer or any physical feature of premises occupied by the employer place the disabled person at a substantial disadvantage in comparison with persons who are not disabled'. For example, the employer may need to consider installing a disabled toilet, or reassigning a newly-disabled employee to work he can do, letting him return to work initially on light duties, or letting him work from home. The employer should not delay taking appropriate steps, as this may in itself be discrimination. For a case where an employer allowed an insulin-dependent diabetic employee to continue his driving duties, but restricted them for safety reasons and on medical evidence, see *Jones* v. *Post Office* [2001] EWCA Civ 558.

If an employer finds that disability is preventing an employee doing his job properly or at all he must, before dismissing him, consider any reasonable adjustment that would resolve the difficulty. It makes no difference whether the employer caused the injury.

An employer with fewer than 15 employees is exempt from claims relating to disability discrimination before 1 October 2004.

6.22 MANUAL HANDLING INJURIES

See also the manual handling questionnaire on the accompanying CD-ROM.

Manual handling claims are typically for soft tissue injuries of the back, and are based on parallel allegations of negligence and a breach of the Manual Handling Operations Regulations 1992. If the claimant says that his symptoms started while or very shortly after he handled a significant load, an orthopaedic surgeon is very likely to say that they were triggered by the manual handling. If the claimant can show that the injury would not have occurred but for his employer's breach of MHOR, his claim will succeed to some extent.

However, if the load that caused the injury weighed less than an everyday object such as a baby or a bag of shopping, the defendant will be reluctant to accept that his breach of duty caused all the claimant's suffering, and may be able to show that the breach merely accelerated the onset of symptoms (see **section 11.9**).

'Manual handling' under MHOR is 'any transporting or supporting of a load (including the lifting, putting down, pushing, pulling, carrying or moving thereof) by hand or by bodily force'.

'Load' includes inanimate objects and 'any person and any animal'.

MHOR require employers:

- So far as is reasonably practicable, to avoid the need for employees to undertake any manual handling operations at work that involve a risk of their being injured. One must ask whether the task needed to be done at all, and whether a machine could have done it. This risk of being injured need not be substantial, and might even be slight as long as it is 'real'. See *Koonjul*, later in this section. The risk of injury need not be from the manual handling itself, but from something the claimant encountered while manual handling, such as a slippery patch of ice as in *King* v. *RCO Support Services & Yorkshire Traction Co* [2002] EWCA Civ 314, or a circular saw as in *Sherlock* v. *Chester City Council* [2004] EWCA Civ 201.
- Where there is no reasonably practicable alternative, to carry out a suitable and sufficient risk assessment, taking into account various specified factors.
- To take appropriate steps to reduce the risk of injury to the lowest level reasonably practicable.
- To take appropriate steps to provide employees carrying out manual handling operations with a general indication, and where practicable to do so with precise information, on the weight of each load. In *Swain* v. *Denso Marston Ltd* [2000] ICR 1079 an employee thought that a roller he was unbolting was hollow. When he took off the last bolt its actual weight (20kg) took him by surprise and he was injured. The duty to give a general indication of the weight of each load is not qualified by the words 'when reasonably practicable'. Therefore the employer had a strict duty to give the employee a rough idea what it weighed. As the injury had been caused by a failure to do so, the claim succeeded.

Employers are also required to train employees in the correct postures and techniques for lifting. The common law duty to provide a safe system of work generally requires that an employer supervise employees, loads, equipment and the workplace to make sure that the safe system they have devised is being obeyed.

The Court of Appeal said in *Koonjul* v. *Thameslink Healthcare Services* [2000] PIQR P123 that an 'element of realism' must be used when dealing with these claims. The claimant's case was that she had sustained a back injury while making a child's bed. The job had to be done by hand. Did it involve a risk of injury? The Court of Appeal found that MHOR could not require a precise valuation of the risk involved in carrying out everyday activities, with precise warnings to each employee. Hale LJ said:

> . . . to bring the case within the obligations of regulation 4 . . . there must be a real risk, a foreseeable possibility of injury; certainly nothing approaching a probability . . . in making an assessment of whether there is such a risk of injury, the employer is not entitled to assume that all his employees will on all occasions behave with full and proper concern for their own safety . . . However, in making such assessments there has to be an element of realism. As the guidance on the regulations points out . . . 'full assessment of every manual handling operation could be a major undertaking and might involve wasted effort'.

See also *Alsop* v. *Sheffield City Council* [2002] EWCA Civ 429, a claim by a dustman who had slipped and fallen while pulling a wheelie bin. The claimant had chosen to pull the bin up a 30 degree ramp from the pavement to the road, rather than wheel it a short distance on the flat to where the pavement met the road. He argued that the accident was caused by a lack of training, but 'There would have been no more for the [defendant] to do than to inform their operatives to use their common sense.'

The guidance mentioned in *Koonjul* is the Health and Safety Executive publication *Guidance on Regulations – Manual Handling Operations Regulations 1992*. At the heart of this is an illustration showing maximum weights for manual handling in various postures. The weights are from 3kg (woman, stooping) to 25kg (man, standing upright). The courts generally accept that breach of the guideline weights is a breach of MHOR. The illustration must be interpreted in the light of MHOR and the guidance booklet. The illustration is readily available in free HSE leaflets and at **www.hse.gov.uk**.

An employer should allow his employees to handle heavier weights than these only if 'a more detailed assessment [of all factors including the health and fitness of the workers] shows that it is appropriate to do so'.

One cannot expect workers to cope with handling the guideline weights in all conditions. The factors to consider are the same as those the employer should examine in the risk assessment. See Schedule 1 to the 1992 Regulations. Paraphrased, and with a few additions suggested by past claims, the factors are whether:

- Work involves holding load away from the worker's trunk. If the employee is lifting items on and off a rack, he will be able to stand close to it and lift safely unless, for example, boxes or sacks have been placed on the floor in front of it and he cannot step right up to the rack.
- Work involves stooping while lifting. As can readily be seen from the HSE illustration, employees should not be expected to lift small objects weighing more than 10 kg by bending forward to pick them up off the ground. The employer should install racking or a worktop so that the objects are at a convenient height.

- Work may involve twisting while lifting. See *O'Neill* v. *DSG Retail Ltd* [2002] EWCA Civ 1139.
- Work involves lifting while seated, which particularly affects supermarket checkout operators. There is now HSE guidance on checkout design.
- Work involves reaching upwards.
- The load had to be raised or lowered through a large vertical distance. It is often possible to avoid this by installing a loading dock, or using vehicles with tail-lift hoists, or having workers fill containers at a convenient height which are then put up on shelving by a fork lift truck.
- Strenuous pushing or pulling is involved. Injuries quite often occur when otherwise acceptable loads get jammed, and the worker has to jerk them free of a conveyor or stack.
- There is a need to carry the load some distance after lifting it. This should be avoided by designing the workplace in an efficient manner, so that each stage in an assembly process is next to the following one, or so that delivery lorries do not have to park any great distance from the workplace. If a load has to be shifted some distance, it should be carried on a conveyor belt or a fork lift truck, or failing that a trolley or a sack truck moving over a smooth floor.
- The load may shift (e.g. slide inside a container) unpredictably.
- The work involves frequent or prolonged lifting and handling.
- There is insufficient time for rest and recovery.
- The work rate imposed by a process is too fast, for example, items arriving on a conveyor belt that must be cleared at speed.
- The load is bulky, unwieldy, slippery, difficult to hold.
- The load is dangerous or unpleasant (sharp, hot, toxic, smells bad, prone to slop or smear).
- Working is in a confined space or with limited headroom.
- Working is on an uneven or slippery surface, for example, a courier van with a litter of parcels sliding around on the floor. Tripping over something while laden is a major cause of back injuries.
- The working area contains ramps or steps.
- The working area is very hot, cold, humid.
- The working area is windy (particularly important if working with sheet material that can act as a sail).
- The working area is badly lit.
- The worker is small or a young person; unfit or injured; or a pregnant woman.
- The worker has not been properly trained.
- The worker has to wear personal protective equipment that makes tasks harder.

What sort of things should be covered in manual handling training? Amongst other things:

- weight limits, in particular the maximum weight that an employee should attempt to lift on his own;
- test lifting (lifting one corner of a load to assess its weight);
- using mechanical equipment to help when possible (sack trucks, trolleys, hoists, conveyors);
- breaking down overweight loads, or bulky loads, or seeking help to move them;
- lifting with both hands unless item is very light;
- lifting in a stable posture with feet apart;
- bending the knees so that the back can be kept straight;
- keeping the load close to the body;
- not rushing;
- not stretching or over-reaching;
- not twisting when lifting (but turning around by using the feet instead);
- keeping floors clear, lighting on unless there is plenty of daylight, and loads not blocking employee's vision, in order to reduce the risk of tripping;
- watching out for loads that may have an off-centre balance point (e.g. TV sets and computer monitors);
- bringing any problems (from uneven floors to pressure of work) to the attention of managers;
- telling manager at once of a health problem that affects ability to do normal lifting and handling, even if he thinks he would say 'carry on'.

In *O'Neill* v. *DSG Retail Ltd* [2002] EWCA Civ 1139 the claimant was the manager of the defendant's consumer goods warehouse. He had seen a manual handling leaflet, and four posters about manual handling were displayed at his workplace. However, unlike his subordinates, he had not received any practical training, and had not seen the company training video. He suffered a severe spinal injury while moving a number of microwave ovens that weighed about 15kg each. A workmate called out to him while he was holding one at waist height, and he instinctively twisted around without moving his feet, in order to hear better. The training video was based on a risk assessment that identified exactly this risk, and was partly designed to stop workers reacting instinctively during manual handling. The claim succeeded.

A training programme should have a good student-tutor ratio; should include practical exercises; and should have an exam at the end. All too often the training is just sitting in the canteen watching a video. For an idea of the content of a good training course, obtain a copy of the National Back Pain Association booklet *Lifting and Handling: An Ergonomic Approach* (see **Appendix 4** for contact details) (**www.backcare.org.uk**).

A manual handling claim can be based on a long period of handling loads that were always below the guideline weight. It is much more difficult to succeed with such a claim than with one that identifies a single incident involving an overweight load. Even trade union law firms shy away from them, rightly expecting difficulty with the medical evidence. The claimant's medical expert may say that the problem was caused by work, rather than sports, weekend activities or simple deterioration, but it will not be hard for the defendant to obtain medical evidence that says the opposite. It is a great deal harder for claimants to provide information about all the lifting done over the previous years than to provide detail about one incident.

A claim based on endless repetition of a task is regulated not by the Personal Injury Protocol but by the Pre-action Protocol for Disease and Illness Claims, and will have all the usual problems of an industrial disease claim.

As to manual handling claims by nurses, see *Woolger* v. *West Surrey & NE Hampshire HA* (1993) *The Times* 8 November, *Simon* v. *Royal London Hospital NHS Trust* (APIL Newsletter, February 2002), *Knott* v. *Newham Healthcare NHS Trust* [2002] EWHC 2091 (QB), *Bohitige* v. *Barnet Healthcare NHS Trust* [1997] EWCA Civ 1039, the Royal College of Nursing BackCare book *The Handling of Patients*, and the HSE's booklet *Manual Handling in the Health Services*.

Other manual handling guidance relating to specific industries such as farming and water cooler supplies is available from the HSE.

6.23 PERSONAL PROTECTIVE EQUIPMENT

The common law and the Personal Protective Equipment at Work Regulations 1998 (PPE) require employers to provide appropriate protective clothing and equipment. This may include boots, gloves, helmets, goggles, filter masks, positive-pressure respirators, lifejackets, reflective jackets or body armour.

The Regulations require an employer to provide suitable equipment, taking account of both the risk and the wearer. The PPE apply in any situation where suitable equipment would reduce the risk of a task that exposes workers to any more than life's usual level of risk. It is not a defence to say that it was not usual practice in the industry to provide a particular sort of protective equipment (*Henser-Leather* v. *Securicor Cash Services* [2002] EWCA Civ 816).

Regulation 7 requires employers to maintain protective equipment 'in an efficient state, in efficient working order and in good repair'. This imposes a strict duty, so a claim will succeed if work equipment was not efficient, even if the employer could have done no more to ensure its safety and efficiency (*Stark* v. *The Post Office* [2000] EWCA Civ 64) (see **section 6.8**).

However, that does not mean that the equipment has to protect against unforeseen risks, of a different nature to those against which the equipment was supposed to offer protection. A steel toecap boot is designed to protect against impact, not against frostbite during extreme weather conditions that the employer had, quite reasonably, not foreseen in his risk assessment (*Fytche* v. *Wincanton Logistics* [2004] UKHL 31).

Regulation 10 requires the employer to ensure that workers actually use the equipment. Merely issuing the equipment to the employee without checking that he is using it is not enough to defeat a claim if he is injured because he does not use it. For the same reason an employer cannot generally argue that there was no point providing PPE as the claimant would not have used it. See *Henser-Leather* v. *Securicor* (earlier in this section).

The PPE regulations are often displaced by specific regulations, such as those relating to asbestos, lead, radiation and aspects of the construction industry.

6.24 DEFECTIVE WORK EQUIPMENT

An employer has a common law duty of care to provide his employees with the equipment necessary for the safe performance of their work. He will be liable in negligence if injury is caused by inappropriate or defective equipment, or a lack of training in its use. In a claim based on negligence, it must have been reasonably foreseeable that inappropriate or defective equipment or training might cause some injury. Apart from his common law duty of care, an employer also has statutory duties relating to equipment.

The Employers' Liability (Defective Equipment) Act 1969 relates to injuries suffered by an employee in the course of his employment as a result of a defect in equipment provided by his employer for the purposes of the employer's business. If the defect is 'attributable wholly or partly to the fault of a third party (whether identified or not)' the Act deems the injury to be the result of the negligence of the employer. The employer will be liable to compensate the employee, even if he could not have discovered the defect. The Act applies to all equipment from aircraft to paving slabs (*Knowles* v. *Liverpool City Council* [1993] 1 WLR 1428).

There is a good chance that a guiltless employer caught by the Act can claim a full indemnity from the supplier from whom he bought the goods, relying on breach of contract or negligence and CPR Part 20. In the wake of the Provision and Use of Work Equipment Regulations 1998 the 1969 Act lost much of its importance.

The Health and Safety at Work Act 1974 as amended by the Consumer Protection Act 1987 imposes a statutory duty in respect of articles and substances used at work. The duty is imposed on designers, manufacturers, importers, suppliers and installers. The duty is to ensure that articles and substances used at work are as safe and without risk to health as it is reasonably practicable to make them. Breach of the duties contained within HASAWA itself may lead to prosecution of the employer, and perhaps a compensation order in the criminal courts, but cannot be used to found a civil claim for damages.

However, a civil claim can be based on regulations made under HASAWA. The Provision and Use of Work Equipment Regulations 1998 (PUWER) impose statutory duties in the selection and maintenance of work equipment, and training so that employees use it safely. See the text of the regulations themselves, and the HSE's Approved Code of Practice and Guidance Notes.

The main provisions of PUWER are that work equipment must be 'so constructed or adapted as to be suitable for the purpose for which it is used or provided'; and every employer must 'ensure that work equipment is maintained in an efficient state, in efficient working order and in good repair'.

'Work equipment'? In PUWER this includes everything from hammers and knives, through microphones and photocopiers, woodworking machinery and ladders, to vehicles and aircraft. The definition includes equipment provided by the employee himself. The employer has a duty to check that it is suitable, and that it works.

PUWER does not cover substances except in the sense that they may have leaked from defective equipment, and does not cover structural elements of buildings. Structures are covered by the Workplace (Health, Safety & Welfare) Regulations 1992.

'Suitable'? The court should take all the circumstances into account, then stand back and ask itself by reference to the facts existing immediately before the accident whether the equipment was suitable (*Palmer* v. *Marks & Spencer plc* [2001] EWCA Civ 1528). In *Wright* v. *Romford Blinds & Shutters* [2003] EWHC 1165 (QB) the claimant fell off the roof rack of a van while loading it. The roof rack was a suitable method of carrying loads, but was not suitable as a working platform as it had no toe board or guardrail to prevent a slip and fall. In *Yorkshire Traction* v. *Searby* [2003] EWCA Civ 1856 the claimant was a bus driver, and was punched by a passenger while at the wheel. The claim failed on the facts, but absence of a bandit screen could mean that a bus is not suitable work equipment.

'Efficient'? The duty to maintain work equipment in an efficient state is not qualified by the words reasonably practicable. If equipment causes injury because it is not efficient, the defendant cannot escape liability even if he took the greatest possible care in selection, maintenance and training (*Stark* v. *The Post Office* [2000] EWCA Civ 64).

However, in *Green* v. *Yorkshire Traction Co Ltd* [2001] EWCA Civ 1925, the Court of Appeal refused an argument based on *Stark*. The claimant was a bus driver who had slipped on a wet step while getting out of the bus on a rainy day. His case was: 'For it to be properly maintained the step would at all times have had to be in a state where no one would slip on it.' The court refused to accept that the step was not maintained in an efficient state merely because some water had got onto the step either from passengers' coats or from their feet.

If the claimant can show how he was injured by work equipment, because the work equipment was not safe and efficient, he need not prove what was wrong with it, or what could have been done to make it safe and efficient (*Nimmo* v. *Alexander Cowan & Sons Ltd* [1968] AC 107).

In any claim relating to defective work equipment, it may help to ask whether staff in the maintenance section can say anything useful. If the workplace is unionised, the trade union safety representative or shop steward should be able to help with this enquiry. In a non-unionised workplace, do not count on getting any support from the claimant's colleagues.

6.25 UNGUARDED MACHINERY

The Provision and Use of Work Equipment Regulations 1998 impose a duty on employers to take 'measures . . . which are effective' to keep any part of a person away from dangerous parts of machinery, or to stop such machinery moving before any part of a person enters a danger zone.

A strict duty to place fixed fences around all moving parts would make a drill or a grinding wheel unusable. Under PUWER the employer is required to take measures which are practicable, and which depend on various factors dealt with in the Regulations and Guidance Notes. The employer's options are fixed guards, failing which he may use other guards or protection devices, or failing that jigs, holders or push-sticks, so that whatever comes into contact with moving parts or blades it is not the operator's fingers.

For example, take a circular saw. A typical saw bench consists of a flat work surface, in which there is a slit through which projects part of a vertical circular blade with a diameter of 30cm or so. A fixed guard able to keep all fingers away from the blade would also prevent the saw cutting a plank as thick as a finger. For general use, the blade should instead have a spring-loaded guard which lifts out of the way as a plank is fed into it. The operator should be instructed to use a system of electrically-driven rollers to send the plank past the blade. If he is pushing the plank past the blade by hand, the danger arises when his hand starts to approach the blade. He should be instructed either to change his grip and start pulling from the other end, or at least use a disposable push-stick instead of his fingers.

6.26 WORKPLACE TRIPS AND SLIPS

These claims are usually based on breach of an employer's statutory health and safety duties, and negligence or breach of the duty of care of any occupier of premises under the Occupiers' Liability Acts.

The Workplace (Health, Safety and Welfare) Regulations 1992 (WorkplaceHSW) apply to nearly all workplaces and impose both strict and qualified duties on employers. If an employee was carrying out a manual handling operation when he tripped or slipped, the Manual Handling Operations Regulations 1992 will also apply. This is so even if the manual handling itself caused neither the fall nor the injury (see **section 6.22**).

The main strict duties are: Regulation 5(1): 'The workplace and the equipment, devices and systems to which this regulation applies shall be maintained (including cleaned as appropriate) in an efficient state, in efficient working order, and in good repair.' Regulation 12(1): 'Every floor in a workplace and the surface of every traffic route shall be of a construction such that [it] is suitable for the purpose for which it is used' and in particular floors shall have 'no hole or slope, or be uneven or slippery so as, in each case, to expose any person to a risk to his health and safety'.

'Efficient'? If something is not efficient, even the most careful employer will be in breach of a strict duty to keep it so (*Stark* v. *The Post Office* [2000] EWCA Civ 64) (see **section 6.8**). In *Jaguar Cars* v. *Coates* [2004] EWCA Civ 337 the claimant tripped on some sound, clean, dry, level, well-illuminated steps, which were quite ordinary except that at 19 inches deep, each step was fractionally deeper than usual. The trial judge found that the extra depth of the steps meant it was foreseeable that a careless person might trip. The Court of Appeal found that the steps were nonetheless efficient.

'Suitable'? In *McGhee* v. *Strathclyde Fire Brigade* [2002] ScotCS 16 the judge said that a floor was suitable if, immediately prior to the accident, there had been no real risk of a pedestrian slipping or tripping and thereby suffering an injury. In *Koonjul* v. *Thameslink Healthcare Services* [2000] PIQR P123 the Court of Appeal approved this approach. A floor or traffic route is suitable unless it presents a real risk of injury, although the risk may be slight.

In *Palmer* v. *Marks & Spencer plc* [2001] EWCA Civ 1528, Schiemann J said:

> I do not consider that the existence of this small rise means that it should be regarded as rendering the floor unsuitable for the purpose for which it is used, namely leaving or entering the shop. Another way of putting the point is to say that this degree of risk in this situation does not fall within the concept of constituting a risk to health and safety as used in this regulation. The court should take all the circumstances into account, then stand back and ask itself by reference to the facts existing before the accident whether the floor was suitable, or whether it was uneven to the extent of exposing persons to a risk to their health and safety.

'All the circumstances'? The nature of the alleged defect; the reason it was there; the sort of people who were exposed to it; and whether it had previously caused any problems. If it had existed for some time before the claimant's accident, in a heavily-used area, this is likely to be the most important factor.

Turning to qualified duties, the main ones under WorkplaceHSW are to ensure, so far as is reasonably practicable, that 'waste materials shall not be allowed to accumulate in a workplace except in suitable receptacles' and that 'every floor in a workplace and the surface of every traffic route in a workplace shall be kept free from obstruction and from any article or substance which may cause a person to slip, trip or fall'.

'Reasonably practicable'? An employer can satisfy a duty of care qualified by these words by taking appropriate steps to prevent accidents. He is not required to take steps that are grossly disproportionate to the risk (see **section 6.8**).

Trip claims

The claimant in *Palmer* was injured when she tripped over a weather bar that stuck up ⅓ inch at the threshold of an exterior door. There was a good reason for the existence of the bar. It was in a well-lit area. It had been there for two years before the accident. Each time the store's shift changed 20 to 25 people had walked over it, and no other accident or complaint had been reported. This kind of 'slight rise occurs almost everywhere in [our] everyday lives. The ordinary person wouldn't regard walking about every day as a risk to their health and safety and nor would the employer in constructing the floor'. The claim failed even though the hazard was next to some steps and might cause somebody to fall down them.

The claimant in *Jaguar Cars* v. *Coates* tripped while walking up a set of four steps leading from the works car park. The steps were sound, had been there for some years, and were used by about 100 employees a day without any previous accident or complaint. The claimant argued that the employer was negligent and in breach of reg.5(1) WorkplaceHSW as the steps were somewhat deeper than usual; and in breach of reg.12(5) which says 'suitable and sufficient handrails and, if appropriate, guards shall be provided on all traffic routes which are staircases except in circumstances in which a handrail can not be provided without obstructing the traffic route'. The Court of Appeal said that the foreseeability of a trip did not necessarily mean it was negligent not to fit a handrail. These steps were efficient and had posed no real risk if used with due care and attention. There was no breach of reg.12(5) as these steps were not a staircase.

Slip claims

In *Jacob* v. *Tesco Stores* [1998] EWCA Civ 1793 the claimant was employed by the defendant, and slipped on spilt liquid at an unused checkout. On scanty evidence the court concluded that the spill had probably been on the floor for some time. Under *Ward* v. *Tesco Stores* [1976] 1 WLR 801 the occupier of a supermarket has a common law duty to watch for spills and clean them up swiftly, and when the claimant proved she had slipped on a spill there was an evidential burden of proof on the defendant. The employer also had a statutory duty, as far as reasonably practicable, to ensure that all floors were 'kept free from any substance likely to cause persons to slip'. The defendant had instructed all employees that if they saw a spill during the day they should stand over it and send for a cleaner. There was at least one cleaner on duty all day, but the cleaners stayed in their room until called. The Court of Appeal found that they should have been instructed to carry out regular patrols looking for spills.

In *Furness* v. *Midland Bank plc* (CA 10 November 2000) the claimant slipped on a few 10p-sized droplets of water on the smooth tiled surface of a staircase. The staircase was in an office, and gave access to the stationery store and ladies' toilet. There was no history of spillages on the staircase, so the claimant's employer had no *Ward* v. *Tesco Stores* duty to watch for spills and clean them up swiftly. The employer did carry out inspections from time to time and the staircase was cleaned every day. The claim was brought on the basis that the employer was in breach of the qualified duty, above, as it should have instructed the staff to keep an eye out for spills and clean them up at once. The Court of Appeal felt that it was 'absurd' to suggest that such an instruction would have achieved anything at all, and said 'this really was just one of those unfortunate things that can happen without fault on anybody's part'.

The facts of *McGhee* v. *Strathclyde Fire Brigade* were that the claimant slipped at the foot of some stairs, on a floor of smooth, worn terrazzo tiles that had been polished that day and buffed 40 minutes before the slip. The court accepted on these facts that there had been a low but real risk of slipping. The claim succeeded.

In cases where somebody other than the defendant or one of its employees might have placed the slippery substance on the floor, the defendant can escape liability for breach of a qualified duty if it can prove that it operated as effective a system as was reasonably practicable for regular and thorough examination and cleaning of the floor. If the claim relates to part of the employer's premises to which the public did not have access, however, it can only be an employee who placed the slippery substance there. In that case, the employer will often be vicariously liable for making the floor slippery, however often it checked the floor.

If the floor is slippery as a necessary result of a work activity and those at risk are part of a specialist team that knows the routine, there may be a lower duty on an employer to provide warnings than if the same slippery surface were in an area to which the public have access, such as a supermarket (*Prosho* v. *Royal Devon & Exeter Healthcare Trust* [2001] 12 CL 407).

It is normal practice in any trip or slip case for a defendant to allege that the claimant contributed to the accident by his own negligence in 'failing to look where he was putting his feet'. In a workplace case, the courts are reluctant to make a heavy deduction where an employee is injured because his employer was in breach of statutory duty. If the claimant himself was guilty of no more than simple 'inadvertence of the sort that is to be expected of employees,' there may be no deduction (*White* v. *Lord Chancellor's Department* [1997] EWCA Civ 2451).

6.27 INDUSTRIAL DISEASE CLAIMS

Space precludes more than a brief comment on industrial diseases. Later, there are some specific points about work related upper limb disorders (WRULDs) and occupational stress (see **sections 6.28** and **6.29**).

Other claims for industrial diseases relate to:

- Harmful substances. These may be solid, liquid, vapour or gas. Solvents and dust are the usual culprits. They cause a range of conditions from dermatitis and asthma, through chronic bronchitis, emphysema and heart conditions, to cancer and death.
- Exposure to noise, causing deafness.
- Exposure to radiation.
- Vibration, causing Vibration White-Finger (VWF) and Hand/Arm Vibration Syndrome (HAVS).

Because these claims are expensive and uncertain, it is expensive to buy the after-the-event legal expenses insurance one would need to tackle them on the basis of a conditional fee agreement. It is difficult for a general personal injury practitioner to run occasional industrial disease claims without making a loss on them. Most are dealt with by a handful of firms that specialise in trades union and insurance work, know the right experts and barristers to use, and have a library of data collected from obscure archives and occupational medicine journals.

Stages of knowledge

An employer has no absolute duty to prevent industrial disease. When a substance or process is first used, employers go through various stages of knowledge. At first, no harm is suspected. Then the innocence of the substance/process is doubted by some. At this stage there is still no right to compensation for disease caused by exposure.

Then a very large employer with its own medical department collects enough data to recognise that there is a real risk. At this stage, the very large employer may be liable if injury results because it fails to give health warnings to workers and carry out health monitoring. From the time when the very large employer realises there is a risk that can and should be reduced, it will be liable if injury results because it failed to take reasonable steps to avoid the risk. See, for example, the VWF case *Armstrong and others* v. *British Coal* [1998] EWCA Civ 1359. Proving the date this stage was reached can involve reading literally tons of documents.

The next stage is that even small employers know or ought to know there is a risk, and are negligent if they do not take reasonable steps to avoid it. This stage generally arrives shortly after the HSE publishes guidance on the subject, and may arrive at different dates for different employers within the same industry. See the VWF case *Doherty* v. *Rugby Joinery* [2004] EWCA Civ 147.

Finally, legislation imposes a statutory duty on all employers to take steps to reduce the risk, usually giving a transitional period during which industry must find alternatives to the dangerous substance or process. Industrial disease legislation got under way over 100 years ago. The best-known example is the Control of Substances Hazardous to Health Regulations 2002 (COSHH).

Causation

An employee may be exposed to the same dangerous substance or process for many years. He cannot claim until it becomes apparent that the exposure has caused an injury (*Merlin* v. *British Nuclear Fuels plc* [1990] 2 QB 557 and *Fairchild* v. *Glenhaven Funeral Services Ltd* [2002] UKHL 22).

Many industrial diseases (WRULD, asthma, dermatitis) may be caused by things outside the workplace, making it hard to prove that the defendant employer's negligence was to blame.

Even if the claimant's disease was clearly caused by something he encountered only in the workplace, some of the exposure may have been legal. The claimant may be unable to show that his injury was caused entirely by the defendant's negligence or breach of duty. To cover this situation, the courts have devised the material contribution test (see **section 4.4**).

Vulnerable workers

Some diseases are caused by substances and processes that are harmful to only a small percentage of the workforce. WRULDs and occupational stress are good examples. An employer has a duty to take special care of employees he knows to be at risk of injury. His task is often made harder by the reluctance of workers to announce that they have work-related symptoms. An employer must avoid discriminating against a disabled worker or candidate, but may have a duty of care to dismiss a vulnerable worker. He has a duty to warn employees if the job has an inherent, specific risk of injury. On all these points, see **section 6.19**.

Procedure

Industrial disease claims are very different from general personal injury claims, a point highlighted by the existence of a separate Pre-action Protocol. Any claim, work-related or not, 'where the injury is not the result of an accident but takes the form of an illness or disease [unless it was] solely caused by an accident or other similar single event' is covered by the Pre-action Protocol for Disease and Injury Claims. For an up-to-date copy, go to the website of the Department for Constitutional Affairs at **www.dca.gov.uk**.

These claims are often dealt with as group actions. The court gives overall conduct of the generic issues, in other words those common to all the claims, to one or two law firms. It is more or less compulsory to join in (CPR Part 19 and *Taylor* v. *Nugent Care Society* [2004] EWCA Civ 51). To check whether any particular disease is being dealt with in this way, contact the Law Society's Multi Party Actions Information Service on 0870 606 2522, or search for Group Litigation Orders on the Court Service website at **www.courtservice.gov.uk**.

In some cases, national compensation schemes have been set up, for example under the Pneumoconiosis etc (Workers Compensation) Act 1979. The Department of Trade and Industry Coalhealth compensation scheme covers claims by those employed by British Coal after 1954 (1949 in Scotland) and who have developed problems with chronic bronchitis, emphysema, exacerbation of asthma, carpal tunnel syndrome or VWF. Those who missed the final application dates may be able to bring a civil claim in the usual way.

Other compensation schemes have been created on the initiative of individual insurers and employers, such as the Inland Revenue's WRULD scheme, and the industrial deafness scheme set up by Iron Trades Insurance and the shipbuilding industry.

Interesting case law

The following cases are relevant:

- *Stokes* v. *Guest Keen & Nettlefold (Bolts & Nuts) Ltd* [1968] 1 WLR 1776. Scrotal cancer from mineral oil.
- *Thompson* v. *Smiths Ship Repairers* [1984] 1 QB 405. Industrial deafness.

- *Fashade* v. *North Middlesex Hospital NHS Trust* (2000) *Solicitors Journal* 15 December. Glutaraldehyde sterilising solution.
- *Holtby* v. *Brigham & Cowan (Hull) Ltd* [2000] EWCA Civ 111. Asbestosis.
- *Allen* v. *British Rail Engineering Ltd* [2001] EWCA Civ 242. VWF.
- *Fairchild* v. *Glenhaven Funeral Services Ltd* [2002] UKHL 22. Mesothelioma from asbestos.
- *Dugmore* v. *Swansea NHS Trust* [2002] EWCA Civ 1689. Anaphylactic shock from latex dust.

6.28 WORK-RELATED UPPER LIMB DISORDERS

These are also known as repetitive strain injuries (RSI). Like all cases of industrial disease, they present the difficulties mentioned in the previous section. WRULD is caused by factors that are quite normal in the workplace but can cause injury if taken to extremes. For example, typing and word processing.

It affects only a small percentage of any workforce, and it is impossible to identify all vulnerable employees in advance. Workers with early symptoms do not necessarily realise that they have a serious problem. They may believe, quite rightly, that their job will be at risk if they mention arm and hand problems. WRULDs may cause lifetime disability if not caught and treated in time. It is therefore very important that employees recognise the significance of early symptoms such as niggling pains in their wrists and shoulders. In many of the successful claims, the key point was that the employer did not warn the employee what precautions to take or what symptoms to watch for.

WRULD claims are usually based on both negligence and breach of statutory duty. In negligence, an employer's duty is to take reasonable care to reduce the risk of injury. He has no absolute duty to prevent injury. There is a common law duty where the employer knows that the job has 'an inherent, specific and not insignificant risk of [causing] an industrial disease or condition' to tell job applicants workers right at the start so they can decide whether to take up the job (*Mountenay* v. *Bernard Matthews plc* [1994] 5 Med LR 293).

Statutory duties are more important than negligence in these claims. The Health and Safety (Display Screen) Regulations 1992 require an employer to make a suitable risk assessment of workstations, and reduce health and safety risks to the lowest extent reasonably practicable. Workstations must comply with the specific requirements in the Schedule. Every employer must provide suitable equipment, suitable training, and must 'plan the activities of users at work [so] that their daily work on their display screen equipment is periodically interrupted by . . . breaks or changes of activity'. The HSE has produced a Code of Guidance on the Display Screen Regulations.

In addition, the Manual Handling Operations Regulations 1992 apply, requiring every employer as far as reasonably practicable to avoid the need for his employees to undertake any manual handling operations at work which involve a risk of them being injured; to carry out a suitable and sufficient risk assessment; and to reduce the risk of injury in unavoidable tasks to the lowest level reasonably practicable (see **section 6.22**).

Regulation 4 of the Provision and Use of Work Equipment Regulations 1998 requires every employer to ensure that work equipment is 'so constructed or adapted as to be suitable for the purpose for which it is used or provided'. Regulation 5 of PUWER requires every employer to 'ensure that work equipment is maintained in an efficient state, in efficient working order and in good repair'. Regulation 7 requires an employer to provide training where the equipment is likely to involve a specific risk to health. Regulation 9 requires him to provide general training (see **section 6.24**).

The Management of Health and Safety at Work Regulations 1999 require employers to carry out risk assessments including assessing the risk of occupational stress; health monitoring where there is 'a reasonable likelihood that a disease or condition may occur under particular conditions of work'; and assessing the capabilities of each employee.

The Workplace (Health, Safety and Welfare) Regulations 1992 require an employer to keep the workplace in an efficient state, in efficient working order and in good repair, to make workstations suitable, and to provide suitable seating.

Classic WRULD scenarios are:

- Offices that bring in new IT systems, requiring large amounts of typing to transfer files from the old system to the new.
- Operations centres of banks, where staff have no duties other than data entry (no answering telephones, waiting by FAX machines, filing, just typing eight hours a day). These centres often produce weekly productivity figures showing the number of keystrokes made by each worker, and bonus payments or even continued employment depend on a high score.
- Poultry factories, where chickens are gutted and trussed.

The claimant must always show excessive stress on the injured limbs. Unless the defendant admits liability or has been found liable for WRULD suffered by other employees doing identical work, the claimant must prove how much he did, and how much is too much. There is now caselaw relating to WRULD in most industries, and one can extract rules of thumb such as that 10,000 keystrokes a day is too much. HSE publications can also help. See, for example, *Upper Limb Disorders in the Workplace and Work Related Upper Limb Disorders – A Guide to Prevention* (1990). Unless the claimant can negotiate a settlement by finding compelling material here, he will need an ergonomics expert to say whether the work was excessive.

Some hand surgeons are more likely than others to accept that a WRULD was caused by work activities.

A large employer may well have obtained an ergonomics report to see whether its processes create any risk of WRULD. The claimant should be able to see this unless the dominant purpose for which it was produced was the conduct of actual or anticipated litigation (see **section 20.4** and *Ball* v. *The Post Office* [1995] PIQR P5).

In *Mountenay* v. *Bernard Matthews plc* [1994] 5 Med LR 293 poultry processing workers had a range of upper limb disorders. The court accepted that before any of the claimants had started work for the company it was or should have been clear to the company that some of the work processes were capable of causing upper limb disorders in the minority of workers who were susceptible. The employer should have given very clear warnings and reminders to all workers who might be affected, telling them what symptoms to watch for, and emphasising the need to report any symptoms to the company at once. Workers should also have been rotated between risky and non-risky jobs.

Foster v. *National Power* [1997] LTL 7 May, involved two tennis elbows and one epicondylitis suffered by a clerical worker who spent four and a half hours a day for about a year moving individual pages from one stack of paper to another. The judge accepted that the injuries had been caused by repetitive work at high speed, in a bad posture, under pressure. The simultaneous occurrence of the three problems tended to confirm that the condition was the result of over use, as did the disappearance of the problems when work finished.

In *Pickford* v. *ICI* [1998] UKHL 25 the claimant was a secretary whose work included typing, but she spent less than 75 per cent of her time typing. She complained of writer's cramp, a reasonably well-recognised condition but one having no objective physical signs. The court accepted the defendant's argument that her condition was a psychiatric one that was merely associated with work, and not caused by it. In any case she had been at liberty to vary her work activities and take breaks. Her injury had not been foreseeable. The claim failed.

In *Amosu and others* v. *Financial Times Ltd* (1998) LTL 31 July the court considered that the claimant journalists had over medicalised their fears about the introduction of a new editing system. Their duties did not consist entirely of typing. As journalists they also had to use the telephone, read books and articles, etc. They failed to establish that they suffered from the physical problems they alleged.

In *Alexander* v. *Midland Bank* [1999] EWCA Civ 1918 five bank employees used a computer keypad, operated by the right hand only, to encode data. They were supposed to achieve a certain number of keystrokes per hour. Staff were urged on to achieve higher speeds by calls over a loudspeaker, a board that showed the high achievers, and redundancies. Rest breaks were 10 minutes per two hours, and there was a no talking rule. The employees complained of diffuse fibromyalgia, the symptoms of which are almost entirely subjective. This was a physical condition of some sort, not a psychosomatic condition, and had been caused by repetition, pressure and lack of breaks.

The main diseases involved are:

- Tenosynovitis. Cause uncertain, but may be effect of rapid repetitive movement, unaccustomed use. Treatment – non-steroidal anti-inflammatory painkillers (NSAIDs), ultrasound, rest.
- De Quervain's tenovaginitis (or washerwoman's thumb). Cause uncertain, but may be effect of excessive use of wrist especially in wringing motion. Treatment – steroid injection, possibly surgical release.
- Trigger finger/trigger thumb. Cause uncertain, but may be effect of rapid repetitive motion. Treatment – steroid injection, possibly surgical release.
- Tendonitis (of back/side of forearm). Cause uncertain, but may be effect of rapid repetitive movement. Treatment – rest, NSAIDs, possibly surgery.
- Carpal tunnel syndrome. Has various causes, including fluid retention as with the menopause, pregnancy, the pill, obesity or a blow causing injury to the wrist. Treatment – steroid injection, diuretics, splints worn at night, surgery (which is straightforward and may be immediately effective).
- Tennis elbow/golfer's elbow (epicondylitis). May be caused by over-use, or a single sharp blow, or problems in the cervical spine. Treatment – ultrasound, steroid injection, possibly surgery. Not generally accepted as a work-related injury.

See the British Orthopaedic Association's *Working Party Report on Occupational Causes of Upper Limb Disorders* (1990).

The above are all recognisable conditions with recognisable symptoms. Most forms of RSI produce clear clinical signs in the form of visible localised swelling, crepitus (a grating, crunching noise when the affected joint is moved), and even hard lumps.

There is a problem with diffuse RSI of the hands and forearms. Diffuse RSI may not produce any detectable symptoms apart from pain and fatigue. Many doctors believe that, if there is no localised swelling or crepitus, RSI is either all in the claimant's mind or malingering. A few hand surgeons take a particularly strong view and are much sought after by defendants in need of an expert witness. Medical science is advancing. For an interesting discussion, see *Alexander* v. *Midland Bank* [1999] EWCA Civ 1918. Claims for diffuse RSI are more likely to succeed if colleagues doing the same job have already succeeded with RSI claims based on objective, clinically detectable symptoms.

RSI can be caused by factors outside the workplace (such as knitting, canoeing or playing the saxophone). It may be possible to prove that the employer was negligent and that the claimant is suffering RSI, but not that the one caused the other. Some medical experts regularly accept that RSI can be caused by work, others do not. Where there are known to be two schools of thought, the parties should not agree to instruct a joint medical expert. If they do, the case will stand or fall depending on which expert is chosen, with no opportunity for the judge to decide which evidence he prefers. The claimant may obtain a report unilaterally, and then obtain another if the first one is not what he wants (see **section 20.10**).

The amounts awarded by the courts for RSI have not, in general, been generous. Few claims reach £20,000, and the record to date seems to be about £250,000 where there is long-term disability and a need for care and assistance.

6.29 OCCUPATIONAL STRESS

The problem with occupational stress claims is that the claimant has been made ill by conditions that merely made his colleagues miserable. They bent, he snapped. An employer is entitled to assume that his employees are coping with the ordinary pressures of work unless he is told that a particular employee is not coping.

A claim against the employer may be based on:

- Negligence.
- Breach of statutory duty.
- Breach of contract, usually breach of a term implied into the claimant's employment contract by the common law, such as the trust and confidence or reasonable support terms (see **section 6.11** and *Gogay* v. *Hertfordshire County Council* [2000] EWCA Civ 228).
- Employment and discrimination legislation. If the matters complained of amount to unlawful discrimination, it well may be that the claimant would do better to bring a discrimination claim in the Employment Tribunal. If the employer has committed a sufficiently fundamental breach of the employment contract, the employee may be able to leave and claim unfair dismissal and/or wrongful dismissal. He may be able to bring a civil claim for damages for injury sustained in the course of employment, and a Tribunal claim relating to the way in which his employment ended. Again, see **section 6.11**. If the employer's unfair treatment of the employee made him ill and thus made dismissal inevitable, he may have a cast-iron case for unfair dismissal (*Edwards* v. *Governors of Hanson School* [2001] UKEAT 314/99/1101).
- If the defendant intended to injure the claimant, trespass against the person or harassment (see **section 4.6**).

An employer has no duty to prevent stress or unhappiness. They are part of life, and certainly part of many jobs. Too much stress can cause a recognisable psychiatric disorder. This is potentially compensatable, but there is no absolute duty for an employer to prevent injury.

The Management of Health and Safety at Work Regulations 1999 require employers to carry out risk assessments including assessing the risk of occupational stress; health monitoring where there is 'a reasonable likelihood that a disease or condition may occur under particular conditions of work'; and assessing the capabilities of each employee.

Since 1995 an employer has had a common law duty to prevent mental injury to employees who are simply being ground down by work. The duty is to take reasonable steps to reduce the risk of psychiatric injury when the employer knows or ought to know that an employee is at real risk of psychiatric injury. If the employer fails in this duty, and the failure causes injury, the employee is entitled to damages for negligence (*Walker* v. *Northumberland County Council* [1995] 1 All ER 737).

This leaves the courts with a wide discretion. Should the employer have realised that the claimant was the one in a hundred who could not cope? Should he have realised that there was a real risk of injury? Were there reasonable steps that could have been taken? Would they have worked? The appeal courts have set the compensation threshold very high.

A common situation is that the claimant has been off sick after a nervous breakdown brought on by overwork, the employer fails to take reasonable steps to improve the system of work when he comes back, and he therefore suffers another breakdown. The employer probably will not be liable for the first breakdown, but may be for the second one (*Young* v. *The Post Office* [2002] IRLR 660).

There is a stigma to psychiatric problems, and people do not usually rush to say: 'I think I'm going off the rails'. In the conjoined appeals in *Hatton* v. *Sutherland* [2002] EWCA Civ 76, *Barber* v. *Somerset County Council*, *Jones* v. *Sandwell* and *Bishop* v. *Baker Refractories* the Court of Appeal said of occupational stress:

> Unless he knows of some particular problem or vulnerability, an employer is usually entitled to assume that his employee is up to the normal pressures of the job . . . Generally he is entitled to take what he is told by or on behalf of the employee at face value . . . an employee who returns to work after a period of sickness without making further disclosure or explanation to his employer is usually implying that he believes himself fit to return to the work which he was doing before.

If a stressed worker just struggles on, it is unlikely that the employer should have foreseen a breakdown. The Court of Appeal said 'in view of the many difficulties of knowing when and why a particular person will go over the edge from pressure to stress, and from stress to injury to health, the indications must be plain enough for any reasonable employer to realise that he should do something about it'.

Presumably, it will not be plain enough if the employer merely notes uncharacteristic absences from work; uncharacteristic loss of punctuality;

tension or conflict with colleagues. These do not necessarily show that the worker is suffering from occupational stress.

Barber v. *Somerset County Council* [2004] UKHL 13 is a useful case when one seeks the point at which a claim will only just succeed. The claimant was a senior teacher with a very good attendance record, who had been signed off sick for three weeks with stress and depression. The management team should have recognised this as a clear warning and 'made [sympathetic] inquiries about his problems and seen what they could do to ease them, in consultation with officials at the County Council's Education Department, instead of brushing him off unsympathetically . . . or sympathising but simply telling him to prioritise his work'.

In a badly organised workplace one may find obvious hazards that one might reasonably expect any employer to eliminate, such as exposure to a risk of injury from aggressive members of the public, faulty equipment, a poor environment (hazardous, noisy, ill-lit), or bullying. As to bullying at work, see *Barlow* v. *Borough of Broxbourne* [2003] EWHC 50 (QB), *Horkulak* v. *Cantor Fitzgerald* [2003] EWHC 1918 (QB) and *Wong* v. *Parkside Health NHS Trust* [2001] EWCA Civ 1721.

The courts do not expect work to be fun. Most workers are exposed to some degree of stress from tight deadlines, interruptions and conflicting demands; personality clashes, backbiting and undermining by colleagues; and having to do things they were not trained for. These can all be highly stressful. If a worker is vulnerable, they may cause a psychiatric disorder. However, a foreseeable risk of injury to the claimant does not necessarily mean it was reasonable for the employer to take any steps to eliminate these stressors.

The courts take the view that any employer ought to be aware of HSE publications, such as the Guidance Note Stress at Work 1995. This expressly does not relate to everyday work stresses and pressures, but to 'excessive and unreasonable pressures that pose a risk to health'. See also *Managing the Risks from Workplace-Related Stress* (pp.12–20, Health and Safety Bulletin, December 2000). If the claim is against a local authority, see the 2003 guide produced by the Employers' Organisation for Local Government, *Addressing Stress at Work*.

The Disability Discrimination Act 1995 requires employers to take such steps as are reasonable to assist an employee with a mental impairment, whether the impairment was caused by the job or not (see **section 6.21**). Subject to this, if an employee cannot cope with his job without injury, the only solution may be to dismiss him. Dismissing the troubled employee may be the employer's best defence.

In *Young* v. *The Post Office* [2002] IRLR 660 the claimant had a nervous breakdown due to stress. The employer promised to give the claimant help and supervision to help him cope when he returned from sick leave. He came back, there was a lack of support, the claimant did not tell the employer what this was doing to his stress levels, and he had another breakdown. Finding the employer liable for the second breakdown, the Court of Appeal declined to make any deduction for contributory negligence. If an employer is in breach of duty, the courts will be reluctant to blame a vulnerable worker for failing to keep his employer fully informed.

CHAPTER 7

Uninsured and untraced defendants

Most people are insured against injury claims. Owners and occupiers of buildings tend to be insured for third party risks, often including cover for causing injury while away from the property. Many people have third party cover through holiday or sports insurance, membership of organisations such as clubs, or credit card agreements.

Under the Road Traffic Act 1988 and the Employer's Liability (Compulsory Insurance) Act 1969, road users and employers are required to have insurance or to comply with self-insurance arrangements.

If the claimant was injured by an uninsured or untraced driver, he has a number of safety nets. Under s.151 of the Road Traffic Act 1988 if the driver's insurers avoid or cancel the defendant's insurance policy, they must still pay the claimant. Section 151 requires the claimant to give notice of the issue of proceedings to the relevant insurers (see **section 17.4**). This will not always help the claimant, in particular if the driver obtained his insurance by misrepresentation or non-disclosure.

The owner of a vehicle may be vicariously liable to the victim of somebody he allowed to drive it (see **section 4.8**). Finally, the Motor Insurers' Bureau will compensate victims of uninsured and untraced drivers, as described in **section 7.1**.

There are no safety nets for victims of uninsured employers. The directors themselves cannot be sued for failing to take out compulsory insurance (*Richardson* v. *Pitt-Stanley* [1995] 1 All ER 460). A claimant may need to look long and hard for the insurance company of a vanished company, starting with letters to the defendant's former directors, receiver or liquidator, and any successor company working out of the same premises. The Association of British Insurers runs a scheme under which it circulates details of claims to its members, and they check their records to see whether they are the relevant insurer. The Association of Personal Injury Lawyers prints enquiries about insurers in *PI Focus*, and keeps a database of insurers. Desperate claimants sometimes advertise with a view to tracing the insurers, or use an insurance archaeologist (see **Appendix 4**).

Road and workplace claims aside, where the culprit is uninsured, it may be that somebody else is liable for his torts or breach of contract (vicarious liability of employer, liability of credit card or HP company). Failing that, it may be possible to enforce the judgment against the culprit's property or income as a matter of debt collection.

If the culprit has neither insurance nor assets, the claimant may be entitled to obtain judgment and ask his own house contents insurers to settle it if it remains unpaid. It is certainly worth checking whether the claimant has cover for unsatisfied judgments. This is sometimes called reverse liability insurance.

7.1 MOTOR INSURERS' BUREAU

The Motor Insurers' Bureau (MIB) has several functions. Under the Motor Vehicles (Compulsory Insurance) (Information Centre & Compensation Body) Regulations 2003, it operates the Motor Insurers' Information Centre (MIIC). This provides the Motor Insurance Database, which, if given a registration number, can swiftly identify 90 per cent of vehicles; the vehicle's insurers, their address and policy number; and their UK representative. The MIIC charges £10 per search, but provides free Internet access. See **www.miic.org.uk** and **www.midis.org.uk**.

If somebody is injured in the UK by a driver from abroad, who is insured abroad, the MIB deals with the claim. As far as the claimant is concerned, the MIB acts as the foreign insurer's agent or representative under the Green Card scheme and the Financial Services and Markets Act 2000 (Fourth Motor Insurance Directive) Regulations 2002.

The MIB's most important function is the safety net it provides, under European Directives, for victims of drivers who are uninsured or cannot be traced. It does this under the two Agreements described in **sections 7.2** and **7.3**. Specialist textbooks are available.

The MIB can be expected to reject any claim for any breach of the relevant Agreement, even a trivial breach that causes it no prejudice. The Agreements are extremely demanding, and many law firms have been sued after missing one of the procedural steps. Errors are almost inevitable unless one has a specialist MIB team. Claimant lawyers who want to make a profit should set up a specialist team or turn MIB work away. A few law firms welcome referrals.

The MIB moves premises fairly often so one must check every time one starts a claim (see **Appendix 4**). It has a website with the Agreements, Notes for Guidance and application forms, at **www.mib.org.uk**.

The MIB Agreements apply where the guilty driver should have had third party insurance under Part VI of the Road Traffic Act 1988. Following the Motor Vehicles (Compulsory Insurance) Regulations 2000 such insurance is required before driving on the 'highway and any other road or other public place'. This might include a car park. In some circumstances it might include a beach.

Even if the guilty driver initially appears to be both traceable and insured, one may need to rely on one of the Agreements. Under Clause 13 of the Uninsured Drivers Agreement 1999:

> MIB shall incur no liability under MIB's obligation unless the claimant has as soon as reasonably practicable (a) demanded the information and, where appropriate, the particulars specified in section 154(1) of the 1988 Act, and (b) if the person of whom the demand is made fails to comply with the provisions of that subsection (i) made a formal complaint to a police officer in respect of such failure, and (ii) used all reasonable endeavours to obtain the name and address of the registered keeper of the vehicle or, if so required by MIB, has authorised MIB to take such steps on his behalf.

According to the *APIL Newsletter* for June 2002, the Motor Insurers' Bureau will usually interpret 'as soon as reasonably practicable' to mean that the claimant should demand the information from the defendant within a few days of the accident, and make the complaint to the police within 7–14 days, unless there is a good reason for delay such as that the claimant was heading for the airport for a holiday when the accident occurred, or was seriously injured.

Section 154 requires a driver to say whether he was insured, and give either the details in his certificate of insurance, or the registration mark of his vehicle, the policy number, the name of the insurer, and the period of cover. It is an offence not to do so, punishable by a fine of up to £2,500.

The Agreements and Notes indicate that 'all reasonable endeavours' will include:

> the exchange of names, addresses and insurance particulars between those involved either at the scene of the accident or afterwards . . . corresponding with the owner or driver of the vehicle or his representatives. He will be obliged under the terms of his motor policy to inform his insurers and a letter of claim addressed to him will commonly be passed to the insurers who may reply on his behalf . . . enquiries of the police.

Also, if one knows the vehicle's registration number, 'enquiry of the Driver and Vehicle Licensing Agency at Swansea SA99 1BP as to the registered keeper of the vehicle is desirable so that through him the identity of the owner or driver can be established or confirmed'. See **Appendix 4** for further contact details. To be on the safe side, it is worth also asking any known witnesses whether they can help, notifying one's own insurers, and searching the Motor Insurance Database.

If a driver is identified but is uninsured, the Uninsured Drivers Agreement applies. However, if the driver subsequently drops out of sight, the MIB is likely to say that he was never truly identified, and that it will deal with the claim under the less generous Untraced Drivers Agreement or not at all. The Amended Notes for Guidance to the Uninsured Drivers Agreement 1999 say that if it is 'unclear whether the owner or driver of a vehicle has been correctly identified it is sensible for the claimant to register a claim under both this Agreement and the Untraced Drivers Agreement following which MIB will advise which Agreement will . . . apply in the circumstances of the particular case'.

If the victim was a passenger in the vehicle of the negligent driver, he cannot make an MIB claim if he knew or ought to have known that the driver was uninsured. This would include a situation where the passenger was consciously colluding in the use of an uninsured vehicle but not where the passenger had simply not thought about insurance (see *White* v. *White and another* [2001] UKHL 9). Neither can he claim if he knew that the vehicle was stolen or was being used for criminal purposes or to avoid arrest; or that the driver was under age; disqualified from driving; or not the owner of the car, not the employee of the owner, and did not own a car himself.

In late 2003 the MIB introduced the MIBLES legal expenses insurance scheme. If the guilty driver had no road traffic liability insurer, this provides free legal expenses cover. One simply completes the relevant MIB application form. Where realistic legal expenses cover is already available, a claimant's lawyer cannot justify purchasing legal expenses insurance to back up a conditional fee agreement, and cannot recover the extra costs of doing so.

7.2 MIB UNTRACED DRIVERS AGREEMENT

This applies where 'it is not possible for the applicant . . . to identify the person who is, or appears to be, liable in respect of the death, injury or damage . . .'. This includes hit-and-run cases. It might also include an accident caused by skidding on engine oil or diesel spilt from an unidentified vehicle, or colliding with items shed from a vehicle's load.

If the applicant applies on the official form and otherwise follows the Agreement to the letter, the MIB will pay 'a sum equivalent to the amount which a court would have awarded to the applicant as general and special damages' plus interest and certain legal costs.

In Spring 2003 the Advocate General of the European Commission said that the United Kingdom had committed a 'serious breach of Community Law' in the way it arranged compensation for victims of untraced drivers. The Agreement gave victims no right to sue the MIB for breach of the Directive, and in reality they could not go through the UK courts to make the Department for Transport (DfT) implement the Directive. The Directive also required that compensation be paid for property damage if the vehicle that caused the injury was identified even if the driver was not (i.e. joyrider cases), and that victims should be paid interest and legal costs. The DfT responded by negotiating a new Agreement for accidents occurring after 14 February 2003. The 1996 Agreement continues to apply to accidents occurring before then. The 2003 Agreement does resolve the problems identified by the Advocate General, but includes new pitfalls.

The Agreement states that an application under the Agreement:

> . . . must have been made not later than:
>
> 1. Three years after the date of the event which is the subject of the application in the case of a claim for compensation for death or bodily injury (whether or not damage to property has also arisen from the same event) or
> 2. Nine months after the date of that event in the case of a claim for compensation for damage to property (whether or not death or bodily injury has also arisen from the same event).

The applicant will be time barred if he misses the application deadlines, even if he is a young child or a mental patient (see clauses 2 and 4(3)).

> The applicant, or a person acting on the applicant's behalf, must have reported that event to the police:
>
> 1. In the case of an event from which there has arisen a death or bodily injury alone, not later than 14 days after its occurrence, and
> 2. In the case of an event from which there has arisen property damage (whether or not a death or bodily injury has also arisen from it), not later than 5 days after its occurrence, but where that is not reasonably possible the event must have been reported as soon as reasonably possible.

The Agreement also stipulates that the applicant must produce satisfactory evidence of having made the report 'in the form of an acknowledgement from the relevant force showing the crime or incident number under which that force has recorded the matter'. The claim will fail if the officer failed to log it or the police misfiled the record, even if the complaint was made to a local officer who can clearly remember it.

Property damage is now covered as long as the vehicle is identified. There is a £300 excess.

The common law rule where a claimant receives sick pay from his employer following an accident, and is required to repay the employer out of compensation, is that he need not give the defendant credit for the sick pay. If he does, the defendant gets a windfall and the claimant ends up out of pocket. However, the 2003 Agreement says:

> MIB shall adopt the same method of calculation as the court would adopt in calculating damages but it shall be under no obligation to include in that calculation an amount in respect of loss of earnings suffered by the applicant to the extent that he has been paid wages or salary (or any sum in lieu of them) whether or not such payments were made subject to an agreement or undertaking on his part to repay the same in the event of his recovering damages for the loss of those earnings.

Legal costs payable by the MIB are calculated on a sliding scale. For claims worth up to £150,000, the MIB pays £500 to £3,000 for costs, plus VAT and reasonable disbursements. For claims worth over £150,000 the MIB pays costs amounting to 2 per cent of the compensation.

7.3 MIB UNINSURED DRIVERS AGREEMENT

This Agreement covers a claimant's injury, loss and property damage where this was caused by the driving of a known defendant who had no valid insurance for his vehicle. There is a £300 excess for property damage.

One must apply to the MIB using the official application form. Generally, the claimant must also issue proceedings and obtain judgment against the defendant. When issuing proceedings one should join the MIB as a defendant unless there is good reason not to do so. The Notes for Guidance set out the paragraphs to use in the particulars of claim. Joining the MIB relieves the claimant of some of the burden of keeping the MIB informed as set out below.

Once the claimant has judgment against the guilty driver, and has assigned the benefit of it to the MIB, the MIB will pay it if the driver does not pay it himself within seven days. The judgment may include compensation, interest and legal costs on the usual basis. If the MIB thinks it is worthwhile, it can then try to get its outlay back from the driver.

It is entitled to offset any insurance payments received by the claimant. In a reversal of the usual common law rule, it seems this would include payments from income protection insurance and medical expenses insurance that the claimant took out at his own expense. If one asks the claimant whether he has lost income or incurred any medical expenses, and he says 'no', this may be shorthand for 'yes, but it was covered by insurance'. These losses and expenses should be included in the special damages claim.

Claims under the Uninsured Drivers Agreement 1999 can be a nightmare for the busy personal injury lawyer. Clause 10, for example, says 'MIB shall incur no liability unless the claimant has . . . given notice in writing . . . seven days after . . . the date when the claimant receives notification from the Court that service of the Claim Form or other originating process has occurred'. It is all too easy, especially if engrossed in a trial or away on holiday, for a lawyer to miss that deadline, and have to compensate the claimant himself.

There are half a dozen similar conditions. Clause 11.1 requires the claimant to give prompt notice of 'any amendment to the Particulars of Claim or any amendment of or addition to any schedule or other document required to be served therewith'. Clearly this includes amendments to the schedule of loss. Less obviously, as CPR PD 16.4.3 says: 'Where the claimant is relying on the evidence of a medical practitioner the claimant must attach to or serve with his particulars of claim a report from a medical practitioner about the personal injuries which he alleges in his claim' the claim will fail if the claimant hears from the medical expert with even a trivial amendment to the medical report and does not promptly notify the MIB.

The Motor Accident Solicitors Society (MASS) took judicial review proceedings over the terms of the Agreement, and the MIB settled these by making some concessions. The Agreement itself has not been amended, but the Notes for Guidance now say:

> At the request of the Secretary of State, these notes have been revised with effect from 15th April 2002 and in their revised form have been agreed and approved by MIB, the Law Society of England & Wales, the Law Society of Scotland, the Motor Accident Solicitors Society and the Association of Personal Injury Lawyers. Any application made under the Agreement after this date (unless proceedings have already been issued) will be handled by MIB in accordance with these notes.

The main concessions are:

- Despite Clause 3 of the Agreement, time will not run against a person under a disability.
- Despite Clause 6, it is possible for the claimant to obtain compensation for unpaid care and assistance from relatives, and travel by relatives.
- Despite Clause 8, which requires that service be made by registered or recorded post or by FAX, one can serve documents on the MIB in any of the ways normally acceptable under the CPR.
- The Agreement requires the claimant to notify the MIB of various events within seven days. Where proceedings are issued and the MIB is not joined as a party, the seven-day notice periods are extended to 14 days.

The claimant has a problem if he cannot trace the driver in order to serve proceedings on him. This very seldom happens in general personal injury work, but is common in MIB matters. Uninsured drivers are often feckless and nomadic, and if the claimant loses touch with the defendant, the MIB will seek to deal with the claim under the less generous Uninsured Drivers Agreement instead. Right at the outset, the claimant should ask the MIB to confirm that they will either accept service on behalf of the defendant, or deal with the claim under the Uninsured Drivers Agreement without any need for proceedings to be issued. If they do not give the required confirmation within a month and the claimant does know the defendant's current whereabouts, he should consider issuing and serving proceedings straight away.

If the claimant misses one of the many deadlines but is still within the limitation period, he can probably just reissue the proceedings (see **section 18.1**). A claimant can bring only one action at a time in respect of one accident. Bringing two is an abuse of the process of the court, and so the first set may need to be discontinued before reissuing. Consider *Cachia* v. *Faluyi* [2001] EWCA Civ 998.

7.4 INSOLVENT INSURERS

If the defendant's insurance company is insolvent or has ceased trading, and if the defendant does not seem to have enough assets to pay damages, the claimant may benefit under the Financial Services Compensation Scheme (FSCS) (see **Appendix 4**). See ss. 212–224 Financial Services and Markets Act 2000.

The FSCS is the successor to the Policyholders Protection Board set up under the Policyholders Protection Act 1975. It intervenes when an insurance company becomes insolvent, and either arranges for other insurers to deal with claims, or pays compensation from government funds.

The FSCS pays the first £2,000 of a claim, and then 90 per cent of the balance. In the case of compulsory insurance (road traffic, employer's liability) it pays 100 per cent of the claim. It also takes care of the defendant's liability to pay the claimant's legal costs (*Geologistics* v. *FSCS* [2003] EWCA Civ 1877).

7.5 TRACING AND SERVING DEFENDANTS

Although this is not a procedural textbook, it may help to mention some common problems, and solutions.

Road traffic cases

The general rule is that the claimant must issue and serve proceedings on the defendant, and cannot serve them on his insurers. However, the European Communities (Rights against Insurers) Regulations 2002 say 'without prejudice to his right to issue proceedings against the insured person [the claimant may] issue proceedings against the insurer [of the vehicle and the] Insurer shall be directly liable to the [claimant] to the extent that he is liable to the insured person'. Claimants intending to rely on the 2002 Regulations should note that if the insured caused injury deliberately, or if the insured had induced the insurer to provide cover by making a material non-disclosure, the insurers are not liable to the insured person.

Defendant under disability

If the defendant is under 18 or a mental patient, he cannot be a party to court proceedings. A litigation friend should be appointed before proceedings are issued. A mental patient under the Mental Health Act 1983 is simply a person who is 'incapable, by reason of mental disorder, of managing and administering his property and affairs' (CPR Parts 6 and 21 and the corresponding Practice Directions).

Dead defendant

Section 1 of the Law Reform (Miscellaneous Provisions) Act 1934 says 'on the death of any person . . . all causes of action subsisting against . . . him shall survive against . . . his estate'. The claim is brought against 'The Personal Representatives of the estate of [the deceased defendant].' If nobody has yet been appointed as the deceased's personal representative, the claimant must apply to the court to have this done (CPR Part 19).

Corporate defendant

A cheap and simple internet search of the Companies Register will reveal whether a company of that name exists, its registered office address, whether there has been a change of name, the status of the company (e.g. active), names of directors, and whether the company is solvent, the last accounts filed, etc. **www.companieshouse.gov.uk**.

Bankrupt or insolvent sefendant

In a road traffic case, the defendant's insurers must still pay the claimant (s.153 Road Traffic Act 1988). The Third Parties (Rights against Insurers) Act 1930 allows most claimants to recover compensation from a bankrupt defendant's insurance company directly, rather than by standing in line with the other creditors.

Defendant employer

If the defendant company was the claimant's employer and subsequently sold the business, the correct defendant is usually the purchaser (Transfer of Undertakings (Protection of Employment) Regulations 1981 (TUPE), *Martin* v. *Lancashire County Council* [2000] EWCA Civ 155 and *Bernadone* v. *Pall Mall Services* [2000] EWCA Civ 155).

CHAPTER 8

Criminal injuries

In theory, the victim of a mugging or rape could make a civil claim for damages from the attacker, basing it on trespass against the person. However, the victim may not be able to identify the assailant. If he needs to serve proceedings, he may be unable to locate him. Even if the assailant has insurance for causing injury, it would be contrary to public policy for insurance to indemnify him for the effects of his own wilful acts (*Gray* v. *Barr* [1971] 2 QB 554 and *Churchill Insurance* v. *Charlton* [2001] EWCA Civ 112). The assailant may not have enough income or assets to make him worth suing.

To overcome these problems, there is a compensation scheme under the Criminal Injuries Compensation Act 1995.

The Scheme generally pays less than a civil claim, but is cheap and can be swift. It can be used to prepare and even to fund a subsequent civil claim against the assailant. In the civil claim, the claimant need not give credit for the criminal injuries award. If the civil claim is successful, the claimant will have to repay the criminal injuries award out of his compensation. The assailant will not be ordered to pay the costs of the criminal injuries application. Prior to the CPR he would have been ordered to pay the costs of the civil claim even if the claimant recovered less than he did through the criminal injuries award. (*Oldham* v. *Sharples* [1997] EWCA Civ 960).

8.1 CRIMINAL INJURIES COMPENSATION SCHEME

The 2001 Scheme described in this chapter receives about 75,000 applications a year, about half of which are successful. It is run by the Criminal Injuries Compensation Authority (CICA).

The Scheme provides for an award for pain and suffering according to a tariff, and an additional amount for financial losses if the effects of the injury last longer than 28 weeks.

Case law provides important footnotes to the Scheme. Specialist textbooks are available. For a copy of the Scheme itself, the application form and the essential Guide to the Criminal Injuries Compensation Scheme contact CICA (see **Appendix 4**).

The application:

> should be made as soon as possible after the incident giving rise to the injury and must be received by the Authority within two years of the date of the incident. A claims officer may waive this time limit where he considers that, by reason of the particular circumstances of the case, it is reasonable and in the interests of justice to do so.

The Scheme covers injuries and death caused by:

- A crime of violence (including assaults, arson, poisoning, deliberate running down in a car, encouraging a dog to attack, some sexual offences).
- Trespass on a railway, basically where a railway worker witnesses a suicide.
- Making, helping with or attempting the arrest of a suspected criminal.
- Preventing or attempting to prevent a crime.

A crime of violence under the 2001 Scheme does not necessarily involve deliberate injury. The culprit may have been reckless as to whether he injured the victim. Some crimes of violence require only that the guilty person foresaw that the victim might suffer some injury, however slight (Offences Against the Person Act 1861 and Sexual Offences Act 2003).

If the injury was caused by domestic violence, it is generally a precondition that the assailant be prosecuted; and (if the assailant and victim are both adults) that they stopped living together in the same household before the application was brought and are unlikely to live together again. The CICA will not pay compensation where there is any likelihood that the assailant will benefit from it. For the claimant lawyer, it is worth remembering that a conviction is obtained in only 3 per cent of domestic violence incidents reported to the police. Very often, the complaint is dropped, the couple are reconciled, and a criminal injuries application would fail.

Victims of child abuse and neglect may be entitled to an award, but only for those things that amount to a crime of violence. 'Reasonable chastisement' of a child by its parent or guardian is not a crime of violence. Consider *R* v. *H (reasonable chastisement)* [2001] EWCA Crim 1024. Neither is physical force that a teacher may be entitled to apply to a child under ss.549 and 550 of the Education Act 1996. Child neglect may in some circumstances amount to a crime of violence (*X (Minors)* v. *Bedfordshire County Council* [1995] 2 AC 633).

Sexual offences are not covered if the victim consented to the act that caused the injury, even if aged 12 and very drunk at the time (*R (CD)* v. *Criminal Injuries Compensation Appeals Panel* [2004] EWHC 1674 (Admin)). If the victim did not truly consent, for example if he had a very low IQ and submitted to the advances of a sex offender with whom he was locked in a prison cell, an award may be made. (*EJ* v. *Criminal Injuries Compensation Appeals Panel* [2003] EWCA Civ 234).

There is no need for the assailant to have been convicted. In fact, the assailant is convicted in only about 15 per cent of applications. The assailant may have been too young for prosecution, mentally unfit for trial, or untraceable. It may not even be a problem if the defendant was prosecuted but acquitted. The standard of proof under the Scheme is the civil standard. The applicant need only show on the balance of probabilities that the injury was the result of an offence.

8.2 THE PAIN AND SUFFERING TARIFF

Under the 2001 Scheme, every injury falls into one of about 400 categories, from a sprained wrist to paraplegia. When assessing the value of pain and suffering, each category of injury falls into one of 25 levels of compensation, from Level 1 (£1,000) to Level 25 (£250,000).

The rape victim who is permanently disabled by mental illness gets £27,000. If she were able to make a civil claim for compensation, a court might award her up to twice as much as the tariff allows.

Where the applicant's physical injuries fall into several categories, for example, a broken leg and a broken arm, he gets the full tariff payment for the most serious injury and then a percentage of the tariff figure for the others. This does not apply to awards for minor multiple injuries as described in **section 8.4**.

As with civil claims for compensation, there are restrictions on the extent to which an applicant can claim compensation if he suffers psychiatric injury without physical injury. The restrictions under the Scheme are slightly different to those in civil claims. An award is available for psychiatric injury where the applicant was put in reasonable fear of immediate physical harm to his own person; or where he witnessed an act of violence or its immediate aftermath and he had close ties of love and affection with the victim.

The CICA does consider evidence when assessing the amount of its awards to victims of crime, but it is not the CICA's job to maximise the applicant's compensation by obtaining an exhaustive range of medical reports (*R (Milton)* v. *CICB* [1997] PIQR P74). The CICA is obliged to do only what the Scheme says, but a claims officer 'cannot lawfully elect not to arrange a medical examination if, objectively, the decision he has to make requires one'. If the applicant supplies a medical report, he can expect the CICA to consider it, but not pay for it unless objectively it is a report that the CICA should itself have obtained (*C* v. *Criminal Injuries Compensation Authority* [2004] EWCA Civ 234). In a case of minor injury, the CICA may reasonably decide to value the claim without seeing any medical reports at all.

In *R (Embling)* v. *CICAP* (2000) The Times 15 August the CICA and then the Criminal Injuries Compensation Appeal Panel (CICAP) assessed the applicant's damages on the basis that she had fully recovered from her injuries, when plainly she had not. The High Court said: 'It is, putting it at its lowest, very difficult to see how the Panel, if it had properly directed itself in law, could have come to any view other than that the case was one of "continuing disability".'

In *C* v. *Criminal Injuries Compensation Authority* [2004] EWCA Civ 234 the CICA picked what was plainly the wrong tariff category and awarded £82,000. CICAP increased this to £250,000. The Court of Appeal said 'the review decision was plainly right. It is incomprehensible that it should have taken the CICA over six years to reach this obvious conclusion and make a full award ... the suggestion of maladministration cannot be lightly dismissed'.

8.3 FINANCIAL LOSSES

In addition to the amount payable for pain and suffering under the tariff, the Scheme pays something for lost earnings, or lost earning capacity, but pays nothing for the first 28 weeks of the loss. The maximum rate of loss of earnings is 1.5 times the gross average industrial earnings as calculated by the Department for Education and Employment.

Future loss of earnings is calculated in broadly the same way as in civil claims.

If the applicant has been incapacitated for longer than 28 weeks, the Scheme may pay for medical treatment, nursing care, disability equipment, and special accommodation. The CICA can award compensation for unpaid care provided by relatives, but is unlikely to do so except after very serious injury.

If, as a result of his injury, the applicant receives state benefits, a pension, or insurance payments, the CICA will offset these against his claim. Basically, it deducts benefits from the loss of earnings and care compensation. It takes all benefits into account, including the injury pension of a police officer or fireman.

The CICA is alert to find out what free or subsidised assistance the applicant can get from the National Health Service, social services or charities. It will deduct this from any claim for future care, accommodation, etc.

8.4 ELIGIBILITY

An applicant's injuries must justify at least a Level 1 payment under the tariff. Typical Level 1 injuries are a broken nose; chipped tooth requiring dental treatment; a sprained wrist, ankle or back causing at least six weeks' disability; a broken rib; or an assault beyond ordinary chastisement resulting in bruising, weals, hair pulled from scalp, etc.

Minor multiple physical injuries also attract a Level 1 award, if:

> the applicant has sustained at least 3 separate physical injuries of the type illustrated below, at least one of which must still have had significant residual effects 6 weeks after the incident. The injuries must also have necessitated at least 2 visits to or by a medical practitioner within that 6-week period. Examples of qualifying injuries are grazing, cuts, lacerations (no permanent scarring); severe and widespread bruising; severe soft tissue injury (no permanent disability); black eye(s); bloody nose; hair pulled from scalp; loss of fingernail.

The CICA may withhold or reduce compensation in various situations, for example where:

- The applicant failed to take, without delay, all reasonable steps to report the incident to the police. The CICA says it 'attaches great importance to the duty of every victim of crime to inform the police of all the circumstances without delay . . . if you have not reported the circumstances of the injury to the police and can offer no reasonable explanation for not doing so, you should assume that any application for compensation will be rejected', as in *R (Thompson)* v. *Criminal Injuries Compensation Authority* [1999] EWHC 178 (Admin). Delay in reporting the incident is likely to result, at least, in reduction of the award.
- The applicant failed to co-operate with the police or other authority in attempting to bring the assailant to justice. The applicant will be in trouble if he withheld relevant information for any reason, including fear of vengeance or to protect a friend who was present but whom he considered to be innocent.
- The applicant failed to give all reasonable assistance to the CICA. For example, attending for medical examination, and giving a forwarding address if moving house.
- The conduct of the applicant before, during or after the incident means that it is appropriate to withhold or reduce the award. One might think this means conduct that triggered the assault, or a revenge attack afterwards, but the CICA gives it a very wide interpretation.
- The applicant's character as shown by his criminal convictions (excluding convictions which are spent under the Rehabilitation of Offenders Act 1974) or by evidence available to the claims officer makes it inappropriate that a full award or any award at all should be made. The CICA calculates the reduction for convictions according to a tariff, under which a fine or a community service order for previous offences may not result in any deduction from his compensation, but if he has been imprisoned for more than 30 months for any offence in the recent past, no award will be made, however innocent a victim he was of the crime of violence. In *R (Pearson)* v. *Criminal Injuries Compensation Board* [1999] EWHC 420 (Admin) the award was reduced by two-thirds because of some road traffic offences committed by the applicant three

years before the assault. In *R (Adair)* v. *Criminal Injuries Compensation Authority* (QBD 20 March 2003) the High Court expressed surprise that the CICA deducted 75 per cent from the compensation of a man who had been very seriously injured in an assault and subsequently committed road traffic offences, but refused to intervene.

Until 2000, the CICA rejected claims with no more explanation than that the applicant's own conduct caused or contributed to the incident. This made it very difficult for the applicant to find a law firm willing to challenge the rejection, as they could have little idea what they were trying to prove on the applicant's behalf. In *R (Leatherland)* v. *CICA* [1998] EWHC 406 (Admin) the court said that the CICA had to give 'proper, sufficient and intelligible reasons' for its decisions, and disclose 'at least the gist of the evidence' it intended to rely on, which enables the applicant to decide whether to appeal. The court said that the CICA's practice of disclosing its witness statements only on the day before the appeal hearing was calculated to cause significant procedural unfairness, but this practice continues.

8.5 COSTS AND FUNDING IN CRIMINAL INJURIES

The Scheme says: 'Where an applicant is represented, the costs of representation will not be met by the Authority.' The same applies to appeals to CICAP.

If the applicant cannot afford to pay legal fees, this may be incompatible with his right to a fair trial under Article 6 of the European Convention on Human Rights 1950. However, if it is clear from an early stage that the applicant will receive a substantial award, the courts will expect the applicant to put together a legal and medical team by relying on this as a means of paying them in future (*C* v. *Criminal Injuries Compensation Authority* [2004] EWCA Civ 234).

The CICA does have power to pay travelling expenses, and to pay for medical records or medical reports obtained by the applicant. It may be necessary to apply pressure, by judicial review, if it refuses to pay for reports that are objectively necessary. In a case of catastrophic injury, this may include a report valuing care, equipment and accommodation (see **section 14.16** and *C* v. *Criminal Injuries Compensation Authority*).

The applicant may be able to fund the claim through legal expenses insurance, or trades union help. If not, note that Legal Help (a limited version of legal aid) is available. It will generally provide enough funding to complete the application form. The reader is advised to check the latest position with the Legal Services Commission (LSC), but subject to that the LSC does not recoup its outlays from the CICA award. This makes Legal Help the best method of funding the claim, and eligible applicants should generally be advised to go to a law firm able to offer it.

If the applicant is not eligible for free assistance, one can offer him a conditional fee agreement. A criminal injuries application is not litigation, there is no risk of a hostile costs order, and therefore no need for after-the-event legal expenses insurance.

8.6 APPEALS AND REVIEWS

The Scheme permits the applicant to ask for a review by a more senior CICA claims officer; and the review itself can be appealed to the Criminal Injuries Compensation Appeal Panel, which is independent (see **Appendix 4**).

The time limit for making an appeal is short.

The CICAP chairman was reported as saying in 2002 that CICAP would deny compensation to the applicant if it felt that his representative did not give 'reasonable assistance' before and at the hearing; and in 2003 that all submissions made for the applicant must be 'realistic and capable of being accepted' because if the CICAP suspects any 'try on' it may reject all the submissions.

So a law firm acting for an applicant must deal with an appeal hearing in the same way as a trial, even though there is a fair chance it will not be paid for its work. It may be unwise to send an inexperienced advocate. Have regard to the relevant Scheme and Notes for Guidance, and all the papers provided by the CICAP.

The CICAP Standard Directions require one to supply an up-to-date schedule of loss and full evidence of financial losses; and to prepare and submit a statement of arithmetical agreement and disagreement, based on the Schedule and the CICAP's Counter-Schedule. Consider also sending the CICAP a skeleton argument before the hearing. As when preparing for trial, ensure the CICAP receives a paginated bundle of all relevant papers. This should include an up-to-date statement of state benefits received by the applicant.

It is unlikely that the CICAP will hear oral evidence from an expert witness. If there is a conflict of expert evidence, one should try to resolve it before the hearing, or get the experts to agree a statement setting out exactly what is in issue.

One needs to tell the applicant where and when to go for the hearing, and what to expect. If he does not turn up, his evidence will carry very little weight.

Under some circumstances a CICA or CICAP decision can be examined by the courts through the judicial review procedure under Part 54 of the CPR. If bringing such proceedings, note that there is a Pre-action Protocol for judicial review. For the latest version of the Protocol, go to the website of the Department for Constitutional Affairs at **www.dca.gov.uk**.

8.7 COMPENSATION ORDERS IN THE CRIMINAL COURTS

These are not part of the Criminal Injuries Compensation Scheme but one of the criminal courts' sentencing options under the Powers of Criminal Courts (Sentencing) Act 2000.

Both the magistrates' court and the Crown Court may, when sentencing an offender, order him to pay compensation to the victim of various matters including:

- Assault occasioning actual bodily harm or grievous bodily harm (s.18, s.20 and s.47 Offences Against the Person Act 1861).
- Indecent assault (ss.14 and 15 Sexual Offences Act 1956 and see the Sexual Offences Act 2003).
- Providing rented housing which is a statutory nuisance by reason of damp, etc.

Injuries from road accidents are not covered.

Compensation can be awarded under the 2000 Act for any personal injury, loss or damage. The criminal courts have no power to award compensation to dependants of the victim of a fatal incident, other than bereavement and funeral expenses.

When assessing the value of pain and suffering, the court will use the CICA tariff. However, if the injury is below the CICA's minor injuries level, so no compensation would be payable by the CICA, the court can still award compensation based on Home Department guideline figures.

Magistrates' courts cannot sentence the defendant to pay more than £5,000 compensation for each offence. The defendant must have the money to pay the compensation or the order cannot be made. If he has income but no savings he may be ordered to pay by instalments over a period of years. If he does have the means to pay a compensation order and fails to do so, he may be imprisoned for non-payment.

To obtain a compensation order, ask the prosecutor to request one. Give the prosecutor a medical report and a statement about pain, suffering, loss and expense. The prosecutor has a duty to calculate the extent of the loss, and to present evidence of it to the court (*R (Richards)* v. *Horsham Justices* [1985] 1 WLR 986).

Whenever the court has power to make a compensation order it must consider doing so, and must give reasons if it does not. If the defendant cannot afford to pay both a fine and compensation, the court must lean towards compensation.

These payments are not subject to deduction of state benefits the applicant may have received as a result of his injuries. However they are deducted from any criminal injuries compensation he may receive.

If an assailant is prosecuted for causing actual bodily harm or grievous bodily harm it may not be possible to bring a civil claim against him later (ss.42–45 Offences Against the Person Act 1861).

8.8 CRIMINAL INJURIES COMPENSATION (OVERSEAS) SCHEME

The Ministry of Defence runs the Criminal Injuries Compensation (Overseas) Scheme (CICOS) for the benefit of members of the armed forces and their dependents who are the victims of crimes of violence while serving overseas. Details can be obtained from the Ministry of Defence, Service Personnel Policy (Pensions) (see **Appendix 4**).

CICOS excludes injuries 'as a result of war operation or military activity by warring factions,' for example injury caused by a Serbian tank shell fired into a UN compound in Bosnia. 'It is not for the courts to consider whether the Scheme with its exclusion is a good scheme or a bad scheme' (*R (Walker)* v. *Ministry of Defence* [2000] UKHL 22).

CHAPTER 9

Compensation – the background

The personal injury lawyer's 'bible' is Kemp & Kemp, *The Quantum of Damages*. Published by Sweet & Maxwell, it is available as a heavyweight looseleaf or a CD-ROM. It is updated every few months, and is indispensable.

9.1 GENERAL DAMAGES, SPECIAL DAMAGES

Compensation is divided into general and special damages. The distinction is important because they attract interest at different rates, and because settlement offers are often expressed in terms of general damages or special damages. This is risky, because the distinction between them is blurred.

In casual discussions, most use special damages to mean all financial losses, and general damages to mean everything else. Strictly speaking, general damages include pain and suffering; loss of amenity; risk on the labour market; loss of job satisfaction; loss of congenial employment; loss of marriage prospects; loss of use of vehicle; loss of enjoyment of holiday or club subscription; and any future financial losses (*British Transport Commission* v. *Gourley* [1956] AC 185).

Strictly speaking, special damages are past losses that can be calculated arithmetically. They include damage to property, past loss of earnings, and past expenses such as the cost of medication. They also include the value of past unpaid care and assistance (*Roberts* v. *Johnstone* [1989] QB 878).

If the claimant accepts an offer of £Y,000 for general damages, special damages to be dealt with later, the defendant may take the view that this bars any claim for future financial losses. Rather than frame or accept an offer in these terms, it is better to ensure it is clear which heads of loss the offer is intended to cover.

The claimant is required, when proceedings are served, to include a schedule of loss. Although this is often called a schedule of special damages, it should in fact include 'details of any past and future expenses and losses' (CPR PD 16.4.2).

9.2 PROVISIONAL DAMAGES

The usual rule is that when a claim is settled, it is settled once and for all. A provisional damages order allows the claimant to go back for more compensation if a predicted problem develops within a specified time after settlement.

Section 32A Supreme Court Act 1981 and s.51 County Courts Act 1984 allow the court to make a provisional damages order where it is proved or admitted that as a result of the matters complained of in the action there is a chance that at some definite or indefinite time in the future the injured person will develop some serious disease or suffer some serious deterioration in his physical or mental condition. The order will specify when and in what circumstances the claimant will be entitled to re-open the claim.

'Chance'? The chance must at least be real or substantial. It must be more than merely fanciful, negligible or trivial (*Curi* v. *Colina* [1998] EWCA Civ 1326). Some judges may be satisfied by a 0.5 per cent risk if the feared deterioration would be very serious. It is most unlikely that the court will make a provisional damages order if the risk is near or more than 50 per cent, because it will prefer to make a final compensation order, adjusted upwards to reflect that risk.

'Time'? The court will not leave the defendant exposed to a provisional damages order indefinitely, so the medical evidence must indicate the time within which the deterioration might occur. The order will state how long the claimant has to come back to court.

'Serious'? It is very common after an orthopaedic injury for there to be a risk of osteoarthritis. This is seldom serious enough, as it will seldom cause a clear and separate deterioration going beyond ordinary or continuing deterioration (*Willson* v. *Ministry of Defence* [1991] 1 All ER 638). Osteoarthritis might be sufficiently serious if it would make the difference between the claimant being able to walk and having to get around in a wheelchair; or between being able to work and being dependent on state benefits.

Risks serious enough to justify an award include those of developing epilepsy, blindness, paralysis, or a fatal condition such as mesothelioma. Provisional damages are particularly appropriate where the deterioration would be fatal, because unlike a final settlement, it does not bar a claim by the claimant's dependants. (s.3 Damages Act 1996).

If the claimant is eligible for provisional damages but prefers to have the claim settled once and for all, the court will add a little to his basic damages to take account of the risk. For examples, see the asbestos section in Kemp & Kemp *The Quantum of Damages*. If the deterioration does not take place, he is slightly over compensated. If it does, he is severely under compensated.

The procedure is set out in CPR Part 41 and the corresponding Practice Direction. A claim for provisional damages must be stated in the particulars of claim (CPR PD 16.4.4). After issuing proceedings, the claimant asks the court to make the appropriate order, probably after obtaining the defendant's consent. If proceedings have not yet been issued, and the only reason for issuing them is to obtain a provisional damages order by consent, one can use the CPR Part 8 procedure.

The great majority of claimants, and all defendants, prefer a once and for all settlement.

9.3 INTERIM PAYMENTS

From the claimant's point of view, an interim payment can enable him to survive, emotionally and financially, for long enough to settle the claim for its real value.

The first step is to ask the defendant to make one voluntarily. The defendant may do so out of goodwill. He is more likely to make one if it will reduce the overall cost of the claim. This is particularly likely if it takes the amount in dispute below the Small Claims limit, so that the court allocates the claim to the Small Claims track when proceedings are issued. If a claim is initially allocated to the fast track, an interim payment could result in reallocation to the Small Claims track by reducing the amount in dispute.

Interim payments to enable the claimant to repair or replace his damaged vehicle can minimise a claim for car hire and loss of use.

Interim payments for physiotherapy, private surgery and other treatment can minimise the claim for loss of earnings, pain and suffering, and care.

Payments to make up lost earnings can minimise claims for the cost of borrowing, and in an extreme case the costs of a mortgage repossession action by the claimant's mortgagee.

Any interim payment can minimise the claimant's entitlement to interest. A defendant making an interim payment should state that it is to be offset first against special damages, as a much higher rate of interest is paid on special damages than on general damages (see **sections 10.1** and **10.2**).

However, it may not be to the defendant's advantage to make an interim payment which will enable the claimant to buy care, equipment or accommodation that he is not already getting. If the claimant does without these things pending trial, the court may well conclude that they are not necessary (*Havenhand* v. *Jeffrey* [1997] EWCA Civ 1076). In this situation, clearly the claimant should seek an order for a compulsory interim payment to fund a care regime or buy equipment.

If the claimant is under 18 or incapable by reason of mental disorder of managing and administering [his] property and affairs, interim payments must be dealt with in accordance with directions given by the court and not otherwise; and one needs the permission of the court before a voluntary payment is made (CPR Part 21.11 and CPR PD 25B.1). This applies whether or not proceedings have been issued.

If the claimant's legal costs are being funded by the Community Legal Service (CLS), his solicitor needs the permission of the CLS before he can send on an interim payment.

If the claimant is still receiving state benefits, he will not want an interim payment large enough to take him over the capital limit for the means test unless his lawyer has set up a personal injury trust (see **section 9.16**).

When asking for a voluntary payment, the claimant should give all the information he would be required to provide on applying to the court for a compulsory one (see CPR Part 25.6 and its Practice Direction). In particular, the claimant should:

- Specify the amount he wants, and whether this is before or after deduction of state benefits.
- Disclose enough evidence to give the defendant a clear idea of the value of both pain and suffering and financial losses. The defendant wants to know that if he makes the voluntary payment, he will not be paying more than the claim is worth. More subtly, he will not want to pay so much that the claimant loses interest in achieving a prompt final settlement.
- Indicate why the claim cannot yet be settled finally, and when he expects it can be.
- Say whether he proposes to apply for a compulsory interim payment if the defendant will not co-operate. He should give the defendant a reasonable deadline, say 28 or 42 days. Note that the court will not make an order for interim payment in a Small Claim (CPR Part 27.2).
- Say how making the payment may benefit the defendant.
- Indicate whether he will suffer hardship unless the payment is made. Strictly speaking he does not need to give this information, or tell the defendant what the payment is for, but if he does it may encourage the defendant or, failing that, the court.

If the claimant has received state benefits in respect of the accident, the defendant will deduct an equivalent sum from the interim payment (see **section 9.7**). The defendant must obtain a CRU certificate showing the relevant state benefits.

It is prudent for the defendant to specify that any voluntary payment made to the claimant is an interim payment on account of damages. However, if this is forgotten, the courts will generally treat any extra-contractual payment after an accident as an interim payment rather than a gift (*Williams* v. *BOC Gases Ltd* [2000] EWCA Civ 95 and *Gaca* v. *Pirelli General plc* [2004] EWCA Civ 373).

Many insurance company accounts departments seem to attach a note to all cheques saying that they are in full and final settlement. Before cashing such a cheque for an interim payment, the claimant should ensure he has ample evidence on his file that the defendant knows and accepts that the rest of the claim is continuing.

Compulsory payment

If the defendant does not make a voluntary interim payment, the claimant can issue proceedings and apply to court for a compulsory one, typically of 30–40 per cent of the full value of the claim. Except in the Small Claims track or when trial is imminent, the court will readily grant an interim payment as long as the criteria are met. Note that:

- the claimant must have obtained judgment against the defendant, or the defendant must have admitted liability to pay him damages;
- the court must be satisfied that the claimant is going to obtain judgment against the defendant for a substantial amount of money;
- the claim must be one that will be paid by an insurer, or the Motor Insurers' Bureau, or a public body.

The claimant must follow the procedure in CPR Part 25.6 and its Practice Direction, adducing evidence to show that he will recover damages from the defendant and that the claim is worth substantially more than the proposed interim payment.

Whether an interim payment has been made voluntarily or under a court order, it should not affect the trial. Under CPR Part 25.9, the fact that an interim payment has been made shall not be communicated to the trial judge until all questions of liability and quantum have been decided.

9.4 MULTIPLIERS AND MULTIPLICANDS

To calculate future losses and expenses, assess how much will be lost per year (the multiplicand) and multiply this by a figure based on the number of years the loss will last (the multiplier).

The Court of Appeal in *Cornell* v. *Green* [1998] EWCA Civ 510 described it as 'absolutely essential' that the multiplier/multiplicand method be adopted if at all possible. If the evidence is too sparse for this, the court can value the loss only by plucking a figure out of the air. Such a figure may be described as future loss of earnings, but also as damages for loss of earning capacity (*Smith* v. *Manchesters;* damages for risk on the labour market; or *Blamire* damages after *Blamire* v. *South Cumbria Health Authority* [1993] PIQR Q1). It will be less than the claimant would have obtained on a multiplier/multiplicand basis (see **section 12.1**).

At what point does the evidence become too scanty? In the context of future loss of earnings, see *Cornell* (above), where there was enough evidence, and *McCrae* v. *Chase International* [2003] EWCA Civ 505 and *Willemse* v. *Hesp* [2003] EWCA Civ 994, where there was not.

If the claimant's case is that the accident deprived him of a chance, for example of being promoted, special rules apply (see **section 9.5**).

'Multiplicand'? A future loss or expense may be a loss of earnings or benefits, or a need for care, equipment or accommodation. For example, see **section 13.6** about future loss of earnings.

Any multiplicand must be worked out at current rates. Future inflation can be dealt with only by using the appropriate discount rate when calculating the multiplier. It is not for the claimant to guess how much a nurse will charge in 10 years, or how much a wheelchair will cost in 20 years (*Auty* v. *National Coal Board* [1985] 1 All ER 930).

'Multiplier'? If the claimant is 40 and would have retired at 65, the court is not going to allow him to use a multiplier of 25. The figure must be reduced because of accelerated receipt, that is, the claimant getting the money now and having the opportunity to invest it, buy property with it, etc.

The reduction must be carried out according to the Ogden Tables (*Wells* v. *Wells* [1998] UKHL 27). The Tables are prepared by the Government Actuary. They take account of accelerated receipt and normal mortality rates. The official title is Actuarial Tables with Explanatory Notes for use in Personal Injury and Fatal Accident cases. The Notes discuss when the basic multiplier should be adjusted to take account of other contingencies. The Ogden Tables are available from HMSO for about £12.50; they are printed in several personal injury textbooks, including Kemp & Kemp; and they are available free on the internet at **www.gad.gov.uk**, but perhaps more conveniently at **www.lawinclear.co.uk**.

For most calculations using the Ogden Tables, one simply needs to know the claimant's age and what discount rate to apply. There will very seldom be any need to obtain expert evidence from an actuary. The Notes discuss when actuarial evidence might be necessary, and one should be guided by this (*Prigmore* v. *Welbourne* [2003] EWCA Civ 1687).

Except in fatal cases, one assess the multiplier at the date of settlement or trial. In the 4th Edition of the Ogden Tables, one used Tables 19 to 38 (which relied on population projections using data from mid-1998 and assumed that people would live longer) rather than Tables 1 to 18 (which were based on historical mortality rates) (*Worrall* v. *Powergen* [1999] PIQR Q103). In November 2004, the 5th Edition of the Ogden Tables was released. The 5th Edition is based on mortality rates in 2003, and omits the old Tables 1 to 18.

One of the most frequently used pages of the Ogden Tables is 'Multipliers for Loss of Earnings to Pension Age 65'. Choose the appropriate table for male or female, find the row that corresponds to the claimant's age at settlement or trial, and look along that to the column with the appropriate discount rate. Say the claimant would have retired at 65 but is disabled at 25. The claim is to be settled straight away. The claimant was earning £17,000 a year net. He would have had 40 years of working life ahead of him and expected no promotion. Without discounting, his loss would be 40 × £17,000 = £680,000. From the Ogden Tables, with a 2.5 per cent discount rate, the basic multiplier is 24.79 years, so the claimant's loss is in fact 24.79 × £17,000 = £421,430.

The basic Ogden multipliers take account of inflation and average mortality. Say that because of the defendant's negligence, the claimant will have a lifelong need for £5,000 per annum of home help. The appropriate Table is Multipliers for Pecuniary Loss for Life. Find the basic Ogden multiplier using the claimant's age at settlement or trial and the discount rate. This is the correct multiplier to use unless there is positive evidence that a contingency applies. For example, if there is medical evidence indicating a particular risk that this claimant will die prematurely, a further discount should be made. The court should not follow the old practice of making a further discount for no apparent reason (*Wells* v. *Wells* [1998] UKHL 27).

In a claim for future loss of earnings where the claimant was in robust health at the time of the accident and well established in a stable job, little or nothing should be deducted from the basic Ogden multiplier.

However, if there is evidence that the claimant would have been ill or unemployed even if the accident had not occurred, the Ogden multiplier should be discounted. For a typical example, see *Herring* v. *Ministry of Defence* [2003] EWCA Civ 528. The trial judge found that the claimant's career could be predicted with great confidence, but in calculating the future loss of earnings, the judge took 25 per cent off the basic Ogden multiplier. Effectively, the judge treated it as a loss of a chance case. The Explanatory Notes did suggest a contingency discount of 3 per cent from the basic multiplier because the claimant's intended occupation came in to the *more risky* category. There was no evidence of any other contingency, and the Court of Appeal said that no more than 10 per cent should have been deducted from the basic Ogden multiplier. In fact the Court of Appeal considered the right figure in this case to be 8.5 per cent. The Ogden Tables working party is, at the time of writing, re-examining the discount to be made for contingencies. Even for a *more risky* occupation like mining or police work, 8.5 per cent may prove to be too high.

Other contingencies that would justify a deduction from the basic Ogden multiplier for loss of earnings are that the claimant would have had a career break even if the accident had not occurred, or that he lives in an area of high unemployment and might well have found himself out of work even if the accident had not occurred (*Evans* v. *Pontypridd Roofing Ltd* [2001] EWCA Civ 1657).

It will seldom be appropriate to adjust the Ogden figure upwards. In *Biesheuvel* v. *Birrell* [1999] PIQR Q40 the court increased the multiplier as the claimant would be subject to tax in Holland, and Dutch tax rates are higher than in the UK. In future, a foreign claimant wanting such an increase will need to produce compelling evidence not just of income tax rates, but of the other elements of the cost of living equation, such as the effect of VAT and purchase tax, cost of food and clothing, cost of housing, and the cost of borrowing (*Van Oudenhoven* v. *Griffin Inns* [2000] EWCA Civ 102).

Apart from losses to retirement age and losses for life, the Ogden Tables can be used to calculate a loss that will not start until some years in the future. For example, the amount needed to pay for surgery that will not be needed for another 20 years (see Ogden Table 27).

'Discount rate'? This is set by the Lord Chancellor pursuant to s.1 of the Damages Act 1996. The Damages (Personal Injury) Order 2001 made it 2.5 per cent. See *Setting The Discount Rate – The Lord Chancellor's Reasons* at **www.dca.gov.uk/civil/discount.htm**.

Trial judges must apply the rate that has been set, unless they are satisfied that the case falls outside the range considered by the Lord Chancellor (*Warren* v. *Northern General Hospitals Trust* [2000] EWCA Civ 100 and *Warriner* v. *Warriner* [2002] 1 WLR 1703).

Although the Lord Chancellor's figure was rather more generous than the 3 per cent rate set by the court in *Wells*, it has proved controversial. Being set by reference to the rate for Index Linked Government Securities (ILGS), it is effectively based on the retail cost of a basket of shopping. Critics point out that claims for future loss are mainly for future loss of earnings and the future cost of care, both of which have been rising, for many years, at more than the Retail Prices Index. In the conjoined appeals in *Cooke* v. *United Bristol Healthcare* [2003] EWCA Civ 1370, *Sheppard* v. *Stibbe* and *Page* v. *Lee*, the Court of Appeal very firmly refused to apply a different discount rate. This judgment is criticised by the Ogden Tables working party in the 5th Edition. See paragraphs 15 to 16 of the Introduction, and for a detailed discussion see Appendix A, and a defendants' riposte in Appendix B.

To check for any recent changes to the discount rate, go to the Department for Constitutional Affairs website at **www.dca.gov.uk**.

The court awards damages in full for past losses, and calculates future losses as above. A claimant with a large multiplicand for future losses will often benefit greatly by delaying as long as possible before trial or settlement. Even where there has been inexcusable delay by the claimant in bringing the claim to trial, the court will probably use the multiplier appropriate to the claimant at the date of trial (*Pritchard* v. *J H Cobden Ltd* [1988] Fam 22). The court may impose a penalty for delay, by allowing the claimant less for interest or legal costs.

9.5 LOSS OF A CHANCE

When assessing compensation, the court should value a chance that the claimant has lost because of the defendant's negligence.

When determining liability and causation, the court decides whether the defendant's negligence probably did or did not cause the claimant's injury. If it probably did, he is entitled to full compensation. If it probably did not, he is not entitled to any (see **section 4.4**). However:

> in assessing damages which depend on its view as to what will happen in the future (or would have happened in the future if something had not happened in the past) the court must make an estimate as to what the chances are that a particular thing will or would have happened and reflect those chances, whether they are more or less than even, in the amount of damages which it awards
>
> (*Mallet* v. *McGonagle* [1970] AC 166)

A medical expert should therefore include in his report a 30 per cent chance that a whiplash victim will not make a full recovery, or a 10 per cent risk that a fracture patient will develop osteoarthritis. If the claimant had a 40 per cent chance of being promoted to higher earnings, he should adduce evidence of it.

Loss of a chance calculations may be expressed in terms of the baseline (the claimant's earnings if, as is most likely, he had not been promoted) and the chance itself. In *Doyle* v. *Wallace* [1998] EWCA Civ 1030 there was a 50 per cent chance that, if the accident had not occurred, the claimant would have done a clerical or administrative job. This provided the baseline earnings. But for the accident, the claimant would have had a 50 per cent chance of becoming a drama teacher and earning significantly more. She recovered her baseline loss of earnings, plus 50 per cent of the extra earnings she would have received if she had succeeded in her ambition.

In *Langford* v. *Hebran* [2001] EWCA Civ 361 the court showed itself willing to give some weight to even quite a small chance, as long as it considers it to be real or substantial. If the chance could better be described as fanciful, negligible, trivial or speculative it will be given no weight at all. It is not possible to say from the case law that a 15 per cent chance is real and a 2 per cent chance is never more than fanciful.

Loss of a chance may work to the defendant's advantage. In *Williams* v. *Green* [2001] EWCA Civ 1888 the claimant teacher had been a very strong candidate for promotion, would probably have become a head teacher by 2003 and would have worked until retirement in 2014. The Court of Appeal reduced the award for future loss of earnings by 40 per cent because she had degenerative change in her spine that might have led to early retirement.

If the medical expert says that the claimant will never return to work, the defendant should ask whether he is certain. If he concedes that there is a 10 per cent chance the claimant will return to work, the defendant can seek a discount from the claim for future loss of earnings. Judges do tend to be reluctant to discount damages for this reason, and one should look upon it as a bargaining point, not a certainty.

9.6 MITIGATION OF LOSSES

A claimant has what is often described as a duty to keep the losses caused by the defendant's tort or breach of contract as small as reasonably possible. When acting for a claimant, one must tell him this from the outset. The courts allow a good deal of leeway for delays resulting from pain, depression and lack of knowledge, but if the claimant should have kept his losses smaller, the defendant is entitled to deal with his claim as if he actually did.

The rule in *Liesbosch Dredger* v. *SS Edison* [1933] AC 449 was that the court would disregard a claimant's means when assessing his loss and damage. The defendant was not responsible for any extra loss arising because the claimant could not afford the most cost-effective solution, or could not afford to prevent the damage getting worse. However, see *Lagden* v. *O'Connor* [2003] UKHL 64.

In practice, the claimant's duty to mitigate his losses relates to medical treatment, loss of earnings, and vehicle hire. As to the latter, see **section 14.6**.

As to medical treatment, the claimant should seek medical advice and follow it. If his doctor recommends physiotherapy, he should undergo it even though it is painful, tiring and inconvenient. If he fails to attend without a good reason such as being too busy at work, the medical evidence may possibly say this hampered his recovery. Even if not, the claimant may forfeit the court's sympathy, upon which the outcome of a claim so much depends.

If a medical expert recommends surgery and the claimant does not undergo it, the questions are whether this was unreasonable, and if so what the surgery would have achieved. To establish whether a refusal is reasonable, balance the prospects of successful surgery against the risks. Tactically, the claimant's lawyer should ask the treating surgeon to list all the risks for this purpose, as he will seldom do so when advising a patient. Any surgery involves a small risk of serious infection. Spinal surgery often involves some small risk of paralysis. If the claimant is offered surgery that might go seriously wrong, the court will treat a refusal with sympathy (*Lansiquot* v. *Geest plc* [2002] UKPC 48).

Where the claimant is off work because of an accident, he should go back to work as soon as he is fit enough. If he is offered an opportunity to go back part time or on light duties, he should accept if possible. If he stays off work unnecessarily, the defendant cannot be expected to pay the extra loss of earnings.

If the claimant does a demanding job that he will not be able to cope with for a long time or at all, he must look for some other sort of work, and look into retraining if appropriate.

If the defendant is able to allege, plausibly, that the claimant did not do enough to get back to work, the dispute will turn on two things. The first is the sympathy of the individual judge, which is highly variable although most are prepared to make allowances for claimants who are thrown into an unfamiliar situation and who may be depressed and lacking in confidence. The second is the claimant's folder of mitigation evidence. A fat folder of evidence will be a knockout blow to the defendant's allegation, and can avoid the expense and uncertainty of instructing an employment consultant to give expert evidence. The contents should be collected over a number of years, and consist of:

- job advertisements about which he enquired;
- notes of telephone conversations with employers and the Job Centre;
- unsuccessful applications (the application form, the date of any interview);
- rejection letters;
- correspondence with retraining advisers.

Very few claimants will put together a satisfactory folder without repeated urging and chivvying from their lawyers.

The extent to which the claimant is expected to mitigate depends on social conditions. If he was a senior teacher before his accident and cannot go back to his old work, the judge will probably not expect him to take a job as a lavatory attendant or nightwatchman. He might expect a young ex-teacher to accept work as a shop assistant while finding something better.

If the claimant tries to mitigate his losses by setting up his own business, he should not expect the defendant to pay for losses caused by the failure of the business. Unless the claimant was already self employed at the time of the accident, the court will probably take the start of a new business, or the time when it becomes more than a hobby, to be the end of the period of loss of earnings. Any losses after that date are unlikely, in law, to have been caused by the defendant. One might say that they are too remote from the injury to be attributed to the defendant's negligence.

9.7 STATE BENEFITS AND THE COMPENSATION RECOVERY UNIT (CRU)

The Compensation Recovery Unit (CRU) exists to recoup from the defendant, as compensator, an amount equal to the state benefits that the claimant received because of his injury.

The defendant is usually entitled to deduct the entire sum from the claimant's damages. There can never be any deduction from damages for pain, suffering and loss of amenity. This is sometimes referred to as ring fencing of general damages.

The legislation is brief but complex. See the Social Security (Recovery of Benefits) Act 1997 and Social Security (Recovery of Benefits) Regulations 1997. The CRU's 44-page booklet *Recovery of Benefits & NHS Charges: A Guide for Companies & Solicitors* (Form ZI) can be downloaded from **www.dwp.gov.uk/publications/dwp/2004/z1_apr.pdf**.

A compensator who 'is alleged to be liable to any extent in respect of an accident, injury or disease . . . is liable to pay to the Secretary of State an amount equal to the total amount of the recoverable benefits'. This liability arises when the compensator 'makes a payment . . . to or in respect of any other person in consequence of any accident, injury or disease suffered by the other, and (b) any listed benefits have been, or are likely to be, paid to or for the other during the relevant period in respect of the accident, injury or disease'.

'Alleged to be liable'? The scheme requires the compensator to repay state benefits even if making a nuisance value payment with a denial of liability.

'Total amount'? There is nothing in the Act to permit the compensator to reduce the amount of benefits where he is reducing the damages because of contributory negligence by the claimant.

'Payment'? This includes voluntary or compulsory compensation payments, and both interim and final payments.

'Relevant period'? In a case of accident or injury, this is at most the period of five years immediately following the day on which the accident or injury in question occurred. In a case of disease, it is the period of five years beginning with the date on which the claimant first claims a listed benefit in consequence of the disease.

The relevant period ends when 'a person makes a compensation payment in final discharge of any claim made by or in respect of the claimant and arising out of the accident, injury or disease, . . . or an agreement is made under which an earlier compensation payment is treated as having been made in final discharge of any such claim'.

It follows that only benefits that have already been paid at the time of settlement can be recouped, even where the damages include losses which will be sustained after that. If the claimant is still receiving state benefits as a result of his injuries, it will motivate him to settle swiftly. Likewise, if the claimant is still receiving benefits and the defendant will not be able to deduct from the compensation all that he has to pay to the CRU (usually because he alleges contributory negligence) the defendant may be motivated to settle as fast as possible.

'In respect of the accident?' The injury sustained in the accident must be a contributory cause of the payment of the state benefits, but need not be the sole cause.

'Listed benefits'? The benefits that are covered are listed in the Schedule to the Act. Not all state benefits are recouped by the CRU. However, the defendant may offset the others against compensation anyway (see **section 9.10**).

Benefits come and go. One can check the deductibility of unfamiliar benefits with the CRU (see **Appendix 4** for contact details).

'Certificate of recoverable benefits'? The defendant, or more often his insurer, registers each new claim after receiving the letter of claim, using

Form CRU1. If the claimant's date of birth, National Insurance number, address and employment details were not in the letter of claim, the compensator asks the claimant to provide them.

Section 4(1) of the Act says: 'Before . . . the compensator . . . makes a compensation payment he must apply to the Secretary of State for a certificate of recoverable benefits.' The CRU sends a copy of the certificate to both defendant and claimant. It lists the relevant benefits that the claimant has received.

Under s.5(1), the certificate must specify the amount of each recoverable benefit that the claimant has received (or is likely to receive before the certificate expires), and s.6(1) says: 'A person who makes a compensation payment in any case is liable to pay to the Secretary of State an amount equal to the total amount of the recoverable benefits.'

Most certificates are valid for four weeks and must then be renewed. If the claim is settled within the life of a CRU certificate, the parties are entitled to rely on it. The CRU often wrongly issues a Nil certificate and then corrects the error in the next certificate. If the claim is settled without a valid certificate and the CRU demands payment of more than the parties expect, the compensator will have to bear any loss unless the settlement says otherwise.

'Deduction'? The compensator is entitled to deduct its CRU liability from the claimant's compensation on a like for like basis. See ss.8 and 9 of the Act. To use the language of the Act, where a listed benefit has been paid, and any of the damages can be attributed to that type of benefit, the defendant's liability to the claimant will be discharged if he pays compensation calculated in accordance with s.8, that is, 'The gross amount of the compensation payment, less the sum of the reductions made under subsection 3.'

Under s.8, state benefits relating to income are deducted by the defendant from damages for loss of earnings. They can also be deducted from interest on such compensation (*Griffiths* v. *British Coal* [2001] EWCA Civ 336). The income-type benefits are Disability Working Allowance; Incapacity Benefit; Income Support; Industrial Injuries Disablement Benefit; Invalidity Pension; Invalidity Allowance; Jobseeker's Allowance; Reduced Earnings Allowance; Severe Disablement Allowance; Sickness Benefit; Statutory Sick Pay paid before 6 April 2004; Unemployability Supplement; and Unemployment Benefit.

State benefits relating to care are deducted by the defendant from damages for the costs of care, including damages for the value of gratuitous assistance provided by friends and relatives. Again, see *Griffiths* (above). The care-type benefits are Attendance Allowance; the care component of Disability Living Allowance; and the Constant Attendance Allowance or Exceptionally Severe Disablement Allowance supplement to Industrial Injuries Disablement Benefit.

State benefits relating to mobility (the mobility component of Disability Living Allowance, and Mobility Allowance) are deducted from damages for loss of mobility.

If the claimant was on low earnings, it may not be worth his making a claim for loss of earnings. It follows from *Khiaban* v. *Beard* [2003] EWCA Civ 358 that the claimant is free to decide what losses to claim. The less work done by the claimant's lawyer, the less risk that he will run up legal costs that the defendant is not ordered to pay.

Usually, the compensator can offset all the recoverable benefits from the damages. However, he may have to pay more to the CRU than he can offset. This can arise in two situations. First, where there was contributory negligence by the claimant. Second, where the claimant received benefits after the accident that were not in fact paid in respect of the accident, injury or disease. In other words, the Certificate of Recoverable Benefits assumes that all the post-accident benefits were paid because of the accident, but the medical evidence in the civil claim refutes this.

Reviews and appeals

If the certificate includes benefits that were not paid 'in respect of the accident, injury or disease,' the aggrieved party will want it altered. Depending on whether the compensator was able to deduct all the benefits from damages, this may be the compensator or the claimant. If the compensator is entitled to deduct all his liability from the claimant's compensation, he will not bother to challenge the certificate.

A review or appeal may be needed if the CRU made a mathematical error and demanded too much; or the defendant says that the claimant's injuries were never such as to justify his claiming benefits; or either party says that the claimant's need for benefits was caused by something other than the accident. Typically, the medical experts say that the accident merely accelerated the onset of a condition that would have disabled the claimant anyway after a few years, and the parties want benefits paid after that time to be removed from the certificate.

The CRU may be willing to review the certificate informally. Once the claim has been settled and the sum on the CRU certificate paid off, the aggrieved party can appeal the certificate in hope of a refund. Any refund may go to the compensator or the claimant, or be split between them depending what benefits the compensator offset against damages, and whether the claim was settled as a result of an offer (see **section 16.6**).

Section 11 of the Act says:

> No appeal may be made under this section until . . . the claim giving rise to the compensation payment has been finally disposed of and . . . the liability under s.6 has been discharged . . . regulations may make provision . . . as to the manner in which, and the time within which, appeals under this section may be made . . . as to the procedure to be followed where such an appeal is made. . .

An appeal complying with the regulations must be lodged within one month of the date when the certificate is confirmed or revised, or within one month of settling the claim. One needs to check the regulations with the CRU in advance of any appeal, in case the time limit has altered in the meantime.

If the CRU wants to recoup benefits that one doubts were paid as a result of the accident, and if a successful appeal will get one's client a refund, note that there is nothing to require the Medical Appeal Tribunal to give any special weight to medical reports obtained by the parties but s.12(3) of the Act says: 'In determining any appeal . . . [the Medical Appeal Tribunal] must take into account any decision of a court relating to the same, or any similar, issue arising in connection with the accident, injury or disease in question.' If the amount involved is large enough, it could make it worth going to trial.

Despite arguments to the contrary by the Secretary of State, the tribunal should, when deciding an appeal, consider whether the benefits should have been paid. If they should not have been paid or were not paid as a result of the accident, the appeal will succeed. For this apparently self evident proposition, see the joint decision in *Secretary of State for Social Security* v. *Oldham MBC, Tarmac Roadstone NW, Trefoil Steel Co* and *Yorkshire Repetition Castings (*Social Security Commissioners 15 May 2001).

Section 17 of the 1997 Act says: 'In assessing damages in respect of any accident, injury or disease, the amount of any listed benefits paid or likely to be paid is to be disregarded.' A defendant cannot get around that by saying that the claimant's duty to mitigate his losses means he must pay the mobility element of his state benefits into the Motability scheme (*Eagle* v. *Chambers (No2)* [2004] EWCA Civ 1033).

The claimant may be entitled to claim state benefits after receiving his compensation, and his lawyer must ensure that he does not lose that right unnecessarily (see **section 9.16**).

9.8 DEDUCTION OF INSURANCE BENEFITS

In *Hodgson* v. *Trapp* [1989] AC 807 the House of Lords said: 'If, in consequence of the injuries sustained, the [claimant] has enjoyed receipts to which he would not otherwise have been entitled, prima facie those receipts are to be set against the aggregate of the [claimant's] losses and expenses in arriving at the measure of his damages.' The House of Lords mentioned two exceptions. These were payments received through insurance, and gifts. As to the benevolence exception see **section 9.13**.

If the claimant had the foresight to take out an insurance policy before the accident and as a result of the accident the policy gives him help with his mortgage, or a lump sum for his injury, he gets a windfall. The defendant cannot claim a right to pay less compensation because the claimant's own insurers have already paid up. The claimant paid the premiums, and is entitled to the benefit (see *Bradburn* v. *Great Western Railway* (1874) LR Ex 1 and *Parry* v. *Cleaver* [1970] AC 1).

The insurance exception does not apply to payments from an accident insurance policy taken out and paid for by the claimant's employer for his benefit. *McCamley* v. *Cammell Laird Shipbuilders* [1990] 1 WLR 963 was wrongly decided in this respect. In *Page* v. *Sheerness Steel* [1996] PIQR Q26 the claimant was a member of his employer's contributory pension scheme, which entitled him to the benefit of a permanent health insurance (PHI) scheme. In the event of disability this would provide him with an income of half his pre-accident pay. He did not pay the PHI premiums himself and was not a party to the PHI policy. The court said:

> There is no evidence that the [claimant] would have got more pay but for the insurance, or that the existence of the insurance had an effect on his remuneration . . . it is an essential requirement of the insurance exception that the cost of the insurance be borne wholly or at least in part by the [claimant].

The defendant will be entitled to credit for the sums the claimant received under the policy unless the claimant contributed to the insurance plan by direct payments, or contributed indirectly by accepting a reduced hourly wage, perhaps reflected in a collective bargaining agreement (*Gaca* v. *Pirelli General plc* [2004] EWCA Civ 373).

Turning to private health care insurance, if the claimant had a health care plan at the time of the accident, it probably contained a clause about treatment for injuries caused by a third party, stating that the claimant must repay the insurer's outlays out of damages recovered from the third party. As this is a class of indemnity insurance, the insurer generally has a right of subrogation in any case.

The claimant is entitled to recover the cost of the treatment from the defendant. The question is whether he must reimburse the insurer for its outlays. It is prudent to obtain the claimant's express permission before one reimburses the insurer company on his behalf.

The insurance exception does not apply to property insurance. If a claimant's car is written off in an accident, and his own insurers pay for a new car, he cannot claim the value of the car from the defendant's insurers and keep the money. His own insurers have a right of subrogation. This enables them to claim back from the defendant, in the claimant's name, their outlays in respect of his property.

9.9 DEDUCTION OF SICK PAY

In the public sector, an injured employee may be entitled under statute to receive sick pay after an accident, with a statutory requirement that if the accident was caused by a third party, and the employee recovers damages from the third party, he must repay the sick pay. For example, NHS employees and the National Health Service (Injury Benefits) Regulations

1995. If the claimant has received such benefits, the defendant cannot set them off against the claim for loss of earnings, because if he does and the NHS then carries out clawback, the claimant will be out of pocket.

In the private sector, the position is slightly more complex. If the claimant was entitled to sick pay under his employment contract, the contract may allow him to keep it unconditionally. If so, the defendant is entitled to deduct it from the loss of earnings claim. To put it another way, the claimant must give credit for it. He cannot receive his pay and still claim a full loss of earnings (*Hussain* v. *New Taplow Paper Mills* [1988] AC 514).

However, the employment contract may include a clause requiring the claimant to repay sick pay out of any damages he recovers from a third party. In that case the payment is in the nature of a loan, and the defendant is not entitled to credit for it (*IRC* v. *Hambrook* [1956] 2 QB 641 and *Berriello* v. *Felixstowe Dock & Railway Co* [1989] 1 WLR 695). Claims under the MIB Untraced Drivers Agreement are an exception to this rule.

If the claimant is employed by somebody other than the defendant, and receives sick pay to which he was not entitled under contract and which he need not repay out of damages, the law on deductibility is unclear. The court may accept that this falls within the 'benevolence exception' (see **section 9.13**). If so, the defendant would be no more entitled to set this off against the damages than if it were a Christmas present. The courts are perhaps more likely to say that to the extent the claimant has been paid, he has not lost earnings.

If the employer who paid gratuitous sick pay actually is the defendant, the court will generally treat this as an interim payment (*Williams* v. *BOC Gases Ltd* [2000] EWCA Civ 95 and *Gaca* v. *Pirelli General plc* [2004] EWCA Civ 373).

If an employee receives sick pay net of tax and National Insurance contributions, he is not obliged to repay his employer more than the net amount (*British Railways Board* v. *Franklin* [1994] PIQR P1).

Sick pay is different in kind to pension payments made following medical retirement (see **section 9.12**).

9.10 DEDUCTION OF OTHER BENEFITS

The CRU recoups most state benefits received by the claimant, but not all. Where a benefit is not covered by the CRU scheme, the general rule is that the defendant is entitled to deduct it on a like for like basis: '. . . attendance allowance . . . and the special damages claimed for cost of care are designed to meet . . . identical expenses. To allow double recovery in such a case at the expense of both taxpayers and insurers seems to me incapable of justification on any rational ground' (*Hodgson* v. *Trapp* [1989] AC 807).

Statutory Sick Pay paid on or after 6 April 1994 is not recouped by the CRU. The best view seems to be that the defendant is entitled to deduct it from the loss of earnings claim, subject to any right the employer may have under the claimant's employment contract to claw it back out of any compensation he gets for accidental injury.

Housing Benefit may be paid as a result of an accident, and again the defendant is entitled to credit for it against the loss of earnings claim. In *Clenshaw* v. *Tanner* [2002] EWHC 184 (QB), the defendant benefited to the extent of £17,000.

9.11 DEDUCTION OF REDUNDANCY PAYMENTS

If the claimant is made redundant after the accident, and this is wholly or partly a result of injuries sustained in the accident, the defendant may be entitled to offset all or part of the redundancy payment against the claim for loss of earnings (see *Colledge* v. *Bass Mitchells & Butlers Ltd* [1988] 1 All ER 536).

9.12 DEDUCTION OF PENSION INCOME

Income from an occupational pension that is received before normal retirement age is not deductible from the loss of earnings claim (*Parry* v. *Cleaver* [1970] AC 1). A pension is considered to be a form of insurance because the claimant does not get back what he paid into it. Instead, he gets a return that depends how long he lives after retirement. Pensions are 'the fruit, through insurance, of all the money which was set aside in the past in respect of his past work. They are different in kind' from pay, and cannot be treated as if they are pay.

For a discussion of the case law, see *Smoker* v. *London Fire & Civil Defence Authority* [1991] 2 AC 502, a case in which the defendant was also in effect the employer, and the provider of the pension.

The rule applies equally to state retirement pension that the claimant receives because of the accident before he had intended to retire (*Hewson* v. *Downs* [1970] 1 QB 73).

Pension income received before normal retirement age is not deductible from the loss of pension claim either. Pension income received after normal retirement age is deductible from the loss of pension claim.

As to claims for loss of pension, see **section 13.7**.

9.13 GIFTS TO THE CLAIMANT

A defendant is not entitled to offset against damages any gift the claimant may receive as a result of his injuries. In *Parry* v. *Cleaver* [1970] AC 1 the court described as revolting the idea that a claimant's compensation should be reduced because of the benevolence of his family or the public.

This benevolence exception applies to gifts from family and friends, receipts from disaster relief funds, and may apply to gifts from the claimant's employer.

In *Cunningham* v. *Harrison* [1973] 1 QB 942, the claimant's employer agreed before proceedings were issued to make an *ex gratia* payment to the claimant of £828 a year for life. The employer was not a defendant, and the court said that as it was a purely voluntary payment it would not be deducted from the loss of earnings claim. However, an extra-contractual payment made by the claimant's employer after an accident at work is likely to be treated by the court as an interim payment on account of compensation (*Gaca* v. *Pirelli General plc* [2004] EWCA Civ 373).

9.14 TAX ON COMPENSATION

There is no tax on damages for personal injuries, other than the inheritance tax which may be payable on certain fatal incident claims (see **Chapter 15**). Neither is there any tax on interest on damages, if the interest was part of the settlement or judgment.

However, when the claimant invests his damages in shares, a savings account or property, the investment is subject to tax in the usual way. It makes no difference that the money came originally from a personal injury claim. At the time of writing, the only exception is the annuity part of a structured settlement.

9.15 STRUCTURED SETTLEMENTS

Structures were devised for claimants with very serious injuries, to ensure that their compensation lasts long enough to pay for food, care and housing for life. If compensation is paid to the claimant on a monthly basis for life, it overcomes the following risks:

- The claimant might invest or spend a lump sum unwisely, run out of money and end up dependent on state benefits.
- The claimant might run out of money by living longer than expected.
- The claimant might die earlier than expected, leaving damages intended to meet his care needs as a windfall for his heirs.

A structured settlement enables the defendant to provide the claimant with an income for life either by purchasing an annuity from a life insurance company or (in the case of a government department) undertaking to make periodical payments itself.

A structured settlement, according to CPR PD 40C, is

> . . . an order or agreement in settlement of a claim which includes, or consists of, payment by instalments over a specified period which may be for the remainder of the claimant's life . . . The part of such a settlement which is to be paid by periodical payments attracts tax benefits and statutory guarantees of payment if entered into in accordance with the Damages Act 1996 and the Income and Corporation Taxes Act 1988 [as amended].

Income from the annuity is tax free if the arrangement is of a type approved by the Inland Revenue.

The 1996 Act was amended by the Courts Act 2003, so that a court 'awarding damages for future pecuniary loss in respect of personal injury may order that the damages are wholly or partly to take the form of periodical payments, and shall consider whether to make that order'. The CPR have been amended to press parties to structure more often. Structured settlements will not become the norm in larger cases unless they become cheaper for the defendant than paying a lump sum conventionally calculated to provide enough compensation for the rest of the claimant's life. Given the discount rate set by the Lord Chancellor under the Damages Act 1996, lump sums are generally cheaper. Two insurance companies who had provided the best value annuities for a great many structured settlement annuities decided in 2003 to stop selling them.

When should one consider a structured settlement? As it will tie up a large proportion of the claimant's damages, one can immediately rule out cases where the claimant is financially sophisticated and wants to play with the money, for example, by property development. One can also rule out cases where the claimant wants to buy a house and needs all his damages to do so. If there is a hefty deduction for contributory negligence, the claimant may need access to all his compensation to avoid being dependent on state support. The following gives some guidance in the matter of structured settlements for different levels of compensation:

- Over £150,000. If the claimant is a child, a mental patient or has an uncertain life-span, many claimant lawyers would give at least some thought to a structured settlement.
- Over £250,000. The NHS Litigation Authority has long had a policy of considering a structured settlement in any case worth more than this.
- Over £500,000. Following amendment on 6 October 2003, CPR PD 40C says: 'Parties should raise the question of a structured settlement in respect of future loss with the court during case management in every case where future loss is likely to equal or exceed £500,000, and in any other

case where [it] might be appropriate.' If they do not, they are likely to find that the court raises it of its own motion at the case management conference.

Structured settlements are highly complex. Typically, the parties agree how much compensation the claimant should get as a normal lump-sum settlement. Part of the lump sum is then used to buy an annuity. The claimant gets 60 per cent of his compensation as a lump sum (to be invested in stocks and shares, used to buy a home, and kept ready for any other major purchases). The other 40 per cent buys him an annuity for life. This is a top down settlement.

The alternative is a bottom up settlement, which means the claimant showing how much annual income he will need, and the defendant shopping around to find an annuity that will provide that much income. Given the current discount rate, this is more expensive.

The disastrous performance of with profits endowment policies in recent years shows how desirable it can be to have investments that are guaranteed to perform. The annuity for a structured settlement is usually based on index linked Government securities (ILGS). There is some concern about this, as an annuity created today for a young claimant may need to last until 2090, but the ILGS may not continue beyond 2035. Also, the ILGS is linked to the Retail Prices Index but average UK pay and the costs of care have both been increasing much faster than the RPI for decades. See the conjoined appeals in *Cooke* v. *United Bristol Healthcare* [2003] EWCA Civ 1370, *Sheppard* v. *Stibbe* and *Page* v. *Lee*.

Do not rule out a structured settlement simply because annuities are not currently paying very much interest. The claimant has to invest in something, and no conventional investment has paid very much in the last decade.

Despite the withdrawal of the two main players, a handful of insurance companies still offer annuities that could be used to provide:

- an immediate lifetime income for the claimant;
- a deferred lifetime income to start at a date when it is predicted that, for example, he will lose the assistance of unpaid carers;
- an income for a term certain, for example until the claimant is entitled to draw on his own retirement pension;
- lump sums at intervals, for example, to buy the claimant a house when he reaches 21, or to replace a car at six-year intervals;
- a contingent income, which will not pay anything unless some condition is satisfied, for example, a voluntary carer falls by the wayside, or free local authority care comes to an end.

A properly constructed structured settlement is guaranteed in case the annuity company collapses. See **section 7.4** as to the Financial Services Compensation Scheme, and see s.4 of the Damages Act 1996.

Because of the legal and financial complexity of these arrangements, only a very few accountants nationwide have the expertise necessary to deal with one. Many have been set up by Frenkel Topping & Co, Accountants **www.frenkeltopping.co.uk** (see also **Appendix 4**).

The procedural side is regulated by CPR Parts 21 and 40, and their corresponding Practice Directions, plus the Court of Protection rules if the claimant is 'incapable by reason of mental disorder of managing and administering [his] property and affairs'.

Structured settlements are generally used where the claimant is under 18 or has a mental disorder. Part 21 provides that the court must approve settlements for persons under either disability. Therefore the accountant's report must be good enough to convince the court that the chosen method of setting up the settlement is the best one. The accountant must be paid on an hourly basis, not by commission on the annuity. Nor should the accountant recommend that he personally be involved in future management of the claimant's finances, although the claimant can of course choose who he likes to set up and run the settlement.

When seeking the court's approval to a settlement, it is necessary to submit a written legal opinion taking account of many practical matters set out at PD 40C.5, such as the claimant's need for therapies or changing levels of care in future.

The costs of investigating and setting up the structured settlement are generally paid by the defendant. CPR PD 40C says that 'the reasonable cost of financial advice from an independent financial adviser or accountant and any reasonably necessary advice from a party's medical and legal advisers will be regarded as a cost in the litigation'. In clinical negligence work, the National Health Service Litigation Authority generally offers £3,000 for these costs and fees.

9.16 BENEFITS AFTER COMPENSATION

The claimant will not be able to receive means-tested benefits if either his income or capital go above the current limits. Many claimants lose their right to state benefits when they receive a damages cheque. In a special provision for personal injury claimants, legislation states that their damages will be disregarded by the means test if they follow the correct procedure. The claimant's lawyer probably owes his client a duty to ensure this happens. Consider the tax case of *Hurlingham Estates* v. *Wilde & Partners* [1997] STC 627.

The Income Support means test is used for national and local authority benefits including Income Support, Incapacity Benefit, Working Families' Tax Credit, Council Tax Benefit and Housing Benefit. A very similar test is used for care and accommodation provided by a local authority. See the

Income Support (General) Regulations 1987 (Schedule 10 and regulations 45, 46 and 53), Social Security Amendment (Personal Injury Payments) Regulations 2002, and the various National Assistance assessment of resources regulations.

Beattie v. *Secretary of State for Social Security* [2001] EWCA Civ 498 said that the claimant's income from a structured settlement should not be disregarded by the means test for Income Support, even if it is paid directly to a receiver who uses it to fund the care regime. The effect of *Beattie* was subsequently partly reversed by the Social Security Amendment (Personal Injury Payments) Regulations 2002 and the National Assistance (Assessment of Resources) (Amendment No 2) (England) Regulations 2002.

The Court Administered Funds Disregard applies to damages held or administered for the claimant by the court under CPR Part 21.11 or by the Court of Protection's Public Guardianship Office (PGO) (*Firth* v. *Geo Ackroyd* [2000] Lloyd's Rep Med 312). Formerly the Public Trust Office, the PGO holds funds on behalf of claimants who are incapable by reason of mental disorder of managing and administering their own property and affairs (see **Appendix 4** for contact details).

The Trust Funds Disregard applies if damages are paid into a personal injury trust or special needs trust (Income Support (General) Regulations 1987 and *Bell* v. *Todd* [2000] Lloyd's Rep Med 12). The capital of such a trust is disregarded by the means tests. Payments to the claimant from such a trust may be in the form of income, or of capital, for example to buy a car. Capital payments do not affect means-tested benefits unless they take the money in the claimant's hands over the normal limit for capital. The income from such a trust is ignored for Income Support purposes unless used to pay the claimant's normal expenses of daily living such as food, clothing or footwear, household fuel, rent or rates.

The law and procedure of trusts is complex, and the disregards are subject to change without notice. If incorrectly set up, a trust will be ineffective for means-tested benefits, and may give rise to a lifetime liability to inheritance Tax. An expert's fee for setting up such a trust is likely to be in the region of £500 plus VAT. Advisers who have expressed an interest in this area include Bill Braithwaite QC and Philip Boyd of Counsel; David Coldrick of Wrigleys, Solicitors, author of *Coldrick on Personal Injury Trusts* which is published by Ark Group (**www.ark-group.com**) and Frenkel Topping & Co, accountants (**www.frenkeltopping.co.uk**).

A trustee's powers and duties are governed by the Trustee Act 2000. If a large amount of compensation is involved, consider using a professional trustee who has no personal interest in spending the claimant's money now or benefiting from it after his death. Usually an accountant or a private client solicitor, a professional trustee would charge about £300 plus VAT per year for this service.

Set up a personal injury trust before compensation is received, but if this is overlooked it can (apparently) be done later.

9.17 THE INSOLVENT CLAIMANT

From the claimant's point of view, his right to claim damages is just as much part of his estate as land, cash or shares. If he is adjudged bankrupt and a trustee in bankruptcy is appointed, his estate vests in the trustee under the Insolvency Act 1986.

Some property is excluded from this, basically tools of the bankrupt's trade and essential domestic items.

Also excluded is a right to compensation for 'pain felt by the bankrupt in respect of his body, mind or character . . . [calculated] without immediate reference to his rights of property'. The trustee in bankruptcy 'is entitled to the damages for past and future loss of earnings and is not entitled to the damages for pain and suffering' (*Ord* v. *Upton* [2000] Ch 352).

This does not mean that the claimant has no personal interest in claiming loss of earnings. There may be enough to pay his creditors and the trustee's costs, discharge the bankruptcy, and perhaps leave something over for the claimant himself.

If the claim includes both pain and suffering and other losses, it will all vest in the trustee. If the claim includes little by way of special damages, the trustee may well not want to pursue the claim himself but 'would have to consider carefully his duty to the bankrupt and would probably, if requested, assign the cause of action to him' (*Ord* v. *Upton*). This involves obtaining the consent of the trustee and the approval of the court, and the cost of doing so may be heavy. It seems that the claimant can decide to limit his claim to those items that do not vest in the trustee in bankruptcy (*Khan* v. *Trident Safeguards Ltd* [2004] EWCA Civ 624). One should check with the trustee before settling the claim on that basis, or issuing proceedings, in case the trustee wants to pursue a claim for other possible heads of loss.

From the point of view of the claimant's solicitor, if his client becomes insolvent he may well not get paid. He may be in no better position if his client has legal expenses insurance (*Tarbuck* v. *Avon Insurance* [2002] QB 571). However, the Court of Appeal has since said *obiter* that *Tarbuck* 'should no longer be followed' (*First National Trinity Finance* v. *OT Computers* [2004] EWCA Civ 653).

CHAPTER 10

Interest on compensation

The claimant's entitlement to interest arises under s.35A of the Supreme Court Act 1981 and s.69 of the County Courts Act 1984. It is intended to compensate the claimant for having to wait for his money. No interest is paid on future losses, such as future loss of earnings.

If proceedings are issued and the claimant wants interest, he must state this in the particulars of claim, saying under what statutes or contract he is entitled to it (CPR Part 16.4.2).

The court has a discretion in awarding interest. The main factor is whether the claimant took an unreasonably long time to get the claim to trial (*Spittle* v. *Bunney* [1988] 1 WLR 847). The courts have become tougher on delay since the Civil Procedure Rules 1998. One can be confident that the court will allow full interest for three or four years after the accident. After this, the uncertainty increases.

If there was considerable delay but the claimant had a good reason for it, such as that he was still receiving medical treatment and the outlook remained doubtful for some years, or he was clinically depressed and found it hard to think about the accident or his losses, he should cover this in his witness statements.

General damages and special damages are treated differently. For definitions, see **section 9.1**.

10.1 INTEREST ON GENERAL DAMAGES

This runs from the date when proceedings are served on the defendant, until judgment or assessment of damages. The rate has been 2 per cent per annum for many years and is likely to remain at that rate (*Lawrence* v. *Chief Constable of Staffordshire* [2000] PIQR Q349).

10.2 INTEREST ON SPECIAL DAMAGES

When the claimant issues proceedings, he acquires a right to interest on special damages from the date of the accident to the date of assessment of damages. If he has not issued proceedings, he has no right to interest.

It is generally awarded at half the rate paid from time to time on the court's special investment account (*Jefford* v. *Gee* [1970] 2 QB 130). This is because some special damages arise at the moment of the accident (such as damage to a car or clothing), some in the following weeks (such as relatives' travel to see the claimant in hospital), and some at different times in the coming years. It would be very tedious to calculate interest separately for each item. In effect the court assumes that on average the losses occurred halfway between the accident and trial.

If a very large item of special damages occurred at or within a very short time of the accident, the claimant should claim interest on it at the full special account rate. Likewise, if his special damages claim consists entirely of earnings lost in the first year after the accident, and the claim is being settled after two or three years, it is fairer to the claimant and more logical to calculate the interest at the full special account rate from halfway through the period during which he lost earnings (*Prokop* v. *DHSS* [1985] CLY 1037).

The Law Society's *Gazette* publishes an annual ready reckoner table in late September or early October, courtesy of Mr R M Nelson-Jones, solicitor. Just read the figures off the table.

10.3 INTEREST IN FATAL INCIDENT CLAIMS

The Law Reform (Miscellaneous Provisions) Act 1934 allows the deceased's estate to claim damages that the deceased himself could have claimed during his life. If the deceased survived the injury long enough to have had a right to claim loss of earnings, arguably the estate should be entitled to interest on this at the full special investment account rate from the date of death to the date of judgment.

The Fatal Accidents Act 1976 gives a right to claim a statutory sum for bereavement. The court is likely to award interest at the full special investment account rate from the date of death to the date of judgment (*Prior* v. *Hastie* [1987] CLY 1219).

The 1976 Act also gives dependants a right to claim for what the deceased would have given them but for the death – the dependency. They can expect interest at half the special investment account rate in respect of losses to the date of trial (*Cookson* v. *Knowles* [1979] AC 556).

Both statutes give a right to claim for funeral expenses. Usually, funeral expenses attract interest at half the special investment account rate, although one could argue for the full rate as this loss arises almost immediately after death. If liability is clear, the claimant should request an interim payment for funeral expenses early on, and it makes sense for the defendant to pay at once. Interest then becomes irrelevant.

10.4 INTEREST AND CRU RECOUPMENT

If the claimant received state benefits as a result of his injury, the defendant is entitled to deduct an equivalent amount from the compensation before it ever reaches the claimant.

Section 17 of the Social Security (Recovery of Benefits) Act 1997 says: 'In assessing damages in respect of any accident, injury or disease, the amount of any listed benefits paid or likely to be paid is to be disregarded.' In *Wadey* v. *Surrey County Council* [2000] UKHL 24 the House of Lords said: 'The effect of s 17 . . . in the context of the scheme which the Act lays down, is that the amount of any listed benefits paid or likely to be paid during the relevant period must be disregarded in the assessment of interest on the damages which are to be assessed without taking account of those benefits.' Calculate interest on all the compensation before deducting state benefits.

10.5 INTEREST AND EMPLOYER'S CLAWBACK

As with state benefits, so with sick pay received by the claimant subject to the employer's right to claw it back out of compensation. Calculate interest on all the compensation before taking off the amount to be repaid to the employer (*Davies* v. *Inman* [1998] EWCA Civ 1606).

10.6 INTEREST FOLLOWING SETTLEMENT

When judgment is entered either by consent or at trial, the claimant becomes the owner of a judgment debt and he is entitled to interest at the prescribed rate. For the High Court, see s.17 Judgments Act 1838. For the county court, see s.74 County Courts Act 1984, which applies to judgments for £5,000 or more. If judgment is entered for liability only, interest does not start to run until damages are assessed (*Thomas* v. *Bunn* [1991] 1 AC 362).

When a claim is settled without judgment, for example with a Tomlin Order, the claimant has no statutory right to interest from the settlement until the damages are actually paid. In a large claim, the claimant should consider making it a term of the settlement that the defendant pay interest at the rate prescribed by the Judgment Debts (Rate of Interest) Order 1993 if it takes him longer than 14 days to send a cheque for the agreed compensation. At the time of writing, the rate under the Order is 8 per cent.

CHAPTER 11

Pain and suffering

Compensation for pain and suffering is part of general damages. It is often spoken of in one breath with loss of amenity, and together they may be referred to as PSLA. As to loss of amenity, see **Chapter 12**.

As with any element of a claim, the claimant must prove his pain and suffering. In a Small Claim, he may do this with a witness statement describing pain, aching, restricted movement and any inability to do work, housework or leisure activities. Otherwise, he will rely on a report from a medical expert, backed up by a witness statement and occasionally photographs.

One can prepare a fairly accurate statement if the claimant keeps a pain diary. It is probably best if the claimant restricts himself to writing entries of 15 to 25 words, once a week for the first month, and then monthly until his condition stabilises. A typical entry might be: 50 per cent recovered; neck still stiff and painful; main problem now is reversing the car; sleep occasionally disturbed. Many arguments about symptoms that apparently started some time after the accident could be avoided if the claimant, in his first pain diary entry, mentioned all the parts of his body apparently affected by the accident.

The courts have created case law that amounts to a tariff by which injuries can be valued. Despite various attempts to turn this into one compact table, valuing a claim accurately still means doing it the hard way (see **section 11.1**).

There is no single correct value for a particular injury. All one can say is that the value of the claim falls in a bracket, say £750–£1,250 or £40,000–£50,000. The position within the bracket depends on the extent of the claimant's loss of amenity, but rather more on the way the particular judge feels about the particular claimant. On appeal, the trial judge's valuation will stand unless it is outside the bracket. The appeal courts often comment on the advantage enjoyed by the trial judge, that he actually saw and heard the claimant.

When valuing general damages, the leading reference book is Kemp & Kemp, *The Quantum of Damages*, published by Sweet & Maxwell. Other reference sources may be helpful, but Kemp & Kemp is indispensable. It has many summaries of quantum judgments, in categories such as Spine below neck and minor injuries.

The overwhelming majority of injuries are minor. Nothing is paid for the shock and shaking up of a minor car shunt at the traffic lights, unless there was also some recognisable physical injury. (*Nicholls* v. *Rushton* [1992] SJ 627). The minor injuries section of Kemp & Kemp notes awards of compensation for some truly trivial injuries, but a judge may well take the view that the victim of an accidental pinprick should not waste the court's time claiming for something *de minimis*. If the injury is minor, the main question is whether it is worth less than the Small Claims limit. Such claims are dealt with, if at all, on an altogether different basis (see **Chapter 21**).

11.1 USING CASE LAW

When valuing an injury, the author's own approach is to write a summary of the main points, with no more detail than is provided in Kemp & Kemp's case summaries, and then find about 15 cases that involved broadly similar injuries. For example:

> Claimant aged 25. Whiplash injury to neck in car accident. Office worker. Three days off work. Considerable discomfort for two months after accident, and considerable pain for the first week of this. Greatly aggravated by typing, which she had to do for 4–5 hours per day. To cope with this she had to take painkillers at 9am on work days, despite which after the first 20 minutes the pain was enough to affect her concentration. During the first month she had to lie down all evening after a work day. Her husband took care of all housework and cooking during this period. After two months, she resumed all sporting and leisure activities.

One should try to find case summaries from the last 10 years, as the court's attitudes change over time. The author finds it helpful to make a list in order of value, as follows:

Case ref:	Parties:	Value/Date:	Seriousness:	Value today:
ABC123	*Roe* v. *Doe*	£1000/01.01.03	+	£1100
DEF345	*Smith* v. *Bloggs*	£950/31.12.02	=	£1000
GHI456	*White* v. *Black*	£850/01.02.03	–?	£900
JKL789	*Katz* v. *Dog*	£825/01.03.03	–	£865

One adjusts older cases for inflation to date, using the Retail Prices Index (*Wright* v. *British Railways Board* [1983] 2 All ER 698). If the case was worth more than £10,000 as at 23 March 2000, make a *Heil* v. *Rankin* adjustment (see **section 11.2**). Kemp & Kemp contains handy ready reckoners, and they are available online at **www.picalculator.co.uk**.

When deciding whether a case summary involves more or less serious injuries than the claim one is valuing, the two main points are the severity of the claimant's pain and disability, and its duration. How long was the victim off work? How long was he off housework? And sport? Permanent residual symptoms such as aches or stiffness add considerably to the value of a claim, even if they are at nuisance level and the claimant is able to do all his pre-accident activities. It may help to ask oneself whether one would rather have had the injuries in the case summary one is reading, or the injuries the claimant actually had.

The author finds that when completing the seriousness column, it is usually possible to find some inconsistency in the judgments. Having completed the list, keep it on the file as it is likely to come in handy when reporting to the client, pointing out to the opposition that the case they are relying on is inconsistent with the general trend, and having costs assessed.

One should try to find cases involving somebody of roughly the same age and pre-accident health as the claimant. This is especially important with an elderly claimant with permanent disability. If one cannot find a case where the claimant not only suffered similar injuries but was elderly, one can proceed as in *Nutbrown* v. *Sheffield Health Authority* [1993] 4 Med LR 187. One assesses the correct figure for a person in the prime of his life (£50,000 in that case) and then adjusts to reflect the claimant's age, health and fitness before and after the accident, and if appropriate his post-trial life expectancy and deprivation of the last years of his life. The courts do not seem attracted by the idea of a purely mathematical deduction based on the victim's life expectancy. If the deduction had been a mathematical one based on a life expectancy of 80, the claimant in *Nutbrown* would have got £8,000, but in fact got £25,000. It is quite easy to find cases involving elderly claimants which the judge has valued at more or less the same amount as if the claimant had been doomed to suffer for 60 years.

If the claimant has suffered multiple injuries, it is seldom appropriate to value each one and simply add them together. The suffering overlaps, so one deducts an aggregation discount of 10–30 per cent. This calculation is seldom explicit in quantum reports. Kemp & Kemp contains at least one report including the trial judge's calculation (see *Bennett* v. *Hewitt* (13 April 2000).

In any claim worth over £5,000, or involving scarring, psychiatric problems, multiple injuries or pre-existing disability, one might consider obtaining counsel's opinion on the value. This is often more cost effective than asking colleagues for a second opinion. It is best to ask counsel to supply not just a figure, but the names and references of the cases he relies on. With one's client's permission, one can disclose counsel's advice to the opponent. Many solicitors and legal executives are reluctant to differ with a barrister.

11.2 *HEIL* V. *RANKIN* ADJUSTMENT

In March 2000, in *Heil* v. *Rankin* [2000] EWCA Civ 84, the Court of Appeal increased the amount to be awarded for pain and suffering from then on.

Until 10 or 15 years have gone by, it will still be necessary to refer to pre-*Heil* v. *Rankin* cases when valuing pain and suffering. When relying on an older case one must do the following. Using the Retail Prices Index, adjust the value of pain and suffering for inflation from the date of judgment to 23 March 2000. If this produces a figure greater than £10,000, adjust with the *Heil* v. *Rankin* formula to give the correct figure as at 23 March 2000. Finally, adjust for inflation from 24 March 2000 to the present day.

The *Heil* v. *Rankin* formula is: £ + [(£ − 10,000)/420,000 × £] where £ is the value of pain and suffering in that particular old case at 23 March 2000. This produces a sliding scale:

Value before *Heil* v. *Rankin*:	Value after *Heil* v. *Rankin*:
£10,000	£10,000
£15,000	£15,178
£20,000	£20,476
£30,000	£31,428
£100,000	£121,428
£150,000	£200,000

11.3 JUDICIAL STUDIES BOARD GUIDELINES

An attempt by a team of judges to turn thousands of quantum cases into one accessible tariff has produced the Judicial Studies Board Guidelines for the Assessment of General Damages in Personal Injury Cases. The Guidelines are available on their own as a slim paperback, or as part of other books such as Kemp & Kemp. They are easy to use, but rather a blunt instrument.

The Guidelines: 'are not in themselves law ... the law is to be found elsewhere in rather greater detail' (*Arafa* v. *Potter* [1994] PIQR Q73).

> The Judicial Studies Board Guidelines are a reliable and valuable tool but they do not have the force of law nor any special authority and should only be used in addition to relevant caselaw . . .[and in the Court of Appeal] the parties are in my opinion entitled to something more than just a comparison with the Guidelines . . .
>
> *Reed* v. *Sunderland Health Authority* [1998] EWCA Civ 1552)

11.4 TYPES OF MEDICAL EXPERT

Most accidents produce only musculo-skeletal injuries. The best expert for these claims is a consultant orthopaedic surgeon, except in Small Claims where one might use a GP or even rely entirely on the claimant's witness statement.

The lowest grade of doctor is the houseman, and it is never worth obtaining a report from one of these very junior doctors. The next step up is a registrar. A senior registrar is one step short of being a consultant. It is best to pay the extra and get a consultant's report. Doctors are 'Dr', surgeons are 'Mr'.

Is it ever worth instructing the claimant's GP where the claim is worth more than the Small Claims limit? Say the claimant had minor injuries and has already made a complete recovery. It is evident that pain and suffering are worth £2,000 at most. No doctor will be able to say more than 'The claimant says he pulled a muscle, couldn't work for a week but was OK within 3 months. That sounds about right and is not inconsistent with his medical records.' The claimant's GP will often charge well under £100 for a report, including accessing the claimant's records.

The argument against instructing the claimant's GP is that he probably will not fully understand the procedure for expert evidence, hence the pro forma on the accompanying CD-ROM. If it is necessary to go back to him several times with questions and amendments, the saving will prove to be an illusion. Also, there is a small but real risk in the fast track that an expert witness will be needed to give oral evidence at trial, and a busy GP is likely to be very irate if it happens to him.

There are now many GPs who, rather then dealing just with their own patients, offer a service as general medico-legal experts. They often charge £250 or so for a report. For only a little more it is possible to get an authoritative report from a consultant.

It is normally better to go to a consultant orthopaedic surgeon than an A&E consultant. The A&E consultant may not be able to give an authoritative prognosis, although if a report is needed quickly, he will probably provide one in weeks rather than months.

If acting for a claimant who has an injury about which there are known to be several schools of medical thought, it is vital that one instructs an expert from the right school. As finding such an expert can be hit and miss, one should if possible avoid instructing him jointly with the defendant (see **section 20.11**). Also, instruct a senior specialist. If the court has to choose between the evidence of two experts, it is likely to accept the opinion of the most senior, as in the prolapsed intervertebral disc case *Miller* v. *Lothian Primary Care NHS Trust* [2004] ScotCS 159.

For epilepsy (often demonstrated by fits, fainting or blackouts after a head injury) one needs a neurologist. Neurology seems, in some areas of the country at least, to attract unsympathetic individuals whose usual advice to a patient is 'pull yourself together'. A neurologist is not necessarily the best expert to start the ball rolling in a case of brain injury. Use a top neuropsychologist instead. For neurological injuries, for example to the brachial plexus, you need a neurosurgeon.

As to psychologists and psychiatrists, see **section 11.11**.

11.5 MEDICAL REPORTS

With the help of a medical dictionary, medical reports tend to be self explanatory except when they relate to the injuries that are discussed later in this chapter.

From the claimant's point of view it is vital that the medical report that he uses to settle the claim should contain a prognosis, or prediction of how he will fare in future. If the claimant still has pain and suffering when he first sees the medico-legal expert, at that point he probably has a good statistical chance of complete recovery but some chance of permanent symptoms. It is often impossible to predict that the claimant will suffer long-term problems until two or three years after the accident, by which time 90 per cent of sufferers have already made a full recovery. If instructed too early, a good medical expert will suggest that he sees the claimant again for a final report after another 12 or 18 months. A lesser expert may either make no comment on the future or say that the claimant will probably get better.

Osteoarthritis can be caused or brought on by an accident. It may be called osteoarthrosis, long-term degenerative change, deterioration of the joints, or just long-term problems. If acting for the claimant, it is as well to ask the surgeon whether there is a risk of osteoarthritis if the injury damaged the articular surface of a joint, damaged the cartilage that is supposed to protect a joint, or caused significant spinal problems.

If there is any risk for the future, the court needs to know. A 30 per cent chance that a whiplash victim will not make a full recovery, or a 10 per cent risk that a fracture patient will develop osteoarthritis, or a 2 per cent risk of epilepsy may affect the compensation (see **section 9.5**). For a recent example, which in fact worked in favour of the defendant, see *Williams* v. *Green* [2001] EWCA Civ 1888.

If there is a risk of serious deterioration, such as epilepsy, blindness, paralysis, cancer or death, the claimant's lawyer should find out whether his client wants to claim provisional damages. If so, one should obtain a supplemental medical report (see **section 9.2**).

Often, a medical report will say that the accident only brought forward a medical problem that the claimant would have had anyway. Cases of accelerated onset are particularly common with neck and back injuries. The claimant is entitled to compensation only for the pain and suffering caused by the accident, and one needs to know the time by which onset has been accelerated. This can be little more than guesswork by the medical expert. If there is a continuing loss of earnings, there might easily be a £50,000 difference between three years' acceleration and five years'. Consider getting another medical report.

If an orthopaedic report suggests that the claimant responded in a surprising or inconsistent way to tests, or 'hyper-related' to examination, he may not want to disclose it to the defendant. This expert is saying that there is no sufficient physical explanation for at least some of the claimant's symptoms. He may be implying that the claimant is malingering. There are other similar phrases '. . . no organic basis for this complaint . . .' or ' . . . high degree of functional overlay . . .'. The claimant has to decide whether to try another orthopaedic surgeon/neurologist, or to accept that there is a psychiatric element and approach a psychologist, psychiatrist or consultant anaesthetist (see **section 11.10**).

Since 2003 VAT has been payable on medico-legal reports, whether dealing with liability or causation, and whether prepared on the basis of an examination or from the notes (*D'Ambrumenil* v. *Commissioners of Customs & Excise* ECJ C-307/01). A medical report is exempt only if it is intended for the protection, maintenance or restoration of human health.

11.6 OBTAINING AND UNDERSTANDING MEDICAL RECORDS

For a claimant, medical records are seldom useful except in clinical negligence work, but the Civil Procedure Rules 1998 expect that the medical expert will see them, and the defendant's team may well want to see them. Medical experts are seldom willing to obtain them directly, and expect the claimant's lawyer to do this for them.

To obtain the records, first get the claimant's written consent. It is best to use the consent form agreed by the Law Society and British Medical Association (BMA), but note that each form relates to one health professional. For GP, orthopaedic, physio and psychiatric records, one needs the claimant to sign four copies of the consent form. There is a copy on the accompanying CD-ROM. The latest version can be obtained from the Law Society website at **www.lawsociety.org.uk**.

One generally obtains records from the claimant's GP and the medical records officer of any hospital at which the claimant was treated. Write to them enclosing a signed consent form. To avoid delays, use a standard letter that anticipates the usual queries. There is a suggested letter on the accompanying CD-ROM. In clinical negligence claims, there is a different system based on the Law Society's Protocol for Obtaining Hospital Medical Records.

Records made by ambulance crew, physiotherapists and hospital occupational therapists are seldom needed. They tend to be held separately by the relevant department, rather than by the hospital's medical records officer. Records made by community occupational therapists are very seldom needed. They are held by the local authority's Social Services department.

If the claimant received private medical advice or treatment (e.g. from a dentist, or from an orthopaedic surgeon who saw him privately through BUPA or PPP) then the records relating to that consultation or treatment will be held by the treating dentist or surgeon, not by the hospital where the treatment took place.

X-ray and scan images are meaningless except to medical experts, awkward to store, unless kept as digitised files on a computer, and expensive to post. Because of restrictions on what a hospital is allowed to charge, the hospital may have to subsidise requests for copy images out of its healthcare budget. If an X-ray or scan has been taken, the written records will include a brief report from a radiologist stating what it shows, and one's medico-legal expert will usually be happy to rely on this. In a case worth less than (say) £5,000 one will very seldom need to obtain any actual images. In a more valuable case, one should obtain any relevant imaging. Most medical records officers willingly provide a list of images so that one can select the ones to be copied, and it takes very little time to check the list and delete images that, by the date and part of the body, clearly cannot be relevant.

Imaging may be held by the hospital medical records department if taken on the NHS, or by the treating doctor if taken privately. There is an additional problem with MRI and other images taken with very expensive scanners, in that they may have been taken by a private company. If the company is separate from the hospital, one must write them a separate letter.

Some hospitals are quick and efficient. Some are incredibly disorganised and slow. It will help with hospitals if one includes the reference number they gave the claimant (the hospital number).

Some record holders simply ignore requests for records. If gentle persuasion does not work, one can either give up or switch to threats. The NHS complaints procedure applies. With GPs, who are the usual culprits, try mentioning the possibility of a complaint to the General Medical Council. It may possibly work to threaten dentists with the General Dental Council. There are sanctions for failure to comply with the Data Protection Act 1998, so try suggesting to a defaulter that one may be forced to complain to the Office of the Information Commissioner. See **Appendix 4** for all contact details.

Small Claims are an exception to the usual practice with medical records. As the loser does not have to pay for the winner's costs of obtaining them, they are seldom obtained.

To obtain medical records of military personnel, one must write to the correct address (see **Appendix 4**) with a consent form signed by the claimant quoting his full name, address and telephone number; date of birth; service number; unit; date of discharge; whether a war pension has been applied for; date of accident; hospitals attended.

Having got the records, one seldom has time to do more than glance through them and send a set off to the medical expert. In a fairly large claim it is as well to read at least the typed correspondence in the records. In a very large claim, or in the event of a dispute, one needs to read and understand all the records. This requires a medical dictionary such as the popular one by Churchill Livingstone with its anatomical diagrams; the *British National Formulary* for drug details; and a dictionary of medical abbreviations such as that available at **www.lawinclear.co.uk**.

11.7 THE COST OF MEDICAL RECORDS

Many doctors and hospitals will not only greatly overcharge for records, but refuse to hand them over until one has paid in advance. Do not give in to this.

The rules are clear, and are laid down by the Data Protection Act 1998 (replacing the Access to Health Records Act 1980). The 1998 Act covers all records, whether paper or electronic. The maximum fee that can be charged by a doctor or hospital for providing copies of paper and electronic records is £50, with no additional charge for copying or postage. Records appears to include film images.

Note that some of the agencies that offer to find medical experts for lawyers will, as part of the service, obtain medical records. They may be willing to allow postponement of payment for records for 12 months or so.

11.8 WHIPLASH INJURIES

Medical reports may talk of a hyperextension-hyperflexion injury, meaning that the neck extends and then flexes beyond its normal range of movement. This causes an injury to the soft tissues of the neck. It can be caused by a fall but is particularly associated with road traffic accidents. In the classic rear end shunt scenario, the victim is sitting in a stationary car at the traffic lights when hit from behind by another vehicle.

Whiplash is the most common road traffic injury. The most obvious symptom is severe pain and stiffness around the third and fourth cervical vertebrae. The initial severe symptoms fade, and most victims make a 95–100 per cent recovery within 12 weeks. Unless there are significant symptoms for longer than a month, or considerable financial losses, a whiplash claim is unlikely to be worth more than the Small Claims limit.

Whiplash is a considerable problem because some victims suffer chronic pain and stiffness; it is impossible to predict whether a particular claimant will be in this group; opinions differ as to how far chronic neck pain is a physical or psychiatric problem; and there are very often no objectively verifiable symptoms. A whiplash victim may have muscle spasm that can be felt by an examining doctor, but this is certainly not present in all cases (Hohl M 1975 *Soft Tissue Injuries of the Neck* Clinical Orthopaedics 109:42–49). As a result, there is an extreme range of views amongst both lawyers and doctors, from those who believe anything any claimant says about whiplash to those who believe it always settles within 12 weeks. There may be a bitter and costly disagreement over the extent of the claimant's disability, indeed over whether he is disabled at all. The state of the medical art is such that unless the claimant wearies of litigation, or is caught doing something he claims he cannot do, or encounters a particularly stubborn medical expert, his claim will succeed.

If whiplash is caused by a very low-speed road accident, the main issue at trial may be whether the accident could have caused the alleged injury. A 40 mph impact may cause the head to decelerate at 46G, which is enough to cause extensive tearing of muscle. A 20 mph impact can certainly cause significant whiplash injuries. But can an impact speed of 5–10 mph cause significant injury? After all, one can experience and enjoy quite violent collisions in fairground dodgem cars with hard seats and no head restraints. There may be a dispute about both the speed of the vehicles and what that meant for the claimant.

Can the issue be resolved by expert evidence about the accident itself? Skid marks, especially if the vehicles were cornering, may allow a fairly accurate estimate of the speed of at least one of the vehicles. The nature and extent of the vehicle damage may help, but is not a very good guide to the speed at which the vehicles were travelling, as damage depends very much on the weights, speeds, design of vehicle shell, and direction of impact. An engineer will seldom claim to know the impact speed to the nearest 15 mph. Until late 2004, it was very rare to find that a defendant obtained expert evidence from an engineer in a whiplash case. Since then many insurers have started serving expert reports in low-impact whiplash cases saying that the accident could not possibly have caused injury. If the court feels that the claimant is honest it will prefer his evidence. See *Armstrong* v. *First York*, CA (17 January 2005, not yet reported).

In US courtrooms, whiplash arguments have long revolved around the Dv or Delta velocity. This is the change in velocity of the victim as a result of the impact. If the victim's car were embedded in concrete before the defendant's vehicle hit it at 40 mph, the exposed part of the car would end up as mere twisted metal and the claimant would be cut by flying glass, but he would not suffer a whiplash injury as the Delta velocity would be nil. Conversely, imagine the claimant in a small rigid car which is hit from behind by an articulated lorry doing 12 mph. The car is almost undamaged but accelerates like a tiddleywink. The claimant's body goes with the car, and his head catches up a moment later. The key to a whiplash injury is not impact speed but (if the victim's car was stationary at the time) how far up the road the car was shunted.

In the UK, a whiplash claim will stand or fall depending, quite simply, on whether the orthopaedic experts accept, based on descriptions of the accident, that it caused the injury described by the claimant. Most laymen would doubt that an accident could cause significant injury unless it causes a certain amount of vehicle damage. Any claim to have suffered a significant neck injury in an impact at 5–10 mph will be received with scepticism by most doctors. In practice, a claimant will be in difficulty if he tries to blame significant suffering on an accident that merely scuffed the paint on his car. He will be on firmer ground if the bumper was cracked. He will generally be believed if the bodywork was bent. He is in a very strong position if he sustained his injury in a high-energy impact, proven by extensive vehicle damage and corroborated by minor injuries. Few experienced lawyers would try to pin down an orthopaedic surgeon about the conclusions he drew from descriptions of the accident, but where there was significant vehicle damage it is definitely worth the claimant's lawyer describing it in the letter of instruction. It will be interesting to see how the current trend develops. Until 2004, the author had read well over 2,000 orthopaedic reports in whiplash cases without ever seeing Delta velocity mentioned. UK orthopaedic surgeons do quite often mention the impact speed, and they occasionally refer to aggravating factors. These include the following:

- The impact was from behind. Some research indicates that a rear end shunt is twice as likely to cause whiplash as a head-on impact.
- The impact caused the vehicle to spin violently.
- There were multiple impacts, in the sense that the first collision pushed the claimant's vehicle into something else.
- The impact occurred at a moment when the claimant was looking over one shoulder. The tearing of muscle fibres may be much greater in these cases.
- The impact occurred at a moment when the claimant was leaning forward. As the seat accelerates forward, the claimant in effect sits back in his seat, but when his body is stopped by the seat back, his head keeps on going.
- The claimant was in a seat without an effective head restraint. This may mean that he had a head rest, but it was not properly adjusted and made the injury worse by acting as a pivot at the base of the skull. Impact causes a passenger's body to ride up several inches, so the proper position for a head rest is higher than one might think.
- The claimant still had, at the time of impact, lingering symptoms from a previous whiplash injury (see *Pearce* v. *Lindfield* [2003] EWCA Civ 647).

Depending on the violence of the collision, there may be accompanying minor injuries in the form of:

- Seat belt bruising on the chest and hips. Wearing a seat belt prevents or reduces many injuries, but increases the frequency and severity of whiplash injury.
- Impact of the side of the head on the side window if the impact was partly from that side.
- Often, bruising to the shins, knees, ankles or hands as they strike the parcel shelf or steering column.
- Occasionally, impact of the head on the steering wheel (this is possible even when wearing a three-point seat belt as the body can rotate forwards on the side away from the upper seat belt attachment).
- Occasionally, lacerations to the face or hands from broken glass.

If the accident was very minor, the defendant will not be happy if the claimant produces a medical report that blames him for a long period of disability. If the claimant's report is from a GP, the defendant will not feel that it is authoritative and will want to challenge it by obtaining his own report from an independent orthopaedic consultant. However, if the claimant starts off with a report from an orthopaedic consultant, the defendant is somewhat less likely to want to obtain his own report. Very few claimants are dishonest, so a defendant's best hope of reducing a large whiplash claim is to show that it is an acceleration case, in other words that the claimant would eventually have suffered similar symptoms even if the accident had not occurred. The claimant need not necessarily agree to be examined by the defendant's medical expert (see **section 20.10**).

Where whiplash symptoms persist after three years, there is some question how far they are the result of the accident itself, and how far they are caused by a supervening Chronic Pain Syndrome (see **section 11.10**). The distinction can be important.

It is very useful to know the usual and unusual symptoms, so that one is in a better position to respond when the claimant describes his own experiences. For example, can a whiplash injury produce low back symptoms two weeks later? Or pain in the jaw?

The signs and symptoms of moderate or severe whiplash are set out below, with the acute stage first.

Acute stage

Acute 1

In most cases, almost at once, a feeling of being dazed or bewildered, and within a few hours, a headache, typically at the occiput or back of the head, extending when bad into the temples and forehead. The dazed feeling fades over a few hours but may still be present at a low level a week after the accident.

Acute 2

Pain and stiffness in the back of the neck, although it is common for the victim of a whiplash injury to feel no pain in the minutes after impact. The pain starts gradually. In most cases the pain and stiffness will be experienced in full within 12 hours of the accident, but sometimes there is little sign of it for 24 or even 48 hours, and the symptoms may continue to get worse for as much as a week after the accident. The classic pain distribution is from the top of the shoulders, through the trapezius, to the base of the skull extending about 3 inches to each side of the spine. The pain may radiate up into the back of the head and occasionally the jaw. Usually there is a dull aching pain all the time, which in the first days or weeks is too severe to be ignored at any time. There is usually also a sharp pain from time to time in the back of the neck.

The pain and stiffness restrict all movements of the victim's neck, often causing him to keep his neck rigid and rotate his whole upper body in order to look more than a few degrees right or left. For the average person, the normal ranges of movement of the neck are flexion (chin towards chest) of zero to 45 degrees, where zero is a normal standing position; extension (as if to look straight upwards) zero to 45 degrees; lateral flexion (ear towards shoulder) zero to 45 degrees; rotation (as if to look over shoulder) zero to 60 degrees on each side.

The victim will typically find that he cannot sit in one posture for more than 10 to 15 minutes without getting too uncomfortable, but then on moving finds that he has stiffened up and has to mobilise slowly to keep the pain to a minimum. The pain is worse on moving after a period of immobility, or when the claimant's body is jarred by taking an awkward step, or hitting a bump in a vehicle.

Driving a vehicle is particularly difficult because it involves using the shoulders when turning the wheel; using the neck to look right and left; and sitting immobile.

The pain and stiffness is exacerbated by exactly the posture and actions required to type at a keyboard, so an office worker may be worse off than a whiplash victim who is able to keep mobile.

Acute 3

In about 30 per cent of cases, there is pain across the back of the shoulder(s) and in about 20 per cent of cases, pain between the shoulder blades, possibly accompanied by muscle spasm.

In about 30 per cent of cases, pain will be experienced in the low back from strained tissues there. This may take a week to reach a peak, and in the first two weeks it may be masked by more severe pain from the neck.

In about 15 per cent of cases there is tingling and/or numbness in the little fingers and ring fingers. When this occurs it is not constant, but happens several times a day for perhaps 5–15 minutes each time. Occasionally, there is also pain or tingling in the forearm, in the dermatomal distribution described below.

In about 15 per cent of cases there is pain in the arms and/or hands, or a feeling that the arms are heavy or tired. In the short term, this can be the result of a nerve trapped in the neck. If the symptoms persist for a long time, this feeling of weakness in the arms may be explained as the body's adaptation to neck pain aggravated by heavy lifting, in order to discourage lifting.

Occasionally there is vertigo.

Rarely, vague visual disturbances occur. There is no blurring of the vision, but a patient may say 'my eyes feel a bit odd,' and feel that he needs to look at something carefully in order to be sure he is seeing correctly, or that it seems to take longer to go from focus on a close object to focus on a far one. This is likely to last no more than a week.

Rarely, there is pain and audible clicking in the joint of the jaw. Tempero-mandibular joint injury is accepted by a substantial minority of doctors to be a possible direct consequence of a whiplash accident.

In a few cases, tinnitus occurs.

If the victim had twisted around to look over his shoulder or to reach for something in the back of the vehicle at the moment of impact, there may be injury to the ligaments and muscles of the trunk and arms, and some experts would also expect a facet joint injury in the low back.

Chronic symptoms

The classic long-term symptoms from a whiplash injury are as follows.

Chronic 1

There is pain in the same distribution as for acute pain. This will be a dull, aching pain, but if the sufferer carelessly overdoes things, he experiences severe aching or the sharp pain of muscle spasm. In the more serious cases the pain distribution will radiate out into the shoulders. The pain will be variable. It may be severe at times, particularly the morning after a day when the victim took too much exercise. There will usually be times when there is no pain, for example, when lying down. Driving a car and working at a keyboard are likely to exacerbate the pain after a short time. The patient is likely to be experimenting from time to time with heat pads, osteopathy, chiropractic, acupuncture, aromatherapy, Shiatzu massage, etc.

Chronic 2

Stiffness of the neck. The range of movement of the neck may be reduced by about one-third in each direction. If extension of the neck is particularly painful, it may point to a facet joint injury. Sitting, standing or lying in one position for longer than 20 minutes will allow the neck to stiffen in that position, so that the sufferer has to be very careful when he starts moving again.

Chronic 3

There may be intermittent tingling in the little finger and ring finger of each hand.

Chronic 4

In the very long term, there may be wasting of the muscles at the back of the neck because the patient avoids any activity that might require him to exercise them. A few surgeons test for this by asking the patient to stand upright, placing his hand at the back of the patient's head, and asking him to press back against the hand while the surgeon uses his other hand to feel the bulk of the tensed muscles (see **section 11.10**).

Chronic 5

It is likely that there will be anxiety and depression. If these started not long after the accident, at a time when the patient was still unable to work because of pain, and do not seem merely to continue a pattern established before the accident, it is likely that the medical experts will attribute them to the accident. Depression, in particular, delays recovery as the sufferer may spend most of the day in bed rather than mobilising his neck. It is seen as a reasonable excuse for failure to attend for physiotherapy. It is closely associated with Chronic Pain Syndrome.

Chronic 6

Stomach problems may occur (from discomfort, through heartburn, diarrhoea and nausea, to peptic or duodenal ulcer) caused by painkillers.

Recovery

The rates of recovery from whiplash vary a great deal depending who carried out the research, and where. The following is a rough average. Just over half of whiplash victims suffer some chronic symptoms, usually very minor and intermittent. Nearly all make a good enough recovery to return to all work and leisure activities within six months at most. There is some evidence that symptoms continue to improve five or even eight years after the accident, but a medical report produced three years after the accident will generally say that any ongoing symptoms are likely to be permanent.

In perhaps 5 per cent of cases the patient never recovers sufficiently to return to work, or struggles on for a time before giving up work as in *Sandry v. Jones* (2000) *The Times* 3 August. Some research indicates that this is particularly likely where the patient reports not only pain and stiffness in the neck, but also pain in the arms and/or low back pain.

Some patients who have very severe whiplash symptoms in the first hours or weeks make a complete recovery. Others who had only moderate symptoms suffer permanently. There is little or no correlation between acute and long-term symptoms. Symptoms of whiplash are prone to recur unexpectedly when the patient seems all but recovered. The cautious claimant lawyer will advise any whiplash sufferer with continuing problems to delay settling his compensation claim until nearly three years after the accident.

Diagnosis and treatment

Whatever causes chronic symptoms after whiplash, it cannot be seen on medical imaging. There is probably a substantial psychiatric element. There are different schools of medical thought. For the lawyer, it is well worth knowing some anatomy.

The spine consists of cylindrical bones (the vertebrae), stacked one on top of each other and separated by tough, flexible intervertebral discs. Some medical experts state that these act as shock absorbers; most say they do not.

Projecting from each vertebra towards the surface of the back are a central peg of bone and two bony wings. The central peg is what can be felt just under the surface of the back. The wings on each vertebra articulate with those on the adjoining vertebrae to make the facet joints (or zygapophyseal joints) that stabilise the spine. The vertebrae form a hollow, flexible column, held together by ligaments and wrapped in muscles, down the centre of which runs the spinal cord. At each intervertebral joint are the nerve roots, from which nerves leave the spinal cord to control skin sensation and muscle power in parts of the body at that level and below.

As to skin sensation, each nerve root serves a band of skin about 5cm wide. The bands served by the nerves that leave the spine at the level of the ribs wrap around the chest, horizontally or thereabouts. The nerves that emerge further down the spine supply roughly vertical parallel bands of skin that sweep down the legs to the feet. This is known as the dermatomal distribution, and can be seen in any atlas of anatomy and in the appendices to the *Churchill Livingstone Pocket Medical Dictionary*.

As to muscle power, the nerves emerging from the spine supply the muscles in a similar but more complex pattern known as the myotomal distribution. For example, the nerves emerging from the spine at the 5th and 6th cervical vertebra (C5 and C6) operate the biceps and deltoid muscles, which are also supplied by peripheral nerves coming from the brachial plexus.

If a nerve root is irritated or compressed, it will produce characteristic symptoms of pain or numbness in the parts of the body served by the nerve in question, and perhaps weakness and suppression of reflexes if that part of the body is a limb. The upper cervical nerve roots serve the back of the head. The nerve roots from C5 to C8 serve the arms and hands. If a surgeon suspects nerve root compression in the neck, he may test for it by pressing down on the top of the patient's head (axial loading), extending the neck, compressing the jugular vein, or having the patient cough. If it is present, the report may talk of radicular pain. It may be caused by pressure from bone, or pressure from a disc in which case the report may talk of discogenic symptoms.

In thin individuals, the facet joints lie close to the surface of the back, but usually they are buried under several centimetres of muscle, and the other parts of the spine are buried even deeper. When long-term symptoms occur after a whiplash injury, many doctors subscribe to the view that this is usually the result of injury to the vertebral facet joints. The typical pattern of shoulder pain after a whiplash injury is thought by many experts to conform not so much to the dermatomal distribution as to radiation from the facet joints, described in Bogduk & Marsland *The cervical zygapophyseal joints – a source of neck pain* (1988) Spine 13:610–617. If a diagnostic nerve block of the medial branch of the cervical dorsal ramus stops the pain temporarily, this tends to confirm a facet joint injury. A surgeon may then try injecting local anaesthetic into the facet joint. This is a common and fairly safe procedure. In a severe case a surgeon may use a radiofrequency lesion to create a more long-term effect by overheating the nerve. This may give pain relief for six months, at some risk of affecting adjoining nerves.

The following summary of treatment for whiplash is for interested lawyers. Please do not treat it as medical advice:

- Non-steroidal anti-inflammatory drugs/pain-killers such as ibuprofen.
- Maybe rest for the first few days, but seldom for any longer than that as too much rest can lead to loss of neuro-muscular tone and condition, and cause long-term pain. The classic soft surgical collar is not capable of immobilising the neck, although it may be a reminder to the patient that he should not move it hastily. Both soft and hard collars are now believed by many doctors to do more harm than good after the first week or so.
- Maybe ice packs in the first 48 hours.
- After 72 hours, heat from a heat lamp, heat pad, etc.
- Ultrasound, which heats deeper structures.
- Mobilisation of the neck by the patient himself, or manipulation of the neck by a physiotherapist. If administered by a physiotherapist, it is likely to be painful. The court would expect the patient to co-operate with this. Physiotherapy during the first six weeks will almost certainly reduce the symptoms. After that, any reduction may well be temporary, lasting only a day or so. It is not likely to produce a dramatic recovery. Early and thorough physiotherapy is often very beneficial. Since NHS physiotherapy is often neither early nor thorough, many insurers have arrangements with private therapists so that claimants can be offered free treatment.
- Chiropractic treatment. This is highly effective in a high proportion of cases, but not always effective. It is likely to cause at least a temporary improvement in symptoms lasting 12–24 hours after each treatment. See Woodward, Cook, Gargan & Bannister *Chiropractic Treatment of Chronic Whiplash Injuries* (1996) J Bone Joint Surg 27(9) 643–645.

- Sometimes, prescription of antidepressant medication such as amitriptylene or dothiepin.
- Infrequently, if pain has continued for more than three months, giving the patient a TENS (transcutaneous electrical nerve stimulation) device to use at home. This is a small box that applies an electrical current to the skin via electrodes. It can reduce pain, but is effective only for a minority of patients who try it. If it works, the effects often last only while the device is attached and for 15–30 minutes or so after it is removed. A patient who benefits from a TENS machine should claim the cost of the machine, batteries, depreciation, electrodes and contact gel.
- Rarely, manipulation under anaesthetic by an orthopaedic surgeon. The benefits from this are questionable and there is some risk.
- Rarely, steroid and anaesthetic injections into the facet joints of the neck. This procedure is unpleasant and has some risks. Many doubt the value of this treatment. See Barnsley *et al*, *Lack of effect of intra articular corticosteroids for chronic neck pain in the cervical zygapophyseal joints* (1994) 330 New England J Med 1047–1050. The same is true of injections into the facet joints of the low back (see **section 11.9**).
- Surgery. Very rare, and only if there is clearly a serious fracture, prolapsed disc or similar problem. Considerable risks have to be balanced against uncertain benefits.

The claimant with chronic pain from whiplash may undergo medical imaging, perhaps arranged by the defendant if the claim looks like being expensive. The options are plain X-ray, computerised tomography (CT) scanning, and magnetic resonance imaging (MRI). None of these will show small tears and scars in the soft tissue. Injury to the facet joints is difficult or impossible to detect with any sort of imaging. Imaging may also fail to reveal some injuries to intervertebral discs.

Imaging often shows that the claimant has degenerative changes in the vertebrae or discs that must already have been there at the time of the accident. Degenerative change in the spine is a normal part of ageing. Where it involves osteophytes or hypertrophic facet joints that impinge on the nerve roots, it is called cervical spondylosis. The medical experts may accept that these would shortly have caused some or all of the symptoms even if the accident had not occurred. The problem is that medical imaging of people with no neck pain very often shows a great deal of degeneration in the cervical spine; and imaging of people who report symptoms that suggest cervical spondylosis very often shows little or no abnormality.

Ordinary X-rays give a good image of degenerative changes to the vertebrae. They do not give a good image of soft tissue, and do not give a good image if one bone is shielded by another as often occurs within the spine. X-rays are ionising radiation, and are to be avoided unless medically necessary. There is not only little correlation between pain and deterioration seen on imaging, but also very little correlation between a whiplash injury and the subsequent progress, shown on X-ray, of degenerative disease in the cervical spine.

CT scanning consists of multiple X-rays that show a set of slices through the body. They do not give a good image of soft tissue, although they may show a prolapsed intervertebral disc. They may reveal fractures that were hidden on a plain X-ray. For CT scanning, the patient is loaded into a cylinder while lying on a stretcher. Depending how much of the spine is to be examined, and the distance between each slice, CT scanning may involve a large amount of ionising radiation. CT scans of people without any spinal problems very often show abnormalities, and a result showing no abnormality does not mean that there is no injury. See Weisel *et al*, *A study of computer-assisted tomography: The incidence of positive CAT scans in an asymptomatic group of patients* (1984) Spine 9 549–551.

MRI scans use radio waves in a strong magnetic field. They are the single most important method of identifying injury to soft tissues, particularly to the intervertebral discs. Although MRI scans are helpful, they give many false positive and false negative results. According to some research, MRIs of people who have no neck pain show significant problems with the intervertebral discs or the spinal canal in 50 per cent of those over 40 and 25 per cent of those under 40. MRI scans of people who do have neck pain frequently show nothing abnormal. See Pettersen *et al*, *MRI and Neurology in Acute Whiplash Trauma: No Correlation in Prospective Examination of 39 cases.* See also Boden *et al Abnormal Magnetic Resonance Scans of the Cervical Spine in Asymptomatic Subjects* (1990) 71A Bone & Joint Surgery 1178–1184.

11.9 MILD TO MODERATE BACK INJURIES

Over half of all musculo-skeletal disability is caused by back pain from injury or disease. Back pain is the most frequent chronic disabling condition in patients under 45 years old. At some time in their lives, 60 per cent of the population will experience disabling back pain. In nearly all cases it is the low back, the lumbar spine, that is affected.

In litigation, the usual culprits are manual handling at work, bad posture at a keyboard, road traffic accidents, direct impact, and indirect impact from a jarring fall. Most major injuries to the public, and over 30 per cent of major injuries to workers, are the result of simply falling over. For example, slipping or tripping and landing on one's bottom. Rugby players may doubt that a slip or trip resulting in a fall on the spot can cause a significant injury, but anybody handling employer's liability claims in the multi-track will encounter claimants who successfully blame a mere slip or trip for early medical retirement. Chronic back pain may be best considered as a separate syndrome, requiring different treatment to acute back pain (see **section 11.10**).

Most low back pain is caused by minor strains, requiring two to five days' rest. The other main possibilities are prolapsed intervertebral disc (the slipped disc); degenerative change in the spine; spondylolisthesis, a congenital condition that may never cause symptoms unless provoked by an accident; facet joint injury; disease (rheumatoid arthritis, ankylosing spondylitis, various forms of cancer); and pregnancy. It is easy to suffer from a back condition without knowing it. If somebody who has never had a bad back does some heavy lifting at work and then his back is never right again, he is likely to feel that the lifting was to blame. He may be right, but his claim depends completely on the medical evidence, which depends to a surprising extent on guesswork.

Pain cannot be measured, there may be no objective signs of a low back injury, and the reasons for back pain are not well understood. In up to 80 per cent of low back injuries no definite diagnosis is made, because symptoms, medical imaging and pathological findings do not correspond. (Wall, *Causes of Intractable Pain* (1986) 12, 969–974). Medical imaging of people with no back trouble shows in almost 40 per cent of cases that they have a prolapsed intervertebral disc so large that a surgeon would want to operate if they had pain. On the other hand, many people who are disabled by back pain have normal scans (Deyo, *Magnetic Resonance Imaging of the lumbar spine* (1994) New England Journal of Medicine 331: 115–116, and Jensen *et al*, *Magnetic Resonance Imaging of the lumbar spine in people without back pain* (1994) N Eng J Med 331: 69–73).

Swedish research found objective evidence, such as muscle spasm or something visible on imaging, in only half of people absent from work with back pain (Valfors, *Acute, sub-acute and chronic low back pain: Clinical symptoms, absenteeism and working environment* (1985) Scand J Rehabil Med Suppl 11, 1–98).

Readers will find a brief description of the vertebrae, nerve root involvement (radicular pain), dermatomal distribution and facet joint injury in **Section 11.8**. Flexion of the spine means bending forwards, and extension means bending over backwards. In the low back, the flexible lumbar spine is attached to the inflexible sacrum or tailbone. This concentrates stresses at the lumbo-sacral joint (L5/S1). Low back problems tend to be at L5/S1 or at the L4/L5 joint just above it. A prolapsed intervertebral disc, degenerative change or spondylolisthesis may irritate or compress the roots of the nerves that exit the spine in this area, causing nerve root pain.

Nerve root involvement will cause pain at the root itself, and radicular pain. In the low back the latter nearly always takes the form of sciatica, which is felt in the buttocks and down the back of the legs, often going below the knee. There may be numbness and occasionally weakness in the same distribution. Where the nerve root is compressed or irritated, spinal flexion provokes severe, sharp sciatic pain, and so do straight leg raising

(SLR), coughing, sneezing and laughing. Reaching down in the morning to put on shoes and socks is so painful that the victim has to ask somebody else to help. Nerve root involvement at L5/S1 may impair the patient's ability to flex his knee or ankle, or to raise his big toe. Nerve root involvement in the low back may suppress the ankle jerk reflex, and the patellar or knee jerk reflex. There may be pins and needles along the outer edge of the foot.

There follows a description of typical acute and chronic symptoms of the major low back problems. As with whiplash, where symptoms become chronic, and particularly when they persist year after year, there will be a question how far they are a direct result of the accident itself, and how far they are caused by a supervening Chronic Pain Syndrome. This distinction can be important, particularly when deciding what medical expert(s) to instruct (see **section 11.10**).

Prolapsed intervertebral disc

Between each of the vertebrae is a disc of soft tissue, with a leathery outer casing or annulus that contains a nucleus of jelly. The classic prolapsed invertebral disc (PID) occurs when the annulus is ruptured and some of the jelly escapes to impinge on nerves in the spine. The escaped (sequestered) jelly absorbs liquid and expands for 24 hours, causing increasing pain as the nerves are compressed more and more.

It takes a very violent incident to rupture a healthy disc, and the adjoining bones may break first. However, as we get older, the annulus degenerates and becomes more likely to rupture. A prolapsed disc is common, and especially in older people it may not cause pain. In Britain up to 10 per cent of working men, mainly between 20 and 45, have pain from disc abnormalities. An accident can cause a degenerate disc to rupture, but if the disc is in very poor condition it may rupture when one gets out of bed, or reaches into the fridge for a pint of milk, or even when one sneezes. Only 12 per cent of all sufferers blame their PID on an accident.

One school of thought amongst orthopaedic surgeons is that an accident that causes a significant strain to the spine can cause a disc prolapse that would, probably, never otherwise have occurred. Some of these surgeons also take the view that an excessive loading or flexion of the spine can create a fissure in the wall of the disc which produces little trouble at the time but can open up to permit a major disc prolapse even six months later, with no significant symptoms before.

Many other surgeons consider that a prolapse cannot be caused by violence unless the disc is so degenerate that it would have given way at any moment. If the court accepts that view, and that something else would very soon have caused the disc to prolapse, a PID claim is worth very little.

Many surgeons take the view that if a prolapse is triggered by a trauma it will happen there and then, followed by severe symptoms within 48 hours at most. Another school of thought holds that trauma may cause a fissure in the annulus, leading to disc prolapse a month or even three months later. For a concise discussion, see *Miller* v. *Lothian Primary Care NHS Trust* [2004] ScotCS 159. In *Miller* the dispute was resolved in favour of the 48 hours school of thought, but it might have gone the other way had the pursuer's team instructed a more senior orthopaedic expert.

CPR PD 35.2.2 says 'where there is a range of opinion on matters to be dealt with in the report [an expert witness should] summarise the range of opinion and give reasons for his own opinion'. Few experts interpret this as meaning they should volunteer that another school of thought exists, although they may admit it exists if presented with a report from an expert who belongs to the other school.

The symptoms of prolapsed intervertebral disc are as follows, starting with the acute phase.

PID Acute 1

When a disc prolapses, it will produce the characteristic initial symptoms of immediate moderate pain from the damaged disc itself. This is nearly always at L5/S1 or L4/L5, and is likely to be enough to make the patient stop what he was doing and have a rest for a while.

PID Acute 2

The pain increases over 24 hours with low backache and pain extending into the outer side of one buttock. It may become severe, and remain severe and constant for a week or two, with some relief when the patient lies down. Pain and stiffness from the disc itself, rather than nerve root pain, restricts straight leg raising (SLR) perhaps to as little as 20 degrees. If SLR of one leg causes pain in the other leg, this strongly suggests a PID.

PID Acute 3

A day or two after the injury, nerve root pain starts to radiate down the leg in the dermatomal distribution, perhaps going beyond the knee.

PID Acute 4

The first few weeks are usually the worst, and the victim may find that he needs help to get out of bed, and has to crawl when he needs to go the lavatory. If his bedroom is upstairs, it will often be necessary to bring his bed downstairs for the first five or six weeks. The symptoms are often at their worst for the first five or six weeks after the trauma, and during the first two or three weeks in particular the patient may have to stay in bed because of the pain. The pain during this period is so bad that the patient has difficulty getting to sleep and wakes up several times every night.

The severity and duration of the pain depends on type and location of the prolapse, and also on the patient, his age, and his job. Generally, if a prolapsed disc keeps the patient off work, it will do so for two to six months. The pain will eventually clear up on its own, but surgeons are often keen to offer a surgical solution. The great bulk of all back surgery is for PID, in the form of a microdiscectomy to remove sequestered material. Although not without risk, it stops sciatica in 90 per cent of cases and generally also reduces the back pain. Chronic symptoms are as follows.

PID Chronic 1

There is tenderness if the area around the lumbo-sacral joint is pressed with a finger or tapped with the fist.

PID Chronic 2

There is intermittent severe pain like a toothache, usually at L5/S1 or L4/L5 but spreading into the outer half of one buttock. The patient finds that he cannot sit for more than 20 minutes or so without standing up for a while. Walking uphill is painful. Some dull back ache most of the time, but the patient will have some pain free times. Severe pain when he moves suddenly, twists his back, or takes an awkward step that jars his back. There will be times when he has no pain for two to three days, and other periods when he has severe pain for at least part of every day. Leaning over to one side (lateral flexion) is not limited except at extremes where it pulls on tender areas at the injury site.

PID Chronic 3

Nerve root pain radiates from the buttock down the back of one leg, often below the knee and sometimes as far as the foot. It is frequently felt as a sharp pain, shooting down the leg intermittently like an electric shock. It limits SLR to 40 degrees or so. Coughing and sneezing make it worse. There may be weakness of the muscle that raises the big toe.

PID Chronic 4

In the morning, stiffness in the low back may mean that it takes the patient some time to progress gradually from lying in bed to standing up.

PID Chronic 5

There may be loss of the normal lumbar lordosis so that when the patient stands and is viewed from the side, instead of there being a normal concave curve in the low back, it appears flat.

Degenerative change in the spine

Most people aged 35 and over, and many athletic people in their 20s, have some degenerative change in the low back. This may irritate or compress a nerve root. A great many of these people will have no symptoms, or nothing that they would mention to a doctor, until they have an accident. As in the cervical spine, there is a very poor correlation between degenerative change seen on medical imaging and pain reported by the patient. If there is nerve root involvement, it is generally at L5/S1, and symptoms start when the patient has a road accident or does some awkward heavy lifting. Typical signs and symptoms are as follows.

Acute 1

Back pain occurs around the lumbo-sacral joint, often lasting for many months. The patient cannot sit or stand for more than 20 minutes or so without changing position. There are probably periods when he has no pain for two to three days, and other periods when he has severe pain for part of every day. The pain is likely to affect the patient at night when he is trying to sleep, so he takes painkillers or sleeping tablets half an hour before going to bed. Twisting the spine (so that the hips stay still, but the shoulders rotate) is painful. Leaning over to one side (lateral flexion) is not limited except at extremes where it pulls on tender areas at the injury site.

Acute 2

Nerve root pain occurs as with PID. SLR provokes pain in the buttocks and/or legs. Extension of the spine is also painful. The pain is worse on lifting and carrying loads, and is made worse by coughing and sneezing.

Acute 3

There is tenderness if the area around the lumbo-sacral joint is pressed with a finger or tapped with the fist.

Chronic 1

The acute signs and symptoms continue.

Chronic 2

There may be loss of the normal lumbar lordosis.

Spondylolisthesis

Ten per cent of the population have spondylolisthesis, and amongst those who play contact sports the figure can be as high as 50 per cent. It occurs where there is a defect in the bones of the spine so that one of the vertebrae in the low back is able to slip forwards or backwards. As with the other conditions just mentioned, the patient may not have noticed any problem until an accident caused immediate pain. Signs and symptoms are as follows.

Acute 1

There is pain at L5/S1, perhaps radiating around the pelvis, made worse by activity and relieved by resting.

Acute 2

There is nerve root pain as described above, made worse by standing and stooping, and relieved by lying down. There are periods when the patient has no pain for two to three days, and other periods when he has severe pain for part of every day.

Chronic 1

Acute signs and symptoms continue.

Chronic 2

There may be loss of the normal lumbar lordosis.

Low back strain

These injuries are rather like whiplash. Generally the patient recovers in full in one to six months. Where a road traffic accident causes disability that lasts over six months, back strain is the third most common reason after fractures and whiplash (Galasko *et al*, *Long term disability following road traffic accidents* (1986) Transport & Road Research Laboratory, Research Report 59, Department of Transport).

A back strain may also be caused by manual handling or a fall. It may affect intervertebral discs, facet joint capsules, muscles and ligaments. Unlike the conditions described above, it does not cause nerve root pain.

The medical report may speak of motion segments, each of which consists of soft tissues (the disc, muscles, ligaments and capsules) with a vertebra above and below. Flexing or extending any one motion segment will cause pain within it, and perhaps also referred pain elsewhere.

A ligamentous strain generally gets better on its own in a few weeks, but a violent accident may cause chronic problems by tearing the supraspinous and interspinous ligaments, the ligamentum flavum, or the inter-transverse ligaments; or injuring the facet joint capsules.

It is fairly common to come across a case where a claimant has had a succession of injuries, each making a low back strain worse before it has had time to recover. The court will apportion the blame between multiple tort-feasors as in the whiplash case *Pearce* v. *Lindfield* [2003] EWCA Civ 647. Signs and symptoms are as follows.

Acute 1

The injury site itself is immediately tender, and discomfort increases over a few minutes or hours to severe local pain. In one third of cases the patient experiences this severe pain immediately. If injured while lifting a heavy load, he may report that he had such pain in the affected area that he felt faint or dizzy and had to sit down for a bit, and was unable to finish his working day so he went home. A sympathetic doctor would accept that a violent car accident caused a low back strain if the patient first reported back pain at any time in the first two weeks, especially if the accident caused other injuries that might initially have masked the back pain. For the first three or four days the patient may be unable to stand even briefly, and may for example have to crawl along the floor in order to get to the lavatory. The pain decreases daily, but more slowly after the first three or four days. After the first week or two, the patient will probably have no pain while resting, although his back may be more tender when relaxed. Pain restricts all movements of the back. The patient usually experiences worse pain when he is standing upright unless he can shift position frequently.

Acute 2

There may be occasions of very severe pain when muscles in the back, perhaps over an area as large as a fist, go into spasm. This can be very frightening for the patient, who feels unable to do anything other than lie down on his back with his lower legs propped up on cushions. This may occur every six or eight weeks, causing him to take strong painkillers and lie in bed for several days.

Acute 3

A strain affecting the facet joints may produce a diffuse ache of referred pain deep in the buttocks and the muscles at the back of the thighs. It is worse after exercise. Where a patient reports pain radiating down the leg, he is very likely to develop chronic back pain. (Helsing *et al, A Prospective Study of Patients with Acute Back and Neck Pain in Sweden* (1994) Phys Ther 74(2), 116–124).

Chronic 1

There is aching at the injury site nearly all the time, particularly first thing in the morning, so that it takes him 15 minutes or so to get going in the morning. Pain on standing still for more than 10–20 minutes, or walking for more than 15–30 minutes. If the patient has to do too much bending, lifting or walking, his back pain will get worse as the day goes by, becoming a severe aching pain.

Chronic 2

Stiffness and pain occur on sitting for longer than 20 minutes, especially at the wheel of a car. This is eased by walking about. Often, pain if the patient lies on his back on a firm mattress, so he may place a folded quilt on top of the mattress and lie on that.

Chronic 3

Spinal movements are restricted by pain. Forward bending is often restricted. Twisting the spine and leaning over to one side (lateral flexion of the spine) are limited at extremes where these movements start to pull on tender areas at the injury site.

Chronic 4

There is referred pain extending into one or both buttocks, where it may feel like a toothache, and into the back of the thighs, with increased pain on walking uphill, bending backwards or straightening up after bending forwards. Typically the patient will say that if he does too much, say by carrying too much shopping, he will pay for it with increased pain immediately afterwards and also the next day.

Chronic 5

The patient suffers from depression.

As with whiplash, if these symptoms continue for three years, they may well be permanent. The treatment for low back strain is the same as for whiplash. Again, the best therapist may be a chiropractor (Meade, Dyer, Townsend & Frank's *Low Back Pain of Mechanical Origin: Randomised Comparison of Chiropractic and Hospital Outpatient Treatment* (1990) Br Med J 300:1431–1437).

Facet joint injury

As with whiplash, many doctors consider that where there is no distinct injury but the patient complains of long-term pain, he may have a facet joint injury, consisting of soft tissue injuries and possibly small bony injuries of the vertebral facet joints. These cannot be seen on medical imaging, and not all doctors accept facet joint syndrome as a possible diagnosis. The following suggest that a patient has facet joint syndrome:

- Tenderness when pressing or tapping the area over the facet joints, although if these are deeply buried in muscle or fat it is hard to tell.
- Muscle spasm in the area of the injured joint.
- Pain that is more or less continuous and radiates into the buttock and/or leg, although not strictly in the dermatomal distribution. The pain is worse on spinal extension, especially if the patient is asked to twist his back at the same time; when the patient straightens his spine after stooping forward; and when walking uphill.

As in whiplash, an orthopaedic department or pain clinic may try steroid and anaesthetic injections into the facet joints of the affected part of the spine. This procedure is unpleasant and has some risks, but may provide pain relief for several weeks or months. As with injections into the cervical facet joints, the benefits are doubted by many (see Carette *et al*, *A Controlled Trial of Corticosteroid Injection into Facet Joints for Chronic Low Back Pain* (1991) N Engl J Med 325(14) at 1002–1007). If the injections work, the patient may be offered a more long-lasting but riskier solution, in the form of radio frequency lesion.

Tactics

In a case of PID, the defendant probably knows which orthopaedic surgeons subscribe to his preferred school of thought, and he may ask the claimant to instruct one of them jointly. The claimant should not agree to instruct a joint medical expert in a low back claim. If there is a jointly-instructed expert, the case will stand or fall depending on who is chosen. If there are two orthopaedic surgeons with opposing views, the judge can decide which evidence he prefers. If the claimant approaches the wrong expert the first time he can try again with another one, but if he obtained the report jointly with the defendant he will find this difficult.

A useful question for the defendant to ask the medical expert in any back injury claim is 'Given the nature of the force that caused the injury, and the demands of the claimant's everyday life, how long would it have been before the same force was applied anyway?' An awkward step while shopping can trigger back symptoms in a vulnerable person. Even if the claimant was not particularly vulnerable, he may have been a keen rugby player or rucksack-carrying member of the Territorial Army who encountered forces like those in the accident every weekend. The defendant may be able to treat it as a mere acceleration case, causing injury and loss for a year or five, rather than for life.

If the back problems were not inevitable, the defendant may be entitled to a discount because there was a substantial chance that they would have occurred, as in *Williams* v. *Green* [2001] EWCA Civ 1888. If the claimant's medical history included a pre-accident bout of sciatica, there is a good chance that he would have had more whether or not the accident had occurred. If he had had two such bouts, there was an even chance that he would have another, and the more he has the more likely it becomes. Back pain is also quite likely in and for six months after pregnancy. Most pregnancies cause some back pain, and some cause sciatica.

Most orthopaedic surgeons are reluctant to carry out tests designed to trap malingering claimants, or to report the outcome of such tests except in the most oblique way. Both claimant and defendant lawyers need to know about the Waddell tests, and distraction testing in particular. Professor Gordon Waddell FRCS has described a range of tests that may, by causing the patient to report pain when there is no reason for it, reveal 'illness behaviour'. Illness behaviour does not necessarily mean malingering. Indeed, the literature cited below indicates that some illness behaviour is quite normal when a patient has suffered pain and disability for an extended period. However, if the patient has more than one or two Waddell signs, this suggests either a psychiatric element or outright malingering. Some of the signs are more apt than others to show malingering.

Tests include:

- Tenderness to light touch. In the absence of a Complex Regional Pain Syndrome, there is no reason for a back pain sufferer to feel discomfort if the surgeon touches his skin lightly, especially over extensive areas of the back. It should not cause pain if the surgeon lightly pinches up a cigar-sized roll of the patient's skin.
- Inappropriate distribution of pain and numbness, that is, not in the dermatomal distribution or facet joint distribution. The classic inappropriate sign is for the patient to complain that the whole limb is painful or numb. This is often known as glove or stocking distribution.

- Pain in the lower back when the patient stands and the surgeon presses down on his head. May be referred to in a medical report as axial loading or loading of the vertex. Axial loading may provoke pain if there is nerve root involvement in the neck, but should not do so if the problem is in the low back.
- Pain in the lower back on simulated rotation. The patient stands, and keeps his feet in one place while the surgeon holds his hips and rotates them. Although the body is turned to face in a different direction, the spine is not being twisted at all, so there is no reason for the patient to feel back pain.
- Straight leg raising (SLR or sciatic stretch test). The surgeon tests how far the patient can lift his leg while lying prone on a couch. He should be able to lift it the same amount when sitting or standing. This may be known as the flip test, because if the patient is sitting, when it reaches a point where it provokes nerve root pain he will flip over backwards. Variants include the sciatic stretch test, Bragaard test, bowstring test, search for Lasegue's sign, and femoral stretch test.
- Inappropriate weakness test, for example when the patient says he cannot press his big toe downwards.
- Theatrical presentation. The patient gives an exaggerated account of the accident and his suffering since; makes slow, hesitant or laboured movements while dressing and undressing for examination or climbing onto the examination couch; cries out loudly with pain during the examination; puffs and groans as if asking for sympathy; looks as if he might fall over at any moment, and seems always on the point of grasping nearby furniture to support himself. Such presentation might also include walking with an ostentatious limp; displaying a bottle of painkillers, anaesthetic patch, a lumbar corset or a TENS machine; or pausing to get his breath back every 50 yards down the street.
- Inappropriate responses when completing a questionnaire, such as the McGill University Pain Questionnaire. For example, if the patient says he never gets any respite from back pain.

For more information see Waddell, McCulloch, Kummel & Venner, *Non-organic physical signs in low back pain* (1980) 5 Spine 117–125 and *Chronic Low Back Pain, Psychologic Distress and Illness Behaviour* (1980) 9 Spine 209–213; Waddell, Pilowsky and Bond, *Clinical Assessment and Interpretation of Abnormal Illness Behaviour in Low Back Pain* (1989) Pain 39:41–53; Waddell, Somerville, Henderson and Newton, *Objective Clinical Evaluation of Physical Impairment in Chronic Low Back Pain* (1992) 17 Spine 617–628; and Greenough, *Recovery from low back pain. 1–5 year follow-ups of 287 injury-related cases* (1993) 254 Acta Orthop Scan Suppl 1–34.

11.10 CHRONIC PAIN SYNDROME

If the claimant develops Chronic Pain Syndrome as a result of injuries caused by the defendant, this is not so remote from the defendant's negligence that he can resist paying compensation for it. In *Lucy* v. *Mariehamns* [1971] 2 Lloyds Rep 314 a night watchman was struck on the face and body by a large quantity of warm hydraulic oil under pressure. This caused his eyes to be itchy for a while. The symptoms from the accident would have lasted a week with a normal person. Because the claimant had a mental quirk, he suffered genuine pain for years, and was entitled to damages for all the suffering caused by the accident. In the past, the courts used the term anxiety neurosis, but today they use the medical terms described below.

Disability is generally the result of pain rather than fused joints or missing limbs. Medical science cannot say to what extent there is a physical cause for pain. It is defined by the International Association for the Study of Pain as 'an unpleasant sensory and emotional experience associated with actual or potential tissue damage or described in terms of tissue damage'. The emotional component means that people experience pain in different ways, just as people experience a relationship or a painting in different ways. It is not possible to measure an emotion.

The amount of pain depends not only on the strength of the sensory element, but also on the importance attributed to it. The extent of disability depends how much the sufferer fears pain. Humans disregard pain to some extent if exalted by fighting, sport or sex, but the human imagination is prone to dwell on injuries. An accident victim often suffers unnecessary disability through fear that activity will worsen the injury, or at least will cause pain. Accident victims who behave in a very self-protective manner are, ironically, much less likely to get better.

In dealing with a physical injury, orthopaedic surgeons try to identify and cure the physical problem, or at least make it cause less pain. If the patient then develops Chronic Pain Syndrome, effective treatment becomes a matter not of propping him up with a succession of drugs and therapies and the hope that a cure will be found, but of helping him to come to terms with the pain so that he can live an independent and fulfilling existence. Chronic Pain Syndrome is not an injury that has failed to recover, but an illness in its own right, with its own symptoms and its own medical specialists. See Grady & Severn's *Key Topics In Chronic Pain*, Bios Scientific Publishing.

In practice, the limited funds of an NHS hospital may mean the patient does just get drugs and anaesthetic injections. Particularly if the claimant accepts that there is a psychiatric element to his pain, private therapies aimed at changing his outlook may be more effective. Private rehabilitation can be funded by an interim payment.

Chronic Pain Syndrome is generally a mixture of physical and psychiatric problems.

To start with the psychiatric component, the courts award compensation for recognised psychiatric disorders (see **section 11.11**). Several are relevant to chronic pain. The American Psychiatric Association *Diagnostic and Statistical Manual* (DSM-IV) defines Pain Disorder. This causes 'significant distress or impairment in social, occupational or other important areas of functioning. Psychological factors are judged to play a significant role in the onset, severity, exacerbation or maintenance of the pain. The pain is not intentionally produced or feigned'. A Pain Disorder sufferer may put a lot of time and effort into seeking a cure. The pain may lead to inactivity, social isolation and depression. It is frequently associated with sleep disturbance, mainly in the form of delayed sleep onset, frequent awakenings, sleep that does not refresh, and decreased sleep time. It may be the result of anxiety and depression. Many accidents cause anxiety, especially about the apparent inability of the doctors to achieve a cure. The money worries resulting from an accident can cause or exacerbate anxiety. DSM-IV also defines Conversion Disorder, which involves deficits affecting voluntary motor or sensory function that suggest a neurological or other medical cause but cannot be explained by a medical condition.

The World Health Organisation *International Classification of Mental & Behavioural Disorders* (ICD-10) speaks instead of Persistent Somatoform Pain Disorder which causes persistent distressing severe pain which cannot be fully explained by a physical disorder or physiological process; and Somatization Disorder.

Depression causes pain. About half of those receiving treatment for depression report pain in the face, head or back, which has no apparent cause and ceases as the depression fades. If an individual has pain, he will experience it more severely if he becomes depressed. Nervous or anxious individuals, and those who were already under stress from family, work or money are particularly likely to suffer chronic pain.

Pain causes depression. It seems that chronic pain and depression are caused to some extent by the same mechanisms. Antidepressant medication helps reduce both. Where whiplash injury produces long-term disability, there is a good chance that the victim already has signs of anxiety, insomnia, lack of confidence and depression as early as three months after the accident. (Gargan, Bannister *et al*, *The Behavioural Response to Whiplash Injury* (1997) J Bone & Joint Surgery 79–B 523).

Where a patient has back pain for more than three months, he is likely to complain of some problems that are inconsistent with the injury suffered. See **section 11.9** for a discussion of the Waddell signs in the context of back pain. Given that there is usually a psychiatric component, it is perhaps no surprise that Chronic Pain Syndrome sufferers frequently report pain, numbness, etc., that fit no logical pattern. This is a common part of illness behaviour, a person's way of communicating, consciously or unconsciously, a perception that his health is disturbed. The more sympathy it attracts, the more blatant it will become. A great many genuine claimants report some problems that have no apparent medical basis, and both doctors and experienced judges expect this. However, too much inconsistency is often a sign of deliberate exaggeration.

Although there will generally be a psychiatric element, some patients with chronic pain may have an entirely physical problem, for example, a facet joint injury as discussed in the context of whiplash and low back injuries. Other theories held by at least a sizeable minority of medical opinion state that chronic pain can be caused by physical changes that are difficult or impossible to demonstrate. Neuronal sensitisation involves anatomical changes in the central and peripheral nervous system, caused by continuous stimulation of a pain fibre. Symptoms of tenderness at points remote from the back pain may indicate that the patient has a myofascial pain syndrome characterised by nodes of abnormal tissue which act as trigger points for pain. Other possible physical causes might be obstruction of veins; fibrosis in and around nerves; atrophy of neurons within nerve roots; damage to pain receptors; or chemical changes. Some suggest that unexpected symptoms can occur when nerve fibres that normally carry other sensations (touch, position sense, etc.) become rewired to pain centres so that movement and light touch cause pain.

How does all this affect the conduct of a compensation claim? Nearly all claims start with a report from an orthopaedic surgeon. The first warning of Chronic Pain Syndrome is likely to be a comment in the report that the claimant has functional overlay. This covers everything from pure suffering to outright malingering. A claimant lawyer has to be cautious about asking an orthopaedic consultant to clarify whether he feels the claimant is genuinely suffering. An unsympathetic answer may damage the claim a good deal. It may be best to postpone clarification until a different expert has confirmed that the claimant has Chronic Pain Syndrome. When acting for the claimant, naturally one would rather go to trial relying on evidence that there is a physical cause for the client's disability, so the first response if one's own medical expert says there is functional overlay is to consider approaching a more sympathetic orthopaedic surgeon without disclosing what the first one said. This may be possible (see **section 20.15**).

If it is the defendant's expert who says there is no physical reason for all the pain, the claimant must consider whether the report may be attacked. Pain cannot be measured except by asking the patient how much it hurts, so what does this adverse opinion mean? Perhaps the claimant gave some inconsistent response to medical examination. If the expert's view is based on the results of distraction testing, that is pretty convincing (see **section 11.9**). However, a report stating that there is nothing much wrong with the claimant often means no more than that the expert did not like him or trust him. Personal impressions are very important in orthopaedic reporting, hence the frequency with which claimants are described in reports as 'this pleasant man'. Like any interview, a medical examination can go sour if the subject turns up late and unwashed, talks too much or too little, avoids eye contact, thinks too long before answering simple questions, 'doesn't understand' what the expert is asking, gives vague or unhelpful answers, or is caught in what might be a mocking smile.

Every experienced personal injury lawyer has encountered something like the very sound orthopaedic expert who took against an unwashed claimant to the extent that he simply dismissed repeated complaints of chronic severe rib pain. Then when a different expert finally carried out a simple X-ray, it turned out that the ends of a broken rib had failed to unite.

Initially the claimant should ask his own expert to help frame a few questions to put to the hostile expert, for example whether he concedes that it is normal for a person with chronic pain to give some inconsistent responses to medical examination, and whether experts who subscribe to other schools of thought about pain might well consider the claimant to be genuine. CPR PD 35.2.2 says 'where there is a range of opinion on matters to be dealt with in the report [an expert witness should] summarise the range of opinion and give reasons for his own opinion'. Thereafter, one must see what can be achieved in without prejudice discussions between the experts, or by cross-examining the hostile expert at trial as to his impression of the claimant.

If the claimant needs to approach the claim on the basis that he had a physical injury with supervening Chronic Pain Syndrome, he should obtain medical evidence about the latter as early as possible. The later he leaves it, particularly if he has to issue proceedings before he has it, the more risk that the court will refuse to admit this evidence (*Cassie* v. *Ministry of Defence* [2002] EWCA Civ 838). It is unlikely that an orthopaedic surgeon can deal with chronic pain issues.

The best experts to give medical evidence for the claimant with Chronic Pain Syndrome are usually a consultant anaesthetist in charge of a pain clinic and a psychiatrist or psychologist to comment on concurrent depression and overlay. Pain clinics cannot afford to have every patient come back every few months for temporary pain relief. They want patients to learn to live with the pain, feel they are coping, and be useful members of their families and of society. A consultant anaesthetist may recommend that the claimant and partner attend for cognitive behavioural therapy or go to Back School in order to learn to relax, avoid negative thoughts, set goals for themselves, and pace themselves to achieve those goals. This sort of rehabilitation is completely effective in 20 per cent of cases of low back pain.

A pain clinic consultant wants to encourage his patients to be independent, and will not be keen to produce a report stating that the claimant is already functioning as well as he is ever likely to. No consultant anaesthetist, whether or not actually treating the claimant, is likely to recommend that he be given the opportunity to become dependent on special care, equipment or accommodation. However, a claimant with chronic pain may be just as disabled as one with a missing arm or a spinal lesion. If the claimant will apparently need care, equipment or accommodation, the claimant's lawyer may have them costed by a different expert.

From the defendant's point of view, although he has to take his victim as he finds him, he can reduce the compensation if he can show that the claimant would have had pain and disability anyway. The claimant may have had symptoms of Pain Disorder for years before the accident. Look for medical record entries showing many previous visits to the doctor with different aches and pains for which no physical basis was ever found, and correspondingly large amounts of sick leave from school and work. Put this evidence to the medical expert(s). They may conclude that the accident produced only a temporary exacerbation of an existing condition; or accelerated the onset of a problem that would otherwise have occurred some years later.

11.11 PSYCHIATRIC INJURIES

A court may feel more sympathetic to an accident victim who suffered more because of greater personal sensitivity, and may therefore go towards the higher end of the damages bracket when valuing that person's pain and suffering. Except in this way, the courts do not award extra damages for normal human reactions such as distress, disgust, fear, grief or horror. Normal emotion in the face of a very unpleasant experience is not compensatable.

However, further damages may be awarded if the accident causes a recognisable psychiatric disorder (*Hinz* v. *Berry* [1970] 2 QB 40). In practice this usually means one of the disorders described in ICD-10 (World Health Organisation *International Classification of Mental & Behavioural Disorders*) or DSM-IV (American Psychiatric Association *Diagnostic and Statistical Manual*). Recognisable psychiatric disorders include the four syndromes previously mentioned, see **section 11.10**. They also include phobias; depression amounting to a major depressive episode, Post Traumatic Stress Disorder (PTSD), Adjustment Disorder, and Acute Stress Disorder (ASD).

Adjustment Disorder involves sleep disturbance, anxiety and significant emotional difficulties such as irritability. It usually settles within six months but may become chronic, especially where the victim is making a personal injury claim. Acute Stress Disorder may be caused by a threat to a person's life or physical integrity. ASD symptoms last up to four weeks and consist of intrusive, vivid flashbacks to the incident, hyper arousal such as being over-alert and easily startled, and a tendency to avoid circumstances that may prompt intrusive memories. Pathological Bereavement and Complex Post Traumatic Stress Disorder, neither of which can be found in ICD-10 or DSM-IV, are also recognised in medico-legal work.

There is no magic to a diagnosis of Post Traumatic Stress Disorder. The symptoms of PTSD consist, more or less, of ASD symptoms persisting for longer than four weeks. Again, then, intrusion, avoidance and hypervigilance. A psychiatric condition is not formally PTSD unless it substantially satisfies a long list of criteria in the current version of ICD or DSM. For example, currently the claimant must have been exposed to an extreme traumatic event that involved actual or potential injury or death for himself or others. Some might consider an attack by a couple of Rottweilers to be an extreme traumatic event capable of causing PTSD, but not an attack by a poodle, even if the victims suffered identical physical and psychiatric injuries. A condition may narrowly fail to satisfy the PTSD criteria but nonetheless be extremely distressing and hard to treat. DSM gives clear guidance that an Adjustment Disorder should be diagnosed in such circumstances.

If an accident causes physical injury and also a few bad dreams and a few weeks of feeling low, anxious and unable to concentrate, this may just satisfy the definition of ASD. If so, the court might award £250 or £500 more compensation. If the court feels the psychiatric symptoms fall short of being a recognisable psychiatric disorder, it might decide to move closer to the top of the bracket when assessing damages for the physical injury, perhaps to the extent of £250 or £500. It would be disproportionately expensive to obtain a specialist medical report. The claimant can say everything relevant in his witness statement. Some law firms screen clients for psychiatric disorders by getting them to fill in the same sort of self-assessment questionnaire used for this purpose by psychiatrists.

Road accidents very often produce significant travel anxiety. Typical symptoms are gripping the steering wheel so hard that the knuckles go white, keeping the entire body tense throughout a trip, being very aware of other vehicles and as a passenger, 'braking' with the foot on an imaginary brake pedal, grabbing the dashboard if taken by surprise, constantly telling the driver to slow down or bringing his attention to possible hazards. The sufferer probably avoids car travel as much as possible, so it can be quite disabling. Treatment in the form of Cognitive Behavioural therapy or EMDR may be available on the NHS but coverage across the UK is patchy. There are frequently long delays and treatment is regularly disrupted by movement or sickness in staff. Private treatment is expensive, but usually effective if not delayed for too many years. It may be offered by the defendant at no cost to the claimant, or funded by an interim payment. These therapies should be backed up by remedial driving lessons given by a driving instructor with relevant experience. If there is a local driver training facility at which the claimant can try getting back behind the wheel without being exposed to traffic, this may be very helpful. For example, there is Devon County Council's facility at Westpoint, Exeter, which consists of a few acres of tarmac laid out like a typical road system.

It would be worth obtaining a specialist medical report if the claimant has moderate psychiatric injury as defined by the JSB Guidelines. This means the claimant has problems with:

- ability to cope with life and work;
- relationships with family, friends and those with whom he comes into contact;
- the extent to which treatment would be successful;
- future vulnerability;

but with marked improvement by the time of trial, and a good prognosis. Subject to inflation, the Guidelines value this at £3,000 to £9,500.

When obtaining a medical report, one will instruct either a clinical psychologist or a consultant psychiatrist. Psychiatrists have a medical qualification that entitles them to prescribe medication, and are perhaps more likely to know the rules governing expert witnesses. Psychologists generally charge less. If there is a conflict of expert evidence, one can expect a psychologist to be as authoritative as a psychiatrist of equal experience. The question is not so much 'does this case need a psychologist or a psychiatrist', but 'of my favourite psychologists/psychiatrists, who is the best person to deal with this claimant?'.

In law, a claimant who suffers psychiatric injury because of the defendant's negligence is generally barred from recovering compensation unless he was a primary victim. He is a primary victim if the defendant caused him both physical and psychiatric injury. The defendant has to take his victim as he finds him, and the claimant is entitled to compensation for all physical and psychiatric injury caused by the accident, even if the latter arose only because the claimant was especially vulnerable (*Brice* v. *Brown* [1984] 1 All ER 997). A psychologically vulnerable claimant may be said to have an eggshell personality.

The claimant is also a primary victim if he was involved in an accident that might foreseeably have caused physical injury but did not. He is entitled to recover compensation for pure psychiatric injury. The question is whether he was within the range of foreseeable physical injury, or danger zone, for example *Page* v. *Smith* [1996] AC 155, in which the claimant had a minor road accident that caused no physical injury but triggered myalgic encephalomyelitis (ME). He was awarded compensation for this injury, which the court considered to be psychiatric. He was not required to prove that it was reasonably foreseeable that a person of reasonable fortitude would have suffered pure psychiatric injury in the circumstances of this accident.

The definition of primary victim includes a person who the defendant, by his negligence, put in fear for his own safety (*Dulieu* v. *White* [1901] 2 KB 669). In such cases the question is whether it was reasonably foreseeable to a person in the defendant's position that his breach of duty might put a person of normal fortitude in such fear of immediate personal injury to himself as to suffer shock-induced psychiatric illness. There is no need for the claimant to show that he was actually in danger. However, the court may take a restrictive view by finding, as it did in *Hegarty* v. *EE Caledonia Ltd* [1997] EWCA Civ 934, that the claimant's fear was neither rational nor foreseeable. Mr Hegarty had a close up view of massive explosions that destroyed the Piper Alpha oil rig and its crew. One huge fireball destroyed a rescue vessel and nearly engulfed the ship he was on, but stopped after covering half the 100m that separated the claimant from the rig.

In *Young* v. *Charles Church (Southern) Ltd* [1997] EWCA Civ 1523 the Court of Appeal accepted that a claimant who was in physical danger himself but did not realise it was nonetheless a primary victim.

Rescuers may be primary victims if they go to disasters to provide rescue, comfort or medical treatment and are within the danger zone. Somebody who arrives on the scene when all danger is evidently over is not a primary victim however much horror he sees. Giving trivial or peripheral assistance is not enough to make somebody a rescuer. The courts expect members of the emergency services to be hardened to horrifying sights (*White* v. *Chief Constable of South Yorkshire Police* and *Frost* v. *Chief Constable of South Yorkshire Police* [1998] UKHL 45). The courts will, in truly exceptional circumstances, class a helper who was not in danger as a rescuer (*Chadwick* v. *British Railways Board* [1967] 1 WLR 912), but see *White*.

Those not classed as primary victims may be entitled to recover compensation for psychiatric injury as secondary victims, but in *Alcock* v. *Chief Constable of South Yorkshire Police* [1992] 1 AC 310 the House of Lords restricted this. The claimants in *Alcock* had either lost or feared they had lost family members at the Hillsborough disaster. Some had watched it unfold on TV, but it was not shown in detail. Two were in the stadium at the time, but not where the disaster occurred. One of them gave assistance in the aftermath. This was not enough to make them primary victims. All these claims failed, because the court required secondary victims to show that:

- The accident itself, and not grief at having lost a friend or relative, caused them to suffer a recognisable psychiatric disorder.
- It was reasonably foreseeable that a person of normal fortitude would suffer pure psychiatric injury as a result of their involvement with the accident (*McFarlane* v. *EE Caledonia Ltd* [1994] 2 All ER 1).
- They each had a special relationship with a primary victim. This requires that he had particularly close ties of love and affection with the victim. *Alcock* suggests a rebuttable presumption that a parent/child or husband/wife relationship is close enough. A friend, brother or sister relationship would not usually be close enough, but it is a question of fact in each case. The claimant should be ready to adduce evidence of a loving relationship.
- They were present at the event or its immediate aftermath (the proximity test). This test would be satisfied if the claimant was standing beside a relative who was hit by a speeding car. It would barely be satisfied if the

claimant was called to a hospital to see his spouse and three children who had been brought in with severe injuries, and with one child dead, after being in a horrifying accident that occurred two hours earlier (*McLoughlin* v. *O'Brien* [1983] 1 AC 410). Two hours from the incident is getting close to the end of the immediate aftermath. Three hours may be too long.

- They perceived the events sufficiently directly. This generally means that the claimant saw something horrifying with his own eyes.
- The psychiatric injury was caused by a single horrifying event, something which created 'sudden awareness, violently agitating the mind'. Someone watching his son die in hospital fairly quietly over a 14-day period is not enough (*Sion* v. *Hampstead Health Authority* [1994] 5 Med LR 170). It may be enough if it happens over 36 hours and the child has fits while dying (*Walters* v. *North Glamorgan NHS Trust* [2002] EWCA Civ 1792).

These requirements have attracted much academic criticism. They have no medical basis. Their effect is to deny compensation to many, and to require traumatised victims to give detailed evidence about intensely distressing things. In *Galli-Atkinson* v. *Seghal* [2003] EWCA Civ 697 the claimant's evidence included exactly what view she got of her daughter's tattered corpse. Some consider the secondary victim rules to be incompatible with the European Convention on Human Rights 1950.

In any case of pure psychiatric injury where the claimant may be a secondary victim of negligence, one needs to read the cases cited above carefully and see also *Vernon* v. *Bosley* [1996] EWCA Civ 1217.

The secondary victim rules apply only to accidental injury. If the defendant caused pure psychiatric injury by a deliberate act, the claim would be based on trespass as in *Wilkinson* v. *Downton* [1897] 2 QB 57 (see **section 4.6**).

11.12 COVERT VIDEO SURVEILLANCE

If the defendant has good reason to suspect that the claimant is exaggerating his disability, and the claim is worth a lot of money, he may organise covert surveillance. This generally costs £1,000 per attempt, seldom succeeds, and can do the defendant more harm than good. It is done only where there is very good reason to suspect that the claimant is deliberately exaggerating his disability.

The possibility of surveillance worries or angers many perfectly genuine claimants. Nobody likes the thought of being shadowed, or filmed from a darkened van while out shopping, or pottering in the garden. A claimant may be unable to work, but otherwise able to live an apparently normal existence if he can avoid spending too long in one posture, heavy lifting, or making certain movements.

A video may do a great deal of damage if seen by an inexperienced judge who shares the fairly common expectation that if a person is disabled, there will be obvious signs. In fact, the person who looks fairly ordinary is more likely to be genuine than one who puffs and grimaces, walks with a stick and an obvious limp, and keeps stopping to get his breath back.

It can be damaging if a video shows the claimant doing something his witness statement says he cannot do. The claimant's lawyer must be careful not to phrase the witness statement in too positive a way. If one simply asks a typical claimant whether he can do something he may say 'no', when the full answer is 'not really, but I can do some on a good day if I'm careful'. Anyway I don't want people to see me as a useless burden, always asking for help. If I let myself feel like that I can be very hard to live with. I'd rather get on with it myself and pay a penalty in pain the next day'. Consider section D of the injuries questionnaire on the accompanying CD-ROM.

The claimant's lawyer should not agree to have the case tried in the lower reaches of the county court. The District Judge has an unlimited jurisdiction to assess damages under CPR PD 2B. However, it is seldom appropriate for him to do so in a complex case (*Sandry* v. *Jones* (2000) *The Times* 3 August). If the defendant intends to adduce a video tape at trial to cast doubt on the claimant's medical evidence, it probably means that the case is suitable for the High Court, where the judge is likely to have the necessary time and experience.

From the defendant's point of view, especially if the claimant is one of his employees, it is common to hear rumours that a disabled claimant has been seen carrying bulging shopping bags or going hiking in rough terrain. It is fairly common to receive a report from one's orthopaedic surgeon suggesting that there may be deliberate exaggeration. Many surveillance fees can be wasted on such rumours before deciding that most are not worth pursuing. A more specific rumour that the claimant is running a garden maintenance business might well justify surveillance; as would a comment by the orthopaedic surgeon that the claimant ran up the steps to his consulting rooms, or had paint in his hair and ingrained grease on his hands.

A malingerer generally fakes symptoms to deceive the whole world including his family. It is highly unlikely that anybody claiming to be disabled spends his leisure time dancing or weightlifting. He leads an undemanding life that is generally consistent with what he says about his disability. A video surveillance attempt will last only a day or two. It might take many days before something revealing is filmed. To succeed, a surveillance video must show the claimant doing something clearly inconsistent, that he cannot explain away by saying: 'I was having a good day, that day.'

The following activities are particularly revealing: climbing in and out of a car; looking over the shoulder to reverse a car; looking right and left before crossing the road; carrying something heavy without troubling to get help or split it into several smaller loads; running, especially up stairs; walking over rough terrain; working in the front garden if this involves spending a lot of time bending.

The most frequent time and place for covert surveillance is a day when the claimant has a medical appointment with one of the defendant's medical experts. The defendant knows the claimant is going out that day, where he is going, that he will have to use a car or public transport, and maybe walk some distance on foot. In *Hesketh* v. *Courts plc* (later in this section) the defendant's surveillance operatives were able to scrape acquaintance with the claimant because the defendant organised hotel accommodation for him the night before the appointment.

For a completely successful use of video evidence see *Afzal* v. *Chubb Guarding Services Ltd* [2002] EWHC 822 (QB). For a moderately successful case see *Ford* v. *GKR Construction* [2001] 1 All ER 802. Much more often the defendant's team feels that their video evidence clearly shows the claimant doing something he had clearly said he could not, and even the claimant's medical expert shows a few doubts, but the court feels that the video is entirely compatible with the medical evidence.

Care is needed if surveillance is not to become a disaster for the defendant. Enquiry agents who carry out covert surveillance may be ex-army intelligence or ex-police and can be too helpful. Many forms of surveillance are criminal offences. Defendants cannot legally intercept mail, carry out telephone tapping, or take old correspondence from the claimant's dustbin. They are asking for a defamation claim if they approach the claimant's neighbours to ask if he goes out jogging when he says he has to walk with a stick.

It is legitimate to phone a claimant at different times of day to see whether he is always absent during working hours, and to trail him with a video camera when he goes shopping. It may be legitimate to get a pretty girl to pretend to have a puncture outside the claimant's house to see if the claimant will offer to change the wheel for her. It is not legitimate to enter the claimant's property and film through his windows; tip over his dustbins in order to film him picking up rubbish from his path; get into his home by pretending to carry out door-to-door market research; dress up as a deliveryman and leave a large heavy parcel on the claimant's doorstep; or befriend him, get an invitation to his house, and go fishing with him as in *Hesketh* v. *Courts plc* (QBD 14 May 2001).

A defendant's lawyer is controlled by professional rules that prevent him being a party to anything unprofessional, dishonest or illegal. A solicitor could be censured or struck off if he became too deeply implicated in the activities of an overzealous enquiry agent. Ensure that you explain all the rules to enquiry agents. So that they have little incentive to break them, do not instruct them on a payment by results basis.

Before the Human Rights Act 1998, the court would not exclude a relevant video merely because it was obtained illegally. Under Article 8 of the European Convention on Human Rights 1950 the claimant has a right to privacy and family life. Insurance companies have a right under the First Protocol to protection of their property. The court will balance these rights when deciding whether video evidence is admissible. The trial judge in *Hesketh* refused to admit the surveillance video into evidence because it had been obtained with 'subterfuge and double-dealing . . . a snare or a trap' and therefore would have been incompatible with Convention rights. In *Jones* v. *University of Warwick* [2003] EWCA Civ 151 the Court of Appeal did allow the trial judge to see a video that had been obtained by getting into the claimant's house under false pretences with a hidden video camera, but said that the trial judge might impose costs penalties on the defendant, and that had the circumstances been more outrageous the defence might have been struck out.

Once proceedings have been issued, the defendant must comply with the ordinary rules of disclosure, and a video is a document like any other. If it was obtained too late to comply with the usual timetable, it will usually be in the interests of justice for the court to give the defendant leave to rely on it, as long as it does not amount to trial by ambush (*Rall* v. *Hume* [2001] EWCA Civ 146). The claimant's team needs time to decide whether the evidence is in fact inconsistent with the claimant's medical evidence, or can be explained on the basis that the claimant was having a good day. If the defendant discloses the video so late that giving leave would disrupt the timetable and delay trial, the court may well refuse leave.

One cannot assume that the court, even at the Royal Courts of Justice in the Strand, will have facilities to play video evidence at trial. It may be necessary to take a VCR, several TVs, extension leads and a remote control.

CHAPTER 12

Loss of amenity

A claimant who has been affected significantly more than the average person should in theory get extra compensation. The court can achieve this by choosing a figure towards the top of the pain and suffering bracket. In exceptional cases the court will award a specific extra sum to compensate a claimant who has lost more than most. For example, a claimant who suffered 18 months' delay in her plan to become a professional violinist (*Bollard* v. *Simmonds*, £1,000 in 1998), or lost 18 months of amateur show jumping and horse training (*Hunn* v. *McFarlane*, £3,000 in 1996). Both cases are in Kemp & Kemp *The Quantum of Damages*.

Loss of use of a car, and loss of enjoyment of a holiday, golf club subscription or sports equipment each represent a loss of amenity. One cannot say that any of them represent a financial loss or expense as a result of the defendant's negligence. They are part of general damages (see **section 9.1**).

The following types of loss of amenity are always treated as heads of loss in their own right, and the claimant who seeks compensation for them must state this in the particulars of claim.

12.1 RISK ON THE LABOUR MARKET

Compensation for risk on the labour market is also known as loss of earning capacity or, perhaps most often, as a *Smith* v. *Manchester* award. As the Court of Appeal said in *Cornell* v. *Green* [1998] EWCA Civ 510 the latter expression is used in several different ways, The classic situation is:

> where the [claimant] has been able to resume his previous job at the same remuneration but possibly with diminished prospects of promotion, and certainly with diminished prospects of ready and satisfactory alternative employment if, for whatever reason, his current employment comes to an end.

Smith v. *Manchester* compensation in this sense may be awarded if there is a substantial or real risk that the claimant will lose his present job before the end of his estimated working life. The court will consider how likely this is, and how much chance the claimant would have of getting another job at the same pay. The risk must be more than fanciful, negligible or trivial, but this does not mean that a claimant cannot get *Smith* v. *Manchester* compensation unless he is more likely than not to lose his job (*Moeliker* v. *Reyrolle* [1977] 1 WLR 132).

The value of this head of loss is hard to predict, and depends as much on the judge as on the strength of the evidence. It is very difficult to appeal a classic *Smith* v. *Manchester* award as 'there is no rule of thumb which can be applied' (*Foster* v. *Tyne & Wear* [1986] 1 All ER 567). As to evidence, can the claimant get a letter from his employer to confirm that his job is not secure, for whatever reason, without starting his employer thinking whether or not to dismiss him? Would his injuries make it difficult or impossible for him to find work elsewhere? The court will be influenced by the claimant's age, qualifications and work experience; how long he had been with the employer; how long he could be expected to work (in the police, armed forces and tough manual jobs it is very unusual to work until 60); the claimant's disabilities and how a prospective employer would see him; and whether the claimant might decide to resign for some good reason. If the claimant can get evidence concerning the nature and prospects of the employer's business, this would be most helpful. One does occasionally get a frank response when asking the claimant's employer whether he thinks there is a real risk that his business may shrink or collapse.

It is seldom worth spending more than 30 minutes of fee earner time trying to collect evidence for a *Smith* v. *Manchester* claim. The claimant can say a paragraph about it in his statement, and there is also the medical report. If the employer does not want to co-operate, it is not practical to make him. The Court of Appeal in *Watson* v. *Mitcham Cardboards Ltd* [1982] CLY 78 was happy to support a *Smith* v. *Manchester* award, worth £470 in today's money, without any evidence other than the medical report and the claimant's statement.

If obtaining a report from an employment consultant in support of a loss of earnings claim, ask him to comment specifically on risk on the labour market. As a report is likely to cost £750 or so, it is seldom worth getting one to deal only with risk on the labour market. In any case the court would generally prefer to make up its own mind about the claimant's attractiveness to employers rather than hear an employment consultant's guess.

An award for risk on the labour market in the classic sense is often approximately six, or 12 or 24 months' net earnings. There is a useful table of cases in Kemp & Kemp, *The Quantum of Damages*, with awards mostly between £1,000 and £10,000.

The Disability Discrimination Act 1995 (DDA) has had some impact on claims for risk on the labour market, particularly where the claimant works for a large organisation which has many internal opportunities to find sedentary or part-time work for employees who develop disabilities. The DDA requires employers to put considerable effort into finding suitable working arrangements for existing employees and job applicants alike, and the defendant's argument is that this reduces risk on the labour market. However, this sort of legislation is very difficult to enforce even amongst those employers to whom it does apply. Certainly, there is still widespread sexual and racial discrimination in the workplace despite decades of regulation under the Sex Discrimination Act 1975 and Race Relations Act 1976. The court is likely to accept that in reality disabled people are still at a great disadvantage when competing for work.

The expression *Smith* v. *Manchester* is also:

> sometimes used to refer to any case where there is . . . particular difficulty in quantifying loss of future earnings . . . [for example] after injury to a child or to a young woman with no clear pattern of employment and earnings who at the time of the trial is not working, and even if uninjured would not be working but raising a family
>
> (*Cornell* v. *Green* [1998] EWCA Civ 510)

Smith v. *Manchester* in this sense are used to compensate a claimant for loss of future earnings where there are too many variables, or not enough evidence, to calculate the loss using multiplier and multiplicand. The court does not altogether pluck a figure out of the air when valuing this head of loss. It should be guided by previous similar cases. The figure will generally be much lower than would be produced by multiplier and multiplicand (see **section 13.6**).

In *Cornell* itself, the trial judge's *Smith* v. *Manchester* figure was £30,000, but on a successful appeal by the claimant, he recovered £220,000 on a multiplier/multiplicand basis. For cases where the appeal went the other way, see *McCrae* v. *Chase International* [2003] EWCA Civ 505 and *Willemse* v. *Hesp* [2003] EWCA Civ 994.

Although the multiplier/multiplicand basis is generally used where the claimant will probably suffer a loss, it can also be appropriate where the claimant is at risk of a loss, or has lost a chance of gaining something. See **section 9.5**.

12.2 LOSS OF JOB SATISFACTION

This is also called loss of congenial employment. As with *Smith* v. *Manchester* damages, this head of loss is hard to predict but receives helpful coverage in Kemp & Kemp. See in particular the commentary on *Blamey* v. *London Fire Authority* (16 December 1988).

If the claimant enjoyed his career and is forced by his injuries to change to work with unsocial hours, no promotion prospects, boredom or low status, he should be compensated for this. Job satisfaction is subjective. A few jobs offer status or glamour. The uniformed services provide camaraderie and perhaps excitement. Dancers or musicians may earn little but find their jobs fulfilling, and may have spent decades in training.

Typically awards are around £5,000, but can be £1,000 to £10,000. It is not possible to guarantee that the court will award anything, especially if the claimant had been in the job only a short time.

12.3 LOSS OF LEISURE TIME

This is a rare head of loss. Awards are occasionally made to claimants who are forced by injury to give up one job, find another, but have to work more hours to make the same money (*Hearnshaw* v. *English Steel Corporation* (1971) 11 KIR 306 (CA) and *Brewster* v. *National Coal Board* (19th March 1987, QBD)).

12.4 LOSS OF MARRIAGE PROSPECTS

This claim is very rare. It is mainly used as a claimant's riposte where the defendant seeks to reduce a claimant's loss of earnings claim by alleging that but for the accident (s)he would have had a career break to get married and have children. The claimant in return claims that as the defendant has destroyed the marriage prospects he should pay damages for the financial advantages the marriage would have brought (*Hughes* v. *McKeown* [1985] 1 WLR 963).

This head of loss is hard to sustain unless there is evidence that, when injured, the claimant was on the point of marriage to a wealthy person, and that the marriage was cancelled because of those injuries (*Aloni* v. *National Westminster Bank* (20 May 1982, Kemp & Kemp) where £75,000 was awarded).

Alternatively, the claimant may be able to prove that (s)he is from a culture where failure to marry is a disaster, and (s)he no longer has any marriage prospects (*Bakhitiari* v. *The Zoological Society of London* (5 December 1991, Kemp & Kemp) where potentially £10,000 might have been awarded.

If the claimant wishes to claim under this head, this must be stated in the particulars of claim (see **section 17.3**).

CHAPTER 13

Loss of earnings and pension

The defendant is entitled to credit for certain benefits and sick pay the claimant receives as a result of the accident, but not for loans or gifts (see **sections 9.7–9.13**).

The tax and NI figures used to illustrate this chapter are for the tax year April 2004–2005. A full set of rates, including an archive of rates for past years, is available on the Inland Revenue website at **www.inlandrevenue.gov.uk**.

13.1 NET LOSS OF EARNINGS

Whether the claimant was employed or self employed, he is entitled to compensation for loss of net, or take home, pay. To calculate this, one makes certain deductions from gross pay:

- Income tax (*British Transport Commission* v. *Gourley* [1956] AC 185).

  First, calculate the individual's earnings from employment, profits from self employment, and taxable income from any other source such as interest on savings. From the total, deduct allowances and reliefs. The basic personal allowance is £4,745 p.a. Higher personal allowances apply to those aged 65 to 74, and those aged 75 or over. There are special allowances for married couples, parents, the blind, and those who take in lodgers. The most important tax relief is that for pension contributions.

  After deducting the appropriate allowances and reliefs, calculate the amount of income tax in bands. The first £2,020 of taxable income is taxed at 10 per cent; from £2,021 to £31,400 it is taxed at 22 per cent; and any taxable income over £31,400 is taxed at 40 per cent.
- National Insurance contributions (NICs) (*Cooper* v. *Firth Brown* [1963] 2 WLR 418). Employees pay NICs at source. The employer deducts Class 1 contributions from each pay packet. Employee's NICs are calculated on all gross earnings including commission and bonus. The rate in 2004–2005 is nil for earnings up to £91 per week; 11 per cent on earnings from £91.01 to £610 per week; and 1 per cent on earnings exceeding £610. (An employer is also liable to make a separate payment of employer's National

Insurance. These NICs are not included in gross pay, so there is no need to consider them when calculating net pay.)

The self employed pay NICs quarterly. They pay Class 2 contributions at a flat rate of £2.05 per week. They also pay Class 4 contributions at 8 per cent on profits between £4,745 p.a. and £31,720 p.a; and 1 per cent on profits over £31,720.

- Compulsory pension contributions, if any (see *Dews* v. *National Coal Board* [1988] AC 1). If an employee has a contributory pension through work, his monthly contribution will be deducted from his pay packet before he gets it. Strictly speaking one should deduct this from the 'loss of earnings' claim and reintroduce it if making a claim for pension loss. However, claimants generally end up in the same position if they neither deduct it nor bother with a claim for pension loss. In practice, this is what usually happens (see **section 13.7**).

The claimant is not generally required to deduct the cost of travelling to work. In *Dews* the court said it would be appropriate to deduct if it is exceptionally high, for example a wealthy businessman's costs of commuting from the Channel Islands to London by helicopter. This is not a rule of law, but a guideline to prevent the calculation getting bogged down in detail. If the defendant deducts travelling expenses from the loss of earnings claim and the trial judge accepts this, the Court of Appeal will not overturn his decision (*Eagle* v. *Chambers (No2)* [2004] EWCA Civ 1033).

In cases of catastrophic injury where the claimant is also seeking the cost of a care package that includes the cost of his accommodation, food, heating, laundry, etc., the defendant is entitled to deduct the value of these from the figure for loss of earnings (see **section 14.16**).

Whether in claimant or defendant work, one does not aim for perfection, but for adequate results with the minimum work. As far as possible, one works entirely with net figures, to avoid the need to spend time apportioning losses between different tax years and calculating deductions. If it is necessary to start from gross figures, as when the calculation is based on a rate of pay that the accident prevented the claimant ever receiving, an accurate calculation may involve a great deal of work. Payslips may show half a dozen peculiar deductions and additions, for example, shift work; trade union dues; hard lying allowance; overseas or hazardous duty pay; variable bonus; overtime at time and a half; overtime at double time; section leader allowance; training allowance; pay in lieu of holiday. Perhaps one can get somebody in one's firm's accounts department to work out the net figures, or a numerate but junior fee earner.

If one cannot delegate a loss of earnings calculation to somebody competent and cheap, how accurate does it need to be? Defendant lawyers need only check that the claimant's figure is approximately correct. If they spend much fee earner time checking figures precisely, they may be able to reduce the loss of earnings claim by £300, but at the expense of a £500 increase in the client's costs bill. Claimant lawyers are in a similar position, in that the client probably has to bear any shortfall between their total costs and those the defendant has to pay. Note the proportionality principle at CPR Part 44.5. One cannot always justify spending enough time to achieve total accuracy. One cost-effective solution is to use software to calculate the deduction. For example, there is the Horwath Clark Whitehill forensic accountancy toolbox, which may be downloaded free of charge from **www.hcwtoolbox.co.uk**.

It is best to calculate the loss as precisely as possible if cutting corners is inconsistent with one's firm's attitude; if the loss of earnings is £100,000; if one acts for the claimant and the defendant lawyer has shown signs of being difficult; and perhaps also if one has to issue proceedings.

13.2 EMPLOYEE'S LOSS OF EARNINGS

The claimant must prove his net loss of earnings. One needs the following information:

- Actual pre-accident earnings, usually for 13 weeks before the accident. So that both sides can check the calculation, it is best to get the employer to supply the gross figures and deductions for each week or month, rather than just the total net figure.
- The start and finish dates of the period of loss, that is, the period during which the employee's pay was affected by the accident. This is likely to be longer than the period of absence from work. If the claimant is an employee paid a month in arrears and was off sick for three weeks following an accident in the middle of January, the period of loss extends up to pay day at the end of March. If, when he returned to work, he was on light duties and so continued to lose overtime, the period of loss will finish when his pay packet returns to normal.
- Actual earnings during the period of loss, again gross and net, week by week. If the claimant received some earnings during the period of loss, he must give credit for them.
- To reassure the defendant that the claimant's pre-accident earnings were truly representative of normal pay, his actual earnings for a few months after he returned to normal pay.

The claimant may be able to provide a bundle of payslips covering the entire period, in which case one can make the simple calculation:

(Pre-accident net average × Period of loss) – Post-accident net earnings = Loss of earnings

Employees pay tax on the PAYE (pay as you earn) basis, which requires employers to deduct tax at source from each payment as it is made. Employers deduct tax from all pay except that which the employee's tax coding tells them should be tax free. The Inland Revenue tax coding takes account of any fringe benefits such as private use of a company car, the individual's personal allowance, and tax relief for any contributions an employee makes to his employer's pension scheme. Employees are sometimes entitled to a modest amount of tax relief for expenses such as work clothing or subscriptions to professional bodies (Income Tax (Earnings & Pensions) Act 2003). If the amount an employee can earn without paying tax is £4,745, his tax coding is probably L474.

Employers deduct tax in a way that assumes the employee will continue to earn money at the same rate all year. If the employee's income dips, he pays too much tax, so he is entitled to a tax rebate. A rebate can either be made at the time by adjustment of the tax coding, or as a lump sum based on the employee's end-of-year tax return. Tax codes do not take account of damages for loss of earnings, so the claimant is not only fully reimbursed by the defendant for his loss of earnings, he also gets a windfall tax rebate. The defendant is entitled to credit for this against the loss of earnings claim (*Hartley* v. *Sandholme Iron Co* [1975] QB 600). However, in most cases, the work involved in calculating the true tax position is disproportionate to the amount it would save the defendant. Certainly it is very rare for a defendant to take the point.

If the claimant was off work for more than a month or so, the simple calculation above is probably not enough. One needs extra information from the employer. With this extra information one can adjust the loss of earnings figure upwards if:

- During the period of loss the claimant received sick pay, but the defendant is not entitled to credit for it as the claimant must repay it to his employer.
- The pre-accident pay figure is unrepresentative, because the 13 weeks was a period of low pay. Some employees work seasonally. The construction industry has a long period of inactivity in winter. In that case you might need to find the average earnings over a longer period than 13 weeks. Perhaps 26 or 52 weeks would be fairer.
- Pay rates increased during the period of loss, or the claimant would, but for the accident, have been put on different duties and therefore paid at a higher rate.
- The claimant lost a bonus that would have been paid to him either for simply being there at Christmas, or for having a good attendance record during the year.

A defendant expects to receive generous estimates of loss. Optimism is one thing, but exaggeration by a claimant is likely to be rewarded with a costs penalty (CPR Part 44). As a matter of professional conduct the claimant's lawyer must not present a calculation to the defendant that he knows to be too high. Extra information is needed to adjust the loss of earnings claim downwards if:

- Figures for 13 weeks pre-accident earnings reflect a period of unusually high overtime, for example, the Christmas period or a summer rush (so find the average over 26 or 52 weeks as above).
- The claimant would have been absent or on short time anyway during the period of loss, whether for illness, maternity leave or any other reason.

If acting for the claimant, it always makes sense to ask him to provide a set of payslips for the period starting 13 weeks before the accident. There are usually some missing, but these payslips may provide enough information for the claimant's lawyer to assess a defendant's Part 36 offer if it arrives before full pay data are received from the employer. One can do an immediate rough and ready calculation to advise the claimant whether to take the offer seriously.

If the claimant provides an incomplete bundle of payslips, one may be able to fill in the gaps by comparing what he was actually paid in the week/month either side of the gap with the totals of pay to date and tax and NI to date set out elsewhere on the payslip.

The 'to date' totals began at zero at the start of the employer's accounting year. This is usually April, but one can check with some quick arithmetic. If a payslip does not have a date, or the date is illegible, it probably does have a legible entry saying Week X or Month Y. Again, this relates to the employer's accounting year. If this started on 6 April, Week 23 is about 15 September. Apart from payslips, the claimant may be able to supply a P60 showing pay during the previous tax year, or a P45 showing pay to the end of employment. The claimant's lawyer need not do this detective work if the employer supplies pay information before the defendant makes an offer.

Generally, the claimant's lawyer asks his client to let him know when he returns to normal earnings. When this day comes, he asks the claimant's employer to provide a week-by-week breakdown of pay starting 13 weeks before the accident and ceasing when the claimant went back to normal earnings. This means one need only trouble the employer once, and need not calculate loss of earnings twice where once will do. It is appropriate if the claimant is not off work for very long, and gets enough sick pay to pay his mortgage and bills. However, if the claimant is heading for financial hardship, or the loss of earnings will clearly carry on for some time, obtain earnings information from the employer after (say) three months, and present it to the defendant with a request for a voluntary interim payment. When one acts for the claimant if there is time, it is worth asking the client whether he is in dire financial straits. A surprisingly large number of claimants prefer getting overdrawn and borrowing money from friends and family to phoning their lawyer for an interim payment.

When one asks employers for pay information one finds they are, with rare exceptions, quick, very helpful and make no charge for providing actual pay figures, or extra information about post-accident pay rate changes. Do not expect an employer to keep pay records forever. Some dispose of records after a very few years. If the employer is taken over or ceases trading, records may disappear, so obtain them early on.

If the claimant's case requires extra information about post-accident pay rates and the employer is unhelpful, a simple solution may be to invite the defendant to accept that the claimant's post-accident earnings would have increased in line with inflation, which is generally taken to mean the Retail Prices Index. Ready-reckoners to help adjust for the RPI are available online, for example at **www.picalculator.co.uk** or at **www.hcwtoolbox.co.uk**.

They are also printed in various books including Kemp & Kemp *The Quantum of Damages*, Butterworths' *Personal Injury Special Damages Statistics*, and Sweet & Maxwell's *Facts & Figures*. If this is too simplistic, the claimant's lawyer needs to ask him whether he knows somebody willing to act as a comparable earner, as discussed later in this chapter.

The claimant's tax office will have records of his pay and former employers, with dates. The National Insurance Contributions Agency can provide a list of previous employers and dates (see **Appendix 4** for details). Most government bodies dispose of records after two to three years, keeping only a summary.

It sometimes happens that the claimant cannot get enough evidence to prove his past loss of earnings pound for pound. For example, he may have done high-paid casual work pumping concrete on construction sites. These jobs are handed out on a very informal basis by agents or gangmasters who may have no education, scarcely any records and no love for lawyers. If there really is not enough evidence to put before the court, the judge may still be willing to award a lump sum for these past losses if he feels there must be something in what the claimant says (see **section 12.1**).

Apart from the earnings themselves, the claimant is entitled to compensation for the value of any lost fringe benefits:

- *Company car*. The value of this benefit depends on the deal the claimant got. Some employers give the employee the car, petrol, road tax and insurance and allow unlimited private mileage. Maybe the claimant had to pay his employer something per mile for private mileage. In the case of *Aboul Hosn* v. *Trustees of the Italian Hospital* (QBD 10 July 1987, Kemp & Kemp), the court accepted that the private use of a company car could be valued using the tables of costs provided by the AA. In today's money and in the particular circumstances of *Abdul Hosn* the annual value of this benefit was £5,800. If the claimant is a young high flyer, this could mean a claim of nearly £150,000 just for losing his company car. Tax on company cars is currently calculated in a way that works to the claimant's advantage, and one can argue that if the claimant claims only the taxable benefit, he understates his loss.

- *Allowances* such as an employer may pay for lodgings and travel. These are worth claiming only if the claimant got such good allowances that he used to make a profit, in which case they would be taxable. Claim the amount of allowance received, less the actual cost of lodgings or travel.
- *Free use of facilities*, for example, a serving soldier enjoys free or reduced cost accommodation, use of well-equipped gym facilities, and a subsidy towards boarding school fees for his children. The claimant should seek the replacement cost of these facilities. Membership of a private gym is expensive.
- *Private healthcare schemes*. An employee's remuneration package may include free cover with an organisation such as BUPA or PPP. If he loses this cover because he loses his job, and does not obtain equivalent free cover from a new employer, he should obtain a quote from the healthcare company and claim the full amount of the loss.
- A *permanent health insurance* (PHI) policy to protect the employee's income if he is ill or disabled. Value as for private healthcare.
- *Pension* (see **section 13.7**).

An employment consultant may need to be consulted as expert witness if there is any question about:

- How the claimant's career would have developed but for the accident. He can probably comment on the career paths for an employee in a particular industry, and pay in that industry.
- How easy it is to find a job in a particular industry.
- How a prospective employer would perceive this claimant as a job applicant.
- Whether this claimant with this disability will ever find work, and the rate of pay if he does.
- How long it will take this claimant to find work.
- Whether there is any real risk that the claimant may lose his job, and if so whether his disability will make it harder for him to find a new one. This might support a loss of amenity claim for risk on the labour market.

The problem with employment consultants is that the court may feel it can make up its own mind on the above without hearing expert evidence. The court may refuse to admit expert evidence, or admit it but not order the defendant to pay for it. Reports by employment consultants are seen fairly often in high-value claims proceeding in the multi-track. They typically cost £750 or more, so they are never appropriate for the Small Claims track, and seldom in the fast track.

Clearly, one should try to avoid using employment consultants if there is a realistic alternative. The busy personal injury lawyer can easily write a letter of instruction to an expert, but may not have time to find and consider statistics or pin down potential comparable earners. If he spends much time on this, the loser will be reluctant to pay for it at £150 per hour. The following are possible alternatives to instructing an employment consultant.

If the claimant was an established employee of an efficient employer like the army or Marks & Spencer, the employer can probably provide enough information about his career but for the accident. If the claimant alleges that he is unemployable, much the best way of proving it is to produce a fat file of unsuccessful job applications and re-training (see **section 9.6**). If it is difficult to show what the claimant would have earned but for the accident, he may be able to suggest a willing person to act as comparable earner (see **section 13.5**). Another solution is to write to local employers in the particular industry asking them for information about pay and opportunities. If one writes to 15 employers at random, probably three will write back. Finally, the official New Earnings Survey (NES) and its successor the Annual Survey of Hours and Earnings (ASHE) are very useful publications that show actual earnings for a great many employees. They can be seen in several heavyweight personal injury publications including Kemp & Kemp, or online at **www.lawinclear.co.uk**.

Although popular with the courts, the NES and ASHE have limitations. They cover employees only. In a firm of solicitors, an equity partner may earn four times as much as an employed solicitor of the same age. Likewise, a self-employed office cleaner might earn twice as much as a cleaning contractor's employee. The NES does not have regional variations, but one may need a figure for Knightsbridge or the Rhondda. For example, a solicitor may well earn ten times as much in the City as in the High Street of a county town. The NES and ASHE categories do not include all trades and professions. How much does a fire extinguisher salesman earn? How much does a computer games writer earn?

If the claimant gets an employment consultant's report, in a large claim the defendant may want to riposte by getting its own report. The court is likely to allow this, but the claimant is not obliged to undergo a home visit by the defendant's employment consultant. If he needs to ask the claimant anything, he can do so by post (see *Larby* v. *Thurgood* [1993] ICR 66).

13.3 SELF-EMPLOYED PERSON'S LOSS OF EARNINGS

A self-employed person's loss is not his loss of gross profit/turnover. It would have cost him something to achieve that turnover. If he was running a shop, he had to buy stock and pay rent, rates and insurance. If he was running a taxi, he had to pay for fuel, servicing and insurance. Neither is it his loss of drawings, as a person can draw more than a business produces for several years before it folds. The loss is the reduction in his net profit after tax and National Insurance.

The self employed pay tax under Schedule D, the amount being calculated from a tax return they must file within nine months of the end of the tax year. They can choose the start date of their accounting year. To make calculations simpler, most choose 6 April. Tax is charged on the profits of the accounting year that ends in the tax year. The tax paid by the self employed relates mainly to income they have already received. So that they can pay the bill, they must set aside part of their income as it is received. This is difficult for those whose incomes have been disrupted by an accident.

If a claimant receives a tax credit because the accident causes his earnings to drop below their expected level, the defendant is entitled to deduct this from the loss of earnings claim (*Hartley* v. *Sandholme Iron Co* [1975] QB 600). In practice tax credits are very seldom considered by claimant or defendant.

The self-employed can deduct, from their gross income, expenses that are wholly and exclusively incurred for business purposes. The main expenses are rent and rates, staff wages, materials, insurance, fuel, advertising, maintenance, bookkeeping and accounts. Those who run a business from their homes may be entitled to deduct a proportion of household expenses such as telephone, heating and lighting. They are also entitled to tax relief for losses, purchase of business equipment via an annual write-down known as capital allowances (depreciation), and interest paid on business loans.

A self-employed person may be registered for VAT. At present this is compulsory when his turnover reaches £58,000 p.a. He must charge VAT on goods and services he supplies, but is able to reclaim the VAT he pays on his own business purchases.

The claimant must prove his net loss of earnings. Necessary information is:

- actual pre-accident turnover and expenses (usually proved by producing trading accounts and tax assessments for three years before the accident);
- the number of weeks/months for which earnings were affected, that is, the period of loss;
- actual profits and expenses during the period of loss;
- tax coding;
- actual earnings for the year after he returned to normal pay, to reassure the defendant that the pre-accident earnings are truly representative of normal pay.

Say the claimant is a self-employed gardener, working alone and with minimal standing expenses such as rent or insurance. The above figures are enough, and a simple calculation of his losses is:

(Pre-accident net average × Period of loss) – Post-accident net profits = Loss of earnings

The simple calculation is seldom appropriate with a self-employed claimant. It can be very difficult indeed to calculate these losses. It may be necessary to instruct a qualified accountant with forensic experience.

Self-employed people often have chaotic accounts, which are inadequate even for tax purposes. The claimant may have to get an accountant to sort them out as best he can. One cannot expect the defendant to pay for this when costs are assessed.

If there is any risk that the claimant will need to use records kept by a major customer, the Inland Revenue, etc., he should obtain them as soon as possible. Most such records are destroyed after three years.

There is often a conflict between the parties if the claimant discloses earnings information with gaps. The defendant is under pressure to accept evidence with a few gaps or to find a compromise, because the courts tend to give the claimant the benefit of many doubts. It is, after all, the defendant's fault that the claimant was suddenly confronted by losses, and by the need to prove what he was earning during a particular part of his trading year.

There are other reasons why the defendant should not spend too long trying to obtain evidence to fill in all gaps in the earnings evidence. Except in Small Claims, any request for more evidence will cause the claimant's lawyer to run up extra legal costs that the defendant must probably pay. Any delay in settling the claim will, if the claimant is still receiving state benefits, make the defendant liable to pay more to the CRU, and if he is alleging contributory negligence he may not be able to offset all of this against the compensation (see **section 9.7**). Of course, both parties are at risk if it is unclear whether the court will find the claimant's evidence convincing. If it takes some imagination to bridge gaps in the claimant's evidence, it is in both parties' interests to use it.

If one needs to show how the claimant's business would have developed but for the accident, the best evidence will be from a comparable earner (see **section 13.5**). If this cannot be obtained or needs corroboration, approach an ordinary local accountant who does the books for several firms of that sort. He can say how long they take to get established, and what they can expect to earn. Many such accountants are unqualified. This is no problem, as long as he knows the trends for local businesses. There is a fine line between instructing such an accountant as a professional to give factual evidence of local trends, and instructing him as an expert witness to give opinion evidence. If he is instructed as an expert he must comply with the many requirements of CPR Part 35.

Sole trader

A typical example is the person who works in his own shop. He may have a trading name, but his profits and losses are all personal to him. If he is on sick leave, he loses income, but his standing expenses (rent, rates, insurance, depreciation) continue at the same level. His wages bill may increase if he has to ask staff to work longer hours to cover for him, or if he has to employ somebody to do certain jobs that otherwise he would have done himself.

The claimant must prove his losses. The first step is to prove actual pre-accident earnings over the three years before the accident. Although ideally one would like these figures on a month-by-month basis, this would require a great deal of extra labour with carrier bags full of crumpled invoices. In most businesses, expenses are incurred in occasional hefty outlays, rather than smoothly, and some will be incurred in advance or arrears. In some businesses the same applies to receipts. One generally settles for year-by-year figures.

Problems arise when the claimant's pre-accident earnings are not an accurate guide to what he would have earned if the accident had not occurred. If the accident caused only a month or so of sick leave this seldom arises, but adjustments are usually needed when a self-employed person is off work for four months or more.

Adjustments may be needed if the business had marked seasonal variations, in which case the claimant's lawyer may need to ask him to prepare week-by-week figures for receipts going back several years. If profits were improving, the income for the period of illness may have been higher than the previous months, but not as high as it ought to have been. If the business did a few large contracts every year, rather than many small ones, there will be no clear trend and the claimant must try to prove the loss of individual contracts. If the disability caused a period of loss much longer than the actual sick leave, one must look closely at trends before and after the accident. If a sole trader is off work for six months he will probably have to re-start his business from scratch.

Take a roofer, seriously injured at the end of his second year as a self-employed person and off work for five years. His gross receipts were £6,000 in the first year of trading, £13,000 in the second. In each year his business expenses (advertising, vehicle, scaffold hire, protective clothing) amounted to 25 per cent of his receipts. His friend, who has been a roofer in the next town for many years, has gross receipts of £35,000 p.a, and his business expenses amount to 20 per cent of this. The claimant believes that in his third year of trading, he would have received £25,000 and spent 23 per cent of this on expenses. In his fourth year of trading and thereafter, he thinks he would have earned the same as his friend. The period of loss is not five years but seven, because he had been trading for two years at the time of the accident, and it is reasonable to suppose that once he re-starts his business it will take him two years to return to that level of work.

The best evidence would be a witness statement from the claimant's roofer friend, attaching his trading accounts for the last five years. If the claimant cannot produce comparable earner evidence, a report from a local accountant, or any relevant pay statistics, all his lawyer can do is present the claim in an attractive way and bear in mind that if the court does not find enough evidence to carry out a multiplier/multiplicand calculation, it will make a much lower award (see **section 12.1**).

One of the simplest solutions to any claim for loss of self-employed earnings is for the claimant to take on a paid replacement, that is, a temp to do his job for him. This can work if the business is able to run for an extended period with somebody merely sitting by the till taking money from customers. The loss of earnings claim will consist simply of the temp's wages, less the tax saving the claimant made by incurring this business expense. Generally, however, there is not enough income to pay a temp; or the cost of the temp would be so great that it does not make economic sense; or the claimant could not, especially from his sick bed, recruit anybody who could do a reasonable job.

If a friend of the claimant's steps in to give voluntary assistance, keeping his business going while he is off sick, can one claim for the helper's time? If the assistance is provided for pay, under a contract with the claimant or his business, the claimant can recover for any consequent reduction in his own net income. If assistance is provided for free, he cannot recover anything for it (*Hardwick* v. *Hudson* [1999] EWCA Civ 1428).

Partnership

Most of the issues are the same as for a sole trader. However, if the claimant traded in partnership with others, note that he is entitled to compensation for the dip in his profit share, not for the overall loss of profit of the business as a whole. The other partners have no cause of action against the defendant for injuring the claimant (s.2 Administration of Justice Act 1982 and *IRC* v. *Hambrook* [1956] 2 QB 641).

If there is no partnership deed or it is silent as to division of profits, s.24 Partnership Act 1890 assumes that profits should be shared equally amongst the partners. In *Kent* v. *British Railways Board* [1995] PIQR Q42 the claimant was a partner in a tea shop she ran with her husband. They had agreed with the Inland Revenue that 60 per cent of the income would be attributed to him, 40 per cent to her. She was injured by the defendant's negligence. The Court of Appeal confirmed that she could claim only for her own loss but held that as, in reality, the claimant and her husband contributed equally to the business she was entitled to 50 per cent of the loss.

The partners may be able to rearrange the partnership agreement promptly after the accident, so that all the loss falls within the claimant's profit share (*Ward* v. *Newalls Insulation Co Ltd* [1998] EWCA Civ 287).

If a partner is no more than a nominee for tax purposes, part of a legitimate tax avoidance scheme who took no part in the business, the court may be willing to look at the reality behind the scheme. Again, see *Ward* v. *Newalls* (above).

Limited company

A company is a separate legal entity, which has no rights of its own to claim compensation from the defendant for causing injury to the claimant. The claimant can recover only his personal share of the loss. This will be made up of lost salary, bonus and pension as a director or employee; and lost dividends and lost share value if he was a shareholder in the company. Particularly in a small company, the shares may have no value. The claim is for what the claimant personally would have received after tax and National Insurance.

For a case where the claimant was effectively sole owner of the company, see *Bellingham* v. *Dhillon* [1973] QB 304.

If the claimant is off for a relatively short time and somebody is hired to do his job temporarily, the claimant is entitled to claim the cost of the temp if he was personally responsible for paying it. If the company paid it, all one can do is look at what this did to the company's profits, and whether this caused the claimant to receive less by way of salary and dividend.

13.4 ILLEGAL EARNINGS

The issues here are whether the claimant's income was entirely legal, had an incidental illegal element, or was from an illegal source such as benefit fraud or theft. In the latter case, the doctrine *ex turpi causa non oritur actio* applies. 'If a plaintiff . . . asserts as part of her case that she would have committed criminal acts and bases her claim upon such an assertion, she cannot recover in a court of law on that basis' (*Hunter* v. *Butler* (1995) *The Times* 28 December).

Far more often, there is nothing necessarily illegal about the way the claimant earned a living, but there was some incidental tax evasion. The question is whether the claimant intended from the outset to perform the contract in a substantially illegal way (*Colen* v. *Cebrian (UK) Ltd* [2003] EWCA Civ 1676).

The court may be satisfied that the claimant's real earnings were higher than he disclosed to the taxman, and award compensation based on the real earnings (*Duller* v. *S E Lines Engineers* [1981] CLY 585). However, there is a risk that the court will be very ready to find that the claimant was telling the truth in his tax return and not in his Schedule of Loss. Also, if the claimant loses the sympathy of the court it may exercise its discretion against him, for example when valuing his pain and suffering.

The defendant or the judge may tell the Inland Revenue what the claimant has been up to. Indeed, the claimant's lawyer may be obliged to report his own client. See the Law Society's guidance on the Proceeds of Crime Act 2002 at **www.lawsociety.org.uk**.

The defendant must not threaten to report the claimant as a means of getting him to settle for less. That might well amount to blackmail, which is both a criminal offence and enough reason to strike off a solicitor.

13.5 COMPARABLE EARNERS

Sometimes it is too difficult to calculate what the claimant would have earned but for the accident. A mathematical calculation may involve too many variables, such as business trends, variable overtime, different pay for different contracts, lost chances of promotion and missed bonuses. The solution is the comparable earner or comparator; somebody who actually earned the amounts the claimant would have received if he had not been injured. If the claimant is an employee, an appropriate comparable earner probably works at the same premises, in the same job the claimant was doing, and probably earned the same as the claimant in the three months before the accident. If the claimant is self employed, a comparable earner probably has a business of the same size, type and geographical location, and with the same attitude to advertising and borrowing.

If he really is comparable, a single comparator is probably enough although it is better for the claimant to have two.

If there were redundancies at the claimant's workplace after the accident, and he would have been laid off even if the accident had not occurred, he cannot claim for earnings lost after that point unless he can show that his injuries prevented him getting a new job. The most convincing evidence of this is to take a dozen of his former colleagues as comparators and track them in a successful search for work.

Claimant lawyers generally ask the client to suggest suitable comparable earners, and to provide their names and addresses. If the client cannot manage this, one must approach the employer directly. The Data Protection Act 1998 means one must either obtain the written consent of a suitable comparable earner in advance, or (in the case of a large organisation where there are many people doing the same thing) ask the employer to supply anonymised details. In *Rowley* v. *Liverpool City Council* (1989) TLR 16 October the employer was the defendant, and the court took the view that the claimant was entitled to details of three comparable earners. The employer can call the comparable earners 'Employee A', 'Employee B' and so on if he wants to protect their privacy. *Rowley* was decided under the old RSC Order 24 r2.5, but still makes sense under the Civil Procedure Rules 1998.

13.6 FUTURE LOSS OF EARNINGS

As with any loss, it is for the claimant to prove his claim. If he provides enough evidence for a mathematical calculation, the court will use the multiplier/multiplicand approach. This involves deciding the net annual loss (the multiplicand), and multiplying it by a figure based on the number of years for which the loss will last (the multiplier). The multiplier is calculated using the Ogden Tables and a discount rate, and may be adjusted to take account of contingencies such as that the claimant worked in a troubled industry (see **section 9.4**).

The courts have, from time to time, felt able to make detailed predictions on very lean evidence. In *Cassell* v. *Riverside Health Authority* [1992] PIQR Q1 and 168 the court decided that an eight-year-old boy would probably have become a solicitor with a City firm, and would have earned an average of £35,000 a year. A multiplier of 10 was chosen for various out-of-date reasons, so he was awarded £350,000 for future loss of earnings.

For other classic examples see:

- *Taylor* v. *Bristol Omnibus* Co [1975] 2 All ER 1107.
- *Janardan* v. *East Berkshire Health Authority* [1990] 2 Med LR 1.
- *Stefanovic* v. *Carter* [2001] PIQR Q55. 'The judge was faced with a difficult task on vestigial discovery and very little hard evidence.'
- *McCrae* v. *Chase International* [2003] EWCA Civ 505. The claimant's evidence was wholly inadequate.

Where it seems that the claimant has lost some future earnings but there is not enough evidence for a mathematical calculation, the court will generally make a much lower lump sum award (see **section 12.1**). As a last resort, the claimant may argue that the multiplier/multiplicand approach can be applied, based on the national average wage. In 2003 this was £27,300 for men in full-time employment, and £20,600 for women.

If the claimant is able to return to work but his injuries prevent him doing overtime, or prevent him doing his old job so he has to take a lower-paid one, he may claim a partial loss of earnings. The figure is what he would have earned, less what he can reasonably be expected to earn in future (residual earning capacity). It is possible for a person to be physically and mentally fit for some work, but still have no residual earning capacity because in reality he will not be offered a job. The usual reason is age, a situation likely to continue well after age discrimination is outlawed in 2006.

The easiest multiplier/multiplicand calculations involve a claimant who was an established employee and would have received no pay rises except annual ones to reflect the cost of living. There is a single multiplicand, which is the amount the claimant would, but for the accident, have been taking home at the date of settlement or trial. The multiplicand must not be adjusted in an attempt to predict future inflation (*Auty* v. *National Coal Board* [1985] 1 All ER 930). Find the multiplier in the Ogden Tables, and the task is done. The Ogden Tables take account of future inflation to some extent, via the discount rate.

However, one may need to take account of a probability that the claimant would have been promoted or changed jobs. An 18-year-old claimant filling shelves at the local supermarket would almost certainly have found something better in due course. He might have gone back to college and got a degree. He might have stayed at the supermarket and become a manager. A first step is to ask the claimant to provide a detailed *curriculum vitae* and say how he thinks his career would have developed but for the accident. The only simple solution is for both claimant and defendant to accept that he would have fitted into one of the categories in the New Earnings Survey or its successor, the Annual Survey of Hours and Earnings. This is usually too simple to be fair, and instead a sophisticated prediction is necessary, based on the claimant's own qualities, qualifications, work history, ambitions, and the reality of life in his chosen career.

With luck, the claimant had been with the same large and efficient employer for some years at the time of the accident. Such an employer may be able and willing to provide a career projection that: 'Mr Smith would have been promoted to Grade 3 in 2010, then to Grade 4 with special allowances in 2014, and Grade 5 in 2017. He would have retired at 2030.' However, few employers are stable or helpful enough to volunteer such a prediction. The claimant's lawyer must turn the client's musings into a realistic career projection, and if possible get the employer to endorse it in a witness statement. Any career projection should be corroborated by the claimant's *curriculum vitae* and other evidence such as:

- Exam certificates. For a young claimant, school reports.
- References from current and previous employers.
- His personnel files from current and previous employers.
- A statement from the claimant's employer at the time of the accident to say how the claimant was seen (confident? organised? reliable?) compared to his peers, and how far he would have gone in the industry.
- A statement from another employer in the industry to say how far the claimant's qualities might have got him.
- Letters from employment agencies about the career structure, opportunities and level of competition within his chosen industry.
- If the claimant did something analogous to employment in his spare time (Territorial Army, St John Ambulance) a statement or records from the organiser.
- Job advertisements showing the level of opportunity in the claimant's chosen industry, ideally from a magazine aimed specifically at that industry.

One might consider instructing an employment consultant if the claim is valuable, or if preparing the career projection and evidence would cost more in fee-earner time than a consultant would charge.

The career projection provides the multiplicand(s). Say the claimant is 18, and would have worked for a total of 47 years to age 65. Initially, he would have spent 27 years as an assistant manager on £30,000 p.a. Then from the age of 45 he would have been a senior manager on £40,000 p.a. until retirement. There are two multiplicands. The multiplier for future loss of earnings is based on the number of years for which the loss will persist, slightly discounted by the Ogden Tables. The Tables allow one to calculate a multiplier for a loss extending up to retirement at 55, 60, 65, 70 or 75. In this example, the multiplier might be 27.19 years. With two multiplicands, one has to divide the multiplier between the 47 years they cover.

Explanatory Note A:23 to the 5th Edition of the Ogden Tables says: 'The Tables do not provide an immediate answer when . . . for instance . . . promotion was likely to be achieved. It may be possible to use the Tables to deal with such situations by increasing the [multiplicand] . . . or it may be appropriate to split the overall multiplier into two or more parts and apply different multiplicands to each.' Several methods were considered on 26 January 2000 by the High Court in *Warren* v. *Northern General Hospitals Trust*, a case that went to the Court of Appeal and reported at [2000] EWCA Civ 100.

One popular solution is the simple split multiplier. Apportion the multiplier between the multiplicands by applying 27/47 of the multiplier to the first multiplicand, and 20/47 to the second one. This solution fails to allow for the fact that more of the multiplier is used up in the earlier period, in the sense that things that are expected to happen between 27 and 47 years in the future are more uncertain than things that are expected to happen next week. One reason for using a lower figure for the multiplier than the actual number of years the claimant has to work or live is accelerated receipt. The other reason is that in the distant future, the claimant may well succumb to unemployment or death. One might say that more of the multiplier is used up in the earlier period. The simple split multiplier thus works to the detriment of the defendant, although seldom enough to make it worth disputing.

A judge might have a stab at redressing this balance, for example by making the division 32/47 and 15/47. A more sophisticated approach is to consider the two periods separately, using Ogden Table 27 to take account of deferred receipt of damages relating to the later period, and reducing the multiplier for the second period to reflect contingencies, such as that a man in his 50s or 60s might well take time off work because of ill health, or might decide not to work until 65 after all.

The defendant may want any multiplier adjusted downwards if there is evidence that the claimant might not have worked consistently until retirement even if the accident had not occurred. This may be because the claimant had an erratic work record, or was in poor health before the accident occurred, or because he was working in an unstable industry. See the discussion of contingencies at **section 9.4**.

If, at the time of the accident, the future held several routes for the claimant (he might have got a university place, he might have been made sales manager) these can be valued even if they were possibilities rather than probabilities (see **section 9.5**).

13.7 LOSS OF PENSION

There are two main categories of pension. In a defined contribution (or money purchase) scheme, the claimant pays in a particular amount of his earnings each month, and the size of his pension depends on what his pension trustees manage to do with his investment. Under the tax regime we have had for the last few years, this person's pension loss claim will often be nil. If he receives compensation for the lost earnings from which he would have made his pension contributions, and for any pension contributions his employer would have made, he can invest in a tax-efficient fund and buy himself a pension. In 2004, for example, a claimant could invest up to £7,000 a year in an ISA, or up to £3,600 a year in a stakeholder pension even if he had no earnings. An investment that grows tax free and can be realised tax free may be more tax efficient than a pension.

The claim is simply for the pension contributions that the claimant and his employer did not make. He is entitled to interest on damages, and this will more or less make up for the way in which his pension fund would have grown if he had made the contributions at the right time.

Note that when calculating a loss of earnings, one claims the net loss. Strictly speaking this means deducting from the loss of earnings claim the amount that would have been deducted from the claimant's pay and put into his pension scheme (*Dews* v. *National Coal Board* [1988] AC 1). If this is done, this amount can then be reintroduced into the Schedule of Loss as the claim for loss of pension. However, a claimant with a contributory works pension ends up in the same position if he neither gives credit for pension deductions in the first place nor bothers with a claim for pension loss. This is what most claimant lawyers do.

The other category of pension is the defined benefits (or final salary) scheme, which pays a definite amount on retirement, usually calculated as a proportion of the employee's final salary. It is mainly government employees who have these schemes, for example the NHS, police, fire brigade and armed forces pension schemes. If the accident caused a young claimant to be medically retired from this sort of job, the pension loss alone could be worth £100,000.

Factors when calculating this loss are:

- whether the claimant would have continued working for that employer anyway until the age at which he was guaranteed maximum pension;

- whether he would have been promoted and would therefore have received a larger final salary;
- whether he would, but for the accident, have taken a lump sum by way of commutation (as this can result in a larger claim for pension loss).

As time goes by it may also become necessary to consider whether the economy will be able to afford to pay these benefits in future, as the number of pensioners increases and the workforce dwindles.

The difficulty is to work out when it is worth spending £500 to £1,000 on an accountant's report. If supplied with the raw materials, an accountant could tell you whether it is worth obtaining a full report. Some will do so for free, others might charge £125 or so, and this might be deductible from the cost of a full report. A handful of specialist personal injury barristers are willing to do a detailed pension loss calculation as part of their advice on quantum, if given the raw materials.

The raw materials consist of the pension trust deed; the start date of the claimant's pensionable service; the date when he would have retired but for the accident, and what he would have been earning at that date; the date when he will actually retire and what he will be earning at that date; whether the claimant receives an incapacity pension following premature medical retirement, and how much; and whether the claimant took an advance payment of retirement pension by commuting part of it for a lump sum on premature medical retirement. When one talks of earnings in this context one means pensionable salary, which will be defined by the trust deed, usually as gross basic pay at the date of retirement. Ogden Tables 15 to 26 provide multipliers for loss of pension commencing age 50, 55, 60, 65, 70 or 75.

If an accountant's report is obtained, it must be from a qualified accountant with experience of forensic work. He must know the law relating to pension calculations, which is set out in the cases of:

- *British Transport Commission* v. *Gourley* [1956] AC 185.
- *Parry* v. *Cleaver* [1970] AC 1 (deduction of incapacity pension from pension loss claim).
- *Auty* v. *National Coal Board* [1985] 1 All ER 930.
- *Pidduck* v. *Eastern Scottish Omnibus* [1990] 2 All ER 69.
- *Smoker* v. *London Fire & Civil Defence Authority* [1991] 2 AC 502.
- *Longden* v. *British Coal* [1997] UKHL 52 (deduction of commuted pension payments).
- *Wells* v. *Wells* [1998] UKHL 27.
- *Worrall* v. *Powergen* (1999) *The Times* 10 February.
- *Wakefield* v. *Secretary of State for Social Security* (2000) *The Times* 29 February.

CHAPTER 14

Other losses

The claimant is entitled to compensation for any losses suffered by him personally, or expenses incurred by him, if they were caused by the accident and are not too remote from it (*British Transport Commission* v. *Gourley* [1956] AC 185). Any expenses must be reasonably necessary, and reasonable in amount.

In a few cases, the claimant is entitled to damages for things that are not his personal losses, such as the cost to relatives of giving up work to care for him, or doing his share of the housework.

Most of the losses listed in this chapter are special damages. Strictly speaking, loss of use of a vehicle or golf club subscription, loss of enjoyment of a holiday and any sort of future loss are general damages.

14.1 RTA – DAMAGE TO VEHICLE

Following a road traffic accident, each driver should invite his own insurer to inspect the damage to his vehicle before it is repaired or scrapped. It is prudent for each driver to take photographs of his vehicle to show its general condition and the nature and extent of the damage and, if he blames the other driver to any extent, to offer the other driver's insurers a reasonable opportunity to inspect the vehicle before it is repaired or scrapped.

The vehicle damage claim may either be for the excess on the claimant's insurance, if the vehicle was repaired under the claimant's own fully-comprehensive policy of insurance; or for the cost of repairs, if the claimant paid for them himself. This generally means he did not have fully-comprehensive insurance, but people do sometimes pay for repairs themselves to avoid damaging their no claims discount. The claimant is entitled to the cost of carrying out repairs that were necessary to restore the vehicle to its pre-accident condition (*Dimond* v. *Lovell* [2000] UKHL 27). If the claimant does not have fully comprehensive insurance and cannot afford to have the repairs done, he should tell the defendant. The defendant may step in to get the claimant mobile again. The claimant will, by keeping the defendant informed, at least strengthen any claim he may make for car hire or loss of use.

A vehicle is a write off, or beyond economic repair, if the cost of repairs is more than the vehicle was worth. The defendant is liable to pay its pre-accident market value. To be more accurate, the claimant is entitled at most to the cost of replacing the damaged car with a comparable one as at the date of the accident (*Liesbosch Dredger* v. *SS Edison* [1933] AC 449). By comparable, the courts do not mean exactly the same. Some people are very attached to their cars and expect a defendant to pay for months of car hire while they trawl the dealers and newspapers trying to find an exact replacement. The court is concerned that the claimant gets enough compensation to buy a comparable vehicle, and does not care about its exact colour and model.

In *Liesbosch* the claimants' dredger was sunk by collision. The claimants were entitled to the cost of buying a comparable dredger, adapting it so that it functioned in the same way as the old one, and transporting it to where they had been using the old one.

Insurers use vehicle valuation tables to calculate a vehicle's pre-accident market value. They may do this directly, by having the tables on the claims handler's desk, or indirectly by having the vehicle valued by an automotive engineer. The engineer may be employed by the insurer, as in *Bandegani* v. *Norwich Union Fire Insurance Society* [1999] EWCA Civ 1445. There is no rule that an employee cannot give expert evidence, but where an expert has an interest in the outcome, the court must be alerted to this as early as possible (see **section 20.7**). The court is likely to react to any sign that a tied expert does not understand his duty to advise impartially. In *Bandegani* the District Judge at trial disregarded the claimant's evidence that he had bought the car for £1,500 only four months earlier, but the Court of Appeal found that it created a rebuttable presumption that the car was worth about £1,500. The defendant's engineer claimed it was worth £900 but this was inadmissible as the defendant had failed to follow the procedure relating to expert evidence. The Court of Appeal noted that, at least in a Small Claim, the court can assess the value of a vehicle without needing to hear expert evidence.

The main vehicle valuation tables are:

- *Glass's Guide*. Used by the trade, very expensive, available from Glass Information Services, The Old Saw Mill, Cooks Corner, Crowborough, East Sussex TN6 1TQ.
- *Parker's Car Price Guide*. Cheap, revised monthly, covers cars aged up to about 10 years old, can be bought from any large newsagent. The latest edition can be seen free on the internet at **www.parkers.co.uk** but one needs to know the value of the car at the date of the accident. Many personal injury or claims offices buy a copy for their library every three months or so and hang onto it for four or five years.

These guides provide values for each model of vehicle in categories such as A1, good, fair and trade. There is often a dispute over the correct category for the claimant's vehicle. It depends on the elapsed mileage, the condition of the paintwork and trim, the condition of the interior, tread left on the tyres, etc. If the vehicle was the claimant's pride and joy, pre-accident photos of it may resolve the dispute in his favour.

Where a vehicle has been written off, the defendant is entitled to credit for the value of the wreckage (known as its salvage value) on the basis that the claimant can dispose of it for that amount. An insurance company will, therefore, typically offer to pay the claimant 'the value of the damaged vehicle assessed at £1,500 less salvage of £100'. Until 2000 one could be pretty sure that a vehicle had some salvage value, even if it was only £15 for an old car. Because of European Union laws on environmental pollution, a scrapyard is now more likely to charge for disposing of an old or severely damaged car than pay the owner any salvage money.

The claimant may have bought the car on hire purchase and be bound to carry on paying even though it has been destroyed. This does not affect what the defendant must pay (*Chubb Cash Ltd* v. *John Crilley* [1983] 1 WLR 599).

14.2 RTA – RECOVERY AND STORAGE

If the claimant's vehicle was taken to a garage by its recovery vehicle and kept there pending repairs or disposal, the garage may charge him for recovery and storage. If the garage is paid for carrying out repairs, or is allowed to retain wreckage with some salvage value, it probably will not charge for recovery and storage.

If there is a dispute over liability or over whether the vehicle is a write off, a very large storage bill can build up before it is resolved. The claimant should ensure that the defendant knows that a storage charge is accumulating. The defendant should consider making arrangements to remove the vehicle to free storage elsewhere. The defendant may propose that the claimant take it elsewhere, but this is unlikely to make the court decide that the defendant, if liable for the accident, is not liable to pay for all storage fees. Few claimants have facilities for economic transport and storage of a damaged vehicle, especially if it is shedding oil and broken glass.

Problems can arise if the claimant does not tell the defendant that a long delay has arisen with the repairs, during which the garage charges (say) £100 a week for storage. If the vehicle's pre-accident value was £500, the storage bill ends up at £1,500, and the claimant did not keep the defendant informed, a robust District Judge may divide the storage bill between them 50:50.

The claimant's duty to mitigate his losses does not stop at keeping the defendant informed. Where storage charges are building up, the claimant should chase both the garage and his own insurers to prevent unnecessary delay in getting the vehicle repaired or scrapped. If the claimant can, he should ideally try to have the vehicle stored somewhere free but, as previously mentioned, the court will probably expect the defendant to pay for all storage and transport.

As evidence of the recovery and storage claim, the claimant will need receipted invoices from the garage. If he has lost them, he will need a letter from the garage.

14.3 RTA – LOSS OF STANDING EXPENSES

The claimant's duty to mitigate his losses requires him to claim refunds of road tax and car insurance where appropriate.

If a car is written off but the owner still has the tax disc, the Driver and Vehicle Licensing Agency will give him a refund of the unexpired months if he applies using a form available at a Post Office counter.

The claimant's own insurance company will probably suspend his car insurance, or give him a refund for the unused period of the car insurance policy, if he notifies them promptly that the vehicle is off the road. The claimant will still be slightly out of pocket, as the refund will be calculated on a sliding scale rather than *pro rata*.

The claimant did not incur the expense of car insurance or road tax after or because of the defendant's negligence, he merely lost the benefit of them, so any claim would be for loss of amenity. The legal costs involved in pursuing the defendant to pay any shortfall would be disproportionate to the amount claimed. The claimant should be prepared to bargain, or just drop the claim, rather than insisting on the full amount.

14.4 RTA – LOSS OF FUEL IN THE TANK

Even with a family car, a full tank of fuel may be worth £60. This will be lost if the tank was ruptured or the vehicle was written off, and the claimant is entitled to damages in this regard.

Unless he happens to have a fuel receipt timed shortly before the accident, the evidence will all be in his witness statement. There is a good chance that the court will accept what he says.

14.5 RTA – REDUCTION IN VALUE OF VEHICLE

If a vehicle has been skilfully repaired after an accident but is less valuable on the open market because it is not in original condition, the court may award extra compensation (*Payton* v. *Brooks* [1974] RTR 169). *Payton* has been criticised on the basis that the claimant will not suffer a loss unless he actually sells the vehicle at a loss. If he keeps it for his own use until it is scrapped, or by waiting patiently until he finds a purchaser who does not mind the repair, he suffers no loss. *Payton* situations seldom arise, but the case is worth bearing in mind if the damaged vehicle was a vintage car in original condition.

If the claimant's car has been repaired but not skilfully, that is a matter between the claimant and the repair garage. As between the claimant and the defendant, the loss is probably too remote to be attributed to the defendant's negligent driving.

14.6 RTA – VEHICLE HIRE OR LOSS OF USE

While his vehicle is off the road as a result of accident damage, the claimant may hire a replacement. If the accident was caused entirely by the negligence of the defendant, the defendant will generally be ordered to reimburse the actual cost of vehicle hire, or if the claimant simply did without a vehicle for a while, to pay a conventional sum for loss of use. The former represents special damage, but a 'loss of use' claim is part of general damages. If the vehicle was off the road for three weeks and the claimant hired for two of them, he has a loss of use only for the one week when he did not hire.

Any repair takes time. Delays occur while insurers decide whether they will pay and whether the repair estimate is reasonable, and also when the repair garage has to wait for manpower and parts. It may be many months before the claimant has his vehicle again. This may result in a very large claim for vehicle hire or loss of use, perhaps exceeding the value of the vehicle itself, and naturally the defendant will be reluctant to pay. If properly advised at the outset, it is easy for a claimant to proceed in such a way that any dispute is resolved in his favour.

Fully comprehensive insurance

From the claimant's point of view, he should always notify his own insurers of any accident, and if he has fully comprehensive insurance and relies on it, the repair process is very easy. The claimant's own insurers tell him how to go about the repair, and the repair can proceed as soon as they authorise it. The claimant will have to pay the garage the equivalent of his insurance excess, and his own insurers will fund the rest. The question of liability can be dealt with later. If the defendant's insurers eventually admit liability or are adjudged liable, they will send the claimant a cheque for the excess, and the claimant can notify his own insurers so that they reinstate his no claims discount (NCD). The defendant's insurers may reimburse the outlays of the claimant's insurers direct. The lawyers concerned are very seldom informed about this.

If liable for the accident, the defendant must pay for vehicle hire or loss of use for the time it would reasonably have taken the claimant's insurers to process the claim, and for the time it would reasonably have taken a garage to carry out the repair. If the claimant's insurers take an unreasonably long time to process the claim, the claimant can look to them for compensation for vehicle hire or loss of use during the excess time (*Kingfisher Care Homes* v. *Lincoln* [1998] EWCA Civ 446).

As to delays by the repair garage, the courts will generally require a liable defendant to pay for all car hire or loss of use despite any such delays. Theoretically 'the insurers of the defendants should seek a contribution from the repairers for any unjustified length of repair' (*Clark* v. *Ardington* [2002] EWCA Civ 510).

Third party insurance only

If the claimant takes the view that the defendant was entirely responsible for the accident, he will usually want to have his vehicle repaired or replaced at the defendant's expense. It takes time for the defendant to notify his insurers of the accident, for them to send him a claim form, for him to complete and return it, and for the insurers to decide what to do about the repair.

If the claimant intimated a claim straight away, complied swiftly with any request for information, and ensured that the vehicle was kept available for inspection by the defendant's engineer, and if the defendant is liable for the accident, the court is likely to order the defendant to pay for vehicle hire or loss of use for the entire period until the repair was completed.

However, there are various situations in which things can go wrong for the claimant, so if he can afford to have the vehicle repaired or replaced, he should do so rather than rely on having the defendant pay a hefty sum for vehicle hire or loss of use.

The defendant will not be fully liable for the rental unless he is fully liable for the accident. Liability is hard to predict if the defendant has not already admitted liability. If there is 25 per cent contributory negligence, the defendant has to pay only 75 per cent of the claimant's car hire charges.

In *Clark* v. *Ardington* [2002] EWCA Civ 510 the Court of Appeal indicated that a person whose vehicle is damaged is entitled to rent an equivalent vehicle unless he is, for example, abroad or in hospital and unable to drive the rented car, but it emphasised that 'mitigation requires reasonable steps to be taken. Whether that has been done is a question of fact which depends on the circumstances . . . the need for a replacement car is not self-proving'. This leaves it open for a hard-line District Judge to take the view that a claimant did not really need a car, and should have got around on foot or by public transport while his own vehicle was off the road, and therefore is not entitled to recover the cost of car hire from the defendant. If the claimant needed a car because he lived too far to walk to the shops, there was no convenient public transport for him to commute to work, or he had small children in need of transport, these matters should appear in his witness statement.

He should shop around for a good price, not only for the car hire rate but also for the collision damage waiver he will be offered. The CDW tops up the insurance on the hire vehicle to fully comprehensive, and is surprisingly expensive. The Association of British Insurers (ABI) publishes a list of hire rates it considers to be reasonable. If the claimant can show that the local market rates were, at the time, higher than the ABI rates, the actual local rate will prevail. This may be referred to as the spot rate.

If the claimant does rent a replacement vehicle, he should rent a modest one. It should certainly be no larger or more prestigious than his own. He may not be justified in insisting on a sports car or a Mercedes merely because his own damaged car was of that sort. If he needs a prestige car because he is a businessman who needs to impress clients, he must explain this in his witness statement. If he has no objective need for a prestige car, he should rent an ordinary car. In *Clark* v. *Ardington* the Court of Appeal approved the decision of one claimant to rent a Vauxhall Vectra until his damaged sports car was repaired. The court commented that 'upon the facts it would not have been reasonable for him to insist upon a replacement sports car'.

The claimant should ensure that his own vehicle is repaired or replaced swiftly, and keep the hire as short as possible. This may mean ringing insurers and garage to keep the repair process moving along.

The claimant should avoid entering a credit hire agreement if he can. These agreements often end in arguments with the defendant (see later in this section).

If the hire company offers to deliver the car to the claimant at the start of the hire period and collect it at the end, he should ask himself whether it is more reasonable to pay a delivery and collection fee or use a bus or taxi to get to the hire depot himself (*Clark* v. *Ardington* (above)).

Credit hire

Some car hire companies offer hire on credit after an accident. Claimants find this attractive because they are told that the defendant will have to pay for it; or even that it is free. The hire company's motivation is that, in return for accepting delayed payment, it can charge a higher rate for the vehicle than the normal local rate. It also charges for the credit facility, and may seek to charge for extras it insists on bundling with the deal, typically claims handling charges. The claimant signs a car hire agreement, and also a credit agreement giving him 12 months to pay. Very often, the claimant has to use a lawyer chosen by the car hire company for his personal injury claim.

For the claimant, problems arise with credit hire in various situations:

- the claimant could have afforded ordinary car hire at a lower rate, but did not bother to shop around as he found the credit hire deal so attractive;
- he was offered a free courtesy car but turned it down because he had a 'free' credit hire car;

- the hire rate and/or the cost of credit were excessive even for credit hire;
- there is a dispute about the enforceability of the credit agreement.

For the defendant, the main problem is of having to pay more than the market rate for vehicle hire. The defendant can sometimes avoid paying by taking technical points about the amounts and enforceability of credit hire agreements, but at considerable cost in legal fees. A more comprehensive solution for insurers is to use their bulk purchasing power to organise a favourable hire deal, and offer it to the claimant as soon as possible.

In *Dimond* v. *Lovell* [2000] UKHL 27 the House of Lords said that a claimant who could afford to hire a car while his own was being repaired could not expect the defendant to pay the extra charges involved in credit hire. He was entitled to recover only the market rate for hiring a vehicle. The defendant did not have to pay 'for the additional benefits which the accident hire company has provided'.

In *Clark* v. *Ardington* the Court of Appeal stated that a claimant who could not afford to hire a car while his own was being repaired is justified in taking a credit hire car even if the hire rate was more than for non-credit hire. He is entitled to recover, from the defendant, the higher rate charged by the credit hire company, provided it is a reasonable rate to charge for credit hire. The court warned defendants against trying to make detailed enquiries as to what the claimant could have afforded at the time.

Defendants counter attacked in *Lagden* v. *O'Connor* [2003] UKHL 64. They argued that the rule in *Liesbosch Dredger* v. *SS Edison* [1933] AC 449 requires the court to disregard a claimant's means when assessing his loss, so it should make no difference if the claimant is unemployed, in poor health and cannot afford to rent a car. The House of Lords unanimously said that *Liesbosch* was out of date in this respect. The defendants also objected to paying the claims handling charges that the credit hire company bundled with the actual hire. A majority of the House found that 'he had no choice but to use the services of the credit hire company and that, if he was to make use of those services, he had no way of avoiding the additional benefits which were provided to him'. There was no deduction. The House failed to agree on a rule of thumb so that one can decide without going to court who can afford to rent, and who cannot. Lord Hope said 'in practice the dividing line is likely to lie between those who have, and those who do not have, the benefit of a recognised credit or debit card'.

Disputes also arise when the defendant argues that the credit hire agreement is unenforceable because it does not comply with the Consumer Credit Act 1974 or the Consumer Protection (Distance Selling) Regulations 2000. These agreements are, on the face of it, both regulated consumer hire and regulated consumer credit agreements under the Act, and therefore required to comply with the Act's demands. The Act has many technical requirements, such as that those who sell agreements to the public on behalf of the creditor should be licensed credit brokers and that the consumer be given a cooling off period within which to change his mind after signing. If a regulated agreement fails to meet the requirements of the 1974 Act it is unenforceable against the hirer unless it is exempt. Today's credit hire agreements generally are exempt agreements. *Dimond* v. *Lovell* indicates that if the hire charge is to be paid in not more than four payments 'within 12 months' the agreement can be an exempt agreement under the Consumer Credit (Exempt Agreements) Order 1989.

In *Clark* v. *Ardington* the Court of Appeal considered the credit hire agreements used by Helphire Ltd. The defendant alleged that the agreements were unenforceable because:

- the entire Helphire scheme was a sham to bring long-term credit apparently within the definition of an exempt agreement (contrary to the 1974 Act);
- the hire agreements were consumer hire agreements and unenforceable as they lasted longer than the 12 weeks permitted by the Act;
- the hire agreements were also regulated consumer credit agreements and were unenforceable as they did not in reality require payment within 12 months.

The court described the Helphire scheme as complex and opaque but said it was not a sham; that the 12-week limit for credit hire agreements related to the time for which the consumer had the car, not to the amount of time he had to pay; that on a true construction of Helphire's credit hire agreement it did require the hirer to pay the total sum in not more than four payments within the 12 month limit (and it was up to Helphire whether or not it actually demanded this payment in any particular case, or whether the payment was made by a linked insurance policy taken out by the claimant at the same time as he entered the hire agreement itself). The agreements were exempt and valid.

Note also the Consumer Protection (Distance Selling) Regulations 2000, which came into force on 31 October 2001. The regulations require the car hire company to give full written details of the agreement, including a cooling off period, unless the agreement was made face to face, and it will often be possible to show that the agreement did not comply.

Under s.65(1) of the 1974 Act if a regulated consumer credit agreement is improperly executed, the creditor needs a court order before he can enforce it against the debtor. Section 127(3) says that the court shall not make such an order unless there is a document, signed by the debtor, that contains all the terms of the agreement. If the agreement is unenforceable, the debtor gets an unintended free gift of whatever was being lent. Under the Human Rights Act 1998 it is unlawful for a court to act in a way that is incompatible with rights guaranteed by the European Convention on Human Rights 1950.

Under Article 1 of the First Protocol, even credit companies have a right to protection of their property. However, in *Wilson* v. *First County Trust Ltd* [2003] UKHL 40 the House of Lords found that unenforceability for purely technical reasons was not incompatible with Convention rights. This was not a credit hire case but there are parallels.

Loss of use

If the claimant did not hire a replacement for all the time his own vehicle was off the road, he is entitled to compensation for loss of use for the time when he was deprived of it. The conventional approach until 2003 was to award £10/day for loss of use of a car, a little more if the claimant walked with a stick, or less if he lived near the shops and was easily able to get lifts to work.

In the House of Lords case of *Lagden* v. *O'Connor* [2003] UKHL 64 Lord Scott said .' . . the claim will be for general damages and a fair approach to quantum would be to award a sum based upon the spot rate hire charge for a comparable vehicle'.

To see how far the conventional approach has changed in the wake of *Lagden*, one needs to keep an eye on cases reported in *Current Law*, or its electronic equivalent *Current Legal Information*. Both are published by Sweet & Maxwell.

14.7 DAMAGE TO CLOTHING

If, as a result of the defendant's negligence the claimant's clothes, crash helmet, spectacles, wristwatch, jewellery or accessories were damaged in the accident, cut off at the hospital or lost, he is entitled to compensation. He should keep the damaged items. This may help to sort out arguments about value later. Often the defendant's insurers will pay on a new for old basis, but they do not have to. They have to pay the cost of replacing the damaged item with an item in pre-accident condition or, the cost of repairs, whichever is less (*Liesbosch Dredger* v. *SS Edison* [1933] AC 449).

A motorcycle crash helmet can cost £300, and should not be worn again after any significant impact.

Used clothing seldom has any value in today's society, but the courts seem to consider it good practice if the claim is set out in these terms:

- Jeans 6 months old Purchase price £45 Ripped Amount claimed £25
- Shoes 3 months old Purchase price £80 Bloodstained Amount claimed £65

With jewellery, repairs can often be carried out at a fraction of the price of replacement, and the insurers will expect the claimant to look into this, or to use their own approved repairer.

14.8 EXTRA TRAVEL

By the claimant

A person can claim for getting back home from the hospital, or travel to medical appointments, driving around trying to find a new car, taking the bus into town as his injuries prevented him walking, and so on. Each trip must have been reasonably necessary. He cannot claim for travel to see his lawyer, except perhaps by adding it to the claim for legal costs once the claim settles.

By relatives and friends

They have no right to claim compensation from the defendant, but as with care and assistance provided by relatives, it is routine for the claimant to claim on their behalf for the expense of travelling they did on his behalf, or for what he paid them.

Travel by relatives and friends typically consists of journeys to visit the claimant in hospital, to look after his house in his absence, or to ferry him to the doctor and back. Each trip must have been reasonably necessary. Most judges will accept a claim for daily 30-mile round trips to keep a victim company in hospital. Twice-daily trips of that length would not often be accepted, unless the victim is young and distressed. In general see *Hunt* v. *Severs* [1994] 2 All ER 385. It follows from this case that no claim can be made for travel by the culprit himself, even if he is a friend or relative.

Evidence and calculation

For journeys made by private car, the claim is based on a mileage rate. Petrol receipts are not particularly useful. The claimant should put together a list of all the extra journeys, for example:

- January to March 2002. 37 trips by car to Anytown Royal Infirmary, 8 miles round trip, 296 miles.
- April to June 2002. 6 trips by car to GP in Market Street, 1½ miles round trip, 9 miles.

Claimants often claim 40p/mile, on the basis that this is roughly the rate used by the civil service and local authorities when their employees use their own private cars for official business. These figures include standing expenses such as insurance, road tax, depreciation, etc. which the claimant would have incurred anyway. There is an argument that the claimant should receive only 20–25p/mile for travel because AA tables indicate that this is enough to cover fuel and wear and tear. Some judges prefer to award only the cost of the petrol. However, consider *Pritchard* v. *Cook* [1998] EWCA Civ 900, a case in which the defendant's breach of contract forced the claimant to travel some distance to get the engine of his car fixed. Although he bought the car in his private capacity, not in the course of trade, the Court of Appeal said that the AA mileage rate for those doing work for the AA, then 62p/mile, 'clearly was shown to be a reasonable figure' although higher than the Lord Chancellor's Department's mileage rate.

For journeys made by bus, train or taxi, the claimant should ideally produce a ticket or receipt for each trip, and a list stating the purpose of the trip. In practice claimants tend to have evidence for less than half the journeys made. A claimant lawyer should beware of spending too much time making up for this deficiency by going through medical records to prepare a list of physio or chiropractic appointments. A defendant may be tempted to offer reimbursement only for the trips for which a receipt is provided, but the typical District Judge would probably order him to pay for all or most of the alleged trips.

14.9 LOSS OF EARNINGS BY FRIENDS AND FAMILY

As with time and money they spend looking after the claimant and ferrying him to medical appointments, the claimant's family and friends have no right to claim compensation from the defendant, but it is routine for the claimant to claim on their behalf. As with unpaid care and assistance, he does so on the basis that he wishes to reimburse them (see **section 14.16**).

Loss of earnings by friends and relatives must be proved in the same way as the claimant's own loss of earnings. It must have been reasonably necessary that the loss be incurred. For example, if a single parent is injured by the defendant's negligence, a relative may have to take time off work to look after the children. The court will generally award the lower of the loss of earnings and the value of the care provided.

In *Kirkham* v. *Boughey* [1958] 2 QB 338 a High Court judge considered the loss of earnings incurred so as to visit the claimant in hospital was too remote from the injury to be compensatable if the sole justification for the visit is the comfort or pleasure which it gives the claimant. See also *Walker* v. *Mullen* (1984) *The Times* 19 January. Many judges today would distinguish these decisions where possible.

14.10 COST OF MEDICAL TREATMENT

The NHS provides treatment and nursing and does not charge the patient for treatment, but may charge the defendant.

The claimant may purchase therapies privately, in particular chiropractic, osteopathy and treatment for travel anxiety.

There is an increasing tendency for defendants to organise and pay for such therapies directly.

The defendant and the state

If the claimant was injured in a road traffic accident and received emergency treatment, s.158 Road Traffic Act 1988 provides for payment of an emergency treatment fee to the treating doctor, and s.157 requires the defendant to pay for the cost of subsequent treatment. As regards NHS hospitals, both of these sections have been replaced by the Road Traffic (NHS Charges) Act 1999.

The Compensation Recovery Unit administers a scheme under the 1999 Act that requires a person paying compensation for personal injury or death, as a result of the use of a motor vehicle on a road, to pay NHS hospital charges for medical treatment. The required payment is set out in a certificate issued by the CRU. Payment is to be made within 14 days of the date when compensation is paid. The total amount payable by the compensator was originally capped at £10,000, then £30,000, then £33,000 for incidents occurring on or after 1 April 2003. The CRU's 44-page booklet *Recovery of Benefits & NHS Charges: A Guide for Companies & Solicitors* can be downloaded from **www.dwp.gov.uk/publications/dwp/2004/z1_apr.pdf**.

The defendant and the claimant

The claimant is entitled to recover from the defendant the cost of any medical treatment reasonably needed as a result of the defendant's tort or breach of contract.

The effect of s.2(4) of the Law Reform (Personal Injuries) Act 1948 is that the claimant is entitled to opt for NHS or private treatment as he sees fit. This applies equally to past and future treatment, but if the claimant seeks the cost of future private treatment that he could just as well get on the NHS, the court will consider whether in fact he is likely to buy it privately. If treatment will be required over many years, it is not possible to be certain whether the NHS will provide it, and it may be appropriate to award the claimant half its value (*Woodrup* v. *Nicol* [1993] PIQR Q104).

If the treatment has already been paid for by medical expenses insurance (MEI) the question is whether the premiums on the policy were paid by the defendant. The defendant is not entitled to benefit from insurance purchased by a claimant (*Bradburn* v. *Great Western Railway* (1874) LR Ex 1 and *Parry* v. *Cleaver* [1970] AC 1). Therefore the defendant must pay for the treatment regardless, unless perhaps the claim is by an employee against his employer, and the MEI was arranged by the employer. There may be an analogy with permanent health insurance (PHI). A defendant who organised PHI for the claimant is entitled to credit for payments made under it unless the claimant contributed to the insurance plan (*Gaca* v. *Pirelli General plc* [2004] EWCA Civ 373). However, most MEI insurers require the claimant to repay them out of his compensation. If the claimant has to repay the MEI insurer he should not give credit to the employer, as he would end up out of pocket.

Can a claim for private medical treatment include alternative therapies? This largely depends on whether the claimant's medical expert is willing to endorse the treatment by saying that it was appropriate and effective for the claimant. Chiropractic is recognised as a highly effective treatment for whiplash and low back pain (see **sections 11.8** and **11.9**). Osteopathy is also firmly established. It is common for defendants to fund a course of chiropractic or osteopathy, in the hope that the claimant will get better.

Many defendants will fund a course of acupuncture, or at least pay for it after the event if the claimant reports that it helped. There has not yet been a widespread randomised controlled trial to show whether acupuncture really works, but observations by many doctors at pain clinics, and by some orthopaedic surgeons, suggest that it is helpful.

It can be difficult to persuade doctors or the court of the benefits of hypnotherapy or massage, and even more difficult with what might be called fringe therapies such as homeopathy, reflexology and iridology. The claimant should see these costs as a bargaining counter, not as a reason for going to trial.

If the claimant requires physiotherapy, chiropractic, osteopathy or treatment for travel anxiety, it is worth asking the defendant whether it is willing to organise and pay for the treatment.

When costing something that will be required over a period, such as long-term physiotherapy, apply the multiplier/multiplicand approach using the Ogden Tables (see **section 9.4**). If the claimant seeks damages to enable him to pay for treatment that will not be needed for some years, such as an operation, the defendant is entitled to a discount for accelerated receipt. See Ogden Table 27.

If the claimant is disabled, the local authority may provide care and accommodation, and will charge the patient according to his capital or income. The crucial difference between this and NHS treatment is that s.2(4) of the 1948 Act does not apply. This creates complex problems (see **section 14.21**).

14.11 COST OF REHABILITATION

Pain management may be available through an NHS pain clinic or Back School. Otherwise, the claimant must largely rely on the private sector. Private rehabilitation is very expensive, but can save the defendant a lot of money and let the claimant live a fairly independent domestic life so that his family are able to support him without expensive paid help; avoid the mental problems caused by frustration and hopelessness; get some pleasure out of life; and go back to work or start re-training for other work.

A rehabilitation programme may aim at improvement in one or all of the following:

- ability to disregard pain, or function despite pain;
- ability to bathe, dress, use toilet, eat;
- continence of bladder and bowels;
- mobility indoors (including transfer to and from bed, toilet, shower, coping with stairs, using a wheelchair);
- mobility outdoors (including coping with transfer to and from vehicle, coping with kerbs and doors, using a powered wheelchair);
- communications (including speech, comprehension of others, reading and writing, using telephone and e-mail);
- social adjustment (social interaction, emotional control, adjustment to disability);
- cognitive functions (planning and problem solving, memory, orientation in time and space, paying attention, awareness of risks).

Organising rehabilitation involves asking the medical experts whether it is appropriate and who could provide it; approaching the provider for comments and quote; clearing it with the claimant; and asking the defendant to fund it. From the point of view of the claimant's lawyer, there is great satisfaction to be gained by organising rehabilitation for a client.

Making up for the deficiencies of the NHS is not really part of a lawyer's job description, and many claimant lawyers are intensely annoyed when defendant lawyers publicly accuse them of not going far enough in organising rehabilitation. When they do try to organise it, they often find that defendants refuse to fund the rehabilitation without a court order for an interim payment, and in any case the extra work exposes the claimant's lawyer to an increased risk that the defendant will dispute his claim for legal costs.

Insurers increasingly organise rehabilitation themselves. A voluntary Code of Practice on Rehabilitation has been agreed between claimant and defendant lawyers. Claimant lawyers who subscribe to it have a duty to consider, from early in the claim, whether the claimant is in immediate need of aids, adaptations, surgery, therapy, or retraining for employment. They should rely on medical advice and consultation with the claimant, his family and treating doctors. They should then notify the defendant.

Defendants who subscribe to the Code of Practice have a duty to notify the claimant's lawyers as soon as possible if they consider the claimant to be a suitable candidate for rehabilitation. The need for, and extent of, rehabilitation is to be assessed by an independent medical expert. The Code of Practice can be seen on the public website of the Association of Personal Injury Lawyers, **www.apil.com**.

The medical process of rehabilitating accident victims is carried out by a multi-disciplinary team at a specialist centre, ideally headed by a consultant in rehabilitation medicine. The doctor treating the claimant should be able to suggest a centre.

14.12 COST OF DRUGS AND DRESSINGS

If this expense was reasonably incurred as a result of the defendant's negligence, is reasonable in amount, and can be proved, the claimant is entitled to recover the full cost. If he can provide a full set of receipts, he should do so. If, as usual, the claimant has receipts for only half the outlay most District Judges would still award him most of the amount claimed.

People on a low income or over 60 are, at the time of writing, entitled to free prescriptions. The defendant need not pay for an expense that was incurred unnecessarily.

If a person has to pay for prescriptions, it is possible to purchase an annual pre-payment certificate. If the claimant has to buy more than a dozen prescriptions in a year, pre-payment will save money. If he can mitigate his losses by pre-paying he should do so, but it is very rare for a defendant to refuse to pay more than the claimant would have spent had he bought a pre-payment certificate.

14.13 EXTRA POSTAGE AND TELEPHONE CALLS

It is common to see a claim for £15–20 for telephone calls made to keep employers and relatives informed, and to liaise with doctors and garages. It is customary for a defendant to accept this without dispute and without a request for a breakdown of the figure.

14.14 LOSS OF A HOLIDAY

If the claimant has booked a holiday and, as a result of injuries caused by the defendant, he cannot go or cannot enjoy it, he has a claim. It is not possible to say that he incurred a financial loss or expense as a result of the defendant's negligence, so these claims are for loss of amenity, which is part of general damages.

If the claimant cannot go on the holiday and cannot get a refund from the holiday company, the court is likely to award him the entire value of the holiday. *Current Law* contains fairly frequent examples of District Judge awards where the claimant went on a pre-booked holiday but did not enjoy it, as in *Marson* v. *Hall* [1983] CLY 1046 where the claimant and her family took a pre-arranged holiday in Florida six months after the accident. She was awarded £1,000 out of the total holiday cost of £6,000.

If, when the claimant booked his holiday, he took out cancellation insurance, so his own insurance refunded the entire cost of the holiday, he is entitled to claim the cost of the holiday from the defendant without giving credit for the refund. The refund cannot be set off against the loss of enjoyment claim, because the courts do not permit a defendant to enjoy the benefit of insurance taken out by a prudent claimant, and because deduction is only permitted on a like for like basis. (*Bradburn* v. *Great Western Railway* (1874) LR Ex 1, and *Parry* v. *Cleaver* [1970] AC 1).

Claimants frequently try to claim the cost of the cancellation insurance itself. This is typically £50, paid when booking the holiday. It is hard to see how this claim could be sustained. Not only was it incurred before the accident, but also the claimant has already enjoyed the benefit of it.

14.15 COST OF BORROWING

A claimant who has had to take out or extend a loan or overdraft because of an accident often claims the lender's arrangement fee and the loan interest from the defendant, and the claim is often settled.

Several cases from the Commercial and Admiralty courts indicate that interest and loan costs are too remote to be recoverable, for example *The Borag* [1981] 1 WLR 274. In routine personal injury work the court does not usually take this view. It seems to follow from *Lagden* v. *O'Connor* [2003] UKHL 64 that the cost of a loan is at least potentially recoverable.

Before taking out a loan or incurring an overdraft, the claimant should ask the defendant to make an interim payment. This deprives the defendant of the argument that he would promptly have made an interim payment, and the cost of borrowing was therefore wasted.

The claimant can prove the loss by producing the loan agreement and a full set of bank statements.

14.16 CARE AND ASSISTANCE

The claimant must show why he needs care and assistance as a result of the injuries caused by the defendant. These claims are generally valued according to the number of hours of care provided. The claimant must justify both the hourly rate at which he values them, and the number of hours. He is entitled to compensation for care and assistance provided by paid carers, or by unpaid family and friends, but the hourly rate for the latter is lower.

Care includes helping the claimant get washed and dressed, and get around indoors and out. Originally, the basis of care claims was that 'the [claimant's] loss . . . is not the expenditure of money to pay for the nursing attention. His loss is the existence of the need for those nursing services' (*Donnelly* v. *Joyce* [1974] 1 QB 454). However, the House of Lords later said 'the underlying rationale of English law is to enable the voluntary carer to receive the proper recompense for his or her services' (*Hunt* v. *Severs* [1994] 2 All ER 385), a case which has had very striking consequences.

The claimant is also entitled to damages for assistance if he is unable to do his normal domestic tasks (*Daly* v. *General Steam Navigation* [1981] 1 WLR 120).

If damages for unpaid care are intended to reward the carer, the claimant can be no more than trustee of those damages. Six years after *Hunt* the general view was that 'it is not apparently a trust that the Court will seek to enforce' (Crane J in *Bordin* v. *St Marys NHS Trust* [2000] Lloyds Rep Med 287). However, the Court of Appeal has since said that an award of damages for unpaid care does create a trust 'which the court can . . . enforce' (*ATH* v. *MS* [2002] EWCA Civ 792), sometimes cited as *H* v. *S* [2002] EWCA Civ 792. The full implications of the unpaid care trust have not, at the time of writing, been addressed in a judgment. If the claim includes unpaid future care, it is worth discussing the implications with counsel. Provisionally, the position is as follows.

If the claimant receives damages for past unpaid care he can simply pay the money straight to the carer, or the carer can say that he does not want it. Either of these discharges the trust.

As to damages for future unpaid care, there is no easy solution. The best view seems to be that for every day the claimant receives some of the care to which the damages relate, he holds a further fraction of the fund on trust for the carer. Eventually, he will hold it all on trust for the carer, and if he fails to pay, the carer can sue him. Until that day, he holds the balance as trustee for the defendant. The defendant is entitled to call for part repayment if the situation changes in such a way that the claimant will not need all the care to which the award relates. This may be because he dies early, starts to get more state help, or achieves an unexpectedly high level of independence through treatment or equipment. Strictly speaking, as a trustee the claimant must keep trust accounts and does not have a free choice as to investment. He cannot use trust money to fund medical treatment, or put it towards buying a house. If the trust is to be taken seriously, he will need ongoing advice from both a trusts lawyer and an accountant about his obligations, and should consider claiming the cost of this from the defendant.

To avoid creating one of these problematic trusts, the claimant's lawyer should if possible settle the claim on the basis that all future care will be provided by commercial carers. Where compensation is recovered for unpaid care, the claimant's lawyer should strictly speaking advise his client of his duties as a trustee, or at least tell him that he may have such duties and should seek advice. The claimant's lawyer may well owe a professional duty of care to the carer as well as to his own client. If the court does not trust the claimant to reward the carer, it may take control of the trust money as in *ATH*.

The defendant will resist any move to value all future care on a commercial basis, because care provided by an unpaid carer costs the defendant much less. To the defendant, an unpaid care trust is a very secondary consideration.

If the defendant has any interest in reclaiming unspent trust money, he should when making an offer specify how much of it relates to future unpaid care. Having regard to Article 8 of the European Convention on Human Rights 1950 (respect for privacy and family life) and to their own public image, insurers may consider setting up a cost-effective system to alert them if the claimant dies or his circumstances change. They may also wish to consider overhauling the way they value contingencies for accounting purposes.

As to the standard of care and assistance that a claimant is entitled to expect, he can recover damages to pay for what is 'reasonably necessary to alleviate his injury and diminish his disability' (*Rialas* v. *Mitchell* (1984) 128 SJ 704). This standard exists in the courts, but does not have a parallel in the world of healthcare and social services. The only way to get a feeling for it is to search Kemp & Kemp *The Quantum of Damages,* the *Journal of Personal Injury Law* and APIL's *PI Focus* for a dozen recent cases involving broadly similar injuries. It can be difficult to find a case summary that sets out how compensation for care and assistance was calculated. A serious case is likely to allow extra care to enable the claimant to go on holiday, and respite care to give his family the occasional break, but not to allow constant outings or even much companionship for a bedridden claimant.

In larger claims, especially those where the claimant will continue to need care and assistance in the future, consider getting a report from a 'costs of care' consultant. One must bear in mind that the court may not order the defendant to pay the whole £500–£1,000 charged by such an expert. If the claim includes more than 3,000 hours of gratuitous assistance, few claimant lawyers would try to get by without such a report. Costs of care experts are usually occupational therapists (OTs), nurses or intelligent disabled people. The names of the same few experts appear again and again in the law reports. If one instructs an inexperienced expert, there is a risk that they will recommend the amount of care normally available from social services (too little) or think they have a blank cheque to specify an ideal amount of care (too much).

Note that the amount of care and assistance usually depends on the amount of specialised equipment the claimant has and on his accommodation. If you obtain a report on equipment after obtaining one on care, the care report will have to be revised to take account of the proposed equipment. To avoid this wasted time and money, get a combined care and equipment report from an expert qualified to comment on both. That rules out most nurses. The best expert is an OT who has worked in a social services care in the community team, or a lay expert who suffers from a similar disability.

Section 5 of the Administration of Justice Act 1982 says 'in an action . . . for damages for personal injuries any saving to the injured person which is attributable to his maintenance wholly or partly at public expense in a hospital, nursing home or other institution shall be set off against any income lost by him as a result of his injuries'. In other words, if there is a claim for loss of earnings, the defendant is entitled to a discount from it for the proportion of the claimant's earnings that, if the accident had not happened, would have been spent on normal domestic outgoings that are provided as part of a care package. The amounts involved are usually trivial, but s.5 is worth remembering if there is a loss of earnings claim and the claimant spent a long time in hospital or a rehabilitation centre, receiving free food, drink and accommodation (*Jenkins* v. *Grocott and Hoyte* [2000] PIQR Q17).

If the claimant seeks both full loss of earnings and a comprehensive care and accommodation package that does not fall within s.5, the common law situation is similar (*Lim Poh Choo* v. *Camden & Islington Area Health Authority* [1980] AC 174).

Once the judge has found that the claimant needs a private care regime, it is for the defendant to show that the NHS or social services will give the claimant free laundry, incontinence supplies, chiropody, etc. For a case in which he failed to do so, see *Eagle* v. *Chambers (No2)* [2004] EWCA Civ 1033. If the claimant is to receive care or housing from his local authority, the situation is more complex. One cannot assume that he will still receive it after he gets his compensation (see **section 14.21**).

To calculate the value of future care and assistance, one uses the multiplier/multiplicand approach. The multiplicand consists of the net annual expense on care, at today's hourly rates, and the multiplier is taken from the Ogden Tables using the Lord Chancellor's discount rate (see **section 9.4**). Although this discount rate may give the claimant only half the money he needs to fund a lifetime's care, the court will insist on it. See the conjoined appeals in *Cooke* v. *United Bristol Healthcare* [2003] EWCA Civ 1370, *Sheppard* v. *Stibbe* and *Page* v. *Lee*.

If the claimant will need care and assistance over a long period, his circumstances are likely to change, requiring the use of several different multiplicands. For example, he may need unpaid care valued at £2,000 a year for two years while he is still of school age and receiving a lot of state support, then £10,000 a year for 15 years until his parents become too old to care for him, and then commercial care valued at £40,000 a year. Consider the circumstances listed at CPR PD 40C. If there are several multiplicands, one needs to divide the multiplier between them. For a discussion of split multipliers, see **section 13.6**.

If the claimant needs care and assistance, he should not try to struggle by without it until trial. If he does, it provides the defendant with a convincing argument that care and assistance are not reasonably necessary (*Havenhand* v. *Jeffrey* [1997] EWCA Civ 1076). The claimant's lawyer must identify what the claimant needs, and apply for an interim payment to fund the care regime. When the care regime has been set up, it will quickly become apparent whether any changes are needed to make it work.

14.17 CLAIMS FOR COMMERCIAL CARE

The claimant may need help from one or more of a nurse, nursing auxiliary, carer or home help.

A qualified nurse costs about twice as much as the others, but may be needed for assistance with a catheter or stoma, for manual evacuation of the claimant's bowels, or for management of medication, especially if injected. If the claimant spends all day in bed or in a wheelchair he is at risk of pressure sores, and should have frequent skin checks from somebody with a 'nursing eye', especially if he is elderly or completely immobile.

In some cases the claimant may also need help from therapists, for example physiotherapy or speech and language therapy. Although these will be costed on the same basis as any other form of commercial care and assistance, one needs the medical expert to confirm that the therapy is needed, and how often the claimant should have it.

If the claimant reasonably requires paid help and has reasonably obtained this from a specialist employment agency, the court will order the defendant to pay the agency rate. Apart from the pay of the nurse or carer, income tax and employee's National Insurance, this includes employer's NI, employer's liability insurance, travelling expenses, holiday pay, and 20–40 per cent agency commission plus VAT thereon.

The agency rate is usually determined by reference to the BNA or Crossroads rates. BNA provides both trained nurses and lower grades. It is not the cheapest agency, but has branches everywhere and a central office that is happy to provide (for a fee) local pay rates for compensation claims. Sweet & Maxwell's *Facts & Figures* contains BNA rates for London, Newcastle and Cardiff. See **Appendix 4** for contact details of BNA's head office.

Crossroads is a charity whose rates for home carers are quite popular with the courts. Like BNA, it charges a fee for providing its rates (see **Appendix 4**).

Naturally, the defendant would prefer to value the claim on the basis of what the nurse will earn, not the agency rate. There are many good reasons for using an agency rather than trying to recruit carers directly. Without an agency, the claimant would need to advertise in order to get enough applicants. A claimant with disabilities is not in the best position to carry out a vigorous and careful campaign of recruitment and interviewing. Many of the best staff are not available for direct employment as they work only through agencies. Agencies weed out carers who are incompetent or dishonest. The carer will not necessarily be employed by the agency, but if he is the agency will deal with employer's liability insurance, PAYE payroll, health and safety training and risk assessment.

14.18 CLAIMS FOR UNPAID CARE

It has long been accepted that the claimant is entitled to damages for personal care provided by family and friends, with or without hope of payment. Past unpaid care is often described as gratuitous assistance.

As to assistance other than care, in *Daly* v. *General Steam Navigation* [1981] 1 WLR 120 the Court of Appeal approved claims for 'loss of house-keeping capacity,' where family and friends step in to make up for the claimant's inability to do housework.

The principle has since been applied to assistance with child care, gardening, painting and decorating and other DIY, for example in *Worrall* v. *Powergen* [1999] PIQR Q103 and *Pritchard* v. *J H Cobden Ltd* [1988] Fam 22.

Compensation for unpaid past care and assistance is part of special damages, and attracts interest on that basis (*Roberts* v. *Johnstone* [1989] QB 878).

For a decade, defendants relied on the Court of Appeal judgment in *Mills* v. *British Rail Engineering Ltd* [1992] PIQR Q130. This endorsed care awards 'only in recompense for care by the relative well beyond the ordinary call of duty for the special needs'. It seemed that a care award would be made only if the care provided went 'distinctly beyond the ordinary regime of family life' and the case was a 'very serious' one. However, see *Giambrone* v. *JMC Holidays* [2004] EWCA Civ 158 in which child claimants with food poisoning were cared for by their parents at home for periods ranging from weeks to months. The care included child-minding, being at the bedside to provide comfort and support, giving medicine, helping to the lavatory, changing soiled bedding, cleaning up after an accident. The trial judge awarded £150–£275 per child for this, and the Court of Appeal rejected the argument that *Mills* v. *BREL* 'presents any binding authority for the proposition that such awards are reserved for very serious cases'. The Court of Appeal held that the damages should be relatively modest as 'the care is being rendered in a family context'.

It follows from *Donnelly, Hunt* v. *Severs* and *ATH* v. *MS* that there is no need for a contract whereby the claimant agrees to reward the carer. Arguably, a defendant can resist an unpaid care claim if there is evidence that the carers would refuse payment. However, he cannot do so merely by showing that the claimant will not reward the carer unless the court makes him (*ATH* v. *MS* [2002] EWCA Civ 792).

A special problem arises where the defendant is the carer. Say a woman is injured by her husband's negligent driving and he cares for her afterwards. Damages for unpaid care and assistance are 'to enable the voluntary carer to receive the proper recompense for his or her services' (*Hunt* v. *Severs* [1994] 2 All ER 385). Compensation paid by the defendant's insurers is, in law, paid by the defendant himself. The courts do not award compensation for unpaid care provided by the defendant, as to do so would be to require the defendant to compensate himself (*Hunt* v. *Severs*). This is unfortunate if the claim is settled on the basis that the defendant will continue to care for the claimant in future, but the time comes when he is unwilling or unable to do so. The claimant will not then be able to afford to buy care.

If the parties try to evade the rule in *Hunt* v. *Severs* by entering a contract whereby the defendant agrees to provide care and the claimant agrees to pay for it, the court would probably see this simply as a sham. The claimant's lawyer therefore has the very awkward task of finding out how likely it is that the defendant will fall by the wayside. Does he still find the relationship satisfactory? Has he had any extramarital affairs yet? Does he think he will stay indefinitely? Does she? The questions may be more tactful, but that would be their general trend. One can then take account of this risk by valuing future care on the basis that it will probably be provided by commercial carers after a certain date.

The starting point when valuing gratuitous assistance is the commercial hourly rate in the claimant's local area. When a judgment mentions the commercial rate, it usually means the gross rate earned by an employed nurse or carer working in the claimant's area of the UK. However, the expression is sometimes also used to mean the total rate charged by an employment agency for providing a nurse or carer. In this handbook, the former is called the commercial rate, and the latter is called the agency rate.

There are several ways to find the commercial rate. Rates from BNA are given in such a way that make it possible to see how much BNA pays its agency staff in that area. The Government's annual NES and its successor ASHE are also very helpful, as it sets out the average earnings of nurses, nursing auxiliaries, care assistants and cleaners/domestics, but only for employees and only as a UK average. The NES and ASHE can be seen in several heavyweight personal injury publications including Kemp & Kemp, or online at **www.lawinclear.co.uk**.

The gross weekly figures from the NES 2003 were as follows:

- Nurses £484.90 (male) or £457.50 (female). Use this rate if the unpaid carer actually did the tasks of a trained nurse.
- Nursing auxiliaries and assistants £302.50 (male) or £274.50 (female).
- Care assistants and home carers £296.00 (male) or £268.40 (female).
- Cleaners, domestics £271.80 (male) or £221.10 (female). Use this rate if the assistance consisted of simple, undemanding housework.

The courts usually award the commercial rate less a 25 per cent discount. Case law is inconsistent about the percentage and the reason. The reasons most often given are that if the carer were earning the money in the usual way he or she might have to pay tax and National Insurance on it and/or that the carer had ties of love and affection to the claimant. Examples from the cases are:

- *Housecroft* v. *Burnett* [1986] 1 All ER 332: less 18%
- *Maylen* v. *Morris* (21 September 1998, CA, formerly in Kemp & Kemp): less 25%

- *McCamley* v. *Cammell Laird Shipbuilders* [1990] 1 WLR 963: less 14%
- *Lamey* v. *Wirral Health Authority* [1993] CLY 1437. An exceptional amount and quality of unpaid care, which was valued by the court at more than the commercial rate.
- *Nash* v. *Southmead Health Authority* [1993] PIQR Q156: less 33.3%
- *Fairhurst* v. *St Helens & Knowsley* [1995] PIQR Q1: less 25%
- *Page* v. *Sheerness Steel* [1996] PIQR Q26. The Court of Appeal accepted that the trial judge had been within his discretion not to make any discount for tax and NI.
- *Burns* v. *Davies* [1999] Lloyds Rep Med 215: less 20%.
- *Evans* v. *Pontypridd Roofing Ltd* [2001] EWCA Civ 1657. The Court of Appeal was 'not persuaded that the reasons for making a discount which may be regarded as normal should result in a discount greater than 25 per cent' but would not say that this ought to be a general rule.

If the unpaid carer had to give up a paid job to provide the care, the courts will generally value gratuitous assistance at the lower of the actual net loss of earnings and the commercial rate for the care provided, less 25 per cent or so (see *Fitzgerald* v. *Ford* [1996] PIQR Q72 and *A* v. *National Blood Authority* [2001] EWHC 446 (QB)).

A modest claim for gratuitous assistance can be proved by including details in the claimant's quantum witness statement, and in a witness statement from the main carer. This is generally enough if the care is all in the past. If the claim is substantial, one should ask the medical expert to say whether the claim was reasonable. If claiming more than 750 hours of gratuitous assistance, the claimant should give some thought to getting an additional report from a costs of care expert.

14.19 EQUIPMENT CLAIMS

If a device is reasonably necessary to enable a claimant to live a more independent life, and to recapture some of the pleasure of life he enjoyed before the accident, he is entitled to damages to enable him to buy and run it. Generally, one finds out what equipment the claimant needs by obtaining a report from an occupational therapist. If a lawyer commissions an equipment-only report complying with CPR Part 35, it will probably cost £350, and be admissible at trial as expert evidence.

If the claimant rings up social services and asks them about equipment above and beyond what they will give him, they will probably arrange an assessment and list of recommendations for £50, which one can then claim as part of special damages. The report will not be admissible as expert evidence, but the claimant can explain in his statement how he implemented the recommendations, and whether they were successful.

Wheelchairs are available in both manual and powered versions, for use indoors and out, operated by occupant or attendant. The claimant should not buy a wheelchair without first being assessed and preferably trying it. There will be a specialist centre nearby, run either by the local authority or the Disabled Living Foundation (see **Appendix 4** for contact details).

Wheelchair accessories are necessary for safety, visibility, comfort, wet weather and carrying things.

A scooter may be required for outdoor mobility, as long as the user is capable of walking short distances.

Modified road vehicles can give wheelchair access via a ramp or tail-lift hoist; or with special controls they can allow a disabled claimant to drive using his hands and left foot, or just his hands. To try specialised and adapted road vehicles, the claimant could contact a local mobility centre via the Forum of Mobility Centres at **www.justmobility.co.uk/forum**.

An alternative may be the cost of a more expensive but otherwise ordinary vehicle. The claimant may have to buy and run a large estate car in order to have room to carry a powered wheelchair and loading ramp, and if he previously had a small car (or bicycle) he can claim the extra expense. If the claimant can drive a small car as long as he has automatic transmission and power-assisted steering, note that there are now several small economical cars that have both these facilities, so there may be no extra cost.

Personal care equipment may include special baths, hydraulic hoists to get the claimant in and out of an ordinary bath, and a wide range of smaller items such as dressing aids and nail-scissors with long cranked handles. Any bath hoist that, when fully lowered, leaves the claimant's bottom perched several inches above the bottom of the bath seems to the author to be impractical. There are much better designs for no more money.

Kitchen equipment ranges from variable-height work surfaces to one-handed graters so that a disabled owner can carry out some or all kitchen tasks independently.

Special chairs and beds may be required, which provide electric posture control, and change height to help a disabled user get up or to assist carers to position him for certain care activities. Postural support will be necessary if the claimant cannot sit upright unaided.

Physiotherapy equipment ranges from big foam wedges to position a severely disabled person on the floor, to a standing frame for a paraplegic, or a tilt table for a quadriplegic.

A TENS machine may be helpful for pain relief. These provide an electric current through electrodes applied to the skin, and they are quite effective for some people.

The claimant may need pressure relief (antidecubitus) items to go in the bed and wheelchair, such as pads, cushions, and quilted garments to prevent the onset of pressure sores. Plastic sheets, and absorbent pads may be necessary to protect bedding from the effects of incontinence.

For getting around the house hoists, stair-lifts, through-floor lifts and ramps enable transfers to and from wheelchairs, beds, baths and vehicles. Environmental controls, usually through a computer, let the claimant operate his own TV, curtains, lights, heating and front door lock.

Specialised leisure equipment could help, such as a copyholder to keep the claimant's book open at a comfortable height, or a book-holder with automatic page-turner for a quadriplegic claimant. Specialised computer input devices, from special keyboards to predictive text devices operated by breath, chin or voice may be necessary, along with communications aids such as electronic speech generators to help the claimant chat to visitors, and an intercom link to the front door.

The claimant may require an alarmcall device to wear in order to summon assistance in the event of a fall or other emergency.

Replacements for mattresses and clothes ruined by incontinence, and incontinence supplies, together with a tumble drier and a second washing machine to cope with extra laundry will be needed by some and new carpets may be required to replace those ruined by wheelchair use.

If the claimant can no longer play football with his mates or go skiing, the cost of equipment for new pastimes of computer gaming or internet use, wheelchair archery, fishing, etc. could be included. By using the internet, a housebound claimant can be a participating member of a larger society rather than a mere TV watcher.

A claimant may reasonably need a mobile phone and contract, so that he can summon assistance if his car breaks down. The court these days may think that the claimant would have had a mobile phone anyway. The same applies to breakdown recovery services such as the RAC or AA.

The initial purchase price of these things may be considerably less than the total future cost of consumables, maintenance and subscriptions, and depreciation. As to consumables, TENS machines need batteries, electrodes and contact gel; ventilators need filters and sterilising fluid; wheelchairs need batteries and tyres, and if a powered wheelchair is to be used out of doors, it would be as well to include the cost of third party insurance and theft insurance. As to maintenance, powered wheelchairs need maintenance contracts and regular servicing. Alarmcall systems and mobile phones require payment of a subscription or tariff. Depreciation is calculated by finding the annual cost (so if the item will last five years, the annual cost is 20 per cent of the purchase price) and applying a multiplier from the Ogden Tables in the usual way.

To see how the court dealt with the future costs of owning a car, refer to *Woodrup* v. *Nicol* [1993] PIQR Q104. For an example of equipment in a case of brachial plexus injury, see *Duffy* v. *Shaw* (1994) *Daily Telegraph* 8 December. For an example in a case of arm amputation, see *Pinnington* v. *Crossleigh Construction* [2003] EWCA Civ 1684.

14.20 ACCOMMODATION CLAIMS

A claimant might need some of the following:

- Ramps for wheelchair access to his front and back doors.
- Handrails by doorsteps, by the step up to a patio, or beside the bath.
- Banisters if it is unsafe for the claimant to use stairs without.
- Stair-lift, or a through-floor lift if he needs to travel in a wheelchair or if the stairs are too awkward a shape to fit a stairlift.
- A downstairs toilet so that he needs to go up and down stairs only to go to bed.
- More extensive rearrangement to permit the claimant to have single-level accommodation with bedroom, shower and WC, living room, kitchen/dining room all on one level.
- Walk-in or wheel-in shower if difficulty getting feet up over a step.
- Larger bath, bath hoist/seat if unable to sit down in bath and get up unaided.
- Special lavatory (combining lavatory, bidet and hot-air dryer) if the claimant has difficulty wiping his bottom.
- Removal of thresholds and widening of doorways, because normal corridors are generally too narrow to permit the claimant to use a wheelchair, even one manually propelled by the user, without considerable effort and damage to the wallpaper.
- Front door intercom and remote door lock release.
- Central heating, insulation and double glazing if the claimant needs a higher ambient temperature because of his enforced sedentary lifestyle.
- Dry, level access to garage or car parking.
- Improvement of paths.
- Dry storage for wheelchairs, suitable for charging batteries safely.
- Extension to provide accommodation for a night-sleeping carer.
- Redesigned kitchen with new units, new appliances to permit independent activities in kitchen.
- Soft play area if claimant has a low mental age, so he can be left unsupervised for a few minutes.
- Multi-sensory room (glitter balls, bubble and light displays, sounds, puffs of air, curtains) if profound handicap.

If the claimant intends to install a few handrails and a new shower unit, he can probably persuade the court that the changes are necessary by producing photographs, and he can cost the work by producing receipts or estimates.

If the claimant wants to install a downstairs toilet, ramps and stairlift, he can probably prove the need for the change by getting the orthopaedic surgeon to comment, and prove the value of the change by getting a few quotes from local builders and stairlift firms.

If significant changes are needed (new kitchen, new garage with ramp access, annexe for live-in carer, through-floor lift) the claimant will probably need a report from a costs of care consultant and quotes from builders. He may need an architect's report. A specialist architect will be familiar with many of the features of particular injuries, such as a paraplegic's need for a good deal of space to manoeuvre a wheelchair, provision of accommodation for live-in carers and night-sleepers, no slopes in excess of 1:15, and an air temperature of about 21° centigrade. RIBA keeps a list of architects with a special interest in housing for the disabled (see **Appendix 4** for contact details).

It may be cheaper to buy and adapt a new property. A move to a new property will be justified if the existing accommodation is 'wholly inconvenient and inappropriate,' or a move is 'essential' (*Moriarty* v. *McCarthy* [1978] 2 All ER 213). On the balance of probabilities, the move must be 'appropriate and necessary in the light of injuries and disabilities sustained.' (*George* v. *Pinnock* [1973] 1 All ER 926).

In *Roberts* v. *Johnstone* [1989] QB 878 the court set out the approach to take when claiming compensation for the purchase of a new property. The idea is that if the defendant had to buy a house for the claimant, it would eventually become a windfall for his heirs. Therefore the claimant is not entitled to the whole capital cost of buying a property. He should take the cost of buying the new, suitable accommodation (less the sale price of the old house), multiply this by a percentage rate of return to produce the multiplicand, and then apply to that a multiplier based on the number of years for which the money will be tied up. The rate of return is the same as the discount rate used with the Ogden Tables (see **section 9.4**) and Lord Lloyd's speech in *Wells* v. *Wells* [1998] UKHL 27.

The same applies to the cost of adapting the property once bought. If the adaptations enhance the value of the property, they are to be dealt with on the *Roberts* v. *Johnstone* basis. Where the alterations do not enhance the value of the house, their cost will presumably be added to the damages (*Willett* v. *North Bedfordshire Health Authority* [1993] PIQR Q166).

Roberts v. *Johnstone* is a great incentive to the claimant to do whatever he can to cope with the limitations of the old property, perhaps by using more care and equipment. Unless he receives substantial compensation for other things (pain and suffering, loss of earnings) he will not be able to afford the new property.

14.21 VALUE OF LOCAL AUTHORITY SERVICES

Local authorities provide home help, personal care, accommodation and basic disability equipment through their social services departments, and often charge recipients for these services.

Sections 21 to 26 of the National Assistance Act 1948 relate to provision of accommodation by local authorities to persons aged 18 or over who by reason of disability are in need of care and attention which is not otherwise available to them. Other legislation which may be relevant depending on the age of the claim includes the Chronically Sick & Disabled Persons Act 1970; the National Health Service Act 1977; the Health & Social Services & Social Security Adjudications Act 1983; the Children Act 1989; the National Health Service & Community Care Act 1990; the Care Standards Act 2000; the Health & Social Care Act 2001 and the various National Assistance assessment of resources regulations. The complexity of the legislation is such that, where a difficulty arises, one is likely to need the help of personal injury counsel with some relevant experience.

Recoupment

A local authority may be entitled to claw back its outlays in respect of services provided to an accident victim. The National Assistance Act 1948 says it cannot do so if the claimant is unable to pay either from capital or income. A claimant who simply receives his compensation as a lump sum will have the means to pay for any local authority accommodation he has received. However, he can probably deal with his damages in such a way that both capital and income are ignored by the local authority means test (see **section 9.16**).

If the local authority makes a justifiable claim for clawback relating to home help, care and equipment that the claimant needed because of injuries caused by the defendant, the claimant can generally include the amount to be recouped in his compensation claim.

Note s.5 Administration of Justice Act 1982 says 'in an action . . . for damages for personal injuries any saving to the injured person which is attributable to his maintenance wholly or partly at public expense in a hospital, nursing home or other institution shall be set off against any income lost by him as a result of his injuries'.

Will local authority services continue after compensation is received?

The local authority means test may require it to ignore the claimant's damages when deciding whether to provide care, but many social services departments would, if they could, take account of the care he purchases privately. For example, the claimant is receiving 10 hours' assistance per week from social services. His case against the defendant is that he needs a total of 30 hours per week. He starts purchasing 20 hours' care per week. Social services then want to stop their own contribution because the claimant is now receiving more than the 10 hours per week they consider necessary. Under the National Assistance Act 1948 (Choice of Accommodation) Directions 1992 as amended, the Secretary of State requires social services to give their clients some freedom of choice, and in particular to arrange for care more expensive than they would normally fund as long as there is a third party willing and able to pay the difference. If such Directions apply to the claimant's particular circumstances, he should look to the defendant to pay only the 20 hour top-up. If the Directions do not apply or are further amended, he should claim the whole 30 hours a week from the defendant.

Can the defendant insist that the claimant relies on local authority services?

Under s.2(4) of the Law Reform (Personal Injuries) Act 1948 the claimant may recover the cost of private treatment from the defendant even if he could have obtained identical treatment free of charge from the NHS, but this does not apply to local authority services.

The claimant may well prefer to make his own care and accommodation arrangements, which would enable him to choose where he lives; purchase a higher level of care; change carers he does not like; and change the hours when care is provided. The defendant may prefer to see him in a local authority care home, which would be cheaper. The outcome will always depend on the facts of the case, but the courts generally prefer to give the claimant the ability to choose his own surroundings and companions, and there will always be some question how long free services will stay free. Consider *Moser* v. *Enfield & Haringey Area Health Authority* (1983) 133 NLJ 105; *Rialas* v. *Mitchell* (1984) 128 SJ 704; *Willett* v. *North Bedfordshire Health Authority* [1993] PIQR Q166; *Campbell* v. *Mylchreest* [1998] EWCA Civ 60; *Firth* v. *Geo Ackroyd* [2000] Lloyd's Rep Med 312; *Crookdake* v. *Drury* [2003] EWHC 1938 (QB); and *Sowden* v. *Lodge* [2003] EWHC 588 (QB).

For a particularly lucid and up-to-date analysis of what the Court of Appeal described as this 'difficult and developing area of the law,' see the conjoined appeals in *Crookdake* v. *Drury* and *Sowden* v. *Lodge* [2004] EWCA Civ 1370.

14.22 COURT OF PROTECTION COSTS

If the claimant has suffered a brain injury he may be unable to manage his affairs, and may thus fall within the definition of a mental patient. The court will retain and invest his damages, making payments as required. If the damages are substantial, the Court of Protection will administer them. Its fees for so doing are charged at a flat rate, but even so they mount up over a period, especially if the Court of Protection has to appoint a solicitor or accountant as Receiver to look after the affairs of a young accident victim. The court's fees can be claimed as damages, along with the costs of the claimant's Receiver for administering his affairs. See, for example, *Cassell* v.

Riverside Health Authority [1992] PIQR Q1 and 168 and *Wells* v. *Wells* [1998] UKHL 27. Costs and fees might add £50,000 to the compensation.

If the claimant's compensation is to be reduced for contributory negligence, *Ellis* v. *Denton* (QBD 30 June 1989, in Kemp & Kemp) suggests that the claim in respect of fixed fees of the Court of Protection should also be reduced, but a claim for any fees based on the value of the claimant's compensation should not be reduced as that would amount to a double deduction. *Cassell* suggests that *Ellis* v. *Denton* is not good law.

At the time of writing, the Court of Protection and the definition of mental incapacity are about to be overhauled, and considerably changed. For the latest news, go to the website of the Department for Constitutional Affairs at **www.dca.gov.uk**.

14.23 INVESTMENT MANAGEMENT

Advice on the way to invest damages is expensive. It may cost as much as 20 per cent of the original investment. Whether the claimant intends to obtain this himself, or the Court of Protection will obtain it on his behalf, he cannot recover the cost of that advice from the defendant (*Page* v. *Plymouth Hospitals NHS Trust* [2004] EWHC 1154 (QB), and *Eagle* v. *Chambers (No2)* [2004] EWCA Civ 1033).

CHAPTER 15

Fatal incidents – an outline

Although fatal incident claims are based on two very short statutes, they are difficult. Several specialist textbooks are available.

Most claims depend on both the Law Reform (Miscellaneous Provisions) Act 1934 and the Fatal Accidents Act 1976, and are brought in a single set of proceedings, by the deceased's personal representative on behalf of the deceased's estate and dependants.

The claim is based on the usual principles of liability, and the compensation will be reduced if the deceased's own negligence contributed to his injuries or death (s.1(1) Law Reform (Contributory Negligence) Act 1945 and s.5 Fatal Accidents Act 1976).

As to the time within which a claim can be brought, see ss.11 and 12 of the Limitation Act 1980. The time limit for a fatal accident claim is three years from the date of death. If the victim's 1934 Act claim became time barred during his lifetime, or the 1934 Act or 1976 Act claim became time barred after the death, it may still be possible to make a claim (see ss.12 and 33 of the 1980 Act, and *Young* v. *Western Power Distribution* [2003] EWCA Civ 1034).

If the deceased had already started a claim during his lifetime, and this has been settled or judgment has been given, it bars a fatal accident claim (see s.1(1) if the 1976 Act). However, if the claimant received only provisional damages during his lifetime, this does not bar the dependants' claim (s.3 Damages Act 1996).

Damages under the 1934 Act may be subject to inheritance tax (see s.171 of the Inheritance Tax Act 1984). Damages under the 1976 Act are not subject to tax.

If the victim is still alive, there can be no fatal accident claim even if his life hangs by a thread. Neither is the victim entitled to any compensation merely because he is expected to lose some months or years of life (s.1 of the Administration of Justice Act 1982). However, he may still have a lost years claim for things that he would have been able to provide to his dependants but for the reduction in his life expectancy (*Pickett* v. *British Rail Engineering Ltd* [1980] AC 136 and *Phipps* v. *Brooks Dry Cleaning* [1996] PIQR Q100).

15.1 LAW REFORM (MISCELLANEOUS PROVISIONS) ACT 1934

The deceased's estate can claim:

- Compensation for the deceased's pain and suffering until death. If he had already issued proceedings in respect of the fatal incident before he died, the personal representative applies to the court for leave to take over the proceedings and amend them to add a claim under the Fatal Accidents Act as described in **section 15.2**.
- The deceased's loss of earnings until death.
- Any other losses suffered by the deceased during his lifetime as a result of the incident, such as vehicle damage or a need for terminal nursing care.
- Funeral expenses, if paid by the estate. If the dependants paid them, they are part of the 1976 Act claim.
- Any cause of action to which the deceased himself was entitled during his life. If the deceased was entitled to repayment of a loan, or compensation for personal injury or unfair dismissal, his estate can claim in his stead. If the deceased had already issued proceedings, the estate can take them over.

If the deceased is killed instantly or dies within days of the incident, the 1934 Act claim will generally be for funeral expenses only.

Any compensation obtained through a 1934 Act claim goes into the estate. It is then divided between the beneficiaries of the will, or under the intestacy rules.

15.2 FATAL ACCIDENTS ACT 1976

A claim may be based on 'death . . . caused by any wrongful act, neglect or default'. If the death was the result of an assault, the assailant may be untraceable or without funds to pay damages. One should consider applying to the Criminal Injuries Compensation Scheme. For bereavement, the Scheme may pay more than a 1976 Act claim.

The claim is made on behalf of the bereaved, and on behalf of the dependants of the deceased, for:

- Fixed sum for bereavement for 'the wife or husband of the deceased, and (where the deceased was a minor who was never married) of his parents, if he was legitimate, and of his mother, if he was illegitimate'. For claims arising before 1 April 2002 the sum was £7,500 (Damages for Bereavement (Variation of Sum) (England & Wales) Order 1990). For claims arising after that date it is £10,000 (Damages for Bereavement (Variation of Sum) (England & Wales) Order 2002). The fixed sum is apportioned between those who are eligible.

- The dependency, which is intended to compensate those who would to some extent have been dependent on the deceased. Their dependency is their share of the deceased's income, plus the value of services he would have provided. Most relatives are eligible if they would in fact have been dependent on the deceased to some extent. Since the Administration of Justice Act 1982, common law partners are eligible.
- Funeral expenses if paid by the dependants rather than the estate.

To be a dependant, an individual must not only fall into a recognised category of relative but be able to prove that, but for the death, that individual had a reasonable expectation of benefiting from money or services provided by the deceased (*Franklin* v. *South Eastern Railway* (1858) 3 H&N 211). The benefit might have been a regular payment, or a regular service such as childcare or redecorating the house. It might have been a one off, for example if the deceased intended to pay for his daughter's wedding.

It may be unclear how much support the deceased would have given to a dependant, for example if the deceased was heading towards redundancy, or he and the dependant were heading for divorce. A fanciful, negligible or trivial expectation of benefit is ignored. If the dependant had a real or substantial chance of benefiting from the deceased, he will be entitled to some compensation for loss of a chance. For some examples of the courts' approach see *Shepherd* v. *The Post Office* (1995) The Times 15 June; *Dalziel* v. *Donald* [2001] PIQR Q44; and *Davies* v. *Taylor* [1974] AC 207.

The usual dependants are the deceased's spouse and children. They have the strongest claims. Not only is it highly likely that they would in fact have benefited from the deceased if the accident had not occurred, they also had a right in law to insist on the deceased's support had he lived.

As to the services dependency, the case of *Cox* v. *Hockenhull* [1999] EWCA Civ 1579 is interesting. The deceased had taken care of most of the family's housework and all its clerical work. Although she had been 58 years old and was so seriously disabled that her husband had to spend at least 35 hours a week caring for her, the court valued her lost services at £7,500.

If the deceased was a mother the surviving parent may make up for the loss of her services by getting unpaid help with the children from relatives, or he may bring in a paid carer. He should try to get by with the reasonable minimum help. If he does not earn enough to pay for childcare, he may justifiably give up work and claim loss of earnings. The courts have indicated that one should not approach the loss of a mother by bringing in a full-time housekeeper/nanny except for the children's earliest years (*Spittle* v. *Bunney* [1988] 1 WLR 847).

If the child has been adopted by the time the claim is settled, his new parents have a duty to maintain him, and this will greatly affect his dependency claim (*Watson* v. *Willmott* [1991] 1 QB 140).

The dependency consists of the annual loss of net income and services (the multiplicand), multiplied by a figure based on the number of years for which the loss will last but discounted according to the Ogden Tables (see **section 9.4**). In fatal incidents this multiplier is calculated from the date of death, not the date of trial (*Cookson* v. *Knowles* [1979] AC 556). However, see notes 22 and 24 in the Introduction to the 5th edition of the Ogden Tables, and section D of the Explanatory Notes to the 5th edition.

One can find the multiplier very simply using the Tables, if one knows the period for which the dependency would have lasted, the discount rate set by the Lord Chancellor, and whether there should be any further discount for contingencies. Contingencies are discussed in the Explanatory Notes to the Ogden Tables. A child's dependency usually lasts until the age of 18, but there may be evidence that the child would have continued to be dependent until it had finished at university, as in *Corbett* v. *Barking etc Health Authority* [1991] 2 QB 408.

Having found the multiplier in the Tables, split it between the multiplicand(s) that applied between the death and settlement/trial, and the multiplicand(s) predicted to apply during the years after settlement/trial.

One may need several multiplicands to reflect changes in the circumstances of the deceased or the dependants. For example, there are three multiplicands for the post-trial period if the deceased was a salesman, would have been promoted to assistant sales manager two years after the date of trial, and to general manager 10 years after that. One calculates the multiplicands using the rates of pay for assistant manager and general manager that prevailed at the date of trial. One leaves it to the Ogden Tables to predict what inflation might do after that. For a discussion of the way to split the multiplier between the multiplicands, see **section 13.6**.

As to the income dependency, the dependants would not have benefited from the whole of the deceased's income. Some of it would have been spent on food, clothing, etc, for the dependants. Some of it would have gone on things enjoyed by the entire family including the deceased, the most obvious examples being the family home and car. However, some would have been spent purely on the deceased, and that part must be excluded. One method would be to calculate the family's outgoings item by item, using a fatal incident questionnaire such as that on the accompanying CD-ROM. However, it is seldom necessary to do this. It would be difficult and distressing for the dependants to work out how much was spent on the deceased's tobacco, newspapers, food, shoes, etc. To avoid the need for this, the courts provided a rule of thumb in *Harris* v. *Empress Motors* [1984] 1 WLR 212. If the deceased was exceptionally thrifty or extravagant, it may be best to use the questionnaire. Otherwise, the income dependency is the deceased's income minus a conventional percentage.

Where the deceased was the sole breadwinner and there are no dependent children, the conventional deduction is 33.3 per cent of the deceased's income. If the deceased was the breadwinner and there were dependent children, one deducts only 25 per cent for the period during which the children would have been dependent. If both deceased and partner were earning, one takes their total income, deducts 33.3 per cent, and then deducts the partner's income.

Section 4 of the Fatal Accidents Act 1976, as amended by s.3(1) Administration of Justice Act 1982 says that: 'In assessing damages in respect of a person's death in an action under this Act, benefits which have accrued or will or may accrue to any person from his estate or otherwise as a result of his death shall be disregarded.' Section 4 has a very wide effect, requiring one to ignore the benefit of life insurance policies and inheritance. It applies to benefits in kind as well as in money.

It can produce odd results. For example, take a farmer who is sole owner of his farm. The farm generates the family's income. He is killed in an accident, his life insurance pays off the mortgage, his wife inherits the farm. She continues farming it. Her mother and sister come round to help with childcare and housework. With no mortgage to pay, the family's net income is much higher as a result of the death, and the wife owns a very valuable asset free and clear. Her claim under the 1976 Act, however, disregards the insurance and the inheritance. She can claim for a large part of the deceased's earned income, and for the loss of his labour on the farm and his help with childcare and housework. Consider *Wood* v. *Bentall Simplex* [1992] PIQR P332.

Where a dependent child loses one parent and the child is cared for voluntarily by a relative, the dependency includes the value of that care as in *Stanley* v. *Siddique* [1992] 1 QB 1. If the child's parents had separated some time before the incident, the caring parent dies, and the child goes to live with the other parent who would have provided no care but for the accident, the situation appears to be the same. However, the surviving parent had a duty to care for the child. It is not clear how far that care will be disregarded under s.4. Consider *ATH* v. *MS* [2002] EWCA Civ 792 and *L* v. *Barry May Haulage* [2002] PIQR Q35.

Another problem arises where a dependant claims loss of a chance to benefit from the deceased's occupational pension, but actually does receive a pension from the deceased's occupational pension scheme as a result of his death. This will not generally be ignored under s.4 (*Auty* v. *National Coal Board* [1985] 1 All ER 930). However, if the deceased was already supporting himself and his spouse from an occupational pension at the time of the accident, ignore the pension that she receives from the employer as a result of the death (*Pidduck* v. *Eastern Scottish Omnibus* [1990] 2 All ER 69).

CPR Part 37.4 says: 'After deducting the costs not recovered from the defendant any amount recovered otherwise than as damages for bereavement shall be divided among the dependants in such shares as may be directed.' The court will make this division unless the parties have agreed how it should be done. There are no strict rules about how the division should be carried out. If there are children and a surviving spouse, generally the spouse gets most of the compensation and the children get token amounts. CPR Part 21.10 requires one to obtain the court's approval to any settlement on behalf of minor children, whether or not proceedings have been issued.

15.3 FATAL INCIDENTS AND THE CRU

Because of the rule as to fatal incident multipliers in *Cookson* v. *Knowles*, CRU Circular 01/01 says that claims under the Fatal Accidents Act 1976 'are all for future losses; therefore the claims are exempt from recovery for CRU purposes . . . although . . . charges must be recovered for NHS purposes . . . [but in] a claim under the Law Reform (Miscellaneous Provisions) Act 1934 . . . the recovery of benefits must be pursued'.

CHAPTER 16

Settlement offers

Either party can make a liability offer, for instance to share liability 50:50 between claimant and defendant; or a cash offer to settle the whole claim, or part of it, for £X. If the offeree rejects the offer but eventually fails to beat it, he is likely to pay a costs penalty. Typically, the offeree will be ordered to pay all the costs of the action from the date when he could have settled the claim by accepting the offer.

An offeror wishing to ensure that his offer carries a costs penalty will follow the procedure in Part 36 CPR. A Part 36 offer has various automatic consequences in terms of costs and interest.

An offer made before proceedings are issued will be taken into account when the court decides who pays the legal costs, especially if made in the Part 36 form (CPR Part 36.10.1).

The claimant should not make or accept an offer whereby he accepts any liability without first considering whether he needs to make it part of the deal that the defendant abandons any counterclaim, or without checking with his own insurers whether such a settlement will affect his no claims discount.

Acceptance of an offer generally creates a binding contract. The parties can forget the matters on which the contract is based, and simply enforce the contract itself. However, if either party is a minor, there can be no contract until the court approves the settlement under CPR Part 21.10 (*Drinkall* v. *Whitwood* [2003] EWCA Civ 1547).

A Part 36 offer will be treated as 'without prejudice save as to costs' (CPR Part 36.19). A without prejudice offer is privileged, so if it is not accepted, it cannot be brought to the attention of the trial judge until he has dealt with liability and quantum. One can mention it to the judge when only the legal costs remain to be determined (CPR Part 36.19.2 and Part 52.12.1).

A trial or appeal may have to be abandoned if without prejudice material is cited in a witness statement or statement of case, included in the trial bundle or in any appeal bundle, or mentioned to the judge at trial.

16.1 SETTLEMENT IS FINAL

When there have been proceedings in a court or tribunal, and judgment has been given, or they have been dismissed on withdrawal by the claimant, the claim is settled once and for all. The matter is *res judicata*. Also, a claimant who could with reasonable diligence have raised a matter in those proceedings cannot raise it in subsequent proceedings (*Henderson* v. *Henderson* [1843–1860] All ER 378).

If a settlement is reached without proceedings, it will be on the express basis that it is in full and final settlement of all claims.

In either case, if the claimant fails to get well as predicted, or suffers further unexpected losses, he cannot re-open the claim. The exception to this rule is an award of provisional damages (see **section 9.2**).

The rule in *Henderson* can have unfortunate results after a road accident if the guilty driver issues proceedings and the victim's insurers instruct solicitors who successfully beat off the claim but do not ask the court to take account of the victim's own injuries by way of counterclaim. The court will not consider it relevant that the victim, deprived of a claim against the guilty driver, will not necessarily be able to fall back on a claim against the solicitors for professional negligence (*Wain* v. *Sherwood* [1998] EWCA Civ 905).

If the claimant issues proceedings for his uninsured losses, without including his own insurer's outlays, he risks depriving them of their legal right to recover their outlays. Consider *Buckland* v. *Palmer* [1984] 1 WLR 1109. In practice, insurers seldom want their outlays included. They prefer to await the outcome on liability and then settle their outlays directly with the other side's insurers. They do this not under threat of legal proceedings, but under a memorandum of understanding.

The rule in *Henderson* applies to both court and Employment Tribunal proceedings (*Sheriff* v. *Klyne Tugs (Lowestoft) Ltd* [1999] EWCA Civ 1663).

A claimant who has settled his claim with one of several tortfeasors may seek to avoid the rule by bringing fresh proceedings against the others. This will seldom, if ever, be possible: *Jameson* v. *CEGB* [1998] UKHL 51, a claim relating to fatal asbestos exposure where the deceased unwisely settled the claim with his employers before he died, and his family wanted to revive the claim by suing the occupiers instead.

16.2 THE FORMALITIES OF PART 36

CPR Part 36.2.4 says: 'A Part 36 offer or a Part 36 payment may be made at any time after proceedings have started. . .' In this section, this is referred to as a true Part 36 offer. If such an offer is made, and the offeree does not accept it but fails to beat it, he will pay an automatic penalty in costs and interest (see **sections 16.3** and **16.4**).

One may also make a pre-action offer. It will not have automatic costs consequences but CPR Part 36.10.1 says 'the court will take that offer into account when making any order as to costs'. A pre-action offer should be in the form required by CPR Part 36.10, which says it must be 'expressed to be open for at least 21 days' and must 'otherwise comply with [Part 36]'. If it is the defendant who makes the offer, he should offer to pay the legal costs incurred by the claimant between the outset of the claim and 21 days after the date the offer was made. If the claimant subsequently issues proceedings, the defendant must generally protect his position by paying the sum into court as a Part 36 payment within 14 days of service of the claim form (CPR Part 36.10.3). This may not be necessary if the defendant plainly has enough money to back up his offer, as in the conjoined appeals in *Crouch* v. *Kings Healthcare NHS Trust* and *Murry* v. *Blackburn NHS Trust* [2004] EWCA Civ 1332.

The formalities for a true Part 36 offer are in CPR Part 36.5 and CPR PD 36. Subject to any recent changes, an offer must be in writing, signed by the offeror or his legal representative, and must state:

- That it is a Part 36 offer or payment notice.
- Whether it relates to the whole of the claim or to part of it, for example just loss of earnings.
- Whether it takes account of any counterclaim. If the offer takes the counterclaim into account, the counterclaim stops if the offer is accepted, and in the case of a defendant's offer the claimant is entitled to his costs relating to defence of the counterclaim (CPR 36.13.3).
- Whether it includes interest, or give details about interest under CPR Part 36.22.2. Unless the offer says otherwise, it will be taken to be inclusive of interest up to the last date when it could be accepted without the permission of the court (CPR Part 36.22).
- That it remains open for acceptance for 21 days from the date it is made (not from the date it is posted).
- That it can be accepted after that time only if the parties agree liability for costs, or the court gives permission.

It is worth setting out how the offer relates to any interim payment already made, and to any funds already in court, so that all parties can see at a glance the size of the total offer. For a typical claimant's offer letter, see the accompanying CD-ROM.

There are further rules for offers by defendants. If proceedings have been issued, and the defendant makes a cash offer it is not a true Part 36 offer unless he pays the money into court (CPR Part 36.3.1) although see *Crouch* and *Murry*. A payment into court must be accompanied by:

- An N242A payment notice complying with CPR Part 36.6.2 and CPR Part 36.23 concerning CRU recoupment of state benefits, as to which see **section 16.6**.

- A certificate of service as required by CPR PD 36.4.1.
- A CRU certificate listing recoverable benefits as required by CPR Part 36.10.2.

The defendant sends the funds to the Court Funds Office accompanied by the documentation required by CPR PD 36.4.2.

The only situations where the CPR provides that the defendant need not pay the funds into court are where the offer is made by reference to an interim payment, for example on the basis that the defendant does not intend to pay the claimant more than he already has; or under CPR Part 36.2.3 where the defendant has applied for a CRU certificate and is waiting for it to arrive.

A Part 36 payment is effective when the payment notice is served on the offeree in accordance with CPR Part 6, but a Part 36 offer is made when received by the offeree (CPR Part 36.8.1 and Part 36.10.5). Therefore an offer is effective as soon as the offeree has a written copy, even if it was sent by FAX or e-mail to an offeree who refuses to accept service by those means (*Charles* v. *NTL Group Ltd* [2002] EWCA Civ 2004).

If the offeree is legally represented, any Part 36 offer, payment notice or notice of acceptance must be sent to the legal representative (CPR PD 36.11.1).

To avoid any suggestion that one's Part 36 offer did not reach the offeree, it is best to send it by post and FAX. In case of a similar problem with a payment notice, make a note to chase the claimant a few days later so that he acknowledges having been served.

'An offer to settle which is not made in accordance with Part 36 will only have the consequences specified in that Part if the court so orders and will be given such weight on any issue as to costs as the court thinks appropriate' (CPR PD 36.1.3). The court will usually overlook trivial irregularities in an offer, so the offeree who rejects a clear and reasonable offer can expect to suffer the usual costs consequences of Part 36: *Neave* v. *Neave* [2003] EWCA Civ 325, in which the offer was said to be open for '21 days from today' but still carried a costs penalty.

Even offers that hopelessly fail to comply with Part 36 may have some effect on costs, as under CPR Part 44.5 the court must, when deciding who pays the costs, consider 'the efforts made, if any, before and during the proceedings in order to try to resolve the dispute'. However, if the offeree fails to beat the offer only because the offeror made or topped up an offer less than 21 days before the start of the trial, the court will very seldom penalise him (Hunt J in *Spilsbury* v. *Martin International* (QBD 20 February 2002)).

16.3 PART 36 OFFER BY THE DEFENDANT

Pre-action offers do not automatically have the consequences set out in this section, but the court is likely to impose a similar outcome (CPR Part 36.10.1).

Acceptance of a true Part 36 offer or payment in full settlement within 21 days ends the claim. The claimant serves an N243A notice of acceptance under CPR PD 36.7.6, the proceedings are stayed, and under CPR Part 36.13, the claimant is 'entitled to his costs of the proceedings up to the date of serving notice of acceptance . . . Costs under this rule will be payable on the Standard basis if not agreed'. If the sum was paid into court, a court order is needed for payment out, and the order will deal with the costs (CPR Part 36.18.2).

A claimant may accept an offer out of time with the defendant's consent, or with the court's permission. The defendant will usually let the claimant accept on terms that the defendant is liable for costs incurred by the claimant up to the latest date when he could have accepted without needing permission. If the defendant has done a good deal of work since the 'latest date,' he may insist on a contribution to his costs. If the claimant is willing to make this contribution, the defendant cannot justify preventing the claimant from accepting out of time unless significant fresh evidence has come to light in the meantime. If he refuses to settle the claim merely because he has changed his mind, he can expect to pay a costs penalty himself. As to withdrawing an offer, see **section 16.7**.

If the claimant accepts a Part 36 offer or Part 36 payment by the defendant, CPR Part 36.13.4 says that costs 'will be payable on the Standard basis', so the court has no discretion to award Indemnity costs (*Dyson Ltd* v. *Hoover Ltd* [2002] EWHC 2229 (Ch)).

If the claimant does not accept the defendant's offer, this may affect the way legal costs are determined at the end of the claim. If the claimant subsequently beats (betters) the offer, the defendant must pay his legal costs in the usual way. If the claimant fails to beat the offer he will pay a penalty. The defendant pays the claimant's costs up to the last date when the claimant could have accepted the offer; but 'Unless it considers it unjust to do so, the court will order the claimant to pay any costs incurred by the defendant after the latest date on which the payment or offer could have been accepted without needing the permission of the court' (CPR Part 36.20).

16.4 PART 36 OFFER BY THE CLAIMANT

It seems likely that in future a claimant will face costs penalties if he does not make a realistic settlement offer before he issues proceedings.

Pre-action offers do not automatically have the consequences set out in this section, but the court is likely to impose a similar outcome (CPR Part 36.10.1).

If the claimant offers to settle for a certain sum and the defendant accepts this within 21 days, it brings the compensation claim to an end. The defendant serves a notice of acceptance under CPR PD 36.7.6, the proceedings are stayed, and 'the claimant will be entitled to his costs of the proceedings up to the date upon which the defendant serves Notice of Acceptance' (CPR Part 36.14). All that remains is to agree how much the defendant pays towards the claimant's costs.

A defendant may accept an offer out of time with the claimant's consent, which is usually given on terms that the defendant pays the claimant's reasonable legal costs to the date of acceptance. The claimant should not withhold his consent without very good reason.

If the defendant does not accept, the offer makes no difference unless the claimant goes on to beat it. If the claimant betters his own Part 36 offer at trial, then unless the court considers it unjust to do so it will award him his costs on the standard basis up to the latest date when the defendant could have accepted the claimant's offer without leave, and also:

- Interest on the compensation at up to 10 per cent over base rate for some or all of the period starting with the same latest date. Note that the amount of interest is discretionary. A successful claimant will get the maximum 10 per cent over base if the defendant behaved particularly badly.
- Costs on the indemnity basis from the latest date.
- Interest on those costs at up to 10 per cent over base rate.

Note the wording of CPR Part 36.21. It gives these advantages to a claimant only if 'at trial (a) a defendant is held liable for more; or (b) the judgment against a defendant is more advantageous to the claimant than the proposals contained in a claimant's Part 36 offer'. Neither summary judgment nor a negotiated settlement is a trial, but the court does have a general discretion under CPR Part 44.3 to consider all the circumstances, and could award indemnity costs where the claimant beats his own offer other than at trial (*Petrotrade Inc* v. *Texaco Ltd* (2000) *The Times* 14 June CA).

16.5 AUTOMATIC COSTS CONSEQUENCES

It is a keystone of the CPR that Part 36 should produce a simple and predictable outcome as described in the two previous sections. Where the usual costs consequences of Part 36 would be unjust, the court can disapply them, but it will be reluctant to do so.

The burden of proving that the normal outcome of Part 36 would be unjust is on the party seeking to overturn it. The court will consider all the circumstances, including dishonesty, exaggeration of the claim, making an offer so unrealistic that it hampered negotiations, and delay. The court may disapply Part 36 to avoid conferring its benefits on a party who unsuccessfully challenged 'every element of [the claim] which seemed remotely open to challenge,' implied that the claimant was dishonest or careless, and thereby considerably extended the duration of the trial by arguably aggressive cross-examination (*Johnson* v. *Gore Wood* [2004] EWCA Civ 14).

If the offeror obtains evidence at the last moment which prevents the offeree beating a Part 36 offer, the court may penalise him if with due diligence he could have obtained it earlier (*Ford* v. *GKR Construction* [2001] 1 All ER 802).

If one party improperly alleges that the other party is dishonest and is unable to prove it, this may cause the court to disapply the usual Part 36 costs rules (consider *Burgess* v. *British Steel* [2000] All ER (D) 32).

The circumstances the court will consider if asked to disapply Part 36 expressly include 'the information available to the parties at the time when the Part 36 offer or Part 36 payment was made; and the conduct of the parties with regard to the giving or refusing to give information for the purposes of enabling the offer or payment into court to be made or evaluated' (CPR Part 36.21.5). The Pre-action Protocol states 'if [a Part 36] offer is made, the party making the offer must always supply sufficient evidence and/or information to enable the offer to be properly considered'. If an offer is made when the offeree is waiting to hear from the offeror with evidence without which he cannot assess the strength of the claim, he should point this out and assert that the offer cannot have any costs consequences until the evidence is provided. See the Court of Appeal's comments in *Ford* v. *GKR Construction*. One should not run this argument if the information is less than vital.

An offer by a claimant to settle his case for 100 per cent liability is a mere tactical device, and will not bring the claimant any benefit under Part 36 (see **section 16.7**).

CPR Part 36.23.4 says 'a claimant fails to better a Part 36 payment if he fails to obtain judgment for more than the gross sum specified in the Part 36 payment notice'. Say the defendant offered £10,000 at a time when the claimant had received no state benefits. The claimant did not accept the offer but then became dependent on state benefits for six months. Eventually he got judgment for £12,000 gross of state benefits, but the defendant was entitled to deduct benefits worth £3,000 that were received after the date of the offer. The net compensation received is therefore £9,000. The real effect of rejecting the offer is that the claimant ended up with £1,000 less compensation. In this case, he has technically beaten the offer, but the court may well disapply Part 36.

16.6 SETTLEMENT OFFERS AND THE CRU

The Compensation Recovery Unit (CRU) recoups from the defendant as compensator a sum equivalent to the state benefits received by the claimant. The defendant is entitled to deduct these recoverable benefits from corresponding heads of damages. Benefits for income can be offset against damages for loss of earnings, and mobility and care benefits can be set off against damages for loss of mobility or the cost of care. Benefits can never be offset against damages for pain and suffering, which are said to be ring fenced. If the damages are reduced for contributory negligence, or the benefits are inflated because the CRU has demanded repayment of benefits that were not paid in respect of the accident, injury or disease, the defendant may have to pay more to the CRU than he can deduct from the damages. Either party may appeal a CRU certificate after settlement, and this may produce a refund under Regulation 11 of the Social Security (Recovery of Benefits) Regulations 1997. For more background, see **section 9.7**.

If a party simply makes a global settlement offer, it is not possible to tell how much of it relates to benefits from which the defendant is entitled to deduct state benefits. As regards Part 36 payments made by the defendant, CPR Part 36.23.3 says that the payment notice must state the gross amount of compensation before CRU deduction, the name and amount of the benefit, and that the sum paid in is the net amount after the benefit is deducted. For the wording, see CPR PD 36.10.3. Any offer, whether by claimant or defendant, should specify how much relates to heads of loss from which the defendant is entitled to deduct benefits. If it does not, the offeree cannot know the real cost or benefit of the offer. He should request clarification. Under CPR Part 36.9.1 a request for clarification of an offer should, strictly speaking, be made within seven days.

A defendant has to be careful how he phrases a settlement offer, in case he accidentally overcompensates the claimant or loses the benefits of Part 36.

CPR Part 36.23.4 says '. . . a claimant fails to better a Part 36 payment if he fails to obtain judgment for more than the gross sum specified in the Part 36 Payment Notice'.

CPR Part 36.23.3 requires the payment notice to state 'the name and amount of any benefit by which that gross amount is reduced in accordance with s8 and Schedule 2 to the 1997 Act'.

In *Hilton International* v. *Smith* [2001] PIQR P197 the claimant sought compensation for accelerated onset of spinal symptoms. He had received over £40,000 by way of state benefits for his injury. The defendant intended to offer the claimant £6,000. The payment notice recited the total from the CRU certificate as £40,124.58, and ended by saying: 'The gross amount of the compensation payment is therefore £46,124.58.' This made it virtually impossible for the claimant to better the offer as defined in Part 36.23.4. The claimant accepted the offer, and the defendant paid £6,000 to the claimant and the £40,000 to the CRU. The defendant was then entitled to appeal the CRU certificate, and did so on the basis that the benefits had not been paid because of the claimant's injuries. The appeal was successful, and a £40,000 refund arrived. The claimant asked the defendant to hand over the money. The county court ordered the defendant to do so, and its appeal to the High Court was unsuccessful. The terms of the payment in had been absolutely clear and there was no reason to suppose that the claimant knew, when accepting the offer, that the defendant was making a mistake.

CPR Part 36.23 apparently allows a compensator to make a Part 36 payment that takes account of the whole value of the CRU certificate, even if that produces a net payment (typically in a case of contributory negligence) that is less than the claimant's entitlement to general damages. However, the courts emphasise that the compensator has a duty to assess general damages fairly, and to ensure that they are not eroded by deduction of state benefits.

In *Williams* v. *Devon County Council* [2003] EWCA Civ 365 there was a CRU certificate of £15,000. The defendant paid in £10,000. Adding the CRU figure gave a gross offer in the payment notice of £25,000. The claimant went to trial. After a deduction for contributory negligence, she got £23,000 including £7,000 for loss of earnings. The defendant was entitled to offset state benefits only against loss of earnings. After offset of benefits, the claimant ended up with £16,000 in her pocket. On a common sense basis, she had beaten the payment-in. On a literal interpretation of CPR Part 36.23, she had not. Should she have her costs regardless?

The Court of Appeal in fact found that there had been no contributory negligence, but took the opportunity to say that under CPR Part 36.23.3:

> the amount by which the sum is reduced must be no more than the amount appropriate for the head of damages against which the benefits can be off-set . . . In the present case no attempt had been made [by the offerors to do this. The offerors] . . . were clearly arguing that there was contributory negligence, and that the period for which they were liable for lost earnings was substantially shorter than that which [the offeree] was claiming [which meant that the amount on the certificate was more than they could offset] . . . the amount of recoverable benefits had clearly not been 'reduced in accordance with s.8 and Schedule 2' . . . It was not a proper and therefore effective Part 36 payment.

16.7 ACCEPTING AN OFFER

A Part 36 offer as to liability can save a great deal of time and money. If liability can be agreed without trial, the claimant can enter judgment for damages to be assessed, and the court will reconsider the procedural timetable laid down by the Allocation Directions.

A party may propose a 95:05 or a 90:10 settlement to avoid the expense of investigating liability. In *Huck* v. *Robson* [2002] EWCA Civ 398 the claimant offered to settle his claim on a 95:05 basis, and was entitled to the usual benefits of making a Part 36 offer which the defendant failed to beat. An offer to settle for 100 per cent liability would have been merely a tactical device, but a 95:05 offer demonstrated a real and meaningful intention to settle.

If the claimant agrees liability at anything less than 100 per cent, it will affect his relationship with his own liability insurers. Before making or accepting such an offer, the claimant must consider whether he needs to make it part of the deal that the defendant abandons any counterclaim, and must check with his own insurers whether such a settlement will affect his no claims discount (NCD). Particularly if he wants to make a 95:05 offer for tactical reasons, he may be able to agree with them that his NCD will be unaffected by the settlement.

A Part 36 offer as to quantum is more easily dealt with. If the offeree wishes to accept in full and final settlement, and acts within 21 days of the offer, he simply files and serves N243A notice of acceptance as required by CPR PD 36.7.6. The notice sets out the claim number, the title of the proceedings, and the offer or payment the party is accepting. It is signed by the party or his legal representative. On receipt, the court stays the proceedings. The defendant discharges his CRU liability. The only remaining issue is legal costs, to which the claimant is automatically entitled under CPR Part 36.13.4.

If settlement terms have been agreed but the offer was not made under Part 36, or includes terms which the court has no power to order, or the claimant wants to accept it out of time, one cannot use the notice of acceptance procedure. One could agree a Tomlin Order, as on the accompanying CD-ROM, with the other party. This provides for proceedings to be stayed, and so avoids the heavy costs penalties that the court would impose on a claimant who disrupted a trial list by failing to tell it that the claim has settled. The claimant should make it a condition of settlement that the defendant pays his costs. If one settles a claim without any reference to costs, one is taken to have waived any claim for costs. If the claimant receives his damages and costs before a Tomlin Order is agreed, he can discontinue instead (see CPR Part 38).

Occasionally, fresh evidence comes to light before an offer is accepted. The offeror races to withdraw the offer, and the offeree races to accept. As a matter of contract law, the offeror may withdraw the offer at any time up until it is accepted (*Scammell* v. *Dicker* [2000] EWCA Civ 352). If a party seeks to accept an offer more than 21 days after it was made, note that CPR Part 36.11.2 says: 'If the parties do not agree the liability for costs the claimant may only accept the offer of payment with the permission of the court.' This apparently gives the defendant plenty of time to withdraw his offer while the claimant is waiting for permission. The same applies where the defendant needs permission to accept an offer by the claimant, because the offer should 'provide that after 21 days the offeree may only accept it if the parties agree the liability for costs; or the court gives permission' (CPR Part 36.5.6).

However, a Part 36 payment is more than just a contractual offer, and may be taken out of court or reduced 'only with the permission of the court' (CPR 36.6.5). Permission is not readily given (*Flynn* v. *Scougall* [2004] EWCA Civ 873).

16.8 OFFERS IN SMALL CLAIMS

'A Part 36 offer or a Part 36 payment shall not have the consequences set out in this Part while the claim is being dealt with on the Small Claims track unless the court orders otherwise' (CPR Part 36.2.5. See also CPR Part 27.2).

A claim is not a Small Claim until the claimant has issued proceedings and the claim has been allocated to track. Costs Practice Direction 15.1 says: 'Before a claim is allocated to [track] the court is not restricted by any of the special rules that apply to that track.' However, in *Voice & Script* v. *Alghafar* [2003] EWCA Civ 736, the Court of Appeal said 'where, if sought, an allocation would have been made to Small Claims track the normal rule should be that the Small Claims costs regime for costs should apply'.

If the claim has not yet been allocated and the defendant makes an offer which he states is pursuant to Part 36, the claimant may take this as a concession that the case is not suitable for the Small Claims track, and seek his costs in full on the standard basis as in *Dean* v. *Griffin* [2000] CL 443. However, *Voice & Script* cannot be said to encourage this approach, and CPR Part 36.2.5 does envisage a Part 36 offer being made in the Small Claims track.

The court may be willing to impose a modest penalty on a claimant who fails to beat a defendant's offer in a Small Claim, such as depriving the claimant of his costs as in *Coady* v. *Hawkins* (1998) CL 489.

CHAPTER 17

Issuing proceedings – an outline

Before issuing proceedings, the claimant must ensure that he has complied with the Pre-action Protocol, and that he has given the defendant enough information and time to consider liability and quantum, and to make a settlement offer (see **Chapter 3**).

If the claimant can make a reasonable settlement offer to the defendant, he should do so before issuing proceedings. It is likely that the courts will in future penalise claimants who do not.

17.1 COURT TRACKS

Most personal injury claims are brought in the county court. Under CPR Part 26, the court allocates each claim to one of three tracks when a defence is received. Allocation depends mainly on the financial value of the claim. Each track has its own rules, and its own timetable for progress to trial.

Generally, any civil claim worth £5,000 or less is a Small Claim. Under CPR Part 26.6.1, personal injury claims are an exception:

> The Small Claims track is the normal track for any claim for personal injuries where . . . the financial value of the claim is not more than £5,000; and . . . the financial value of any claim for damages for personal injuries is not more than £1,000 . . . [and in this context] 'damages for personal injuries' means damages claimed as compensation for pain, suffering and loss of amenity and does not include any other damages which are claimed.

The main point about Small Claims is that each party bears its own legal costs, win or lose. The speedy and informal Small Claims track holds many surprises for those who usually deal with larger claims. The Lord Chancellor's Department announced on 10 November 2004 that it may raise the Small Claims track limit in 2005, perhaps to £5,000 (see **Chapter 21**).

Under Part 26.6.4:

> the Fast Track is the normal track for any claim . . . for which the Small Claims track is not the normal track; and . . . which has a financial value of not more than £15,000 . . . [provided that] the trial is likely to last for no longer than one day; and

> . . . oral expert evidence at trial will be limited to . . . one expert per party in relation to any expert field; and . . . expert evidence in two expert fields.

One day is five hours of court time. A fast track claim will usually come before the judge for trial about 9–12 months after proceedings are issued.

Under Part 26.6: 'The Multi-Track is the normal track for any claim for which the Small Claims track or the Fast Track is not the normal track.' Multi-track claims are dealt with in more or less the same way as those in the fast track, but the courts allow slower progress to trial, and the use of more expert evidence. The main feature that distinguishes the multi-track is the Case Management Conference (CMC) at which the court will make searching enquiries. Anybody attending on a CMC must be very well prepared. Consider whether the directions made by the court so far have been complied with, in particular as to disclosure, and whether any further directions are needed, especially as regards expert evidence. Have a list of availability dates for all witnesses, including the reasons why any dates are given as unavailable. Be ready to answer any questions about the nature and extent of the issues that must be resolved at trial. For prompts, see the Complex Case Checklist on the accompanying CD-ROM.

If the claim is a heavyweight, consider whether it should be brought in the High Court. Personal injury proceedings worth £50,000 or more may be issued in the Queen's Bench Division of the High Court. If issuing in the High Court, indicate at the bottom of the front page of the claim form why this is appropriate on grounds of value, complexity, etc. (CPR PD 7.2.4). If one attempts to issue proceedings worth less than £50,000 in the High Court, it will generally transfer them to the county court. The High Court, but not the county court, has jurisdiction to deal with an allegation that legislation is incompatible with the Human Rights Act 1998. In the High Court, there is a better chance that case management and the trial itself will be dealt with by a Master and judge who really understand personal injury work. This is particularly likely if one issues proceedings in the Central Office (the Royal Courts of Justice (RCJ) in the Strand, London WC2) rather than a district registry. CPR PD 29.2.6 provides that claims suitable for trial in the RCJ include, amongst others, professional negligence, fatal incidents, malicious prosecution, false imprisonment and claims against the police. The RCJ has some rules and terms of its own. To find out about the 'Bear Garden', the 'Floating List' and other mysteries, see the Queen's Bench Guide at **www.courtservice.gov.uk**.

When the court assesses the financial value of a claim for allocation purposes, under CPR Part 26.8.2 it will 'disregard . . . any amount not in dispute'. This means amongst other things any 'specific sum claimed as a distinct item and which the defendant admits he is liable to pay' or for which he has offered a sum that has been 'accepted by the claimant in satisfaction of any item which forms a distinct part of the claim' (CPR PD 26.7.4).

Typically, the defendant will agree and pay the entire claim for vehicle damage soon after an accident, and he may do the same for other items if it means he can get the amount in dispute below the Small Claims limit.

17.2 ISSUING PROCEEDINGS

One needs an N1 claim form, particulars of claim, schedule of loss, medical report, response pack, letter from defendant's solicitors confirming they will accept service, and cheque for the issue fee. If representing the claimant under a conditional fee agreement then one needs an N251 Notice of Funding, and a Notice of Issue of Certificate if representing the claimant under public funding. Court forms, including the N1A Notes For Claimant on Completing A Claim Form, can be obtained free from a court office or downloaded from the Department for Constitutional Affairs website at **www.dca.gov.uk**.

The N1 claim form

CPR Part 16.2 and 3 apply. When stating the value of the claim, one must be realistic. It determines the amount of the issue fee, and may well act as a cap on the compensation (*Maguire* v. *Molin* [2002] EWCA Civ 1083). Give the claimant's actual address, even if his address for service is his solicitor's address. Under brief details of claim say something like: 'Damages for personal injuries, loss and damage arising out of a road traffic accident caused by the negligent driving of the defendant on [date].'

CPR Part 16.2.1(*c*) requires one to complete the statement of value so that the court knows which track is the usual one for the claim. There is a choice of '. . . not more than £5,000'; or '. . . more than £5,000 but not more than £15,000'; or '. . . more than £15,000'. One must also say whether the 'amount that the claimant expects to recover for pain, suffering and loss of amenity is [not] more than £1,000'. When calculating value for this purpose CPR Part 16.3 says that one should disregard interest, costs, contributory negligence, any counterclaim, and CRU clawback. On the back of the form, delete as appropriate to show whether the particulars of claim are included, to follow, or attached in the usual way.

Particulars of claim

See **section 17.3**.

Schedule of loss

'The claimant must attach to his Particulars of Claim a schedule of details of any past and future expenses and losses which he claims' (CPR PD 16.4.2). This is often known as the schedule of special damages. If one must issue proceedings without having precise figures for a head of loss, give an estimated figure and say what prevents one giving a final figure. For example: Amount to be advised on receipt of a therapist's quote, or . . . following disclosure by the defendant.

The schedule must end with a statement of truth complying with CPR PD 22. This was not so before 8 December 2003, but the CPR have been amended. It is prudent for the claimant's lawyer to have the claimant himself sign the statement of truth, rather than sign it on his behalf. For a typical schedule, see the accompanying CD-ROM.

Medical report

'Where the claimant is relying on the evidence of a medical practitioner the claimant must attach to or serve with his particulars of claim a report from a medical practitioner about the personal injuries which he alleges in his claim' (CPR PD 16.4.3). If one has reports from medical experts in two disciplines, attach them both.

Forms and notes

The following are required: N9 Response Pack and Acknowledgment of Service, with N1C Notes for Defendant, N9C Admission Form and N9D form for defence and counterclaim. These are to advise and assist the defendant. They can be downloaded from **www.dca.gov.uk**.

Letters from solicitors

If the defendant has instructed solicitors to accept service of these proceedings, a copy of a letter from the solicitors confirming this is required. One can serve proceedings on nominated solicitors only if they have given written confirmation that they are instructed to accept service (CPR Part 6.4.2 and *Smith* v. *Probyn* [2000] EWHC 136 (QB)). Where they have given this confirmation, one must serve them and not the defendant (*Nanglegan* v. *The Royal Free Hampstead NHS Trust* [2001] EWCA Civ 127). There is an exception if the defendant is a limited company, as the claimant can serve in the ways permitted by the CPR or rely on the Companies Act 1985 and serve the company at its registered office (CPR Part 6.2.2 and *Murphy* v. *Staples Ltd* [2003] EWCA Civ 656).

Cheque for the court fee

This can be from £30 to £1,700 depending on the value of the claim. If the claimant has a low income, he may be exempt from paying court fees. For the latest information, see **www.courtservice.gov.uk**.

Notice of Issue of Legal Aid, or N251 Notice of Funding

A prudent claimant will serve these on the defendant himself, and not rely entirely on the court to do it for him.

17.3 PARTICULARS OF CLAIM

This document is the claimant's statement of case. Statements of case are the formal documents in which each party states its arguments. There are strict rules about both content and layout, mainly in CPR Parts 5 and 16, and CPR PD 5 and 16. If a party omits to state a point in his statement of case, he cannot argue it at trial except by amending. Once the particulars of claim have been served on the defendant, they cannot be amended without the permission of the defendant or the court (CPR Part 17 and CPR PD 17, and CPR PD22.1.2). There is a good deal of case law on this topic.

The costs regime imposed by the CPR is an incentive to law firms to do without counsel as far as possible, but few law firms have the heavyweight textbooks (costing £300 to £3,000) that would enable them to draw up all their own statements of case in personal injury work. Most get around this by recycling tried and tested precedents for routine claims, and instructing counsel to draw up the statements of case in very high-value claims, and in those that involve breach of workplace statutory duties, breach of contract; trespass to the person; nuisance; claims against the police; clinical negligence; the Admiralty jurisdiction; claims that rely directly on European Union law or the Human Rights Act 1998; claims involving international conventions such as the Convention on Limitation of Liability for Maritime Claims 1976, the Warsaw Convention for the Unification of Certain Rules Relating to International Carriage by Air 1929, the International Convention concerning the Carriage of Passengers and Luggage by Rail or the Convention on the Contract for the International Carriage of Passengers and Luggage by Road; and some fatal incident claims.

'If practicable, the Particulars of Claim should be set out in the Claim Form' (CPR PD 16.3.1). In personal injury cases they are usually too big to fit, and must be supplied as a separate document.

Statements of case should by typed on durable A4 paper with a 3.5cm margins. Each paragraph and page should be numbered. All numbers, including dates, should be given as figures not words (CPR PD 5.2). Start with the court's heading (In the . . . County Court, Case no . . . Between . . . claimant and . . . defendant) (CPR PD 16.3.8). Under that, give a title (Particulars of Claim) so that the reader can identify the document at a glance. In clinical negligence claims, the words clinical negligence should be inserted at the top of every statement of case (CPR PD 16.9.3).

Use short paragraphs. Try to avoid mixing, in the same paragraph, facts which the defendant is likely to agree and those he is likely to dispute. It makes life easier for the court if the particulars of claim start with a paragraph or two of facts about the accident that can all be agreed in the first sentence of the defence.

Particulars of claim are essentially a concise statement of the facts upon which the claimant relies (CPR Part 16.4.1). They may be struck out if they do not contain a coherent set of facts and disclose a legally recognisable claim (CPR PD 3.1.4).

Coherent set of facts

This should include date; time; place; what happened; why the defendant was to blame; and what injury, loss and damage the defendant caused. Give sufficient but not excessive detail. 'Make clear the general nature of the case . . . no more than a concise statement of the facts is required . . . excessive particulars can . . . obscure the issues. . .' (*McPhilemy v. Times Newspapers* [1999] EWCA Civ 1464). The amount of factual detail is a matter of legal fashion. There are some typical examples on the accompanying CD-ROM.

One can refer in the statement of case to any point of law on which the claim is based (CPR PD 16.13.3). Except that one cites any statutory duty that the defendant is alleged to have broken, one states facts, not law. One states law by saying 'the defendant is vicariously liable for the negligent driving of Fred Bloggs,' but facts amounting to the same thing if one says 'At all material times the defendants employed the said Fred Bloggs who drove the said van in the course of his employment with the defendant.'

Do not state evidence: 'The defendant knew or should have known that the claimant was underneath the vehicle at the time' not 'and the claimant knows this because he had just asked the claimant if he needed anything in town and the claimant had said from under the vehicle that he didn't.' Evidence is delivered in the witness statements. However, a plan or photograph may be attached if it will make it much easier for the court to understand the allegations (CPR PD 16.13.3).

Do not state anything for which there is simply no evidence. One can include an allegation based solely on the claimant's testimony but one cannot include mere speculation.

Legally recognisable claim

Most claims rest on an allegation that the defendant's negligence caused the claimant's injury, loss and damage. Some claims are based on breach of contract, breach of the duty of care of an occupier of premises under the Occupiers' Liability Acts, or breach of statutory duty. It is normal in these cases to state a backup allegation of negligence. It is normal, in cases of vicarious liability, to proceed against both employee and employer. However, one must beware of complicating a claim by adding unnecessary allegations that run up costs, as this is likely to result in a costs penalty. It is rare today to allege nuisance in a personal injury claim (see **section 4.1**).

One must state the facts upon which the claim depends. If alleging vicarious liability, state it as above. If the claimant was injured on premises and relies on the Occupiers' Liability Acts, one states that 'the defendant was at all material times the occupier of the said premises,' and that the claimant had been 'invited by the defendant to enter the premises as a visitor,' or as appropriate (see **section 4.5**).

The capacity of the defendant may be an essential part of the claim, If the claimant tripped on a broken paving slab and is suing the local council, one needs to allege that it was 'at all material times the highway authority for the said pavement' (see **section 4.3**).

The relationship between the parties may be vital, especially if the claimant can rely on a breach of statutory duty by the defendant only if he was employed by the defendant. For example, 'At all material times the claimant was employed by the defendant under a contract for service as a manual labourer.' If appropriate, state that the injury occurred while the claimant was in the course of his employment (see **section 6.6**).

In a fatal incident claim, one must give 'particulars pursuant to statute' (see CPR PD 16, the Law Reform (Miscellaneous Provisions) Act 1934 and the Fatal Accidents Act 1976). The claimant must say in what capacity he brings the claim (usually administrator of the deceased's estate); which statute he relies on; whether the claim is for the benefit of the estate and/or the dependants; and the date of birth of any dependant. One must give details of the grant of probate or letters of administration, and describe the dependency claim.

One may need to state knowledge or constructive knowledge. One alleges that the defendant knew something (for example, knowing that the claimant was underneath the vehicle at the time) or that he should have known something (for example the defendant knew or should have known that if petrol is heated to this extent it will explode) (CPR PD 16.8.2). State why the defendant knew or should have known this fact.

If the claim is based on breach of statutory duty, one states not only which paragraphs of the relevant regulations were applicable, but also the facts that made them applicable. For example, the said premises were at all material times a quarry within the meaning of the . . . Regulations, and the said Regulations applied.

The claimant may have a good idea what defences will be raised in due course, but he should not try to anticipate them in the particulars of claim. In particular, note that regulation X might require the defendant 'so far as is reasonably practicable to avoid the need for his employees to undertake any manual handling operations at work which involve a risk of their being injured'. The claimant should never state that the defendant failed to comply with the said duty as far as reasonably practicable. The claimant wants the defendant either to forget to raise this as a defence, or at least by raising it so bear the burden of proving that he had done all that was reasonably practicable to comply with Regulation X. Instead he states: 'In breach of the said duty the defendant failed to avoid the need for the claimant to undertake the said manual handling operation' (see **section 6.8**).

The claimant should generally avoid making positive allegations as to exactly what the defendant should have done to comply with his duty. 'I cannot believe that Parliament intended to impose on the injured workman . . . the obligation to aver with the necessary particularity the manner in which the employer should have employed reasonably practicable means to make and keep the place safe for him. . .' (*Nimmo* v. *Alexander Cowan & Sons Ltd* [1968] AC 107). Unless the claimant states what should have been done, he can reserve his position until the defendant has set out his own views.

Other requirements

If the defendant was convicted of a criminal offence arising out of the incident, the claimant should state the conviction in the particulars of claim, and state to which issue it is relevant (CPR PD 16.8.1).

If the defendant has already admitted liability for the accident, the claimant should state this. If the defendant has also admitted that the breach caused the injury and damage, he will state that too. The distinction is important, as 'Nothing short of a clear admission of liability, both of negligence causing the accident and of damage resulting from the accident caused by the negligence, is enough to . . . entitle the [claimant] to judgment' (*Rankine* v. *Garton* [1979] 2 All ER 1185).

If the claim is based on breach of contract, attach a copy of the contract (CPR PD 16.7.3).

Any human rights element must be stated (CPR PD 16.15 and CPR PD 19.4A).

Turning to quantum, one must include the claimant's date of birth, and brief details of the claimant's personal injuries (CPR PD 16.4.1). One attaches to the particulars of claim, or serves with it, medical evidence under CPR PD 16.4.3, and in the text of the particulars of claim one should refer to the report by author and date.

If there is any unusual loss of amenity, it should be stated (see **Chapter 12**). Certainly one should state any claim for risk on the labour market, loss of job satisfaction, loss of leisure time, and loss of marriage prospects (see **sections 12.1–12.4**).

If the claimant wants provisional damages, these must be stated as required by CPR PD 16.4.4. The same applies to aggravated and exemplary damages (CPR Part 16.4.1).

CPR PD 16.8.2 says: 'The claimant must specifically set out the following matters in his particulars of claim where he wishes to rely on them in support of his claim . . . any facts relating to mitigation of loss or damage.' This is not generally read as an invitation for the claimant to state that he has made an attempt to mitigate his losses, still less to give details of his search for a new job. The best view is perhaps that a claimant complies with PD 16.8.2 if he mentions only those mitigation attempts that failed so badly they increased his losses.

A request for interest on damages stating why the claimant is entitled to it (CPR Part 16.4). Unless the claimant has a contractual right to interest, he is entitled to it under s.35A of the Supreme Court Act 1981 and s.69 of the County Courts Act 1984.

Prayer

It was conventional, before the CPR, to include a 'prayer' for damages towards the end of the particulars of claim. Many claimant lawyers still do so, adapting the prayer to modern times by repeating the Statement of Value from the N1 Claim Form. For example:

AND the claimant claims:

(1) Damages not exceeding £5,000 where the amount which the claimant expects to recover as general damages for pain, suffering and loss of amenity exceeds £1,000

(2) Under paragraph . . . hereof interest for such periods and at such rates as to the court shall seem just.

Completion

Finish with a signed statement of truth complying with CPR PD 22. '[I believe][The claimant believes] that the facts stated in these Particulars of Claim are true' (CPR PD 16.3.4). It is much better to have the claimant sign this than for the claimant's lawyer to sign it. Include the claimant's address for service (CPR PD 16.3.8) and the signature of the lawyer or law firm who drew up the document (CPR PD 5.2.1).

17.4 GIVING NOTICE OF PROCEEDINGS

In road traffic cases, the claimant should serve notice on the defendant's insurers so as to obtain the protection of s.151 Road Traffic Act 1988. If the defendant's insurers avoid or cancel his insurance policy, this generally lets the claimant recover the damages from the insurer directly. Notice must be served before or within seven days after the commencement of the proceedings.

Even verbal notice may be enough in a relatively small claim, but it is far better to give 'clear and timely notice . . . preferably in writing, and probably by sending to the insurers or their solicitors a copy of the claim form' (*Nawaz* v. *Crowe Insurance Group* [2003] EWCA Civ 316).

If the accident was caused by an uninsured driver, the MIB notice requirements go much further than s.151. Under the MIB Uninsured Drivers Agreement 1999 one must give written notice of issue of proceedings to the MIB or any relevant insurer not later than 14 days after issue, confirming that proceedings have been commenced by claim form and enclosing particulars of claim, copy correspondence, etc. (see **section 7.3**).

17.5 THE DEFENCE

The defence is the defendant's statement of case and his response to the particulars of claim. A defendant will very seldom write his defence on the Admission, Defence and Counterclaim form supplied in the court's Response Pack. It will be a separate document, on the same principles as the particulars of claim. See CPR Parts 15 and 16, and the corresponding Practice Directions. For a typical example, see the accompanying CD-ROM.

A defence must be filed at court (CPR Part 15.2) and served on every other party (CPR Part 15.6). It must generally be filed 14 days after service of the particulars of claim, or if the defendant filed an acknowledgment of service, 28 days after service of the particulars of claim. (CPR Part 15.4). The defendant and the claimant can agree an extension of this time by up to 28 days (CPR Part 15.5). No further extension can be agreed even if the claimant is willing. If the defendant realises that any further extension is needed, he must at once apply to the court.

A defendant must not file a defence simply to buy time, or to defend a claim to which there is no real defence. Both of these amount to unreasonable behaviour such that costs may be awarded against a defendant even in a Small Claim, and a costs penalty may be imposed in the fast track or multi-track.

The defendant must state 'which of the allegations in the Particulars of Claim he denies; which allegations he is unable to admit or deny but which he requires the claimant to prove; and which allegations he admits' (CPR Part 16.5.1).

If he simply denies all the allegations without saying why, the court may strike this out as a bare denial (CPR PD 3.1.6). If a competent defendant lawyer serves a bare denial, it reveals that the defendant has not given his lawyer adequate instructions. It may well mean that he has vanished without trace.

If the defendant intends to put forward a different version of events from that given by the claimant he must state his own version (CPR Part 16.5). If he does not deal with an allegation, and the allegation is not inconsistent with the version of events the defendant is putting forward, he is taken to agree it (CPR Part 16.5.5).

The defendant may refer to any point of law on which his defence is based (CPR PD 16.13.3). He must state anything that he wishes to set up as a positive defence, such as that:

- The defendant's vehicle was stationary when the claimant's vehicle collided with it.
- The defendant had done all he should to comply with a statutory duty that required him, for example, 'so far as is reasonably practicable to avoid the need for his employees to undertake any manual handling operations at work which involve a risk of their being injured' (*Nimmo* v. *Alexander Cowan & Sons Ltd* [1968] AC 107 and *Bowes* v. *Sedgefield District Council* [1981] ICR 234).
- The claim is time barred (CPR PD 16.13.1) (see **Chapter 18**).
- The claimant has already reached full and final settlement with the defendant.
- There have already been proceedings before a court or tribunal at which the claim was, or should have been, dealt with, so under the rule in *Henderson* v. *Henderson* no further claim can be brought (see **section 16.1**).
- The claim is based on the claimant's own crime, and the maxim *ex turpi causa non oritur actio* provides a complete defence, as in *Cross* v. *Kirkby* (2000) *The Times* 5 April in which a hunt saboteur had been injured with his own baseball bat.
- The claimant's losses are of illegal earnings because they were based on tax evasion, or because he got his job by making a fraudulent health declaration, and *ex turpi* provides a defence to that part of the claim (see **section 13.4**).
- The claimant has presented his claim dishonestly. An allegation of malingering is a serious allegation of fraud. The defendant must not state the facts and leave the court to draw the inference of fraud, but specifically allege fraud in the defence. However, if a party does so without having reasonably credible material establishing a prima facie case of fraud, his lawyer may face a wasted costs order (*Medcalf v. Weatherill* [2002] UKHL 27). Even in the smallest claims, the court takes such an allegation very

seriously. If the allegation is made in a Small Claim, it will usually be allocated to the fast track (CPR PD 26.8.1).
- The defendant is not a joint and several tortfeasor, and should not be required to pay more than a proportion of the damages (see **section 4.5**).
- The claimant's own carelessness was partly responsible for the accident or his injuries, and the defendant claims a discount for contributory negligence (see **section 4.14**).
- The claimant has failed to mitigate his losses (see **section 9.6**).

If the defendant has obtained a medical report and proposes to rely on it, he should attach a copy (CPR PD 16.12.1).

If a medical report is served with the particulars of claim, the defence should state whether the defendant agrees what it says, disputes what it says (and if so why), or neither agrees nor disputes it but has no knowledge of the matters it describes (CPR PD 16.12.1). The same applies to the schedule of loss. If the defendant disputes it, he should do so in a counter-schedule, preferably echoing the layout of the schedule (CPR PD 16.12.2).

The defendant may dispute the Statement of Value in the Claim Form (CPR Part 16.5.6). It can save him a great deal of money if he persuades the court to allocate what is apparently a fast track claim to the Small Claims track, or what is apparently a large claim to the fast track.

A defence must be verified by a statement of truth complying with CPR PD 22.

If the defendant alleges that another party is liable with him, or instead of him, he will usually want to join that party to the proceedings in order to obtain contribution or indemnity under the Civil Liability (Contribution) Act 1978, or to escape liability altogether. The procedure is set out in CPR Part 20 and CPR PD 20. The defendant should if possible deal with this at the same time as he serves his defence (see **section 4.17**).

17.6 COUNTERCLAIMS

In a typical road accident there is damage to the defendant's vehicle, as well as the claimant's. If the defendant was injured or did not have fully-comprehensive insurance for his vehicle damage, he may be prompted to make a counterclaim under CPR Part 20. The claimant must respond swiftly by filing and serving a defence to counterclaim (CPR Part 15.4).

The claimant is probably insured for any liability that may arise, but must notify his own liability insurers immediately. They will usually instruct the claimant's own lawyer to deal with the defence to counterclaim on their behalf.

A counterclaim is not set off against the claimant's compensation. Therefore if liability is divided 50:50, the claimant recovers 50 per cent of his damages and the defendant gets 50 per cent of the value of the counterclaim.

The normal costs order where there is claim and counterclaim is as follows. If liability is divided between the parties, the defendant pays the full costs of the claim including the costs of resolving the liability issue, but as the Part 20 claimant he is entitled to the costs that relate purely to his counterclaim. If the claimant fails completely, the claimant normally has to pay all the costs. If the claimant accepts a settlement offer made by the defendant, the claimant is entitled to his costs relating to defence of the counterclaim (CPR 36.13.3).

17.7 UNDER 18 OR MENTAL DISABILITY

A person who is under 18, or is a mental patient as defined by the Mental Health Act 1983 is said to be under a disability. This affects litigation in various ways. See CPR Part 21 and the corresponding PD 21, which lay down general rules and cover the appointment of a litigation friend to conduct proceedings on behalf of the person under a disability. See also CPR Part 6 as to service of proceedings on a child or mental patient; CPR Part 40 on structured settlements, which one should be particularly ready to consider when settling a claim for a claimant under a disability; and the Court of Protection Rules 2001 which deal with mental patients, the Court of Protection, and the appointment of a Receiver to control a patient's finances.

Under s.94(2) of the 1983 Act the court has power to manage a person's estate if 'after considering medical evidence [it] is satisfied that a person is incapable, by reason of mental disorder, of managing and administering his property and affairs, and a person as to whom [it] is so satisfied is referred to . . . as a patient'. At the time of writing, both the Court of Protection and the definition of mental incapacity are shortly to be overhauled. For the latest news about the Mental Capacity Bill 2003, go to the website of the Department for Constitutional Affairs (**www.dca.gov.uk**).

The 1983 Act and the CPR both use a subjective test of incapability. The more complex the claimant's affairs, the more likely it is he will be incapable of managing them. However, an inability to grasp the finer points of a complex claim does not amount to mental incapability, and the court will not necessarily accept a consultant psychiatrist's view that the claimant is incapable (*W* v. *L (mental health patient)* [1973] 3 All ER 884 and *Masterman-Lister* v. *Jewell & Home Counties Dairies* [2002] EWCA Civ 1889).

An adult is presumed to be mentally competent until proven otherwise, but if one is acting for a claimant who is very elderly or has suffered a head injury, one must be alert for signs of incapability. For example, emotional outbursts, inconsistent instructions, difficulty in obtaining instructions, or hints from his family. If alerted that the claimant may be mentally incapable, one should ask him for permission to obtain a medical report about his mental state. Unless one can say that the defendant's negligence has made the claimant mentally incapable, this will have to be done at the claimant's own expense. If the claim is of modest value, one might obtain the report from the claimant's GP. If not, one will need to instruct a consultant psychiatrist. If the claimant refuses to attend and pay for a psychiatric examination, a difficult situation arises. One may wish to discuss the position with the Law Society's professional ethics department.

The BMA and the Law Society jointly author a slim book called *Assessment of Mental Capacity – Guidance for Doctors and Lawyers*, which is available from the Law Society bookshop, (tel) 0207 320 5640, **www.lawsociety.org.uk**.

CPR Part 21.10 says 'where a claim is made by or on behalf of [a claimant under a disability] no settlement compromise or payment and no acceptance of money paid into court shall be valid . . . without the approval of the court'. A claimant under a disability cannot give a good receipt for damages. Neither can his representatives. Unless the court procedure is followed, the defendant may end up compensating the claimant twice.

CPR Part 21.10 allows a party to back out of an agreement on liability or quantum if one party to the agreement is under a disability and the court has not yet approved the terms (*Dietz* v. *Lennig Chemicals* [1969] 1 AC 170 and *Drinkall* v. *Whitwood* [2003] EWCA Civ 1547).

To obtain the court's approval, see the procedure in CPR Part 21.10 and PD 21. Arguably, if the court's approval is necessary, even a claim worth less than the Small Claims limit should be allocated to the fast track. Consider *M (a minor)* v. *Liverpool City Council* [1994] CLY 3774 and *K* v. *Grocutt* [2001] 2 CL 49. If the only reason for issuing proceedings is to obtain the court's approval to a settlement, the claimant can use the swift procedure under CPR Part 8.

Most personal injury claims are fairly small. A defendant will generally prefer to pay a child's compensation straight to his parents in return for their signing a parental indemnity form. The claimant's lawyer must not be a party to a breach of CPR Part 21.11, which says: 'Where in any proceedings . . . money is recovered by or on behalf of or for the benefit of a child or patient; or . . . money paid into court is accepted by or on behalf of a child or patient, the money shall be dealt with in accordance with directions given by the court under this rule and not otherwise.'

In the case of a child (and a mental patient if the fund is up to £20,000) the court usually deals with damages by investing them itself, paying out when the child reaches the age of 18 or when money is needed for a particular purpose. The court will seldom release money for a child's normal living expenses. If the child wants a pony, that might result in a payment-out. If the fund is only £500 or so and the claimant's parents strike the judge as being trustworthy, he may simply pay it out to them to hold for the claimant until he is 18.

In the case of a mental patient, funds of more than £20,000 are usually handled by the Public Guardianship Office (PGO) for the Court of Protection, and funds of more than £30,000 are always handled by the PGO (see **Appendix 4** for contact details). If the claimant's mental disability is the fault of the defendant, the claim for special damages should include the management costs of the Court of Protection. However the fund is held, the claimant's lawyer needs to ensure that it is disregarded for the purpose of means-tested benefits (see **section 9.16**).

The court looks after the affairs of a mental patient, via a Receiver who is generally a close relative of the patient. The Receiver's task is to decide what the patient needs and request payments from the funds in court. Even if an honest and businesslike relative is available, it may be best to instruct a solicitor or accountant to act as Receiver for the first few years (*Eagle* v. *Chambers (No2)* [2004] EWCA Civ 1033). A professional Receiver is likely to charge at least £3,500 per annum for his services. He can and should be insured in case he makes off with the funds.

CHAPTER 18

Outline of limitation

18.1 LIMITATION ACT 1980

A claim must be settled, or proceedings issued, within the limitation period. For accidental injury this is usually three years from the date of the injury. Beyond this time, the claim is time-barred. This does not mean that the claimant's right is extinguished, except for claims brought under the Consumer Protection Act 1987. However, the claimant's remedy will be barred if the defendant is entitled to rely on a limitation defence and so states in the defence.

Time seldom runs against claimants who were, at the time of the accident, under 18 or incapable by reason of mental disorder of managing and administering their property and affairs (s.28 Limitation Act 1980). Claims brought under the Consumer Protection Act 1987 are an exception, under s.11A of the Act.

There are several specialist textbooks on limitation. A new Limitation Act, making extensive changes, is expected shortly, but in the meantime the law is contained in the Limitation Act 1980.

Most personal injury claims are covered by s.11 of the 1980 Act, which applies to 'any action for damages for negligence, nuisance or breach of duty [whether statutory or contractual] . . . where the damages claimed by the plaintiff for the negligence, nuisance or breach of duty consist of or include damages in respect of personal injuries. . .'. Any action must be brought within 'three years from . . . the date on which the cause of action accrued, or . . . the date of knowledge (if later) of the person injured'.

The claimant's date of knowledge is when he knows that he has suffered a significant injury; that it was attributable to the defendant's act or omission; and the identity of the defendant (s.14 of the 1980 Act).

The court has a general discretion under s.33 of the 1980 Act to extend the three-year time limit, taking into account the length of, and reasons for, the delay; the effect of the delay on the evidence in the case; the conduct of the defendant after the cause of action arose, including his response to the claimant's reasonable requests for information; the duration of any disability of the claimant arising after the accrual of the cause of action; the extent to which the claimant acted promptly and reasonably once he knew he might have an action for damages; and the steps, if any, taken by the claimant to obtain medical, legal or other expert advice together with the nature of any advice he received.

Sections 14 and 33 have been closely examined in many stale cases of clinical negligence, industrial disease, child abuse and educational failure. See in particular *Spargo* v. *North Essex District Health Authority* [1997] EWCA Civ 1232, *K R & others* v. *Bryn Alyn Community Homes* [2003] EWCA Civ 85, and *Adams* v. *Bracknell Forest* [2004] UKHL 29.

Note that if the claimant issued proceedings within the limitation period, and needs to re-issue them against the same defendant outside the limitation period, s.33 will very seldom apply (*Walkley* v. *Precision Forgings Ltd* [1979] 2 All ER 548). This situation arises where the claimant issued proceedings but failed to serve them before they expired; or served them without giving notice as required by the MIB Uninsured Drivers Agreement or s.151 Road Traffic Act 1988. Although *Walkley* has attracted much criticism, it appears that it is not contrary to Article 6 of the European Convention on Human Rights 1950 (see *Young* v. *Western Power Distribution* [2003] EWCA Civ 1034). It may be possible to avoid the effect of *Walkley* by arguing that the first proceedings were not valid, as in *McEvoy* v. *AA Welding & Fabrication* [1997] EWCA Civ 2921; the second proceedings are technically against a different defendant, as in *Shapland* v. *Palmer* [1999] EWCA Civ 1061 or *Piggott* v. *Aulton* [2003] EWCA Civ 24.

Section 2 of the Limitation Act 1980 applies to claims based on trespass. An action 'shall not be brought after the expiration of six years from the date on which the cause of action accrued'. Again, time does not generally run against a person under a disability. Section 33 does not apply to these cases, and this basically prevents a claimant proceeding with child abuse claims against the actual abuser if the claimant has reached the age of 18 plus six without issuing proceedings (*Stubbings* v. *Webb* [1993] AC 498). It appears that this different limitation period for trespass cases is not incompatible with Article 14 of the European Convention on Human Rights 1950 (*Stubbings* v. *United Kingdom* [1996] ECHR 44).

It has long been established that a defendant may waive the right to rely on a limitation defence, and that parties may enter into an agreement whereby the defendant waives this right. However, the court will not accept that he has done so unless he gave very clear confirmation, upon which the claimant must usually have relied to his detriment (*Seechurn* v. *Ace Insurance* [2002] 2 Lloyd's Rep 390). A defendant cannot be deprived of his right to rely on a limitation defence 'merely because he has continued to negotiate with another party about the claim after the limitation period had expired and without anything being agreed about the manner in which the claim was to be resolved if negotiations broke down' (*Hillingdon Borough Council* v. *ARC* [2000] EWCA Civ 191).

18.2 OTHER TIME LIMITS

Although the general time limit on applications to the MIB is three years, under the Untraced Drivers Agreement 2003 if the applicant is to recover for property damage he must report the incident to the police within five days, and lodge the application within nine months, and even if there is no property damage claim the incident must be reported to the police within 14 days. Time under the Untraced Drivers Agreement does run against victims under 18 and mental patients (see **section 7.2**).

Under the Uninsured Drivers Agreement 1999 certain steps must be taken as soon as reasonably practicable (see **section 7.3**).

If the accident occurred overseas, on board ship, in the air, at the airport, or on an international road or rail journey, the Limitation Act may well not apply. Time limits may be shorter than the usual three years, or not be capable of extension.

If the claimant is entitled to make a claim for unfair dismissal or discrimination, the time limit for an application to the Employment Tribunal is a matter of months (see **section 6.20**).

Human rights proceedings under the European Convention on Human Rights 1950 have a basic one-year time limit, with discretion to extend. Applications to the European Court of Human Rights are made when all remedies through the UK courts have been exhausted, and must be made within a period of six months from the date on which the final UK decision is taken.

Criminal injuries compensation is paid within a statutory scheme. The applicant must report the incident to the police promptly. The application should be made as soon as possible, and in any case within two years of the injury (see **Chapter 8**).

There is a six-year time limit on claims under the Protection from Harassment Act 1997, see **section 4.6**.

If, having obtained judgment against the defendant in a personal injuries claim, the claimant has to rely on his rights against the defendant's insurers under the Third Parties (Rights against Insurers) Act 1930, it seems that for limitation purposes this is not a claim for 'damages in respect of personal injuries' (*Burns* v. *Shuttlehurst* [1999] 1 WLR 1449).

CHAPTER 19

Outline of legal costs

Legal costs is a very large topic, and in a personal injury handbook it can only be touched upon. For a concise introduction, see O'Hare & Browne's *Civil Litigation*, published by Sweet & Maxwell. John O'Hare is a costs judge and Master of the Supreme Court Costs Office.

The loser generally pays the winner's legal costs. Technically, costs means

> fees, charges, disbursements, expenses, remuneration, reimbursement allowed to a litigant in person under Rule 48.6, any additional liability incurred under a funding arrangement, and any fee or reward charged by a lay representative for acting on behalf of a party in proceedings allocated to the Small Claims track
>
> (CPR Part 43.2.1)

Additional liability is essentially the success fee and legal expenses insurance premium payable by the loser where the winner was represented under a conditional fee agreement (see **section 19.1**).

The expression 'costs and disbursements' distinguishes between a party's profit costs (solicitor's fees) and disbursements paid for by the party or his solicitor, such as court fees, medical report fees, and the cost of a copy of the police accident report.

The Small Claims track is an exception to the loser pays rule, the loser having only a very limited liability for the winner's costs (see **Chapter 21**).

19.1 CONDITIONAL FEE AGREEMENTS

Conditional fee agreements (CFAs), were introduced by statute in the 1990s to cushion the blow when legal aid was withdrawn for most personal injury claims. Legal aid is still available in some situations (see **section 1.2**).

A solicitor who represents a claimant under a CFA gets paid nothing if the claim fails, and generally has to pay the disbursements out of his own pocket until the end of the claim. If the claim succeeds he gets his base costs and a success fee on top. The success fee is a percentage of the base costs, up to 100 per cent for very risky claims. The unsuccessful defendant has to pay the base costs and the success fee, and will also be liable to reimburse the claimant for the cost of an after-the-event (ATE or AEI) legal expenses insurance policy.

CFAs are governed by very detailed regulations about the contents of the agreements and about what the claimant must be told. Defendants are naturally unwilling to pay the success fee and ATE premium. This has produced a great deal of satellite litigation in the last 10 years, often on very technical points. The Court of Appeal put the brakes on with *Hollins* v. *Russell* [2003] EWCA Civ 718, saying that a CFA is unenforceable only if there is a materially adverse effect on the client or on the proper administration of justice. The courts have also set benchmarks for success fees.

From 1 June 2003, CPR Part 45.15 says that in road traffic accidents that occurred on or after 6 October 2003 the success fee will be 12.5 per cent if the claim settles, or 100 per cent if it goes to trial. This may be varied in a claim worth over £500,000 (see also **section 19.3**). In employer's liability cases relating to injuries sustained before 1 October 2004, other than road traffic and industrial disease cases, CPR Part 45.20 provides for a basic success fee of 25 per cent, or 100 per cent if it goes to trial.

Otherwise, the court assesses the success fee for itself, according to the criteria in Costs Practice Direction 11.8. In a very straightforward claim, a success fee of 5 per cent of base costs may be appropriate, to allow for what the court in *Callery* v. *Gray* [2001] EWCA Civ 1117 described as 'the wholly unexpected risk lurking below the limpid waters of the simplest of claims'. *Halloran* v. *Delaney* [2003] EWCA Civ 1258 indicates that 5 per cent is appropriate if prospects of success are 'virtually 100 per cent'. A success fee of 25 per cent may be appropriate for a housing disrepair case as in *Bowen* v. *Bridgend County Council* [2004] EWHC 9010 (Costs) (see **section 5.6**). In *Abrew* v. *Tesco Stores* [2003] EWHC 446 (QB) the Supreme Court Costs Master approved a 50 per cent success fee for a claim involving a slip in a shop (see **section 5.4**).

Success fees are assessed at the very start of the case, before the claimant knows whether the defendant will admit liability. The courts are now getting very keen on stepped success fees, which start off with a high percentage success fee on the assumption that liability will not be admitted, but provide for a change to a much lower percentage if it is.

ATE insurance should cover the claimant for the risk that he might lose and have to pay the defendant's legal costs. It generally also protects the claimant against having to pay for his own disbursements if he loses. ATE insurance is bought on the open market, and can cost £10,000 or more in a heavyweight clinical negligence case. At the time of writing, typical premiums in routine cases are £350–£450 for road traffic, and £750–£900 for employer's liability (excluding industrial disease). However much the claimant actually paid for his ATE insurance, the defendant has to reimburse him only for a reasonable amount. This is relevant where the ATE insurer has bundled other services with the insurance. 'Bells and whistles' that may be included in a luxury ATE policy may include cover for:

- The costs of the claimant's lawyer if the claimant loses. The legislation did not intend both to give the claimant's lawyer a success fee if he wins and to insure his costs in case the claim fails.
- Deferral of the premium so it need not be paid until the end of the claim.
- The risk that the premium may not all be allowed if the court carries out a detailed assessment of the costs properly payable by the defendant.
- The services of a claims manager from a company that exists to advertise for claimants and sell their details to solicitors.

In exceptional cases, the court will assess the correct amount for an ATE premium. It will do so according to Costs Practice Direction 11.10. In practice, the court's starting point is the amounts previously approved by the courts in similar cases. Bearing in mind swings in the ATE market, the court will be most impressed by recent cases.

Funding is still a very fast moving and technical area, and the ATE market is still unstable. ATE insurers demand detailed and regular information about the progress of claims. It took a lot of time to comply with the old legal aid system, but the head of a personal injury department today can easily spend one third of his time on CFA compliance. Claimant lawyers have suffered enough catastrophic outcomes in the last few years to show that many are not spending enough time on compliance. To keep up to date, one can subscribe to the Law Society's bi-monthly magazine *Litigation Funding*.

19.2 COSTS IF PROCEEDINGS WERE ISSUED

If the claim settled after proceedings were issued, the court has jurisdiction over costs and disbursements. It will order the loser to pay most or all of the winner's costs. It may express its displeasure over delay or misconduct by ordering the winner to pay part of the loser's costs. The court's discretion is exercised within fairly narrow confines created by the CPR and case law.

The court's costs officer carries out a detailed assessment of costs after a multi-track trial or other hearing lasting more than one day; if the party receiving the costs is legally aided, a child or a mental patient; or if the claim settles without a hearing and the parties are unable to agree costs.

The judge will carry out summary assessment of costs at the end of a fast track trial, in which case the order will deal with the whole costs of the claim; and at the end of any other hearing that lasted not more than one day. In other words the judge assesses the costs there and then, under CPR Part 44.7 and Costs Practice Direction 13.

Where summary assessment is to take place, a party that seeks any contribution towards its costs must file an N260 Statement of Costs at court, and serve copies on the other parties (Costs Practice Direction 13.5). Attach evidence of counsel's fees and any disbursements. Note that the court has power, at a final hearing, to deal summarily with any additional liability under a conditional fee agreement. If acting under a CFA, justify the success fee by attaching to the N260 a copy of the N251 Notice of Funding; copies of every estimate of costs filed during the claim; a copy of any earlier N260s; a statement of reasons for the percentage increase of the success fee, including a copy of the risk assessment by which the percentage of the fee was calculated; and justify the ATE insurance premium by attaching a copy of the certificate showing the nature and extent of the cover and the amount of the premium.

The N260 should be filed and served 'as soon as possible and in any event not less than 24 hours before the date fixed for the hearing'. In fact the court will not reject it outright if it is handed in on the day of the hearing, but it may well be less sympathetic to the costs calculation (Costs Practice Direction 13.6 and *McDonald* v. *Taree Holdings* [2001] EWCA Civ 312). If one serves the N260 well before the hearing, there may be time to agree the claim with the other party.

19.3 COSTS IF PROCEEDINGS WERE NOT ISSUED

If proceedings were not issued, a successful claimant is entitled to expect the defendant to pay most or all of his costs, but a successful defendant has no such right.

Generally, the claimant is entitled to the costs and disbursements actually run up by his solicitor on his behalf. This is automatic if the claim settled on prompt acceptance of a Part 36 offer (CPR Part 36.13.4, see **sections 16.3** and **16.4**). Otherwise, the claimant must make it an express condition of the settlement that the defendant pays his reasonable costs and disbursements, not just his compensation.

If the defendant offers to pay compensation but will not accept the principle that he is liable to pay costs, the claimant can only reject the offer and issue personal injury proceedings in the usual way. Such disputes are rare.

More often, a dispute arises over the amount of the costs the defendant should pay, in which case the claimant can issue proceedings using the simpler costs-only system (CPR Part 44.12A). If the claimant issues such proceedings, the defendant can make an offer to settle the costs claim under CPR Part 47.19. Unless the offer says so, it will not be taken to include the costs of the costs negotiations, nor of the Part 8 assessment proceedings themselves (*Crosbie* v. *Munroe* [2003] EWCA Civ 350).

In 2003, amendments to CPR Part 45 introduced a system of fixed costs for road traffic accident cases worth £10,000 or less (CPR Parts 45.7 to 45.14, and Costs Practice Direction 25A). The system applies where the claim is worth more than the limit for the Small Claims track, the accident occurred on or after 6 October 2003, and the claim settles before proceedings are issued. The claimant is entitled to claim the following from the defendant:

- basic costs payment of £800, plus
- 20 per cent of compensation from £0 to £5,000, plus 15 per cent of compensation exceeding £5,000 up to £10,000, plus
- if the claimant lives or works in London and the work was done in London, an additional 12.5 per cent, plus
- disbursements according to the table at CPR Part 45.10, that is, the cost of obtaining medical records, a medical report, a police report, an engineer's report or a search of the records of the DVLA, an ATE legal expenses insurance premium, and any other disbursement that has arisen due to a particular feature of the dispute. If the claimant is under a disability, he is also entitled to counsel's fees and the court fee for seeking the court's approval to the settlement under CPR Part 21.10.

The claimant is also entitled to:

- A success fee if the claimant was represented under a conditional fee agreement (see **section 19.1**).
- In exceptional cases, further costs awarded by the court under CPR Part 45.12. If the claimant seeks these further costs and gets more than a 20 per cent increase on the fixed costs, he is also entitled to the costs of claiming the further costs. Otherwise, he will probably find that the CPR Part 45.12 procedure costs him more than he gains by it. The claimant should try to agree a figure with the defendant before following this procedure. If everything is agreed except payment of a particular disbursement, or payment of the success fee, the claimant should use the costs only proceedings system in CPR Part 44.12A procedure.

This system is designed to achieve an overall balance, but will seldom equal the precise amount of work done by the claimant's solicitor on any individual case. Sometimes he will be overpaid, sometimes underpaid. If he wants to keep the overpayments he must state this in the agreement with the client. Otherwise the rules of professional conduct require a solicitor to account for it to the client.

19.4 COSTS SHORTFALL

Although the loser generally pays the winner's reasonable legal costs and disbursements, he very often pays less than the total run up by the winner's team. Unless the successful claimant is protected by legal expenses insurance or an agreement with his solicitor, any costs shortfall will be deducted from his compensation. If the shortfall is so large that it wipes out the compensation altogether, the balance comes out of the claimant's insurance or pocket.

Costs to be paid by a party to his own lawyer are calculated on the indemnity basis, which includes everything that was done as long as it was reasonable. Any doubts are resolved in favour of the recipient.

Costs to be paid by one party to another are calculated on the standard basis, which is less generous. The burden of proof is on the recipient to show that his costs were reasonably incurred and are reasonable in amount. The paying party gets the benefit of any doubts. The standard basis requires not only that each item be reasonable, but also that the costs be proportionate to the claim itself. CPR Part 44.5 gives seven factors to be considered when deciding what is proportionate and what is not. PD 44 says:

> The relationship between the total of the costs incurred and the financial value of the claim may not be a reliable guide . . . in any proceedings there will be costs which will inevitably be incurred and which are necessary for the successful conduct of the case . . . thus in a modest claim the proportion of the costs is likely to be higher than in a large claim, and may even equal or possibly exceed the amount in dispute.

See also *Lownds* v. *Home Office* [2002] EWCA Civ 365 and *Jefferson* v. *National Freight Carriers* [2001] EWCA Civ 2082.

The court may order one party to pay the other's costs on the indemnity basis, if the paying party is a defendant who failed to beat a Part 36 offer, or the paying party's conduct was very unreasonable. This does not necessarily mean unfair, dishonest or oppressive. It could mean raising several pointless technical arguments, or failing to admit liability in a clear case until six days before trial, where the accident occurred five years earlier (*Craig* v. *Railtrack* [2002] EWHC 168 (QB)).

In many situations, particularly of misconduct by the winner, the court will split the costs between winner and loser. Under CPR Part 44.5, if costs are assessed by the court it considers all the circumstances, including:

- The conduct of the parties. This includes conduct before, as well as during, the proceedings. Note in particular the extent to which the parties followed any relevant Pre-action Protocol; whether the parties made reasonable attempts to settle the claim; whether it was reasonable for a party to raise, pursue or contest a particular allegation or issue; the manner in which a party dealt with a particular allegation or issue; and whether the claimant exaggerated his claim. A party who fails to disclose relevant documents, thereby preventing his opponent from making a realistic offer, can expect a costs penalty (*Ford* v. *GKR Construction* [2001] 1 All ER 802).
- The amount or value of the claim.
- The complexity of the claim, or the difficulty or novelty of any issues it raised.

- Where the work was done, as different courts have different local rates.
- Whether a party has succeeded on part of his case, even if he has not been wholly successful.
- Any payment into court or settlement offer that is drawn to the court's attention. Note in particular the effect of CPR Part 36, described in the chapter on settlement offers (see **Chapter 16**).

19.5 CHALLENGING A COSTS CLAIMS

Both claimants and defendants need to be aware of chinks in the receiving party's armour. Very briefly, when considering liability for costs, the following will be relevant.

Did the receiving party have a contract to pay his own solicitor's costs? The indemnity principle says that the paying party cannot be required to indemnify the receiving party for costs that the receiving party himself has no obligation to pay. There are statutory exceptions for legal aid and conditional fee agreements. The practical relevance of the indemnity principle is that the loser cannot be required to pay for work done or disbursements incurred before the receiving party entered into a contract with his solicitor as to how the work was to be funded; and may not be obliged to pay anything at all if the contract is unenforceable.

Did the receiving party give proper notice that the claim was funded by the Legal Services Commission or under a CFA? If he had legal aid, Notice of Issue and perhaps also Notice of Amendment should have been served. If he had a CFA, the Practice Direction Protocols says at para 4.A.1: 'When a person enters into a funding arrangement . . . he should inform other potential parties to the claim that he has done so.' Para 4A.2 says that this 'applies to all proceedings whether . . . a pre-action protocol applies or otherwise'. The word proceedings includes negotiations leading to settlement before proceedings are issued (*Crosbie* v. *Munroe* [2003] EWCA Civ 350). When proceedings are issued under a conditional fee agreement, the claimant must give notice to the defendant preferably using court form N251, the notice of funding. The claimant is not entitled to his success fee for any period in the proceedings for which a notice of funding has not been served (CPR Part 44.3B(1)c).

The amount of the success fee is regulated by the CPR in road traffic and most employer's liability cases (see **section 19.1**). In other situations, the defendant will want to see the claimant's solicitor's risk assessment from which the success fee was calculated. Particularly if liability had already been admitted when this was done, the defendant will want to see whether the risk assessment was carried out in a reasonable way.

The amount of the ATE premium must be reasonable (see **section 19.1**). The defendant will want to see a copy of the insurance certificate showing the nature and extent of the cover and the amount of the premium.

Was the receiving party represented under a CFA when he could and should have relied on legal expenses insurance? The claimant's solicitor must enquire whether any such cover is available. He must carry out a fairly thorough hunt for it even in a claim of modest value. If he does not, and it turns out that legal expenses cover was in fact available, the paying party will not be liable for any additional liability arising out of the CFA (*Sarwar* v. *Alam* [2001] EWCA Civ 1401). In *Sarwar* the claimant found out at the end of the claim that the defendant driver's legal expenses cover extended to the claimant, because the claimant was his passenger at the time of the accident. Given the terms of this particular legal expenses policy (which reserved to the insurers the right to 'full conduct and control of any claim') the claimant was not bound to rely on it and was entitled to have his costs paid by the defendant. However, if the defendant's policy had offered the claimant a transparently independent legal service, the position would probably have been different.

The same applies to CFAs given when the claimant could and should have had legal aid (see **section 1.2**).

Did the receiving party commit a significant breach of the Pre-action Protocol, for example by refusing to make proper disclosure or greatly exaggerating the claim? Particularly if he thereby prevented the paying party from making a prompt and accurate settlement offer under Part 36, the paying party may argue that he should pay a costs penalty (see **Chapters 3** and **16**).

Did the claim settle when a Part 36 offer or payment was accepted? In that case the basic costs consequences are automatic (see **sections 16.3** and **16.4**). However, if the automatic costs consequences would be unjust, the court may vary them (see **section 16.5**).

Is the receiving party seeking costs at the hourly rate appropriate for a file of this complexity, and in this geographical area? As to complexity, the question is whether the file was handled by the right grade of fee earner. The courts recognise four categories:

(a) Solicitors with over eight years' post-qualification experience including at least eight years of litigation experience.
(b) Solicitors and Fellows of the Institute of Legal Executives with over four years' post-qualification experience including at least four years' litigation experience.
(c) Other solicitors and Fellows of the Institute of Legal Executives and fee earners of equivalent experience.
(d) Trainee solicitors, paralegals and other fee earners.

If a routine file was handled by a Grade A fee earner, one can argue that the file, or at least some aspects of it, should have been handled by a Grade B or C. However, it is fair to say that a senior fee earner may get through work much faster than a junior colleague.

As to the geographical area, hourly rates vary from court to court, the highest ones being in London. The appropriate hourly rate is not necessarily the one for the court where proceedings were issued. It is probably the rate for the court nearest the receiving party's solicitor's office, although if a party from Carlisle chooses to instruct solicitors in the City of London to deal with a routine road traffic accident near his home, he cannot expect to recover the London rate from the loser. Approved rates are in the Court Service's Guide to the Summary Assessment of Costs, which is online at **www.courtservice.gov.uk/cms/5454.htm**.

The paying party will consider whether the receiving party's lawyer spent too much time on the file. If the defendant is paying, he may wish to see a copy of the claimant's solicitor's case plan, prepared under the guidance in *Lownds* v. *Home Office* [2002] EWCA Civ 365 (see **section 1.3**).

The paying party will want to see evidence of any disbursements, for example a copy of a doctor's fee note for providing a report. It will ask itself whether the claim includes disbursements which seem excessive (for example £300 for a report by a GP), disbursements which did not assist with the claim, or disbursements that has never previously been heard of, such as a medical report that was not disclosed in the litigation.

Did the receiving party pay a court fee at a time when the Certificate of Recoverable Benefits indicates that he was exempt on grounds of income? See court leaflet EX160 / 160A.

Is the claim governed by special rules? There are now fixed costs for most road traffic claims (see **section 19.3**).

Is the claim one which the claimant could not, when issuing proceedings, reasonably have expected to be worth more than the Small Claims limit? Or which would, if issued, have been allocated to the Small Claims track? Then the no costs rule applies (see **section 21.3**).

Is it a Claims Direct claim? This should be apparent from the costs claim. If not, it may be indicated by an ATE legal expenses insurance premium of £1312.50 or £1569.75; a payment to Medical Legal Support Services Ltd (MLSS) of £395 plus VAT, a payment to Poole & Co of £72.50 plus VAT, and medical evidence provided by Mobile Doctors. Apart from the cost of the medical evidence, defendants are not liable to pay much of this. Consider the Claims Direct test cases at [2002] EWHC 9002 (Costs) and [2003] EWCA Civ 136.

Is it an Accident Group (TAG) claim? This should be apparent from the costs claim. If it is not immediately obvious, it may be indicated by the words TAG Protect, an ATE premium of £840 or £997.50; an AIL fee (Accident Investigations Ltd) of £310 or £320; medical fees billed by either the Mobile Doctors or Expedia agencies; and a fee from Rowe & Cohen of £40 plus VAT. Various rules apply to these cases, in particular that the AIL fee is essentially a referral fee contrary to the Solicitors Introduction & Referral Code, and not payable by the defendant. Consider the Accident Group test cases [2004]

EWCA Civ 575, also reported as *Sharratt* v. *London Central Bus Co*. You may also need to refer to other TAG cases at [2003] 1 All ER 353, [2003] EWCA Civ 718, [2003] EWHC 9004 (Costs) and [2003] EWHC 9020 (Costs).

Many costs challenges consist simply of a global offer in respect of the receiving party's costs, with the unspoken intention of paying all the disbursements, but knocking 25 per cent off the profit costs. Depending how busy the receiving party is, how close he is to the end of his financial year, whether he has been to detailed assessment before and knows the ropes, and whether he has had any hair-raising experiences at detailed assessment, the receiving party will probably accept a discount somewhere between 7.5 per cent and 20 per cent – 25 per cent is for the desperate.

CHAPTER 20

Evidence in personal injury claims

20.1 HEARSAY

Hearsay evidence is a 'statement made, otherwise than by a person while giving oral evidence in proceedings, which is tendered as evidence of the matters stated' (s.1 Civil Evidence Act 1995). If witness X says at trial 'the police officer had told me he saw a fire raging on the stairs' in order to prove his own state of mind, this is not hearsay. It becomes hearsay if adduced as evidence that there was a vigorous fire on the stairs. It will always be hearsay if adduced in evidence as a written statement, without calling the maker to give direct oral evidence at trial.

If one reads a written statement, or even a transcript of oral evidence, one cannot easily assess whether the author was telling the truth or was certain of what he said. One can get a good idea of the witness and his evidence only by hearing him, asking him questions and seeing how he responds. Therefore, compared with direct oral evidence, hearsay is always of lower cogency. In other words a witness's written statement has less weight or value than his oral evidence. It is less persuasive.

Some hearsay is better than others. It depends whether the statement is thorough and makes sense; whether it has any obvious gaps or inconsistencies, whether it was prepared at the time of the incident or later; whether the witness appears to be independent of the parties or has any personal interest in the outcome of the trial; and whether there is a good reason for not calling him to give evidence (see s.4 of the Act). International travel is so cheap and easy today that it is no longer a good reason for not calling a witness to say that he will be on holiday at the time of trial, especially if he is in Europe. With the spread of video conferencing facilities, it may be that the witness can give direct oral evidence at trial despite being on the other side of the world (CPR PD 32).

One may wish to rely at trial on a witness's statement, rather than call him to give evidence in person, for many reasons. Perhaps he can give evidence only on one minor point and one wishes to avoid the expense of having him lose earnings for several days while he waits at court. It may be that his evidence is about some technical point that he cannot now be expected to remember, such as the wages he paid to the claimant four years ago.

It may be that one would very much like to call a witness to give evidence, but one has to rely on his written statement instead for the good reason that the witness is very ill, in prison, dead, or on an expedition in an inaccessible jungle. Note that a judge may be willing to visit a bedridden witness and take his evidence on commission.

Whatever the reason, if one tries to rely on a written statement instead of calling the witness it is likely to make the other side suspect that one is afraid he will not come up to proof (i.e. simply fail to tell the desired story) or will give away some undesirable fact when the other side has an opportunity to cross-examine him. This is the reason for the hearsay procedure under CPR Part 33 and CPR PD 33.

After proceedings have been issued and a defence delivered, the court will allocate the claim to track and make directions. In the fast track, it usually directs that there be simultaneous exchange of witness statements in 10 weeks (CPR Part 28 and CPR PD 28). If one does not intend to call the maker of a statement to give oral evidence, one serves a copy of his signed statement accompanied by a Part 33 Hearsay Notice. This gives a reason why the witness will not be called. The other party then has 14 days to respond, for example by applying to the court for permission to call the witness itself. If one fails to comply with the Part 33 procedure, the court may refuse to admit the hearsay evidence. In that case it will seldom adjourn the trial, and if it does it will be at the expense of the party who failed to comply.

The following are either not hearsay as defined, or are admissible without the need to follow the hearsay procedure because of exceptions in the 1995 Act:

- A contemporaneous note, that is, one made by a witness at or about the relevant time. This is hearsay if adduced in evidence, but not if merely used by the witness to refresh his memory while giving evidence.
- A letter or statement made by a witness out of court showing that the witness made a previous inconsistent statement. This is not hearsay if adduced merely to show that he has been inconsistent.
- Evidence that the other party made an informal admission out of court, the classic example being 'I'm sorry, I just didn't see you' (s.1 of the Act).
- A map or other published work (s.7 of the Act).
- Documents forming part of the records of a business or public authority (s.9 of the Act). Any such document may be received in evidence without further proof, so long as a certificate is produced, signed by a suitable officer of the company or authority. Typical examples include a record held by the Department for Work and Pensions of the dates and

amounts of state benefits claimed; and pay records from the claimant's employer.
- The Ogden Tables. See s.10 of the 1995 Act.

Note that a letter from the claimant's employer estimating what the claimant would have earned but for the accident goes beyond the s.9 business records exception. If the parties cannot agree the letter, the party wishing to rely on it must embody what it says in a formal witness statement, and either call the maker to give evidence or follow the hearsay procedure.

One can rely upon written statements at interlocutory applications, for example for an interim payment, without following the Part 33 procedure (CPR Part 33.3).

20.2 *RES IPSA LOQUITUR*

Literally, the thing speaks for itself. 'These three words are used to encapsulate a common sense reasoning process which is no more or less profound for being expressed in Latin. In any given case either . . . the facts speak for themselves, or they do not' (*Carroll* v. *Fearon* [1998] EWCA Civ 40).

It is often said that in a situation of *res ipsa loquitur*, the burden of proof shifts from claimant to defendant. In fact the claimant always bears the burden of showing that his version of events is correct, and if he cannot, his claim will fail. However if he can prove:

> facts which raise a prima facie inference that the accident was caused by negligence on the part of the defendants, the issue will be decided in the [claimant's] favour unless the defendants by their evidence provide some answer which is adequate to displace the prima facie inference. In this situation there is said to be an evidential burden of proof resting on the defendants'
>
> (*Henderson* v. *Henry E Jenkins & Sons* [1970] AC 282)

In practice, *res ipsa* is shorthand for situations of the following kind. The claimant was injured when a tool fell from the defendant's premises as he walked past. He has no idea what caused it to fall, and cannot positively say that it was not dropped by a trespassing hooligan. If he can show that the injury was caused by something that was under the defendant's sole management and control, and if the event was one that would not normally occur without negligence, the court may be willing to find the defendant liable in negligence unless the defendant can show that he exercised all reasonable care and skill; or that the accident would have occurred even if he had done; or can give an alternative explanation of what happened which exonerates him and is not merely wishful thinking.

The classic application of *res ipsa loquitur* is where the claimant is injured when he slips on a spill in a shop. For a discussion of *Ward* v. *Tesco Stores* [1976] 1 WLR 801, see **section 5.4**. It may operate to make a defendant driver liable for injury caused by mechanical failure in his vehicle (*Henderson v. Henry E Jenkins & Sons* [1970] AC 282). Very rarely, it will apply in a road traffic accident, as in *Widdowson* v. *Newgate Meat Corp* [1997] EWCA Civ 2763.

The courts have in the past accepted that something was under the defendant's sole management and control even if it was possible that a third party might have intervened, as long as there is no evidence that any third party actually did. However, see *Fryer* v. *Pearson* (2000) *The Times* 4 April.

20.3 CONVICTIONS AND CAUTIONS

Evidence of a party's character or convictions is not generally admissible in a civil trial. However s.11 Civil Evidence Act 1968 says: 'In any civil proceedings the fact that a person has been convicted of an offence by a court in the United Kingdom is admissible to prove where relevant that he committed that offence and he shall be taken to have committed it unless the contrary is proved.' Evidence of convictions relating to other accidents would not be relevant as defined by the Act.

If, as a result of a road accident, the defendant is convicted of driving without due care and attention and drunk driving, this can be used in support of a civil claim that the accident was caused by his negligence. The due care conviction reverses the burden of proof in the civil trial, so that the defendant has to prove that he was not negligent. If the defendant does not admit liability after being convicted, the claimant should obtain documentation from the relevant magistrates' court. If the defendant pleaded not guilty there will be a full trial transcript, which is likely to be expensive; and a certificate of conviction. If he pleaded guilty, there will be only a certificate of conviction, which is often free although there may be a small charge.

If the defendant was prosecuted but acquitted, this is not fatal to a negligence claim. To achieve a conviction, one has to show beyond a reasonable doubt that the defendant was guilty, whereas in a civil claim one need only show on the balance of probabilities that he was negligent. This is a much lower standard.

No prosecuting body has a policy of full enforcement. The HSE nearly always prefers to persuade and warn offenders. The police may prefer the alternative of a caution, based on Home Office circular 18/1994, *The Cautioning of Offenders*. A caution is not a conviction, and therefore does not fall within s.11 of the 1968 Act, but note that a caution cannot be given unless the person to be cautioned admits the offence.

A conviction may bar a civil claim for assault (s.42–45 Offences Against the Person Act 1861 and *Wong* v. *Parkside Health NHS Trust* [2001] EWCA Civ 1721).

If the claimant issues proceedings and wishes to rely on the defendant's conviction in support of his claim, he must state it in the particulars of claim (CPR PD 16.8.1).

20.4 DISCLOSURE

Pre-action disclosure

Both parties are required to disclose relevant documents, even before proceedings are issued.

The Personal Injury Protocol requires the claimant, when sending his letter of claim to the defendant, to provide 'copies of the essential documents' that he relies on. If the defendant responds to the letter of claim by denying liability for the accident, the Protocol requires him to provide copies of liability documents to the claimant. If either party fails to comply with the Protocol, he may pay a penalty later, in costs or interest. The court might well penalise either party for withholding crucial liability or quantum documents until after proceedings were issued, if the other party shows that the claim would have settled beforehand if they had been disclosed promptly.

The Personal Injury Protocol contains a Standard Disclosure List, setting out categories of documents that are likely to be relevant to liability in particular cases. There is a copy of the main categories on the accompanying CD-ROM, and a full copy of the List can be seen with the CPR and Protocols at **www.dca.gov.uk**.

Unfortunately for the claimant, the Protocol does not say that the defendant must always provide copies of all documents in the Standard Disclosure List. Instead it requires the defendant to disclose 'documents in his possession which are material to the issues between the parties and which would be likely to be ordered to be disclosed by the court, either on an application for Pre-Action Disclosure or on disclosure during proceedings'. As to what documents these might be, see the rest of this section.

An application for Pre-action Disclosure under CPR Part 31.16 enables the court, before personal injury proceedings have been issued, to make an order requiring potential parties to give sight of their documents. The procedure is potentially useful to claimants, but it is expensive and the outcome is uncertain. For the law and procedure see CPR Part 31, s.33 Supreme Court Act 1981 and s.52 County Courts Act 1984. The parties to the application are known as applicant and respondent. The applicant will have to bear the costs of searching for and copying documents, and will usually bear the costs of the application itself (CPR Part 48.1.2). However, the respondent may have to bear the costs of the application if it resisted unreasonably, and especially if it did so with a view to obstructing justice (*Bermuda International Securities* v. *KPMG* [2001] EWCA Civ 269), in which the costs of the application were in fact ordered to be costs in the case in the main action, if one ever commenced. The costs of such an application may be well over £1,000, and if this is likely to be disproportionate to the claim, one should not apply.

Before making the application, the claimant should ask the defendant to make voluntary disclosure. The request should be in writing, giving the defendant a reasonable time to comply, describing precisely what the claimant wants, how he knows it exists, why it is relevant, and what he expects to achieve with it. The request should say whether or not, if the defendant fails to provide the document, the claimant will make an application for Pre-action Disclosure.

An application for compulsory Pre-action Disclosure is made under the procedure at CPR Part 23, that is, by Notice of Application with supporting evidence. This should consist of a statement by the applicant to which is attached copies of any relevant documents. The statement should deal with the following:

- How the applicant knows that the document sought exists, or why he thinks it is likely to exist.
- That the applicant and respondent are likely to be parties to subsequent proceedings, which will for our purposes be for personal injury. The applicant does not have to show it is likely that PI proceedings will be issued. It is enough to show that the respondent may well be a party if the contemplated PI proceedings are issued (*Herbert Black* v. *Sumitomo Corp* [2001] EWCA Civ 1819). It will normally be sufficient if the court is satisfied that the PI claim is 'properly arguable and . . . [has] a real prospect of success' (*Rose* v. *Lynx Express* [2004] EWCA Civ 447). It is not enough if the PI claim as it stands is so weak that it is liable to be struck out (*K* v. *Secretary of State for the Home Department* [2002] EWCA Civ 775).
- If PI proceedings were issued, the respondent would have to disclose the document. 'It follows from that, that the court must be clear what the issues in the litigation are likely to be, i.e. what case the claimant is likely to be making and what defence is likely to be run' (*Bermuda International Securities Ltd* v. *KPMG* [2001] EWCA Civ 269). The applicant must explain what issue turns on the document, and why it would be discloseable if proceedings were issued. The applicant should give enough evidence of the value of the claim for the court to see that it would not be allocated to the Small Claims track.
- Pre-action Disclosure is desirable to dispose fairly of the anticipated PI proceedings, to assist in resolving the dispute without issuing proceedings, or to save costs. There must be 'a real prospect' that Pre-action Disclosure will achieve at least one of these (*Herbert Black* v. *Sumitomo*).

It will help the application if, in his witness statement, the applicant shows that he himself has complied with the Pre-action Protocol, he has made reasonable demands for the documents but these have been refused or ignored, and he cannot get hold of the information in the document from another source. Note that the applicant might be able to obtain liability documents from the police, the Health and Safety Executive, his trade union, a national governing body that keeps records of an individual's training, or the manufacturer of equipment involved in the accident. He may be able to obtain quantum documents from his own attic or bank.

The Personal Injury Protocol says that the rules about disclosing documents are not designed to encourage fishing expeditions, that is, requests for documents that the applicant merely hopes might show he has a valid claim. One useful test is whether the applicant is able to draw up particulars of claim without seeing the document. If he can, he should attach them to the application. If not, there is a good chance that he is fishing to see whether he has a claim.

The applicant should provide the court with a Statement of Costs, which it will use when deciding what costs the opposition should pay if the application succeeds. It is useful also to give the court a draft unless order. This should comply with CPR Part 31.16.4, and provide for the respondent to disclose the documents within X days, that he pay the applicant's costs of the application forthwith, and in default that he be debarred from adducing any evidence on that point, or defending the claim.

If the respondent wants to resist the application, he may argue that the documents provided give the court no jurisdiction to make the order. He would have difficulty persuading the court that the applicant and respondent are unlikely to be parties to proceedings, but may be able to show that the document would not have to be disclosed even if proceedings were issued, or that he certainly will not settle the claim unless proceedings are issued, so disclosure would be better dealt with in the usual way, after issue.

Failing this, the defendant may be able to persuade the court that it should not exercise its discretion in favour of the applicant because he could have got enough documentation from somewhere else, or has not made any clear allegations of negligence, or is making too wide and woolly a request for disclosure. '. . . The more diffuse the allegations . . . and the wider the disclosure sought, the more sceptical the court is entitled to be' but a clear and precise request might succeed 'even where the complaint might seem somewhat speculative or the request might be argued to constitute a mere fishing exercise' (*Herbert Black* v. *Sumitomo* [2001] EWCA Civ 1819).

Defendants very seldom apply for Pre-action Disclosure, preferring to protect their position by requesting the document and stating that they cannot settle the claim without sight of it. If the claimant runs up extra costs by refusing to disclose it, particularly if he issues proceedings unnecessarily, he can expect a substantial costs penalty. However, if the claimant issues proceedings, then discloses the disputed document, enabling the defendant to make a Part 36 payment that the claimant accepts, CPR Part 36 simply says 'the claimant will be entitled to his costs of the proceedings up to the date of serving notice of acceptance'. A typical busy defendant will probably not ask the court to reverse the usual costs consequences of Part 36 (see **section 16.5**).

Disclosure during action

Once proceedings have been issued, a defence received, and the case has been allocated to the fast track, the court will usually make a direction under CPR Part 28.3 and CPR PD 28, requiring the parties to make Standard Disclosure under CPR Part 31.6. This involves supplying the opposition with an N265 List of Documents and copies of the listed documents. Each party is required to disclose:

- any documents which are in his possession, or have been in his possession, or which he is entitled to obtain;
    - upon which he intends to rely to prove part of his case;
    - or which tend to prove part of his case or part of the other side's case;
    - or which tend to disprove part of the other side's case, or part of his own case.

A party making disclosure needs to spend only a reasonable and proportionate amount of time looking for documents (CPR Part 31.7). The obligation is only to disclose what can be found during a reasonable search. If the court is asked to decide whether the search was reasonable, it will balance the difficulty of the search against the importance of the document.

It is up to the disclosing party himself to say whether a document is relevant. If he does not wish to rely on the document himself, and takes the view that it does not help his opponent, he need not disclose it. Unless the opponent knows what this document says, he cannot challenge the decision.

Neither party has to disclose documents that are protected by privilege. A document prepared before litigation was contemplated cannot be privileged, whatever its purpose. Once litigation is contemplated, there are several forms of privilege. Attempts to settle are generally privileged as they are expressly or impliedly made on a without prejudice basis (see **section 3.4**). A document may also be protected by litigation privilege or legal advice privilege.

Litigation privilege is broad, protecting documents prepared in contemplation of litigation. Communications with agents (including eyewitnesses and expert witnesses) for the purpose of litigation are generally privileged.

Litigation privilege may protect a witness statement taken by a defendant from one of its employees, if the dominant purpose for which it was produced was for use in the conduct or in aid of the conduct of actual or anticipated litigation. *Linstead* v. *East Sussex, Brighton & Hove Health Authority* [2001] PIQR 356 related to a witness statement by a midwife who had been involved in the claimant's labour. The statement had been prepared after the claimant intimated a claim, in order to send it to the defendant's solicitors. It was clearly protected by litigation privilege, and this did not amount to an infringement of the claimant's right to a fair trial under Article 6 of the European Convention on Human Rights 1950.

Litigation privilege will seldom protect an internal accident investigation report. These are typically prepared partly to defend a claim in case the injured person brings one, and partly to reduce the risk of future accidents. In *Waugh* v. *British Railways Board* [1980] AC 521 the House of Lords found that an important purpose of the defendant's accident investigation had been to take action for safety reasons. It could not be said that the dominant purpose of the report was to prepare for litigation, so it was not protected by litigation privilege. After a workplace accident, the Management of Health & Safety at Work Regulations 1999 require an employer to carry out an accident investigation. This seems to rule out an argument that the investigation's dominant purpose was to assist in litigation.

Legal advice privilege is very narrow. It protects confidential communications between solicitor and client in the course of a solicitor-client relationship formed for the purpose of obtaining advice or assistance with a view to, or in the course of, litigation.

Typical privileged documents are correspondence and memos of conversations between lawyer and client; advice from a barrister; and medical reports and witness statements which one is not ready to disclose.

If the other party makes disclosure in accordance with directions and one considers that they have made an incomplete and inadequate job of it, one may apply for Specific Disclosure under CPR Part 31.12. The application may be unsuccessful, and then the applicant will have to pay a hefty costs bill. Before making the application, one should make a written request to the other side, giving him a reasonable time to comply. If the information one requires may well be dealt with in the other party's witness statements, consider postponing the application until after exchange of witness statements.

These applications often allege that the respondent has waived privilege in the document, by accidentally including it in a List of Documents or copying it to the other side. A party 'may inspect a document mentioned in a statement of case, a witness statement, a witness summary, or an affidavit' (CPR Part 31.14). However 'Where a party inadvertently allows a privileged document to be inspected, the party who has inspected the document may use it or its contents only with the permission of the court' (CPR Part 31.20). The court will not give permission if the mistake was obvious, and '. . . a mistake is an obvious mistake either where the particular solicitor in fact realised that the particular document or documents had been disclosed by mistake or where the hypothetical reasonable solicitor would have realised that such a mistake had been made'. The recipient has no duty to ask whether privilege had been deliberately waived (*Breeze* v. *John Stacy* [1999] EWCA Civ 1625 and *Al Fayed* v. *Commissioner of Police of the Metropolis* [2002] EWCA Civ 780).

As to documents given to an expert and mentioned in his report which is then disclosed to the other side, see the summary of *Lucas* v. *Barking, Havering & Redbridge NHS Trust* in **section 20.5**.

Each party to litigation has a continuing obligation to make disclosure. A discloseable document must be disclosed even if received only after the formal List of Documents has been sent (CPR Part 31.11).

If a document is disclosed and the other side doubts that it is authentic, it must object by serving a notice under CPR Part 32.19 requiring its authenticity to be proved at trial. Otherwise the party is deemed to admit that the document is authentic. That does not mean he admits that it is accurate.

In order that one avoids calling the maker of a document to give evidence, one should try to agree the document with the other side before trial. This applies to sketch plans, police accident reports, photographs, videos, statements of earnings supplied by the claimant's employer, witness statements and medical reports. To say that a copy document is agreed usually means only that it is an accurate copy, not that one accepts that its contents are true.

20.5 DISCLOSING MEDICAL RECORDS

A claimant's medical records may contain material irrelevant to the accident that he is very unwilling to have publicised. However, to make a personal injury claim he must generally disclose all the records, not only to the doctor instructed by his lawyer, but to lawyers and claims handlers on both sides. The BMA/Law Society consent form for disclosure of medical records includes text intended to overcome the claimant's reluctance. There is a copy on the accompanying CD-ROM. For the latest version including the Law Society and BMA logos, go to **www.lawsociety.org.uk**.

A claimant lawyer may well refuse to act for an accident victim who will not disclose his medical records. Without sight of the records one cannot properly advise the claimant about the value of the claim and therefore about whether to accept a settlement offer. One cannot tell whether it is reasonable for the Legal Services Commission or legal expenses insurer to support the claim. If one intends to act on a 'no win, no fee' basis, it is not possible properly to estimate whether the claim will succeed and therefore whether one will get paid.

The defendant will be keen to see the claimant's medical records because they may suggest that the injury was not caused in the way the claimant says; or that the claimant has unrelated medical problems which might have kept him off work, or given him a need for care and equipment, even if the accident had not occurred. The records may also indicate that he failed to mitigate his losses by attending for treatment or physiotherapy.

The general rules of disclosure are described in the previous section. In addition, the Pre-action Protocols expect that when a medical expert is instructed he will see the records. If he does not, his report will be limited, and this will look suspicious to the defendant and the court. The claimant cannot resist disclosing his medical records on the basis that the records are not in his control under CPR Part 31.8, because he is entitled to ask his doctors to provide him with copies.

Until 2002, case law was developing towards a blanket rule that medical records should always be disclosed to the defendant. In *Dunn* v. *British Coal* [1993] 1 ICR 591 the defendant wanted disclosure of medical records to its medical expert, who was to examine the claimant who alleged a continuing disability which was responsible for a continuing loss of earnings. The Court of Appeal said: '[Claimants] almost always consent [to disclose their medical records]. If they do not and they withhold their consent unreasonably the defendant can apply for a stay of the action until [he] does consent.'

In *Hipwood* v. *Gloucester Health Authority* [1995] PIQR 447 the Court of Appeal indicated that where liability, causation and quantum were all in issue and there is continuing disability, all the claimant's medical records are likely to be relevant and discloseable. As a general rule they should be disclosed to both the defendant's lawyer and his medical expert. If the claimant resists disclosure on the basis that they were not relevant, the defendant's lawyer should discuss this with the medical expert, and if appropriate apply to the court. The District Judge or Master could then inspect the medical records himself '. . . and enquire of them if they seriously suggested that a disease, whatever its nature, suffered 20 years ago but completely recovered from was of any relevance'.

In *Bennett* v. *Compass Group & British Ceramic Research* [2002] EWCA Civ 642 the claimant had low back pain following a fall, and had served a medical report that referred to her medical records. CPR Part 31.14 at that date said 'a party may inspect a document mentioned in . . . an expert's report'. The District Judge had already made a direction requiring the claimant to give the defendant a consent form allowing them to approach her treating doctors to obtain copies of her medical records from them directly. The claimant had no objection to disclosing all her records but objected to the defendant obtaining them directly and so appealed. The Court of Appeal said that a claimant should be allowed to retain control over his own medical records and a District Judge should very seldom direct the claimant to give direct access to the defendant. In more general terms, the Court of Appeal approved *Dunn* v. *British Coal*. It said that under CPR Part 31.14 and the general rules of disclosure the defendant was entitled to see the records. The court appeared to indicate that the claimant's medical records fall within standard disclosure under CPR Part 31.6. Ordinarily the appropriate order will be that the claimant should permit inspection of the relevant documents. Pill L.J. said that where the claimant is organising disclosure of the records himself he may decline to disclose part of the records, for example if they are irrelevant or disclosure of them would be disproportionate. If the defendant wishes to challenge that, the District Judge or Master can see the records and decide.

CPR Part 31.14 has been amended since *Bennett* v. *Compass Group* and now says 'a party may inspect a document mentioned in a statement of case, a witness statement, a witness summary, or an affidavit'. The list included an expert's report, but this has been revoked and the paragraph now ends: 'Subject to Rule 35.10.4, a party may apply for an order for inspection of any document mentioned in an expert's report which has not already been disclosed in the proceedings.'

Experts are required by CPR Part 35.10 to 'state the substance of all material instructions, whether oral or written, on the basis of which the report was written'. CPR Part 35.10.4 says that instructions to an expert are not privileged against disclosure, but 'the court will not . . . order disclosure of any specific document . . . unless it is satisfied that there are reasonable grounds to consider the statement of instructions given under paragraph 3 to be inaccurate or incomplete'.

In *Lucas* v. *Barking, Havering & Redbridge NHS Trust* [2003] EWCA Civ 1102 the Court of Appeal said that the primary purpose of CPR Part 35.10.4 was to encourage a party to give his expert all material instructions by ensuring that he did not waive privilege in so doing. A secondary purpose was to prevent the other party starting a lengthy argument about it. *Lucas* was not about medical records, but about a witness statement and an earlier expert's report, both of which were privileged from disclosure. The claimant had given them to his expert as part of his instructions, and the expert had set out substantial parts of the witness statement and earlier report in his statement of instructions. The claimant did not want to disclose the rest of these documents. The defendant's application for disclosure was refused, there being no grounds to believe that the statement of instructions was inaccurate or incomplete. *Lucas* and CPR Part 35.10.4 are relevant to medical records too. 'If a party wishes to inspect documents referred to in the expert report of another party, before issuing an application he should request inspection of the documents informally, and inspection should be provided by agreement unless the request is unreasonable' (CPR PD 31).

20.6 WITNESSES AND WITNESS STATEMENTS

When interviewing a witness and preparing a statement, there is some scope for legal skill but one works within a matrix of professional ethics. The answer to any troubling point that one fears might embarrass oneself or one's client, is either 'It's forbidden' or 'It's compulsory.' Any witness's evidence must be the truth, the whole truth and nothing but the truth, and a lawyer's overriding duty is to the court. A lawyer must present his client's case in the best light, but if one goes too far one may end up in the witness box, facing an investigation for professional misconduct, or paying a wasted costs order under CPR Part 48.7 and Costs Practice Direction 53.

> While a discreet and prudent attorney may very properly ascertain from witnesses in advance of trial what they in fact do know, and the extent and limitations of their memory, as a guide to his own examinations, he has no legal or moral right to go further. His duty is to extract the facts from the witness, not to pour them into him; to learn what the witness does know, not to teach him what he ought to know
>
> (In the matter of Titus B. Eldridge and attorney (1882) NY 161. An American case, often cited)

For authoritative comments on what to do and avoid, refer to the *Guide to Professional Conduct of Solicitors 1999*, Law Society, and the *Code of Conduct for the Bar in England & Wales*. One must not instruct an enquiry agent to interview witnesses on one's behalf unless they can be trusted to observe these principles. See the comments of Toulson J in the Admiralty case *Aquarius Financial Enterprises* v. *Certain Underwriters at Lloyds* (2001) 151 NLJ 694. The *Guide* and *Code* can be seen at **www.lawsociety.org.uk** and **www.barcouncil.org.uk**.

The evidence contained in a statement must be, quite simply, what the witness can remember. Some witnesses are very willing to alter their story to suit other evidence, hence the usual direction that the parties exchange witness statements simultaneously. One must give a witness no encouragement and little opportunity to tailor his evidence. The first step with any witness, whether or not he is a party, is to get his own entire story down in full, uncontaminated. Ideally, one must get it typed up and signed by the witness before he has any idea what facts must be proved for the claim to get off the ground, before he sees the police accident report, before he hears what other witnesses have said, and before he sees the statements of case. One must be careful not to influence a witness at interview, for example by asking questions that suggest one wants a particular answer, or by telling him what facts have been agreed between the parties.

If the witness does not express himself clearly, one can suggest that what he just said could neatly be summarised by using a particular adjective or phrase, but one must ensure that he does not agree the suggestion only because he is overawed by one's suit and qualifications. Ask him whether he is entirely happy with it. Perhaps suggest some alternatives. 'You've told me that you saw the red car going towards the junction. You've told me that you just can't say how fast it was going. I'll put that in your statement, but can we see if it's possible to narrow it down a bit? For example could the red car have been going at 5mph? Or 50mph? You think it was somewhere between the two? Can we narrow it down a bit more? . . . And was there anything unusual about the speed the car was doing, or was it just what you would have expected?'

One can advise the client about the relevant law, as long as one is not working with him to create false evidence. The best guarantee of this is to have taken a full signed statement from him already. There will seldom be a good reason to describe the legal framework of the claim to any other witness.

One must take particular care if trying to find out what any witness thinks about anybody else's version of events. The appeal courts have several times criticised lawyers in the strongest terms for allowing a witness's evidence to become contaminated. The parties cannot negotiate if they do not personally appreciate the strengths and weakness of the case, so one is allowed to put it to one's client that what he is saying seems inconsistent with other evidence, or even that the court may find his story hard to believe. He will need to see copy accident reports, witness statements and statements of case. It will very seldom be appropriate to copy these documents to any other non-expert witness, and never before taking that witness's statement.

Do not get personally involved with a witness. Avoid telling a witness about the claimant's suffering, as this is likely to influence his evidence. Do not offer inducements to witnesses. Clearly it would not be appropriate to offer him £50 to give a statement, or take him out to dinner. If a witness says that he will give a statement only if he does not have to go to court, one cannot promise this. If his evidence is very straightforward, one may be able to tell him that it is highly unlikely he will have to give evidence. There is always a risk that one may have to call him, or that the other party will do so under CPR Part 32.5.

One must be cautious about approaching the other party or his witnesses oneself. As a matter of professional ethics, a solicitor must not communicate with the other party if he is represented by a solicitor. An unrepresented defendant may sometimes be happy to be interviewed by the claimant's lawyer, but this may end with his insurers refusing to indemnify him. If one acts for the claimant and wishes to interview the defendant, one should ask his insurers for permission. This may be granted on the basis that they attend the interview.

There is no property in a witness, hence the notes to Principle 21.10 of the *Guide to Professional Conduct of Solicitors*: 'It is permissible for a solicitor acting for any party to interview and take statements from any witness or prospective witness at any stage in the proceedings, whether or not that witness has been interviewed or called as a witness by another party.' However, the notes give various practical warnings. The other side will be suspicious if one interviews their witness, especially if he changes his story after being interviewed, and will react strongly to any suggestion that one tried to influence him. To avoid such problems, the notes suggest offering to have the other side's lawyer present at the interview, failing which one can 'record the interview, ask the witness to bring a representative and ask the witness to sign an additional statement to the effect that the witness has freely attended the interview, and has not been coerced into giving the statement or changing his or her evidence'.

Some insurance company claims handlers make a practice of ringing claimants and arranging to go and see them. There is no rule to prevent this, even if the claimant is represented by solicitors.

The main witness statements will be from the claimant and defendant themselves. One prepares formal statements for all non-expert witnesses as laid down by CPR Part 32 and CPR PD 32.17–25. If a statement has not been prepared, filed and served in accordance with these rules and any directions, the court may refuse to hear evidence from that witness.

Witness statements must be on durable A4 paper, with 3.5cm margins, typed on only one side of the paper, with numbered paragraphs and numbered pages. All numbers, including dates, are to be in numerals. The most important formality is the signed statement of truth under CPR PD 22. Generally, the court will receive a statement in evidence if one has overlooked a formality, but an unsigned statement may well be unsigned because it does not reflect the witness's views.

CPR PD 32.18.1 requires one to state various matters about the witness (name, address, occupation or description such as unemployed or housewife, whether a party to the proceedings or employed by a party). It is useful to state the relationship between the witness and the party for whom the statement is being made. If the party was giving the witness a lift when the accident occurred and they are otherwise strangers, it is well worth saying so. An independent witness is generally more credible than a party's friend, relative or work colleague.

Paragraphs should be kept short, so that the court can, if invited to do so, immediately go to the sentence under discussion. For an example of the content of a liability witness statement, see the accompanying CD-ROM.

The court is interested in the facts perceived by an eyewitness and not his opinions. The only significant exception to this relates to estimated sizes, ages, speeds and distances as these are inevitably a matter of opinion, as are comments on road conditions, lighting and the effect of fog, rain, etc. A witness statement must not usurp the court's job of interpreting the evidence. Do not say: it was blatantly the van driver's fault. It is probably acceptable to say: I remember thinking he's going way too fast and I bet he can't stop in time. The court is interested in the opinions of expert witnesses, to whom different rules apply as discussed in the next section.

'The witness statement must, if practicable, be in the intended witness's own words' (CPR PD 32.18.1). However, nobody wants to read a transcript of a two-hour interview. Drawing up a statement involves producing a concise summary in a logical order, perhaps with sub-headings.

One is not bound to put into the statement everything the witness said. The notes to Principle 21.01 in the *Guide to Professional Conduct of Solicitors* say one 'must never deceive or mislead the court [but] a solicitor who knows of facts which . . . would assist the adversary is not under any duty to inform the adversary or the court of this to the prejudice of his or her own client'. One puts in all the evidence that the witness might reasonably be expected to give in answer to examination in chief, which is to say the questions one would ask him at trial. One is not bound to include all the information he might give under cross-examination, that is, when answering the other side's questions at trial. However, one must not leave something out if this twists the sense of what remains. Say after asking a witness all the questions one plans to raise at trial, one incautiously says: 'Anything else you'd like to tell me?' and he responds: 'Yes, your client reeked of alcohol'. The effect of omitting this from the statement may, in some situations, be to deceive the court. One may need to discuss a problem of this sort with counsel. If one cannot fairly omit the point from the witness's statement, it may be best not to call that witness.

One should never put anything into a statement that a witness did not say, however confident one is that he would agree to it. Rather than risk alienating the witness, one should always ring him up and check.

If one knows that something a witness said is false, one cannot put it into his witness statement. However, it is for the court, not the lawyers, to decide whether something is false. One may suspect that it is, or even be morally certain of it, but one will very seldom know it is unless the witness actually says so. If a witness admits that he intends to mislead the court, one cannot help him do so. The notes to Principle 21.13 in the *Guide to Professional Conduct of Solicitors* say if a client admits he has 'misled the court in any material matter . . . the solicitor must decline to act further in the proceedings, unless the client agrees fully to disclose his or her conduct to the court'. If a client makes statements that are inconsistent with what he has said before, it would not justify refusing to act for him unless it is clear that he is attempting to put forward false evidence to the court. See the notes to Principle 21.21.

In any personal injury claim, a great deal depends on the court's impression of the claimant. This is formed largely from his witness statement. The courts like honest, straightforward, accurate, concise, fairly stoical individuals. One may need to explain to a client that it is actually unhelpful to describe pain and suffering in too much detail.

If one can make a witness accept in cross-examination that he has given evidence about something he did not see, or that is clearly wrong, he will look like a liar or an idiot. Avoid simplistic drafting. If including anything which one knows the witness is not certain about or did not himself see, qualify it with words such as: I am fairly sure that. . . or: at the moment of impact I had looked away for a second, but . . . .

If a witness statement contains material that the maker did not personally observe, it is merely a matter of information and belief. The statement must make it clear if it contains any such matters (CPR PD 32.18.2). Usually, they will be either opinion evidence, which is inadmissible and should not be included, or hearsay which is much better dealt with by taking a statement from the original speaker.

The Bar Council's Written Standards encourage one to explain to a witness what a statement is, and to remind him from time to time. One might say, when sending the statement out for signature: 'The enclosed draft statement is your evidence, and it is vital that you are completely happy with it. Do not sign it unless it accurately describes what you can remember. I am happy to make any necessary changes. Please tell me if you think that I have left out anything significant, or if you feel that the statement is phrased in a misleading way'. Occasionally, one may need to mention to a witness that signing a statement of truth without an honest belief in its truth may result in proceedings against him for contempt of court (CPR Part 32.14 and CPR PD 22.3.8).

It is good practice to prepare two statements for the claimant, one on liability and the other on quantum. With two statements, it is easier to make tidy amendments, and one avoids the risk of burying the court in information when one makes an application or attends for assessment of damages to which only one of these aspects is relevant.

Should witness statements be disclosed before issuing proceedings? Ideally, well before issuing, the parties will have identified the matters in dispute, and obtained all their evidence on liability and quantum. The Court of Appeal has said that it is of paramount importance that the parties settle if possible, rather than issuing proceedings. It follows from the Personal Injury Protocol and CPR Part 44 on costs that the claimant should generally give the defendant enough information to settle the claim long enough before he issues proceedings. However, it is usual for the parties to exchange witness statements simultaneously, so that a party cannot take unfair advantage by secretly revising its statements after seeing those of the other side. Before issuing proceedings, the claimant should ideally send draft particulars of claim to the defendant and try to agree simultaneous mutual exchange of all witness statements. If the defendant is unwilling to exchange all its statements within a reasonable time, the claimant should consider making unilateral disclosure of his own quantum statement at least 21 days before he issues proceedings. In the author's view, this makes sense even if liability is denied (see **section 3.2**).

After proceedings have been issued and a defence delivered, the court will allocate the claim to track and make directions. In the fast track, it usually directs that there be simultaneous exchange of witness statements in 10 weeks (CPR Part 28 and CPR PD 28). If one fails to serve witness statements in time, the court may refuse to admit the evidence of those witnesses. The more surprises in the statements and the longer the delay, the more likely this is. For an example in a pedestrian trip case, see *Stroh* v. *London Borough of Haringey* [1999] EWCA Civ 1825.

One should not disclose a statement by a witness that is not really required. As there is no property in a witness, the other side can approach one's witnesses to find out if there are any gaps in their statements. Also, if one discloses a statement but does not call the witness to give evidence, the other side may decide to call him themselves under CPR Part 32.5.

One should not call a witness to give evidence at trial if he is not really necessary. Cases are blown out of the water every day because the claimant calls a witness to give evidence about one self-evident thing, and the witness gives unexpected evidence about something else too.

20.7 EXPERT EVIDENCE

An expert witness has experience, and usually training, that goes beyond the court's own knowledge. He is permitted to give opinion evidence, stating what conclusions can be drawn from the facts.

The court takes account of his opinions but is not bound by them. It makes its own findings from all the evidence. However, where medical experts give persuasive and unchallenged evidence that the claimant has a particular condition such as disabling depression, a court or tribunal cannot simply decide that this is wrong because he does not look depressed to them (*Kapadia* v. *Lambeth London Borough Council* [2000] All ER (D) 785).

Expert evidence is not needed in matters the court can assess for itself, such as whether a floor is slippery enough to be dangerous. If the court needs to decide the effect of an accident on the claimant's pre-existing back injury, clearly it will want guidance from a medical expert. If it is considering what a disabled claimant is likely to earn in future, it is less clear that it needs guidance from an expert employment consultant. The court has a duty to restrict expert evidence to that which is reasonably required to resolve the proceedings (CPR Part 35.1).

Expert evidence is regulated by CPR Part 35 and the corresponding Practice Direction. 'It is the duty of an expert to help the court on the matters within his expertise. This duty overrides any obligation to the person from whom he has received instructions or by whom he is paid' (CPR Part 35.3). 'An expert should assist the court by providing objective, unbiased opinion on matters within his expertise, and should not assume the role of an advocate' (CPR PD 35.1.3).

Unfortunately, there are still experts doing personal injury work who clearly like or dislike every claimant merely because he is a claimant, and overlook vital points such as that the claimant saw his doctor about a serious health problem the week before the alleged accident. The courts are patient with experts. If an expert is challenged about an oversight and duly amends his report, he will get away with it. If he dismisses a relevant fact, brazenly saying: this does not change my opinion, the court may feel that he does not understand his duty to the court. If an expert does not understand this duty, the court will refuse to consider his evidence. See the discussion in *Stevens* v. *Gullis* [1999] EWCA Civ 1978.

If an expert is apparently competent and understands his duty to the court, the fact that he is friendly with, or even employed by, one of the parties does not bar him from giving expert evidence (*Field* v. *Leeds City Council* (2000) *The Times* 18 January). However, if an expert has an interest in the outcome of the case, the court should be told of this as soon as possible (*R (Factortame Ltd)* v. *Secretary of State for Transport* [2002] EWCA Civ 932). The court will be alert for evidence of bias, and may give less weight to a report from a tied expert.

Before the CPR, a claimant lawyer would dot every i and cross every t in a personal injury case. This might mean that in a case worth only £15,000 one would obtain expert evidence from a liability expert, orthopaedic consultant, neurologist, psychologist, plastic surgeon, costs of care expert and forensic accountant. At the end of the claim, a successful claimant nearly always obtained an order that the defendant pay for all expert reports that were reasonably obtained and reasonably priced. Today, the defendant is unlikely to be ordered to pay for this many reports except in a complex case of truly catastrophic injury. The vast majority of claims are settled on the evidence of one expert witness per side, usually an orthopaedic surgeon.

The evidence an expert gives must involve some genuine expert input, or it is not admissible. Thus, the evidence of an accident reconstruction expert will not be admitted if he merely reads the witness statements and jumps to a conclusion without making any site visit, measurements or calculations. See the discussion in *Liddell* v. *Middleton* [1996] PIQR P36.

Consultant orthopaedic surgeons who are experienced in medico-legal work understand the needs and preferences of the courts, and are aware that their opinions may be dissected by lawyers and their peers. They generally make well-informed, diligent and courteous experts, able to discuss their own uncertainties calmly. Experts who do little court work may delay unduly, offer opinions that ignore half the evidence, and resent questions.

Should one disclose one's expert evidence before issuing proceedings? Ideally, well before issuing, the parties will have identified the matters in dispute, and obtained all their evidence on liability and quantum. The Court of Appeal has said that it is of paramount importance that the parties settle if possible, rather than issuing proceedings. It follows from the Personal Injury Protocol and CPR Part 44 on costs that the claimant should generally give the defendant enough information to settle the claim long enough before he issues proceedings. Under the Personal Injury Protocol, if the defendant admits liability after receiving the letter of claim, the claimant should send him copies of any medical reports received. On issuing proceedings, the claimant will generally attach his medical evidence to the Particulars of Claim (CPR PD 16.4.3.) and the defendant should do the same when serving the Defence (CPR PD 16.12.1). Otherwise it is usual for the parties to exchange expert evidence simultaneously, so that a party cannot take unfair advantage by secretly revising its evidence after seeing that obtained by the other side.

After proceedings have been issued and a defence delivered, the court will allocate the claim to track and make directions. In the fast track, it usually directs that there be simultaneous exchange of expert evidence in 14 weeks (CPR Part 28 and CPR PD 28).

Neither party is entitled to rely on any expert evidence, written or oral, in any track, unless a direction specifically authorises it. (CPR Part 35.4 in the fast track and multi-track, and CPR Part 27.5 in the Small Claims track). In the fast track, the court will not allow an expert to appear in court and give oral evidence 'unless it believes it is necessary in the interests of justice to do so' (CPR PD 28.7.2). Except in cases of really trivial injury, the claimant can be sure of getting permission to rely on the written report of a medical expert in one speciality, usually orthopaedics. He cannot be absolutely sure, even in a large claim where it is very important to him, of getting permission to rely on reports from medical experts in two different specialities such as orthopaedics and psychiatry. This is especially the case if the report of the second expert is received somewhat late and risks disrupting the court's timetable for progress to trial (*Cassie* v. *Ministry of Defence* [2002] EWCA Civ 838).

For all these reasons, one must use expert evidence with caution. One must sometimes say to a client something like:

> We don't yet have any expert evidence that abc. To prove this point, we need a report from an expert in xyz, which will cost about £350. I think it will help us prove abc, and if it does it will add £X,000 to your claim. I also think that at the end of the day, the court will order the defendant to pay for it. However, the court may feel that the cost of the report is disproportionate to what it achieved. If so, or if the report does not support your case, the cost will come out of your compensation. Please tell me whether or not to obtain the report.

As to medical experts, see **sections 11.4** and **11.5**.

20.8 LIABILITY EXPERTS

Say one's client is a building labourer who fell from a scaffold platform because he leant against a second floor guard-rail that unexpectedly hinged outwards. It was necessary to have a gate in the guard-rail so that materials could be passed through it by a crane and set down on the platform. The question is whether the gate was hinged, locked and marked in the right way. If one gets a report from an expert witness it will be fairly expensive. In an unusual discipline, one may have to use an unknown expert with a risk that he will produce an unsatisfactory report. In any case the court will not order the defendant to pay for the report if the claimant could have gone down a different and cheaper route.

The claimant's initial approach is to ask the defendant to admit liability. If he will not, but any judge is likely to feel that liability is obvious, the claimant might decide to rely on photographs and plain common sense. He might back these up with a page from a scaffolding textbook obtained from the building studies department of the local technical college. In a less clear-cut case, one should try to find a regulation, code of practice or guideline issued by the Health & Safety Executive, the British Standards Institution or the Construction Industry Training Board.

When considering the following cases, note that the courts have become much less willing to admit expert evidence, or to order the loser to pay for it, since the CPR.

Relevant cases include:

- *Dale* v. *British Coal Corporation (No 2)* (1992) 136 Solicitor's Journal LB 199. The Court of Appeal said 'where it is necessary to show that a prudent employer should have taken precautions not taken by the defendants, there should normally be expert evidence'.
- *Liddell* v. *Middleton* [1996] PIQR P36. The Court of Appeal said '. . . in industrial accidents an expert may well be needed to explain complicated machinery or to give evidence of practice and safety procedure. . .'.
- *Hawkes* v. *London Borough of Southwark* [1998] EWCA Civ 310. Another Court of Appeal case, in which the court said forcefully that it did not need to hear from an expert to know either that carrying a heavy door up a flight of stairs posed a significant risk of injury, or that the risk might have been avoided by having two people carry the door.

Trip and slip cases

An expert's report will seldom be really necessary in these cases, and many judges would refuse to admit it as evidence.

Relevant cases include:

- *Pridham* v. *Hemel Hempstead Corporation* (1971) 69 LGR 523. An engineer has nothing to contribute when the court is deciding whether a highway authority carried out inspections of roads and pavements at reasonable intervals.
- *Dibb* v. *Kirklees Metropolitan Borough Council* [1999] EWCA Civ 1180. A tripper case involving a steep, narrow defective pavement in which the Court of Appeal seems to have found the evidence of the claimant's expert very useful.
- *Nessa* v. *Walsall Metropolitan Borough Council* (CA 18 December 2000, unreported). The claimant had slipped while leaving a car park by walking down a one-in-four tarmac slope. The slope had been there for 20 to 30 years with no report of any previous accident. The District Judge had refused to let the parties rely on expert evidence. In the Court of Appeal Mantell LJ said, and Sir Ronald Waterhouse agreed, that 'This was a case, in my view, which called out for such evidence, if not demanded it. The judge was left with the very difficult task of making up his own mind about the dangerousness or otherwise of this slope without any assistance from an outside source.' It is to be wondered how may other judges would take this view today.

Road accident reconstruction consultants

Many judges are hostile to the use of these experts, and the Court of Appeal in *Liddell* v. *Middleton* [1996] PIQR P36 described a 'regrettable tendency' for parties to instruct experts unnecessarily, and said 'in road traffic accidents it is the exception rather than the rule that expert witnesses are required'. All the major law firms continue to make regular use of these experts in a small percentage of multi-track cases, and a smaller percentage of fast track cases.

Occupational health and safety consultants

It is not generally necessary to have expert evidence about whether a task could be said to have involved a risk of injury (*Liddell* v. *Middleton*). However, deciding whether an employer had done all that was reasonably practicable to comply with a statutory duty involves assessing how likely this sort of accident was to occur, how serious it would be if it did, what extra safety measures could be taken, what they would cost in money, and what they would cost in time and inconvenience probably does require expert evidence.

Where expert evidence is needed after a workplace accident, any health and safety consultant can deal with injuries arising from trips, falls and manual handling. Most can tackle fork lift truck accidents. However, a claim for occupational asthma may require evidence from a health and safety consultant with a particular interest in the safe use of chemicals in the workplace and in dust and fume extraction, or perhaps a consulting engineer.

Consulting engineers

One who offers a service to lawyers can probably deal with all the stock claims, such as trips, falls and manual handling. If the claimant has been let down by a lift, blown up in a ground-based electrical installation, or scalded by boiling zinc at a galvanising works, you may need an engineer who specialises in the relevant process.

If the claimant has a WRULD apparently caused by production line work, one probably needs an ergonomics expert.

If toxic fumes poisoned the claimant, one may need both a chemical pathologist to say whether the symptoms were caused by the fumes and a consulting engineer from the industry in question to explain how it was that the claimant came to be exposed to them, and whether this shows a breach of statutory duty.

Other experts

If a horse kicked the claimant during a riding lesson, one may need a horse expert with solid experience of riding schools and the appropriate qualification from the national governing body.

20.9 FINDING AN EXPERT

Some experts are more impressive than others. The opinion of a professor of orthopaedic surgery at a teaching hospital will generally be more influential than that of an ordinary consultant orthopaedic surgeon half his age.

If the issue is one of effective vehicle brakes, the court may well be much more impressed by a fleet engineer with 30 years' relevant experience than by a newly qualified automotive engineer, even if the latter has an MSc and the former an HND.

When choosing between the conflicting evidence of two experts, their qualifications and professional standing are important but the main thing is the quality of their evidence and reasoning as demonstrated to the court (*Transco* v. *Griggs* [2003] EWCA Civ 564).

An expert who has given up doing any practical work in favour of doing pure forensic work has a limited shelf life. If it is more than three or four years since he last had any hands-on experience, it casts a shadow over his opinions.

Ideally, the expert will know CPR Part 35 and PD 35. If not, he must be willing to act on what one tells him about them, and in particular to turn work around swiftly. See **section 20.10**. If considering instructing an expert who may be inexperienced, ask how many times he has given evidence at trial. If the answer is none, has he been on a training course, or at least read a textbook on expert practice?

Try to find somebody who has already stood in the witness box as expert a few times. One curse of personal injury claims is the expert who will agree anything with the other side's expert if it means that he stays out of the witness box.

Unless instructing an expert one knows well, it is worth getting a quote first, to cover the cost of the expert's investigation and report. What would he charge for giving evidence at trial? Most experts have a daily rate for this. Check the expert's terms of business. If one asks him to attend trial and give evidence, the chances are this will be cancelled on short notice. Will he charge a cancellation fee? Typically, an expert will charge 100 per cent of his daily rate if given less than 48 hours' notice of cancellation, and 50 per cent of it unless he is given seven days' notice.

Any law firm doing personal injury work will have its own directory of approved experts, and probably a system that fee-earners are required to use when a new expert is needed. A few experts, mainly those who are seldom used, are one or more of professionally incompetent; lazy; dogmatic; partisan; shifty, arrogant or bemused in the witness box; hard to contact; and intellectually or financially dishonest. When considering a new expert, it is really necessary to know how they have been rated by lawyers who have seen them in action. The following are potential sources of good experts (see **Appendix 4** for contact details):

- Association of Personal Injury Lawyers. APIL maintains an excellent database of experts in many fields, their performance rated by APIL members. Free to APIL members.
- In a case of clinical negligence, Action against Medical Accidents has a database of experts in a wide range of highly specialised fields, rated by performance.
- There are also dozens of agencies set up to introduce expert to lawyer, some of which provide experts with training, and rate them according to feedback from lawyer clients. Perhaps the best known is the Academy of Experts.
- There are also several directories of expert witnesses.

Failing this, try the professional body of the relevant discipline, for example the Institute of Electrical Engineers.

Many personal injury lawyers get their clients through intermediaries such as the claims companies which one sees advertising on TV, car hire companies and various legal expenses insurers. Some of these organisations impose, tactfully or not, their own system for selecting expert witnesses, and thereby make a secret profit. The system discourages lawyers from using their favourite local experts.

20.10 COMMISSIONING AN EXPERT'S REPORT UNILATERALLY

This section and the four subsequent ones describe the procedure in claims governed by the Personal Injury Protocol. The procedure in claims to which the Clinical Negligence and Disease and Illness protocols apply is slightly different.

The procedural rules are in the Pre-action Protocols, the Protocols Practice Direction, and CPR Part 35 and PD 35, all of which can be seen on the Department for Constitutional Affairs website at **www.dca.gov.uk**.

There is also the *Code of Guidance for Experts & Those Instructing Them*, produced by the Academy of Experts and distributed by them without charge (see **Appendix 4** for contact details). The *Code* was favourably mentioned by Lord Woolf in *Peet* v. *Mid Kent Healthcare* [2001] EWCA Civ 1703. It is worth a look, but if it conflicts with the CPR, the latter prevails.

One may instruct an expert jointly with the other side, but this section looks at the position where the expert is instructed unilaterally. Typically, the claimant instructs an expert first, well before issuing proceedings, and the defendant decides on seeing the report whether to get its own report from a different expert. The Protocols Practice Direction says: 'If an expert is needed, the parties should wherever possible and to save expense engage an agreed expert.' The mutually agreed expert, instructed unilaterally, is very different to the jointly instructed expert.

'Before any party instructs an expert he should give the other party a list of the name(s) of one or more experts in the relevant speciality whom he considers are suitable to instruct' (Personal Injury Protocol 3.14). If the other party wishes to indicate an objection to an expert he must do so within 14 days, unless the claimant proposed an expert in his letter of claim in which case the defendant's 14 days does not start to elapse until the time for acknowledging the letter of claim has expired (Personal Injury Protocol 3.16). If the other party objects to all the proposed experts, the parties may instruct experts of their own choice but the court reserves the right to decide whether they acted reasonably.

If the other party does not object to the proposed expert within the 14 days, he is not entitled to rely on his own expert evidence on that topic unless the first party agrees, the court so directs, or the first party's report has been amended and the first party is not prepared to disclose the original report (Personal Injury Protocol 3.18).

Whether one acts for claimant or defendant, it is a good idea to propose one's own experts before the other side does. Claimants usually nominate two or three medical experts in the letter of claim. If the other party gets his proposal in first, few courts would penalise one for instructing your own choice of expert after objecting to all the proposed experts without giving reasons. The proposer may demand the objector's reasons, but the Protocol does not require one to give them. Whether one's objection is to the expert's personality or qualifications, it would be very unwise to do so. Expert witnesses are more than usually likely to sue for defamation.

From the defendant's point of view, if the claimant proposes several experts, the defendant should object to all but one even if he has no desire to instruct an expert himself and is perfectly happy for the claimant to instruct any of the proposed experts. This restricts the claimant's ability to change experts if he does not like the first report he gets (see **section 20.15**).

There is a suggested letter for instructing a medical expert in the Personal Injury Protocol, and a slightly amended version on the accompanying CD-ROM. When drafting a letter of instruction to a medical expert, do send him the medical records and any relevant witness statements, and check whether he understands the need to comply with the court's timetable. One must ensure from the outset that he is willing and able to be prompt in producing his report, providing clarification, dealing with any updating report, cooperating in a without prejudice discussion to resolve conflicts with the other side's expert, and attending for trial if necessary (see **sections 20.13** and **20.14**).

Given the court's attitude to listing, he should be willing to drop everything, including holidays and professional commitments, to attend at trial. When providing the court with an expert's availability dates, it is not enough to say that he will not be available between certain dates. One must tell the court why, or it may well list the trial for that time anyway (*Rollinson* v. *Kimberley Clark* [1999] EWCA Civ 1587).

One should not send an expert anything for which one might wish to claim privilege, such as a witness statement that has not yet been signed, a statement by a witness one may prefer not to call, a report by another expert that one may not wish to rely on, or a barrister's opinion. If the expert relies on the document in producing his report he should refer to it and the other side will want to see it. CPR PD 31.7.1 says 'inspection should be provided by agreement unless the request is unreasonable'. Following *Lucas* v. *Barking, Havering & Redbridge NHS Trust* [2003] EWCA Civ 1102, the court probably will not order a party to disclose a privileged document merely because it was sent to the expert, but a dispute over disclosure can increase the costs stakes a great deal. If the expert does not need to see a document, one should not send it to him, and if he does one should get it in a version one is happy with and disclose it to the other side.

One must not press an expert to come to a particular conclusion, or instruct him on a conditional fee basis so that he is paid only if his evidence wins the claim (*R (Factortame Ltd)* v. *Secretary of State for Transport* [2002] EWCA Civ 932).

What if there is a dispute over the facts upon which the expert will be reporting? The expert must eventually be told that there are two versions of events. The question is whether one should tell him at the outset. Liability experts should generally have both versions before them at the outset. Indeed, their task is usually to advise which version is correct.

However, when instructing a medical expert for the claimant, one should avoid if possible telling him at the outset that the claimant is alleged to be lying about the accident or his symptoms. In most cases, a doctor's opinion depends mainly on what the patient tells them and on his own, humanly fallible, assessment of whether the patient is lying or exaggerating. Doctors hate being taken for a ride by patients, and any suggestion that a claimant is dishonest will make a medical expert very alert for suspicious signs during the examination. He will be prone to interpret a few second's delay in answering, uncertainty in an answer, or even a lack of eye contact, as evidence that the claimant is evasive or dishonest. In a situation like this the claimant's lawyer should instruct the medical expert unilaterally and tell him only the claimant's version of events. When the report has been disclosed to the defendant, the latter can ask the expert to assume that the defendant's version of events is true and advise accordingly.

The letter of instructions is not 'privileged against disclosure but the court will not, in relation to those instructions . . . order disclosure of any specific document. . .' unless there are reasonable grounds to consider that the expert, in his report, failed to set out all the 'material instructions, whether written or oral, on the basis of which the report was written' (CPR Part 35.10.3 and 4).

If the expert refers in his report to a document that has not been disclosed to the other party, this no longer gives the opposition an automatic right to see it. CPR Part 31.14.1 has been amended to change this. Neither does it necessarily mean that the statement of instructions is incomplete. Complete does not mean exhaustive. Experts are not required to repeat all their instructions or the entire contents of documents upon which they rely. Neither does a party generally waive privilege over a document by giving a copy to his expert. See *Lucas* v. *Barking, Havering & Redbridge NHS Trust* [2003] EWCA Civ 1102, in which the claimant's expert referred in his report to an undisclosed witness statement and an undisclosed earlier expert report. The Court of Appeal refused the defendant's request for sight of these documents as there was no evidence that the statement of instructions was inaccurate or incomplete. The primary purpose of CPR Part 35.10.4 was to encourage a party to give his expert all material instructions by ensuring that he did not waive privilege in so doing.

If one chooses to rely upon a report, one must disclose not only the report itself but any side letters, supplemental reports and messages received from him that contain any of his opinion (e.g. I haven't mentioned this in my report, but there are things which make me think that the claimant must have had serious health problems before the accident). However, the court has no power to order disclosure of earlier draft reports by that expert, unless the report relied on is apparently partial or incomplete (*Jackson* v. *Marley Davenport* [2004] EWCA Civ 1225).

20.11 COMMISSIONING A REPORT FROM A SINGLE JOINT EXPERT

The parties may voluntarily go one step further than agreeing an expert as described in the previous section, and instruct a single joint expert (SJE). If they do not, the court has the power at CPR Part 35.7 to direct the parties to use an SJE. This power is not often exercised at present.

For the litigator, the main point about an SJE is that since the parties instructed him together, they will receive his report simultaneously. A party cannot simply suppress the report if he does not like it. An SJE's opinion will probably decide the issue on which he reports. It is prudent for a lawyer to ask his client before agreeing to instruct an SJE. Say the claimant and the expert dislike each other on sight, and the expert produces a hostile report. The claimant will not be happy if he finds that his lawyer needlessly committed him to relying on that expert's opinion.

If the claimant proposes some well-known experts as SJE the defendant usually agrees, making it a condition that the report should be from a particular expert. The defendants may agree to pay half the fee pending settlement or trial. Claimants should note that some defendant lawyers will agree to pay part or all of the fee, but when they are sent the expert's bill they refuse to pay until the claim settles.

Where the parties opt for a jointly instructed expert, by convention the claimant drafts a joint letter of instruction and asks the defendant to agree it.

The letter is very like the usual unilateral letter, but should tell the expert that after his duty to the court he owes a duty equally to claimant and defendant. The letter must tell him to whom he should send his bill. Conflict may arise if the defendant wants to amend the letter, usually to draw a medical SJE's attention to certain points in the medical records. Neither party should be too alert to quibble about the draft letter or any supplemental instructions sent by the opposition, as the court will assume that the expert is robust and impartial.

If the parties cannot agree a joint letter, they will probably give up the idea of using an SJE unless one has been imposed on them by the court. One should ideally have a joint letter of instruction, but it is not compulsory. 'Where the court gives a direction under rule 35.7 for a single joint expert to be used, each instructing party may give instructions to the expert' (CPR Part 35.8.1, and see also *Daniels* v. *Walker* [2000] 1 WLR 1382). The court has no power to order that there be a single letter of instruction (*Yorke* v. *Katra* [2003] EWCA Civ 867).

A party cannot have any dealings with an SJE without keeping the other party fully informed (*Peet* v. *Mid Kent Healthcare* [2001] EWCA Civ 1703). The best way to ensure the other party is informed is to keep all communications with the expert in writing and send them copies. One must avoid discussing a case with an SJE by telephone, although certainly one can ring him to check what dates he will be available for trial.

The Court of Appeal has said that although it will not always be appropriate to instruct an SJE, especially in very large cases, it will usually be helpful (*Daniels* v. *Walker* [2000] 1 WLR 1382). Unless there is a reason for doing otherwise, experts should be instructed jointly (*Peet* v. *Mid Kent Healthcare* [2001] EWCA Civ 1703).

Practitioners are not quite so enthusiastic. In a survey on SJEs carried out by the Law Society in 2003, virtually all personal injury solicitors had used one at least once, although there was marked reluctance to use them in the multi-track. In the fast track, 88 per cent of respondents were generally happy with the quality of the SJEs they had encountered, and they listed many good points including efficiency, convenience, certainty, objectivity, clarity, speed of settlement. However, things can go badly wrong in an individual case. Of the Law Society's respondents, 55 per cent had experienced problems with at least one SJE, for example the expert who took a stand and refused to change even when faced with overwhelming evidence. If a party considers an SJE to be unsatisfactory, his struggle to reform or replace the expert can run up a lot of costs, often to no avail.

Many practitioners would prefer to avoid using an SJE in the following circumstances:

- Any liability expert unless the claim is of only moderate value.
- A medical expert if there is a dispute over the facts on which he will be reporting.

- A medical expert where there are known to be two schools of thought about the way an injury can be caused (as with RSI and prolapsed intervertebral disc) or where only a sympathetic expert is likely to think there is anything wrong with the claimant (as with diffuse RSI, Chronic Pain Syndrome, and mild traumatic brain injury/post concussional syndrome). See *Oxley* v. *Penwarden* [2001] CPLR 1, a case where there were two schools of thought about a vascular condition that led to amputation; and *Miller* v. *Lothian Primary Care NHS Trust* [2004] ScotCS 159, where one school of thought about prolapsed intervertebral disc was represented by a more senior and specialised expert than the other.
- The costs of care expert. Their qualifications are often humble, and if the claimant is permanently disabled the costs of care will make up a very large proportion of the total claim.

20.12 AN INDEPENDENT REPORT FOR THE DEFENDANT

If he has already been examined by his own preferred expert, the claimant may be reluctant to attend for examination by a new expert on behalf of the defendant. A defendant should not necessarily see this as sinister. The examination will be inconvenient, may be painful, and certainly will not help the claimant because if it results in a favourable report, the defendant will not disclose it. Can the defendant compel a reluctant claimant to attend for a medical examination with a new expert? He can apply pressure by refusing to negotiate. If proceedings have been issued he can apply for an order staying the proceedings until the claimant attends. The question is whether the court would grant the order.

Assuming that the existing report is not from a single joint expert, the position is as follows.

In the Small Claims track it is unlikely that the court would back the defendant if he wants to obtain his own medical report, where the claimant has already been seen by one doctor and does not want to be examined again. Even if the claimant attends voluntarily, there is a fair chance that the court will refuse to give the defendant leave to rely on the new report.

In the fast track, the situation may turn on paragraph 3 of the Personal Injury Protocol. If the claimant proposed to use a particular expert and the defendant failed to object to the proposal within a few weeks, the defendant is not entitled to rely on his own expert evidence unless the claimant agrees, the court so directs, or the first party's expert report has been amended and the first party is not willing to disclose the original report. Towards the top end of the fast track and in the multi-track, one would expect the judge to permit the defendant to obtain his own report anyway, unless he leaves this so late that it risks disrupting the court's timetable for progress to trial as in *Calden* v. *Nunn* [2003] EWCA Civ 200.

If the court considers it appropriate for the claimant to undergo medical examination by the defendant's expert and the claimant fails to comply, it will stay those parts of the claim to which the examination is relevant (*James* v. *Baily Gibson & Co* [2002] EWHC Civ 822 (QB)). If the examination is relevant to issues at the heart of the claim and the claimant repeatedly fails to attend, the claim will be struck out (*Jassim* v. *Grand Metropolitan* [1999] EWCA Civ 595).

The position is different if the existing report is from a jointly instructed medical expert. The defendant will be given permission to rely on a report from a different expert in the same field only if he has good reason to object to the report by the existing expert (*Daniels* v. *Walker* [2000] 1 WLR 1382). If the defendant has no good reason, the claimant should not agree to see a different expert (see **section 20.15**).

When the claimant agrees to see the defendant's medical expert, he should do so on condition that the defendant pays his reasonable expenses. Rail tickets, travelling expenses, overnight accommodation and loss of earnings may add up to £300 or more. Many claimant lawyers have experienced severe delays and disputes over payment and now refuse to advise any clients to attend for examination unless the defendant pays these expenses beforehand.

If the claimant attends for medical examination by the defendant's expert and concludes that the report will be hostile, can he order the expert, as a matter of medical ethics, not to disclose it to the defendant? No (*Kapadia* v. *Lambeth London Borough Council* [2000] All ER (D) 785).

20.13 CLARIFYING AND CHALLENGING A REPORT

There are detailed requirements as to the form and content of expert's reports at CPR Part 35 and PD 35. The court may refuse to admit evidence from an expert whose report does not comply with these rules. Briefly, the report must list the expert's qualifications, be addressed to the court and not to the party who instructed the expert, contain a statement setting out what instructions, documents and records the report is based on, contain a signed statement of truth in the form required by the latest amendment of CPR PD 35.2.4, and include the statement 'I understand my duty to the court and have complied with that duty.' This refers to the overriding duty to give the court the expert's 'objective, unbiased opinion' (CPR Part 35.3 and CPR PD 35.1.3).

Each party is entitled to ask written questions of an expert, whether an SJE or instructed by the other party (CPR Part 35.6 and PD 35.5). Written questions to an expert 'may be put once only . . . within 28 days of service of the expert's report; and . . . must be for the purpose only of clarification of the report unless in any case . . . the court gives permission; or . . . the other party agrees' (CPR Part 35.6.2). The other party should agree to late questions or questions going beyond clarification if the court is likely to give permission, which it will do in practice if it is in the interests of justice that the answers be given.

Say the expert has omitted to give a prognosis, and the other party asks for one; or the defendant wants to ask the claimant's expert whether the injuries would have been less severe if the claimant had been wearing a seatbelt; or whether the claimant's pre-accident history of degenerative change means he would have had some of the neck symptoms even if the accident had not taken place. Strictly these are not requests for clarification, but the court will order the expert to deal with the point. It is legitimate to invite the expert to amend or expand the report to ensure accuracy, internal consistency, completeness, relevance, and clarity. The party who originally instructed the expert cannot object to a question merely because the answer is unlikely to help their case. An expert is not for the sole use of one party (*Mutch* v. *Allen* [2001] EWCA Civ 76). Note CPR PD 35.5.2: 'Where a party sends a written question or questions direct to an expert, a copy of the questions should, at the same time, be sent to the other party or parties.'

What if claimant and defendant each have their own experts to advise on the same point, and there is a significant difference of opinion between them? Once proceedings have been issued, the court may under CPR Part 35.12 direct that there be a discussion between experts, resulting in a statement of issues on which they agree, issues on which they disagree, and reasons for any disagreement. As CPR Part 35.12.says that the discussions themselves shall not be referred to at trial unless the parties agree, they are generally known as without prejudice discussions. If proceedings have not yet been issued, the parties should organise such discussions on their own initiative. They are usually carried out by phone. It is legitimate, and often prudent, for the lawyers to agree an agenda for the discussion consisting as far as possible of leading questions – questions with yes or no answers. Usually one of the experts is hard to get hold of. The keener of the two experts will rapidly tire of chasing the evasive one. The court will expect the claimant to ensure the discussions take place. The parties cannot attend the discussions. In exceptional circumstances the court may allow them to tape-record the discussions instead, for example if there is good reason to fear that, face to face, one expert will dominate the other (*HH & R* v. *Lambeth, Southwark & Lewisham Health Authority* [2001] EWCA Civ 1455).

Peet v. *Mid Kent Healthcare* [2001] EWCA Civ 1703 says there will seldom be any need to test the evidence of an SJE by cross-examination at trial. This suggests that one will seldom be allowed to.

If one receives a report from the other party that seems to show bias on the part of their expert, the court will probably expect one to respond initially by reminding the expert of his duty to the court and asking whether he considers it appropriate to amend the report. If he does not, or if the bias is so gross that the situation seems hopeless, consider making immediate application to the court for an order that evidence from this expert be inadmissible. The court will balance the extent of the apparent bias, and the effect on costs and on the trial date of either instructing a fresh expert or proceeding without.

In *Pearce* v. *Ove Arup Partnership* [2001] EWHC 455 the claimant's expert witness was allowed to give evidence. The judge found he had come 'to argue a case. Any point which might support that case, however flimsy, he took . . . [He] bears a heavy responsibility for this case ever coming to trial, with its attendant cost, expense and waste of time . . . I consider it necessary to refer [his] conduct to his professional body, the RIBA'. This expert's professional body, in the event, did not agree with the judge.

An expert witness may be ordered to pay costs of litigation if by his evidence he causes significant expense to be incurred, and does so in flagrant disregard of his duties to the Court (*Phillips* v. *Symes* [2004] EWHC 2329 (Ch)).

20.14 UPDATING A MEDICAL REPORT

The Part 36 system of settlement offers is the keystone of the CPR. One cannot calculate how much to offer without a very good idea of the medical position. So that claims can be settled before proceedings are issued, the CPR requires one to put all one's cards on the table at an early stage. The claimant would often prefer to prevent the defendant getting enough information to make a worrying offer until he is quite ready for trial. However, it follows from the Personal Injury Protocol and CPR Part 44 on costs that the claimant should generally disclose medical evidence long enough before he issues proceedings (see **section 3.2**).

Once proceedings have been issued, 'No party may call an expert or put in evidence an expert's report without the court's permission' (CPR Part 35.4.1). 'A party who fails to disclose an expert's report may not use the report at the trial or call the expert to give evidence orally unless the court gives permission' (CPR Part 35.13).

When a defence is delivered, the court will allocate the claim to track and make directions. In the fast track, it does so under CPR Part 28 and CPR PD 28, and the usual directions are for disclosure of documents in four weeks, exchange of witness statements in 10 weeks and exchange of experts' reports in 14 weeks. The court will, at the same time, fix the trial date or trial period, which will be 30 weeks after directions if the court has space. One must try to get the medical evidence in time to exchange it as directed. The court will seldom be much concerned about a missed directions deadline, unless the delay, and the time the other side needs to respond when one does comply, put the trial date at risk. 'Litigants and lawyers must be in no doubt that the court will regard the postponement of a trial as an order of last resort' (CPR PD 28.5.4).

Those who disclose a medical report late because they failed to tell their expert how long he had to prepare the report will often be refused permission to rely on it. Certainly a party who flouts the directions timetable for tactical reasons is likely to suffer. 'It is quite wrong for trials to be delayed, and for the possibility of making an effective Part 36 offer to be rendered nugatory, because of the late service of an expert's statement' (*Baron* v. *Lovell* [1999] EWCA Civ 1977).

In personal injury work, some last-minute changes to medical evidence may be inevitable. In *Baron* v. *Lovell*, Brooke L.J. referred to the familiar problem of the back or neck injury where symptoms generally settle within two years, but 'In a minority of cases they continue to cause trouble for about five years. If one is extremely unlucky, they go on causing significant pain and other difficulties on a lifelong basis.' Because it is impossible to predict who will suffer long term problems, a doctor seeing the claimant within the first two years is likely to predict a full recovery, and it is only when symptoms continue beyond that time that he starts to predict long-term problems. The claimant may then have to change his approach to the claim, serving fresh medical evidence and quantum witness statements, and recalculating his financial losses. This happens fairly often. If proceedings are already under way, the claimant is likely to need the court's permission to amend the particulars of claim, alter the directions timetable and rely on medical evidence served out of time. He must apply for permission as soon as possible once he realises it will be needed (CPR PD 28.4.2).

He may well not get permission, especially if the medical evidence means that he needs to try a different tack. In *Cassie* v. *Ministry of Defence* [2002] EWCA Civ 838 the claimant suffered spinal injuries in a fall at work. Liability was agreed, but not quantum so the claimant issued proceedings. Four years after the accident, he appeared to have recovered fully, but after another two years he began to suffer quite severe back problems and had to give up work. A joint orthopaedic report was obtained, which said there was no organic basis for the back pain. Then the claimant saw a psychiatrist because he was depressed, and this led to a psychiatric report that indicated that the pain was genuine. On that basis, the claim was worth perhaps £300,000. The District Judge refused to let the claimant rely on the psychiatric report, which was obtained somewhat late, and at trial he was awarded £26,000. The Court of Appeal backed the trial judge but described the case as worrying and difficult, and one judge said: 'I am uneasy as to whether justice, in these circumstances, has been done.'

Some evidence of the claimant's pain and suffering will be given not in a medical report, but in his own witness statement. The Court of Appeal in *Baron* v. *Lovell* also said: 'If a claimant's symptoms are continuing, this must be made clear in the witness statements served on his side. It is not legitimate to serve out of date statements and then hope to be allowed to update them in a radical way just before the trial.'

20.15 CHANGING TO A DIFFERENT EXPERT

Say one commissioned a report from an expert unilaterally, and when it arrives it is very disappointing. Its contents may suggest that the expert is sloppy or biased, or the expert may have taken so long to produce the report that one cannot afford to have him on the team. More likely, the report simply does not give the opinion one hoped for. Can one keep quiet about the report and get a fresh report from a different expert? It depends whether one acts for claimant or defendant, and whether the other side knows one has obtained a report already.

If the claimant proposed three experts without objection from the defendant and obtained the first report without telling the defendant which expert he intended to try, the defendant will not know that the claimant rejected it and got a fresh report from one of the other two experts. The truth may emerge when the claimant seeks his costs and the defendant understandably refuses to pay for a report that was never disclosed.

If the defendant learns that the claimant has a report, he will want to see it. However, the report is privileged unless the expert was jointly instructed. The court cannot directly order a party to disclose a report. It is up to him to decide whether he wants to rely on it (*Carlson* v. *Townsend* [2001] EWCA Civ 511).

If the defendant has obtained a medical report that he finds disappointing and wants to instruct a fresh expert, the prudent claimant should not agree to be re-examined until the defendant has given a very good reason. The claimant should insist on seeing the defendant's first report to satisfy himself that the reason is a good one, but the defendant will not wish to disclose any report that undermines the defence.

If proceedings are issued, one needs the court's permission to rely on the evidence of any expert. One gets this by attaching Dr A's report to the Particulars of Claim, and citing Dr A as the proposed expert in the Allocation Questionnaire. If one then wants to rely on Dr B instead, the court will want to know why. The court will give permission to change experts only for very good reason. One good reason would be if the expert evidently does not, despite having it explained to him, understand the nature of his duty to the court.

If a party wants to change experts after proceedings have been issued, will he have to disclose the report of the first expert? Probably, despite *Carlson*. Where a party refuses to disclose the report of the first expert, the court can take the report of the fresh expert with a pinch of salt (*Jenkins* v. *Grocott and Hoyte* [2000] PIQR Q17). The court may make permission to rely on a report from a second expert conditional on disclosure of the first report. This is particularly likely if the second expert's report was obtained in breach of the Protocol (*Beck* v. *Ministry of Defence* [2003] EWCA Civ 1043).

If a party does not like the report from his original expert, should he get a fresh report before or after asking the court's permission? One will be better able to persuade the court if one already knows that the new expert will say something different and useful, but CPR PD 28.4.2 says it is 'essential that any party who wishes to have a direction varied takes steps to do so as soon as possible'. The courts have criticised, and refused permission to, parties who have obtained fresh reports without telling the other side what they were doing (*Calden* v. *Nunn* [2003] EWCA Civ 200. CPR PD 28.4.2). If a change of expert, and the need for the other side to respond to it, would risk derailing the timetable leading to trial, one 'must be in no doubt that the court will regard the postponement of a trial as an order of last resort' (CPR PD 38.5.6).

If the parties instructed the expert jointly, they may not be bound by his report if they have good reason to dislike it when it turns up. In *Daniels* v. *Walker* [2000] 1 WLR 1382 a single joint expert recommended that the claimant receive full-time care. The defendant's team felt that part-time care would be sufficient, and wanted leave to rely on a report to that effect from an independent expert. The judge refused. This being a heavyweight case, and the difference between full-time and part-time care being worth a great deal of money, the Court of Appeal did give the defendant leave. If one is unhappy with an expert's report the court will probably expect one to initially try to resolve the problem by written questions. Only if this fails should one obtain a report from a further expert. If the claim is of only moderate value, do not count on getting leave to rely on it.

In *Cosgrove* v. *Pattison* (2001) The Times 13 February the court indicated that it will, when deciding whether to allow the evidence of a further expert witness, consider the nature of the issues, the number of issues, the reason for requiring a new expert, the amount and importance of the particular issue at stake, the effect on the trial of permitting one party to call separate expert evidence, any delay likely to be caused to the proceedings, any other special features, and the overall justice to the parties. One might add to this list whether the party seeking leave has otherwise complied with the Pre-action Protocol.

CHAPTER 21

Small Claims

On 10 November 2004 the Government produced a report entitled *Tackling the Compensation Culture*. This strikes the author as a very revealing title, since the report itself admits that 'accident claims . . . are not soaring. The trend has been reasonably static for the last four years – indeed they fell by 9.5 per cent in the year to March 2004'. The report looks at the Small Claims limit and says that the Government 'accepts the [Better Regulation] Task Force's recommendation to undertake research into the benefits and costs of raising it'. If the Small Claims limit is raised to £5,000 as proposed, it will have a huge effect on both accident victims and law firms. Most of the former who are not represented by solicitors will no longer be able to find one to act for them; and many law firms will lose the bulk of their personal injury caseload.

By 1999, 87 per cent of defended civil actions in the county court were Small Claims. However, very few personal injury claims worth less than the Small Claims limit ever get off the ground. This is because they require special knowledge, and the Small Claims financial limits are lower for personal injury than for other civil claims.

As Professor A Baldwin pointed out in his report, *Lay & Judicial Perspectives on the Expansion of the Small Claims Regime* (2002), 'almost no PI cases are heard as Small Claims'. To quote the court's leaflet EX 301 *Making a Claim*, 'if your claim is for a sum over £5,000 . . . it is advisable to seek the help of a solicitor . . . personal injury claims can be more complicated and it may be preferable to get some professional help and advice no matter what the value of your claim is'. If a layman does want to bring a PI Small Claim on his own and has time to learn how to do so, how can he draft particulars of claim, value his pain and suffering, or respond to the defendant's rejection of some of his claimed losses? Will he find a medical expert willing to prepare a report in a claim that might go badly wrong? Without legal expenses cover, how much risk is there that he will face a hostile costs order for unreasonable behaviour?

The point of Small Claims is that they are less formal than the fast track, and the loser makes only a small contribution to the winner's costs. Subject to any increase in the financial limit for Small Claims, under CPR Part 26 and

CPR PD 26 a personal injury claim will be allocated to the court's Small Claims track if pain, suffering and loss of amenity are worth less than £1,000; and the whole claim including pain, suffering and financial losses such as uninsured vehicle damage is worth less than £5,000.

There are cases where the courts have valued injuries lasting only two weeks at £1,000, but as a rule of thumb, injuries are worth less than £1,000 if the claimant had significant symptoms for less than a month.

21.1 THE SPECIAL PROBLEM OF SMALL CLAIMS

The no costs rule in Small Claims more or less prevents parties having full legal advice and representation. If a claimant receives full service from a law firm, there is a good chance that their costs will wipe out most or all of his compensation. Even trade union and legal expenses insurance cover seldom allow a law firm to do much more for the claimant than write a couple of letters.

It is important for both claimant and defendant to identify a probable Small Claim as early as possible, and deal with it accordingly. There is not much point chasing the other side to disclose documents in a Small Claim, and the claimant cannot afford to have a lawyer do serious research on legal issues.

One cannot escape the no costs rule by settling the claim before it is allocated to track. In *Voice & Script* v. *Alghafar* [2003] EWCA Civ 736 the Court of Appeal said 'where, if sought, an allocation would have been made to Small Claims track the normal rule should be that the Small Claims costs regime for costs should apply'.

Most claimant law firms simply refuse to act for personal injury clients with Small Claims. If turning a claimant away it is good public relations, and good risk management, to hand him a leaflet summarising the rules on limitation of actions, a list of possible special damages, and a leaflet about Small Claims. In the latter, one could say that the claim appears to be a Small Claim, and so is an exception to the usual rule that the defendant has to pay the successful claimant's legal costs; if a lawyer represented the claimant, the costs would certainly make a large hole in his compensation; he might very well end up out of pocket; and most other law firms would say the same. If he finds that he has significant symptoms for more than a month, or that he has financial losses worth much more than £4,000, he should come back because probably it is not a Small Claim after all. He should check whether he has legal expenses insurance which might entitle him to some legal advice; failing which he could consider bringing a Small Claim himself, with the help of leaflets from his local county court or a website (for example, **www.lawinclear.co.uk**).

When a claim is first intimated, it is seldom apparent to the defendant that it is a Small Claim. The defendant carries out whatever investigations into liability seem appropriate. The true value of the claim emerges when the claimant sends a detailed description of symptoms, or discloses a medical report. If the claim is a little above the Small Claims limit the defendant can often make a payment or an open offer to bring the sum in dispute below the limit.

When the value of the claim is apparent, the defendant should point out to the claimant or his lawyer that it is a Small Claim at best. If the claimant is not legally represented, the defendant's lawyer can write to him directly, describing the costs risk to which he will be exposed if he issues proceedings. If the claimant is represented, it may change his lawyer's views quite sharply.

From the defendant's point of view, Small Claims become a real threat if the claimant issues proceedings. Most defendants then pass the claim to solicitors. In the absence of any special deal, the defendants then become liable to pay legal fees that they cannot recover from the claimant even if they defeat his claim. Initially, the fees will be for drawing up a defence and completing the allocation questionnaire. Later comes the hearing itself. Preparation for and advocacy at a hearing could be worth over £1,000. A party can ask for the hearing to proceed in his absence, but defendants generally prefer to be represented. If the claim is worth only £1,000 or so, the defendant has strong motivation to settle.

21.2 ALLOCATION TO TRACK

A claim is not certainly a Small Claim until it has been allocated to the Small Claims track, and its value is only one of several factors considered in the allocation process. However, it is most unlikely that a personal injury claim worth less than the Small Claims limit will be allocated to the fast track rather than the Small Claims track.

Each of the following is, on its own, worth less than £1,000 unless the court is in a generous mood:

- two black eyes and feeling of being shaken up for a month;
- cuts and bruises, but a swift recovery and no trace of scarring after three months;
- sprained ankle where the victim had two weeks off work but made a full recovery within two months;
- whiplash injury involving a week off work and 99 per cent recovery in less than one month;
- fracture of bone in hand or foot involving a week off work, full recovery in less than one month.

A claimant who wishes to stay within the Small Claims limit may expressly limit the value of his claim to that amount (*Khiaban* v. *Beard* [2003] EWCA Civ 358).

When assessing the value of a claim for allocation purposes, the court will disregard any sum not in dispute. CPR PD 26 directs the court to disregard as not in dispute a specific sum claimed as a distinct item that the defendant admits he is liable to pay, or for which he has offered a sum that the claimant has accepted. However, if the claimant values an item at £2,000 and the defendant has offered to pay £1,000, the sum in dispute is still £2,000.

The court has a discretion on allocating the case, and might allocate to the fast track purely on grounds of complexity. However, CPR PD 26 specifically states that 'accident claims . . . are generally suitable for the Small Claims track,' and see the pre-CPR workplace claim *Afzal* v. *Ford Motor Co* [1994] 4 All ER 720. A small claim based on clinical negligence or trespass to the person may be too complex for the Small Claims track.

A claim worth less than the Small Claims limit may be allocated to the fast track if the defendant, on receiving the proceedings, makes a counterclaim under CPR Part 20 that takes the total in dispute over the Small Claims limit; or serves a defence alleging that the claim is fraudulent (CPR PD 26.8.1).

The court's approval is required before a claim can be settled on behalf of a claimant under a disability, that is, one who is under 18 or a mental patient. These cases may well be allocated to the fast track. Consider *M (a minor)* v. *Liverpool City Council* [1994] CLY 3774 and *K* v. *Grocutt* [2001] 2 CL 49.

The fact that the claimant is willing to settle for less than the Small Claims limit does not mean that he is not entitled to his costs on the standard basis if the claim was objectively worth more than the limit. Unless the claimant has expressly limited the value of his claim the test is whether, at the time he issued proceedings, the claimant could reasonably have expected to be awarded more than the Small Claims limit (*Afzal* v. *Ford Motor Co* [1994] 4 All ER 720).

Say the claimant accepted £875, a sum fairly close to the Small Claims limit at the time. That does not necessarily mean the claimant could reasonably have expected to recover more than £1,000, but it is certainly something the court can take into account. Consider *Smith* v. *Vauxhall Motors* [1996] EWCA Civ 669, in which the claimant settled her claim for £375 but recovered her costs.

21.3 LEGAL COSTS IN SMALL CLAIMS

The winner in a Small Claim is entitled to ask the court to award him some fixed costs under Part 27.14. The amounts are set out in CPR PD 27. At the time of writing a successful claimant is entitled to:

- The court fees he paid. There will seldom be any fee other than the issue fee, and an allocation fee if the claim is worth more than £1,500 in total.

- If the claim is for a specified sum of money and a solicitor drew up and issued the proceedings, a small amount for solicitors' fees, calculated from the table at CPR Part 45. A claim for repairs to a vehicle is for a specified sum of money, unless it includes a claim for compensation for pain and suffering.
- The expenses of witnesses for turning up at the hearing, consisting of up to £50 per witness per day for loss of earnings if they have to take the day off work (or up to £50 for a baby sitter if the witness is a housewife and mother), plus reasonable travel and overnight expenses. The witness must be able to prove what net earnings he lost, so an employed person should get a letter from his employer. A self-employed person should have a copy of his last trading accounts, and be able to explain why he could not make up for the lost time by working a Sunday instead. If the evidence of the witness was not really necessary, or it would have been just as good to rely on a written statement from the witness, the court may not allow witness expenses.
- Up to £200 per expert witness. In practice, in a Small Claim there will be only one expert. This will usually be the claimant's GP, whose medical report covers all the injuries. See the *pro forma* report on the accompanying CD-ROM.

Note that CPR Part 27.14 does not require the defendant to reimburse a successful claimant for the cost of photos or plans, a police accident report, or copy medical records.

The amounts above are what the loser must pay the winner. If a party commissions medical evidence that costs more than £200, the fixed costs rules do not make him any less liable to pay the doctor's bill. Likewise, a party who calls a witness to the hearing must be ready to reimburse him for his actual losses and expenses, whatever they are.

21.4 EXCEPTIONS TO THE NO COSTS RULE

A party may pay more than these fixed costs if the case is allocated to a track other than the Small Claims track, or if he behaved unreasonably.

Even in Small Claims, under CPR Part 27.14.2 the court may apply a costs penalty to a party who is guilty of unreasonable behaviour. District Judges have a wide discretion, and the Lord Chancellor's Department did not respond the author's requests in 2004 for information about the frequency and size of these penalties nationwide. The following may represent unreasonable behaviour:

- failing to comply with the Pre-action Protocol, particularly if the party was represented by a solicitor;
- exaggerating the claim beyond normal optimism;

- bringing a claim that is hopeless from the start, especially if by issuing proceedings the claimant hoped to make the defendant pay him something just for nuisance value;
- giving dishonest evidence, where the court finds that it simply could not be true;
- changing his story halfway through, or giving verbal evidence that conflicts with his own witness statement (*Owen* v. *Burnham* [2001] 8 CL 56);
- ignoring directions or orders, particularly if he was legally represented;
- failing to turn up for the hearing without making arrangements for it to be dealt with in his absence;
- after allowances have been made because he did not have a lawyer, presenting his case at a hearing in such a way that it takes days, not hours (*Hayes* v. *Airtours Holidays Ltd* [2001] 7 CL 64);
- in the case of a defendant, failing to state why the claim was defended until formally serving a defence (*Northfield* v. *DSM (Southern) Ltd* [2000] 9 CL 56);
- purporting to defend a claim to which there was no real defence.

21.5 PROCEDURE IN SMALL CLAIMS

Briefly, the Small Claims track is designed to give a swift and relatively easy route to a hearing. CPR Part 27.2 disapplies many formalities, including Part 18 requests for further information; Part 25 interim payments; Part 31 on disclosure of documents; Parts 32 and 33 on the form and content of witness statements, and rules of evidence generally; most of Part 35 on the form and content of expert's reports; Part 36 on settlement offers and payments; and Part 39 on trial bundles. Small Claims end in a hearing, not a trial.

The court will, on allocating a case to the Small Claims track, give standard directions in accordance with CPR PD 27, Appendix A. These provide for limited disclosure.

Very little of CPR Part 35 applies to Small Claims. The court will not accept verbal evidence from medical or other experts. Written reports only are acceptable. There is no automatic right to put written questions to the other side's expert. The parts of CPR Part 35 that do apply are 35.1, which permits the court to restrict expert evidence; 35.3, which provides that the expert's main duty is to the court, not to his client; and 35.8, which provides for single joint experts. CPR Part 35.4 states that 'no party may call an expert or put in evidence an expert's opinion without the court's permission' and is disapplied by CPR Part 27.2, but Part 27.5 says: 'No expert may give evidence, whether oral or written, at a Hearing without the permission of the court.' Note that the standard directions do not grant this permission.

The claimant does not necessarily need any medical evidence in a Small Claim. Paragraph 2.11 of the Personal Injury Protocol says: 'If proceedings have to be issued, a medical report must be attached to those proceedings.' However, this misrepresents the position: see CPR PD 16.4.3. Where the claimant has already recovered from a minor injury, a doctor could do little more than summarise the relevant medical records (if any) and recount what the claimant says. There are plenty of cases in the textbooks, and even in the law reports, that were decided by the courts on the basis purely of the claimant's own statement, perhaps supported by medical records or photographs of the injuries (*Payne* v. *Hunt* [2001] 7 CL 165).

APPENDIX 1

List of documents

Please see below for a list of the documents on the accompanying CD-ROM. These documents are illustrations. Please do not use them as precedents without first checking them against the latest edition of the Civil Procedure Rules 1998 and the relevant Pre-action Protocol. One can do this on the website of the Department for Constitutional Affairs at **www.dca.gov.uk**

1. Letter of claim
2. Standard disclosure list
3. Letter instructing medical expert
4. Pro forma for claimant's own doctor
5. Consent form for medical records
6. Letter requesting medical records
7. Claimant's Part 36 offer letter
8. Particulars of claim – No. 1
9. Particulars of claim – No. 2
10. Schedule of loss
11. Typical defence
12. Witness statement – liability
13. Tomlin order
14. Complex case checklist

APPENDIX 2

List of questionnaires

Please see below for a list of the questionnaires on the accompanying CD-ROM. Note that in every case one needs to ask the client to check as soon as possible whether he has insurance to cover legal costs. He may have this as an add-on to a car, house contents, travel, business or sports insurance policy, as a member of a club, association or trade union, or hidden in a credit card agreement.

The claimant might be covered if somebody in his family is a trades union member or has legal expenses insurance. If he was injured as a passenger in a car he may be covered by the driver's legal expenses insurance, even if it was the driver's fault he was injured.

1. Initial enquiry questionnaire
2. Road accident
3. Pedestrian tripping accident
4. Pedestrian slipping accident
5. Accident at work – general
6. Manual handling at work
7. Fatal incident losses
8. Injuries, minor to catastrophic

APPENDIX 3

Personal injury law on the internet

The Government's full Statute Law Database will shortly go online. It is widely hoped that it will be made freely available to all. Combined with the existing free services, it would mean that most source material needed by lawyers would be available free, fully updated, at the click of a mouse. Follow its progress at **www.dca.gov.uk/lawdatfr.htm**

Most personal injury source material from the last 10 years can already be found free on the internet, at the sites listed below.

There are two professional sites that provide a wide range of information and training for the personal injury lawyer. The author of this handbook is very much involved with **www.lawinclear.co.uk** which contains a guide to law and practice, and hyperlinks to take the reader to the full text of cases, legislation, practice rules, guidance notes, etc. For a free trial, or to contribute an article, please go to the website.

The excellent Association of Personal Injury lawyers has a public site at **www.apil.com** and a professional site at **www.apilonline.com**

Employment law overlaps considerably with personal injury. There is an excellent professional website, the brainchild of another Law Society handbook author, at **www.emplaw.co.uk**

As to free online material, the latest updates of the Civil Procedure Rules 1998, Protocols and Practice Directions are at **www.dca.gov.uk**

Statutes and statutory instruments from 1987 onwards can be found at **www.hmso.gov.uk**

For case law since 1995 try **www.bailii.org** or **www.lawreports.co.uk** (which has a section dedicated to employment law cases) or **www.parliament.the-stationery-office.co.uk**

Welsh legislation started to diverge from English following the Government of Wales Act 1998. This may come to affect personal injury. **www.wales-legislation.hmso.gov.uk**

You can find court forms, court fees, Group Litigation Orders, the *Queen's Bench Guide* and some case law at **www.courtservice.gov.uk**

The Law Society has *The Guide To Professional Conduct Of Solicitors 1999*, and guidance on money laundering and the proceeds of crime, at **www.lawsociety.org.uk**

The HSE's smaller documents can be found at **www.hse.gov.uk** and larger ones can be purchased through **www.tso.co.uk**

APPENDIX 4

Useful contact details

Academy of Experts
3 Gray's Inn Square
London
WC1R 5AH
Tel: 0207 430 0333
www.academy-experts.org

Action against Medical Accidents (AvMA)
44 High Street
Croydon
CR0 1YB
Tel: 0208 686 8333
www.avma.org.uk

APIL
11 Castle Quay
Nottingham
NG7 1FW
Tel: 0115 958 0585
www.apil.com

Army Medical Records Directorate
Royal Army Medical College
Millbank
London
SW1P 4RJ

Association of Child Abuse Lawyers (ACAL)
Tel: 01932 264988
www.childabuselawyers.com

BNA
Head Office
The Colonnades
Beaconsfield Close
Hatfield
Herts
AL10 8YD
www.bna.co.uk

Crossroads Association
10 Regent Place
Rugby
CV21 2PN
www.crossroads.org.uk

Compensation Recovery Unit (CRU)
Durham House
Washington
Tyne & Wear
NE38 7SF
Tel: 0191 225 2005

Court of Protection's Public Guardianship Office (PGO)
Archway Tower
2 Junction Road
London
N19 5SZ

Criminal Injuries Compensation Authority (CICA)
Tay House
300 Bath Street
Glasgow
G2 4LN
Tel: 0800 359 3601
www.cica.gov.uk

Criminal Injuries Compensation Appeals Panel (CICAP)
11th Floor, Cardinal Tower
12 Farringdon Road
London
EC1M 3HS
Tel: 0207 549 4600
www.cicap.gov.uk

Disabled Living Foundation
380–384 Harrow Road
London
W9 2HU
Tel: 0207 289 6111
www.dlf.org.uk

Driver and Vehicle Licensing Agency (DVLA)
Swansea
SA99 1BP
Tel: 0870 240 0010
www.dvla.org.uk

Financial Services Compensation Scheme (FSCS)
7th Floor, Lloyds Chambers
1 Portsoken Street
London
E1 8BN
Tel: 0207 892 7300
www.fscs.org.uk

Frenkel Topping & Co, Accountants
Frontier House
Merchants Quay
Salford Quays
Manchester
M5 2SR
Tel: 0161 886 8000
www.frenkeltopping.co.uk

General Dental Council
37 Wimpole Street
London
W1M 8DQ

General Medical Council
178–202 Great Portland Street
London
W1N 6JE

InSolutions (Insurance archaeologist)
Tel: 01603 207470

Medical Directorate General Naval
Room 10, Royal Army Medical College
Millbank
London
SW1P 4RJ

Ministry of Defence, Service Personnel Policy (Pensions)
Room 5/84
Northumberland Avenue
London
WC2N 5BL

Motor Insurers Bureau (MIB)
Linford Wood House
6–12 Capital Drive
Linford Wood
Milton Keynes
MK14 6XT
Tel: 01908 830001
www.mib.org.uk

National Back Pain Association
(NBPA) (BackCare)
31–33 Park Road
Teddington
Middlesex
TW11 0AB
www.backcare.org.uk

National Insurance Contributions
Agency
Special Section A
Long Benton
Newcastle upon Tyne
NE98 1NX

Office of the Information
Commissioner
Wycliffe House
Water Lane
Wilmslow
SK9 5AF

P G Video
Tel: 0845 644 3119

RAF (Medical)
Room 034
Building 248
RAF Insworth
Gloucestershire
GL3 1EZ

RIBA
66 Portland Place
London
W1N 4AD
Tel: 0207 580 5533

Symbiosis Forensic Systems
47 The Parade
Royal Priors
Leamington Spa
CV32 4BL
Tel: 01926 436930
www.symbiosis.com

Index

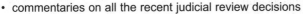

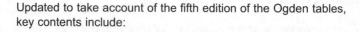